THE JAPANESE MAIN BANK SYSTEM

The Japanese Main Bank System

Its Relevance for Developing and
Transforming Economies

Edited by

MASAHIKO AOKI

and

HUGH PATRICK

OXFORD UNIVERSITY PRESS
1994

Oxford University Press, Walton Street, Oxford OX2 6DP
Oxford New York
Athens Auckland Bangkok Bombay
Calcutta Cape Town Dar es Salaam Delhi
Florence Hong Kong Istanbul Karachi
Kuala Lumpur Madras Madrid Melbourne
Mexico City Nairobi Paris Singapore
Taipei Tokyo Toronto
and associated companies in
Berlin Ibadan

Oxford is a trade mark of Oxford University Press

Published in the United States
by Oxford University Press Inc., New York

British Library Cataloguing in Publication Data
ISBN 0–19–828899–9

Library of Congress Cataloging in Publication Data
Data available
ISBN 0–19–828899–9

Set by Hope Services (Abingdon) Ltd.
Printed in Great Britain
on acid-free paper by
Biddles Ltd.
Guildford & King's Lynn

CONTENTS

PART I THE JAPANESE MAIN BANK SYSTEM

Data series in the tables are indexed. A reference list follows
each chapter.

LIST OF FIGURES

LIST OF TABLES

FOREWORD

The World Bank's research programme is intended to provide information and guidance to the Bank's member countries and to its own operational staff on different development processes and policies as they apply across a wide range of countries. The topics covered are also wide-ranging.

It is in this context that a considerable amount of research has been done under a Program for the Study of the Japanese Development Management Experience financed by the Policy and Human Resources Development Trust Fund established at the World Bank by the Government of Japan. The programme is managed by the Studies and Training Design Division of the World Bank's Economic Development Institute.

Under this programme the Japanese development experience has been given close attention, especially the early post-war experiences that helped transform the country from a wartime command economy to a market economy which has yielded today's economic superpower. The programme analyses the key features of the Japanese financial system and its evolution, with particular reference to the main bank system of long-term relationships among the banks and their borrowers. It also examines the role of the Japanese state as agent for development and the implications of the Japanese experience for the comparative understanding of the state in other developing countries.

Until now, very little has been published outside of Japan about the relationship among banks, borrowers, and government—a potentially important topic for economies undergoing financial reforms and restructuring of the interface between the public and the private sectors. *The Japanese Main Bank System* is intended to help policy-makers and analysts better understand the issues they may currently be facing as they attempt to develop efficient and effective financial systems. The book describes, analyses, and evaluates the Japanese main bank system, and examines its relevance as a model for the developing market economies and transforming socialist economies.

The authors offer their findings and conclusions to readers in the developing world for their consideration as they seek solutions to the challenges they confront.

Michael Bruno
Vice President, Development Economics and Chief Economist
The World Bank
Washington DC

ACKNOWLEDGEMENTS

This study is the result of a World Bank sponsored project that has involved a large number of people, each of whom has contributed in a special way to this final product. Our deepest thanks go to Hyung-Ki Kim, Division Chief, Studies and Training Design Division, Economic Development Institute, World Bank, whose initiative and project management were essential throughout. We worked well together, and pleasurably so. We are also of course particularly indebted to our colleagues who wrote the chapters.

The scholars and practitioners who participated in this project met in an initial planning session and in two intensive workshop sessions to review chapter drafts in what was a labour-intensive but intellectually rewarding project. We, and they, benefited from the expertise, insight, and constructive comments made by the other participants in our meetings: Noritaka Akamatsu, World Bank; Jenny Corbett, Nissan Institute of Japanese Studies, University of Oxford; Monsoor Dailami, World Bank; Dennis deTray, World Bank; Ronald Gilson, Stanford University; Koichi Hamada, Economic Growth Center, Yale University; Christian Harm, New York University; Thomas Hellman, Stanford University; Akiyoshi Horiuchi, University of Tokyo; Kensuke Hotta, Managing Director, Sumitomo Bank; Millard Long, World Bank; Diane McNaughton, World Bank; Ronald McKinnon, Stanford University; Hideaki Miyajima, Waseda University; Junichi Nishiwaki, Mitsubishi Research Institute; Mitsuaki Okabe, Wharton School, University of Pennsylvania; Ryuko Okazaki, Research and Statistics Division, Bank of Japan; Tetsuji Okazaki, University of Tokyo; Joseph Pegues, World Bank; Gerald Roland, Free University of Brussels; Tsutomu Shibata, Japan Development Bank; Xavier Simon, World Bank; Marilou Uy, World Bank; Dimitri Vittas, World Bank; Ernst-Ludwig von Thadden, University of Basel; and Ayako Yasuda, Stanford University.

Most of the funding for this project was provided by the World Bank. Additional funding was provided by the Center on Japanese Economy and Business and the Japan Relations Studies Program at Columbia University, and by the Economy of Japan Program of the Center for Economic Policy Research at Stanford University. We benefited from the project administration by staff at our two institutions, especially Kaori Kuroda and Shin Umezu at Columbia and Deborah Carvalho and Sharon Latimer at Stanford. Latifah Alsegaf at the World Bank ably and amiably assisted Hyung-Ki Kim and us throughout.

To turn a manuscript into a book requires a great deal of effort which all too often authors only inadequately appreciate. We are indebted to

Hilary Hodgson, whose copy-editing turned the material, written by scholars from a number of countries, into British English in an Oxford University Press format; Jenny Corbett, who, applying her expert knowledge, kindly reviewed the copy-edited manuscript; and, for painstaking editing, Larry Meissner. Andrew Schuller and Anna Zaranko shepherded the book through the publication process at Oxford University Press, for which we thank them.

Masahiko Aoki
Hugh Patrick

CONTRIBUTORS

Editors

MASAHIKO AOKI is Henri and Tomoye Takahashi Professor of Japanese Studies in the Department of Economics, and director of the Economy of Japan Program of the Center for Economic Policy Research at Stanford University. He serves as editor-in-chief of the *Journal of the Japanese and International Economy*, is president-elect of the Japan Association for Economics and Econometrics, and a fellow of the Econometric Society. Awarded the Japan Academy Prize in 1981, he has previously been on the faculty of Harvard University and Kyoto University. He contributed to and co-edited *The Japanese Firm: Sources of its Competitiveness* (Oxford, 1994). Among his many other publications is *Information, Incentives, and Bargaining in the Japanese Economy* (Cambridge, 1988), which has been translated into six languages and awarded a number of prizes.

HUGH PATRICK is R. D. Calkins Professor of International Business, director of the Center on Japanese Economy and Business and co-director of the Pacific Basin Studies Program at Columbia University. He is also chair of the International Steering Committee of the Pacific Trade and Development Conference series (PAFTAD). He has previously been professor of economics and director of the Economic Growth Center at Yale University, and visiting professor at Hitotsubashi University (Tokyo), University of Tokyo and University of Bombay. Among other works, he is the general co-editor of the three-volume series *The Political Economy of Japan*, and served as project director, editor, and contributor to *Pacific Basin Industries in Distress*, which won the 1992 Masayoshi Ohira Prize, and *The Financial Development of Japan, Korea, and Taiwan* (Oxford, 1994).

Other Contributors

THEODOR BAUMS is Dr. jur., professor of law at the University of Osnabrück, Germany, and director of the Institute of Commercial and Enterprise Law. He is the author of a number of works on corporate law, banking and finance law, and anti-trust in both Germany and Europe, as well as *Relationships between Banks and Firms in U.S. Banking Law* (1992, in German). His work on international issues includes, as co-editor, *Institutional Investors and Corporate Governance* (1994).

V. V. BHATT is a consultant to the World Bank, where he has held a number of positions, including chief of the Public Finance Division.

Previously he was the chief executive of the Industrial Development Bank of India, an advisor to the Reserve Bank of India, and has served as a director of several other financial institutions. He has written extensively on development strategies; his most recent book is *Financial System, Innovations, and Development.*

JOHN Y. CAMPBELL is Otto Eckstein Professor of Applied Economics at Harvard University, and a research associate at the National Bureau of Economic Research. He was Class of 1926 Professor of Economics and Public Affairs at the Woodrow Wilson School, Princeton University, and has served as co-editor of the American Economic Review. He is widely published in his specialties of macroeconomics and asset pricing.

YASUSHI HAMAO is an associate professor of finance at the Graduate School of Business, Columbia University. Previously, he was on the faculty of the University of California, San Diego. Awarded a 1991–92 Batterymarch Fellowship, which recognizes prominent young scholars in finance, his research is in the areas of asset pricing and corporate finance.

TOSHIHIRO HORIUCHI is a professor at Kyoto Sangyo University. Previously, he was on the faculty of the Institute of Economic Research at Kyoto University, with the Japan Center for Economic Research, and a senior marketing researcher with a Kyoto-based consulting company. He has been a visiting fellow or professor at the Robert Schuman Center, European University Institute; Siena University; London School of Economics; and the Research Institute of the Ministry of International Trade and Industry (Japan).

TAKEO HOSHI is an assistant professor at the Graduate School of International Relations and Pacific Studies at the University of California, San Diego. A PhD from the Massachusetts Institute of Technology and Fulbright Scholar, he is the co-author of *The Economic Implications of Japanese Financing Patterns* (forthcoming).

ANIL KASHYAP is an associate professor of business economics at the Graduate School of Business, University of Chicago, a Faculty Research Fellow at the National Bureau of Economic Research, and an associate fellow in the Research Department of the Federal Reserve Bank of Chicago. Previously, he was a staff economist for the Board of Governors of the Federal Reserve System. He has also published work on monetary policy and the sources of business cycles.

DONG-WON KIM is a professor of economics at the University of Suwon in Suwon, Korea. In 1993–94 he was a visiting scholar at the Salomon Center, Stern School of Business, New York University. He has been a special research fellow at the Korea Institute of Finance (KIF) in Seoul. He has written many papers on financial reform in Korea for the

Bank of Korea, Korea Development Insitution (KDI), Korea Economic Research Institute, and KIF, and is a contributor to *The Financial Development of Japan, Korea, and Taiwan* (Oxford, 1994).

GARY LOVEMAN is an associate professor of business administration at the Graduate School of Business Administration, Harvard University, where he teaches service management in MBA and executive programmes. Since 1991 he has been involved in field study of enterprise reform and small business development in Poland, and is the author of *Starting Over: Economic Renewal in Post-Communist Economies* (forthcoming).

SANG-WOO NAM is a senior fellow at the Korea Development Institute (KDI), Seoul, and served as its president during 1991–93. Previously, he was a lecturer at Korea University, on the staff of the World Bank, and a counsellor to the deputy prime minister of Korea. He has written several books on finance, and numerous papers and articles on finance and macroeconomic issues.

FRANK PACKER is an economist in the International Finance Department of the Federal Reserve Bank of New York. An MBA from the University of Chicago and a PhD from Columbia University, he spent four years doing research at the Industrial Bank of Japan, the University of Tokyo, and the Bank of Japan. He has worked as an analyst for the Office of Technology Assessment, US Congress, and published several articles on the main bank system and bankruptcy in Japan.

YINGYI QIAN is an assistant professor of economics at Stanford University, and a consultant to the World Bank. He is co-founder of the Chinese Economist Society (USA) and has served as its president. Born in Beijing, he has an MPhil from Yale University and a PhD from Harvard University. In addition to his work on China specifically, he has published on theoretical aspects of economic efficiency, egalitarianism, and development.

J. MARK RAMSEYER is Professor of Law at the University of Chicago, where he teaches courses on corporate law and Japanese law. Prior to taking his position at Chicago, he taught on the law faculty of the University of California, Los Angeles, was a Fulbright scholar in Japan, and worked for a law firm in Chicago. He has also taught at Harvard University and, in Japan, at Tokyo, Hitotsubashi, and Tohoku Universities. His books include *Ho to Keizaigaku* (*Law and Economics*), which was awarded the Suntory Cultural Foundation Prize in Political Economy.

CLARK W. REYNOLDS is a professor of economics at the Food Research Institute, Stanford University, and was the founding director of the Americas program, now the North America Forum, at Stanford University. He has held visiting appointments at a number of European and Mexican universities. He has published work on many aspects of developmental economics, including, as a co-author, _A Case for Open Regionalism in the Andes_ (1994) and, as a co-editor, _US-Mexico Relations: Labor Market Interdependence_ (1992), and is currently writing a sequel to _The Mexican Economy: Twentieth Century Structure and Growth_ (1970).

PAUL SHEARD is International Cooperation (Osaka Gas) Associate Professor of Economics at Osaka University and Lecturer in Economics at Australian National University. He has been visiting scholar and visiting assistant professor at Stanford University, and visiting scholar at Osaka University and the Bank of Japan. He has published widely on Japanese corporate organization and finance, and is the editor of _International Adjustment and the Japanese Firm_ (1992).

SATOSHI SUNAMURA is currently a Senior Managing Director at Barclays Bank plc in Tokyo. A member of the Japanese Society for International Development as well as at the Japanese Institute of Negotiation, he has previously served as a Senior Special Advisor to the World Bank, and in the mid-70s as a chief manager at the Overseas Economic Co-operation Fund. A former director and general manager of the Bank of Tokyo, where he had served 32 years including assignments at Headquarters, London, Hong Kong and Melbourne. In particular, he played a major role during 1985–90 on the Third World Debt Issues representing the whole Japanese banking community, which include the roles of Chairman or Vice Chairman at the International Bank Advisory Committees for Trinidad Tobago, Venezuela, Mexico, Brazil, Philippine, Vietnam, etc. He has made a variety of speeches on international financial topics and some are published. He is a graduate of Kyoto University (Economics) 1959 and trained in Oxford and London.

JURO TERANISHI is a professor of economics at the Institute of Economic Research, Hitotsubashi University, Tokyo. He is the author of a number of works on finance and development, including, in Japanese, _Money, Finance and Economic Development in Japan_, which won the _Ekonomistu_ Prize and Nikkei Prize in 1982, and _Financing and Industrialization of Developing Economies_ (1991). In English, he contributed to, and is co-editor of, _The Japanese Experience of Economic Reforms_ (Macmillan, 1993), which won the 1994 Masayoshi Ohira Prize, and wrote a chapter for _The Financial Development of Japan, Korea, and Taiwan_ (Oxford, 1994).

KAZUO UEDA is a professor of economics at the University of Tokyo. He has written many papers on the Japanese economy, especially its microeconomic aspects and its money and financial markets. He is the author of _Japanese Monetary Policy under the Large Current Account Surplus_ (in Japanese).

INTRODUCTION

The world is in a period of rapid economic change—in structure, behaviour, policies, and institutions. These transformations are perhaps nowhere more profound than in the systems of national and international finance. The forces at work embody an evolutionary process in many countries, overlaid with new policy approaches to new and enduring issues, as well as discontinuously transformational forces, where planned socialist economies are embarked on the transition to market economies.

The motivations of this book, and the collaborative project sponsored by the World Bank on which it is based, are two-fold. One is from the perspective of analysts and policy-makers concerned with the development of efficient and effective financial systems in various developing market economies and transforming socialist economies. The architecture of a country's financial system depends on its own heritage, existing institutions, goals, and policies. Yet no system develops in a vacuum, nor should it. Policy-makers, institution-builders, and analysts can learn from the experience of other countries; after all, most of the problems of financial institution-building and financial reform are generic and the successes and failures of others provide important lessons. The Japanese experience is particularly relevant but not always well understood.

Accordingly, this is the second purpose of this book: to describe, analyse, and evaluate the Japanese main bank system, and to examine its relevance as a model for developing market economies and transforming socialist economies. Banks have played a dominant role in post-war Japan, especially in the era of exceptionally rapid growth from the mid-1950s to the mid-1970s when the business need for external financing of its burgeoning investment was particularly strong. Large Japanese banks developed particularly close and distinctive relationships with their large industrial clients, and with each other, which substantially reduced the cost and increased the quality of monitoring and of rescue of firms in distress.

This main bank relationship was initially a practitioner's term describing a set of arrangements that had developed without an explicitly distinctive legal or regulatory basis. It is appropriately analysed as an especially intensive manifestation of relationship banking. The term 'Japanese main bank system' as used in this book refers to a more or less informal set of regular practices, institutional arrangements, and behaviour that constitute a system of corporate finance and governance, especially for large industrial firms typically listed on the stock exchange, but applying in principle and practice in less complete ways to medium and small firms as well. These relationships were not exclusive, in that corporations also borrowed from other banks and banks lent to firms that had main bank relationships with other large banks. However, certain monitoring functions of the firms are exclusively delegated to their main banks. These arrangements are an integral component of the main bank system, which can be broadly considered as a nexus of relationships involving firms, various types of banks, other financial institutions and the regulatory authorities (the Ministry of Finance and the Bank of Japan).

Two basic issues of the financing of economic development are how best to provide external funds for the business sector, the engine of growth, and relatedly, how to monitor the behaviour and performance of these corporate borrowers under an effective system of corporate governance. Internally generated funds are essential but inadequate where firms and economies are growing rapidly. A fundamental choice is between a securities market-based system of external finance, primarily for large businesses, through competitive issue of equity, bonds, and commercial paper; and a banking-based system of loans, short term and longer term. The securities market system, often termed the Anglo-American model, has dominated much academic and policy thinking about financial systems. The bank-based system of corporate finance, monitoring, and governance—more recently termed by some the Japanese-German system—provides an alternative analytical model of direct policy relevance. While the dichotomy between securities market and bank systems of corporate finance is analytically important, the reality is that advanced industrial countries combine both so that differences are less extreme in practice than in theory. Nonetheless, in designing a financial system and creating the appropriate incentives and institutions, the choice of model is of central importance.

A basic conclusion of this study is that banking-based systems in most cases are the most appropriate for industrial financing until a rather late stage of a country's economic and financial development. The real world is characterized by imperfect information, which is costly to generate and is unequally shared between borrowers and lenders. The cross-country historical evidence, and the case of Japan, indicate that under certain conditions banks are better (or less expensively) able than securities market institutions to evaluate the credit-worthiness of borrowers and the viability of new projects, to monitor the ongoing performance of firms, and to rescue or liquidate firms in distress. The identification of such conditions is a major objective of this volume and the collective project on which it was based.

Scholarly knowledge and understanding of the basic features, characteristics, and performance of the Japanese main bank system, and efforts to incorporate it into a rigorous theoretical framework, are relatively recent and new. What are the basic characteristics of the main bank system, theoretically and empirically? What are its roots; how did it develop? What was its role in its heyday of exceptionally rapid growth? What institutional mechanisms and government policies supported its activities? How has the system performed? What are its strengths and weaknesses? How has the main bank system changed and what is its appropriate role, as deregulation, liberalization, and internationalization of Japan's financial markets have proceeded over the past two decades and a vigorous new issue securities market has dramatically emerged? What does the asset bubble of the late 1980s, with its dramatic increases in land and stock prices and its subsequent bursting, imply for future main bank relationships, especially in the light of heavy non-performing loan burdens afflicting all banks?

While we cannot pretend to answer these questions completely, this project has made a quantum leap forward. It has succeeded in substantially deepening both our theoretical and empirical understanding of the Japanese main bank system. This has been possible because the project incorporated many of the world's best scholars on the Japanese main bank system as writers and commentators; the results of their individual and cooperative efforts are reflected in the following pages.

This introduction is just that: a reader's guide to, though by no means a summary of, the chapters that make up the substance of this volume. The book is divided into two parts: Part I, The Japanese Main Bank System, consisting of ten chapters; and Part II, The Comparative Context: Relevance for Developing and Transforming Economies, consisting of seven chapters.

PART I

In the first chapter, Aoki, Patrick, and Sheard provide an analytical and empirical overview of the Japanese main bank system in order to provide a common conceptual framework for the other studies in the book. They provide the first analysis and discussion of the comprehensive range of activities which define the multi-dimensional set of main bank-industrial client relationships contingent on the financial state, size, history, and ownership structure of the firm. This substantially expands earlier, narrower, definitions based on the criteria of bank loan share and equity ownership of corporations. It also describes as integral elements of the main bank system the relationships among major main bank players which reciprocally delegate monitoring functions among each other, and the government regulatory structure which supports such relationships. The chapter provides two further contexts: where the Japanese case fits into a typology of financial systems and especially of banking systems; and the historical development of Japan's financial and banking systems, classified in five phases from the formation of modern banking institutions in the 1870s to the present. The primary focus is on the main bank system in its heyday, namely the rapid growth period from the mid-1950s to the mid-1970s; this focus appears in most of the remaining chapters as well, since that experience seems particularly relevant for developing market and transforming socialist economies today.

The Japanese main bank system, which came into being in the early post-World War II period, was not created *de novo* by government fiat or bank-business decisions. It had important historical antecedents as the pre-war banking system and industrial system (including zaibatsu) evolved. War-time consolidation, increasingly strong government policies to force bank lending to munitions industries as the highest priority, and the emergence first of autonomous loan syndicates and then of designated bank-company financing ties were the crucible from which the main bank system was forged in the turmoil of the early post-war Occupation and chaotic conditions. Teranishi in Chapter 2 addresses these and related issues in new and insightful ways, in the context particularly of the changing needs for corporate monitoring and the ways in which this was done as the financial and industrial system evolved over time. The historical context of the post-war development of the main bank system is further addressed in a number of other chapters in both parts of this volume.

Government policies toward the financial system and especially the banking system were crucial in creating a post-war environment in which the main bank system developed and flourished, as Ueda examines in Chapter 3. System safety was accorded high priority. Incentives favoured banking; the disincentives for corporate bond issue were severe. Competition was constrained by market segmentation, restrictive entry barriers, and ceiling interest rates on deposits, loans, and the few other financial instruments allowed. Nonetheless, the system was rather competitive among incumbents, and effective loan interest rates were adjusted upwards by the differential use of compensating balance and other mechanisms. There was some credit rationing and creation of interest rate subsidies and rents, yet the regulatory system was on the whole objective, fair, and honest. Importantly, the regulatory framework maintained considerable bank autonomy in decisions on which firms and even industries to lend to. The Ministry of Finance and Bank of Japan served not only as regulators but as promoters, supporters and, where necessary, as rescuers of financial institutions (mostly small) in distress.

Every system of corporate finance requires mechanisms for the monitoring of corporate performance and behaviour, including information collection and some ability to influence decisions where financial and managerial interest diverge. Aoki in Chapter 4 considers three conceptual stages of monitoring: *ex ante*, in which potential new projects and/or new clients are evaluated, in part to overcome problems of adverse selection and in part to cope with possible coordination failure among industries; ongoing (*interim*) monitoring of the performance of a firm and its projects, early identification of potential difficulties, and the overcoming of moral hazard problems arising from divergence of interests between lenders and borrowers; and *ex post*, to verify the results and in particular to exercise control over the firm when poor performance has resulted in firm distress. While these monitoring functions are dispersed among a range of institutions in a securities market system, they are concentrated to the main bank in Japan. Such institutional arrangements for monitoring were particularly effective at the stage of development of the Japanese economy during the high growth period. They were also closely related to, and complemented by, the ways in which corporate governance was structured. Japanese management maintains considerable autonomy in normal circumstances, but severe financial adversity triggers the shift of corporate control to the main bank. In this case, the main bank decides whether to rescue or liquidate, contingent on various factors. This *ex post* flexibility is one of the important consequences of the integration of monitoring functions.

One of the most important institutional features of the Japanese financial system has been the creation and significant role of a small number of long-term credit banks, private and governmental, to provide longer-term loans to finance business fixed investment. The relationships between the large commercial banks and the long-term credit banks has been important; long-term credit banks provided a superior credit-worthiness analysis capability in loan syndication as well as serving as a neutral counterbalance to the inward-looking aspects of group-affiliated city banks. In addition, long-term credit banks serve as the main bank for some firms; in particular, the Industrial Bank of Japan is one of the top main bank players together with six of the city banks. These roles of the long-term credit banks, and the mechanisms by which they obtained their funds which made their lending possible, are incisively treated in Chapter 5 by Packer.

One of the most important, and most distinctive, characteristics of the main bank system is the role the main bank plays when its major client is in severe distress, requiring rescue, reorganization and restructuring, or liquidation (though for large firms typically not through the bankruptcy courts). Sheard in Chapter 6 builds upon and extends the analysis of Chapters 1 and 4 on why the main bank is a highly efficient performer of these services, what the incentives are for it to do so, what the restructuring process entails, and what the main bank is prepared to do (or not do). He carefully describes the restructuring process, and, importantly, provides extensive empirical evidence on how large firms in distress have been handled by their main banks both in earlier years and, more recently, with the aftermath of the land and stock market collapses from 1990, which created and exposed not only a plethora of non-performing loan problems but some notable cases of firm mismanagement and fraudulent behaviour.

In a stimulating, controversial, and important analysis, Ramseyer in Chapter 7 addresses the issue of whether the main bank system of ongoing transactions with corporate clients really is built on implicit (insurance) contracts of expected obligations to rescue at times of distress. He argues instead that main bank behaviour rationally reflects narrowly defined self interest, but in a legal and regulatory environment different from the United States, where the doctrine of equitable subordination prevents a bank lender from taking the lead in a restructuring since it would thereby lose its preferred creditor status. In contrast, Japanese banks are not penalized by intervening in distressed firms, so they cannot credibly threaten to abandon badly performing firms as long as management has not engaged in fraudulent or hostile behaviour. This suggests possible inefficiencies in the main bank's involvement in rescue. Ramseyer also analyses how the regulatory environment prevented the development of a Japanese domestic bond market and generated other benefits for banks. He makes the key point that legal rules matter, and national differences in laws and their implementation are a major component of any sensible analysis of policy choices in developing an effective financial system.

In Chapter 8 Horiuchi treats two important aspects of the main bank system, the effect of firm size and status on the nature of its main bank relationship and *de facto* loan syndication, mainly to larger firms. Both topics are based on valuable survey data which he and his collaborators assembled. The main bank system as usually conceived refers essentially to the financing and governance arrangements for Japan's 1,500 or so large industrial corporations listed on the stock exchanges. Yet virtually every firm, large or small (namely the 120,000 firms with assets of $8 million or more), claims it has a main bank relationship; and banks and other financial institutions acknowledge having some form of main bank relationship with many of these smaller unlisted firms. Yet there are substantial differences between these relationships, partly stemming from the traditional policy of loan market segmentation between large and small firms. Horiuchi finds that main bank relationships between small firms and smaller local financial institutions are becoming more flexible and less stable, as those firms try to avoid the exercise of dominant influence by a single local financial institution, and as city banks increase their competitive efforts to penetrate into local loan markets. The chapter also discusses the historical evolution and actual functioning of *de facto* syndication of loans to corporate clients, with the main bank taking the lead in short-term financing and typically working together with a long-term credit bank for term loan syndicates. Syndicates diversify risk (to borrower as well as lender), while allowing the concentration of ongoing monitoring in the main bank under a system of reciprocal delegated monitoring.

One of the most critical problems in, and indispensable elements of, bank management is how to develop a capable staff able in practice to implement the monitoring and other functions required by the main bank system (and indeed virtually any form of financial intermediation). The lack of such human capital—persons with skill and experience in evaluating the viability of projects and the ongoing credit-worthiness of firms—has been identified as one of the major problems in financial reform in other countries, especially in transforming socialist economies. This project was fortunate in being able to incorporate as a chapter writer a Japanese former senior banker with more than 34 years of international management experience in a major Japanese bank. Sunamura in Chapter 9 provides a detailed and careful explanation of how banks train up their managerial personnel over time, and how they develop a close and enduring relationship with major clients through a variety of mechanisms. These include the formation and maintenance of client-specific teams involving staff at different levels (though personnel may rotate), seconding of young bank staff for a year or two at a company, and the dispatch of retiring senior bank managers to become full-time senior employees of client firms. He argues that arrangements to develop skilled bankers in major Japanese banks are not culture-specific; they can be created in other environments. Even so, the degree to which the bank and staff members engage in this human capital investment through on-the-job training and other means clearly is enhanced by implicit long-term employment commitments on both sides.

The Japanese securities market for new issues of corporate bonds, equities, and commercial paper grew dramatically in the 1980s, from an initial small earlier base. Among the causes of this changing pattern of external finance for some (but by no means all) large Japanese corporations, two were particularly important. First, by the 1970s rapid economic growth had made Japan the world's second largest market economy, with European levels of per capita income; concomitantly, flourishing large firms became low credit risks. Second, deregulation and internationalization of the financial system made it possible for an increasing number of large corporations to bypass the persistent highly restrictive domestic corporate bond market by issuing Eurobonds, many with equity conversion or warrant provisions. These new opportunities reduced the dependence of many large corporations on bank loans, and seemingly reduced the closeness of the relationship with their main bank. While that has been true in some cases, the story in fact is more complex; the relationships have changed, but have not necessarily weakened. Campbell and Hamao in Chapter 10 trace these changes in corporate finance, and provide a new empirical analysis which demonstrates that those firms having stronger ties with main banks in the early 1980s showed only modest changes in capital structure throughout the decade. It was 'unaffiliated' firms with weak main bank relationships in the early 1980s that have dramatically reduced their reliance on bank debt in favour of equity and equity-related debt instruments. Moreover, firms with strong main bank relationships often turned to their main bank to facilitate bond issuance; while 'unaffiliated' firms initially used (and paid for) bank guarantees, over time they have increasingly been able to issue non-guaranteed bonds.

PART II

As already noted, the two basic objectives of this book are to define and analyse the Japanese main bank system and to examine its relevance as a model for developing market economies and transforming socialist economies. Part II addresses the issue of relevance by providing comparative analyses from the perspectives of other countries. After all, the financial problems and issues Japan has faced are common to most countries. Three general points: what is most relevant about Japanese institutions, policies and experience depends importantly upon a country's own specific conditions and objectives; accordingly, borrowing from the Japanese model requires appropriate modification of details; and the essence is the substance, not simply the form, of institutions and policies.

The overall structure of this part is as follows. In Chapter 11 Patrick provides a general overview of the relevance of the Japanese financing experience for the developing market economies and transforming socialist economies. In the next chapter Baums provides the first comprehensive, up-to-date analysis available in English of the relationships among large German banks and large industrial corporations. This chapter is significant not only in its own right, but because Japanese and German banking are often lumped together as one model; while this is appropriate at a broad analytical level, there are major differences in the details of the arrangements, especially with regard to corporate governance. The following five chapters illuminate the issues from the perspectives and in the light of the experiences of three developing market economies—Korea, India, and Mexico, and two transforming socialist economies—China and Poland.

The studies of the Japanese main bank system in Part I appropriately focus primarily on micro issues of corporate finance, monitoring by the main bank, and corporate governance. To some extent they also address broader issues of the overall architecture of the Japanese system, its structure, and the financial policies of the government. Patrick's overview study (Chapter 11) explicitly provides this broader Japanese setting in order to address those generic policy issues of financial development facing all countries, how Japan dealt with them, and what lessons can be derived. Particular emphasis is placed upon the financing of large industrial enterprises and the main bank system, consonant with the purposes of this project. Issues include the Japanese experience in control over inflation and macroeconomic stability; the priority given to banking in financial intermediation; bank system safety; competition policy; ceiling interest rates and credit rationing; long-term directed credit for the fixed investment of priority industries; and information asymmetry, monitoring, and restructuring, in which the main banks specialize. Financial systems in many developing marketing economies and transforming socialist economies face three major practical problems: soft budgeting (whereby non-viable enterprises continue to receive loans and accumulate debts they cannot pay off); rent-seeking (corruption), both individual and institutional; and scarcity of human resources to carry out project evaluation, credit-worthiness analysis, and ongoing monitoring. He addresses these and other issues in arguing that the Japanese main bank system is a good model for other countries.

Given the analytical importance of the German model of universal banking, it is surprising that relatively little empirical research on the subject has appeared in English. Baums makes an important contribution in Chapter 12. The major German banks, particularly the Big Three, own significant shares in some, but by no means all, major German industrial corporations, and serve both as their commercial and investment bankers; however, major firms tend to rely predominantly on internal sources of funds. The banks can play a significant corporate governance role by controlling shareholder proxies and by serving on the company's outside Supervisory Board, but apparently are not involved in operating decisions of management. The Supervisory Board's function is to select top management and, if need be, replace it. The investment banking role, the control over proxies, the higher percentage of company share ownership allowed legally and put into practice, and the leadership role on the outside board (together with worker representatives) distinguish German banking from Japanese. Importantly, in Baums' evaluation the actual control exercised by the Big Three banks is considerably less than stereotypically depicted.

How Korea financed its extraordinarily successful economic development is an important topic in its own right. Korea has a financial structure in form rather similar to Japan. Moreover, in the mid-1970s it implemented a version of what might be considered an earlier form of the Japanese main bank system. However, the substance of government policies and, as a consequence, banking and business practices, have been very different. Put simply, the governmental authorities dominate the decisions concerning the allocation of bank loans to large industrial companies, which typically are organized into family-controlled, powerful business groups (*chaebol*); the banks are little more than instruments of credit control and information gathering for the government. Nam and Kim in Chapter 13 provide a new analysis of these patterns, with special emphasis on the government programme to designate specific banks as lead banks for each of the business groups. They make clear the still-limited role of the banks as autonomous allocators of credit and effective monitors in more than the information-gathering sense. Having made clear the differences between the Korean lead bank system and Japanese main bank system, they leave open the question of how the Korean banking system will evolve.

India represents a quite different case. The financial structure is somewhat similar to Japan, and there are three types of lead banks; however, banks are government owned, decision making has been rather bureaucratic, and coordination among commercial banks and long-term development banks has been weak. As Bhatt in Chapter 14 so well puts it: 'The lead banks have some of the characteristics of the main bank system in Japan; however, the institutional and policy framework has been quite different from that in Japan during 1950–70 and these differential characteristics in this framework in India seem to have affected adversely the functioning of the lead bank systems.' Bhatt describes and analyses the weaknesses and problems of banking in India, notes the 1991–92 deregulation and liberalization measures, and derives policy lessons based on the respective experiences of India and Japan.

Mexico is another story. Having nationalized the banks in 1982, the government since the late 1980s has deregulated interest rates and carried out other market-oriented financial reforms and, significantly, in 1991–92 sold the banks to business group holding companies with more diversified ownership and regional participation, while enacting new rules for prudential regulation and for conditions of monitoring, control and governance. Reynolds in Chapter 15 traces the process which led first to the decisions to nationalize the banks and then, as one important component of the Salinas government market-oriented economic reforms, to reprivatize. This new organization of Mexico's financial sector faces many of the same problems and opportunities as the Japanese main banking system. However, a commercial bank in Mexico is only one, albeit important, component of a business-controlled financial group, and it is too early to determine where within the group the monitoring, information-sharing, and control functions will be located. Reynolds clearly describes this rather complicated new structure and the safeguards built into it to prevent moral hazard, preferential access by insiders, and related potential problems, and explicitly notes similarities and differences with respect to the Japanese main bank system.

China is important both in its own right and as the outstanding case of economic reform to achieve a socialist market economy prior to fundamental political change. The transformation objectives as well as processes have been quite different from those in the former socialist East European and Soviet Union states. As economic reform has proceeded apace the economy has grown rapidly, and the role of markets increased substantially over the past decade. Qian persuasively argues in Chapter 16 that reform of China's commercial banking system, such as it is, should be at the core of China's financial restructuring, including the creation of various types of financial institutions analogous to the Japanese financial structure to fund local, smaller, non-state enterprises in what is a dynamic, fluid, rapidly changing economic environment. However, China first has to solve its deficit-ridden state enterprise soft-budgeting problem, since deficits are now covered by a continuation of fiscal budget deficits and specialized government bank policy loans. To be effective, commercial banking to finance (profitable) state enterprises has to be separated from policy lending, and appropriate incentives need to be created for bank managers. Japan's main bank system offers a good model, but in light of the proclivity to soft budgeting, it will be essential to develop a credible commitment *not* to rescue non-viable enterprises and bad projects.

The Poland case study by Hoshi, Kashyap, and Loveman (Chapter 17) is the most explicit of all the country studies in linking financial reform in Poland to Japan's experiences, especially in war-time and the early post-war period. While of course there are major differences, there are also important similarities in the problems Japan then faced (and solved) and Poland now faces: government control over the financial system, rapid inflation, a huge bad debt overhang plaguing enterprises and banks alike, and the need to shift the production structure from munitions to civilian goods. They argue that Poland has no viable alternative to a bank-based financial system, and that the Japanese main bank model of relationship banking, with its incentives for intensive monitoring involving information gathering and exchange, is preferable to the Anglo-American banking model. The Japanese post-war solution of separating old assets and liabilities from new ones on bank balance sheets, and dealing with the former by asset revaluations to market, write-downs, and cancellation of 'old' bank capital provides a useful guide as Poland, like the other transforming socialist economies, struggles with its bad debt problems. As Polish enterprises become economically viable, a new system of Polish banks will be able to take on the rescue or liquidation function when an enterprise is in distress, as in the Japanese main bank system. To achieve that will require the creation of credibility that henceforth banks will not bail out unviable firms (the soft-budget problem) and that the government will not force them to, together with the development of bank capacity to assess enterprise credit-worthiness and to engage efficiently in restructuring (or liquidation) efforts, and have the autonomy to make and impose its decisions.

These introductory paragraphs on each of the succeeding chapters only touch the surface of analyses and presentation of empirical evidence in what is a set of deeply and richly nuanced studies of great analytical and policy interest and relevance. We invite you to read further, carefully.

Masahiko Aoki
Hugh Patrick

PART I

THE JAPANESE MAIN
BANK SYSTEM

1

The Japanese Main Bank System: An Introductory Overview

MASAHIKO AOKI

HUGH PATRICK

PAUL SHEARD

'Main bank' is a practitioners' term used by financial institutions, corporations, and regulators, as in 'Bank X is the main bank of Firm Y' or 'Firm Y has Bank X as its main bank'. Although there is widespread agreement among practitioners regarding which banks and firms have a main bank relationship, there is no formal or legal definition of a main bank. The traditional academic definition is that a main bank relationship is a long-term relationship between a firm and a particular bank from which the firm obtains its largest share of borrowings. That definition is too restrictive. We regard the provision of bank credit as one of several aspects of the relationship between a main bank and the firm, although traditionally it has been a key one. Another important aspect is the role played by the main bank in corporate monitoring and governance. The main bank not only provides loans, it holds equity and, in the eyes of capital market participants and regulators, is expected to monitor the firm and intervene when things go wrong.

The term 'main bank system' as used in this book refers to *a system of corporate financing and governance* involving an informal set of practices, institutional arrangements, and behaviours among industrial and commercial firms, banks of various types, other financial institutions, and the regulatory authorities. At the core is the relationship between the main bank and the firm. This relationship has many aspects, the importance or intensity of which vary considerably both across firms and across time, and depending on circumstance for a given firm: these include reciprocal shareholdings, the supply of management resources and the dispatch of directors, and the provision of various financial services, notably loans and other credits, trustee administration, guarantee and, recently, underwriting of bond issues, operation of payment settlement accounts, foreign exchange dealings, and investment banking and advisory services relating to the issue of securities and to corporate acquisitions and divestments.

The authors thank Theodor Baums, Jenny Corbett, Koichi Hamada, Takeo Hoshi, Anil Kashyap, Frank Packer, Dimitri Vittas and other participants in project workshops for helpful comments on earlier drafts. We also thank competent research assistance received from Ayako Yasuda and Nariyasu Yamazawa at Stanford University.

But also important in shaping the system are the relationships between the main bank and the firm's other financiers, between the latter and the firm, and between the regulatory authorities and all of these actors, but particularly the main banks.

What we conceive of as the main bank system had its genesis in the period spanning the build-up to, and aftermath of, World War II, and it continues as an integral part of the Japanese financial system and industrial organization to the present time. As would be expected in light of the startling developments and immense changes that have occurred in the Japanese economy over the post-war period, the main bank system has evolved in a dynamic fashion, and has had to adapt in response to both endogenous changes in corporate behaviour and to more exogenous changes in the regulatory and economic environment. The period that roughly corresponds to the high-growth era from the early 1950s to the early 1970s can be seen as the heyday of the main bank system. This is the period when firms were growing rapidly and were hungry for investment funds, and when financial markets were heavily regulated. Having a good main bank relationship with one of the major banks, or, if a smaller firm, with one of the regional banks, was the cornerstone of corporate financial strategy, and was virtually essential for corporate success.

Since the mid-1970s, the foundations of the main bank system as it operated in the regulated high-growth era have been shaken, as financial markets and international capital transactions have been slowly but surely deregulated and as the investment and external financing needs and capabilities of large corporations have undergone dramatic shifts. The 1980s saw: wide variation emerging in firms' demands for investment funds and levels of internal funds; firms developing and experimenting with increasingly sophisticated treasury functions; a dramatic shift in corporate finance as firms turned from bank borrowings to issuance of market securities, often through overseas (Euro) markets; and a shift in the direction of bank lending as the banks became caught up in, and indeed helped to fuel, a dramatic rise in equity and asset values (the so-called bubble economy) to 1990.

If the main bank system was only or mainly a bank-firm lending arrangement, these changes might have signalled the beginning of its breakdown; and the longer sweep of history may still judge this to be so. But the main bank plays a wider role in corporate financing than just lending. The main bank system is central to the way in which corporate oversight and governance is exercised in the Japanese capital market, aspects which have been brought into even sharper focus by the events of the 1980s and early 1990s. All capital markets require institutional mechanisms for monitoring and evaluating the performance of corporate managements, to which stewardship over the savings and assets of countless individuals in the economy has been entrusted. Capital markets also require the capacity to intervene, if need be, to effect changes in the way corporate assets are utilized and managed and to bring poorly performing managers to account, such a possibility serving as a useful check on managerial discretion. In post-war Japan, the main bank system has been the main pillar of corporate monitoring and governance, compensating for the lack of more arm's-length market-oriented means such as the take-over mechanism, and probably obviating a need for them to develop. It is yet to be seen whether this aspect of the main bank system has been significantly eroded in the recent development of financial markets mentioned above. In spite of the increasing securitization of corporate financing, the core of reciprocal stockholding between the financial institutions and firms remains stable and there is no sign of the development of an active take-over mechanism. The financial system, regarded not as a simple intermediary of the flow of funds but as a complex system of financing *and* monitoring, may be more robust in periods of change because of its interdependencies with other institutional elements of the economy.

The purpose of this chapter is to provide a common conceptual framework and context for the chapters that follow. The first section identifies the major characteristics of the main bank system and analyses how it operates as a nexus of relationships among firms, financiers, and regulators. In the second section, the context of the main bank system is examined in two respects: where the Japanese main bank system fits into a typology of financial systems and how the main bank system has been shaped by the historical development of the Japanese financial system.

THE MAIN BANK SYSTEM AS A NEXUS OF RELATIONSHIPS

In this section, we characterize the main bank system not just as a system of industrial financing based on bank lending, but as one involving a nexus of relationships comprising three elements: (1) a multitude of financial, informational, and managerial relationships observed between the typical Japanese firm and its partner bank; (2) a unique reciprocal relationship among major banks; and (3) relationships between the regulatory authorities—the Ministry of Finance (MOF) and the Bank of Japan (BOJ)—and the banking industry. (This section relies heavily upon results of joint research undertaken by Aoki and Sheard 1992.)

Matrix Representation of Main Bank-Firm Relationships

Almost every Japanese company has what it calls a main bank relationship—both large companies and small—according to a survey of some 110,000 companies with annual sales of ¥1 billion or more (about $1 billion) (Shukan Daiyamondo, 1987). Similarly, virtually every Japanese bank, large or small, serves as the main bank to some degree for at least some companies. However, the strongest main bank relationships, and the central focus of this book, is on the relationships between large firms and large banks.

Conceptually, main bank relationships should be distinguished from the loose forms of corporate groupings of large firms that have attracted attention in the literature and in US-Japan policy debates. These corporate forms, known as *kigyo shudan* (enterprise group) or financial *keiretsu* (affiliated group), are groups of major corporations from diverse industrial, commercial and financial sectors, connected by interlocking shareholdings, a common main bank relationship, a certain degree of (reciprocal) business transactions, and at least for core firms, common membership in a presidents' club. (See Aoki, 1988, chapters 3.1 and 6.2; and Gerlach, 1992, for descriptions of the institutional features and functions of enterprise groups (financial keiretsu).)

While the member firms of enterprise groupings have the affiliated city bank in the same group as their main bank, even those firms not affiliated with any grouping, including firms of smaller size, normally maintain a main bank relationship with one of the principal commercial banks. They may be either city banks of the Big Six groupings (Dai-ichi Kangyo Bank, Fuji Bank, Mitsubishi Bank, Sakura Bank, Sanwa Bank, Sumitomo Bank), long-term credit banks (particularly the Industrial Bank of Japan), less significant city banks (Daiwa Bank, Tokai Bank, Tokyo Bank, Asahi Bank, Hokkaido Takushoku Bank), or smaller regional banks in the case of regionally based listed firms and small or medium firms. There is no legal definition of city banks. They are customarily understood to be those commercial banks having headquarters in a major metropolitan area and a nation-wide network of branches. See Table 1.5 below for historical changes in city bank membership. In a small but not negligible subset of cases, a firm purposefully maintains a main bank relationship with two or three banks, as shown by the fact that the banks are allocated precisely the same loan balances (and loan share) and usually have the same (or close to the same) shareholding.

A common approach has been to define the main bank as the bank that has the largest share of loans to the firm, assuming that this position is relatively stable over time. Focusing exclusively on the loan relationship, however, can be misleading and at best captures only one aspect of the main bank relationship. It is not rare for a firm to borrow more from a trust bank or a long-term credit bank than from the bank that would be regarded among practitioners (including the firm itself) as the firm's main bank. This can happen when the group affiliated trust bank provides significant loan volume but does not assume the main bank role, or when special project term finance is involved. A more troublesome fact is that a definition based on loan shares does not apply to the recently growing number of firms that do not have any bank borrowings. Many such firms can still be characterized as having a main bank relationship or at least as operating within the purview of the main bank system.

We introduce a comprehensive way of characterizing main bank relationships by identifying five important aspects of the relations between a firm and its main bank, the importance or intensity of which may differ contingent on the financial state and life-cycle stage of firms at a given point in time. The central idea of main bank relations being multi-faceted and as implicitly defining a wealth-contingent corporate governance system is summarized in Figure 1. We first discuss the five main dimensions of the main bank relationship, and then consider how the relationship in each dimension is affected by the financial state of the client firm.

		Financial State of the Firm			
		Excellent	Favourable	Normal	Critical
	α		(•)	•	◉
Nature of	β	(•)	•		
Main Bank	γ	•	•	•	•
Relations	δ	•	•	•	•
	ε	(•)	(•)	•	◉

α : Bank loans

β : Bond issue related services (trustee administrator in the case of domestic issues and co-lead management in the case of Euro issues)

γ : Shareholding

δ : Payment settlement accounts

ε : The supply of management information and resources

• : -- indicates this role performed in this financial state

◉: -- indicates this role performed strongly in this financial state

(•): -- indicates this role performed weakly in this financial state

Fig. 1.1 The Matrix Representation of Main Bank Relations

Bank Loans (α)

Bank loans have been and continue to be the dominant source of external financing for the non-financial corporate sector, as shown in Table 1.1. Throughout the period until 1986, borrowings from private financing institutions—city banks, regional banks, long-term credit banks, trust banks, credit associations and cooperatives, and insurance companies— comprised more than 70 per cent (slightly below that level in 1978 and

1979) of total external sources of funds for the non-financial corporate sector. After a decline during the late 1980s asset bubble, the dependence on borrowed funds, including those from public financing institutions— the Japan Development Bank, the Export-Import Bank of Japan, various public finance institutions for small businesses—increased again to more than the 70 per cent level in the early 1990s. Borrowed funds persist as the core of corporate financing in Japan.

When the firm borrows, the main bank typically provides the largest single proportion of the firm's borrowing (from private financial institutions). The main bank to large listed firms is normally one of the city banks or the Industrial Bank of Japan. Table 1.2 provides data on the share of loans for the 991 manufacturing firms listed on the stock exchange between 1977 and 1991, assuming that the main bank is identifiable with a city bank with the largest loan share. The main bank typically supplies both short-term and long-term loans, its share in total lending amounting to around 15 per cent. On average, the firm may have secured a significant fraction of long-term investment loans from other sources, notably long-term credit banks, trust banks, and insurance companies. Having the largest share of short-term loans, rather than the size of the overall loan share, is thought to be the hallmark of the main bank, as this is what defines its pivotal oversight role in the ongoing financing of the firm and at times its ability to obtain and exercise leverage over the firm's operations and management. Over the 1977–91 period, the main bank provided about 20 per cent of all short-term loans and about 40 per cent of the short-term loans provided by city banks.

The main bank monitors its client quite intensively, both on its own behalf and for the other lenders, thus avoiding costly duplication of monitoring costs. While this delegation of monitoring often occurred through formal loan consortia in the early post-war period, it gradually became more informal and tacit. One may say that currently the main bank in each case leads a *de facto* loan consortium (see Chapter 8 by Horiuchi).

Bond-Issue Related Services (β)

The main bank plays an important role in domestic and international bond issues. When a firm issues bonds in the domestic market, the main bank performs legally required trustee administration (*jutaku gyomu*) for bond holders. Data on 109 cases of domestic convertible bond issues in the six-month period from October 1988 through March 1989 show that the main bank was the number one trustee in 84 cases (77 per cent) and number one, two or three in 105 cases (96 per cent). City banks were not allowed to underwrite bonds prior to April 1993, when rules were changed to allow eventual entry. Trustee administration involves the assessment and custody of collateral, and, when necessary, calling, chairing and setting the agenda of the creditors' meeting. The position of the

TABLE 1.1 External Funding Sources of the Non-Financial Corporate Sector: 1965–92

(billion yen)

| | Total | Equity | Bonds | | Borrowing | | | Foreign Debt |
			Domestic	Overseas	Private Institutions	Public Institutions	Commercial Paper	
1970	11191	980	346	10	8617	805		4310
1971	16068	842	642	−4	12485	908		1189
1972	17998	1206	354	−27	15193	845		427
1973	16914	1185	779	−37	13591	1447		−52
1974	15891	831	541	29	11558	1482		1147
1975	16855	1161	1287	325	12827	1923		−670
1976	17163	934	661	298	13248	1639		380
1977	13259	1079	647	144	10256	1646		−514
1978	12933	1148	747	142	8724	1340		830
1979	13596	1368	901	396	8338	1962		628
1980	18313	1440	563	214	13359	1939		7602
1981	21159	2112	1050	299	16289	2578		−1175
1982	23122	2045	632	892	17279	2280		7
1983	22664	1564	298	1286	17903	1585		27
1984	25411	2229	857	1420	19953	1329		−379
1985	29772	2017	681	2346	22997	1010		739
1986	33415	2205	1579	2587	26285	553		202
1987	42675	4124	2364	3760	25772	1955		2999
1988	54193	5225	1607	4282	30112	3863	7587	1513
1989	72971	10124	1463	9513	37797	6515	3780	3777
1990	66740	4438	3130	3768	39031	6739	2696	6934
1991	38319	1277	3633	6516	23938	6365	3362	−95
1992								
1–3	2765	207	911	588	−24	558	−2690	1745
4–6	3722	53	1277	66	−312	66	−238	−168
7–9	10614	154	1157	−667	6637	−667	359	17

Source: Bank of Japan, flow of funds data.

TABLE 1.2 Loans Shares of Financial Institutions to Listed Firms in Manufacturing

(per cents)

Fiscal Year	Long-Term Credit Banks	City Banks	(Main Bank)	Trust Banks	Regional Banks	Life Insurers	Others
LONG-TERM LOANS							
77	19.9	11.7	6.0	22.8	1.3	15.1	29.2
78	20.3	11.6	6.0	22.8	1.3	15.0	29.0
79	20.3	11.6	6.0	22.4	1.2	14.8	29.6
80	20.1	12.1	6.2	22.0	1.2	14.9	29.7
81	20.0	13.3	6.7	21.7	1.3	14.5	29.3
82	20.0	13.8	6.8	21.1	1.4	14.2	29.4
83	19.9	13.9	6.9	20.7	1.5	13.9	30.1
84	20.1	14.3	7.0	19.8	1.8	13.4	30.7
85	19.8	14.3	7.1	19.6	2.1	13.0	31.2
86	19.8	16.6	8.0	19.3	2.5	12.8	29.0
87	21.4	17.2	8.6	19.1	2.5	12.6	27.2
88	21.4	17.5	9.1	18.3	2.5	12.8	27.4
89	21.9	18.6	9.6	16.5	2.6	12.8	27.7
90	20.6	18.9	10.3	15.5	2.9	15.1	27.0
91	19.0	17.4	9.5	14.9	2.8	18.8	27.1
SHORT-TERM LOANS							
77	4.7	60.0	24.2	5.2	13.6	0.3	16.2
78	5.5	59.0	24.0	5.7	13.4	0.4	16.0
79	6.4	59.5	23.6	6.3	13.1	0.4	14.3
80	6.3	58.7	23.1	6.4	13.2	0.3	15.1
81	6.2	57.1	22.4	6.4	13.5	0.2	16.5
82	6.5	55.5	21.9	7.0	14.3	0.3	16.4
83	6.9	53.5	21.1	7.5	14.8	0.4	16.8

84	7.5	52.5	21.2	8.1	15.0	0.5	16.5
85	8.1	52.4	21.3	8.8	14.6	0.5	15.6
86	9.2	51.5	20.9	9.2	14.0	0.5	15.7
87	9.1	50.5	20.4	9.4	14.0	0.5	16.5
88	8.9	49.1	20.0	9.3	14.0	0.5	18.1
89	9.2	49.8	20.3	10.0	13.6	0.7	16.7
90	8.7	46.4	19.5	9.4	13.1	0.8	21.6
91	7.3	46.5	19.5	8.9	14.0	0.8	22.5
TOTAL							
77	14.5	28.9	12.5	16.5	5.7	9.8	24.6
78	14.7	29.5	12.8	16.3	5.9	9.5	24.0
79	14.5	31.5	13.3	15.7	6.2	8.8	23.2
80	14.2	31.9	13.3	15.4	6.3	8.7	23.5
81	14.0	32.4	13.5	15.0	6.7	8.2	23.7
82	13.9	32.7	13.6	14.7	7.2	7.9	23.5
83	13.7	32.7	13.6	14.4	7.8	7.5	23.8
84	13.6	33.8	14.2	13.8	8.5	6.8	23.4
85	13.4	35.2	14.8	13.7	9.0	6.1	22.6
86	13.7	36.5	15.3	13.7	9.1	5.7	21.4
87	14.0	37.4	15.6	13.3	9.4	5.3	20.7
88	13.7	37.0	15.7	12.8	9.6	5.2	21.7
89	14.0	37.9	16.1	12.5	9.4	5.3	20.9
90	13.2	36.0	15.8	11.7	9.2	6.2	23.7
91	12.3	34.2	15.0	11.4	9.2	8.4	24.4

Main Bank = the city bank with the largest loan share at each firm. The table covers 991 firms.

Source: Data are from NEEDS (Nikkei, Economic Electronic Databank System).

main bank as the bond issue administrator means it is able to earn significant income in fees. These are 0.13 to 0.25 per cent of face value initially and 0.05 to 0.25 per cent annually until maturity (depending on rating, size of issue, and whether or not there is collateral). In major cases of bankruptcy of listed firms, it has been customary for the trustee banks (main banks) to purchase outstanding bonds at face value.

The main bank purchases a considerable proportion of the domestic bonds issued by client firms, whether domestic or overseas bonds. Table 1.3 shows the bank holdings of domestic bonds issued by non-financial corporations. Banks held more than 50 per cent of domestic bonds outstanding up to 1970 when domestic bond issues were limited to a relatively small number of large corporations such as electric power companies. Since then the relative share of banks in total holdings declined steadily up to 1987, while trust accounts, insurance companies, and the Trust Department of the Ministry of Finance (managing funds from postal savings and public pension plans) increased their shares remarkably in the 1980s. At the end of March 1992, the value of outstanding domestic corporate bonds was 46.9 trillion yen, with banks holding 14.3 per cent, up from their 10.3 per cent share in 1986.

The main bank plays an important role also in the case of overseas bond issues (straight bonds, convertible bonds, warrant bonds), which have been steadily increasing since the beginning of the 1980s (see Table 1.1: equity financing in the table includes convertible and warrant bond issues). In the beginning of the 1980s, a large proportion of overseas issues were guaranteed by main banks (see Chapter 10 by Campbell and Hamao). Unlike the case of domestic public bond issues, the main bank is able to act as co-manager of the bond issue through its overseas subsidiaries, although it has been administratively guided by a 1975 agreement among the Banking, Securities, and International Finance Bureaux of the MOF not to act as a lead manager. Data on 84 cases of overseas dollar warrant bond issues by Japanese firms between October 1988 and March 1989 show there were 5.3 co-managers per issue and the firm's principal transacting bank was involved as a co-manager in 71 cases (84.5 per cent). As well as commission income on the bond issue, the main bank earns fees on the associated foreign exchange transactions. In 1988, 33 per cent of operating profits of city banks came from their international divisions, largely reflecting these kinds of transactions; the corresponding figure for regional banks was 12 per cent.

Stockholding (γ)

The main bank maintains a substantial stockholding in the firms to which it acts as main bank, usually at, or close to, the level permissible by law. The Japanese Anti-Monopoly Law allows banks to hold up to 5 per cent of a firm's stock (prior to 1987 up to 10 per cent) on their own account.

TABLE 1.3 Bank Holdings of Domestic Corporate Bonds

Fiscal Year	Absolute Value (trillion yen)	Relative Share (%)
53	0.1	74.7
54	0.2	75.7
55	0.2	73.8
56	0.2	68.0
57	0.2	69.0
58	0.3	68.9
59	0.4	67.0
60	0.5	53.8
61	0.6	52.7
62	0.7	52.6
63	0.7	52.5
64	0.8	51.5
65	1.0	56.5
66	1.1	56.4
67	1.2	55.7
68	1.4	55.7
69	1.5	54.6
70	1.6	51.2
71	1.7	46.0
72	1.7	41.0
73	1.8	36.9
74	1.9	33.9
75	2.1	30.9
76	2.0	26.5
77	1.9	23.0
78	1.8	20.7
79	1.9	19.6
80	2.0	19.4
81	2.1	18.6
82	2.0	16.5
83	1.8	14.4
84	1.7	12.6
85	2.0	11.0
86	2.1	10.3
87	5.0	14.7
88	5.3	14.2
89	5.4	13.3
90	5.8	13.6
91	6.7	14.3

Bank of Japan, flow of funds data.

The main bank usually is in the top five shareholders of the firm and is normally the top shareholder among banks. According to interview evidence, special significance in the minds of practitioners attaches to the top shareholding position among banks (other than trust banks). The main bank, in all but exceptional cases, is the top shareholder among banks, although it is not necessarily the top shareholder or even the top shareholder among financial institutions, because insurance companies, manufacturing companies, and individuals associated with a founding or controlling family (directly or through a non-listed firm) often occupy top shareholding positions.

Sheard (1989, p. 402) reports that the main bank, defined as the bank with the largest loan share, was one of the top five shareholders in 72 per cent of cases for firms listed on the first section of the Tokyo Stock Exchange in 1980, and that in only 11 per cent of cases was the main bank not among the top 20 shareholders.

The main bank seldom sells its shares in the market unless it abandons its main bank position. Although the bank's holding is limited to 5 per cent of the stock, the main bank can possibly mobilize, if necessary, shareholdings by the group-affiliated trust bank, insurance company, trading company, and other firms for concerted voting; its potential voting power in case of emergency, as well as its ability to protect a customer firm from hostile take-over, is significant. (On the economic role of cross shareholding in Japan, see Sheard, 1991a, 1994b.)

Payment Settlement Accounts (δ)

Firms operate non-interest bearing payment settlement accounts (*toza yokin* or *kessai koza*) with commercial banks for the purpose of managing cash-flow receipts and payments, in particular the settling of payment of cheques and promissory bills (*yakusoku tegata*), the principal method of payment for inter-firm transactions in Japan. When a firm issues a promissory bill to its suppliers (normally of three months' duration) it typically designates its main bank as the major bank of settlement for its bill. More generally, firms tend to concentrate their cash flow transactions in the settlement account with the main bank.[1]

By observing the movement of payments into and out of those settlement accounts on a daily basis through computer-based channels, the main bank can keep track of changes in the financial position of client firms. This function provides the main bank with an extremely advantageous position in terms of information which no other financial institu-

---

[1] Horiuchi and Murakami (1991, p. 96) provide some survey evidence on this point from a survey of listed and unlisted firms eliciting 457 responses. They found firms in their sample did business with an average of 16.7 banks and used an average of 6.5 for everyday settlement functions. Interviews with bank managers suggest that the degree of concentration on the main bank or banks is quite high, but clear-cut empirical evidence is difficult to acquire.

tion can enjoy. This is probably one of the principal reasons why it is normally city banks (or local banks for smaller firms) that can act as main banks. The main bank also handles a large proportion of foreign exchange business and other banking business of its client firms. The expectation of being able to garner a disproportionate share of various banking business (relative to loan share) constitutes one of the principal benefits of being a main bank.

Information Services and Supply of Management Resources (ε)

The main bank provides various valuable information and investment banking services to its client firms, for instance relating to the acquisition or liquidation of business assets and real estate, or the introduction of potential business partners, often followed by the requisite loan arrangements. The main bank often has its managers sit as directors or auditors on the board of client firms and sends its (mid-career) employees as permanent managers of client firms.[2]

One characteristic of the corporate governance structure of the Japanese firm is that the board of directors is mainly composed of incumbent managers and, in the normal course of affairs, functions as a *de facto* substructure of top executive management. Incumbent managers are, broadly, of two kinds, insiders or so-called life-time employees of the firm who have risen to top management positions through internal promotional hierarchies and outsiders, ex-employees of other organizations (such as banks, affiliated companies, or government ministries and agencies) who have entered the firm usually at board level, mid-career or late in their career. A third category comprises truly outside directors who serve on the board concurrently, frequently in the capacity of auditor, that is, while holding a regular position elsewhere. Managerial ties of this form, through incumbent managers or concurrently serving directors, are extensively used by main banks.

In 1992, about one quarter (24.4 per cent) of the 40,045 directors of listed Japanese firms were from outside the firm. Of these about one-fifth (21.7 per cent, or just over 5 per cent of all directors) were from banks (*Kigyo Keiretsu Soran*, 1992, p. 86). The banks forming the core of the main bank system—the largest six or seven city banks and the Industrial Bank of Japan—were the main sources of bank directors. Dispatching

---

[2] Under Japanese corporate law, auditors (*kansayaku*) have a wide range of authority, including certifying the validity of accounts, but they cannot interfere with the directors' discretionary decisions. However, in order to prevent the board of directors from making an illegal or seriously unjust decision, auditors have a right to attend board meetings and to have their opinions heard. When they find serious wrongdoing by directors, the auditors can initiate a derivative suit for injunction without putting up security against expenses incurred. In practice, however, auditors are generally seen as being part of, or close to, incumbent management. See Aoki (1984, chapter 11) for a detailed institutional description of the corporate governance structure in Japan.

financial institutions had an average loan share of 21 per cent and average loan rank of 1.95, and average shareholding of 4.6 per cent and average shareholding rank of 3.3 (Sheard, 1994b).

Close management relationships (ϵ) often accompany long-term credit relationships (α). Bank employees on the management track normally terminate their career within the promotional hierarchy of the original employer at a relatively early age, often before age 50, at the bank's discretion, unless they are elite managers selected for promotion to the board. Their employment contracts are switched to the main bank's client firms by agreement between those firms and the main bank, either after they are first dispatched (*shukko*) to those firms for a certain period of time or immediately upon induced early retirement from the main bank. This practice was prevalent even with the largest firms before the mid-1970s when they were more dependent upon bank loans and the bank's bargaining power was relatively stronger, but now seems to involve mainly firms of less than excellent financial states.[3]

The transfer in mid-career of managers from the main bank to its customer firms helps to strengthen the bond between a firm and its main bank and has the equalizing effect of transferring management know-how in the absence of a competitive market for managerial talent. Also, the bank's screening and selection of managers for eventual out-placing has a strong motivational impact on its permanent employees (see Chapter 9 by Sunamura). In this regard, note that the personnel managers of the bank possess strong internal controlling power, and many top executives of city banks rotate through the personnel department in their career. (See Aoki, 1988, chapter 3, for the role of the personnel department in the exercise of internal control in the Japanese firm more generally.

State-Contingent Nature of Relationships

A key conceptual point associated with the characterization in Figure 1.1 is the state-contingent aspect of the main bank's role in the firm's financing, management, and corporate governance. The settlement account and stockholding relations are present in any main bank relationship. How the other main bank functions are combined in the precise relationship between a particular firm and its main bank is contingent upon the firm's financial position. Firms with an *excellent* financial position—E firms—with ample accumulated reserves and surplus funds for investment outside may limit their relationships with the main bank to occasional bond

---

[3] According to a survey by Horiuchi and Murakami (1991, p. 113), about 40 per cent of 457 responding firms stated that their main source of externally hired managers of department head (*bucho*) rank or above was from main banks. Compared with five years before, however, more large firms had decreased their reliance upon the main bank for mid-career managerial employees than increased it (net difference of 3.3 per cent), while more small and medium firms had increased their reliance than decreased it (net difference of 9.4 per cent).

issue services (γ) and payment settlement account (δ), and possibly a (perhaps) symbolic supply of auditor-directors (ε). Matsushita Electric, a representative firm in this category, maintains a main bank relationship with Sumitomo Bank, which holds 4.7 per cent of its stock as the largest shareholder and has a (concurrent) director on its board. In this category, bargaining power is decisively in favour of the firm and the banks compete for possible main bank positions.

By having main bank relationships with E-firms, banks can gain access to profitable business associated with the firm's supplier and dealer networks. It may happen that, reflecting this stronger bargaining power, firms in this category have more than one main bank. For example, Toyota maintains a close main bank relationship with three banks, Sakura Bank, Tokai Bank and Sanwa Bank, although Toyota is conventionally classified as a member of the Mitsui group whose core financial institution is Sakura Bank. These three banks are Toyota's largest shareholders, each holding the maximum possible 5 per cent of stock. As of 1988, two of them had a representative on the board in the capacity of (concurrently serving) auditor.

Firms with a *favourable* financial position—F firms—may require external financing from time to time for funding investment but are able to raise most of this from domestic or overseas securities markets at cheaper capital costs, and like excellent firms they may have little or no sustained long-term bank borrowing. But, in combining all the other relations, the main bank is expected to perform a major monitoring role for bondholders and stockholders. The main bank functions as a gate-keeper for the firm's entry into bond markets, itself frequently holding a large proportion of the issued bonds, and earns substantial income by serving as trustee or manager for mediating bond issues as described above.

Next come firms of a *normal* financial position—N firms—which do not have sufficient internal funds for financing investment and make extensive use of bank borrowing. The main bank plays a leading role in the provision of loan contracts, although its loan share is not overwhelming, and its lending is combined with a non-negligible equity stake and close role in settlements' management. This is the case that historically has been perceived to characterize Japanese corporate finance, which is thought, somewhat misleadingly, to be fading away. In fact, many Japanese firms, some large ones and most smaller ones, are still classified in this category. At the end of fiscal 1990, 63 per cent of listed manufacturing firms were in this category.

At the lowest end of the financial spectrum are those firms in a *critical* position—C firms—which require an additional infusion of funds for continuing operations. The unique position of the main bank in the corporate governance structure manifests itself for firms in this category. The main bank is in a unique business and legal position to influence decisively the fate of the firm in its combined capacities of major stock-holder, creditor, and trustee for bondholders. For firms in this category, the main bank has three options. It may abandon the position of main bank by withdrawing all or part of potentially bad loans before other creditors become aware of the problem, exploiting if it can the advantage conferred upon it by its unique informational position; it may rescue the troubled firm by *ex post* supply of refinancing; or it may decide to bring the case to the court-led bankruptcy procedure of private liquidation by refusing additional financing (see Chapter 6 by Sheard).

Main banks on occasion resort to the first option, specifically *vis-à-vis* smaller firms, but it is likely to cause damage to their reputation as a reliable main bank. Because other creditors are aware of the main bank's incentives, and the main bank's loans can only be recovered at their (or new creditors') expense, in practice the scope for this opportunistic behaviour is quite limited. In the second case, the main bank normally takes over management of a failed firm, sometimes after fierce resistance from incumbent management, and deep main bank involvement (relation ϵ) appears in its strongest form. This option is often quite costly for the main bank because, in leading the rescue operation, the main bank normally bears more than proportionate costs of refinancing, writing off bad loans, and so on, relative to its original loan share, and it sometimes assumes bad loans by other lenders. The main bank may be able to avoid additional costs necessary for rescue operations by simply liquidating a defaulting firm. But doing so is a double-edged sword. The main bank may face fierce resistance from employees who fear the loss of jobs (employment continuation value), and possibly from trade creditors as well, and it loses control over the reorganization process. Particularly if the main bank prematurely liquidates a firm that may have a chance of revival, the main bank may not only lose possible future returns from its recovery, but also may depreciate its own reputational capital.

The rescuing aspect of a main bank's intervention in C-firms has been emphasized in the literature as unique to the Japanese banking system. As discussed in later chapters (especially Chapter 4 by Aoki) it is an institutional arrangement complementary to the system of permanent employment. That is, the rescue of financially depressed firms helps to preserve the firm-specific human assets accumulated in the framework of the lifetime employment system and hence provides incentives for them to be generated in the first place. However, as noted above, the rescue operation is normally accompanied by the take-over of failed management by the main bank. In that respect, the main bank system provides a mechanism for disciplining poor management in the absence of a more active market for corporate control. However, the main bank's intervention or take-over is triggered only when firms are in a critically distressed financial state.

Maintenance of a main bank relationship is important even for E-firms because it helps them to remain largely free from external interventions and monitoring, given the strategic place occupied by the main bank in the network of interlocking stable shareholdings. Thus the main bank system involves a unique contingent corporate governance system in which management control shifts between internal management and the main bank, depending on the financial state of the firm.

Further Extensions

The matrix characterization presented above is, for expository purposes, stylized and over-simplified. Three further dimensions may be added here, however, to capture better the rich detail of the real world.

One is to introduce a more explicit time dimension to allow the whole matrix of main bank-firm relations to be related to the life-cycle of firms and to distinguish between large and smaller firms. The discussion so far has focused on large, listed firms, but main bank relations extend in some form to smaller non-listed firms. While an analogous form of multi-dimensional, state-contingent main bank relationship may exist, its substance differs according to whether the firm is a large well-established listed one or a smaller non-listed one. For smaller firms, the distinction between various financial states may be less relevant. Not having access to public stock and bond markets and, if growing rapidly, needing external funds, most smaller firms will rely heavily on bank borrowing and so will look like normal firms (but with less bond issue) in terms of Figure 1.1. The main bank usually plays less of a rescue-cum-intervention role for small firms in critical states, and apparently feels less of a responsibility to do so. Failing small firms are more likely to be marginal ones in their markets, and the assets at stake more easily deployable in secondary asset and labour markets. It is rational for the bank to allocate its scarce stock of managerial resources, which it has trained to deal with informal corporate reorganizations of projects (failing firms), where the benefit is largest; in general, these will be large listed firms where, although the loan share may appear modest, its absolute magnitude is very large. Horiuchi deals with the comparison of main bank relationships by firm size in more detail in Chapter 8.

A second extension, focusing on large listed firms, considers the ownership characteristics of the firm. The kind of monitoring the main bank will want and be able to carry out may depend on whether there is a large corporate shareholder, that is, whether the firm is an affiliate or subsidiary of another listed firm, whether there is an inside owner-manager, that is, dominating or residual family control over the firm's management, or whether the firm is managerial in the sense that incumbent management comprises professional career managers. At least 10 and perhaps as much as 20 per cent of all listed firms in Japan have founding-family or related figures in senior management and top share-holding positions. Although these inside-owners usually control substantially less than a majority of shares, they are often quite entrenched under normal circumstances. In at least a quarter of cases, the largest share-holder of listed firms is another listed firm, and in at least half of these cases that firm has a shareholding of 20 per cent or more.

The state-contingent role of the main bank depends on the kind of firm. Where there is virtually complete separation of ownership and control and dispersed shareholding, the role of the main bank in corporate governance is likely to be most important and prototypical. If there is a large parent firm, the primary role of the main bank in corporate governance may be overshadowed; for example, in critical states the parent company is likely to play the leading pro-active role, with the main bank's role being facilitating and secondary, unless the parent firm's own financial position is seriously threatened. (For case-study evidence on the existence of such a hierarchy of contingent roles, responsibilities, and risk-sharing, see Sheard, 1991b; for econometric evidence see Kaplan and Minton, 1994.)

With owner-managed firms, the nature of the main bank's monitoring, and its capacity to influence the firm's actions, must be sensitive to idiosyncratic features such as the history and degree of trust in the relationship, personality and ability of the owners.

The third extension of the matrix characterization is to introduce a more explicit time frame. Although the characterization is robust enough to cover the period from 1951 to the present, the relative distribution of firms among different categories has been changing over time. In the period from 1951 to 1975, the heyday of the main bank relationship, less than 2 per cent of listed firms were in the E category incurring no debt (except for trade debits), around 15 per cent of listed firms were in the F category issuing some bond debts, while the majority of the listed firms (some 80 per cent) were in the N category (see Figure 1.2), dependent only upon bank loans (the high proportion of F category on an asset-weighted basis is due mainly to the regulated public utility industry, which was allowed to make frequent bond issues). But after the deregulation and internationalization of bond markets starting in 1975, the composition gradually changed. At the end of March 1989, in the middle of the bubble, as many as 8 per cent of listed firms relied only upon equity financing and about 30 per cent of listed firms raised some or all of their funds from bond markets. However, still about 62 per cent of listed firms were in the N or C category, dependent upon the traditional lending role of the main banks.

Firms in the E and the upper F categories have recently come to diversify their bank relationships, specifically payment settlement accounts (δ), bank shareholdings (γ), and investment banking related services (ϵ),

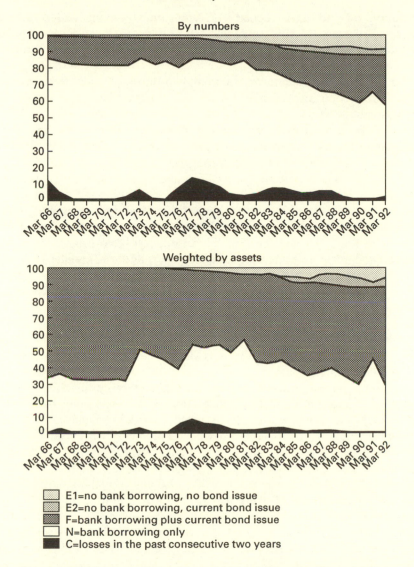

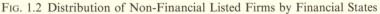

E1=no bank borrowing, no bond issue
E2=no bank borrowing, current bond issue
F=bank borrowing plus current bond issue
N=bank borrowing only
C=losses in the past consecutive two years

FIG. 1.2 Distribution of Non-Financial Listed Firms by Financial States

among several city banks to strengthen their bargaining power. These quasi-main bank relationships are now often referred to by practitioners as multiple core bank relationships. Particularly due to the diversification of payment settlement accounts and increasing marketization of derivative assets, the monitoring capacity of city banks *vis-à-vis* firms of E or F category has clearly declined. But it is certainly premature to see this trend as portending the demise of the main bank system. With the relaxation of traditional regulations segregating banking and securities business domains, the city banks will try to maintain relations with firms by extending their services to underwriting domestic bond issues through their securities subsidiaries.[4]

For firms in the N category, almost two-thirds of listed firms and a larger proportion of unlisted firms, the matrix characterization still remains valid.

It is difficult to distinguish two hypotheses about E firms: one, that they have outgrown or graduated from the main bank system; or two, that while achieving considerable managerial autonomy, they continue to operate in the more broadly conceived main bank (contingent corporate governance) system. One clue is obtained by examining the behaviour of E firms when they need to borrow again because of binding liquidity constraints due to deteriorating economic performance or increased need for investment funds. During the 1965–91 period, 200 listed firms were in the position of having no borrowing at some point; of these, 66 later resumed bank borrowing. Four firms even fell into the C firm category, making losses in two consecutive years. Of the 75 cases where the 66 firms resumed bank borrowing after not borrowing for one or more periods, there were only 10 in which the main bank position, defined as the largest city bank lender, changed (Table 1.4). This indicates that firms maintained stable main bank relationships during periods when they were in an excellent financial state.

To obtain further evidence, we analysed the stability of the top bank shareholder position of all listed firms that do not have any bank borrowings. In 1986, of the 1,724 firms listed on stock exchanges in Japan (excluding banks and property insurance companies), 132 firms (7.7 per cent) were identified as having zero bank borrowings. We examined changes in the top bank shareholder position of these 132 firms. For 82.6 per cent of the firms, the bank that occupied the top shareholding position among banks was also the top shareholder among banks both five years earlier and five years later. In a further 13.6 per cent of cases, the bank so identified was in the top position among banks either five years earlier or five years later, and in most of these cases (9.0 percentage points) the bank was in second place among banks in the year it was not first. That is, there was only a slight change in rank, which could in theory have represented a minor reshuffling among a small set of core main

---

[4] In the MOF's decree implemented on 1 April 1993, a bank subsidiary will not be allowed to be a lead manager for new bond issues by firms with net assets of less than 5 billion yen for which the parent bank is trustee. Initially, the MOF has licensed only two long-term credit banks and the central financial institution for agricultural cooperatives to establish securities company subsidiaries. The aim of these measures appears to be to restrict the main bank's expansion into bond-related business in order to protect securities companies left financially weakened in the aftermath of the bubble. But these restrictions are probably only temporary.

TABLE 1.4 Switching of Main Bank by Once-Excellent Firms

Number of E firms = 200			Number of years in E state													
Transition of state	Firms	Cases	1	2	3	4	5	6	7	8	9	10	11	12	13	14
E ⇒ F	13	16	3	2	4		1	2	1				1	1	1		
MB switching	2	2					1							1			
E ⇒ N	62	71	16	17	8	3	5	8	3	2	1		4	3	1		
MB switching	8	10	4	1	2			1			1			1			
E ⇒ C	4	4	1		2												1
MB switching																	
Total	79	91	20	19	14	3	6	10	4	2	1		5	4	2		1
MB switching	10	12	4	1	2		1	2			1			2			
Per cent	12.7	13.2															

Source: Data are from NEEDS (Nikkei Economic Electronic Databank System).

banks or a temporary, rather than long-lasting, movement in the share-holding order.

The recent changes in the pattern of corporate finance raise questions about the longer-term viability of the main bank's role as a discipliner of poor management. This role of the main bank continues, and it is not clear that it has been significantly weakened (see Chapter 6 by Sheard). Certainly, an alternative disciplinary mechanism, such as a free-wheeling market for corporate control, has not appeared, and is not likely to emerge in the foreseeable future.[5]

On the other hand, as more firms migrate into the E and F categories accompanied by diversification in banking ties, a sort of vacuum is created regarding the monitoring of management of those firms, apart from product market discipline. This may even have been a factor behind some of the reckless financial decision-making seen during the recent bubble. But this does not imply that the problem can be solved simply by trans-planting an Anglo-American take-over mechanism into the Japanese system. The advisability of such a proposal must be based on a careful comparative study of the monitoring characteristics of the main bank system and the market-oriented financial system in relation to other elements of the economy. To do so is beyond the scope of this chapter; the issues are explored further in Aoki's chapter.

Reciprocal Delegation of Monitoring Among Banks

When a firm borrows, the main bank has the largest loan share but it is not the sole lender, although it is considered to have the principal responsibility for monitoring the firm. Thus there is 'exclusivity in monitoring with non-exclusivity in lending' (Sheard, 1994a). Monitoring may be said to be delegated to the main bank; because other banks do not monitor the borrowing firms with the same intensity, they rely largely upon the judgement of the main bank. Both the delegation and the subordination arrangements in the case of financial distress of borrowing firms are reciprocal: for instance, Banks A, B, and C lend to firms i, j, and k, A as main bank to i, B as main bank to j, and C to k. Thus a city bank is concurrently main bank for some of its customers and for other customers is a member of a *de facto* syndicate for which another city bank is the main bank. This relationship has been termed 'reciprocal delegated monitoring' (Sheard, 1994a). In a sense, the whole non-financial corpo-

---

[5] In a recent carefully executed econometric study, Kaplan and Minton (1992) discovered that there was indeed a statistically significant negative correlation between the profitability of large firms and the probability of the dispatch of bank (or corporate) directors to those firms in the 1980s. They maintained that 'the web of relationships in Japan substitutes for the alternative corporate control mechanisms in the US. . . . Recently, several authors have argued that the efficacy of relationships in Japan may be weakening. We conclude by testing for a deterioration in our sample and find little evidence for one.'

rate sector is divided into territories of major banks, although the boundaries sometimes overlap.

The *de facto* loan syndicate led by the main bank is hierarchical both in terms of proportionate loan shares and implicit benefits and obligations. The hierarchy corresponds roughly to the presumed monitoring capacity and position in the segmented financial system and can be hypothetically ranked as follows. Just below the main bank are the trust bank and insurance companies in the same enterprise grouping (*keiretsu*) and the long-term credit bank with the largest share of long-term loans. Next are the other large non-affiliated financial institutions: competitor city, trust, and long-term credit banks. The third tier comprises non-affiliated insurance companies and regional banks and other financial institutions with which the main bank has a fairly close relationship. The lowest tier comprises other smaller financial institutions and foreign banks. The respective shares in syndicate lending seem to be rather stable over time in most instances, with the main bank typically having the single largest share.[6]

Monitoring by financial institutions can be classified into three interrelated, but conceptually distinguishable, functions: *ex ante* monitoring—screening potential investment proposals and checking the capacity of the borrowing firm to implement them; interim monitoring—gathering information on the ongoing business and affairs of the borrowing firm; and *ex post* monitoring—verifying the outcome of investment projects and, if necessary, disciplining failing incumbent managers of the firm by management. A feature of the Japanese system is that these three monitoring functions are integrated in the hands of the main bank. This is in contrast to the Anglo-American securities-based financial system in which they are dispersed among many different specialized agents (see Chapter 4 by Aoki for further detail).

In times of corporate distress the main bank is expected to play the leading role in overseeing or organizing a financial rescue, restructuring, or dismantling of the firm (depending on the severity of the problem and its future prospects), and to bear a disproportionate share of the costs of associated financial assistance (interest deferrals and/or exemptions), loan losses and new funding requirements relative to the syndicate as a whole (see Chapter 6 by Sheard). There is a pecking order in the compensation and exit of *de facto* syndicate members, the general contours of which seem clear but the details opaque, since each case is apparently negotiated separately. It appears that the main bank almost completely bails out the

---

[6] There are 64 regional banks and 68 second-tier regional banks (former sogo banks). City and long-term credit banks can have up to a 5 per cent shareholding in them. Of the 95 listed regional banks in 1991, a city or long-term credit bank was the top shareholder (37 cases) or number two shareholder (26 cases) in two-thirds of them. In 30 per cent of these cases, the bank had dispatched a director to the board (compiled from *Kigyo Keiretsu Soran*, 1991).

smaller financial institutions (third and fourth tiers). Whether it absorbs some of the losses of first- and second-tier members depends on the case; indeed, the non-main bank financial institutions closest to the business client may also take some disproportionate share of the losses. In effect, even if not formally written into loan agreements, the main bank acts as a kind of subordinated lender and provider of management assistance, restructuring or, in the worst case, receivership services towards distressed or failing firms. These features in turn provide strong incentives for the main bank to monitor the ongoing business and affairs of the borrowing firm closely. A main bank has the capacity to monitor because it is a major stockholder and operates major payment settlement accounts for borrowing firms.

Relationships Between Regulatory Authorities and the Banking Industry

Being the main bank involves obligations and responsibilities, which may necessitate bearing extraordinary costs in certain circumstances, especially when client firms are financially distressed. Why does the main bank not behave opportunistically and try to shirk its responsibility to undertake costly operations to rescue financially distressed firms more often? The reason is that banks can anticipate extra profits, which can be called main bank rents, over time when they act as main banks. There are two sources for such rents, one originating in private arrangements and the other created through the design of the regulatory system. Why does competition among banks and new entry not wipe out main bank rents?

Even aside from profits from large loan shares, being able to garner a disproportionately large share of non-lending banking business allows the main bank access to various forms of profitable fees and commissions in what appear to be less than perfectly price-competitive markets. The main bank may also be able to extend its profitable businesses to clients' business partners, such as suppliers and dealers, by capturing their networks of payment settlement accounts. These are some of the reasons why there is hidden competition among city banks to become the main bank even for major firms which do not rely upon bank loans. Indeed, switching of main banks is sometimes observed. But why does it not happen more frequently? (Horiuchi, Packer and Fukuda (1988) provide data on switching.)

There are certain private incentives for both the bank and the firm to comply with the conventions of the main bank relationship. By concentrating its banking business with the main bank and allowing the main bank to hold a stable block of its shares, the firm is effectively submitting itself to the bank's monitoring (a form of voluntary disclosure). By so doing the firm obliges the main bank to render assistance in adversity. Former and incumbent bank managers we interviewed indicated that it was extremely difficult for the banks to default on their obligations if they were given information in advance by the firm indicating that there are potential troubles. The main bank rents in non-critical financial states may constitute a kind of insurance premium against business adversity. On the other hand, the main bank may expect future returns to emergency loan and other expenditures made during the rescue operation, if the firm can credibly commit itself to a continuing relationship with the main bank. The main bank's shareholding may be considered as a device facilitating such commitment (Sheard, 1994b). Thus a part of main bank rents may be considered as originating in private arrangements.

But there could be other arrangements as well. The firm may shop around among banks for a better deal. Banks, knowing the opportunistic behaviour of firms, may compete for client firms on the basis of parallel independent monitoring, ruthlessly leaving troubled firms. If banks do behave in this way, it would certainly be an optimal response for firms as well to drive hard bargains with banks. This sort of reciprocal behaviour could constitute an equilibrium in a one-shot game and its repetition would also become sustainable. It is worth asking under what conditions main bank system arrangements prevail rather than the repetition of this short-term competitive equilibrium, or other possible equilibria.

For the main bank system to be viable and sustainable there must be some kind of regulatory framework for constraining the behaviour of agents, especially main banks and other financial institutions, to be consistent with the implicit rules of main bank relationships, as well as for guaranteeing rents for banks which perform the delegated monitoring function properly. The discretionary regulatory mechanisms operated by the MOF and BOJ have provided an institutional framework within which the main bank system has operated, and may constitute an essential element supporting its viability.

The Convoy System

One of the most important regulatory mechanisms sustaining the main bank system has been the rigid control over new entry to city bank status—an indispensable prerequisite for a bank to be qualified as the main bank for major firms.[7] The number of city banks has been kept quite small since 1953 (not more than 15) and mergers among them have reduced the number to 11, as shown in Table 1.5. The MOF was able to

---

[7] An exception is the Industrial Bank of Japan (IBJ), a long-term credit bank rather than a city bank. The MOF also restricted the number of long-term credit banks to three, and of these only the IBJ and, to a much lesser extent, the Long-Term Credit Bank of Japan (LTCB), have played a prominent role as a main bank. An indicator of this is that IBJ had 47 per cent of long-term credit bank assets in 1991, but accounted for 69 per cent of the firms that had a long-term credit bank as their number one lender, while the figures for LTCB were 33 per cent and 24 per cent respectively, and for Nippon Credit Bank 20 per cent and 8 per cent respectively (computed from *Kigyo Keiretsu Soran*, 1991, pp. 645–48 and 858–59). See Packer's chapter for further analysis.

TABLE 1.5 Changes in the Number of Domestic Branches of City Banks

Year ending 31 March	Dai-Ichi	Nihon-Kangyo	Fuji	Sumitomo	Mitsubishi	Sanwa	Mitsui	Taiyo	Kobe	Tokai	Kyowa	Saitama	Daiwa	Tokyo	Hokkaido
Total in 1957	93	116	182	135	156	182	100		151	174	234		99	35	108
1958	2	0	0	0	0	1	0		—8	0	0		0	—1	0
1959	2	1	1	2	—1	—1	0		—4	—5	—2		0	—1	0
1960	0	—1	—1	0	—1	2	0		2	3	—3		0	4	3
1961	0	4	4	4	0	0	2		1	—1	—1		4	2	2
1962	—	—	—	—	—	—	—		—	—	—		—	—	—
1963	3	4	3	2	3	0	5		3	2	0		—1	—1	4
1964	6	4	—1	3	5	4	5		—2	4	2		6	1	4
1965	32[a]	2	7	3	5	5	3		4	6	—5		4	0	8
1966	7	8	4	25[b]	6	3	10		3	4	—1		4	3	4
1967	—1	2	4	1	2	5	0		3	4	0		3	0	5
1968	—1	0	0	0	0	0	—1		—2	—1	0		2	0	—1
1969	1	0	0	—1	—1	0	17[c]	0	3	0	—1		—1	—1	0
1970	2	—1	—1	2	—1	—1	2	2	2	3	—1		7	—1	7
1971		2	4	2	2	4	—1	2	—1	—1	—1	3	—1	—1	—1
1972		—1	0	—1	—1	—1	—1	2	—1	0	—1	2	—1	0	0
1973		0	2	3	3	0	—3		2	4	—1	4	—1	—1	2
1974		5	—1	—1	3	3	1		—7	0	—1	4	2	0	2
1975		5	4	4	3	3	2		4	3	0	—1	—1	—1	0
1976		6	1	—2	1	1	2		6	4	0	2	—1	0	5

	Dai-Ichi Kangyo			Sakura				Asahi					
1977	1	2	6	2	0	2	6	0	1	2	3	1	2
1978	1	2	3	2	5	4	1	0	0	4	5	2	2
1979	3	0	5	2	4	4	4	6	0	4	4	1	4
1980	1	6	4	4	1	2	0	1	0	2	1	-2	1
1981	1	5	3	4	2	3	1	6	4	4	3	0	1
1982	8	0	2	4	3	4	3	4	3	1	1	0	2
1983	3	7	5	1	3	4	1	2	1	5	5	1	4
1984	3	2	3	5	3	5	0	2	1	1	1	-1	7
1985	1	3	2	5	0	4	-6	2	0	0	1	0	3
1986	1	2	5	7	2	2	0	3	-6	1	1	-1	-2
1987	3	6	97[d]	6	4	3	-3	1	-4	1	1	0	1
1988	0	6	-1	4	3	2	-2	-4	-3	1	2	-1	-3
1989	3	9	-1	8	4	-1	4	-1	0	3	4	0	2
1990	3	11	7	4	14	6	-1	2	2	8	2	1	2
Total in 1991	344	274	325	249	261	194	319	233	222	181	175	32	180

This table was constructed from data on the number of branches of each bank at the end of each fiscal year. Entries for 1957–61 include overseas branches, but beginning with 1962 they do not. For this reason, there is no entry for 1962—it would include not only the net change in domestic branches but also the elimination of foreign branches from the count. As a result of this discontinuity, summing the changes from the total in 1957 to the total in 1991 does not yield the number of domestic branches in 1991. The effect of this is most significant for Bank of Tokyo which, as a foreign exchange bank operating mostly overseas, had a number of overseas branches in the early 1950s. Taiyo had 140 branches, and Saitama 128, when their status was upgraded to city banks.

In general, a large increase in a year includes the results of an acquisition (see notes a–d). For further information on mergers and branch openings before 1971, see Adams and Hoshi (1972, pp. 154–58).

a   Asahi Bank acquired.
b   Kawachi Bank acquired.
c   Toto Bank acquired.
d   Heiwa Sogo Bank acquired.

control new entry to city bank status by restricting the allocation of nation-wide branch licences to incumbent city banks and by only twice allowing entry to the ranks of city banks, both times to large regional banks (Taiyo Bank in 1968 and Saitama Bank in 1969).

In the high growth period (1951–75), the monetary authorities (the BOJ) set low interest rate ceilings on essentially all financial assets, including loans, deposits, bank debentures and corporate bonds. However, effective lending rates were allowed to be above the nominal ceiling because banks were able to require compensating deposit balances from borrowing firms. City banks were able to borrow funds for industrial financing from the BOJ at a favourable discount rate up to an amount set at the central bank's discretion. Bond issues were tightly regulated so that only highly qualified firms (particularly, public utilities companies) could issue bonds on a rotational basis decided by a group of securities houses and banks. The city banks have been prohibited from underwriting bonds issued by firms, but in the period concerned, the bonds were typically purchased by the main banks and other financial institutions (Table 1.3) and some were eligible collateral for central bank loans. The stable monetary and fiscal policies assured that the rate of inflation was moderate and the real interest rates for deposit and lending were positive. This *macro* stability served as an important prerequisite for the *micro* viability and effectiveness of the main bank system, a point discussed further by Patrick in Chapter 11.

The consequence was a convoy system in which all incumbent city banks grew at about the same pace with sufficient rents, the interest rate spread was substantial, and there were no financial institution failures. Thus main bank rents had elements of oligopolistic rents, as well as shares in possible social savings of monitoring costs. But how they were decomposed into the two is a controversial and difficult conceptual and empirical issue (see Chapters 3 by Ueda, 4 by Aoki, and 11 by Patrick). This description of regulations on bond issues and interest rates is most applicable to the period up to the mid-1970s. The impact of the post-1975 deregulations is analysed and assessed by Ramseyer in Chapter 7, and by Campbell and Hamao in Chapter 10.

Direct Inspection and Sanction Mechanisms

The equity shares of banks, particularly those at the hub of the main bank system, are cross-held and dispersed with their major customer firms and with other financial institutions. The largest shareholder, usually another financial institution such as an insurance company, typically holds about 5 per cent. About 90 per cent of a bank's equity, on average, is held in corporate hands, reflecting the fact that most firms own a small bundle of shares (typically a fraction of 1 per cent) in their major transacting banks, particularly the bank that is their main bank.[8] Shareholdings by individuals are not significant, unlike most large US banks. This results in a structure whereby, at the aggregate level, banks are owned by industry, but in practice they are managerially autonomous.

Under this situation, the so-called convoy system might have created serious managerial moral hazard problems. The protection by the authorities was counterbalanced, however, in substantial part by the close supervision and prudential control of the regulatory authorities. The Inspection Division (Kensabu) of the MOF's Banking Bureau, in charge of detecting violations of the Banking Law and the Securities and Exchange Law, can inspect the books of banks at its discretion. If it finds any irregularity in bank business, it has the authority to advise on ways to solve the problems. The BOJ as the lender of last resort closely monitors the daily operations of banks through its Credit and Management Department and regularly conducts on-site examinations through the Supervision Department (Kosakyoku). There is close information-sharing between these departments.

When a bank is judged to be poorly managed and to need drastic organizational and asset restructuring, typically the MOF arranges for a retired high-ranking MOF bureaucrat to enter as a director, sometimes even as the president, just as the firm in distress has to accept bank-dispatched managers. The MOF influences bank decisions concerning dividends payout. Behind the scenes, it usually mediates acquisitions of troubled smaller banks by larger city banks (notable cases are Sumitomo's take-overs of Kawachi Bank in 1965 and of Heiwa Sogo Bank in 1986), mergers of city banks (there have been four such cases in the post-war period, identified in Table 1.5), and more recently, the merger of smaller financial institutions with others in the same category (such as credit associations). These discretionary strategic roles played by MOF compensate for, and probably contribute to, the absence of effective stockholder control over the otherwise autonomous management of banks.

The MOF's discretionary allocation among city banks of new branch licences provided it with strong leverage over these banks. With low deposit ceiling interest rates, expansion of the deposit base became the key element of a long-term profit-maximizing strategy. How many branches they could obtain and in what location became vital concerns for city banks. It is believed the MOF awarded extra new branch offices (in some cases via the acquisition of second-tier regional banks) to city

---

[8] Of the shares of the leading banks (11 city banks, 3 long-term credit banks, and 7 trust banks), 58 per cent is held by non-financial firms and 34 per cent by financial institutions, including other banks. Corporate ownership is 92 per cent and individual ownership only 6 per cent, compared to 72 per cent and 23 per cent respectively for listed firms as a whole. See Sheard (1994b) for further details and analysis.

banks that agreed to rescue major firms whose failure might have caused serious social problems, such as massive lay-offs of employees and the domino-effect of business failures. It was able implicitly to threaten the withdrawal of new branch licensing opportunities to deviant banks. The BOJ coordinated with the MOF in assisting the rescue operations of city banks by extending emergency loans to those banks. These regulatory measures may have smoothed the allocation of main bank rents among city banks over time. They may also have been important in binding main banks to their perceived obligations both *vis-à-vis* distressed firms and other financiers, and in resolving *ex post* coordination problems among banks. Whether such mechanisms led to excessively soft rescues of failed firms that should have been liquidated, or whether they obliged main banks to take responsibility for rescue, is a controversial issue. But we maintain that the regulatory framework has, at any rate, assured city banks of profitability and growth as long as they followed the conventions implied by main bank relationships and reciprocal delegated monitoring arrangements. In that sense, this sanction mechanism may have been an indispensable element of the main bank system.

Who Monitors the Regulators

One remaining question is who monitors the monitor (the regulatory agencies) of the monitor (the main bank). What incentives do the regulatory agencies have to monitor well? The practice of *amakudari* (descending from heaven) seems to play an important role in providing incentives to bureaucrats. Many retired MOF bureaucrats and BOJ executives obtain executive positions at city banks and other financial institutions. This flow of personnel is not limited to the trouble-shooting cases referred to above. Healthy banks are willing to accept ex-bureaucrats for various reasons, including as a means of gaining access to valuable information from, and to exert influence on, the regulatory authorities. As of July 1992, there were 78 former MOF officials and 64 former BOJ officials on the board of directors of the 115 listed banks in Japan. 51 per cent of banks had a former MOF official on their board, 44 per cent had a former BOJ official, and 69 per cent had an official from one or the other (computed from *Kigyo Keiretsu Soran*, 1992, pp. 601–29).[9]

An obvious danger of such practice is that it could induce a moral hazard problem if bureaucrats promote their own ties with specific banks and financial institutions for possible personal (post-retirement) advantage. The system places checks on such behaviour (although it may not completely eliminate the tendency) by minimizing individuals' discretion in arranging post-retirement jobs: the job is arranged by the Personnel Division of the MOF (or the BOJ), not by the individual concerned,

---

[9] For a detailed discussion of the *amakudari* practice as an incentive for bureaucrats, as well as its implications for system performance, see Aoki (1988, chapter 7).

unlike the revolving-door practice in the United States. Thus the incentive for individual bureaucrats to develop ties with particular institutions during their bureaucratic tenure is curbed. Indeed, such attempts would put potential opportunities at risk.

The Ministry provides various post-retirement jobs, differentiated by prestige and income, to their bureaucrats as final prizes in the promotional tournament up to retirement from the Ministry. The bureaucrats compete for better prizes which are awarded according to their contribution to the political stock of the Ministry throughout their careers. How attractive those prizes are is determined in turn by the Ministry's contribution to the growth of the system, since the prizes are ultimately supplied by industries the Ministry regulates. In this way the cycle is completed. The bureaucrats are collectively interested in the continual growth and security of a system sustained by the generation of rents by the institutions that make up the convoy system. Overt individual corruption may not be so high in such a system. Indeed, the moral hazard problem may be more institutional than individual: it has been asserted that the MOF was slow in 1992 and 1993 in resolving the major bad debt situation of eight housing loan corporations since, embarrassingly, major managerial positions were held by ex-MOF officials. Also, there is considerable inertia to institutional change, particularly when it involves financial deregulation and redistribution or dissipation of rents. How this and the moral hazard problem affect the workings of the main bank system are discussed further by Ueda in Chapter 3.

Complementary Role of Long-Term Credit Banks

Japanese financial authorities strengthened financial market segmentation in the early 1950s by creating special financial institutions to make long-term loans to industry. The main government development finance institution was the Japan Development Bank (JDB), although the Export-Import Bank of Japan also made term loans, as the Small Business Finance Corporation did later. Three private long-term credit banks were established by recapitalizing or transforming special long-term credit banks from the pre-war period, of which the Industrial Bank of Japan (IBJ) was the most important.

Until the end of World War II, the IBJ was instrumental in the channelling of public funds (mostly postal savings) to targeted military industries. IBJ was legally a private bank, but it operated under a special law authorizing it to issue bank debentures, and its equity was widely held by other financial institutions. The IBJ had accumulated substantial human resources for monitoring projects and managerial decision-making in firms, but its survival became problematical after the war owing to the depletion of its equity capital and because the occupation forces held it responsible for its role in the planned-economy war effort. Some human resources were transferred to the Reconstruction Finance Bank (RFB—Fukko Kin'yu Kinko), but the RFB was mainly financed by bank debentures underwritten by the BOJ and was considered to be responsible for the explosive post-war hyperinflation. Its activity was suspended in 1949.

The JDB was created as a fully government-owned bank and its operating funds came mainly from postal savings, provided by the MOF's Trust Fund Bureau through its Fiscal Investment and Loan Program. At its inception the JDB employed a large number of ex-managers of IBJ, both directly and via the RFB or IBJ on secondment. The monitoring capacity the JDB inherited from the IBJ was complementary to that of the main banks (see Chapter 4 by Aoki, and Chapter 5 by Packer). JDB lending to such industries as power generation, steel, coal, fertilizer, shipping and shipbuilding reflected strategic judgements from the viewpoint of national economic management, and is regarded as having had an important role in macroeconomic coordination.

Because the JDB and IBJ were able to offer industrial-strategic and engineering-related judgements, the main bank's capacity to observe the managerial competence of their client firms was improved. This extended to the banks' assessment of the clients' capacity to adapt new technologies. In contrast to the apparent lack of communication between the government-owned development bank and commercial banks, as observed in India (see Chapter 14 by Bhatt), there was intense informal communication between the JDB and IBJ on the one hand, and city and other private banks on the other, during the period of high economic growth. This provided the basis for the formation of *de facto* loan consortia for priority industries with lead financing by the JDB, the IBJ, or the main city bank, as the case may be. However, it should be noted that the JDB, unlike the IBJ, never played any specific visible role in the ongoing monitoring or corporate governance of industrial firms, especially concerning rescue operations. That was primarily the task of the main banks. In this sense, too, there was strong complementarity between the monitoring task of the JDB and that of the main banks. The safety net provided by the intense after-loan monitoring by the main banks may have been important in reducing the risks associated with channelling public funds originating in postal savings into large-scale investments in strategic industries.

The IBJ played perhaps an even more important role in the assessment (*ex ante* monitoring) of new projects proposed by large established firms, as well as in providing investment banking services. Indeed the IBJ itself served as a main bank for some firms, particularly large firms in capital-intensive industries (see Chapter 5 by Packer). The IBJ's neutral position *vis-à-vis* the six major enterprise groups helped it to play a brokering role in cross-group mergers, such as the merger between Fuji Steel and Yawata Steel in 1970 that resulted in the formation of the world's largest private steel company, Nippon Steel. The IBJ was able to raise funds on favourable terms in the early years, as it was authorized to issue bank debentures which were purchased by the Trust Fund Bureau and by city banks which could use them as collateral against BOJ borrowing.

The role of long-term credit banks in financing (and probably in monitoring) firms associated with other bank groups steadily declined after the 1960s and has been gradually replaced by city banks. In 1955, the proportion of government funds, including JDB loans, plus loans by private long-term credit banks, to the total new supply of industrial equipment funds reached as high as 54 per cent (8.8 per cent was from city bank loans). But throughout the 1960s and 70s this figure was about 27–31 per cent, while the contribution of city banks steadily increased up to 31 per cent in 1985 (Bank of Japan, Flow of Funds, various editions). The catalytic role of the long-term credit banks in the development of the main bank system cannot be overlooked, however, and is assessed in more detail by Packer in Chapter 5.

THE MAIN BANK SYSTEM IN COMPARATIVE AND HISTORICAL CONTEXT

The characterization of the main bank system as (1) a nexus of main bank-firm relationships, (2) delegation of reciprocal monitoring arrangements among main banks, and (3) discretionary regulatory relationships, is admittedly stylized and static. The remainder of this chapter examines the main bank system in two contexts: its international *comparative* context and its *historical* context.

One important feature of this study is comparative. The purpose of comparison is two-fold: to understand the operation of particular systems by analysing them in the context of the broader set of revealed feasible alternatives, and to understand the features or principles common to seemingly diverse systems. These in turn provide a basis for asking questions about the effectiveness and efficiency of different systems in achieving various goals, and about the possible lessons that can be learned from other systems. Each country has its unique feature.

Countries have differing values, laws, and institutions governing the way in which economic units form and interact, and the historical experience of each country shapes both its values and present policy choices. But countries also share common characteristics. Moreover, they face common problems, generic in nature, which require similar types of decisions on appropriate economic policies and institutional frameworks. They may be able to draw lessons from the experience of others or derive hints in regard to their institutional design and policy-making.

In examining comparative financial systems and potential lessons from the Japanese (main bank) system, we need first to set out what alternative banking systems exist and what their distinctive characteristics are. The next section provides a simple schematic typology of alternative systems.

Typology of Banking Systems

Financial systems are often classified into two types (see, for example, Berglof, 1990; Mayer, 1990; Rybczinski, 1984). One is the neo-classical spot market model of independent, arms-length financial transactions, in which securities markets are well developed and play an important role; this is often referred to as the Anglo-American model of securities-based or capital market finance. The other model is that of a bank-based system of relationship finance—of repeated transactions and more or less close relations between the supplier of funds and the user of those funds, typically bank and firm. The close relations may be solidified by the bank's stable equity holding in the firm to enhance control and commitment. The resurgence of interest in banks as a theoretical and practical alternative model able to compete viably against securities markets has been generated in substantial part by the remarkable economic successes of Japan and Germany, economies in which banks have played leading roles in industrial financing. For this reason, this system is sometimes referred to as the Japan-German model.

For advanced economies, the distinction between a securities-based system and a bank-based system of corporate financing appears sharper in theory than it is in practice, however. In practice, elements of bank-based financing and marketable securities-based financing are found in every financial system, although the weights and functions may differ (see Table 1.6). At an aggregate level, in the post-war period, the largest source of financing of gross real investment of the non-financial corporate sector in every advanced industrial market economy has been from internal sources (retained earnings and depreciation allowances) rather than through the financial system, whether bank loans or new securities issue. More than three-quarters of non-financial corporate financing in the United Kingdom, United States and Germany since 1975 was financed within the corporate sector by retention of profits and depreciation charges, while close to one-half of those was financed likewise in Japan. Moreover, loans have been the predominant form of external finance everywhere except in the United States.

Frequently, the comparative issue is posed as one of efficiency: which system is more efficient, bank-based or securities market-based finance? Posed at a general level, this may not be a very useful question. Difficult conceptual issues arise in discussing efficiency in a comparative institutional context, such as the issue of multiple equilibria that cannot be Pareto-ranked. Which system is better according to some criterion may

TABLE 1.6 International Comparison of Shares of Funding Sources of Non-Financial Corporate Sector: Japan, US, Germany, UK

(per cents)

Japan

	Internal	External	Borrowing	Securities
1962–64	39.4	60.6	46.6	11.0
1965–69	50.1	49.9	43.2	5.6
1970–74	41.6	58.4	50.0	5.7
1975–79	50.6	49.4	41.5	7.5
1980–84	59.0	41.0	35.0	6.2
1985–89	52.3	47.7	32.1	11.0

United States

	Internal	External	Borrowing	Securities
1962–64	76.0	24.0	11.3	7.9
1965–69	67.9	32.1	18.8	13.9
1970–74	55.1	44.9	25.6	18.0
1975–79	69.7	30.3	16.3	14.0
1980–84	74.2	25.8	15.5	9.5
1985–89	85.4	14.6	14.0	-1.3

Germany

	Internal	External	Borrowing	Securities
1962–64	66.5	33.5	22.8	5.0
1965–69	68.8	31.2	20.8	4.1
1970–74	58.5	41.5	28.1	3.2
1975–79	72.6	27.4	22.3	1.6
1980–84	75.4	24.6	21.6	3.0
1985–89	78.6	21.4	16.5	4.9

United Kingdom

	Internal	External	Borrowing	Securities
1962–64	73.2	26.8	16.5	10.3
1965–69	74.1	25.9	14.6	11.3
1970–74	62.2	37.8	34.2	3.6
1975–79	79.1	20.9	16.4	4.5
1980–84	82.5	17.5	16.3	1.2
1985–89	63.0	37.0	26.1	10.9

Source: Flow of Funds Tables

depend subtly on the nature of national institutions, values, and historical experiences. A system that worked well in some country in a particular period may not function well in another country at another point in time. In the real world of imperfect and asymmetric information and transactional frictions, each system embodies different information processing and incentive mechanisms and different mechanisms for monitoring and control, with implications for how problems of adverse selection, moral hazard, opportunistic behaviour, and commitments are handled. Many of the following chapters are devoted to comparing the performance characteristics of various systems in these regards with the Japanese main bank system as a point of reference.

The essence of banking is the collecting of deposits (or borrowing the deposits of others) and the provision of funds, usually in the form of loans to business firms, but in some systems in the form of bonds and equity as well. Typically, the lending relationship involves repeated transactions with specific business borrowers, in which bank evaluation of borrower credit-worthiness is key. It can best be thought of as a bilateral bargaining game over time; the accumulation of knowledge (information), the development of trust, changes in the relative power positions of borrower and lender, and the changing external environment (competitive conditions) shape the bargains struck and restruck over time. The bank monitors the behaviour and performance of its business client to some degree, accumulating information which places it in an advantageous position relative to other potential lenders, but at a cost: information and monitoring take resources, they are not free goods. In this sense, virtually all bank loan transactions can be thought of as less than arm's length and not completely impersonal; in other words, relationship banking is the norm in all banking systems.

Within this general schema, however, bank-business relationships can and do take on a number of different forms. Three dimensions can be used to characterize different types of banking systems. One is the kind of *regulatory regime* in which the banks operate. What kinds of operating restrictions and prudential requirements does the bank face, and how regulated are the markets in which the bank operates? Of particular interest is how bank activities in securities markets are regulated. In some systems, notably in the United States, commercial banks are prohibited by law from carrying out equity transactions on their own account. Elsewhere, as in Japan and Germany, in contrast, banks can and do own equity in firms. The ability or willingness to take leading equity positions in firms seems to be one of the key features distinguishing the Japanese-German from Anglo-American banking systems. Another important regulatory difference pertinent to the emergence of different banking systems is found in the permissible range of bank activity in bond related services such as underwriting. (In Chapter 7, Ramseyer elucidates how regulatory differences in this case crucially define the contrasting behaviours and performances of the Japanese banks on one hand and the American banks on the other.)

A second is the *ownership* structure of the banks themselves. A bank is a deposit-taking institution, but it is also a kind of firm: who owns the bank and ultimately controls its strategic orientation and behaviour *vis-à-vis* the non-financial corporate sector?

A third dimension concerns the *monitoring* role of the bank and its role in corporate governance. We have already distinguished three stages of monitoring by financial institutions, *ex ante*, interim, and *ex post*. In alternative systems, banks may assume responsibility for these respective roles to varying degrees. In the Japanese main bank system, these three monitoring functions are integrated to a considerable extent in the hands of the main banks, whereas in other systems they may be decentralized into the hands of a wider set of capital market agents.

Based on these dimensions we can identify the following five major prototypes of banking systems relevant for our project (Table 1.7).

Socialist State-Owned Mono-Bank System

At one extreme of the spectrum of banking systems is the state-owned mono-bank system in a socialist planned economy. In this system, a free securities market does not exist and financial transactions mediated by the mono-bank are the administrative and accounting consequences of bureaucratically determined real resource allocations. Accordingly, the banks do not perform any autonomous *ex ante* monitoring function. The socialist financial system, given its derivative and essentially primitive nature, has never been held up as an appropriate model for a market economy; as former socialist economies reform and transform, it is of decreasing relevance except as a base point from which to move. Some aspects, however, such as the lack of discipline in *ex post* monitoring, or what Kornai (1980) terms the soft-budget tendency, remain of interest from a theoretical viewpoint as limiting cases of behaviour that might be observed in market economies under certain ownership and regulatory structures. Soft budgeting refers to the tendency for the state-owned mono-bank to refinance inefficient firms and not be committed to punishing them by liquidation or other means (see Chapter 16 by Qian).

Exclusive Group Banking System

Each bank provides a large proportion of (investment) funds to a particular group of firms. As in Korea in the 1960s and 70s, the government may own banks and assign one bank to each business group (*chaebol*) as its lead bank. In Japan in the 1920s, family-owned groups of industrial firms, directly or through a holding company, as in the case of large zaibatsu, owned banks for the purpose of raising investment funds for

TABLE 1.7 Typology of Banking Systems

Banking system	Regulatory relationship with securities market	Control of the bank	Bank's role in monitoring	Bank's role in corporate governance
State mono-banking	No security market	The state	No *ex ante* monitoring, *ex post* 'soft budgeting'	State planner's intermediary
Exclusive grouping	Market underdeveloped	Government or industrial group	No autonomous *ex ante* monitoring idiosyncratic risk	Government's or group's common agency
Main bank	Limited equity holding, no underwriting	Autonomous management, hands-on regulation	Integrated monitoring, recriprocal delegation	Contingent control
Universal banking	Equity holding, underwriting allowed	Autonomous management, hands-off regulation	Parallel integrated monitoring	Shared control (German case) or active control (pre-Glass-Steagall US case)
Arm's length banking	Strictly separated	Market	Decentralized	Hands-off

their firms, as discussed later. The bank acting either as an agent of the government or, more often, as the agent for a group of ownership-affiliated firms is a typical case in developing economies (for example, Mexico before the nationalization of banks in 1982, see Chapter 15 by Reynolds). Since financing is highly preferential, it matters less whether financing is done in the form of securities or loans. In any case, competitive securities markets typically are under-developed because of the exclusivity of financing. Since banks are either state controlled or captured by industrial interests or interests of controlling families, it is unlikely that banks play an autonomous *ex ante* monitoring function or exercise controlling power in the corporate governance of firms. Banks may be exposed to group-specific idiosyncratic risks and susceptible to the soft-budget tendency *ex post*, endangering the prudence of their management and, in more extreme cases, the asset of their deposits.

Main Bank System

The firm borrows or has equity owned by many banks, but the main financier is delegated responsibility for monitoring the firm. The bank and its main client firms reciprocally own equities, although there is a limit imposed on the bank's ownership, and proxy voting by the bank is not permitted. Corporate holdings in the banks are so dispersed that the banks are, in effect, managerially autonomous. In normal times, bank intervention in corporate governance is limited. However, corporate failure triggers a take-over mechanism that sees control rights shift to the bank. The *ex post* monitoring function is exclusively delegated to the main bank, which gives it incentives to engage in *ex ante* and interim monitoring more intensively than other financial institutions. If the main bank tries to shirk its responsibility *ex post*, sanctions may be imposed by the regulatory authorities.

Universal Banking System

The current German system may be the most important example. The regulatory framework allows the banks to engage in commercial banking services, security-related business including underwriting, asset portfolio management, proxy-voting as well as board representation and equity holding on own account. As a result, the bank can integrate the three functions of monitoring to the highest degree (integrated monitoring) in spite of Chinese Walls at lower levels of functional hierarchy, and is likely to take on an active role in the corporate governance of industrial firms. US investment banks earlier this century were similarly actively involved in corporate governance by combining investment banking services and board representation (De Long, 1991), but public concerns with their excessive controlling power and conflict of interests with portfolio management services led to the enactment of the Glass-Steagall Act in

1933, which separated commercial banking from investment banking. The same concerns are often expressed for the current German system, but it is to be noted that potential bank power is counterbalanced by the voice of employees who participate in corporate governance through the system of codetermination (see Chapter 12 by Baums). One difference from the Japanese main bank system is that major banks seem to monitor independently rather than under a system of reciprocal delegation.

Arm's-Length Banking

This system is exemplified by the US system. Commercial banks are prohibited from engaging in equity transactions on their own account, including equity ownership (although a bank holding company can hold non-controlling equity stakes). Combined with the so-called equitable subordination doctrine which subordinates the claims of banks actively involved in the business of failed firms (see Chapter 7 by Ramseyer), the bank's role in corporate governance is limited. Although commercial bank activities are limited in scope and are specialized, the banking system itself is embedded in a broader financial system containing many other types of specialized agents with different monitoring expertise. Therefore, the comparative assessment of the performance characteristics of this banking system can only be done from a broader perspective. While bank management usually has considerable autonomy, ultimate control of corporate governance resides in the equity market, in what is often referred to as the market for corporate control; in cases of distress, as elsewhere, control becomes vested in the regulatory authorities.

Historical Context of the Main Bank System

The second contextual dimension for the Japanese main bank system is that of historical time. Japan's banking system, like any other, developed within a specific historical context. The clarification of the historical conditions governing its emergence, development, and possible transformation, is important for drawing possible lessons for other economies. How and why did it emerge? Before its emergence, what type of banking system prevailed in Japan and how was it transformed into the main bank system? Was it a result of endogenous growth of the financial system? Or was the role of government as an institutional designer critical for its formation? When did the main bank system establish itself? Was the main bank system established because Japan was a developing economy at the time? Is it bound to change as the economy matures? Will it converge to the Anglo-American model as Japan's capital market becomes increasingly integrated into the international capital market? Alternatively, is it flexible enough to adapt to new conditions?

It is useful to place the development of the main bank system in the context of five phases in the development of banking in Japan. The following is partly based on Patrick (1983) and Kato (1957); an excellent analysis with somewhat different phasing appears in Teranishi (1990).

Creation of a Modern Banking System: 1870s–1910s

In the period from 1870 to the first decade of the twentieth century, a modern, market-based financial system was created through the importation and assimilation of the institutions of banking and other modern financial intermediaries. The Japanese system combined elements of the Anglo-American commercial banking system, composed of national banks (*kokuritsu ginko*) authorized to issue bank ˙notes with national bonds as collateral, and later ordinary banks (*futsu ginko*) funded by private capital, with the continental European model of long-term credit banks for industry and agriculture (Nihon Kangyo Ginko founded in 1896, regional Agricultural-Industry Banks, and IBJ founded in 1900) as well as local savings banks and postal savings. Japan established a central bank in 1882, based on the Belgian example, for the purpose of replacing private bank notes with convertible notes. A stock market also emerged and flourished, but as in other low-income developing economies, banks were the predominant source of external finance for corporations.

Evolution of Exclusive Group Banking: 1910–27

After establishment of the Bank of Japan, national banks were gradually transformed into ordinary banks. Ordinary banks grew under a free, competitive, and unregulated market environment up to the 1927 financial crisis. Entry to the banking industry was free up to 1918, and even after 1918, anyone could open a bank if minimum capital requirements were satisfied. As a result, Japan's banking system was very decentralized. The number of banks was 2,001 in 1920 and 1,515 in 1928. As well as the five large zaibatsu banks (Dai-Ichi, Mitsui, Mitsubishi, Sumitomo and Yasuda), which had 24 per cent of total bank deposits in 1925, there were many medium and small banks. Most of the latter were closely connected to a particular group of industrial firms by credit relations and (cross) ownership. Some of the small banks were family owned (12.2 per cent in 1928) and often closely tied to their own firms. In providing long-term investment funds, those banks took a different development route from the British commercial banks. By making long-term loans rather than by underwriting issues of new securities, they were also different from the German Kreditbanken and the American investment banks. As is usually the case in an exclusive group system, the banks were exposed to excessive idiosyncratic risks, accentuated by their lack of *ex ante* monitoring capability and poor incentives. There were 42 cases of bank bankruptcy in the 1927 financial crisis and many of them had large shares of loans to related firms. The IBJ, originally founded as a long-term credit bank, was called on to rescue failing banks and industrial firms, and to intervene in the equity market to forestall further price declines in the aftermath of the crisis.

On the other hand, somewhat surprisingly, relatively large zaibatsu banks did not play such a prominent role in financing related firms in the 1920s. The first tier zaibatsu firms relied more on internally generated funds. In 1930, one of the largest zaibatsu banks, Mitsui Bank, extended only 10 per cent of its loans to member firms, mostly second-tier member firms except for Mitsui Bussan which as a trading company had very large trade finance needs (Teranishi, 1990, p. 325).

Concentration of the Banking System: 1927–50

The banking crisis of 1927, the most serious Japan has ever faced, had a profound effect on policy-makers; it generated a long-term regulatory bias in favour of financial system stability over competition. The 1927 Banking Act enforced the merger of small ordinary banks whose paid-in capital was below the new standard, such banks numbering more than a half of the total. Throughout the 1930s, mergers and acquisitions were promoted through administrative guidance, and during World War II, through coercion. The number of commercial banks was reduced to 625 in 1932, and to 65 in 1945. During this process, the shares of zaibatsu banks in total deposits increased to 45.7 per cent, and in credits to 67.2 per cent. Further, the proportion of loans by zaibatsu banks to zaibatsu member firms also increased substantially.

Particularly significant for the evolution of the main bank system was the promotion of bank consortia for long-term investment loans initiated in the 1930s, and the introduction of the designated banking system in 1944 (see Chapter 2 by Teranishi). The Munitions Ministry planned the production of military equipment as well as the supply of funds necessary for its implementation. For each firm receiving military procurement orders, a single bank was designated and funds were supplied to the firm through that bank. The firm held its deposit and loan accounts with its designated bank, which may be considered as a prototype of the payment settlements account aspect of the main bank relationships. At the end of the war, the designated banking system applied to 2,240 firms, of which 1,582 were assigned to one of the five major zaibatsu banks. Also, the IBJ enhanced its activity of channelling a large amount of public funds (mostly postal savings) into industrial development and accumulated its capacity to monitor projects and firms.

Thus Japan's banking system swung from a relatively decentralized exclusive group banking system to a quasi-state banking system. Traumatic though the changes in this period were, the reduction in the number of banks, the emergence of consortia, and the experiment of the designated banking system were quite important in setting the initial conditions for the subsequent development of the main bank system in the post-war era. In order for reciprocal delegation of monitoring among city banks to be viable, it seems that the number of banks needs to be relatively limited and stable, as this facilitates enforcement through mutual monitoring among banks and the supervision of the financial authority; at the same time, the number needs to be large enough to overcome oligopolistic tendencies and to achieve some degree of workable competition and diversification of risk.

After the war, the zaibatsu were dissolved and holding companies were made illegal. Zaibatsu control over banks was removed. But the Allied Occupation authorities did not alter the basic structure of the financial system nor curb the heavy hand of the government bureaucracy (notably the MOF). Bank stockholding in non-financial firms continued to be allowed, although initially a 5 per cent limit on bank stockholding was imposed. This bank holding was instrumental in maintaining and reviving old zaibatsu company connections based on mutual stockholding, leading to the post-war keiretsu system discussed earlier.

The main post-war financial reforms were to separate the banking and securities industries based on the US Glass-Steagall Act and to privatize the government-controlled long-term credit and foreign exchange banks. But, since the primary function of the private banks had been the provision of long-term credits complemented by the government-related banks, it did not transform the characteristics of the banking system fundamentally. The informal evolution of specialized financial institutions for different purposes—the funding of large business, small business and agriculture—became formalized into a structure of segmented markets and specialized institutions for each: city banks, local banks, mutual savings banks, small business credit associations and cooperatives, and agriculture credit cooperatives and associations.

The stock market was closed in the 1945–49 period when massive stock transfers took place from zaibatsu families, holding companies and major member firms to the government as part of the zaibatsu dissolution process. The government owned an estimated 40 per cent of total stock outstanding in 1947, prior to subsequent sale to individuals. In a way, Japanese industry was, to a remarkable degree, temporarily socialized. Priority in purchasing government-owned stocks was given first to a firm's workers, then to residents of localities in which plants were located. No individual was allowed to purchase more than 1 per cent of the stock of any firm: 29.3 per cent of workers of affected firms purchased 38.5 per cent of the total stock sold by the government. When the stock market opened in 1949, nearly 70 per cent of stock was owned by individuals (see Mochikabu, 1951, chapter 7; Aoki, 1988, pp. 124–27). The stock holding pattern changed from a high degree of socialization to a high degree of dispersion, before inter-corporate holding developed in the 1950s. This experience is interesting because it suggests that the privatization of industry can proceed without the operation of a competitive equity market if there is an effective banking sector.

Heyday of the Main Bank System, 1951–75

In this period, the main bank's role in corporate financing and monitoring was most prominent and pervasive. Around 1951 marked the end of the post-war reconstruction period, particularly as it applied to establishing the architecture of the financial system, and the take-off of the economy's high growth and escalating corporate investment demand. In late 1949, the BOJ mediated the formation of loan consortia by city banks and involved itself in active *ex ante* monitoring of borrowing firms (see Chapter 8 by Horiuchi). But around the time of the introduction of the drastic stabilization policy under the Dodge plan, the BOJ began to recede from this role. In 1951, the Anti-Monopoly Act was revised and the ceiling on bank equity holding in non-financial firms was lifted from 5 per cent to 10 per cent (in 1987 it was reduced again to 5 per cent). With the signing of the Peace Treaty in 1952, the formation of presidents' clubs, instrumental for re-grouping of ex-zaibatsu firms and formation of new financial groupings, was made possible. Also in 1951, the Japan Development Bank was founded as a government-owned development bank specializing in the provision of long-term investment financing, together with the IBJ, which was reorganized in 1952.

In the heyday of the main bank system, a stable system existed in which banks and other financial institutions mobilized and allocated savings in a high-growth economy regulated by controls over loan, deposit, and bond issue interest rates (see Chapter 11 by Patrick). Finance was mildly repressed, in that demand for funds was in excess of supply, as markets did not fully clear at the regulated rates and some credit rationing occurred, but real interest rates were positive; new entry to the banking industry was prohibited, creation of new financial instruments restricted, and markets and financial institution activities segmented. Funds were, in practice, preferentially allocated among large business borrowers. In spite of all these deviations from the neo-classical competitive norm, the economy realized phenomenal growth and the banking system probably deserves at least partial credit. This era may be the most relevant for drawing lessons for developing and reforming economies.

Market-Embedded Main Bank System: 1975–

In 1974, the economy contracted for the first time in the post-war period and industrial firms started to adjust to slower economic growth by restructuring assets and reducing debt burdens, under so-called slim management (*genryo keiei*) drives. From around 1975, large firms began to reduce their reliance on bank borrowing drastically as economic growth slowed, firms invested less, and private saving first came to surpass private investment. Securities markets became a viable source of external financing for an increasing number of credit-worthy large firms, and the banks began to become increasingly active in supplying bond-related and other investment-banking services. (For detailed analysis of corporate financing trends in this period, see Sheard 1992 and Chapter 10 by Campbell and Hamao.)

Massive government bond issues to finance budget deficits caused by increasing social security and other expenditures began in 1975. In order to market national debt issues, the MOF relied upon a consortium of financial institutions, including city banks. This would eventually make it necessary for the MOF to deregulate secondary markets for national bonds and, as an inevitable result of market forces, to deregulate the private bond market and foreign exchange transactions, leading to closer integration with international securities markets (for more analysis, see Chapter 10 by Campbell and Hamao, and Chapter 7 by Ramseyer).

For these and other reasons, 1975 may be considered the year that ushered in a new era of the main bank system. We call this the era of the 'market-embedded main bank system'. In this phase, the main bank system has been modified by the rise in securities market finance (and explosive increases in share prices), opportunities for expansion into international markets, the strengthening of the relative bargaining power of the financially richer firms, and now new and unexpected problems associated with the decline in the value of banks' unrealized stock portfolio capital gains (which are counted as part of Bank for International Settlements Tier 2 bank capital), and with potential real estate loan problems.

CURRENT PROBLEMS AND THE FUTURE

One question is whether the current problems of the Japanese banking system invalidate the relevance of lessons of the main bank system. The asset-inflation bubble of the late 1980s was partially created by the erosion of the coherence and integrity of the regulatory framework. On the one hand, regulations on bond issues had been successively eased since the mid-1970s and the government reduced its deficit financing since the mid-1980s. On the other hand, the city banks were not permitted to engage in underwriting business. With diminishing opportunity for traditional lending and limited in bond-related services during the easy money policy after the 1985 Plaza Accordingly, banks started to increase loans to real estate development companies, to non-bank financial intermediaries, and to industrial companies for their financial and real estate speculations (*zaiteku*—literally, 'financial engineering'), as well as to individuals who were willing to provide land as collateral. The bubble demonstrated that the Japanese, like others, are subject to collective speculative manias. It also painfully demonstrated *ex post* the weakened monitoring capacity of banks in the newly emergent market environment. But we do not think that this implies that the Japanese experience in the heyday of the main bank system is irrelevant for developing and transforming economies which still face the need for the establishment of sound financial systems facilitating economic development.

Nonetheless, the bad loan consequences of the bursting of the speculative bubble will probably result in a relatively weaker banking system in Japan unless there is further deregulation, particularly permitting banks to engage in bond underwriting and related services more liberally, and hence to evolve into universal banking-type institutions. At this moment, the willingness and capability of main banks to rescue companies is under test, and they may well become more discriminating in client selection in the future. The system may be becoming more diversified in the direction of better firms having weaker core bank relationships with multiple banks. In spite of all these factors, however, the Japanese system seems unlikely to shift to the Anglo-American type arms-length banking system in the near future. One reason is the peripheral nature of the equity market, which, partly due to stable shareholding practices, lacks effective monitoring functions to replace those performed by banks. This in turn reflects structural features of Japanese firm organization, notably the operation of a highly internalized employment system, predicated on long-term employment. The main bank system has aspects that cannot be dismissed simply as late development phenomena (see Chapter 4 by Aoki). Main bank relationships will undoubtedly evolve, but the main bank will continue to be an important actor in the Japanese financial system, particularly if it is able to adapt itself to the new market environment.

REFERENCES

ADAMS, T. F. M. and IWAO HOSHI. 1972. *A Financial History of the New Japan.* Tokyo: Kodansha.

AOKI, MASAHIKO. 1984. *The Cooperative Game Theory of the Firm.* Oxford: Oxford University Press.

——. 1988. *Information, Incentives, and Bargaining in the Japanese Economy.* Cambridge: Cambridge University Press.

AOKI, MASAHIKO and PAUL SHEARD. 1992. 'The Main Bank System and Corporate Governance Structure in Japan.'

Bank of Japan. Various editions. *Keizai Tokei Nenpo (Economic Statistics Annual).* Tokyo.

BERGLÖF, ERIK. 1990. 'Capital Structure as a Mechanism of Control: A Comparison of Financial Systems.' In Masahiko Aoki, Bo Gustafsson, and Oliver E. Williamson, eds., *The Firm as a Nexus of Treaties*. London: Sage Publications.

DE LONG, B. 1991. 'The Great American Universal Banking Experiment.' *The International Economy*, January–February.

GERLACH, MICHAEL L. 1992. *Alliance Capitalism: The Social Organization of Japanese Business*. Berkeley: University of California Press.

HORIUCHI, AKIYOSHI, FRANK PACKER, and SHIN'ICHI FUKUDA. 1988. 'What Role Has the "Main Bank" Played in Japan.' *Journal of the Japanese and International Economies* 2: 159–80.

HORIUCHI, AKIYOSHI and QING-YUAN SUI. 1993. 'The Influence of Japan Development Bank Loans on Corporate Investment Behavior.' *Journal of the Japanese and International Economies* 7(4): 441–65.

HORIUCHI, TOSHIHIRO and EIJI MURAKAMI. 1991. 'Wagakuni ni okeru mein banku torihiki jittai: anketo kekka kara mita kigyo kin'yu no sugata' ('The state of main bank transactions in Japan: the shape of corporate finance as seen from questionnaire results'). In Toshihiro Horiuchi, ed., *Jiyuka kokusaika jidai no kigyo kin'yu no henbo: mein banku no kino to hensei (Transformation of corporate finance in the era of liberalization and internationalization: the function and transformation of the main bank)*. Kenkyu hokoku 75. Nihon Keizai Kenkyu Senta (Japan Center for Economic Research).

KAPLAN, STEVEN N. and BERNADETTE ALCAMO MINTON. 1994. 'Appointments of Outsiders to Japanese Boards.' *Journal of Financial Economics* 34.

KATO, TOSHIHIKO. 1957. *Honpo Ginkoshiron (History of Banking in Japan)*. Tokyo: University of Tokyo Press.

KIGYO KEIRETSU SORAN. Various editions. *Kigyo Keiretsu Soran (Directory of Corporate Affiliations)*. Tokyo: Toyo Keizai Shimposha.

KORNAI, JANOS. 1980. *The Economics of Shortage*. Amsterdam: North-Holland.

Mochikabu gaisha seiri iinkai (Holding Companies Liquidation Committee). 1951. *Nihon zaibatsu to sono kaitai (Japanese zaibatsu and their dissolution)*.

PATRICK, HUGH. 1983. 'Japanese Financial Development in Historical Perspective, 1968–80.' In Gustav Ranis and others, eds., *Comparative Development Perspectives*. Boulder CO: Westview Press.

RYBCZINKSI, TAD M. 1984. 'Industrial Finance Systems in Europe, U.S. and Japan.' *Journal of Economic Behavior and Organization* 5(3–4): 275–86 (September–December).

SHEARD, PAUL. 1989. 'The Main Bank System and Corporate Monitoring and Control in Japan.' *Journal of Economic Behavior and Organization* 11: 399–422.

——. 1991a. 'The Economics of Interlocking Shareholding in Japan.' *Ricerche Economiche* 45: 421–48.

——. 1991b. 'The Role of Firm Organization in the Adjustment of a Declining Industry in Japan: the Case of Aluminum.' *Journal of the Japanese and International Economies* 5(1): 14–40.

——. 1992. 'Japanese Corporate Finance and Behavior: Recent Developments and the Impact of Deregulation.' In Colin McKenzie and Michael Stutchbury, eds., *Japanese Financial Markets and the Role of the Yen*. Sydney: Allen & Unwin.

SHEARD, PAUL. 1994a. 'Delegated Monitoring Among Delegated Monitors: Principal-Agent Aspects of the Japanese Main Bank System.' *Journal of the Japanese and International Economies* 18:1–2 (March).

——. 1994b. 'Interlocking Shareholdings and Corporate Governance in Japan.' in Masahiko Aoki and Ronald Dore, eds., *The Japanese Firm: Sources of Competitive Strength*. Oxford: Oxford University Press: 310–49.

Shukan Daiyamondo. 1987. 'Tokushu: Tsuyoi ginko yowai ginko' ('Special: strong banks, weak banks'). 21 February, pp. 16–31.

TERANISHI, JURO. 1990. 'Financial Systems and the Industrialization of Japan: 1900–1970.' *Banca Nacionale del Lavoro Quarterly Review* 174 (September).

2

Loan Syndication in War-Time Japan and the Origins of the Main Bank System

JURO TERANISHI

Although the term 'main bank' was first used in the post-war period, the particular pattern of corporate control which utilizes the monitoring activity of a bank in a loan syndication is an extension of the long-term process of interaction among changes in industrial structure, the evolution of the financial system, changing patterns of business financing, and some historical accidents.

A fascinating phenomenon in this process is the spontaneous and endogenous emergence of loan syndications during 1939–41. This chapter investigates the reasons behind this and the relationship of loan syndications to the post-war main bank system. The first section traces the evolution of the relationship among shareholders, managers and banks from the late nineteenth century; it then seeks to clarify the nature of the corporate monitoring system that comprised the background for the emergence of loan syndication in the war-time period, and eventually gave rise to the post-war main bank system. The second section presents a detailed analysis of the 130 loan syndications existing around 1939, and discusses the reasons for their emergence. The process of institutional transformation that led to the Designated Financial Institution System for Munitions Company Financing Act (Gunji Yushi Shiteikinyukikan Seido) is also examined. The rise of the post-war main bank system is considered in the third section.

Two factors are identified in this paper as the basic elements which give incentives for banks to organize loan syndications and play the role of main banks; the rise of large and unfamiliar financing needs that compel banks to resort to loan diversification by organizing syndications, and the increasing degree of autonomy of corporate managers which necessitates monitoring by banks, and a minimization of monitoring costs by means of the main bank system. It is shown that in the war-time economy, where a drastic change in industrial structure aimed at increasing production of heavy and chemical industries was carried out, the first factor was

The author is grateful to Hugh Patrick, Masahiko Aoki, Jenny Corbett, Akiyoshi Horiuchi, Takeo Hoshi, Hideaki Miyajima and Tetsuji Okazaki for their comments.

dominant in bringing about the mushrooming of loan syndication. The effects of government control on lending, explicit as well as implicit, were most serious for large city banks, which were obliged to resort to loan syndication to diversify risk. There was a trend since the early 1930s for corporate managers to show an increasing degree of independence from shareholder control, and this tendency was intensified under the reign of planning-oriented bureaucrats, the so-called innovative bureaucrats (*kakushinkanryo*), after 1940. However, the banks did not need to play a monitoring role because corporate managers were increasingly put under the direct control of bureaucrats. Bureaucrats found loan syndication a convenient tool for resource mobilization, and transformed it into a system for channelling funds into munition companies after 1944.

In the case of the post-war main bank system, both factors seem to be important. The autonomy of corporate managers reached its height partly because of the disappearance of large stockholders caused by the historical shocks related to zaibatsu dissolution, partly because of corporate managers' pursuit of autonomy by cross shareholding, and partly owing to the dominance of indirect financing in the flow of funds structure. The main bank system was developed as an efficient device for reducing the agency costs of corporate managers. On the other hand, the formation of loan syndication was triggered by another historical shock; the credit crunch caused by the termination of new lendings by the Reconstruction Finance Bank (Fukko-kinyu Kinko) and to the compulsory pumping of funds from local banks. It seems that loan syndication was gradually built into the system as the need for loan diversification increased during the rapid process of catching up in heavy and chemical industries.

PRE-WAR EVOLUTION OF CORPORATE CONTROL
AND FINANCING

Generally and schematically speaking, the changing pattern of corporate control and business financing since Meiji is comprised of three phases. The first, roughly from the 1880s to the 1900s, is the period of internal financing of business firms, and the dominance of large stockholders in the system of corporate control. The second phase, from the period of World War I to the early 1930s, is characterized by outside financing. Large stockholders were still in power, but agency costs owing to outside financing became significant. During the third phase, starting from the mid-1930s, outside financing was accelerated, and the sovereignty of large stockholders was eroded. Managers became increasingly independent, giving rise to a new form of agency costs to the economy. In Figure 2.1, patterns (A-1) and (A-2) correspond to the first phase, pattern (B) to the second phase, and pattern (C) to the third phase. MC denotes monitoring

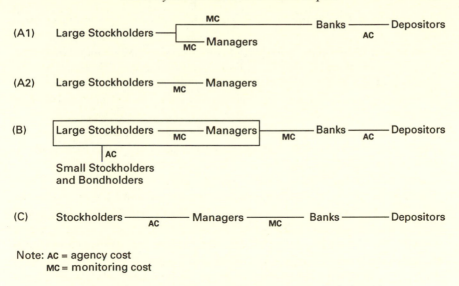

Note: AC = agency cost
      MC = monitoring cost

Fig. 2.1 Patterns of Bank-Stockholder-Manager Relationship

cost and AC is agency cost (in the sense of the distortion of resource allocation that arises whenever agency-principal problems exist due to information asymmetry). When information asymmetry is eliminated by effective monitoring, agency costs disappear, but the economy must bear the resource costs of monitoring.

Internal Financing: Pattern (A-1) and (A-2)

During the first phase, economic development converted Japan from a predominantly agrarian economy to an exporter of light industrial products: the share of employment in the primary sector declined from 70.1 per cent in 1885 to 67.1 per cent in 1910, and the share of manufactured textile products in total exports rose from 8.8 per cent during 1882–91 to 27.7 per cent during 1902–11.

The development of infrastructure, such as railroads and telecommunications, as well as investment in the cotton-spinning industry, was basically financed internally by firms. Zaibatsu, rich family-based conglomerates, expanded their activities by reinvesting profits. Since they were in possession of such highly profitable industries as mining and foreign trade, financing through internal funds was sufficient for the growth of their businesses (pattern (A-2)). Important industries outside the reign of the zaibatsu, such as cotton spinning and railroads, also used internal financing. In this case, however, large stockholders were dependent on bank borrowing for their stock investments (A-2). Shareholders used their shares as collateral for bank borrowing. At the end of 1895, 38.5 per cent of the collateral on lendings of commercial banks (*kokuritsu ginko*) was stock.

To service their bank liabilities, stockholders requested high dividends. Patrick (1967) gives a concise and rigorous description of this aspect of business financing. During the 1880s and 90s, most of the profits of large companies were distributed outside the company, so reliance on internal financing was very low, as shown by the low ratio of retained earnings (reserves) to paid-in capital in Table 2.1. The ratio of net worth to total assets is extremely high for these industries because of the high ratio of paid-in capital. Large shareholders, not business firms, were the major borrowers from the banking sector during this period: in December 1895, only 5.7 per cent of total lendings by commercial banks was to companies, most of the remainder was lent to rich landlords and merchants who were also stockholders of companies.

Although the separation between ownership and management proceeded from this period on, and the composition of managers who were not major shareholders increased steadily (Teranishi, 1990), companies continued to be controlled by large stockholders. Since large stockholders had large enough stakes, it payed for them to monitor management (Schleifer and Vishny, 1986). Take-over was the most important measure invoked to replace inefficient management and, in most cases, large stockholders took the leadership in organizing and directing discussion at stockholder meetings. Majority rule was rarely used: matters were almost always determined by unanimous decision (Kataoka, 1988).

TABLE 2.1 Financing of Railway and Cotton-Spinning Companies

(per cents)

	1890	1895	1900	1905	1915
Railway Companies					
Reserve/Paid-in Capital	—	1.6	2.0	3.6	—
Net Worth/Total Assets	—	91.7	93.2	87.4	—
Corporate Bonds/Total Assets	—	7.0	5.6	1.2	—
Cotton-Spinning Companies					
Reserve/Paid-in Capital	13.3	16.5	11.2	30.5	43.5
Net Worth/Total Assets	74.2	62.3	82.2	87.0	77.4
Sample size	10	20	54	35	31

Note: Sample sizes of railway companies are not available. By 1915 the railways had been nationalized.
Source: Noda (1980, p. 129), Takamura (1971, vol. 2, pp. 16–17) and Sugiyama (1970, pp. 122–23).

Outside Financing and the Emergence of Agency Cost: Pattern (B)

After the 1900s, especially during World War I, the Japanese economy started building heavy and chemical industries. Since these industries required a large amount of investment (non-separability), business firms became increasingly dependent on outside financing. As Table 2.2 shows, the composition of financing by paid-in capital (the major source of financing in pattern (A-1) in Figure 2.1) decreased from 53.2 per cent in 1914 to 42.3 per cent in 1930, while that of reserves (the major source of financing for pattern (A-2)) decreased only slightly from 15.1 per cent in 1914 to 13.1 per cent in 1930.

Outside funds were mainly introduced through bank borrowings by business firms. Many medium-sized banks had common stockholders or managers with particular business firms, and were used as conduits of funds from depositors to these firms. The practice, called organ banking (*kikanginko*), was extremely risky, as it prevented adequate portfolio diversification, and because banks' incentive to monitor borrowing firms properly was reduced, which meant there was a serious agency cost between depositors and banks, as indicated in pattern (B).

Some important groups utilized money and capital markets as sources of outside funds. The conglomerates newly established during this period, called Taisho zaibatsu, used equity finance as a major source of financing. Cotton-spinning companies, the most powerful manufacturing sector in the inter-war period, made use of their high credibility to finance through money markets. Electric utilities and large manufacturing firms obtained long-term funds from corporate bonds, as can be seen in the increasing share of bonds in Table 2.2.

The need for outside financing caused a significant increase in the number of shareholders. Table 2.3 demonstrates this fact for ten large companies. For example, Tokyo Dento (the largest electric utility), saw the number of shareholders increase 14.5 fold from 4,300 in 1916 to 62,300 in 1934. At the same time, the number of shares issued only increased 8.6 fold, implying an increase in small shareholders. A similar phenomenon can be seen for other companies.

Large shareholders still had the power to control companies in pattern (B). There was a significant risk of moral hazard in the form of exploitation of small shareholders and banks. The uncertainty of economic conditions and the muddling of economic policy as an aftermath of the World War I boom were fertile grounds for opportunistic behaviour. In fact, the moral hazard of large stockholders colluding with managers was a serious social problem during this period. Not only was the level of dividends extremely high, but bonus payments to top managers quite frequently amounted to 5 to 10 per cent of profits. Even if a company was in the red, dividends and bonuses were paid by means of false statements of

TABLE 2.2 Financing of Large Firms
(per cents)

	Liabilities		Net Worth	
	Borrowing[1]	Corporate Bonds	Paid-in Capital	Reserves
1914	20.6	11.2	53.2	15.1
1915	16.7	14.2	53.4	15.8
1916	14.9	13.9	50.5	20.7
1917	16.0	11.3	47.9	24.8
1918	17.4	10.3	46.2	26.2
1919	19.3	9.2	43.2	28.3
1920	20.1	6.7	51.3	22.0
1921	18.8	8.0	53.6	19.6
1922	17.6	9.0	53.0	20.5
1923	19.8	10.8	50.6	18.8
1924	18.1	14.4	49.8	17.7
1925	17.4	18.7	46.9	16.9
1926	18.2	19.2	47.5	15.0
1927	19.7	20.0	45.8	14.5
1928	16.4	25.9	44.3	13.5
1929	17.0	26.2	44.1	12.7
1930	18.5	26.0	42.3	13.1
1931	22.8	20.5	45.4	11.2
1932	24.0	19.8	44.8	11.4
1933	23.3	19.0	45.5	12.3
1934	21.4	18.0	47.4	13.2
1935	22.0	16.5	46.7	14.8
1936	24.2	14.4	45.8	15.6
1937	28.4	12.0	44.1	15.5
1938	30.4	11.4	42.5	15.6
1939	33.0	11.9	39.4	15.7
1940	36.5	10.6	37.1	15.8
1941	37.1	11.3	36.0	15.5
1942	43.6	8.9	32.1	15.4
1943	46.6	5.8	30.4	14.4
1950	65.2	4.1	8.5	22.2
1955	58.1	3.8	11.1	27.0
1960	65.1	6.8	14.3	13.9

Note: Based on stock data at the end of business year (generally 31 March) except for 1943, for which data of mid-business year is used. Because of data problems, 1943 adds to 97.2%.
Sample size is 50–75 during 1918–30, about 300 during 1931–43, and about 600 after 1950.
[1] Includes trade credits.

Source: *Jigyogaisha Keieikoritsu no Kenkyu* (Toyo keizai shinposha, 1932) until 1930; after 1931, *Honpo Jigyoseiseki no Bunseki* (Mitsubishi Keizai-Kenkyujo, each year).

TABLE 2.3 Number of Stockholders and Share Distribution of Ten Large Companies

	Tokyo Dento	Daido Denryoku	Nihon Kangyo Bank	Osaka Shosen	Toho Denryoku	Nihon Sekiyu	Nihon Yusen	Kansai Kisen	Nihon Denryoku	Minami Manshu Tetsudo
1915										
Number of shares (a)	1,000	—	200	495	30	400	880	400	—	1,600
Number of stockholders (b)	4.3	—	3.7	5.4	0.3	3.0	4.2	1.8	—	7.6
(a)/(b)	231	—	50	92	102	134	212	217	—	211
1920										
Number of shares (a)	2,480	2,000	800	2,000	90	800	2,000	900	1,000	3,800
Number of stockholders (b)	8.8	14.7	3.8	23.7	0.5	8.3	21.0	5.8	7.5	10.0
(a)/(b)	282	136	212	84	159	97	95	155	134	380
1934										
Number of shares (a)	8,591	3,520	2,175	2,000	4,000	1,600	2,125	1,600	2,800	16,000
Number of stockholders (b)	62.3	37.4	36.5	30.1	30.0	25.3	23.7	22.0	21.1	54.7
(a)/(b)	138	94	60	67	133	63	90	73	133	293
Number of large stockholders[1]	146	30	43	23	63	17	20	29	31	170
Number of shares held by large stockholders (c)	3,477	1,129	404	244	1,017	275	677	788	769	10,970
(c)/(a)(%)	40.4	32.0	18.5	12.1	25.4	17.1	31.8	49.2	27.5	68.5

Note: (a), (b), (c) in thousand.
End of each business year (generally 31 March) except: Nihon Kangyo Bank (end of previous year); Toho Denryoku (entry for 1934 is the end of 1935); and Nihon Denryoku (entry for 1934 is the end of September 1934).
[1] Large stockholders are those owning more than 5,000 shares.

Source: Masuji (1936, pp. 13–32).

settlements or sales of assets. Takahashi (1930) reports a number of incidents of moral hazard by managers and large stockholders.

Until the early 1930s the old zaibatsu firms basically maintained financing pattern (A-2), relying on accumulation of profits. Banks in these zaibatsu groups did not have to lend to group companies, because the zaibatsu had ample internal funds and also because banks tried to avoid the risks of organ banking. This policy was more or less explicit in the case of Mitsui and Sumitomo (Morikawa, 1980, pp. 216, 219).

In sum, the system of corporate control was characterized by two kinds of agency costs. As Figure 2.1 shows, there were significant agency costs between depositors and banks, and between large shareholders cum managers and small shareholders.

The Increasing Independence of Managers: Pattern (C)

The unstable banking system due to organ banking culminated in the Great Financial Crash (*kin'yu kyoko*) of 1927. Thereafter agency costs arising from moral hazard between depositors and banks were significantly reduced. There were three reasons for this. First, after the crash, bank examination by the Bank of Japan (BOJ) and the Ministry of Finance (MOF) was strengthened. Second, the BOJ abandoned the practice of bailing-out ailing banks, which often worsened their moral hazard. Third and most important, a semi-compulsory merger policy was implemented. The minimum capital requirement was raised significantly, and the MOF conducted administrative guidance, quite aggressively urging the merger of banks.

Pattern (C) in Figure 2.1 shows that agency costs arising from moral hazard by banks became quite small after 1930. At the same time, on the real side of the economy, heavy and chemical industrialization was accelerated in the midst of the rapid economic recovery after 1932 and the shift to a military economy after 1937. In order to accommodate these changes, business firms were obliged to resort to outside financing more heavily, especially bank borrowing. In Table 2.2, we can see that the percentage share of borrowing more than doubled between 1931 and 1946.

The effect of these changes on corporate control was, in a nutshell, a shift from pattern (B) to (C). The importance of independent large shareholders declined further, their position eroded by the development of cross-shareholding among business firms. As a consequence, managers became more independent. In terms of agency problems, agency costs arising between stockholders and managers developed for the first time, while those arising from the bank-depositor relationship were significantly reduced.

Old Zaibatsu

A drastic change occurred in the corporate control system of the old zaibatsu. In order to raise funds to adapt to the changing industrial structure, and partly to mitigate anti-zaibatsu sentiments, the self-financing mechanism of pattern (A-2) was abandoned. First, shares held by the families and shareholding companies were offered to the public. Mitsubishi was most active in this respect. Starting with the offering of Mitsubishi Kogyo (1920) and Mitsubishi Ginko (1927) shares, shares of first-line companies, including holding companies themselves, were offered to the public after 1934. Mitsui and Sumitomo were rather cautious in this respect. Mitsui, after offering the shares of Mitsui Ginko for sale to the public in 1917, opened the holdings of a second-line company and those of three affiliates of first-line companies during 1933–34. Sumitomo opened three first-line companies to the public during 1934–37.[1]

Second, and more important, as a device to raise equity capital without diluting group ties, cross shareholding was widely introduced after the early 1930s. In the case of Mitsui, Mitsui Gomei (the holding company) began extensive sales of shares of group companies after 1932. Most of the purchasers were financial institutions in the same group, such as Mitsui Life Insurance, Mitsui Trust, Mitsui Bussan and Taisho Insurance (Kasuga, 1987, pp. 18, 76). In the case of Mitsubishi, after the public offering, overall cross-holdings in the group increased, and the composition changed. This is shown in Table 2.4. The lowest is 5.0 per cent for Mitsubishi Denki, but Mitsubishi Shintaku and Mitsubishi Seiko came to be about 30 per cent held by group companies. With respect to the Sumitomo zaibatsu, cross shareholding was started after 1933, when shares held by Sumitomo Gomei (the holding company) were sold to financial institutions in the group such as Sumitomo Bank, Sumitomo Trust, Sumitomo Life Insurance and Fuso Marine Insurance (Asajima, 1983, pp. 498, 540, 544). Most of the shares sold were in heavy and chemical industries companies strategic for the group.

The result of such cross shareholdings during the years 1930–45 in the zaibatsu group can be seen in Table 2.5, which presents data for immediately after the war. The degree of cross shareholding was already as high as 10 to 40 per cent during the war. It is worth emphasizing that the old zaibatsu had financial motives for using cross shareholdings. In order to complement internal funds, cross shareholding was utilized to tap funds from non-bank financial institutions and other firms within the group.

Third, although during the 1920s and the period before World War I, zaibatsu banks, in order to avoid becoming organ banks, did not have to lend to companies in the same group, this principle was abandoned after around 1930. As Table 2.6 shows, dependence on deposits from group

---

[1] On Mitsubishi, see Mitsubishi Jyuko (1934), Mitsubishi Denki (1937), Mitsubishi Soko (1937), Mitsubishi Shoji (1938), Nihon Kasei (1940), Mitsubishisha (1940), Mitsubishi Seiko (1943). On Mitsui see Hokkaido Tankokisen (1934), Toyo-koatsu (1933), Miike Chisso (1933), Toyo Reiyon (1933). On Sumitomo see Sumitomo Hiryo (Kagaku) (1934), Sumitomo Kinzoku (1935), Sumitomo Densen (Denko) (1937).

TABLE 2.4 Distribution of Shareholding in Companies of the Mitsubishi Zaibatsu Offered to the Public

(per cents)

Company[1]	Date	Owner Family and Holding Company	Other Companies in the Group	Outside Zaibatsu
Mitsubishi Kogyo	Apr. 1920	98.5	0.7	0.8*
(1920 May, mining)	Apr. 1921	61.1	4.0	34.9
	Apr. 1942	43.0	6.5	50.5
Mitsubishi Shintaku	May 1928	22.9	25.2	51.7
(1927 March, trust bank)	Nov. 1937	23.6	29.4	47.0
	May 1942	22.2	29.7	45.1
Mitsubishi Bank[2]	Feb. 1927	96.0	1.0	3.0*
(1928 December,	Apr. 1929	49.0	14.7	36.3
commercial bank)	Dec. 1942	43.9	15.8	40.3
Mitsubishi Jyukogyo	Apr. 1932	98.6	0.6	0.8*
(1934 Summer,	Jul. 1938	49.9	5.4	44.7
machinery)	Jul. 1941	43.2	7.9	48.9
Mitsubishi Denki	Apr. 1932	0.0	87.9	12.1
(1937 February, electric	Oct. 1937	43.2	0.1	56.7
machinery)	Oct. 1944	44.6	5.0	50.4
Mitsubishi Seiko[3]	Aug. 1942	58.3	41.7	0.0
(1942 November, steel)	Dec. 1942	51.0	29.7	19.3
	Apr. 1944	51.0	31.1	17.9

Notes:

[1] The initial public offering date and industry classification are given in parentheses.

[2] The official public offering of Mitsubishi Bank occurred in July 1929, but shares had been sold to employees of the group in December 1928, and the earlier date is considered as the time of the *de facto* offering.

[3] For Mitsubishi Seiko, the time of the public offering is considered to be the date of its merger with Tokyo Kozai, whose shares were already held outside the zaibatsu.

* Indicates persons with close connections to Mitsubishi.

Source: Calculated by the author from tables in Asajima (1986, pp. 274, 280, 287, 296, 310, 316).

companies and lending to them had become an important business for Mitsubishi Bank, as well as Sumitomo Bank, especially during the wartime period after 1937. For Mitsui Bank, owing to a lack of data, the pattern is not clear. However, it is well known that even Mitsui Gomei (the holding company) became heavily dependent on borrowings from group financial institutions during the war, so it seems safe to assume that Mitsui had a similar experience.

TABLE 2.5 Distribution of Shareholding in Zaibatsu Groups Immediately after World War II

Zaibatsu	Number of Companies	Owner Family and Holding Company	Other Companies in the Same Zaibatsu	Outside Zaibatsu
Mitsui				
First Line	10	63.4	11.9	24.7
Second Line	13	35.9	17.2	46.9
Mitsubishi				
First Line	11	30.3	15.3	54.4
Second Line	16	18.4	40.3	41.3
Sumitomo				
First Line	17	27.9	16.5	55.6
Second Line	16	13.2	30.7	56.1
Yasuda				
First Line	20	27.9	17.8	54.3
Second Line	12	17.0	15.3	67.7

Source: Miyajima (1992). Calculated from data in the appendix tables of the Ministry of Finance, *Showa Zaiseishi-Shusen kara Kowa made*, vol. 2.

Finally, it is also well documented that the central decision-making system of the zaibatsu organization weakened during the 1930s. This was especially true of the control the holding company had over decisions relating to investment projects and financing problems. As the internal financing mechanism became eroded and bureaucratic interventions into questions of resource and fund allocation were intensified, it was natural for the zaibatsu organization to become by and large decentralized.

In sum, in the old zaibatsu, the control of families and holding companies was seriously eroded as their supremacy, based on reinvestment of profits, was weakened. The role of independent shareholders gradually declined as cross shareholding became a popular method of financing, managers became more and more independent, and the monitoring of their behaviour became a serious issue.

New Zaibatsu

The dominance of managers is most apparent in the case of the new zaibatsu, which showed a spectacular businesses expansion during the 1930s, based on the introduction of new technology in the heavy and

TABLE 2.6 Deposits and Lendings Relationship within Zaibatsu

	Mitsui		Mitsubishi		Sumitomo	
	(A) Deposits	(B) Lending	(C) Deposits	(D) Lending	(E) Deposits	(F) Lending
1930	9.5	9.6	9.7	17.0	1.8	4.9
1931	5.2	10.8	8.1	12.8	1.8	6.2
1932	8.2	6.9	9.0	17.9	1.8	6.5
1933	8.2	8.5	9.3	21.8	1.8	6.1
1934	7.3	11.6	10.8	20.8	—	6.2
1935	—	—	10.9	24.7	—	3.9
1936	—	—	13.1	23.2	3.1	2.2
1937	—	—	15.0	35.3	2.6	5.0
1938	5.2	11.6	13.5	34.0	—	9.8
1939	3.7	12.6	10.5	46.8	—	12.3
1940	4.0	11.7	12.2	43.7	2.6	14.9
1941	—	—	11.3	43.1	2.7	17.6
1942	—	—	16.0	34.0	2.4	18.4
1943	—	—	—	25.2	—	16.7
1944	—	—	—	48.0	—	—

(A) = Deposits from Companies of Mitsui Zaibatsu as a Percentage of Total Deposits of Mitsui Bank.
(B) = Lendings to Companies of Mitsui Zaibatsu as a Percentage of Total Lendings of Mitsui Bank.
(C) = Deposits from Companies of Mitsubishi Zaibatsu as a Percentage of Total Deposits of Mitsubishi Bank.
(D) = Lendings to Companies of Mitsubishi Zaibatsu as a Percentage of Total Lendings to Mitsubishi Bank and Mitsubishi Trust Company.
(E) = Deposits from Companies of Sumitomo Zaibatsu as a Percentage of Total Deposits of Sumitomo Bank.
(F) = Lendings to Companies of Sumitomo Zaibatsu as a Percentage of Total Lendings of Sumitomo Bank, Sumitomo Trust Company and Fuso Kaijo (marine insurance company).

Source: Kasuga (1987, pp. 83–87), Asajima (1987a, pp. 150–53), and Asajima (1987b, pp. 208–11).

chemical industries. New zaibatsu were managed by owner-founders, but these founders were not content with expanding as family businesses, instead trying quite aggressively to diversify their group activities, and to establish a managerial control system. Several methods were used for this purpose. First, cross shareholding was encouraged. The Riken group was typical of this practice. At the end of April 1937, five major companies in the group owned 51.7 per cent of the shares issued by the group's 23 first-line companies. The Nisso group also used cross shareholding significantly (Udagawa, 1984, pp. 186, 204–5). Second, most of the new zaibatsu, except for Nichitsu, which kept a closed shareholding system based on the extraordinarily large patent income from Chosen Chisso, were keen on the public offering of their shares. By selling shares of group companies at a price higher than their purchase price (face value), the founder obtained funds to invest in new companies. Third, they maintained a relationship with a large number of banks, including the seven major commercial banks, Chosen Bank, and the Industrial Bank of Japan (IBJ).

As a result of these policies, the founders had quite weak positions as shareholders. For example, in the case of Mori, the only new zaibatsu that had a holding company, the holding company held only 15.0 per cent of Nihon Denko and 6.7 per cent of Showa Hiryo, its two major companies.

National Policy Firms (NPF)

The number of state enterprises called national policy firms (*kokusaku-gaisha*, NPF) increased from 27 in 1937 to 154 in June 1941, with total capital of 5.6 billion yen or 15.6 per cent of the 36.2 billion yen total capital of the corporate sector. Although some were production firms, such as Nihon Seitetsu (steel) and Nihon Hassoden (electricity), most were investment or stockholding companies related to the energy industries, the distribution of raw materials, or colonial development, and their rates of profit were quite low. All of the NPF were joint stock companies, but on average more than half of their shares were held by the government, and the power of the stockholder meeting was quite limited. The president and managers were chosen by the government, and all the important decisions, such as changes in the articles of incorporation, disposal of income, issue of bonds or bank borrowing, and merger and dissolution, were effective only with the approval of the government. The NPF were virtually under the control of the related government bureaux. Therefore, whenever a symbiotic relationship occurred between a bureau and NPF managers, who were often former employees of the bureau, monitoring of NPF management was likely to be quite lax.

For example, during the 1920s when high bonuses to managers were a serious social problem, Seiyukai (one of the two leading political parties) proposed that the government's economic planning committee (Keizai

Shingikai) apply the brakes to the practice, pointing to the large payments received by managers of Toyotakushoku, a leading NPF established to develop Korea and the Manchurian region (*Jijishinpo*, 18 September 1928). Toyotakushoku had suffered serious losses due to its easy lending operations in Manchuria since the end of World War I, but the managers continued to take high bonuses without restructuring the firm's huge non-performing loans, in defiance of the recommendations of the Colonial Development Bureau (Kurose, 1988).

Electric Utilities

It is important to mention the corporate control system of electric utilities. Like cotton spinners, these were firms that had high reputations without belonging to any zaibatsu. The reason for the independence of the group seems to be closely related to its shareholding structure. For one thing, most electric utilities had holding companies, with which a cross shareholding structure was established (Masuji 1936, pp. 18–29). For another, among the companies themselves, cross shareholding had taken place. For these reasons, the autonomy of the managers was quite strong and the companies avoided take-over by outsiders, including zaibatsu groups.

Anti-Capitalist Movements

As the dependence on outside financing increased, and cross shareholding became prevalent, the era of the independent large shareholder inevitably came to an end. Shareholders themselves were controlled by other shareholders, and cross shareholding among business firms meant managers became increasingly independent.

Strong anti-capitalist sentiment prevalent during the 1930s also seems to have contributed to the tendency toward managerial autonomy. It is well known that the extensive public offerings of shares held by old zaibatsu was triggered by the assassination of Dan Takuma (director of Mitsui Gomei) in March 1932. The anti-zaibatsu sentiment partly reflected perceived deficiencies in the capitalist market mechanism in the wake of the Great Depression and, more seriously, a result of the influence of Marxist theory and totalitarianism.

The so-called innovative bureaucrats (*kakushin kanryo*) who gathered at the Planning Agency (Kikakuin, established in October 1937) and led the war economy, were possessed of strong anti-capitalist sentiments, and advocated the idea of corporate control that was to give autonomy to managers. Although their idea was not fully realized, partly owing to the opposition of the Ministry of Commerce and Industry (Shoko-sho), which more or less compromised with the interests of the capitalist class, it was partly realized in the control of the dividend rate (Kaisha Rieki Haito oyobi Shikin Yuzu-rei, March 1939), and the establishment during

1938–40 of firm-specific trade unions (*sangyo hohoku-kai*) on the principle of equal partnership among stockholders, managers and employees (Okazaki, 1992). Although the Planning Agency was abolished in October 1943, the concurrent enactment of the Munitions Company Law (Gunji Kaisha-ho) was symbolic in the sense of virtually denying stockholders a role and introducing the dominance of 'production managers' under bureaucratic control in the corporate system.

EMERGENCE OF LOAN SYNDICATION IN WAR-TIME JAPAN

Japan went to war with China in July 1937 and with allied forces throughout the Pacific region in December 1941. Resources were rapidly shifted from consumer goods to heavy and chemical industries related to munition production after 1937, especially during 1937–41. Companies were increasingly dependent on outside financing in order to accommodate the changes. Loan syndication emerged as an endogenous movement within the banking sector around 1939; it was institutionalized and modified after 1941, and especially after 1944, into a tool of fund mobilization for munition production.

War-Time Economy

The mobilization of resources for the sake of war intensified through two stages. During 1937–40, various rationing measures were introduced. Rationing of bank loans for investment purposes was initiated in September 1937 (Temporary Fund Adjustment Act, Rinji Shinkin Chosei-ho) and the compulsory lending system (Meirei Yushi Seido) of the IBJ in March 1939 (Kaisha Rieki-Haito oyobi Shikin Unyo-rei). Lending and security subscriptions over certain amounts had to be approved by the government, and those not directly or indirectly related to expansion of productive capabilities of the munitions industry were not approved. Rationing was extended to cover operating funds, and the compulsory lending system to all banks in October 1940 (Ginko-tou Shikin Unyo-rei). An increasing number of prices were put under control and commodities were rationed starting in April 1939 (Bushi Doin Keikaku).

After December 1940, when the Memorandum of Establishing A New Economic System (Keizai Shintaisei Yoko) was adopted, the economy was pushed into a more totalitarian planned economy form, at least in principle. For each industry, a regulatory board (Tosei-kai) was organized, and the allocation of resources was rigorously set by the planning bureau (Kikakuin) and controlled through the Tosei-kai (Okazaki, 1992). The Bank of Japan Law was amended in February 1942 to allow the BOJ to obey national policy goals, and the Wartime Financing Bank (Senji Kin'yu Kinko) was established in April 1942.

Production reached a peak in 1942. Implementation of the 1943 economic policy had the sole aim of converting existing production resources into munition production—four designated industries (steel, coal, aluminium, and shipbuilding) were affected from March 1943, with aircraft added in November. The Planning Bureau was abolished in October 1943, and the Ministry of Munitions established in November, as the government extended direct intervention into the production of more than 600 manufacturing companies.

Table 2.7 shows the results of the reallocation of resources. The percentage shares of such 'peace' industries as food products, textiles and wood products in employees, lending and production were reduced drastically, while there was a tremendous increase in heavy and chemical industries, especially machinery. It is important to note that the most drastic resource shift occurred during the four-year period from 1937 to 1941. The share of textiles was more than halved from 29.3 per cent to 14.7 per cent, and that of machines more than doubled from 14.4 per cent to 30.2 per cent. As for the lendings of financial institutions and the number of employees, no comparable figures are available. However, the percentage share of lending to manufacturing in the total lending of ordinary banks in June 1933 was 22.4 per cent, while similar figures for all financial institutions in July 1940 and March 1945 were 40.8 per cent and 51.6 per cent respectively. Moreover, the share of employees in the machine industry as a percentage of the total number of employees in manufacturing increased from 20.3 per cent in 1937 to 35.5 per cent in 1941, while the corresponding percentage of gainful workers increased from 28.0 per cent in October 1940 to 50.3 per cent in February 1944.

Loan Syndications Existing in June 1941

The origin of loan syndication in Japan can be traced to the *renmei yushi* of 1930–32. During the deflation caused by the return to gold standard at pre-World War I parity, loan syndications were organized to pump rescue credits to some 20 seriously damaged large companies. The MOF and BOJ guided the system, IBJ and Mitsui Bank were active participants (Mitsui Bank, 1957, p. 422; IBJ 1934, pp. 123–26).

Loan syndication among banks became prevalent after 1939 when banks were still free to allocate their lending, although they were constrained by rigorous specification of lending areas, and when expansion of the heavy and chemical industries, energy, transportation, communication, and mining was the utmost aim of national economic activity.

Examination of the characteristics of firms with syndications in June 1941 provides a key to understanding the economic forces that led to the emergence of the system. The Appendix tables give summary information on the 114 firms for which 130 loan syndication existed at the end of

TABLE 2.7 Distribution of Resources and Output in the Manufacturing Sector

(per cents)

	Employees			Outstanding Lending of Financial Institutions		Value of Production in 1934–36 Prices			
	1932	1937	1941	1941 (Feb.)	1945 (Feb.)	1932	1937	1941	1945
Food Products	14.2	10.5	8.0	3.8	1.5	19.9	15.1	12.2	17.8
Textiles	39.7	30.7	20.3	15.0	7.0	32.6	29.3	14.7	4.6
Lumber and Wood Products	7.2	6.8	7.2	—	—	3.2	2.6	3.1	3.0
Chemicals	7.1	9.7	8.9	14.6	11.8	13.3	17.2	17.5	11.6
Stone, Clay and Glass Products	3.8	4.1	3.8	1.9	0.9	2.4	2.6	2.6	1.8
Iron and Steel	6.0	8.6	9.0	17.6	13.9	8.4	9.4	12.6	12.4
Non-ferrous Metals						3.8	3.1	2.9	5.5
Machinery	11.3	20.3	35.5	36.7	60.2	9.7	14.4	30.2	40.8
Painting and Publishing	4.4	3.0	2.3	—	—	3.0	2.3	1.9	1.0
Electricity and Gas	—	—	—	8.0	2.3	—	—	—	—
Others	5.8	5.7	5.2	2.4	2.4	3.5	3.4	1.0	1.5
Statistical discrepancies	0.5	0.6	2.8	—	—	0.2	0.6	1.4	—

Source: For employees, Mataji Umemura and others (1988), *Long-Term Economic Statistics of Japan*, vol. 2 (*Labor*), table 19 (Tokyo: Toyo Keizai Shimpo-sha); for lending, Bank of Japan (1947), *Senjichu Kin'yu Tokei-yoran*, October; for production, Kazushi Ohkawa and Miyohei Shinohara with Larry Meissner, eds. (1979), *Patterns of Economic Development*, New Haven: Yale University Press.

June 1941. (Nine companies had two syndications, one company had three. Six companies merged into Riken Jyukogyo in July 1941 are regarded as one firm.) The outstanding amount of loans was 1,724 million yen, 8.9 per cent of total lendings of the banking sector.

The following interesting facts should be noted.

Number of Companies by Type of Managing Bank
71 IBJ
 5 IBJ and other banks or trust banks as managers (includes multiple syndications with one managed by the IBJ and the other not; only Toyota Jidosha had actual joint management)
16 Other banks
22 Trust companies

The extent of IBJ involvement is impressive. One reason for this was that the IBJ was regarded as a strategic bank financing the war economy, especially until the Wartime Financing Bank (Senjikin'yu Kinko) was established. The ceiling on the issuance of financial debenture by the IBJ was raised rapidly after 1937. Second, the IBJ had been playing a leading role in corporate bond syndication, and some of its loan syndications began as bridge loans when the underwriting did not go smoothly. Out of 131 companies, 42 also had bond syndications and the IBJ was a manager for 36 of them. The data do not give the names of individual banks except for the IBJ, so it is not possible to check the continuity of the relationship into later periods.

Number of Companies by Type or Group Affiliation
38 National policy firm (NPF)
14 Old and Taisho zaibatsu
12 New zaibatsu
48 Other companies or cooperatives
(The total is 112 because two companies are classified twice: Honkeiko Baientetsu Koji (NPF/Okura) and Manshu Jyukogyo (NPF/Nissan).

Two characteristics are worth noting. First, NPFs comprised the largest group for which loan syndication had been organized. Second, major companies of the new zaibatsu were also recipients of syndicated loans (for example, Hitachi Seisakusho and Manshu Jyukogyo of Nissan, Showa Denki of Mori, Nihon Chisso Hiryo of Nichitsu, and Riken Jyukogyo of Riken).

Among the old zaibatsu, it is interesting that there was only one syndicate for the Sumitomo zaibatsu and only two for Mitsubishi (both for second-line companies), while as many as seven syndicates were organized for Mitsui—including such first-line companies as Mitusi Bussan and Mitsui Kozan, as well as such important second-line companies as Tokyo Shibaura Denki and Kanegafuchi Boseki.

Number of Companies by Rank for Total Assets in 1940
22 Top 100 companies in manufacturing and mining
14 Top 50 companies in transportation, electric and gas utilities

Number of Companies by Industry
18 Chemicals
17 Electric utilities
 4 Food products
13 Metals
14 Machinery
 6 Mining
 9 Textiles
13 Transportation and communication
20 Other

Syndicates were fairly evenly distributed across industries for various reasons. Chemical, metals and machinery were the strategic industries at the time. On the other hand, food products and textiles were the 'sacrificed industries' under the pressure of militarization. In the case of the ten largest cotton-spinning companies, 31 factories were converted into munitions factories, and the machinery and equipment of 19 others was moved to factories already involved in munitions production by the Kigyo Seibirei. It is reported that between September 1941 and March 1942, 12 syndications were organized, of which 7 were related to the textile industry (Nihonkin'yushi-shiryo, Showa-hen, vol. 31, p. 473).

Average Number of Financial Institutions Participating in Each Syndicate
 8.7   Companies with the IBJ as manager bank
10.4   NPF
17.0   Large companies (among top 10 in manufacturing and mining, or transportation, electricity and gas)
 6.9   All syndicates

For large companies, the number of participants was very high, indicating their need to collect large sums of money. The NPFs' requirements also called for a high degree of participation. IBJ-managed syndicates may have had an above-average number of participants because many NPFs were the borrowers. However, calculating the average number for each type of financial institution excluding the NPFs as borrowers, gives us IBJ, 6.7; other banks, 3.1; and trust companies, 2.6. The number of participants in IBJ syndicates is still larger than for other financial institutions, indicating the importance of the financing constraints faced by the IBJ.

The role of a manager in a loan syndicate involves four activities: (1) negotiating with the borrowing company over the lending terms, such as the amount, interest rate, maturity, collateral, and method of payment;

(2) investigating the borrower's economic conditions as well as monitoring its use of the loans; (3) handling communication and intermediation among members of the syndicate; and (4) applying at the window of the BOJ for inspection of loan areas.

In terms of the five roles of a main bank defined by Aoki, Patrick and Sheard in Chapter 1, we have piecemeal evidence that manager banks were not only in charge of organizing bank loans, they also took active roles in bond issue related services, in the supply of management information and resources and, in some cases, in reorganization and liquidation management. As for the management of payment settlement accounts, it seems reasonable to assume that manager banks were also engaged in that role in many cases. However, a shareholding relationship was not usual because of the existence of holding companies, although some of the trust banks increased their shareholding in related companies gradually.

Among the 130 loan syndications, there are 4 in which the manager bank differs among loan syndications of the same company, implying the managing bank was not necessarily fixed. However, all these cases involved co-financing by the IBJ and other financial institutions and, as a half-national bank, the IBJ was fairly neutral with regard to business groups, so it seems safe to assume the manager-bank borrowing-firm relationship was quite stable.

Incentives of Loan Syndication

It seems that a major factor propelling banks to organize loan syndicates was the need to reduce risk by means of loan diversification.

The Temporary Fund Adjustment Act enacted in September 1937, two months after the outbreak of the war with China, had significant effects on the lending behaviour of large banks. Since the lending areas of large banks, especially those of the old zaibatsu, had still been predominantly concentrated in commerce and mining, the urgent requirement to shift lending to munitions production industries caused them serious difficulties. Small local banks could satisfy the requirement by subscribing to corporate bonds, which were marketable and on which information was more available. (In the portfolio of local banks, the ratio of security holdings to outstanding lendings increased from 0.41 in 1933 to 0.63 in 1937, 1.07 in 1941, and 1.88 in 1945.) But large banks, whose customers were firms in heavy and chemical industries, had no other option but to increase lending to them. (For the 11 large banks, the ratio of security holdings to outstanding stocks decreased from 0.72 in 1933 to 0.57 in 1937, 0.60 in 1941, and 0.33 in 1945.) Banks were obliged to lend not only to the newly established heavy and chemical firms, but also to the NPFs in order to show their loyalty to national policy. Lending to NPFs was especially risky because many of them were established not on the basis of a rational calculation of profit opportunity, but rather for the sake of national policy, and because information on them often was not adequately disclosed for reasons of national security.

As the heavy and chemical industrialization based on credit rationing accelerated after 1937, the size of individual bank lending became significantly large. Compared with 1935, lending per account grew three-fold by 1940 (Table 2.8). Loan consortium lending to three companies in the Mitsui zaibatsu during 1940 were 180 million yen for Mitsui Kozan, 36 million yen for Toyo Koatsu, and 100 million yen for Mitsui Bussan (Mitsui Bank, 1957, p. 272). How large these lendings are can be understood by noting that the total deposits of Mitsui Bank in 1940 were 1,589 million yen. This suggests the need for risk diversification was one of the most important reasons for organizing loan syndication at the time.

Among the four old zaibatsu, Mitsui was the most active in resorting to loan syndication. This seems closely related to differences in fund-raising capabilities among banks. From 1936 to 1942, total deposits at Mitsubishi Bank increased by 1,964 million yen from 810 to 2,774, those at Sumitomo Bank by 2,513 million yen from 1,017 to 3,530, those at Yasuda Bank by 2,596 million yen from 929 to 3,525, while the deposits at Mitsui Bank increased by only 1,333 million yen from 859 to 2,190. The reason seems to be that Mitsui was late entering the heavy and chemical industries, and found it difficult to participate in the deposit network of these industries. Another reason might be the small number of branches, as the bank claims in its official history (Mitsui Bank, 1957, p. 270). However, the number of branch offices was almost the same as Mitsubishi, so this is not sufficient to explain the slow growth of deposits. Moreover, it was critical to Mitsui that it failed to make Toshiba a first-line company in 1941 (Sawai, 1992, p. 178).

In July 1937 Japan went to war with China, and in September 1940 ratified an alliance with Nazi Germany and Italy. It is said that the lending behaviour of commercial banks became extremely cautious (IBJ, 1957, p. 449). Table 2.8 shows the rate of increase in commercial bank lending declining after 1939, and in 1941 a drastic reduction was recorded. Profits as a percentage of total assets began to fall after 1937, but continued until 1939 to rise when measured against net worth. Bank stocks, which had shown a sharply rising trend since 1935, fell by 13 per cent from 1940 to 1941.

Whether or not the efficient monitoring of corporate managers was a reason for loan syndication is a subtle question. Although the autonomy of corporate managers was gradually increasing, in the case of the old zaibatsu, they were still under the control of the holding company, or zaibatsu family, so we should conclude that the need to monitor was of secondary importance as an incentive for organizing loan syndication. However, it is worth noting two cases where monitoring was related to the incentive.

TABLE 2.8 Rate of Profits and Bank Lending after 1935

	Increase in Lending (million yen)		Rate of Profit of Large Businesses (after tax net profit) as a percentage of		Outstanding Loans of Commercial Banks		
	Commercial Banks	IBJ	Net Worth	Total Assets	(a) Number of Accounts (thousand)	(b) Outstanding Amount (million yen)	(b)/(a)
1935	259	25	9.1	5.6	992	5,313	5.4
1936	571	20	9.2	5.7	1,031	5,688	5.5
1937	1,029	424	9.9	5.9	967	6,533	6.8
1938	1,057	332	10.0	5.8	917	7,485	8.2
1939	2,502	208	10.2	5.6	847	9,531	11.3
1940	2,488	592	9.8	5.1	769	12,284	16.0
1941	1,640	824	9.1	4.9	—	—	—
1942	2,639	1,029	8.9	4.2	—	—	—
1943	4,588	2,209	8.4	3.8	—	—	—

Note: The term commercial bank refers to ordinary banks.

Source: Goto (1970, Tables 30–2, 58–63 and 95) and *Honpo Jigyoseiseki Bunseki* (Mitsubishi Keizai-Kenkyujo, each year).

First, in the case of the NPF, banks could maintain stronger bargaining power over the borrower by organizing syndication. Since the stockholder meeting was an inadequate method of monitoring NPF managers, and since the managers kept their strong position because they were appointed by the government, collaboration among banks through organizing syndicates was the only efficient means of monitoring these firms. For example, in the case of Toyotakushoku, syndication was an effective tool to reduce the size of requested loans.

Second, in the case of the new zaibatsu, syndication worked as a method of efficient monitoring of the founding management, and the eventual restructuring of the companies under bank control. As the expansionary strategies of the new zaibatsu ran into difficulties for various reasons, all of the founding managers were obliged to resign, and the companies were restructured through the leadership of loan syndicates.[2]

The Designated Financial Institution System

As the war became protracted and the shortage of raw materials and energy became more severe, there was a move toward a more totalitarian planned economy, and direct bureaucratic control over production was strengthened. Loan syndication was gradually transformed by the bureaucrats into a tool for financing munition companies and, at the same time, the independence of corporate managers from stockholders increased, as they were placed under the direct control of bureaucrats instead.

During the second phase of the war economy, from December 1940 to 1942, when innovative bureaucrats introduced iterative planning in the allocation of resources, loan syndication was institutionalized and expected to function as an efficient method of resource reallocation. In August 1941, ten large commercial banks and the IBJ established a loan consortium organization in order to intermediate loan syndication; they were joined by five trust banks in November. This role was inherited by a newly established regulatory board (Tosei-kai) of the financial industry after May 1942.

The institutionalization of loan syndication is a reflection of the shift to a planned economy under the New Economic System introduced in July 1941. Under this system, banking institutions were put under the strict control of bureaucrats. The so-called New System of Financing (*kinyu*

---

[2] For example, in the case of Riken, syndicates even secured an office in the company in order to monitor the rationalization of management and proper accounting (*Ginko-Tsushinroku*, 20 May 1941). Problems encountered include the stagnation of stock prices in 1941, which made it difficult to obtain funds for investment by selling shares of the group companies; the old zaibatsu began to enter the chemical industry, threatening the position of the new zaibatsu; and under the system of planned mobilization, smaller firms (most of them new zaibatsu affiliates) faced difficulty securing resources. Mori left Showa Denko in 1940; Nakano, Nihonsoda in 1940; Okochi, Riken Kogyo in 1942; Ayukawa, Manshusogyo in 1942; and Noguchi fell ill in 1940.

shintaisei) was introduced to establish a Highly Efficient Defence State (*kodo-kokubo-kokka*) (Yamazaki, 1991). However, financial institutions still kept on behaving like private maximizing entities although their independence had been gradually eroded (Fuji Bank, 1952, p. 70). Each bank still maintained the freedom to choose whether to participate in a particular syndication or not, and the assigned loan portion was supplied not in the name of the manager bank, but in the name of each participating bank, as before. A manager bank was chosen for each syndication, so that it was, in principle, not fixed for each company. However, it seems reasonable to believe that the manager bank was virtually fixed for each company in most cases.

During the period from August 1942 to December 1943, the regulatory board of the financial industry (Zenkoku Kin'yu Toseikai) intermediated loan syndications amounting to 13,370 million yen. Outstanding bank loans increased by 9,412 million yen from 23,302 million to 32,714 million. The total flow of loans during the same period is estimated to have amounted to 324,302 million yen.[3]

Since 60 to 70 per cent of loan syndication was related to investment funds, a simple comparison of flow lendings does not necessarily depict the true picture. The BOJ considers almost all lending at the time to have been supplied in the form of loan syndication, so participation in syndicates became an important strategy for individual banks to acquire customers (Bank of Japan, 1986, vol. 4, p. 302).

During the third phase of the war economy, 1943–45, direct bureaucratic intervention in production was intensified. The Munition Company Act of October 1943 stipulated that 'production managers' were to be under the direct control of the government. (1) Managers could disregard the decisions of stockholder meetings with the approval of the relevant minister. (2) They could decline to disclose information with the approval of the relevant minister. (3) Stockholders could not discharge managers without the approval of the relevant minister.

The Designated Financial Institution System for Munition Company Financing was introduced in January 1944 to give managers an even freer hand. Each munition company was assigned one or two banks, one of which was designated as a manager bank based on the history of lender-customer relationships. These banks were allowed to organize loan consortiums. Among the 217 companies covered by the first round designation of munitions companies, a loan consortium was organized for 64 of them. For those companies that already had loan syndicates, consortium members were the same as the members of the loan syndicate.

---

[3] The flow-lending estimate was made by applying the 1939 ratio of year-end outstanding loans to flow lending, multiplied by four-thirds, to the outstanding lending of all banks at year-end 1943. For ordinary banks in 1939, outstanding lending was 9,531 million yen and flow lending was 70,859 million yen, for a ratio of 0.135.

The distribution of manager banks among 217 companies was: IBJ 63, other special banks 10, nine large banks 139, and four local banks 5.

The fixed relationship between each company and the manager bank is no doubt similar to the present day main bank system. However, the two systems are quite different for the following reasons. First, all the loans in this system were supplied in the name of the manager bank, so other banks in the consortium were in practice lending to the manager bank, not to the company. Second, since the financing of munitions companies was an absolute obligation for financial institutions, banks were more or less subordinated to munitions companies, they had no choice but to supply as much funding as was demanded. A monitoring role for the manager bank was not part of the system at all, as is emphasized in Hoshi (1993).

It is important to note that manager banks were not necessarily in charge of the management of borrowers' deposit account. The choice of bank for deposit transactions was left to the discretion of each firm (Bank of Japan, 1972, vol. 34, pp. 397–98). In March 1945, the system was further modified by the Special Law on Munitions Financing (Gunji Yushi-tou Tokubetsu Sochi-ho). Loan syndication was completely eliminated from the system. Instead, each of about 2,000 companies, including non-munitions companies, was assigned one bank, and that bank was given the role of taking care of all its financing needs.

THE MAIN BANK SYSTEM IN THE POST-WAR PERIOD

In the post-war period, pattern (C) in Figure 2.1 was revived in an even stronger form. As the war ended, corporate managers were freed from the direct control of bureaucrats. Although many of them were purged as collaborators in the war economy, the newly nominated young managers were also free of the control of stockholders. First, zaibatsu dissolution as well as the introduction of a wealth tax (*zaisan-zei*) eliminated most of the stock held by holding companies and zaibatsu families. Second, the sale of stock to the public, termed the 'democratization of the security market' (*shokenminshuka*), resulted in the creation of a class of small individual shareholders. Since the stake of a small stockholder is not sufficient to pay for the cost of corporate monitoring, the shocks resulting from post-war reforms intensified the autonomy of corporate managers (Teranishi, 1993b).

Against this backdrop, it seems that the main bank system of the post-war period emerged as banks responded to the following two incentives; first, the necessity of loan diversification; and second, the pursuit of monitoring efficiency.

Loan Syndication

Since the beginning of the war, large corporations had three sources of outside funds: borrowing and bond subscription by the bank with which they maintained a lender-customer relationship; the flow of funds from other banks; and borrowing from governmental or semi-governmental financial institutions. During the war, the second source was syndicated loans and bond syndications, because banks were forced to obey the lending area regulation stipulated in the 1937 legislation (Rinjishikin chosei-ho), while the third source was borrowing from the Wartime Finance Bank (Senjikinyu-Kinko) as well as from the IBJ.

As the war ended, the 1937 legislation on lending area specification was repealed, but a new law, the Rule on the Credit Supply of Financial Institutions (Kinyukikan Shikinyuzu-junshoku), was enacted in March 1947, and although the Wartime Finance Bank was closed, a new institution, the Reconstruction Finance Bank (RFB, also known at the time as the Reconversion Finance Bank, Fukko Kinyu Kinko) was established. While the 1937 legislation had a significant impact on large city banks, the new rule mainly affected small local banks. The large banks had become accustomed to lending to the heavy and chemical industries during the war, so they felt no difficulty obeying rules to supply credit to specified strategic areas: steel, coal, and fertilizer as the first priority; some 60 industries, including non-ferrous metals and energy, as the second.

However, for local banks the rule was not easy to follow, for two reasons. First, funds to specified industries had to be supplied in the form of lending; there was no room given to use corporate bonds, as was possible under the 1937 legislation. Second, funds other than the portion supplied to industries were also controlled by the government, and had to be invested in government bonds (national, local, or RFB), held as reserves, or used for repayment of Bank of Japan borrowing (MOF, 1963, vol. 12, p. 224). There was no room to tap funds through the interbank money markets. In order to help local banks lend to specified industries, the BOJ took on the role of intermediator, actively organizing loan syndications, as requested by large city banks. (The BOJ opened loan intermediation offices in six large cities in May 1947.) The number of cases of intermediation (value of loans in billion yen) was 621 (20.0) in 1947, 2,273 (68.9) in 1948, 2,449 (162.2) in 1949, and 431 (45.5) during January–March 1950. While 75 per cent of lendings by the RFB were investment funds (as of the end of March 1949), 85.5 per cent of loan intermediation by the Bank of Japan was concerned with operating funds (total of the period from 1947 to March 1950). The relative size of RFB loans can be seen from Table 2.9. It can be seen that lending by government and semi-governmental financial institutions amounted to about one-third of the lending of ordinary banks during 1943–49.

TABLE 2.9 Lending by Wartime Finance Corporation, Reconstruction Finance Bank, and Ordinary Banks

(million yen)

End of Month	Industrial Bank of Japan (A)	Wartime Finance Bank (B)	Reconstruction Finance Bank (C)	Ordinary Banks (D)	(A)+(B)+(C)/(D) (%)
1942 Mar.	2,559	—	—	15,662	16.3
1943 Mar.	9,766	306	—	19,034	52.9
1944 Mar.	6,002	999	—	25,054	27.9
1945 Mar.	12,106	2,903	—	40,354	37.2
1945 Sept.	14,649	3,074	—	56,429	31.4
1947 Dec.	—	—	44,210	135,711	32.6
1948 Dec.	—	—	111,159	332,006	33.5
1949 Mar.	17,970	—	131,965	357,096	42.0
1949 Dec.	40,979	—	108,410	588,593	25.4
1950 Dec.	69,158	—	89,895	845,510	18.8
1951 Dec.	102,964	—	79,247	1,286,780	14.2

Note: Data for ordinary banks in 1945 is as of the end of August, and those for IBJ during 1949–51 are the end of March of the following year.

Source: Industrial Bank of Japan (1957); Ministry of Finance (1963, vol. 11, p. 323); Bank of Japan (1947), *Senjichu Kin'yu Tokei-yoran*, October; Bank of Japan, *Economic Statistics Annual*.

However, as a result of the introduction of an orthodox stabilization policy by Joseph Dodge, a Detroit banker advising the Occupation forces, further lending activity by the RFB was suspended in March 1949, the credit supply rule was virtually abolished in August 1949, and loan intermediation by the BOJ was terminated after mid-1950. The size of the interbank call market grew four-fold from 1950 to 1951, as funds of local banks began to flow into city banks by way of the call market. Moreover, in June 1950, the outbreak of the Korean War brought large special procurement demands which caused a tremendous upsurge of economic activity, and the Japanese economy was put on a trajectory of high growth based on heavy and chemical industrialization.

It seems that these circumstances gave large banks the incentive to tap funds of other banks by means of loan syndication. (The importance of BOJ loan intermediation in the rise of the main bank system in the post-war period was first emphasized by Tetsuji Okazaki in a comment on a draft of this chapter.) In order to replace the sudden reduction in RFB and local bank lending to their group companies, and to meet the large financing needs of customers in the heavy and chemical industries, banks were obliged to organize loan syndications.

Corporate Monitoring

In a situation where most of the large banks resorted to *de facto* loan syndication in financing their customers, a reciprocal monitoring arrangement in the form of the main bank system is a natural outcome. Moreover, in the post-war economy, another phenomenon occurred that made monitoring by banks, and the consequent pursuit of efficiency in monitoring, an indispensable element of the financial system. It was the high degree of independence of corporate managers from stockholder control, and the possibility of a rise in agency costs.[4]

We have already touched upon the effects of shocks such as zaibatsu dissolution and the moves to increase the number of stockholders (termed 'security democratization' at the time) on corporate governance immediately after the war. During the process of reorganization of the financial system in the mid-1950s, two important changes made monitoring corporate managers all the more important, and gave rise to the post-war main bank system.

First, is the intensification of cross shareholdings. Although the degree of cross shareholding was rising during the 1930s and thereafter, the disappearance of large stockholders and take-over moves around 1950 made

---

[4] Discussion of the independence of corporate managers from stockholders is held without reference to labour market conditions. Aoki (1988) presents a model of a cooperative game among stockholders, workers, and managers in a broader framework, which takes account of the relationship between the labour and the financial markets. Extension of our model to an Aoki-type framework is an important task left for further research.

corporate managers become actively involved in cross shareholding in order to protect their autonomy. Since banks were also interested in organizing keiretsu groups as their deposit networks in order to tap corporate deposits effectively, cross shareholding was financed by bank loans. The Federation of Corporate Managers (Keidanren) lobbied to revise the Fair Trade Act of 1947 which prohibited the shareholding of other companies in general, and set a limit on the holding of banks in each company at 5 per cent. In 1949, the regulation was changed to prohibit only cross shareholding of competitors, and in 1953, the 5 per cent limit on banks was raised to 10 per cent.

It is important to note the matching of interests between corporate managers and banks in the formation of keiretsu. Managers gained autonomy within the firm, but were monitored by banks. Bank control over borrowers as stockholders was weakened as borrowers resorted to cross shareholding, but banks benefited by the expansion of their deposit base. Moreover, banks themselves were under the strict control of bureaucrats. Since administrative guidance by bureaucrats was applied in accordance with deposit size, and other measures to increase deposits such as branching and the deposit interest rate were regulated, it was vital for banks to expand their corporate deposit bases by means of keiretsu.

The dominance of indirect financing was another factor intensifying the autonomy of corporate managers and making the monitoring arrangement of the main bank system an indispensable ingredient of the post-war financial structure. Although the share of indirect financing had been increasing since the 1930s, the role of indirect finance became predominant in the post-war period for the following three reasons. First, an attempt by the occupation forces to transplant an American-style stock market system was not successful as an immediate remedy for the shortage of long-term funds, for various reasons. The accumulation of financial assets by ordinary asset holders was too low, and security democratization caused difficulties in corporate governance by creating a myriad of small stockholders. Moreover, there seems to have been a technical reason arising from the absence of specialized market-makers for the unsuccessful transplant: occupation forces abolished pre-war trading practices based on futures transactions, but did not introduce an alternative method of price discovery and market-making. Second, the corporate bond market was severely repressed immediately after the war, and a secondary market did not develop until the 1980s. Finally, in order to offset under-development of the securities market, a mechanism of long-term supply of funds by means of indirect financing was introduced: government financing, based on the postal savings system, and the long-term credit bank system, based on the rationing of financial debentures and the preferential supply of BOJ credits, were the main sources of these long-term funds.

In this way, the flow of funds in the post-war period was based mainly on indirect financing, and this seems to have intensified the autonomy of corporate managers because they did not have to take stockholder interests into consideration when financing investment. It is important to note the institutional complementarity between the characteristics of the flow-of-funds structure and those of the corporate monitoring system. The post-war system of the main bank seems to have attained stability as an institution owing to this complementarity. These points are discussed in detail in Teranishi (1993a).

CONCLUSION

I have argued that loan syndication during the early war-time period emerged as a response by banks to the need for risk diversification during rapid reorganization of the industrial structure, and that the post-war main bank system evolved as a response to the credit crunch caused by a sudden termination of directed credits. Moreover, the main bank system was institutionalized as the autonomy of corporate managers intensified, and as the economy was rapidly put on a path of heavy and chemical industrialization based on borrowed technology.

It must be noted that both are phenomena of a generally common trend of accelerated heavy and chemical industrialization since World War I and of the increasing criticism of liberal capitalism and capitalist hegemony. At the same time, one cannot neglect the important roles played by historical shocks related to the war, to defeat, and to subsequent reforms.

Loan Syndications, June 1941

I Industrial Bank of Japan as Manager Bank

Rank¹ A	B	Industry²	Group	BS³	Syndicate Members Banks	Trust Cos.	Company⁴
53	–	machinery	–	no	7	–	Aichi Tokei (64)
::	–	metal	–	no	5	–	Amagasaki Seitetsu (59)
–	::	electricity	–	no	5	1	Chosen Denryoku (31)
–	::	electricity	NPF	no	2	–	Chosen Oryokko Suiryoku Hatsuden (44)
–	::	electricity	–	no	2	–	Chosen Soden (51)
50	–	metal	–	yes	8	–	Daido Seiko (65)
::	–	chemical	–	no	3	–	Dainihon Engyo (19)
–	–	other	NPF	no	8	–	Higashi Manshu Sangyo (8)
–	–	machinery	Nissan	yes	8	5	Hitachi Seisakusho (39)
16	–	mining	NPF, Okura	yes	11	4	Honkeiko Baitetsu-Koji (7)
86	–	machinery	–	yes	6	–	Ikegai Tekko (27)
63	–	chemical	–	no	7	–	Ishihara Sangyo Kaiun (58)
–	–	other	NPF	yes	14	4	Kitashina Kaihatsu (43)
–	–	communications	NPF	yes	14	4	Kokusai Denkitsushin (48)
–	::	paper and pulp	–	no	5	–	Kokusaku Parupkoggo (56)
40	–	textile	–	yes	4	–	Kureha Boseki (4)
–	–	–	–	yes	8	–	Manchurian Government (13)
–	::	electricity	NPF	yes	13	4	Manshu Dengyo (47)

Rank[1] A	B	Industry[2]	BS[3]	Group	Syndicate Members Banks	Trust Cos.	Company[4]
—	—	communications	yes	NPF	13	4	Manshu Denshin Denwa (49)
—	—	other	yes	NPF, Nissan	13	a 4	Manshu Jukogyo (17)
—	—	chemical	yes	—	7	1	Manshu Kagaku (14)
::	—	other	yes	NPF	13	4	Manshu Takushoku Kosha (15)
—	—	mining	yes	NPF	13	4	Manshu Tanko (20)
::	1	transportation	yes	NPF	13	4	Minami Manshu Tetsudo (26)
—	—	mining	no	NPF	8	—	Mosan Tekko-Kaihatsu (36)
::	::	other	yes	NPF	14	4	Nakashina Shinko (70)
61	—	metal	no	—	2	—	Nakayama Seikosho (60)
6	—	chemical	yes	Nichitsu	2	—	Nihon Chisso Hiryo (54)
—	5	electricity	no	—	4	1	Nihon Denryoku (29)
::	::	metal	no	NPF	9	—	Nihon Do Tosei-kumiai (28)
—	2	electricity	yes	NPF	11	a 4	Nihon Hassoden (23)
34	—	metal	no	Furukawa	4	—	Nihon Keikinzoku (41)
::	::	metal	no	NPF	9	—	Nihon Kozai Hanbawi (34)
—	—	food	no	NPF	5	—	Nihon Mikan Kanzume Kogyo-kumiai Rengokai (55)
::	—	metal	yes	NPF	9	—	Nihon Namari Aen Anchimon Tosei-kumiai (40)
—	—	food	no	NPF	9	—	Nihon Nosan Kanzume (42)
1	—	metal	yes	NPF	14	4	Nihon Seitetsu (46)
::	::	mining	no	NPF	9	4	Nihon Sekitan (35)
—	—	other	no	NPF	8	—	Nihon Tekko-genryo Tosei (18)
—	—	food	no	NPF	13	4	Nihon Yushutsu Nosanbutsu (33)
71	—	machinery	no	Nissan	2	1	Nissan Jidosha (50)
20	—	chemical	yes	Nissan	4	2	Nissan Kagaku (53)
90	—	textile	yes	—	1	a 1	Nitto Boseki (9)
—	::	transportation	no	—	3	—	Osaka Kotsu (61)

Company						
Riken (76)	—	8	no	Riken	machinery	:
Riken Denkiseizo (73)	—	8	no	Riken	machinery	—
Riken Gomu (72)	—	8	no	Riken	chemical	:
Riken Kinzoku (71)	—	8	no	Riken	metal	:
Riken Kogaku (75)	—	8	no	Riken	machinery	:
Riken Korandamu (74)	—	8	no	Riken	chemical	:
Sanshin Tetsudo (3)	1	2	no	—	transportation	—
Sansho Kaihatsu (22)	1	6	no	—	other	—
Sansho Tesudo (25)	1	6	no	—	transportation	—
Senman Takushoku (1)	—	6	yes	NPF	other	—
Shinko Jinken (62)	—	2	no	—	textile	:
Shokuryhin Kanzume-seikan Kogyo-kumiai (37)	8	9	no	NPF	food	—
Showa Denko (45)	4	8	yes	Mori	chemical	21
Showa Hikoki (6)	—	7	no	Mitsui	machinery	:
Showa Jukogo (66)	—	9	no	—	machinery	:
Tairen Toshikotsu (38)	—	9	no	—	transportation	:
Taiwan Takushoku (16)	—	9	yes	NPF	other	—
Teikoku Nenrykogy (57)	4	12	yes	NPF	other	—
Teikoku Sanshi (30)	—	9	yes	NPF	textile	:
Tohoku Kogyo (10)	—	7	yes	—	other	—
Tohoku Shinko Denryoku (5)	—	7	yes	NPF	electricity	34
Tokuyama Soda (69)	—	2	no	Sumitomo	chemical	:
Tokyo Ishikawa Zoshensho (2)	—	2	yes	—	machinery	65
Tokyo Shibaura Denki (52)	3	3	yes	Mitsui	machinery	8
Tokyo-Yokohama Dentetsu (12)	2	8	yes	—	transportation	—
Toyota Jidosha (24)	—	b 5	yes	Mitsui	machinery	59
Toyo Kogyo (68)	—	5	no	—	machinery	:

Rank[1] A	B	Industry[2]	Group	BS[3]	Syndicate Members Banks	Trust Cos.	Company[4]
—	—	other	NPF	yes	12	4	Toyo Takushoku (32)
—	—	other	—	no	b 4	2	Ujiden Shoken (63)
—	8	electricity	—	yes	4	2	Ujigawa Denki (21)
—	::	electricity	—	yes	3	—	Yahagi Suiryoku (11)
—	—	other	—	no	9	—	Yamaguchi Keihachi (677)

II Commercial Bank as Manager Bank

Rank[1] A	B	Industry[2]	Group	BS[3]	Syndicate Members Banks	Trust Cos.	Company[4]
—	::	electricity	—	no	1	1	Aigi Suiryoku (85)
::	—	textile	NPF	no	8	—	Dainihon Yushutsu Menshifu Shinko-kumiai (79)
—	45	transportation	NPF	yes	8	—	Dainihon-koku (84)
::	—	metal	—	no	2	3	Fujietsu Kozai (91)
—	—	other	NPF	no	3	—	Hokkaido-chiku Shogyo-kumiai Rengokai (80)
::	—	textile	Mitsui	yes	2	—	Kanegafuchi Boseki (89)
::	—	mining	—	no	1	1	Meiji Kogyo (87)
::	—	other	Mitsui	no	3	—	Mitsui Bissan Bussan (81)
15	—	mining	Mitsui	no	2	1	Mitsui Kazan (82)
72	—	metal	Mitsubishi	no	4	—	Nihon Aruminiumu (90)
::	—	textile	NPF	no	6	—	Nihon Menorimono Oroshisho Kumiai Rengokai (92)
::	—	chemical	—	no	4	—	Nitto Kagaku (77)
::	—	paper and pulp	NPF	no	5	1	Parupu Chosei Kumiai (78)
::	—	chemical	Mitsui	no	2	1	Toyo Koatsu Kogyo (83)
::	—	metal	—	no	4	1	Toyota Seiko (88)
—	—	other	—	no	1	1	Yasukawa Matsumoto Gomei (86)

III Trust Bank as Manager Bank

A	B	Industry	Manager bank	yes/no			Company
—	11	electricity	—	yes	—	4	Dainihon Denryoku (101)
80	—	chemical	—	no	—	4	Denki-Kagaku Kogyo (98)
—	—	chemical	—	yes	—	4	Fuji Shashin Fuirumu (96)
—	—	electricity	—	no	1	1	Jyomo Denryoku (103)
—	—	electricity	—	no	—	4	Kanto Suiryoku (107)
—	—	transportation	Kawasaki	yes	—	2	Keio Denkitetsudo (108)
37	—	transportation	—	no	—	2	Keisei Denkitetsudo (97)
—	—	electricity	—	no	2	2	Kyushu Karyoku Hatsuden (94)
—	—	electricity	—	yes	2	2	Kyushu Suiryoku (109)
10	—	electricity	—	no	1	1	Kyusyu Soden (110)
—	—	electricity	—	no	—	3	Nagano Denki (102)
—	—	textile	Mitsui	no	1	1	Naikai Boshoku (100)
—	—	transportation	—	no	—	3	Nankai Tetsudo (105)
—	24	other	NPF	yes	—	4	Onkyu Kinko (99)
43	—	chemical	—	no	1	1	Rasa Kogyo (104)
—	—	paper and pulp	—	no	1	1	Rengo Shiki (111)
—	—	metal	NPF	no	1	1	Tohoku Kinzoku (113)
—	—	chemical	NPF	no	—	3	Tohoku Shinko Kagaku (95)
—	—	textile	—	no	1	1	Tokyo Jinzo Kenshi (106)
44	—	transportation	—	no	1	1	Tokyo Kosoku-Tetsudo (93)
—	—	machinery	Mitsubishi	no	1	2	Toyo Kikai (112)
—	—	other	—	no	1	1	Ujiden Birudingu (114)

[1] Rankings are by total assets at the end of 1940. Column A is ranking within the mining and manufacturing industries. Column B is ranking within the transportation, gas and electric utility industries.

2 Cooperative and trading companies specialized in a particular industry are classified in that industry, so an industry such as textiles includes not only manufacturers but also such institutions as cooperatives promoting textile exports.

3 Indicates whether company also has a bond syndication.

4 The number in parentheses after the company name is the sequence number in the source for loan syndications.

a Trust bank a co-manager.
b Commercial bank a co-manager.

Source: Loan syndication data are from 'Kyodo Toyushi no Genjo' (*Nihon kin'yu-shiryo, Showa-hen*, vol. 31). Ranking of companies is based on Sangyo Seisakushi Kenkyujo, *Wagakuni Daikigyo no Keisei Hattenkatei* (1976). Group affiliation and industry classification are based on a variety of sources, and are tentative.

REFERENCES

AOKI, MASAHIKO. 1988. *Information, Incentives and Bargaining in the Japanese Economy.* Cambridge: Cambridge University Press.

AOKI, MASAHIKO, HUGH PATRICK and PAUL SHEARD. 1993. 'The Japanese Main Bank System: An Introductory Overview', paper prepared for the joint research project on the Japanese Main Bank System and its Relevance for Developing Market and Transforming Socialist Economies, Stanford University, April.

ASAJIMA, SHOICHI. 1983. *Senkanki Sumitomo Zaibatsu Keieishi (History of Management of Sumitomo Zaibatsu in Interwar Period).* Tokyo: Tokyo University Press.

——. 1986. *Mitsubishi Zaibatsu no Kin'yu Kozo (Financial Structure of Mitsubishi Zaibatsu).* Tokyo: Ochanomizu shobo.

——. 1987a. 'Mitsubishi Zaibatsu.' In Shoichi Asajima, ed., *Zaibatsu Kin'yu Kozo no Hikakukenkyu (Comparative Study of Financial Structure of Zaibatsu).* Tokyo: Ochanomizu shobo.

——. 1987b. 'Sumitomo Zaibatsu.' In Shoichi Asajima, ed., *Zaibatsu Kin'yu Kozo no Hikakukenkyu (Comparative Study of Financial Structure of Zaibatsu).* Tokyo: Ochanomizu shobo.

Bank of Japan. 1972. *Nihon Kin'yushi-shiryo, Showa-hen.* Tokyo.

——. 1986. *One Hundred Year History of the Bank of Japan.* Tokyo.

Fuji Bank. 1952. *Seventy Years History of Fuji Bank.* Tokyo.

GOTO, SHINICHI. 1970. *Nihon no Kin'yu Tokei (Financial Statistics of Japan).* Tokyo: Toyo Keizai Shinposha.

HELLWIG, MARTIN. 1990. 'Banking, Financial Intermediation and Corporate Finance.' Paper presented for the IMF-CEPR conference on European Financial Integration, Rome, 22–24 January.

HOSHI, TAKEO. 1993. 'Evolution of the Main Bank System in Japan.'

Industrial Bank of Japan. 1957. *Fifty Years History of IBJ.* Tokyo.

KASUGA, YUTAKA. 1987. 'Mitsui.' In Shoichi Asajima, ed., *Zaibatsu Kin'yu Kozo no Hikaku kenkyu (Comparative Study of Financial Structure of Zaibatsu).* Tokyo: Ochanomizu shobo.

KATAOKA, YUTAKA. 1988. 'Meiji-ki ni okeru Kabunushi to Kabunushi Sokai' ('Shareholders and Shareholders Meeting in Meiji Period'). *Keieishigaku* 23(2): 33–58 (July).

KUROSE, IKUJI. 1988. '1920 nendai ni okeru Toyotakushoku-Kaisha no Gaishidonyu to Kaigaitoshi' ('Foreign Borrowings and Foreign Investments by Toyotakushoku during the 1920s'). *Kagoshimakeizai-Ronshu* 17(2): 86-109.

MASUJI, YOJIRO. 1936. *Wagakuni Kabushiki-kaisha ni okeru Kabushiki bunsan to Shihai (Distribution and Control of Shares in Joint Stock Companies in Japan).* Tokyo: Dobunkan.

Ministry of Finance. 1963. *Showa Zaiseishi.* Tokyo: Toyo Keizai Shinposha.

MIYAJIMA, HIDEAKI. 1992. 'Zaibatsu kaitai' ('Zaibatsu Dissolution'). In Juro Hashimoto and Haruto Takeda, eds., *Nihonkeizai no Hatten to Kigyosyudan.* Tokyo: Tokyo University Press.

Mitsui Bank. 1957. *Eighty Years History of Mitsui Bank,* Tokyo.

MORIKAWA, HIDEMASA. 1980. *Zaibatsu Keiei-shi no Kenkyu (A Study on the History of Management of Zaibatsu).* Tokyo: Toyo Keizai Shinposha.

NODA, MASAHO. *Nihon Shoken Shijo Seiritsu-shi (An Early History of Security Markets in Japan)*. Tokyo: Yuhikaku.

OKAZAKI, TETSUJI. 1992. 'The Japanese Firm under the Wartime Planned Economy.' Discussion Paper 92-F-4, Faculty of Economics, Tokyo University.

PATRICK, HUGH. 1967. 'Japan 1986-1914.' In Rondo Cameron with others, *Banking in the Early Stages of Industrialization: A Study of Comparative Economic History*. New York: Oxford University Press.

SAWAI, MINORU. 1992. 'Senjikeizai to Zaibatsu' ('War Economy and Zaibatsu'). In Juro Hashimoto and Haruto Takeda, eds., *Nihon Keizai no Hatten to Kigyosyudan*. Tokyo: Tokyo University Press.

SHLEIFER, AUDREI and ROBERT W. VISHNY. 1986. 'Large Shareholders and Corporate Control.' *Journal of Political Economy* 94(3): 461-88 (June).

SHIMURA, KAICHI. 1969. *Nihon Shihon shijo Bunseki (An Analysis of Capital Market in Japan)*. Tokyo: Tokyo University Press.

SUGIYAMA, KAZUO. 1970. 'Bosekigaisha no Tegata-hakko to Shichu Ginko' ('Commercial Banks and Bills Insurance by Cotton Seining Companies'). In Kazuo Yamaguchi, ed., *Nihon Sangyokin'yushi: Bosekikin'yuhen*. Tokyo: Tokyo University Press.

TAKAHASHI, KAMEKICH. 1930. *Kabushikikaisha Bokoku-ron (Moral Hazard of Corporate Companies)*. Tokyo: Banrikaku-shobo.

TAKAMURA, NAOSUKE. 1971. *Nihon Boseki-shi Josetsu (A History of Cotton Spinning Industry in Japan)*. Tokyo: Hanawa-shobo.

TERANISHI, JURO. 1990. 'Financial System and the Industrialization of Japan: 1900–70.' *Banca Nazionale del Lavoro* 174: 309–41 (September).

——. 1993a. 'Financial Sector Reform after the War.' In Juro Teranishi and Yutaka Kosai, eds., *Japanese Experience of Economic Reforms*. London: Macmillan.

——. 1993b. 'Emergence and Establishment of the Financial System in Postwar Japan—Government Intervention, Indirect Financing and the Corporate Monitoring System.' Paper presented at a Seminar on Public Policy during Japan's Rapid Growth, World Bank, Tokyo, 25 January.

UDAGAWA, MASARU. 1984. *New Zaibatsu (Shinko Zaibatsu)*. Tokyo: Nihon Keizai Shinbunsha.

YAMAZAKI, SHIRO. 1991. 'Kyocho Kin'yu Taisei no Tenkai' ('The Evolution of Loan Consortia'). In Toshimitsu Imuta, ed., *Senjitaisei-ka no Kin'yu-kozo*. Tokyo: Nihon Hyoronsha.

3

Institutional and Regulatory Frameworks for the Main Bank System

KAZUO UEDA

Banking is one of the most heavily regulated industries in post-war Japan; thus, with the exception of a few foreign banks, virtually no entry into banking has been allowed. Within the industry, long-term banking and short-term banking have been separated; trust banking services have been provided only by trust banks. Until the late 1970s, most interest rates were set at non-market clearing levels. More important, moral suasion and informal administrative guidelines have been widely used.

This chapter discusses the nature, degree and implications of such heavy government interventions for the performance of the banking sector, especially that of main banks. The implications emerging from the analysis are straightforward. Japanese banks in the late 1940s were in a shaky situation with very low levels of capital and with high operating costs due to a sharp decline in the average size of deposits. The protection provided by a variety of regulations enabled banks to channel funds into targeted industries. Protection was heavier for the larger banks that played the role of main banks. Thus, the existence of government regulation or protection was one of the reasons for the superb performance of Japanese main banks.

The regulatory authorities protected banks essentially in three ways. First, many forms of subsidies were provided, including those arising from interest rate regulations, entry restrictions, and Bank of Japan (BOJ) lending at the discount rate. Second, significant portions of credit risks were borne by the government. Public financial institutions supplied funds jointly with private banks. The trust fund bureau bought large amounts of debentures issued by long-term credit banks. Most important of all, the Ministry of Finance (MOF) and the BOJ rescued troubled banks by any possible means. Third, the flow of funds through the capital market, especially the bond market, was severely controlled.

The decline in management efficiency expected from such heavy protection was minimized by the MOF's guidelines to limit bank expenses. In

The author would like to thank Kensuke Hotta, Sang-Woo Nam, Hugh Patrick, Dimitri Vittas and other participants of the main bank project workshop for helpful comments on earlier versions of the paper.

addition, the high growth of the economy made whatever inefficiencies that existed small relative to the size of the economy or banks assets.

The regulatory environment started to change in the late 1970s as a result of the need to sell large amounts of government bonds. This led to the development of a bond market and to relaxation of interest rate controls. For private banks, decontrol of interest rates meant the disappearance of a significant portion of protection provided by the government. Banks now had to compete more vigorously for profits. Ironically, however, the separation of various types of banking, and that of banking and securities business, imposed serious constraints on the behaviour of banks. The problems now faced by long-term credit banks and trust banks are at least partly a reflection of such a change in the environment.

In the first section the historical evolution of the Japanese regulatory framework for the banking sector is discussed briefly, and it is shown that the framework was essentially constructed during World War II. In the second section, various forms of protection provided by regulations are carefully explained, and then the effects of the protective measures on bank performance are analysed in the third section. The fourth section is devoted to a brief discussion of the recent period in which parts of the regulations were lifted, but the arbitrariness of the sequencing of deregulation created many problems.

HISTORICAL ORIGINS OF THE JAPANESE BANK REGULATIONS

An interesting feature of the Japanese financial system until about the 1920s was that it was mostly free from government regulations. (See, for example, Ueda 1993a for a more thorough discussion of this point.) Financing through equities or bonds was as important as bank lending. There was no separation of banking and securities businesses. However, a series of financial panics and World War II had completely changed the character of the financial system.

The Bank Act of 1927

The Showa financial panic brought about a drastic change in the regulatory environment. The government enacted the Banking Act in 1927, which laid the foundation for bank regulation not only in the pre-war, but also for the post-war period. The act introduced minimum capital requirements, encouraging mergers of smaller banks with larger ones. As a result, the number of ordinary banks decreased from 1,417 in 1926, to 516 in 1933, and to 61 in 1945.

The banking act required all banks to obtain a charter from the Minister of Finance. Opening a new branch also required permission of the minister. The MOF was authorized both to ask banks to report about any aspect of their activities and to carry out bank audits, whenever it wanted, and to dismiss executives or order discontinuation of banking services when necessary. Some of these points, however, were already included in the Bank Act of 1890 and its revision in 1916. In this sense, the 1927 act restated what was in the previous act, introduced minimum capital requirements and strengthened the regulatory power of the MOF.

A significant feature of the bank act was that it did not state the details of bank regulations explicitly. The details were left to administrative guidances. In this way, MOF officials were provided with a large degree of discretion in carrying out bank regulatory policy. In the post-war period, senior MOF officials stated: 'Enforcement by law should be the last resort. Therefore, it would be better to persuade (banks) as patiently as possible relying only on administrative guidances, but not on law' (Satake and Hashiguchi, 1967, p. 13). As a result, a major characteristic of Japanese bank regulation—the high degree of discretion exercised by MOF officials—also originated in the pre-war period.

Formation of the War-Time Financial System

The start of the war with China in 1937 decisively changed the Japanese financial system. Its major function shifted to channelling funds into military industries and to financing large government budget deficits.

Interest rates were regulated to let private banks hold government bonds issued above market prices. For example, administrative guidelines were used to maintain bank deposit rates at levels below the rate on government bonds.

Bank loans were placed at the centre of war-time finance. The government introduced a series of laws to control bank loans. The Temporary Fund Adjustment Law enacted in 1937 stipulated that bank loans for plant and equipment exceeding 100 thousand yen required permission from the MOF, who in turn gave permission for loans favouring military industries. The government also intervened in the flow of funds through the corporate bonds market. The committee on bonds flotation planning organized by the MOF, the BOJ, the IBJ and the economic planning board, strictly controlled new issues of corporate bonds. Effectively, only war-related firms were allowed to issue bonds.

Smaller regional banks without strong ties with military industries channelled funds into large city banks and the Industrial Bank of Japan (IBJ), who in turn lent to military industries. Herein lay the origin of the Japanese main bank system as analysed by Teranishi in Chapter 2. The role played by the IBJ was decisive. It supplied more than 50 per cent of all loans to machinery, chemical and transportation industries (IBJ, 1982, p. 65).

The IBJ collected funds by issuing debentures and by borrowing from financial institutions. Among the financial institutions that supplied funds to the IBJ were the BOJ and the deposit bureau of the MOF, which attracted funds from postal savings (in the post-war period, it was refor- mulated into the trust fund bureau). In addition, the government guaran- teed the bank debentures issued by the IBJ. In effect, this was a scheme to concentrate the credit risk of war-time finance on the IBJ and from there to the government.

THE REGULATORY FRAMEWORK IN THE POST-WAR PERIOD

The post-war financial system, until well into the 1980s, was similar to the war-time system in many respects. Thus, the price mechanism was not playing a major role in resource allocation. Interest rates were heavily regulated. Bank loans were the major vehicle moving savings into invest- ment. Loans to priority sectors were mainly supplied by a small number of large banks. Some of these are still important characteristics of the Japanese financial system.

The government, in addition to interest rates control, used many types of explicit and implicit regulations to protect the banking industry.

The major difference between the war-time and post-war financial sys- tems was the purpose the system was expected to serve. With defeat in the war, the major goal of the financial system shifted to aiding the reconstruction of the economy and later to the promotion of high growth. Bank regulatory policy was also geared to serve such purposes, but at the same time aimed at maintaining the stability of the financial system.

Protection of the banking industry was an important part of policy. This was done in essentially three ways: first, competition was restricted; second, the government assumed significant amounts of risk that would have fallen on private banks in a different system; and third, direct financing of corporate investment was restricted.

Restriction of Competition

Competition among banks was limited by various regulations. New entries into the banking sector were severely limited. Most exceptions have been changes in the form of financial institutions rather than new entries: the merger of Nishinippon Sogo and Takachiho Sogo in 1984, which became an ordinary bank, and the transformation of about 60 Sogo banks into ordinary banks in 1989. Actual new entries include nine foreign trust banks in 1985 and 1986.

Separation of the banking and securities industries, of long-term and short-term banking, and of ordinary banking and trust banking services has been maintained into the 1990s. However, on the assets side, separa- tion of long-term and short-term banking was not strict. City banks have been allowed to make long-term loans. As of April 1993, part of the separation of financial services has been relaxed. For example, long-term banks are now allowed to underwrite corporate bonds and securities companies can enter the trust banking industry, both by establishing subsidiaries.

Opening new branches required permission from the MOF. Short-term changes in the stance of branching regulation were often announced in administrative guidelines. Kobayashi (1978) summarizes the stance of the MOF as follows. Before 1949, branching regulation was carried out by the occupation forces, which allowed new branches for attracting deposits. Between 1949 and 1953, new branches were, in principle, not allowed. Banks were encouraged to streamline or change the location of existing branches. Between 1953 and 1958, branching regulation was further tightened and banks were even encouraged to decrease the number of branches. After 1958, new branches were permitted on a case-by-case basis. Even as of May 1993, city banks are not allowed to open more than one branch every two years. The MOF, however, announced in 1993 that it will essentially abolish branching regulations. (Also see ZGK, 1985.)

In the early post-war period, branching regulation was based on the idea that the number of banks and branches was too large (see Kobayashi, 1978, part 2, p. 40). Therefore, MOF officials thought new branches had to be strictly controlled to avoid excessive competition among banks. However, with the rise in the growth rate of the economy this regulation gave enormous power to the MOF. Tsutsui (1988), by estimating a cost function, shows that the branching regulation was a binding factor in private banks' activities. Some claim that the regulation was more strictly applied to city banks than to regional banks. But this is not obvious. Between 1948 and 1984, the number of city bank branches increased 121 per cent (from 1,363 to 3,006) and for regional banks, 100 per cent (from 3,372 to 6,727).

Interest rates were strictly controlled. During the war, controls were used to let banks hold government bonds and to provide funds for military industries at subsidized rates. In the post-war period, controls created subsidies for priority sectors in the form of low interest rates, which in turn necessitated the control of bank deposit rates.

The government bond rate still played the role of the pivotal interest rate from which many other long-term rates were determined, despite the decreased role of the government as borrower of funds compared with the war period. In the primary markets, once the government bond rate was determined, the bank debenture rate was placed slightly above it, and the corporate bond rate slightly above that. The long-term prime rate was a fixed 0.9 percentage point above the bank debenture rate.

The government bond rate did not reflect market fundamentals. In fact, the major holders of government bonds, private financial institutions, were not allowed to sell them in the secondary market until 1978. Instead, the BOJ bought government bonds from financial institutions one year after issuance. The bond rate was artificially determined by the funding cost of banks, the deposit interest rate, which was in turn determined by the official discount rate. The short-term prime rate was also determined by the official discount rate with a 0.25 percentage point spread.

Not all of these rules were stated in law. For example, the rates on bank debentures and corporate bonds were officially to be determined by the issuer, but were actually determined by the issuer in consultation with the MOF and the BOJ (Koshasai Hikiuke Kyokai, 1980, p. 305). The Temporary Interest Rates Adjustment Law (TIRAL), or guidelines issued by the BOJ, determined the maximum deposit interest rates, which were the actual rates until the mid-1980s. TIRAL also stipulated the maximum rate on short-term bank loans, but not on long-term loans. The actual short-term prime rate, however, was determined by the bank that provided the chair of the Federation of Bankers Association, at the request of the BOJ, and other banks followed the move. The long-term prime rate is also set in a cartel-like manner at a fixed spread above the bank debenture rate. (Dogakinai, 1991, is a useful reference on interest rate determination in Japan both during the high growth period and subsequently.)

There has been some controversy concerning whether or not interest rates were at market clearing levels in Japan. It might seem obvious that they were not. But, for example, the practice of requiring compensating deposits for loans made the effective interest rate more variable than the official rate. Ito and Ueda (1981), however, show that even the effective interest rate was below market clearing levels in the business loan market. In the following, we proceed on the presumption that Japanese interest rates were in general below market clearing levels.

The competition restricting regulations discussed so far must have provided large rents to Japanese banks. It is difficult to estimate the total impact of regulations. A rough estimate, however, of the effects of interest rate controls and related measures on bank earnings is provided below.

Table 3.1 shows estimates of three types of subsidies to the banking sector: low deposit interest rates; BOJ lending at subsidized rates; and issues of bank debentures at subsidized rates. The assumptions used in the estimate are as follows. The deposit rate in the absence of regulation would have been equal to the call rate. But only large depositors would have been paid the call rate. (Interest paid on large time deposits has been gradually deregulated since late 1985, and since then has averaged about 0.2 percentage point below the call rate annually.) The fraction of

TABLE 3.1 Implicit Interest Rate Subsidies and Taxes (billion yen)

1955	1960	1965	1970	1975	1980	1985	1990	Subsidy or taxation due to regulation of:[1]
				City Banks				
2.2	15.8	15.1	60.5	174.9	302.6	149.7	–	Deposit rates
0.3	5.3	15.6	44.2	39.8	66.1	45.7	53.1	Official discount rates
–0.5	–6.0	–23.4	–15.2	–9.3	–	–	–	Bond yields
39.5	76.8	154.5	340.2	451.7	523.8	1,129.0	1,658.6	Profits
				Regional Banks				
2.2	13.3	13.8	48.1	147.2	283.9	143.3	–	Deposit rates
0.0	0.1	0.3	0.9	0.8	1.5	3.4	8.1	Official discount rates
–0.3	–2.2	–7.3	–4.6	–4.9	–	–	–	Bond yields
22.0	53.7	90.0	255.9	372.9	375.6	603.6	788.2	Profits
				Long-Term Credit Banks				
0.8	2.4	8.7	2.7	3.1	–	–	–	Trust Fund Bureau[2]
0.0	0.1	0.4	1.0	1.4	0.1	4.3	9.1	Official discount rate
1.6	13.2	55.1	45.0	53.3	–	–	–	Bond yields
7.8	14.3	24.4	61.6	91.6	107.6	210.9	279.0	Profits

Notes:
[1] Profits are 'current profits' and given for comparative purposes.
[2] Trust Fund Bureau's purchase of long-term bank debentures at non-market prices.

large depositors is assumed to be 38.3 per cent, which is the share of household deposits above 10 million yen in September 1992. Without subsidies, banks would have been required to pay the call rate on borrowings from the BOJ. The market clearing rate on coupon debentures would have been equal to the rate on NTT bonds until 1965, and to the rate on debentures in the secondary market since then. No attempt has been made to estimate the impact of the rate change on the volume of transactions.[1]

The estimates show that the subsidies provided by regulation of deposit interest rates were very large. They often exceeded the after-tax profits of the banks. Of course, a more careful analysis is necessary to determine how the rents were divided between banks and non-financial firms.

The subsidies to the long-term credit banks arising from below market issues of debentures were even larger relative to their profits. About 50 per cent of the subsidies to the long-term credit banks may be seen to have been provided by the city and regional banks. It should be noted that city banks, in return for buying debentures, were allowed to participate in the cooperative financing organized by long-term credit banks. In the case of city banks, the loss on purchases of bank debentures was more or less offset by subsidies provided by the BOJ, as shown by Teranishi (1982). We come back to the subsidies provided by the government in the next section.

Assumption of Risk by the Government

The government reduced the risk borne by private banks by a variety of measures.

The BOJ and the trust fund bureau supplied funds to private banks in the form of BOJ lendings and the bureau purchases of bank debentures. As shown in Table 3.1, the funds were supplied with subsidies. Another implicit subsidy provided by the BOJ was allowing city banks to use the debentures they hold as collateral for BOJ lending. In the early post-war period, the trust fund purchases of debentures were very large at about 30 per cent until 1960. It should be noted that these subsidies went mostly to larger banks, that is, to city and long-term banks.

Cooperative financing with public financial institutions, especially with the Japan Development Bank (JDB), seems to have reduced the credit risk for private banks. Private banks were able to rely on the credit

---

[1] Of course, this is a drastic simplification. The assumption on the share of large deposits is made because it is impossible to estimate accurately the fraction of deposits that would have been paid the competitive rate. Also, we calculate only the subsidies on household deposits. A significant share of corporate deposits with low interest rates were compensatory balances for low loan rates. In this sense, subsidies on corporate deposits should be discussed jointly with subsidies to the non-financial sector arising from below market loan rates. I abstain from this task here. The subsidies on coupon debentures were calculated by summing up the subsidies on debentures issued in the previous five years, including the year of calculation. The other subsidies are only for the year of calculation. Subsidies also existed for discount debentures, but were much smaller than those on coupon debentures.

analysis of public banks. More important, the knowledge they were making loans in accordance with government policy must have been a great relief. Counterbalancing these is the argument that JDB loans appear to be treated on a senior basis in case of financial trouble (see Chapter 5 by Packer). However, in practice, this does not seem to have taken place.

The most important form of risk-taking by the government is its policy of not letting any bank go bankrupt. A troubled bank would be supplied with a BOJ loan or be merged with a healthier bank, in more serious cases. This policy of rescuing any bank is still maintained by the MOF and the BOJ. Some of the recent bail-out attempts provide a good illustration of the role of the government. Take the rescue of a non-bank financial institution, Nichi Jukin.

The Case of Nichi Jukin (Japan Housing Finance)

Nichi Jukin is a non-bank financial institution providing housing loans using borrowings from banks. It has suffered from competition created by the increase in housing loans supplied by city and regional banks. During the late 1980s, Nichi Jukin made many real estate loans which later became non-performing. The seriousness of the problem comes from the size of Nichi Jukin's debt: it is the second largest borrower for Sanwa, accounting for about 0.7 per cent of Sanwa's loans. The total debt of the seven major housing loan companies stood at 13 trillion yen in September 1992, 2.6 per cent of M2+CD, of which about 7 trillion yen is considered to be non-performing (*Toyo Keizai*, 6 February 1993, p. 6).

Nichi Jukin's main bank, Sanwa, was not very active in arranging a rescue plan. Sanwa told *Kin'yu Business* (March 1993, p. 17) that 'rescuing Nichi Jukin in a particular way means rescuing all other housing finance companies in the same way. This would require consideration of factors that go well beyond the responsibility of a main bank.'

The MOF and BOJ, rather than Sanwa, came up with a rescue plan in early 1993. It involves (1) reduction of interest rates to zero for large lenders to Nichi Jukin; (2) reduction of interest rates to 2.5 per cent for other banks and Norin Chukin; (3) reduction of interest rates to 4.5 per cent for small agricultural cooperatives. If the same rescue scheme is applied to all seven housing loan non-banks, the foregone interest would be larger than the current profits for smaller banks, such as agricultural cooperatives. Observers say the whole plan would be based on increased BOJ loans to city, trust, long-term banks and Norin Chukin. Norin Chukin would then lend to smaller agricultural cooperatives. (See *Kin'yu Business*, March 1993; *Kin'yu Zaisei Jijou*, 2 August 1992.)

Restriction of Direct Financing

A different form of protection of banks was provided by the government's policy of restricting the issue of corporate bonds. After the war,

Article 65 of the Securities Transactions Law prohibited banks from participating in underwriting corporate bonds. Some believe major banks have nonetheless played the role of '*de facto* underwriters' (see, for example, Sakakibara and others (1981)).

Between 1949 and 1955, the bond market was controlled by the MOF and the BOJ. The control was temporarily relaxed in 1955–56, a period of loose monetary policy. With monetary tightening in 1957, however, the market was again controlled by the eight bank committee, effectively headed by the IBJ. (The other banks were Mitsui, Mitsubishi, Fuji, Sumitomo, Sanwa, Dai-Ichi, and Kangin, all major underwriters of corporate bonds before World War II.) The committee decided the amounts, rates and issuers of corporate bonds. The purpose was to limit the issue of corporate bonds so that bank debentures and bonds with government guarantee, most of which were issued by public corporations, would not be crowded out. In addition, whatever corporate bonds were issued were expected to be held by the initial investor until maturity. That is, the development of a secondary market was discouraged. An active secondary market would have enhanced the price mechanism, conflicting with the basic premise of the system.

Put differently, instead of letting non-financial firms issue bonds directly, the long-term banks issued bonds for them. There was, perhaps, a good reason for this: the ultimate lenders, households, were not capable of taking large risks or holding long-term instruments. Long-term credit banks, especially the IBJ, possessed a strong credit analysis capability.

Figure 3.1 shows the share of equity and bond financing in the external sources of funds for non-financial firms. The data are supposed to cover

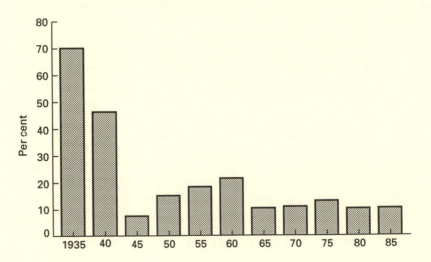

FIG. 3.1 Share of Bond and Equity Finance

all firms, but are collected from suppliers of funds rather than from firms. The share was quite high in 1935, but decreased sharply during the war, and in the post-war period has never reached pre-war levels.

PERFORMANCE OF THE JAPANESE BANKING INDUSTRY

One might expect the strong protection provided by the government to have decreased the efficiency of the Japanese banking industry. This section is devoted to the analysis of such a possibility.

A well-known difficulty in measuring bank performance is that there is no good definition of bank output. Various measures of bank performance have been used, including interest margin, cost-asset ratios, returns on assets or capital. International comparison of these variables should be interpreted with caution unless differences in output mix are controlled for (see Vittas, 1991, for a useful illustration of the difficulty involved). With this in mind, a rough evaluation of the performance of Japanese banks is given below.

Figure 3.2 compares the interest margin (net interest receipts as a percentage of total assets) and the current cost ratio (operating costs as a percentage of total assets) between US money centre banks and Japanese city banks for 1979–88. Clearly, Japanese banks compare quite favourably, especially when one takes into account two factors that increase the US ratios relative to Japan. First, US banks engage in more off balance sheet transactions. Second, though of decreasing significance over time, there has been widespread use of compensating balances in Japan.

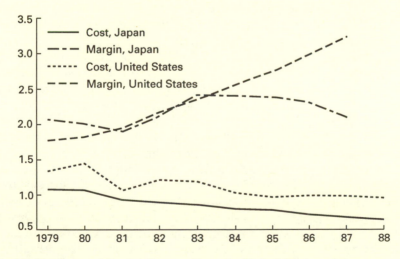

FIG. 3.2 Net Interest Margin, Current Costs for United States and Japanese Banks

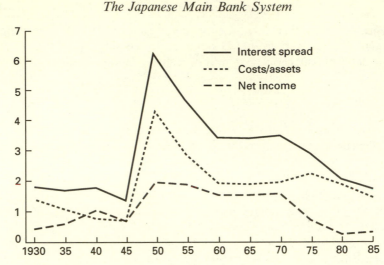

Fig. 3.3 Interest Margin, Current Costs and Net Income (City Banks)

Evidence over a longer time series, however, reveals that in the early post-war period Japanese banks were not as efficient as in the 1980s. Figure 3.3 shows the interest margin, current costs and net income of city banks, all relative to total assets for the period 1935–85. In terms of the cost ratio or interest margin, city banks before the war were as efficient as in the 1980s; but efficiency was sharply lower in the 1950s. Since then, both the cost ratio and interest margin have declined slowly to the current levels. The wide interest margins in the 1950s and 60s reflect both high costs and net incomes relative to total assets. Of course, the wide interest margins were made possible by government regulations on interest rates, especially those on deposit rates.

Why then did Japanese banks suddenly become inefficient right after the war in terms of the measures in Figure 3.3? The reason can be seen from Figure 3.4 which presents the size of deposits per bank relative to GNP, as well as interest margin. It is at once apparent that the war sharply decreased the financial assets of Japanese households and firms. With the decline in the size of deposits, Japanese banks experienced increases in expenses (relative to deposits and assets) and hence had to earn wider interest margins than before. As the stock of wealth increased over time due to high savings rates, the average size of deposits rose, making it possible for banks to operate with narrower interest margins.

How would one interpret such time series movements in the degree of bank efficiency in relation to the strong protective measures given to banks, as discussed in the previous section? It would perhaps be difficult to attribute the jump in costs and interest margins immediately after the war to the introduction of heavy protection for banks. Strong regulation

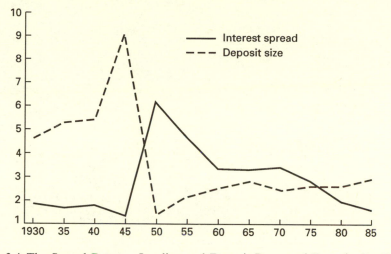

Fig. 3.4 The Spread Between Lending and Deposit Rates and Deposits Per Bank Relative to GNP

Source: The same as Figure 3.3

of the banking sector had already started in the late 1930s, but it did not lead to significant cost increases. A correct interpretation would be that the cost increase was a result of the loss in wealth, and this was a given condition policy-makers and bankers at that time had to face.

Viewed in this way, a more interesting question is why the performance of Japanese banks improved over time, despite the heavy protection given to them. Before turning to this point in the next section, let us consider another perspective on the initial condition of the Japanese banking sector right after the war.

Figure 3.5 presents the capital ratio for Japanese city and regional banks. It can be seen that the ratio declined sharply during the war, remained at low levels early in the post-war period, and has slowly increased since then. Thus, Japanese banks had to operate almost without any capital of their own during the war and early in the post-war period.[2]

Effects of Bank Regulation on Performance

The discussion in the last section suggests that the strong protection given to the banking sector in the post-war period was based on the idea that Japanese banks were very fragile, with low capital and high operating costs, as well as the requirement for them to promote the reconstruction

[2] During the 1970s and 80s, the unrealized capital gains on stocks held by banks increased sharply. Data have been published only for the last few years. When 45 per cent of these 'hidden reserves' are added to capital, as done in the calculation of the BIS ratio, the capital ratio for city banks as defined in Figure 3.5 becomes 7.7 per cent for fiscal 1990.

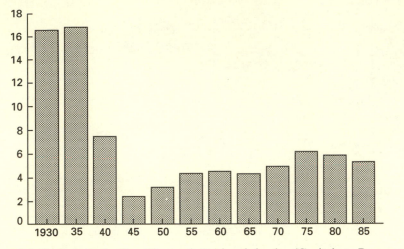

Fɪɢ. 3.5 Capital Ratio for City and Regional banks (Capital + Reserves + Surplus) / Assets

Source: The same as Figure 3.3

of the economy. Heavy protection, however, can easily result in inefficiencies or moral hazard. This section examines some of the reasons why these problems were not very serious.

One of the most important administrative directives used in the postwar period was 'the guidance on current costs'. In 1949 the MOF indicated that current costs should not exceed 90 per cent of current incomes. The target ratio was adjusted downward to 78 per cent in 1952. This was a major part of the MOF's bank regulatory policy until 1967.

According to Kobayashi (1978, part 4, p. 50), the idea behind the guidance on current costs was as follows. Japanese banks were protected by strong policy measures, notably by interest rate controls. The purpose of the controls was to let banks increase capital so that the stability of individual banks, and the banking sector as a whole, would be increased, as well as to provide funds to non-financial industries at low cost. If left alone, banks might use the income to pay increased wages or bonuses and not for increasing the bank's own capital. Kobayashi also notes that in 1954 an attempt was made by the MOF's banking bureau to introduce a deposit insurance system, which was considered to be a more straightforward method of assuring bank stability. The attempt did not succeed as the tax bureau was against it.

Guidance was not applied literally because the current cost ratio was around 80 to 82 per cent on average in the late 1950s (Kobayashi, 1978, part 5, p. 76). But the emphasis placed on the guidance suggests it exerted a significant impact on bank management in terms of containing costs.

Guidance on current costs gave way to the 'uniform accounting principle' in 1967, and was abolished in 1968. This was considered a major move toward encouraging competition among banks. Previously, the MOF applied a rather arbitrary rule in allowing banks to write off bad debts or accumulate reserves for depreciation of real assets owned by banks. The purpose of such a practice was, of course, to give, for example, favourable tax treatment to banks with low profits. But the MOF decided it was no longer necessary to protect banks as heavily as before. A starting point for encouraging competition would be to apply a uniform accounting rule to all banks, so that comparison of bank performance based on balance sheets and income statements could be more meaningful.

Further measures to encourage bank competition were introduced in the 1970s: banks were allowed to compete, if mildly, on dividends; branching regulation was relaxed; and a deposit insurance system was introduced. Moreover, in the official committee to discuss financial reform (Kinyu Seido Chosakai), strong views were expressed on relaxing interest rate controls (Kobayashi, 1978, part 11, p. 65).

Such an historical development of the MOF's bank regulatory policy suggests that it applied both the policy of protecting banks and that of encouraging bank competition, but with increasingly larger weight on the latter, as the post-war period progressed. This must have been an important reason for the good performance of Japanese banks in the second half of the post-war period.

Excessive risk-taking was controlled by a number of measures. In a guideline issued in 1957, city and regional banks were encouraged to hold bank debentures rather than lending long term by themselves, and ceilings were imposed on lending.

Auditing must have played an important role as well. In principle, it only provides *ex post* monitoring of banks; but penalties imposed in problem cases were found to have worked as an *ex ante* constraint on bank behaviour.

For example, a bad loan at a branch, if found, would mean the end of the career of the head of the branch. In more serious cases, when a rescue plan for a bank was required, it was often contingent on an overhaul of directors. Auditing by the MOF is carried out about every three years. For example, in 1958, 25 per cent of city banks and 42 per cent of regional banks were inspected. The frequency of auditing has remained stable over time. In 1990, 33 per cent of city banks and 36 per cent of regional banks were inspected. The BOJ has carried out its own auditing at about the same frequency. The system of bank auditing by both the MOF and the BOJ seems to have the virtue of increasing the coverage of auditing and making it more strict by encouraging competition between the regulators.

In addition, the MOF and BOJ have carried out more informal day-to-day monitoring of banks on the basis of written reports on specific issues and human relationships between the regulator and banks. Most of the large city banks consider it very important to maintain good relations with the regulators. For this purpose, they select some of their most promising young staff to act as MOF and BOJ watchers. The regulators use them to obtain information about the banks or to let the banks know about policy changes as precisely as possible.

In sum, the MOF and BOJ bank regulatory policy was not simply one of protecting banks. Bank protection was judiciously blended with encouragement of competition and punishment in case of trouble.

The honesty of bureaucrats has also been a key factor in the successful development of the Japanese financial system. Chapter 1 by Aoki, Patrick and Sheard discusses at some length the reasons for this. They emphasize the importance of *amakudari* (post-retirement jobs in the private financial sector for bureaucrats) as incentives for honest behaviour. This is certainly a valid argument. Perhaps equally important has been the authority MOF officials have had over the private sector. The authority has derived from the existence of explicit and implicit regulations. Officials have used it mostly in honest ways, because otherwise they would not get promoted to higher positions with greater authority. Behind this virtuous cycle has been, of course, the Japanese life-time employment system.

Another key factor for the good performance of Japanese banks was definitely the performance of the economy. This was already evident in Figure 3.4. The growth of deposits enabled banks to reduce costs. Whatever moral hazard or excessive risk-taking problems that might have existed became trivial compared to fast-growing bank assets. A question remains concerning the extent to which high growth was a result of the high-performing banking sector. The analysis of this question, however, is beyond the scope of this chapter.

FINANCIAL LIBERALIZATION AND BANK PERFORMANCE

Involvement in the so-called bubble economy of the late 1980s and the resulting large accumulation of bad debts have raised questions about the efficiency of Japanese banks. A detailed analysis of this question requires a full-length paper. The following is confined to a discussion of the relationship between the financial liberalization that started in the late 1970s and the events in late 1980s.

Many have attributed the significant financial liberalization that has taken place to the sharp increase in government budget deficits in the late

1970s and the resulting need to sell large amounts of government bonds. (See, for example, Cargill and Royama, 1988, chapter 4.) Perhaps this is basically correct. The foregoing discussion, however, suggests another reason: many of the regulations necessary to protect a banking industry that was very weak at the beginning of the post-war period became obstacles to further improvement of efficiency and had to be removed.

As discussed earlier, bank protection took three forms: discouragement of competition, sharing of credit risks by the government, and the restriction of direct finance. Part, but not all, of the first and third types of regulations were gradually relaxed. Most significant among these was the gradual deregulation of interest rates. The BOJ was no longer able to absorb all the government bonds issued. Unlike the war period, it was impossible to force the public to increase savings for purchasing bonds. Thus, sales of government bonds by financial institutions in the secondary market began to take place in 1978. The long-term government bond rate began to reflect fundamentals, and so did other interest rates. Decontrol of interest rates was also in line with the requirement to narrow the interest margins given to banks as they became more efficient.

Large sales of government bonds inevitably led, if slowly, to the development of the bond market. The high growth of the economy increased stock prices, making the stock market an important place for fund raising. The combination of these two forces led to increasing issues of equity-related bonds such as convertible and warrant bonds. Figure 3.1 gives the impression that bonds and equities were not important even in the 1980s. However, a different picture emerges by looking at larger firms only. Table 3.2 presents the share of equity, bonds, and bank borrowing in the external financing of firms with more than 1 billion yen in equity and listed on stock exchanges. The data are from the 'Financial

TABLE 3.2 Distribution of Sources of
External Corporate Finance

(per cent)

	Equity	Bonds	Loans
1957–59	20.5	11.1	68.3
1960–64	21.2	13.6	65.2
1965–69	8.0	12.1	79.9
1970–74	6.4	10.3	83.3
1975–79	19.6	25.3	55.1
1980–84	30.0	25.1	45.0
1985–88	38.6	51.4	10.0

Notes: Firms with more than 1 billion yen
in equity.
Source: Oba and Horiuchi (1991).

Statements of Principal Enterprises' compiled by the BOJ and cover 638 non-financial firms. They show clearly that bank borrowings decreased sharply in the 1980s with corresponding increases in equity and bonds.

Table 3.3 shows the breakdown of bank loans for plant and equipment purchases by type of bank and by size of borrowing firm. It can be seen that most of the growth in loans took place in loans to smaller firms, even for large banks such as city, long-term and trust banks.

TABLE 3.3 Plant and Equipment Loans by Banks

(billion yen)

Year	City	Regional	Long-Term	Trust
1955	108	44	233	70
	[9]	[13]	[8]	[1]
1960	380	157	802	473
	[43]	[63]	[47]	[19]
1965	833	496	1923	1706
	[179]	[294]	[212]	[62]
1970	2500	1802	3908	4144
	[890]	[1244]	[618]	[330]
1975	9060	6031	7935	8895
	[4946]	[4680]	[1188]	[1687]
1989	57926	29107	13985	13536
	[49726]	[25932]	[4582]	[7235]

Notes:

[1] Loans to firms with capital below 100 million yen.

Source: Bank of Japan, *Economics Statistics Annual,* various years.

Consequently, banks competed vigorously for loans. This led to an enormous increase in land and equity investment-related loans in the late 1980s, as can be seen from Table 3.4. Credit analysis was relatively easy for these loans because it essentially amounted to forecasting future land and equity prices. This seems to have been an important cause of the land and equity price bubble of the period. The problem was more serious for long-term credit and trust banks. They do not possess as many branches or loan officers as city banks and regional banks. This prompted them to increase land and equity investment-related loans by more than other banks. In a sense, they suffered from less than full-scale deregulation of the separation of various financial services.

This raises the question of why the regulators were not able to prevent the price bubble. The quality of bank credit analysis deteriorated in the

TABLE 3.4 Share of Loans to Real Estate
and Financial Industries

	1980	1991
City Banks	8.1	18.9
Regional Banks	6.9	15.8
Trust Banks	17.5	40.5
Long-term Credit Banks	16.7	37.1

Source: Bank of Japan, *Economics Statistics Annual*, various years.

midst of increased competition with equity-related financing. The MOF and BOJ were certainly aware of the huge increase in bank lendings to equity and land-related investment—BOJ (1987) noted that 'behind recent high growth in the money supply are the increasingly speculative activities of firms and households . . . and the fact that banks are aggressively making loans to support these activities' (translation by the author).

They were, however, not able to stop this, given that the general price level was fairly stable and that it was difficult to foresee the subsequent collapse of the bubble and the consequent instability of the financial system. In this sense, macroeconomic policy, rather than bank regulatory policy, was more seriously in trouble.

CONCLUSION

The Japanese financial system in the post-war period originated in the war-time economy. The system in both periods was characterized by heavy government intervention. The war-time financial system was designed to channel funds into military industries. In the post-war period, the government used almost the same system, but to achieve the reconstruction and later rapid growth of the economy.

Government intervention in the banking industry is justified even without such goals. Stability of the financial system is a public good; achievement of stability requires certain regulations. Japanese authorities sought to maintain the stability of the system by protecting banks. This method seems to have worked well, in so far as the reconstruction of the financial system and the promotion of high growth were the prime policy goals.

Now that the policy goal of high growth has been abandoned, the prime reason for government intervention in the financial system must be to achieve stability. The regulations that protected banks have been lifted, but protection is still a major tool used by the policy authority to achieve stability. Attempts to achieve stability have been criticized on grounds of

non-transparency and inefficiency; attempts at liberalization have sometimes led to increased instability. The major problem the policy authority
will have to face is to devise a new method of achieving stability that is
compatible with the free play of the price mechanism.

REFERENCES

Bank of Japan. 1987. 'Jousei Handan Shiryou' ('Quarterly Report on the State of
the Economy'). *Monthly Report of the Research and Statistics Division*, July.
CARGILL, THOMAS F., and SHOICHI ROYAMA. 1988. *The Transition of Finance in
Japan and the US*. Stanford CA: Hoover Press.
DOGAKINAI, SHIGEHARU. 1991. 'Deregulation of Interest Rates.' In *Japan's
Financial Markets*. Tokyo: Foundation for Advanced Information and
Research.
Industrial Bank of Japan. 1982. *Nihon Kougyou Ginkou Shichiju Gonennshi (A 75
Year History of the Industrial Bank of Japan)*. Tokyo.
IWATA, KIKUO, and AKIYOSHI HORIUCHI. 1985. 'Nihon no Ginko Kisei' ('Bank
Regulation in Japan'). *Journal of Economics*, University of Tokyo.
ITO, TAKATOSHI, and KAZUO UEDA. 1981. 'Tests of the Equilibrium Hypothesis in
Disequilibrium Econometrics.' *International Economic Review* 22: 691–708.
KOBAYASHI, KEIKICHI. 1978. 'Sengo Ginkou Gyouseishi' ('The History of Post
War Bank Regulatory Policy'). *Fainansu*, various issues. Ministry of Finance,
Tokyo.
KOUSHASAI HIKIUKE KYOUKAI. 1980. *Nihon Koushasai Shijoushi (History of the
Japanese Bonds Markets)*. Tokyo: University of Tokyo Press.
NAKAJIMA, MASATAKA. 1981. 'Kinri Jiyuka no Seiji Keizaigaku' ('The Political
Economy of Interest Rate Deregulation'). In Kaizuka Shimura and Toyokeizai
Royama, eds., *Kinyu Shouken Kouza*. Tokyo: Toyo Keizai Shinposha.
SAKAKIBARA, EISUKE, ROBERT FELDMAN and YUZO HARADA. 1982. Testimony, 12
March. In Joint Economic Committee, US Congress, *The Japanese Financial
System in Comparative Perspective*. Washington DC.
SATAKE, HIROSHI, and OSAMU HASHIGUCHI. 1967. *Ginkou Gyousei to Ginkou Hou
(Bank Regulatory Policy and the Bank Act)*. Tokyo: Yuhikaku.
TERANISHI, JURO. 1982. *Nihon no Keizai Hatten to Kinyu (The Japanese Economic
Development and Finance)*. Tokyo: Iwanami Shoten.
UEDA, KAZUO. 1993a. 'Nihonteki Shisutemu no Genryuu: Kinyu' ('The Origin of
the Japanese System: Finance'). University of Tokyo.
——. 1993b. 'The Industrial Bank of Japan and Public Financial Institutions.'
University of Tokyo.
VITTAS, DIMITRI. 1991. 'Measuring Commercial Bank Efficiency: Use and Misuse
of Bank Operating Ratios.' Working Paper 806. World Bank, Country
Economics Department, Washington DC.
ZGK (Zenkoku Ginko Kyokai) (Federation of Banking Associations of Japan).
1985. 'Tenpo Gyousei no Hensen to Tenpo Haichi' ('The Development of
Branching Regulation and the Location of Branches'). *Kin'yu*. Tokyo: ZGK.

4

Monitoring Characteristics of the Main Bank System: An Analytical and Developmental View

MASAHIKO AOKI

Transactions involving investible funds between investors (the suppliers of funds in the form of equity or credit) and an industrial firm undertaking a business project entails a substantial degree of information asymmetry and imperfection. First, investors may not be as well informed as the firm regarding the technological and marketing opportunities which define the outcome of a project (the adverse selection problem). Second, managers of the firm themselves may not necessarily be in an advantageous position with regard to information if the financial returns of the project depend upon coordinated undertakings of complementary projects by other firms (the coordination problem). Third, a manager's promise to use the funds for a certain profitable purpose may not be fulfilled because of manager (or worker) incompetence or morally hazardous behaviour hidden behind uncontrollable stochastic events (the moral hazard problem).

To cope with these problems, there need to be mechanisms for assessing the credit-worthiness of proposed projects; tracking the use of funds; distinguishing misuse from temporary bad luck and correcting it; as well as credible commitment to penalizing misuse as a safeguard against future misuse (the commitment problem). Thus, the supply of financial resources requires a substantial degree of concomitant information collection—*monitoring*—by investors before and after the actual investment, as well as their participation in controlling the firm (the corporate governance issue).

Corporate monitoring and control is only possible, however, with special expertise, concentrated resources, and a sufficiently broad scope in terms of cross-sectional coverage as well as time horizon. In capitalist economies a variety of financial intermediaries and agents specializing in corporate monitoring and control have emerged. They include investment

In drafting this paper, the author benefited from joint research with Paul Sheard, and discussion and comments by Elu von Thadden, Ken-ichi Imai, Thomas Hellman, and participants of the project. The research assistance of Ayako Yasuda and Nariyasu Yamazawa is also appreciated. Any error remains the author's responsibility.

and securities houses, commercial banks, long-term credit banks, universal banks, venture capital firms, rating and accounting companies, corporate boards, mutual and pension funds, take-over raiders, bankruptcy courts, and so on. These organizations differ not only in the kind of financial instruments they create, but also in the nature, scope and orientation of information collection, and their roles in the corporate governance structure. A particular set of institutional arrangements webbed by such institutions evolves for each economy. These are conditioned partly by an existing regulatory framework, partly by the historical path, and partly as a response to the prevailing and emergent organizational, technological, and risk-taking attributes of the economy.

Obviously, ways in which information is collected and utilized for investment and corporate control exert different influences on the behavioural patterns of economic agents of both the demand and supply sides of financial intermediaries. Therefore, an institutional arrangement of various intermediaries in a particular financial system may have significant bearings on the performance of the economy in which the system is embedded. The reverse causation also may be possible. The efficiency and effectiveness of a particular financial system may also change over time as the economy progresses. There is thus an important need for a comparative institutional analysis of financial systems.

This chapter is concerned with the question of how the Japanese main bank system copes with the problems arising from information imperfection and asymmetry in financial transactions. More specifically, we ask whether the Japanese main bank system offers significantly different monitoring and controlling perspectives from the Anglo-American securities-based financial system. Are the corporate monitoring and control characteristics of the main bank system an essential ingredient of the Japanese economy which has exhibited a relatively high growth rate (7.7 per cent) over the last 40 years? Even if the main bank system was an effective monitoring device in the high growth period, is it not losing effectiveness in the increasingly market-oriented global environment? Answers to these questions may hinge crucially on an understanding of the relationship of the main bank system with other institutional aspects of the Japanese economy, particularly corporate organizations.

This chapter addresses these questions in nine sections. The first prepares a conceptual framework for a comparative analysis of the monitoring characteristics of financial systems by distinguishing three stages of monitoring: *ex ante* (credit evaluation), *interim* (on-going) and *ex post* (the verification of the financial outcome and action based on it). The second section characterizes the nature of the Japanese main bank system in its heyday as the integration of three stages of corporate monitoring exclusively delegated to the main bank, and implications of this characteristic for the corporate governance structure of Japanese firms are taken up in the third section. The fourth section clarifies the way in which the main bank system complements the particular organizational mode of Japanese firms. The incentives for the main bank to undertake delegated integrated monitoring are analysed in the fifth section, and the sixth examines the benefits and costs of the regulatory framework to make the main bank system viable by the provision of regulatory rents. The seventh section examines how much the establishment and the effectiveness of the main bank system was conditioned by informational and organizational attributes of the Japanese economy during the high growth period and discusses the possible relevance of those attributes to those of developing and transforming economies. The eighth section describes how successive, yet partial, deregulations since the 1970s have impaired the coherence and integrity of the main bank's monitoring functions, facilitating the generation of the bubble in the late 1980s and shaking the foundations of the system. The chapter concludes with a prediction that the Japanese financial system is unlikely to be transformed into the securities-based system of the Anglo-American type, in spite of the increasing securitization of financial instruments; and I suggest a further deregulation that may make the main bank system adaptable to such an environment.

THREE STAGES OF CORPORATE MONITORING

The word 'monitor' is used to mean 'to check or regulate'. In applying 'monitor' to the actions of the suppliers of funds (or their agents) directed towards corporate firms to overcome the problems associated with information asymmetry and imperfection, conceptually, we must differentiate among three kinds of monitoring. The primary distinction is the timing of an action in relation to the transfer of funds from the investor to the firm.

The first stage of monitoring, *ex ante*, refers to the investor's assessment of the credit-worthiness of investment projects proposed by corporate firms and their screening. Generally, this type of monitoring is considered economically valuable as it can reduce the problem of adverse selection in a situation where outside investors are not as well informed beforehand as the inside manager of the firm regarding the profitability and risk potential of proposed projects, the managerial and organizational competence of the firm, and the like. But the future outcome of an investment project may also depend upon the financing of complementary projects undertaken by separate firms. For example, the profitability of a steel plant is affected by the availability of power, which may, in turn, be crucially affected by the construction of a new dam, if the level of accumulation in the power industry is relatively low. Investors who are able to collect a broader cross-sectional range of information may have superior *ex ante* capacity to form judgements than single borrowers.

The second stage, *interim* monitoring, refers to an investor checking the ongoing behaviour of management and the operation of the firm in general, and the use of funds in particular, after the funds are committed. Monitoring at this stage may be a necessary response to the problem of moral hazard arising from situations in which the interests of investors and managers (and the workers) of the firm do not necessarily coincide, so that there are incentives for managers to divert funds to their own interests if investors do not make an effort to uncover such hidden, morally hazardous action.

The third kind of monitoring, *ex post*, refers to the verification of performance outcome (the financial state) of the firm, judgement on the long-run viability of the firm in case of financial distress, and the use of that information for possible corrective or punitive action. The way an investor credibly commits (or does not commit) to a certain action contingent on the *ex post* outcome affects a manager's *ex ante* incentive and interim behaviour. For example, if investors made a credible commitment to punish poor management performance, management would be careful to avoid *ex ante* and interim behaviour that might result in a poor outcome. If investors are not able to make a credible commitment, then management might be tempted to misrepresent the degree of risk in a prospective project and behave inefficiently. The distinctions of the three stages of monitoring are summarized in Table 4.1.

The distinctions among the three stages of monitoring should be regarded as merely conceptual. In practice, they are likely to be intertwined. For example, if the relationship between the investor and the firm are repeatable over time, decisions for new financing are based on the interim monitoring of the previous phase, and the two are difficult to distinguish. New financing may be denied if it is judged that the firm is not financially viable. In this case, an *ex ante* decision is intertwined with an *ex post* judgement. Interim monitoring and *ex post* monitoring may be

TABLE 4.1 Three Stages of Monitoring

Stage of monitoring	Function	Associated problems
Ex ante	Project evaluation credit analysis	Adverse selection, coordination failure
Interim	Watching the management operation of the firm	Moral hazard
Ex post	Verification of financial state and applying punitive and corrective action contingent on the state	Commitment

difficult to distinguish as long as the firm is financially healthy and keeps going. But we will see that the conceptual distinction turns out to be quite useful for comparing the structure and performance of different financial systems.

The monitoring of different stages may be delegated to various financial intermediaries and agents, rather than performed by individual investors, in order to reduce information costs and the costs of duplicating monitoring. Institutional arrangements for such intermediaries may differ across economies, however. For example, the Anglo-American system has developed separate financial intermediaries specializing in particular monitoring functions. *Ex ante* monitoring is performed by investment banks acting as underwriters for large established firms, by venture capital firms for entrepreneurial start-up firms, by commercial banks for conventional smaller firms, and so on. Rating companies may be considered engaged in interim monitoring in that they keep track of the changing financial state of the firm, but their evaluation affects the capacity of firms to raise new funds from capital markets so they also can be considered an important *ex ante* monitoring device in the securities-based financial system. Interim monitoring of management may be most directly performed by the board of directors, which in turn is subject to direct and indirect pressure from major stockholders, as well as a variety of funds managers, market arbitrageurs, corporate raiders.

The court-led bankruptcy procedure constitutes an important *ex post* monitoring device in any financial system. However, the institutionalization of the take-over market (the market for corporate control) may be regarded as the most distinct *ex post* monitoring device for the Anglo-American system and is unparalleled anywhere else. Venture capitalists and LBO (leverage buyout) partners act as disciplinary bodies for entrepreneurial firms and firms going out of the market for corporate control, respectively.

In contrast to the highly decentralized Anglo-American system in which the three stages of monitoring are entrusted to separate specialized intermediaries, the Japanese main bank system in its heyday was characterized as a system in which *the three stages of monitoring of a firm were highly integrated and exclusively delegated to the main bank of the firm.*

MAIN BANK INTEGRATED MONITORING

To identify the kind of institutions performing the critical function of *ex ante* monitoring in the Japanese economy, Table 4.2 provides an overview of the sources of new supplies of industrial equipment funds. In 1955 when Japan's economy took off for a period of high growth, the proportion of funding by government financial institutions (including the Japan

Development Bank, (JDB)) and long-term credit banks (notably the Industrial Bank of Japan (IBJ)) represented about a half of new funding sources. Even during the subsequent period of stable growth (1960-70), it remained around one-quarter. While the proportion of the JDB and IBJ remained almost the same throughout the 1970s and started to decline only in the 1980s, that of city banks has been steadily increasing since the mid-1960s. Although the reliance of an increasing number of firms on bond financing since the late 1980s has attracted wide-spread attention, the overall significance of bond issues in industrial equipment financing has not yet become dominant.

Using Table 4.2 as background, I suggest that long-term credit banks and city banks played an instrumental role as main banks for large firms in *ex ante* monitoring for industrial development through long-term lending, as well as direct and indirect involvement in bond issues. In the earlier period of high economic growth, however, city bank *ex ante* monitoring was complemented in a critical manner by government financial institutions and long-term credit banks. The other private financial institutions, comprising insurance companies, trust banks and banks for small businesses, supplied relatively large shares of equipment funding throughout the period. But the role of trust banks and insurance companies in *ex ante* monitoring has not been autonomous. *Ex ante* monitoring of small businesses was primarily performed by financial institutions for small businesses, complemented by the Small Business Finance Corporation. This chapter is mostly concerned with the monitoring of large firms.

Administratively Mediated Coordination

As a result of their active involvement in financing industrial investment throughout the 1950s, the proportions of outstanding equipment loans by JDB and IBJ at the end of 1960 were 21.7 per cent and 18.1 per cent respectively, in contrast to 15.3 per cent for all city banks combined. The combined share of JDB and IBJ dropped to 22.4 per cent at the end of 1970. One is struck by the magnitude of the involvement of public and private long-term credit banks at the time when the Japanese economy started to take off.

Throughout the 1950s, JDB loans were concentrated in public utilities, particularly the electrical power industry, and marine transportation. Loans for these two industries accounted for 83 per cent of JDB's total outstanding loans at the end of fiscal 1960. IBJ loans were for equipment financing in key manufacturing industries such as iron and steel (13.4 per cent), machinery (12.7 per cent), and chemicals (9.8 per cent), as well as public utilities (18.1 per cent). City banks complemented the long-term financing of the JDB and IBJ by providing operating funds for these strategic industries. They also supplied equipment financing to industries,

TABLE 4.2 New Supply of Industrial Equipment Funds by Source

(billion yen)

1955	1960	1965	1970	1975	1980	1985	Sources
449.5	2,111.5	3,804.2	9,453.3	17,890	20,715	31,491	Total
32.5	341.8	168.4	753.9	953	807	712	Equity
3.5	256.5	228.2	495.3	1,912	1,203	2,832	Debentures
283.1	1,227.6	2,807.1	6,893.0	12,152	15,083	23,629	Loans by private financial institutions (B)
130.4	285.6	531.9	1,310.9	2,873	3,622	4,289	Government funds (C)
							Loans by Private Banks[1]
174.8	603.9	1,323.9	3,724.7	8,436	11,261	19,774	All banks[2] of which:
39.8	202.4	365.3	1,321.1	3,488	4,868	9,776	City banks
113.5	304.8	684.3	1,319.3	2,262	2,402	3,372	Long-term credit banks
							Government Funds, detail
93.4	220.5	309.1	1,164.5	2,433	3,091	3,435	Loans by government financial institutions of which:
48.7	68.6	192.0	330.3	799	646	1,188	Japan Development Bank
20.3	66.0	117.1	332.3	470	798	941	Small Business Finance Corporation
							Percentage Distribution of Total Sources
7.2	16.1	4.4	8.0	5.3	3.9	2.4	Equity
0.8	12.1	6.0	5.2	10.6	5.8	9.0	Debentures
8.9	9.6	9.6	13.9	19.4	23.5	3.0	City bank loans
25.2	14.4	17.9	13.9	12.6	11.5	10.7	Long-term credit bank loans
28.8	34.1	48.0	44.9	35.7	37.7	33.2	Other private financial institution loans
29.0	13.5	13.9	13.8	16.0	17.4	13.6	Government funds

Excludes funds for financial institutions, local government, and individuals.
Notes:
[1] The difference between the total for 'Private financial institutions' and 'All banks' is the total for non-bank financial institutions.
[2] Banking accounts only; that is, excludes trust accounts.

such as textile and fertilizer, that had already achieved world-class competitiveness. (Yasuda, 1993, deals in detail with the complementary roles of JDB, IBJ and city banks.)

Among the industries targeted by the JDB and IBJ, the electrical power industry, comprising nine regional monopolies, occupied a particularly strategic position in the process of taking off. Between 1955 and 1959 these utilities invested a gigantic sum, equal to more than one-third of the total invested in manufacturing (Table 4.3). The mechanism by which the investment and financing decisions were made for the electrical power industry, as well as the role played by JDB and IBJ, is illuminating for understanding the public framework in which *ex ante* monitoring by city banks operated during that period.

TABLE 4.3 Shares of the Electric Power Industry and the Manufacturing Industry in National Investments (progress base): 1955–65

(per cents)

Fiscal Year	Electric Power	Manufacturing
1955	13.1	34.2
1956	12.9	34.4
1957	12.9	34.8
1958	13.2	34.9
1959	13.2	35.6
1960	12.9	37.7
1961	12.6	39.7
1962	12.4	40.9
1963	12.1	42.0
1964	11.6	42.7
1965	11.5	42.5

Fiscal years end 31 March of following year.

Source: NEEDS (Nikkel Economic Electronic Databank System).

Formal investment decisions on the construction of large-scale dams and power plants were coordinated and authorized by the Council of Coordinating Electric Energy Source Development (Dengen Kaihatsu Chosei Shingikai). The Public Utility Bureau of MITI acted as a secretariat for the Council. The funding plan for approved investment projects was discussed at the Industrial Funding Division of the Industrial Structure Council, and then incorporated into the JDB's business plan through the Fiscal and Investment Loan Program administered by the Trust Bureau of the Ministry of Finance (MOF). Throughout the preparatory processes information was exchanged among various public authorities, power companies, private and public long-term credit banks and city banks, important user industries such as steel and ship-building, and academic experts in fields such as economic planning, econometrics, and civil engineering.[1]

The electrical power industry provided important infrastructure for the development of manufacturing, especially because of the acute shortage of energy sources at that time. Therefore, sharing information on demand and supply conditions of the power industry throughout the planning process provided a useful framework for the formation of common expectations regarding medium-term economic prospects. The shared expectations provided not only a useful guideline for specific loan decisions (*ex ante* monitoring) for private banks, but also helped to prevent the economy being trapped in a low equilibrium due to a lack of coordination among industries in investment decisions.

In 1955, the government decided that the JDB should gradually withdraw from its dominant role in investment financing in the power industry. Through the intermediation of the Japanese Bankers Association, consortia of city banks started to increase their funding, either through long-term loans or bond purchases. In 1964, the BOJ decided to make bonds issued by electrical power companies qualify for its discount and market operations. As the priority of public policy changed, the JDB started to shift its lending targets to urban and regional development, as well as more specific, less strategic industries (such as electronics, chemical fertilizer, specific-purpose machinery). Although the role of the JDB in particular, and national planning in general, has steadily declined since the beginning of the 1960s, it is important to keep in mind that throughout the period of high economic growth, the *ex ante* monitoring capacity of city banks was nurtured and developed within a framework of intense knowledge-sharing between public and private sectors, as well as between industry and the banking sector.

Integration of Ex Ante and Interim Monitoring

As indicated in Table 4.2, long-term investment loans by city banks among private financial institutions have not been overwhelming. Further, long-term loans made by main banks (defined as the largest lender among city banks) have recently been around half of such loans by

---

[1] The membership of the Council of Coordinating Electric Energy Source Development in July 1955 included the ministers of Finance, Agriculture, International Trade and Industry, Construction; the directors of the Agency for Economic Planning and the Agency for Local Autonomy; the presidents of the Bank of Japan and the Japan Development Bank; the chair of the Japan Chamber of Commerce and Industry, the Kansai Economic Federation, and the Central Federation of Agricultural Cooperatives; a professor of the University of Tokyo, the director of the Construction Engineering Research Institute, and an executive director for the Central Electric Research Institute.

all city banks (see Table 1.2). The total of loans by other private financial institutions, including trust banks, banks for small businesses, and insurance companies, has far exceeded the loans of main banks (see Table 4.2). In spite of this, since the 1960s the main bank has assumed the leading role in assessing private investment projects for loan purposes; other private financial institutions have relied on the main bank's credit analysis rather than developing their own monitoring capabilities (except for real estate development projects, an area in which the trust banks specialized). Regardless of whether it is the main bank's suggestion or the firm's own decision not to rely exclusively on the main bank as a borrowing source, diversified long-term loan arrangements—that is, the formation of a *de facto* long-term loan consortium—have been made only with the initial lead decision by the main bank to extend a certain critical portion of the required investment funds (see Chapter 8 by Horiuchi).

Other private financial institutions and non-main city banks have been seen as delegating *ex ante* monitoring to the main bank (Sheard, 1989). The ability of the main bank to assume such *ex ante* responsibility, as well as the reliance of other institutions on the main bank's *ex ante* judgement without explicit delegation, are derived from the even greater role of the main bank in interim and *ex post* monitoring.

When the Japanese economy was still catching up in terms of technological capability, an important component of *ex ante* monitoring involved more checking of the managerial and organizational ability of an investing firm to absorb and improve upon engineering know-how developed abroad than assessing the commercial and engineering values of an emergent technology, *per se*. The engineering assessments of imported technologies for large-scale projects were often delegated to the IBJ which was impartial to any financial keiretsu grouping, and had accumulated the necessary engineering and credit analysis capabilities. The city banks were, however, well equipped to assess the organizational and managerial ability of firms belonging to their own groupings.

As shown in Table 1.2, the main bank extends a far larger share of short-term loans than long-term loans, the latter normally being rolled over on maturity. Together with the holding of major payment settlement accounts, this implies that the main bank is deeply involved in the daily transactional operations of customer firms. The holding of major settlement accounts, in particular, amounts to an ability to open the books partially. Such interim monitoring opportunity provided city banks with private information useful for judging the organizational and managerial capacity of borrowing firms. That information is not available to other financial institutions, whose contacts with borrowing firms were less frequent and more tangential.

The link between interim and *ex ante* monitoring was essential also in the case of bond issues. In the pre-1980 period, when overseas bond issuance was highly regulated, domestic bond issues were conditioned on the availability of collateral. After bond issues, the collateral was monitored until maturity by the trustee (jyutaku) administrator assigned at the time of issue. Main banks have normally performed this interim monitoring task for lucrative fees. Although city banks were prohibited from underwriting by regulation (until April 1993), it was almost impossible for firms to issue bonds without prior arrangement with the main banks regarding trusteeship. The securities companies underwriting bonds did not possess the same independent *ex ante* monitoring expertise as investment houses in the Anglo-American system, and they used main bank relationships of issuing firms as the screening device.

Exclusivity of Monitoring

The role of the main bank in *ex post* monitoring has been almost exclusive, as dealt with in detail by Sheard in Chapter 6. There has been an unwritten but well-observed code that when a firm falls into a financially depressed state, it is the responsibility of the main bank to resolve the problem by taking the initiative for either rescuing or restructuring, for court-led reorganization, or liquidation. Further, this rule has been implemented almost without exception by the main banks assuming a larger proportion of the costs of resolving problems than other lenders. JDB loans were normally collateralized, and its claims had priority because it was a public financial intermediary funded by postal savings. The JDB has not played any significant role in *ex post* monitoring except for salvaging the marine transportation industry, which has been in continual depression since the early 1970s and for which city banks never played an active financing role. IBJ has sometimes played a crucial role in dealing with ailing firms, but it did so in the capacity of the main bank and not in lieu of the main (city) banks. In contrast, the main bank would be forced to guarantee the claims of inferior lender institutions, such as agricultural cooperatives and regional banks, in the event of the financial distress of a client firm and, unless the case is brought under bankruptcy procedure, substantial portions of claims by other city banks as well. If additional financing for restructuring is needed, main banks have provided a greater share than normal loans.

Ramseyer (Chapter 7) suggests the possible application of the 'principle of equitable subordination'—the rule that makes claims by lenders involved in the business and affairs of troubled firms subordinate to other claims in a bankruptcy procedure—deters commercial banks in the Anglo-American system from being actively involved in restructuring failing firms. Although a similar rule appears to be imposed *de facto* in the Japanese system, in the context of the delegation of integrated monitoring it appears to motivate the main banks to perform earnest interim and *ex ante* monitoring. The main banks need to prevent client firms from undertaking projects that may place more than the amount of their own lending at risk. The main banks also need to monitor the business and affairs of borrowing firms closely to detect potential problems at the earliest possible time. This motivation encourages other lenders to delegate *ex ante* monitoring to the main bank.

However, one might ask, if monitoring is exclusively delegated to the main bank, why does the credit relationship itself also not become exclusive? Instead, a firm diversifies its borrowing among many financial institutions and the main bank's share of loans is on average less than half. There is an historical reason for this: during the war-time heavy industrialization and post-war reconstruction, the investment needs of representative industrial firms were too large relative to the available financial resources of a single private bank. The formation of consortia was inevitable, as discussed by Teranishi (Chapter 2) and Horiuchi (Chapter 8). There is also a regulatory reason: a city bank's loans to a single firm are limited to 25 per cent of the bank's net worth.

There also seem to be reciprocal incentives for concerned parties to diversify loan relationships. On the firm's side, there may be the fear that reliance on a single bank for investment financing may encourage the bank to intervene in management. By diversifying loan sources, the firm's management may be able to reserve the option of switching the main bank relationship to another bank if the incumbent main bank is too meddlesome. On the main bank side, an exclusive loan relationship may be difficult to terminate, even when it is more efficient to do so. By limiting its own loans to a minority share, the main bank may be able to avoid being completely captured by the interests of the firm and to leave open the option of abandoning failing firms if necessary (Horiuchi and others, 1988).

One important effect of exclusive integrated monitoring, combined with the non-exclusive loan relationship, appears to lie in the increase in the number of potential actions the main bank can implement *ex post*. Feasible actions directed toward financially depressed firms may range from liquidation to court-led reorganization, restructuring under bank management, and simple loan rescheduling. Underwriters and initial holders of bonds cannot commit themselves *ex ante* to such a broad range of options, because, facing liquid secondary markets, they can sell their claims at any time, thereby inducing a change in the identity of maturity date holders. Therefore, the options available *ex post* for bondholders are limited to the one formally stipulated by the legal bankruptcy procedure (see Garcia-Cestona, 1991, for the efficiency implications for the difference). On the other hand, under the exclusive loan relationship observed in many developing economies, including the Japanese economy in the 1920s, it becomes difficult for the banks to refuse to rescue poor partner firms. The viable options available to the Japanese main bank include both liquidation and rescue.

From this perspective, it may be worthwhile to refer to an often-made contention (Mayer, 1988) that the main bank system is a mutual commitment device for a long-term relationship: the main bank can tolerate short-term problems of financially depressed firms, and rescue them at a cost in the short term, while rescued firms reciprocate by making a commitment to deliver future returns and not to desert the main bank after recuperation. Indeed, Hoshi and others (1989) found quantitative evidence to show that main bank relationships have helped financially depressed firms to continue business investments in spite of bad times. However, the outright commitment to rescue may create the reverse commitment problem: that is, dilution of the lender's *ex ante* commitment to punish poorly managed firms. Even if removal of top management is imposed as a precondition for a rescue operation, the certain prospect of a rescue would have adverse incentive effects on the employees of the firm in general. A possible mechanism to cope with this moral hazard problem is discussed in the next section, but it appears premature, at least at the theoretical level, to characterize the main bank system simply as a means of commitment to a long-term relationship.

It seems more reasonable to say that integrated monitoring by the main bank increases the range of actions that can be implemented *ex post*. The implications of this flexibility are not clear *a priori*, however. On one hand, flexibility may facilitate soft budgeting by the main banks (the lack of commitment to punish poor management), letting too many inefficient firms survive. On the other hand, it may contribute to the preservation of valuable organizational resources of good firms that are temporarily distressed, and would be insolvent without *ex post* rescue led by the main bank. The issue of which outcome is more likely under the main bank system must be settled by future empirical studies.

Other Effects of Integrated Monitoring

Another possible effect of integrated monitoring is that it may reduce incentives for the firm to conceal or misrepresent information to the main bank, particularly at the interim stage. The main bank has the option of imposing weak or heavy penalties on management, depending upon the magnitude of the problem. Misrepresentation of information regarding adverse interim events may prolong intervention by the main bank and worsen the situation, thus incurring harsher penalties at a later stage. In order to elicit the main bank's 'gentler' terms of rescue, management is obliged to be honest. The bank managers interviewed for this study were convinced that if the management of a failing company disclosed a problem voluntarily to the main bank at an early stage, it would be extremely difficult for the main bank to shirk its obligation to come to help that company. By concentrating its settlement accounts and other banking business with the main bank, management is effectively submitting itself to the bank's interim monitoring. Voluntary disclosure by the firm may not reduce only interim information-gathering costs for the main bank, but also the costs of implementing *ex post* problem-solving measures.

The last possible effect of exclusive delegation of integrated monitoring is to create a unique corporate governance structure under which the main bank is *ex ante* expected to intervene in management with a high degree of certainty *if* and *only if* firms are financially depressed. This is discussed further in the following section.

THE CONTINGENT GOVERNANCE STRUCTURE

The institutional arrangements of monitoring are closely associated with the ways corporate governance is structured. In the Anglo-American securities-based system, the board of directors, at least theoretically, exercises quasi-independent monitoring and control over management, provided it is not dominated by insiders. Outside board members are themselves major investors or under the direct or indirect pressure of investors. They monitor the business and affairs of the firm, interpret signals sent from financial markets, take the initiative to replace incompetent and poorly performing managers, and accept or reject outside offers for acquisition. With the changes in corporate law in many states to the effect that the board is responsible not only to investors but also to other stakeholders as well, the obligations of the board are becoming somewhat ambiguous. But the general practical (and academic) presumption still remains that the board ought to act in the interest of investors. The increasing activism of some large institutional stockholders, like pension funds for public employees and university teachers, may be encouraging the strengthening of a quasi-independent monitoring role for the board, although fund managers are legally restrained from participating directly on the board.

The Japanese and Anglo-American situations have been in remarkable contrast. The board of directors in Japan is almost entirely composed of inside managers except for a few outsiders (very often representatives from the main bank). A new chief executive officer (CEO) is selected from members of the board by the incumbent or sometimes by the chair, himself a retired CEO. New board members are chosen by the CEO with due regard to the internal balance of power among different divisions. Board membership symbolizes the pinnacle of the internal career track for permanent employees. Because of reciprocal shareholding with financial institutions and other business partners, the incumbent management of publicly held corporations is effectively insulated from hostile take-over. The competitive market for corporate control is almost non-existent.

Thus, management by insiders appears to be self-perpetuating. This observation has prompted some academics to advance the hypothesis that the top management of a Japanese firm represents the interests of permanent employees. This theory is, however, superficial (see Aoki, 1988, chapter 5, for more detailed criticism of this view). It is true that permanent employees are an important constituency of top management. In spite of the apparent centralization of personnel administration, top management itself is subject to reciprocal, internal monitoring by the body of permanent employees. It is not unusual for top managers to be forced to resign if they are on bad terms with the enterprise union of permanent employees. At the same time, it is undeniable that top management must be as concerned with the healthy financial state of the firm as Western managers. It is, in fact, only the mechanism through which the profit motive is enforced on top management that differs from the Anglo-American system.

Weakened profitability of a firm undermines the political basis of top management's relationship with permanent employees because of fear of job insecurity. At the same time, the degree of interim monitoring by the alerted main bank would be intensified. Top management might be forced to take early retirement. Kaplan and Minton (1994) and Mock and Nakamura (1992) have presented quantitative evidence that the correlation between the probability of turnover of top management and the profitability of the firm is, indeed, statistically significant. They showed that low profitability also increases the probability of the appointment of new outside directors who are bankers in the case of publicly traded corporations and managers of parent corporations in the case of subsidiaries.

In the case of a more dramatic financial decline, direct intervention by the main bank is triggered. Top management is forced to leave and a management team dispatched from the main bank assumes full control. At that point, the body of permanent employees no longer is able to exercise semi-autonomous control. What is at stake is the security of their employment, and they are put in a defensive position. This situation can be characterized as tantamount to a temporary take-over of management by the main bank.

The essence of the governance structure of publicly held Japanese corporations may, thus, be characterized as *dualistic* and *contingent*. The structure of governing the selection and policy-orientation of top management is controlled by both the body of permanent employees and the main bank, to which other investors and financiers delegate monitoring functions. The controlling power of both parties is, however, contingent on the financial state of the firm. In the normal or favourable financial states, the controlling power of investors is not explicit, although its presence is always in the minds of top management. When the controlling power of the main bank becomes visible, the position of employees becomes subordinated.

In a way, all effective corporate governance structures may be said to be contingent. In the Anglo-American system, disciplinary action by the board against top management is, in most cases, exercised only when the financial state of the firm has worsened. As long as the financial state of the firm is healthy, take-over raids would not be profitable. However, the contingency aspect appears to be more clearly pronounced in Japan. Who will take over as top management in the event of financial distress is clearly agreed upon *ex ante*. There is no uncertainty about this step, as there is in a securities-based system, while there is much stricter adherence to the rule of 'no external intervention' in the normal state. Also, the Japanese governance structure is unique in the latent monitoring and control exercised by the body of permanent employees in the normal state. The implications of such a dualistic governance structure for corporate behaviour are discussed in Aoki (1988, chapter 5).

COMPLEMENTARITY BETWEEN MAIN BANK MONITORING AND THE EMPLOYMENT SYSTEM

Why have large Japanese corporate firms developed and maintained the contingent governance structure? Aoki (1994a) provides an analytical answer. The article starts with the observation that Japanese firms rely heavily on workers' collective learning, mutual help, lateral cross-functional coordination, and joint responsibilities for tasks. This is in contrast to the dominant mode of internal organization in the West in which jobs are clearly demarcated, and specialized tasks are integrated in hierarchical ordering (see Aoki, 1988, 1990). One possible consequence of Japanese organizational orientation is that 'individual' contributions to the organizational outcome are hard to measure in the short run. This production process may be captured by the concept of a 'team'—in the sense of Alchian and Demsetz (1972). For the rest of this section, therefore, the words 'firm' and 'team', as well as 'employees' and 'team members', are used interchangeably.

In the case of team production, a simple sharing of output among team members leads to free-riding (lack of effort), because team members each might work only to the point where the marginal cost of effort is equated with a share (which is less than one) in their own marginal contribution to organizational output. Suppose management tries to promote reciprocal behaviour among team members to cope with the moral hazard problem, and then monitors team effort, but monitoring is imperfect as a result of limited resources and psychological costs. Some type of external discipline (the so-called budget-breaking) is needed for motivating team members.

Suppose that team production requires some external financing in each period, but the general creditors cannot observe either the level of team member effort or output. However, imagine a financial intermediary called the MB can be created which, for a premium, can perform *ex post* monitoring of team production. That is, it can verify the output and, if necessary, intervene in the management and continuity of the team. Suppose, however, that team members must be guaranteed a minimum income level (say, subsistence) *ex post*. The team may be wound up after the minimum wage payments have been made. In that event, team members suffer a loss of employment value because of imperfections in labour market—they can only get inferior jobs elsewhere. (Implicit in this assumption is the supposition that there is a hierarchy of employment status in the labour market, see Aoki, 1994b.) Under certain conditions, the optimal nexus of contracts among the manager, the team members, the MB, and the general creditors can be shown to have the following analytical property (Aoki, 1994a, Proposition 1).

The range of output states can be divided into three regions: the *high* team-control region, the *low* MB-control region, and the *critical* bankrupt region. In the high team-control region, the firm makes only contractually fixed payments to general creditors, letting team members be the residual claimants (the MB may receive a certain share of the contractual payment in the capacity of a creditor). The residual claimant status is to provide positive incentives for team members. However, such sharing arrangements alone do not prevent free-riding among team members. It is therefore agreed *ex ante* that in the low MB-controlled region, the MB takes over control of output, pays only minimum wages to team members and a fixed contractual payment to the general creditors, and receives the residual. The team goes on to the next period. The residual may be negative in the lower tail of the MB-controlled region. The situation can be identified as a rescue operation by the MB, but such insurance may cause team members to shirk.

Therefore, there must be a third, critical region in which the team is made bankrupt after the payment of minimum wages. As the general creditors cannot observe the level of output of the team, but can witness the bankruptcy, the payment to them may also be lower than under the high or low region. The prospect of the loss of employment value in the event of bankruptcy provides an additional incentive for team members. Comparative static analysis shows that if managers perceive a larger loss in employment value for team members in the event of bankruptcy, they would opt for a contract allowing the MB greater *ex post* intervention, which would in turn elicit greater efforts from the workers to avoid actual bank control and bankruptcy (Aoki, 1994b, Proposition 4). In other words, the imperfect labour market and the main bank contract are complementary monitoring devices for team production.

This model is highly stylized, but it captures the logic by which the contingent governance structure (as an *ex post* monitoring device) is more conducive to controlling the moral hazard problem of team-oriented organizations than the normal debt or equity contract. In this model, the MB ought to be committed to an arrangement to make the firm bankrupt at the lowest critical range of output, but rescue it at a moderately low level of output. To encourage the optimal efforts of team members, the commitment should neither be to rescue uniformly (long-term relationship) nor to punish unequivocally. A variety of options should be left contingent on the level of output. The feasibility of such an arrangement is one of the possible virtues of integrated monitoring. It is to be noted, however, that the described nexus of contracts may become increasingly ineffective as an *ex ante* incentive device as the bargaining power of the MB declines and the premium falls under the threshold point (Aoki, 1994a, Proposition 3).

MONITORING OF MAIN BANK MONITORING

The previous section discussed the incentive effects of the main bank contracts on teams within the Japanese production organization. This section examines incentives for the main bank's delegated integrated monitoring. How is the main bank motivated to undertake *ex ante* and *interim* monitoring when that involves costs? How is the main bank motivated to rescue failing firms when the rescue cost appears to exceed the default value of its own credit? Since other creditors have delegated *ex post* monitoring, they are not able to distinguish between legitimate bankruptcy and an MB's breach of responsibility to honour their claims by rescuing a firm. Why does the main bank not default on the obligation to rescue and liquidate financially depressed firms more frequently? This section tries to clarify why main bank rents may be necessary for the main bank's commitment to the contract.

Suppose a firm's output is possible at only three levels: high, low, or critical, and the probability distribution over them depends upon whether or not the main bank monitors *ex ante* and interim. If it does, the probability of high output becomes higher and that of critical output becomes lower. If the output level is high, the main bank is able to extract a certain level of premium over the normal rate of financial returns in the market (main bank rents). If the output level is low, the main bank has the option of liquidating the firm with a negative rate of premium (equivalent to, say, the difference between the collateral value and the default value of credit), or rescuing it and incurring the costs of meeting the claims of other creditors. If the output level is critical, the main bank has the same options but with an even lower rate of return or higher costs. (These assumptions about main bank returns being contingent on the firm's output state are slightly different from those in the previous section.)

If the firm is not liquidated, then the main bank relationship will continue into the next period, when the main bank will make a new decision on whether or not to monitor. Suppose, however, that when firms in the critical output state are rescued, they shirk in future periods, believing the main bank will not punish them. Then for its part, it is no longer in the main bank's interest to monitor those firms in the future. That is, once the main bank rescues firms in the critical output state, it would be privately optimal for it not to monitor those firms subsequently.

If the expected output of a monitored firm exceeds the actual cost of delegated *ex ante* monitoring, it is *socially* optimal to rescue low, but not critical, output firms *ex post* and to continue to monitor them in subsequent periods. However, rescuing low output firms may be *privately* costlier to the main bank than simply liquidating them, as the main bank has to guarantee other creditors' claims. Further, future returns to the main bank from its rescue operation cannot be secured without continuing its own expenditures on monitoring. Since the true output level is not observable to anyone other than the main bank to which *ex post* monitoring is delegated, the main bank may be motivated for its own purposes to liquidate low output firms, even though such behaviour is socially suboptimal.

In order to counteract such behaviour, let us suppose that penalties are imposed indiscriminately on main banks that liquidate firms, either in the low or critical output state. We examine later how such penalties are imposed. If penalties—reduction of rents—are sufficiently high, the main bank will not liquidate firms of low output. However, a difficulty with this scheme is that if penalties are too high, the main bank may find it costly to liquidate firms at the critical output level, which should be liquidated. Thus, liquidation penalties should be neither too high nor too low. Therefore, the following proposition holds (proof omitted):

If the expected gain from *ex ante* monitoring is sufficiently large relative to the monitoring cost in the current period, there is a range of liquidation penalties under which the main bank always liquidates firms at the critical output level *ex post*, but rescues firms at the low output level and continues to maintain a main bank relationship with them in the next period.

If the conditions are satisfied and the prescribed liquidation penalties are implemented, delegated integrated monitoring becomes incentive compatible for the main bank, even if the true output level of the firm is not observable or verifiable by other creditors. However, if returns to the main bank delivered by firms at the high output level are not sufficiently high, or if no liquidation penalties are imposed, then there may be another, low, equilibrium in which no bank undertakes delegated monitoring *ex ante* or *ex post*, and firms shirk in consequence. The next section discusses how the conditions for high equilibrium can be fulfilled under a certain regulatory framework.

THE BENEFITS AND COSTS OF THE REGULATORY FRAMEWORK

Discussion so far suggests there may be four potential social benefits of the main bank system:

1. Contingent intervention by the main bank in the corporate governance structure, made possible by the main bank's integration of three stages of monitoring, may provide effective external discipline on team-oriented production (discussed earlier, in the fourth section).
2. By delegating monitoring of a firm exclusively to its main bank, the social cost of duplicating *ex ante* and interim monitoring may be avoided.
3. The social cost of myopic liquidation of temporarily depressed, but potentially productive, firms may be avoided by the rescue operation of the main bank (previous section).
4. The social cost of entrapment in low equilibrium (no growth) as a result of the failure to coordinate complementary investment projects among strategically important industries may be avoided (third section).

These benefits may not be possible without their own costs, however. The model in the previous section suggests that the main bank may not be motivated to be honest in delegated monitoring, unless rent is paid for it to maintain good relationships with firms. Although the model indicated the possibility that the fine-tuning of liquidation penalties can realize the gain (benefit 3), in practice, imposition of supra-optimal liquidation penalties may induce soft budgeting among banks, rescuing firms that are socially unproductive. Regarding benefit (4), the issue arises as to whether or not a non-market coordination of investment involves its own cost, for example, as a result of rent-seeking behaviour by industrial firms competing for favouritism. This section discusses whether the regulatory scheme prevailing in the high growth period, summarized in Chapter 1 by Aoki, Patrick and Sheard, may be interpreted as providing a framework for realizing these gains, though possibly with some social costs. In the concluding section, other costs, such as those associated with benefit (2), are explored.

Chapter 1 points out that the regulatory framework for the main bank system is based on five pillars:

1. Keeping the deposit interest rate low, but with a positive real rate.
2. Restricting bond issues to privileged companies and restraining the development of the secondary bond market.
3. Restricting new entry to the banking industry, while barring banks from engaging in the underwriting and brokerage businesses.
4. Managing performance-indexed rewards and penalties to banks, such as branch-licensing, the dispatch of ex-bureaucrats as executives, etc.
5. Administratively guiding the differentiation of lending rates according to the strategic priority of industry and the market performance of borrowing firms, for example, by making trade bills and commercial bills by preferred companies eligible for Bank of Japan rediscounting.

Under (1) (3) and (4), the competitiveness of each city bank is conditioned by its ability to collect deposits, which is in turn affected by the relative size and location of its branches, as well as the number and size of corporate clients for which it manages deposit accounts as the main bank. Suppose the distribution of deposits at the regulated deposit rate among banks is exogenously determined by branch-licensing and banks' historical connections with client firms (this ignores the fierce competition for deposits among city banks). Suppose further that the normal lending rate is anchored to the repressed deposit rate with a normal profit margin—call it the standard rate—and that main banks can raise the effective lending rate to client firms to the competitive level through compensating balances (ignoring any lending rate differentiation). This then, together with the repression of the deposit rate, affords the main banks an opportunity of reaping rents by selecting good client firms. The actual distribution of rents is then partially indexed to the *ex ante* and interim monitoring performance of banks.

When a firm becomes financially depressed, its main bank may liquidate it (or bring it to bankruptcy court) rather than bear the cost of rescuing it. If a single main bank liquidates a number of its client firms, the reputation of the bank as a responsible delegated monitor will be damaged. As consequences: (1) depositors may desert the bank fearing for the security of their deposits; (2) other banks may be reluctant to lend to that bank's client firms fearing for the safety of their credits, because the main bank's willingness to lend no longer signals, through the reputation effect, the credit-worthiness of borrowers; (3) the bank's other client firms may switch their main bank relationships for fear of losing insurance in adversity and losing access to credits from other lenders; (4) the regulatory authority, which is concerned with such social consequences of

bankruptcy as the loss of employment, may penalize the bank that liquidates often. These possibilities imply that liquidation penalties on the
main bank may not be limited to the loss of its defaulted credits. Main
banks naturally take these possibilities into consideration in dealing with
depressed firms.

The existence of main bank rents and liquidation penalties (the reduction of rents) suggests the conditions of the proposition in the previous
section may be met. But there are also counter-arguments or qualifications.

First, even if there are liquidation penalties, there is no assurance that
their actual value lies in the optimal range described by the proposition in
the previous section. They may be too small or too large. Bankers may
believe that potential penalties are very high, given the stigma attached to
firing workers. If so, there may be too many rescues of inefficient firms.

Second, repression of the deposit rate may distort household savings,
although the direction of its impact is not clear. Lower deposit rates
could in theory discourage savings, but Japanese household saving
appears to be relatively interest-inelastic. On the other hand, if a household has a target level of wealth for post-retirement security or for
bequests, it may well respond to the lower deposit rate by increasing its
savings.

Third, the determination of a lending rate is more complicated than
assumed above, and this may have distorted allocational impacts. Instead
of two-level pricing—the standard rate and the competitive rate—banks
vary lending rates according to clients. Throughout the high growth
period, the long-term rate applied to electric utilities by long-term credit
banks provided the minimum (with a spread of 0.9 percentage points
above the interest rate on bank debentures (Suzuki, 1987, p. 147)). The
maximum long-term rate was presumably not set as high as the market-
clearing level, because that would have invited high-risk borrowers who
might have profited from the greater probability of default (the Stiglitz-
Weiss, 1981, adverse selection problem).

One likely scenario was that banks rationed credits among preferred
clients and applied differential rates according to the riskiness of projects
and the relative bargaining power of borrowing firms. The riskiness of
projects and the bargaining power of firms were, in turn, conditioned by
the public priority set by industrial policy and the market shares achieved
by firms. (Here 'rationing' does not imply the Stiglitz-Weiss type stochastic allocation of funds below the market-clearing level. It refers to the discretionary allocation of credits based on *ex ante* monitoring of the main
bank and bargaining between banks and borrowing firms.) The lending
rate applied to preferred firms tended to be lower, but main banks were
able to extract additional gains from relationships with those firms by
other means. For example, main banks were able to profit from holding

firms' major payment settlement and deposit accounts, performing trustee and foreign exchange businesses, having their lending capacity enhanced by the eligibility of firms' bills for BOJ discounting, extending business networks to their suppliers and dealers, and so on. These possibilities suggest main bank rents were possible without repression of the deposit rate, but even if so, they still require regulations restricting the working of competitive bond markets, differential BOJ lending, and the like.

As discussed in the second section, the *ex ante* monitoring capacity of city banks was nurtured at the beginning of the high growth period within a government-industry-bank framework for coordinating the investment decisions of strategic industries. Once a development path was established, investment decisions by the industry and credit decisions by the banking sector were increasingly decentralized. The inter-industry and inter-temporal complementarities among strategic investments made investment in strategic industries more profitable and less risky. Further, the interest rate differentiation among borrowing firms may be considered as a way to distribute the rents made possible by repression of the deposit rate to the banking sector and corporate borrowers. Since preferred rates were given partially on the basis of a firm's market performance, industrial rent-seeking took the form of competition for larger market shares, export promotion, and the like. Corporate borrowers competed over a kind of promotional hierarchy. Since preferred firms were able to borrow at a lower rate, they were presumably able to over-borrow. Growth bias was thus set in the system.

The way the main bank system functioned in the high growth period differs from the neo-classical competitive norm built on the assumptions of perfect information and complete markets. Some authors argue that Japan should, and could, have developed without the repression of the deposit rate and bond markets. In other words, a *laissez-faire* main bank system was possible and preferable. But it is far from clear whether that would have been possible in the real world—where access to information is unequal, markets are inevitably incomplete, and increasing returns and complementarities are abundant. It is possible there are multiple growth paths in such a world. The main bank system as it worked in its heyday seems to have been an important element in complex institutional arrangements which, together, made high growth feasible: whether or not high growth brought higher social welfare *ex post* is a matter of personal judgement. However, because of possible complementarities among institutions, it would have been difficult to change the workings of the financial system alone without affecting the performance of the entire economy. (See Aoki, 1994b, for the 'system effect' of complementary institutions.)

CONDITIONS IN THE HIGH GROWTH PERIOD AND THEIR
RELEVANCIES TO DEVELOPING AND TRANSFORMING
ECONOMIES

This chapter argues that the main bank system was instrumental for the high growth of the Japanese economy in the 1950s and 60s. The following questions may be raised: is the Japanese experience replicable elsewhere; what lessons can one learn from it; or was it a unique experience? To answer these questions directly is not the purpose of this chapter. However, summarized below are four of the important historical and developmental conditions prevailing in that period which made the main bank system an effective vehicle for high growth, and a consideration of their relevance for developing and transforming economies. Generally speaking, the performance of any financial system differs according to the informational, technological, organizational, and other features of the system environment.

(1) The advanced engineering know-how that was useful for new investment in targeted industries had been developed abroad; and its commercial application had already been proved, with a few exceptions (for example, the transistor). Complementarities among investments in these industries were assessed in the public domain, as described in the second section. The focus of *ex ante* monitoring by the banking sector at that time was, therefore, on the managerial and organizational capacities of individual firms to absorb and improve upon know-how available from elsewhere. The integration of *ex ante* and interim monitoring by the city banks was advantageous for this process, because continual interim monitoring provided the city banks with the organization-specific knowledge not available to other financial institutions such as securities houses, and even public long-term credit banks.

(2) In spite of Japan's considerable experience of private enterprise, the capacity to assess the quality and economic feasibility of the most advanced engineering processes was limited, because of international isolation and the suppression of private initiatives during the oppressive environment of World War II, and the subsequent period of social and economic turmoil. The establishment of the JDB and the restructuring of the IBJ as a private long-term credit bank were a response to this limitation (see Chapter 5 by Packer). At the early stage of high growth, the city banks were able to rely upon the project assessment capabilities of the JDB and the IBJ. Also, the mechanism of public planning, as described above, helped the formation and dissemination of valuable macroeconomic forecasts. It reduced the burden of individual assessment of risk. Throughout the 1950s and 60s, the capacity to assess the credit-worthiness of proposed projects gradually accumulated by and spread to the city banks.

(3) There already were a number of established private enterprises with substantial physical and human assets at the beginning of the high growth period, although their financial and economic capabilities had not been valued in global financial markets. Those enterprises were capable of using their physical assets as collateral for bank loans. They also endeavoured to improve imported technology by feeding back their manufacturing and marketing experiences to redesign, as well as promoting the cross-functional coordination of organizational learning (the organizational routinization of improved practices). Such organizational orientation required the long-term association of employees with a particular enterprise, and the practice of so-called permanent employment was firmly established, even at the level of blue-collar workers. The resulting imperfection of the labour market made the threat of selective intervention by the main bank in the event of poor collective performance quite an effective external motivating device.

(4) The high propensity of households to save, and the tradition of strong administrative regulation, made protection of the banking industry by the monetary authorities feasible through the convoy system (see Chapter 1 by Aoki, Patrick and Sheard). Insulation of the domestic capital market from the international market guaranteed that bond issues by better firms did not get entirely out of the control of city banks. The regime of regulated interest rates prevailing in the heyday of the main bank system allowed rents to those main banks that performed delegated monitoring.

The main bank system thus operated under specific and unique historical and developmental conditions. The main bank system and its performance characteristics could hardly be reproduced in different historical environments. However, the experience of the main bank system and examination of its history and environment may suggest some generic lessons as well. Regarding the choice between a bank-based financial system and a securities-based financial system for developing and transforming economies, the following points may be worth examination.

First, the management of securities-based financial systems separates *ex ante*, interim and *ex post* monitoring. Its development therefore requires a substantial degree of specialized monitoring expertise dispersed among investment houses, rating companies, fund managers, and reorganization specialists. In contrast, the bank-based system economizes on the use of scarce monitoring resources through the integration of various monitoring tasks. Developing economies may not need the decentralized specialization of *ex ante* monitoring as much as advanced economies facing the technological frontier.

Second, in developing and, particularly, transforming economies, many potentially valuable firms suffer from debt burdens carried from the past. In that situation, equity financing is not an effective and efficient vehicle for raising new funds, because the prospective residual value is limited. In the same situation, bond financing may make bankruptcy more frequent, as there cannot be a commitment to long-term relationships either on the side of creditors or firms because of the possibility of turnover of securities. A bank-oriented system may be more effective in such a situation. Aoki (1994b) has demonstrated the theoretical possibility that the nexus of contracts, as illustrated in the fourth section, may function as an optimal device for *ex post* monitoring of firms when they are in weak *ex ante* financial positions. It is necessary in this case, however, that the agent for *ex post* monitoring (the MB in the model) operates with a low premium requirement (possibly with state subsidies), while it is firmly committed to punish firms with the poorest performance. The question of how such a monitoring agent can be made to fulfil its obligations, does not seem to be answerable from the Japanese experience, however, because its regulatory framework presupposed that a fairly sound private banking system already existed.

Third, the difficulty of transforming and developing economies may be traced to possible entrapment in bad equilibrium caused by the failure to coordinate cross-industrial investment. Litwaek and Qian (1993) and Dewatripont and Roland (1993) argue that the coordination problem may be resolved by identifying and concentrating investment in leading industries. However, a decentralized securities-based financial system may not be appropriate for such coordination when the accumulation of capital in strategic industries is still poor and information concerning interindustrial complementarities may not be transmitted through the market. A bank-based system, possibly supported by a public development bank, may provide a better coordinating framework. From the Japanese experience, however, it seems there needs to be sufficient exchange of information between the public development bank and private banks so that *ex ante* monitoring capability is diffused. Also, in order not to be trapped by the soft budgeting problem rampant in socialist economies, financing by the public development bank should be limited to the partial funding of initial investment and its claims should be given priority, while the duty of interim and *ex post* monitoring of individual firms should be delegated to private banks operating on the private business principle.

Fourth, the securities-based finance system operates on the principle that the performance of firms is assessed by the market evaluation of their ability to produce residual value. This mechanism is supported by the institution of the joint-stock company (which is necessary to identify the residual claimant) and by competitive markets for labour services (which are necessary to measure the residual value after market-determined wage payments). However, the ownership of ex-state-owned firms, and of new private firms in developing and transforming economies may take various institutional forms in addition to publicly traded joint-stock companies. These include worker-controlled enterprises, cooperatives, closely held limited liability companies, and partnerships. As the model in the fourth section suggests, *ex post* monitoring by the bank-oriented system may be compatible with a variety of ownership arrangements, as the bank's intervention depends only on a firm's poor performance in terms of output.

Fifth, the Japanese main bank system operated within the rigid regulatory control of new entries to the banking industry and branch openings by incumbents. Also, there was a high degree of trust between the main bank and its client firms (voluntary disclosure of interim information and the bank's commitment to help in difficult times). Government regulation, although discretionary, was reasonably neutral in the sense that bureaucrats were prevented from developing personal ties with any particular private financial institutions. The main bank and firms always monitored each other closely and neither was captured by others by *a priori* tie, ownership relationships, or the like. The switching of main bank relationships was not rare. The spill-over of rents to industrial firms was based on performance-related indices, such as market share and export bills eligible for preferential rediscount. However, if the government regulators of a bank-oriented system act arbitrarily in distributing political rents among private banks, and if the bank is captured by the specific interests of particular firms, as is often observed in exclusive relational banking in developing economies, then the banking system would certainly lose its efficacy as a social monitoring device.

DECLINING MONITORING CAPACITY IN A MARKET ENVIRONMENT

The exclusive delegation of integrated monitoring to the main bank was identified as the major monitoring characteristic of the main bank system in its heyday. Since the mid-1970s, however, two pillars of the regulatory framework supporting the regime, regulation of interest rates and of bond issue requirements, have been gradually removed. As a result, firms have come increasingly to rely on bond issues, at home and abroad, while non-competitive rent opportunities for banks have been squeezed. (There is statistical evidence that bank rents have started to decline dramatically since the mid-1970s; see Aoki, 1988.) Meanwhile, regulation over business segmentation by types of financial institution has been largely left intact until recently. It is worth noting that banks were not allowed to underwrite and deal in corporate bonds. Thus, the coherence and integrity of the regulatory framework, which was so effective in the heyday of the main bank system, have been impaired. This section provides an overview of how it has affected the main bank's effectiveness and capacity to offer integrated monitoring, *ex ante*, interim and *ex post*.

Many leading Japanese industries reached the international technological and marketing frontier by the 1990s. Credit assessments of projects on an uncertain technological and market trajectory require sophisticated skills in finance, engineering and market analysis. The long-standing custom of relying on collateral and the regulatory prohibition on banks from the underwriting business have deterred them from accumulating the advanced *ex ante* monitoring capability investment houses and venture capitalist firms in the securities-based system have acquired. The securities houses that relied upon the *ex ante* monitoring capability of banks have gained little experience in monitoring. The lack of *ex ante* monitoring capacity of financial institutions may be irrelevant to large established firms which have accumulated the corporate reputation necessary for raising funds in international bond markets. However, such a lack of experience may have serious adverse effects on the development of innovative small and medium firms that do not possess assets for collateral.

The pitfalls of collateralism were shown most dramatically in the bubble of the late 1980s and its aftermath. After the Plaza accord, there was increasing external pressure on Japan to keep the official discount rate low to stimulate domestic demand as a means of reducing its trade surplus. The Japanese government itself was also inclined to an easy money policy, fearing that high interest rates might induce an even greater appreciation of the yen. On the other hand, the government reduced its deficits and firms performing well drifted away from the banks when financing equipment. In facing the dual reductions of government and business borrowing, the banking sector sought replacement lending opportunities in real estate related businesses. The increasing price of land ignited a general speculative mood. Banks that previously enjoyed a reputation for prudence competed fiercely for lending as long as the loans were collaterized. As Stiglitz and Weiss (1981) argued, however, a collateral requirement alone without proper *ex ante* monitoring of borrowers may have an adverse selection effect. Wealthier borrowers who are able to offer larger collateral might have been willing to take greater risks, some indeed might have simply gambled. The banking sector turned into a cash-generating machine and the collective speculative mania continued until the bubble burst in 1990–92.

The deregulation of bond issues may also have had detrimental effects on the interim monitoring incentives and capacity of main banks. When the firm becomes less reliant on bank loans and is freed from the bank's implicit and explicit intervention, the shirking of managers and workers may not necessarily be bad news for main banks, because that may increase the probability of a firms' return to bank loans. Thus, the main bank may become lukewarm in interim monitoring. Also, the diversification by firms of settlement accounts among multiple banks, and the development of the securitization of loans, diminish the flow of information from firms to city banks and consequently the bank's ability to keep track of the firm's business.

In the case of the impact of deregulation on the main bank's *ex post* monitoring capacity, an implication of the decline of regulatory rents may be significant. The declining rent opportunity for the main bank may remove its incentive to commit itself to costly punitive or rescue operations. The prospect of less intervention by the bank may have positive incentive effects on workers and managers when the bank's power is strong. However, theoretical analysis indicates that, when the bank's power to control has already been weakened below a certain threshold, a further decline in the bank's active role in *ex post* monitoring would trigger a negative incentive effect on inside members of the firm (Aoki, 1994a, Proposition 3).

The emergence of market financing and the use of the market for corporate control are not the same thing, and a monitoring mechanism alternative to main bank surveillance has not appeared. Sales of stock by firms and banks have so far been limited to their peripheral, but not their core, reciprocal holdings. The management of large corporate firms is still effectively insulated from the discipline of a hostile take-over, which I predict will remain so in the near future.[2] However, the bank's role in the contingent governance structure of firms is becoming increasingly inactive; as the balance of power has been tilted in favour of the firm *vis-à-vis* the bank. The legal prohibition of a pure holding company and the role of the internal board, which is unlikely to be modified without external pressure, combine to make the management of those firms virtually free from external discipline, except for the discipline of the product market, which may be slow to operate.

Thus, the partial and inconsistent deregulation starting in the mid-1970s has impaired the integrity of the main bank's monitoring capacity and incentives irreversibly. The main bank system as a social device for corporate monitoring appears to be under severe test.

TOWARDS THE UNIVERSAL BANKING SYSTEM?

How can the weakened main bank system's capacity to monitor be remedied? Should the Japanese financial system convert to the Anglo-

---

[2] In a recently conducted questionnaire survey by the Ministry of International Trade and Industry for the Industrial Structure Council (1993, Data Appendix, p. 43), 93.5 per cent of 584 responding companies replied that the main bank will continue to be necessary in the future, and the highest reason quoted for this (78.6 per cent) was that the main bank will remain as a 'stable stockholder'. Other major reasons included: 'the supply of funds on favourable terms' (55.0 per cent), 'emergency financing at the time of financial distress' (48.4 per cent), 'the provision of information regarding financing and investment diversification' (43.5 per cent).

American type of securities-based financial system with a 'big bang'? Or is it possible in an evolutionary way to adapt the main bank system to a new market environment by changing the present regulatory framework? The 'big bang' approach is unlikely to be effective for three reasons.

First, a path-dependent change in the financial system may be more viable and less costly. As emphasized in the first section, the efficient management of a securities-based system requires the accumulation of human resources specialized in separate monitoring functions at different stages. In Japan, because of the well-established convention of exclusive delegation of integrated monitoring to banks, the specialized monitoring abilities of other financial institutions, such as securities houses, rating companies, venture capitalist firms, and various funds, are much less developed. For example, securities houses have not yet developed their own monitoring capacity as a result of free-riding on banks' *ex ante* screening, yet they enjoy handsome profits from highly regulated brokerage fees. The adaptation of the Japanese financial system to the new market environment may be better realized, at least in a transitional period, by the efficient use of existing human resources. Because of the imperfect workings of the labour market, the accumulation and transfer of human resources from the banking sector to securities-related financial institutions may take place only slowly. This factor makes the path-dependent reform of the bank-based system more realistic.

Second, a quantum leap to the securities-based decentralized financial system, particularly the establishment of an active market for corporate control, may be incompatible with other institutional features of the Japanese economy. In spite of the increasing importance of high-technology industry and the prospects of a gradual increase in the mobility of workers with specialized skills, emphasis on cross-functional coordination, decentralized on-site problem-solving and collective learning will remain important features of Japanese industry and will continue to be a source of competitive advantage for some (Aoki, 1990). In order for such organizational practices to be effective, long-term relationships between workers and managers are desirable. However, the increased value through drastic restructuring by outside raiders is often made possible by a breach of the implicit contracts with workers (Shleifer and Summers, 1988). This implies that the development of a market for corporate control, particularly by hostile take-over, may not be compatible with the dominant organizational practice in Japan.

Third, the earlier summary in the section on conditions prevailing in the high growth period might have suggested that some aspects of the main bank system were applicable only at the developmental stage of the economy; but the main bank system should not be dismissed as a phenomenon of late development. Neither would I predict that the Japanese financial system will move to the 'more advanced' Anglo-American securities-based system. That system is itself in the process of transformation and some aspects of it may be seen as converging with the Japanese-German system. Venture capital firms are reminiscent of Japanese long-term credit banks or city banks in integrating the three types of monitoring. Although venture capital firms are different from Japanese main banks in their specialized *ex ante* monitoring expertise, integrated monitoring may be an effective response to the imperfections and asymmetry of information in highly uncertain fields such as high technology.

Increasing stockholding by institutional investors and their activism in the Anglo-American system may make poor management respond to persuasion and quasi-internal pressure to improve. When such relational investing works, it may save the large costs of take-overs. These had devastating effects on some industries and firms in the 1980s, although there are also cases, such as the chemical and pharmaceutical industries, where the institutionalization of active markets for corporate control contributed to efficient restructuring of the industry (see Chandler, 1992). The take-over mechanism is also becoming less potent for the legal and practical reasons already mentioned in the third section. There may be a danger that managers insulate themselves against investors' interests through collusion with other stakeholders, such as employees. However, as intangible assets, such as in-house training, become important components of the corporate capability, the inclusive governance structure may become conducive to the competitiveness of the firm.

The overhauling of the Japanese financial system seems to lie not in a leap to a securities-based system of the 1980s Anglo-American type, but possibly in the reform of the bank-oriented system, specifically in adapting banks' monitoring capacity to a market environment. It appears imperative for banks to restore and develop an *ex ante* monitoring capacity attuned to the condition of the marketization of credits. A regulatory change of 1 April 1993 permitting banks to engage in underwriting through subsidiaries may represent such a direction. If this path continues, it will help banks transform themselves gradually to a universal banking system which relies more on fees for specialized investment banking services than regulatory rents for revenues. However, the deregulation process seems to be slow, hampering the efficient restructuring of the entire financial system.[3]

If barriers to the penetration of banks and securities houses of each others' business are substantially removed, both institutions would be motivated to develop monitoring capacities for competitive survival. In

---

[3] The impact of the deregulation made effective on 1 April seems to be limited because of various restrictions, such as discretionary licensing of subsidiary opening by banks, the restriction of transfer of personnel between banks and their securities subsidiaries, the prohibition of performing both underwriting and trustee businesses for the same clientele firms, etc.

such an environment, exclusive monitoring by the main bank would be gradually lessened and competition among banks, as well as among investment houses, for profitable fee business may become keener. Long-term credit banks and city banks could continue to play an important monitoring role, taking advantage of the opportunities that still exist for integrated monitoring, even though the degree of integrity is weakened. In the area of *ex post* monitoring, the main bank will continue to play a unique role, although its function may become more like the coordinator of rescue or punitive operations of multiple banks and other financial institutions involved with failing firms. Also, as the labour market becomes more competitive and human resources become more mobile across firms, the form of *ex post* monitoring may increasingly be reorganization and liquidation, rather than rescue.

These predictions remain speculative. However, it is hoped that this chapter has clarified the points that: (1) the performance characteristics of a financial system depend upon the level of development and upon the systematic characteristics of the economy in which it is embedded; and (2) there is probably no financial system that is the most efficient throughout all stages of development and across different economies with diverse characteristics. Recognizing this will make the comparative institutional analysis of financial systems one of the most important research agenda items for understanding the workings of advanced, developing, and transforming economies.

REFERENCES

ALCHIAN, A., and H. DEMSETZ. 1972. 'Production, Information Costs, and Economic Organization.' *American Economic Review* 62: 777–94.

AOKI, MASAHIKO. 1984. *The Cooperative Game Theory of the Firm.* Oxford: Oxford University Press.

——. 1988. *Information, Incentives, and Bargaining in the Japanese Economy.* Cambridge: Cambridge University Press.

——. 1990. 'Toward an Economic Model of the Japanese Firm.' *Journal of Economic Literature* 28: 1–27 (March).

——. 1994a. 'The Contingent Governance of Teams: An Analysis of Institutional Complementarity.' *International Economic Review* 35 (August).

——. 1994b. 'The Japanese Firm as a System of Attributes.' In Masahiko Aoki and Ronald Dore, eds., *The Japanese Firm: Sources of Competitive Strength.* Oxford: Oxford University Press: 11–40.

CHANDLER, A. 1992. 'Competitive Performance of U.S. Industrial Enterprises: A Historical Perspective.'

DEWATRIPONT, M., and G. ROLAND. 1993. 'The Design of Reform Packages under Uncertainty.'

GARCIA-CESTONA, M. 1992. 'Banks and Corporate Finance: Impacts on Firms' Survival.' A chapter in a PhD dissertation, Stanford University.

HORIUCHI, AKIYOSHI, FRANK PACKER, and SHIN'ICHI FUKUDA. 1988. 'What Role Has the "Main Bank" Played in Japan.' *Journal of the Japanese and International Economies* 2: 159–80.

HOSHI, TAKEO, ANIL KASHYAP and DAVID SCHARFSTEIN. 1990. 'The Role of Banks in Reducing the Costs of Financial Distress in Japan.' *Journal of Financial Economics* 27: 67–88.

Industrial Structure Council (of the Japanese Government), Subcommittee for Long-Range Issues. 1993. 'Issues on Self-Reform of the Japanese Economic System for the 21st Century.' June.

KAPLAN, STEVEN N. and BERNADETTE ALCAMO MINTON. 1994. 'Appointments of Outsiders to Japanese Boards.' *Journal of Financial Economics* 34.

LITWACK, J. and YINGYI QIAN. 1993. 'Economic Transition Strategies: Fiscal Instability Can Favor Unbalanced Investment.' Stanford University.

MAYER, COLIN. 1988. 'New Issues in Corporate Finance.' *European Economic Review* 32: 1167–88.

MOCK, R. and M. NAKAMURA. 1992. 'Banks and Corporate Control in Japan.' University of Alberta.

SHEARD, PAUL. 1989. 'The Main Bank System and Corporate Monitoring and Control in Japan.' *Journal of Economic Behavior and Organization* 11: 399–422.

SHLEIFER, ANDREI and LAWRENCE SUMMERS. 1988. 'Breach of Trust in Hostile Takeovers.' In Alan J. Auerbach, ed., *Corporate Takeovers: Causes and Consequences*. Chicago: University of Chicago Press.

STIGLITZ, JOSEPH E. and ANDREW WEISS. 1981. 'Credit Rationing in Markets with Imperfect Information.' *American Economic Review* 71(3): 393–410 (June).

SUZUKI, YOSHIO, ed. 1987. *The Japanese Financial System*. New York: Oxford University Press, 1987.

YASUDA, A. 1993. 'The Performance and Roles of Japanese Development Banks.' Senior Honor Thesis submitted to Stanford University.

5

The Role of Long-Term Credit Banks Within the Main Bank System

FRANK PACKER

The role of banks in financing Japan's post-war growth has been well documented. At the same time, there has been increasing recognition that special relationships between certain banks and their customers—the main bank system—may have lowered various costs associated with bank debt in Japan, and be partially responsible for the extraordinary reliance on bank debt for most of the post-war period.

One problem with the provision of long-term investment financing by commercial banks is that it can put at risk the uninterrupted provision of liquidity services to the population at large. Though economic models often abstract away from this problem with the assumption that banks providing liquidity services have the ability to diversify away the long-term risk of their outstanding loans, regulators have rarely been so sanguine. In general, the United States has depended on the existence of well-developed securities markets to supplement and, in many cases, replace the provision of long-term debt by commercial banks. In Japan, particularly the Japan of the high growth era, the answer has lain rather in the creation of special classes of banks whose principal sources of financing are other than individual deposits. This paper examines one such class of institution, the long-term credit banks.

The long-term credit banks differ from the other principal private suppliers of long-term loans in post-war Japan, the trust banks, in two major respects. One is that because they have access to fixed rate long-term financing, they have been able to make the provision of fixed rate long-term loans their principal business. Secondly, the long-term credit banks do not have an exclusive affiliation with any of the six major corporate groups which lie at the core of the main bank system in Japan. While the trust banks either lent to designated sectors or supplemented the loans of their group's city bank, and as a result have been traditionally weak in credit analysis, the long-term credit banks have built up substantial

The author especially wishes to thank Toshihiro Horiuchi, Robert McCauley, Hugh Patrick, Clark Reynolds, Tsutomu Shibata, and Marilou Uy for detailed comments on earlier versions of the paper. The views expressed are those of the author and do not necessarily reflect those of the Federal Reserve Bank of New York or the Federal Reserve System.

in-house credit analysis capability, and loaned across corporate groups to the principal players in major industries.

Japanese insurance companies have also provided long-term fixed rate loans to industry. At the end of 1980, life insurance companies were providing 5 trillion yen of outstanding industrial equipment loans, compared to 9.6 and 10.6 for the long-term credit and trust banks, respectively (Bronte, 1982, p. 105). Like the trust banks, most insurance companies belong to an industrial group, lend principally to the firms within those groups, and are only rarely the largest lender to any particular borrower.

Interpretations of the role of the long-term credit banks within the Japanese financial system have varied. In views which stress government control over credit allocation, emphasis is placed on the governmental origins of the long-term credit banks and the government's use of them to channel long-term funds to designated sectors. In another view more popular among economists and consistent with the above-mentioned public policy concern, the existence of long-term credit banks, along with their participation in financial consortia, has assured maturity transformation in Japan. (A cogent statement in English of this view, which also emphasizes the Japan Development Bank, is Sakakibara and others, 1982.) Although the two views are not necessarily mutually exclusive, an emphasis on the mechanics of maturity transformation does not rule out lending decisions based primarily on economic considerations.

Neither interpretation explicitly places the long-term credit banks within the system of main bank relationships which has become a defining characteristic of the Japanese financial system. This chapter claims that the existence of long-term credit banks with a neutral stand among the six bank-centred keiretsu has helped to minimize potential drawbacks of the main bank system. They have brought active and knowledgeable participation to the syndication of credits, and provided a source of main bank services to large companies outside the principal bank groups. In coordination with government policy, long-term credit banks have been able to provide services to entire industries in decline and transition, helping to coordinate those efforts that are required across groups.

Long-term credit banks owe much to the suppression of the corporate bond market in the post-war era. Nonetheless, considering their institutional clout in brokering information flows and tie-ups with companies of different groups, as well as their ability to work with main banks and other short-term lenders in all stages of the monitoring process, they have arguably outperformed what might have been expected from the alternative, an unregulated domestic bond market.

The chapter proceeds as follows. In the first section, we review the origins and identify in detail the important legal and institutional features that distinguish the long-term credit banks. It is contended that while the regulatory regime has allowed them to act as main banks to corporations when necessary, the use and exclusivity of the privilege of issuing financial debentures has assured them of a pre-eminent role in long-term finance. In the sections that follow, evidence is provided that this has allowed long-term credit banks to limit the risks taken on by keiretsu banks in cooperative financing, as well as to act as main banks themselves for a significant number of companies.

ORIGINS AND DISTINCTIVE FEATURES OF LONG-TERM CREDIT BANKS

The establishment in Japan of institutions specializing in long-term credit occurred at the turn of the twentieth century, and thus postdate by a few decades the start of Japan's modernization and establishment of a modern banking system. (For a complete discussion and analysis of the development of the Japanese banking system during the Meiji period, see Patrick, 1967, and the sources cited therein.) Prior to their establishment, long-term funding needs had been principally met by the issuance of stock and loans from ordinary banks which were secured by the stocks of the company. These stocks in turn served as collateral for bank bills which were discounted at the central bank, guaranteeing commercial bank liquidity. Concerned that the provision of funds for fixed investment was not proper for ordinary commercial banks, and that the acceptance of corporate stock as collateral was not a proper activity of the Central Bank (IBJ, 1982, pp. 2–3), Meiji oligarch Matsukata had long planned for the creation of special banks, but it took many years to overcome the opposition from private financiers, and to pass legislation enabling the creation of specialized long-term credit banks based largely on the French model.

The Hypothec Bank of Japan (Nippon Kangyo Ginko) was established in 1898 and supplied long-term funds to agriculture and related industries secured by real estate. The law governing the activities of the Hypothec Bank was passed a year earlier in 1897. Another bank, Noko Ginko, which specialized in lending to smaller agricultural businesses, was also established to specialize in loans secured by real estate. This was absorbed into the Hypothec Bank in 1934. In addition to agriculture, the Hypothec Bank made an equal proportion of loans to light manufacturing industries, such as cotton textiles.

In 1901, the Colonial Bank of Hokkaido (Hokkaido Takushoku Ginko) was established to finance the development of Hokkaido, also specializing in loans secured by real estate. In 1903, the Industrial Bank of Japan (IBJ, Nihon Kogyo Ginko) was established to specialize in long-term loans in manufacturing and railways secured by movable property (IBJ, 1982, pp. 4–6; Fukuzawa, 1987, p. 3).

Though privately capitalized, the officers and directors of these banks were appointed by the Ministry of Finance (MOF), and thus they were effectively government institutions. All three of the special banks were allowed to issue debentures as a means of long-term fund raising, most of which were purchased by the Ministry of Finance Deposit Bureau which drew funds from the Postal Savings System.

However, the emergence of these banks did not mean that ordinary banks ceased their long-term lending. The long-term banks were meant to serve as a supplement to ordinary bank lending, and while the quantity of short-term loans the special banks could make was limited, at no time was the maturity structure of the loan portfolio of ordinary banks limited by statutory regulation. In contrast, the French system of long-term credit banks, upon which Japan's system was based, limited the ability of ordinary banks to make long-term loans. Nonetheless, concurrent with the industrialization of the Japanese economy, the special banks emerged as more than supplementary institutions. In particular, as government controls became more pronounced in the war economy, IBJ assumed an ever more central role in managing syndicated financing of the military build-up, a fact which has been touched on elsewhere in this volume (see Chapter 2 by Teranishi; also Hoshi, 1993, table 8).

The institutions specializing in long-term lending suffered a short death, at least in theory, after World War II during the Allied Occupation. In April 1950, all of the special bank laws were abolished and distinctions between all banks apparently eliminated. However, historical accounts relate that more than one year earlier in November 1948, IBJ had already obtained the verbal approval of Occupation authorities to recapitalize as a bank specializing in long-term credit with bond-issuing authority. This was in sharp contrast to earlier policy requiring that special banks make the choice of being either commercial banks or bond-issuing companies. IBJ also had to overcome initial resistance due both to a suspicion of IBJ for its central role in the financing of the war effort and an economic judgement that long-term funds should be raised in the capital market.

Unable to recapitalize, IBJ directors in the last half of 1948 had faced the danger of liquidation or absorption by another bank. The fact that Japanese government support was wavering during this period appears to have contributed to the organizational sense of IBJ as a private institution. Approval was conditioned on, among other things, restrictions on deposit-taking, and the elimination of governmental authority. Consistent with the agreement, IBJ not only recapitalized but proceeded to raise funds under a special new law passed in 1949 which temporarily permitted IBJ to issue debentures up to 20 times capital. (A historical narrative is IBJ, 1957; also, contemporaneous documentation in MOF, 1976, pp. 557–616; personal reminiscences in Hazawa, 1975, pp. 203–23; and drama in a generally accurate historical novel: Takasugi, 1987, vols. 1–2.)

Simultaneous with the abolition of the special bank laws in 1950, a new law was passed which allowed all banks to issue debentures if the sum of outstanding debentures and deposits was less than 20 times capital. Nonetheless, only the former special banks was able to issue debentures as the city banks' many deposits and low capital placed them above the limit (Kinyu Seido Chosakai, 1987, vol. 3, p. 6). By this point, Occupation authorities were clearly favouring the former special banks, as special assistance funds were used to purchase their issues of preferred stock in 1950, in an effort to stimulate long-term financing of industry.

The 1950 law was inevitably a transitional measure. Prior to its passage, there was controversy among the Japanese over the fairness of also permitting Kangyo Bank to issue debentures when only IBJ had agreed to restrictions on individual deposits (MOF, 1983, pp. 599, 603). Not only did this issue remain unresolved, but when the Bank of Tokyo proposed to issue bonds of their own in 1951, (IBJ, 1957, p. 893) a more general concern arose that the indiscriminate permission to issue bonds among banks would lead to confusion and over-supply in the bond market, and adversely affect the supply of long-term finance (MOF, 1983, p. 608). Another important development affecting the future of the bank debenture market occurred during the final stages of the establishment of the Japan Development Bank in early 1951. Due to last-second objections by Occupation authorities, as well as the Bank of Japan (BOJ), it was decided that JDB would not be granted special debenture-issuing privileges as had been previously planned (MOF, 1983, p. 145).

Meanwhile, the current economic situation was also stimulating further discussion of the long-term credit system. In the Korean War boom in 1951, large city banks were overwhelmed by the spiralling funding needs of both their clients and those of the sectors identified by the priority production system, and had increasingly resorted to credit from the central bank to meet funding needs, a phenomenon dubbed the 'overloan problem'. The four designated priority sectors were coal, iron and steel, electric power, and shipping. In 1952, these four accounted for 44 per cent of all Japanese plant and equipment investment, and 70 per cent of all lending for plant and equipment investment from banks went to these industries. In the same year, city banks relied on BOF loans for more than 10 per cent of their funding needs. Despite BOJ assistance, city banks had begun to withdraw loans to other corporations in non-priority sectors for the purpose of meeting the demand of the designated sectors (Kinyu Seido Chosakai, 1987, vol. 3, pp. 7–8).

In response to questioning in the Diet in February 1952, Minister of Finance Ikeda stated that the current financial system was inadequate, and suggested that the establishment of investment banks specializing in long-term finance funded by debenture issuance would perhaps be one solution to the problem (MOF, 1983, p. 609).

The government set up a temporary Financial System Council consisting of representatives of industry, finance, and academia to examine further reform of the institutions for long-term credit in December 1951. After study of various proposals and debate, the Council presented recommendations in February 1952 to the MOF (IBJ, 1982, pp. 144–50; MOF, 1983, pp. 610–13). Following cabinet approval, the MOF submitted a Long-Term Credit Bank Law to the Diet the following month.

The formal explanation accompanying the proposed law stated that newly formed government institutions, such as the Japan Development Bank, could be counted on to perform only a supplementary role to private institutions in the financing of long-term investment. Specialized long-term credit banks would reduce the burden of over-extended city banks in the provision of long-term credit and further the protection of depositors. However, in order to secure the smooth supply of funds to these institutions, these banks would need to have specialized access to the funds, so the 1950 law granting all banks the right to issue bonds up to 20 times capital was to be abolished (IBJ, 1982, p. 148; MOF, 1983, pp. 612–13).

Significantly, the neutral status of the long-term credit banks with regard to the city banks and their particular clients was considered important at the time: it would make more efficient the allocation of long-term capital and facilitate mutually beneficial relations between the long-term credit banks and city banks. It was also considered that neutrality would assure that any indirect government funding of priority sectors that occurred through the long-term credit banks would in turn be provided to the private sector on a basis independent of any particular group affiliation (Takenaka, 1968, pp. 61–62). In contrast, the idea that securities markets should serve as the supplementary source of long-term debt was given little serious consideration. A compelling argument made in Teranishi and elsewhere is that the scarcity of financial capital made the dependence on securities markets impractical for the provision of long-term capital. (For evidence on the scarcity of financial capital in the Japanese economy around 1950, see Teranishi, 1982, pp. 413–17.) This also was the stated belief of the MOF at the time of the promulgation of the long-term credit bank law in 1952 (Takenaka, 1968, p. 60). The postwar experience of high inflation had also left savers (investors) wary of longer-term bonds.

One important aspect of the plan which was discussed at numerous stages of the deliberations was how many long-term credit banks there should be. Due to economies of scale in the provision of long-term credit, and perceived limitations in the demand for bank debentures, the general opinion was that few, rather than many, banks should be established, though a monopoly was to be avoided. In addition to IBJ, the two other former special banks were viewed as prime candidates; however, the Kangyo Bank and Hokkaido Takushoku Bank were unwilling to forgo their commercial banking business for the sake of retaining their debenture-issuing privileges. Instead, they promised to contribute personnel and capital to a newly established long-term credit bank, and preparations for the creation of a new bank were begun with the active assistance of the financial community (MOF, 1983, pp. 598, 608–16).

The Long-Term Credit Bank Law passed the Diet in June, and was enacted in December 1952, while the law permitting debenture issue by all banks was abolished. The IBJ moved immediately to charter itself as a long-term credit bank and, simultaneously, a Long-Term Credit Bank (LTCB) was created out of the long-term lending divisions of the Kangyo Bank and Hokkaido Takushoku Bank. A third bank based on the remnants of the colonial Bank of Chosen (Korea), was chartered as a long-term credit bank in 1957 as Nippon Fudosan Bank, later renamed the Nippon Credit Bank (NCB). The number of long-term credit banks has been fixed for the decades since at three.

The Long-Term Credit Bank Law (1952)

The 1952 law had two major elements: it constrained the scope of business long-term credit banks could perform, and gave them the right to issue financial debentures (something city banks could not do).

Constraints on the Scope of Business

The scope of business that a long-term credit bank may perform is limited by Article 6 of the Long-Term Credit Bank Law. Its principal business is defined as the making of loans, discounting of bills, acceptance of bills, and provision of guarantees with regard to long-term working capital or plant and equipment capital (Article 6.1.1). Long-term credits (defined as longer than six months) for other purposes may be provided only if they are secured by real estate (Article 6.2), and short-term credits for any purpose may be provided only to the extent that they do not exceed the total of the bank's deposits or similar accepted money. In contrast, the city banks are not limited by law in their mix of long- and short-term finance. A long-term credit bank also may act as a trustee for local government and corporate bonds, and perform foreign exchange transactions (Article 6.1.4–5), rights which the city banks also possess. Table 5.1 outlines the law and contrasts it with the 1981 banking law.

The limitation on short-term finance to the quantity of deposits is made the more binding by the fact that unlike the city banks, long-term credit banks, in principle, are not to be deposit-taking institutions. The acceptance of deposits is limited to borrowing customers, companies for which the bank acts as trustee, and government institutions (Article 6.1.3).

The Right to Issue Financial Debentures (Articles 8–12)

Banks chartered under the long-term credit bank law are granted compensation for the above constraints in the form of the right to issue long-term financial debentures with a maturity of five years. These coupon debentures, combined with the prevention of the creation of deposit instruments of similar length by the city banks have been central to the segmentation of short- and long-term finance in Japan. Since November 1991, the long-term credit banks, as well as Norinchukin and Shoko Chukin, have been allowed to issue two-year debentures. This was part of a larger liberalization policy which granted city banks permission to issue three-year large-lot time deposits. The allowed term of the fund procurement of the city banks has only been gradually lengthened. A two-year term deposit was approved in 1971, a three-year quasi-term deposit (with the right of withdrawal after one year) in 1981, and a large-lot three-year deposit in 1991. Loan trusts, the principal source of lendable funds for the trust banks, come in five-year maturities, but operate as variable-rate instruments. The long-term credit banks may also issue discount debentures which are one year in maturity. Both coupon and discount debentures are issued on a monthly basis, and are granted numerous forms of preferential treatment to assure smooth issuance and a secure source of funds.

In addition to the long-term credit banks, three other institutions are allowed to issue financial debentures: the Central Cooperative Bank for Agriculture and Forestry (Norin Chuo Kinko), the Central Cooperative Bank for Commerce and Industry (Shoko Chukin Chuo Kinko), and the Bank of Tokyo. The first two provide funds primarily for small farms and businesses. The Bank of Tokyo's coupon debentures may have a maturity of only three years. Those desiring a more complete English language overview of the bank debenture market are referred to Doi (1990). Table 5.2 compares ordinary corporate and financial debentures.

Article 8 allows debentures to be issued to a limit of 30 times total capital and reserves, far larger than the capital limit of 2 times stipulated for ordinary corporate debentures. (The original limit of 20 was raised in 1981.) These bonds, unlike those of the great majority of Japanese corporations until recently, may be unsecured. The bonds are bearer bonds unless otherwise requested (Article 11.2) which gives them added liquidity, and has facilitated their use as collateral for call money and BOJ borrowings.

Issuing procedures are also much simpler than those required for ordinary corporate bonds. While ordinary corporations cannot start subscription until application is submitted to, and approval granted by, the MOF, bank debenture issuers only have to report the amount and terms (Article 10). This parallels the practice in the US bond market of 'shelf

TABLE 5.1 Important Distinctions of the Long-Term Credit Bank Law

	Long-Term Credit Bank Law (1952)	Banking Law (1981)
Purpose	'. . . to streamline long-term finance, to ensure the proper supervision of long-term credit bank . . . and at the same time contribute to the maintenance of the financial system by means of a functional differentiation of the banking business.' (Art. 1)	'. . . to aim at the maintenance of credit, and smoothness of financing together with ensuring protection of depositors, to ensure healthy and proper management of the banking business, and contribute to the healthy development of the national economy.' (Art. 1)
Definition	'. . . any (juridical) person which intends to engage as its principal business in the lending of equipment capital or long-term working capital through the issuance of debentures instead of through the acceptance of deposits.' (Art. 4.1)	'an institution which is engaged in . . . 1) Receiving of deposits or instalment savings together with lending of funds or discounting bills or notes; 2) Carrying on of exchange transactions.' (Art. 22)
Long- and Short-term Finance	'. . . may make loans, discount bills, guarantee obligations, or accept bills with regard to equipment capital or long-term working capital.' (Art. 6.1.1) '. . . may make loans, secured by real estate, of long-term capital (more than 6 months) other than equipment capital and long-term working capital.' (Art. 6.2)	No distinction made.

	'... may make loans, discount bills, guarantee obligations or accept bills with regard to short-term capital (less than 6 months) within the limits of an amount equal to the total of accepted and other money of a similar nature.' (Art. 6.2)	No similar provisions.
Required Prudential Measures	'... in order to ensure the preservation and collection of its claims ... with regards to long-term capital, ... shall give special consideration to such means as requiring sound collateral or redemption of the loans on an instalment basis.' (Art. 7)	
Limitation on Loans to Single Customers	30% capital and surplus funds. (Supplementary Provisions, Art. 6)	20% of capital and surplus funds. (Supplementary Provisions, Art. 4)
The Acceptance of Deposits and Instalments Savings	'Acceptance of deposits or instalment savings limited to acceptance of those from the State, local public bodies, borrowers, companies for which the bank acts as trustee in the issuance of corporate bonds, and other customers.' (Art. 6, No. 3)	No limitation.
Issuance of Debentures	Up to 30 times capital and reserves. (Art. 8)	Not allowed.

TABLE 5.2 Advantages of Financial Debentures

	Ordinary Corporate Debentures	Financial Debentures
Amount of Issuance	Ceiling for bond issuance is lower of capital and reserves, or net asset value for corporations, up to 2 times capital and reserves for city banks.	Ceiling is 30 times capital and reserves for long-term credit banks. (Art. 8).
Ease of Issuance and Distribution	Subscription may not begin until after application submitted to MOF and approval obtained.	Must only report amount and terms of issue.
	Have to abandon financing when there is a subscription shortage.	Allowed to reduce the amount of issue to the amount subscribed (*gengaku hakko*).
	Most are required to be issued on a secured basis.	Security not required.
	Public issues issued through direct subscription, whereby issuing amount and terms are publicly announced, and investors submit issuer-prepared application forms to designated securities firms, and are allocated a share upon issuance.	Investors can buy and obtain certificates at any time after one month prior to issuance. Subscriptions and application forms unnecessary (*uridashi*).
	Direct subscription must take place through securities firm.	Bank can sell their own debentures.
	Minimum unit of purchase is ¥100,000.	Minimum unit of purchase is ¥10,000.
Liquidity Features	Purchaser registered.	Bearer bonds.
	—	Accepted as collateral for borrowings from the Bank of Japan during high growth era.
	—	Used as target for BOJ market operations during high growth era.
	—	Were commonly used as collateral to raise money in the call money market in the high growth era. Securities companies were allowed until 1965 to post customers' debentures as collateral (*unyo azukari*).
Tax Treatment	Withholding tax on interest of 15–20% from 1967–78. Current withholding tax is 20%.	5% withholding tax on discount bonds from 1967–78. Current withholding tax of 18%.
Yield	—	Discount bonds set a few basis points above the comparable one-year deposit rate (from 1967).

registration', a privilege which has been granted since 1981 to all US issuers of corporate bonds.

Article 11 provides the issuers of financial debentures with another advantage: the capability for reduced issuance (*gengaku hakko*). While, according to the Commercial Code, ordinary corporate bonds issues must be called off when the amount subscribed does not reach the total amount of the issue, financial debenture issues can be adjusted downward depending on the level of subscription, which permits a continuous issuance of financial debentures regardless of unexpected financial conditions.

Finally, bank debentures, unlike other corporate bonds, can be sold without subscription (*uridashi*), whereby investors may buy them at any period during the month preceding the issue, and obtain the certificates immediately upon payment. This allows purchasers to forgo the preparation of application forms, and promotes sales to the general public. Approximately 70 per cent of coupon and all discount debentures are sold in this manner.

The Evolution of the Primary Market for Financial Debentures

The rates on issued coupon debentures are set by an informal cartel consisting of the long-term credit banks, the three other institutions which issue bank debentures, and the trust banks. Changes in the rate follow close consultation with the MOF and the BOF. Trust banks are included in the negotiations as the prospective dividend rate on trust certificates offered by the trust banks is fixed at 0.02 percentage point above the prevailing bank coupon rate; the actual return is variable (Pressnel, 1973, p. 225). Over time, secondary market yields have also come to play a role in determining a rate change, and now the coupon rate is usually revised when the lowest yield on issued debentures differs by 0.2 percentage point or more from the coupon rate.

Since the introduction of a long-term prime rate as the standard minimum rate for long-term loans it has been set at a fixed spread over the debenture rate. This spread started at 1.4 percentage points, moved to 1 point in 1966, and has been fixed at 0.9 percentage point since 1968. Though traditionally the long-term prime has served as the lower limit for long-term lending, since the mid-1980s, discounts from the long-term prime have become less exceptional (Suzuki, 1987, pp. 146–47) In April 1991, city and regional banks individually began to set their own long-term prime rates (linked to the short-term prime), at rates significantly higher than those charged by the long-term credit banks.

Given the fixed spread and the existence of excess demand for long-term investment financing during the high growth era—the well-known city bank practice of rolling over short-term loans suggests firms desired more long-term credit than they got—the profitability of the long-term credit banks depended on the successful issuance of coupon debentures. However, as an integral part of the structure of regulated interest rates the coupons on financial debentures did not reflect equilibrium rates. The subscription rate was below market rates—not only well below the short-term call rate (Shimura, 1980, p. 219), but consistently below the yield on bank coupon debentures in the secondary markets. In such an environment, the generation of demand in the primary market for coupon debentures was not a trivial issue. Teranishi (1982) provides evidence that the long-term credit market was out of equilibrium (pp. 505–15), and a detailed description and analysis of the structure of regulated interest rates during the high growth era (pp. 451–506).

The Era of Trust Fund Bureau Purchases

In the early 1950s, the long-term credit banks depended principally on the debenture purchases of the Trust Fund Bureau (Shikin Unyobu) of the Minstry of Finance. Between 1952 and 1955, the Bureau bought close to half of issued coupon debentures, as shown in Table 5.3.

However, the dependence on the government as the principal purchaser of coupon bonds was destined to be short-lived. In June 1955, the Trust Fund Bureau temporarily ceased the purchase of new issues, and requests were made by the MOF to the local and city banks to compensate with an increase in their own purchases. Reasons for the withdrawal of Bureau participation included the increased burden of purchasing municipal bonds, and the funding of public corporations and the Japan Development Bank (IBJ, 1982, pp. 221–22; sup. vol. p. 372).

Although the Trust Fund Bureau continued to refinance their previous purchases and would, from time to time, make new purchases of financial

TABLE 5.3 Purchasers of Coupon Debentures by Type
(per cent)

	1952–55	1956–65	1966–75	1976–85	1986–90
Government	45.8	14.9	6.6	3.1	1.8
City Banks	31.8	44.7	26.8	10.0	5.3
Regional Banks	18.2	15.7	9.8	9.5	8.9
Other Financial Institutions	3.4	10.3	19.8	18.2	16.6
Individuals	0.8	14.4	37.0	59.2	67.3

Note: Figures are averages of yearly percentages for purchasers of coupon debenture issues. Percentages before 1978 include only coupon debentures issued by long-term credit banks. The category of individuals includes non-financial companies.

Source: Shimura (1980, App., pp. 82–83) for figures before 1978; Bank of Japan, *Economic Statistics Annual*, for subsequent years.

debentures explicitly tied to sector-specific loans, the ratio of their purchases to all coupon debentures issued sharply declined to below 10 per cent of all issues by 1959, and except for a resurgence to 10–20 per cent levels in 1961–63, remained at single digit levels thereafter. As examples, a 1958 purchase of 10 billion yen of long-term bank debentures by the Bureau went to long-term loans to steel and shipping in a predetermined 40/60 ratio. In 1961, a purchase of 5.5 billion yen (followed by 3 billion yen in 1962) occurred for the funding of electric power and steel. In 1963, there was a purchase of bonds tied to 6 billion yen of loans to the machine tool industry (IBJ, 1982, pp. 348, 541).

The Purchases of City Banks and Other Banking Institutions

Accompanying the decline in the importance of Trust Fund Bureau purchases, purchases of issues increased by private banks, in particular the city banks. Between 1956 and 1965, city banks averaged 45 per cent of all purchases of issued coupon bonds. Three principal factors were responsible:

(1) Regulation of Deposit Rates. Although the rates of interest on bonds were not as great as a city bank could have received in providing long-term funds to a company, they were nonetheless always substantially above regulated time deposit rates. This enabled banks to hold bonds at a profit despite their low rates of interest (Shimura, 1980, p. 230).

(2) Cooperative Financing (*kyocho yushi*). A practice evolved whereby city banks could expect financing for their preferred customers from the long-term credit banks in return for their purchases of the coupon bonds. Apparently, a rule of thumb was for the long-term credit banks to make loans to the city bank's preferred customers of approximately double the amount of bond purchases of that city bank (Patrick, 1972, p. 125). City banks could also expect a flow back of deposits from customers able to obtain financing from the long-term credit banks. A similar sort of mechanism was at work encouraging the debenture purchases by the smaller regional banks. In compensation for purchasing bonds, they would be made the agents of long-term credit bank loans to customers in their local region (Shimura, 1980, pp. 254–55).[1]

---

[1] Further discussion of the agency loan system is in the third section of this chapter. Government policy also played a role in financial debenture purchases by regional banks and other financial institutions. When city banks were less willing to buy debentures during tight money periods, the government would encourage the local banks to turn away from the call money markets and buy more financial debentures (IBJ, 1982, p. 545). To provide further incentives for diversification of the long-term banks' fund sources, sogo banks and credit cooperatives were allowed to be representatives of agency loans in 1954 and 1959, respectively.

(3) Access to Bank of Japan Credit. Financial debentures could be used as collateral for BOJ loans upon which city banks remained heavily dependent. For example, as of June 1964, more than 40 per cent of the outstanding Bank of Japan loans were collateralized by financial debentures (Takenaka, 1968, p. 72). When the BOF shifted its emphasis to market operations in the early 1960s as a means of supplying liquidity to the system, coupon debentures were made one of the categories of eligible paper. Thus, as rates in the secondary market meant that issues could be disposed of only at a loss, it was BOJ policy which made the debentures liquid and encouraged the use of coupon debentures by city banks as a reserve instrument. Further, the fact that credit from the BOJ was substantially below market rates implied that the costs of coupon debenture purchases could be effectively recouped in the form of BOJ subsidies.

Ironically, while long-term credit banks were in part created to cure the 'over-loan problem', city bank dependence on the Bank of Japan credit was systematically related to the fund supply of the long-term credit banks during this period. Teranishi (1982, pp. 483–89) has documented that for 1966–77, BOJ subsidies to city banks were approximately equal to what they passed on to all bond issuers in terms of the purchase of over-priced bonds. Approximately 45 per cent of the estimated 'tax' of aggregate bond holdings was due to the holdings of financial debentures, a figure which undoubtedly was greater during the early stages of the high growth period.

Discount Bonds and the Increasing Importance of Individual Investors

In Japanese bond statistics, individuals are aggregated non-financial corporations (and foreign investors). In practice, many corporate purchasers are wealthy individuals who both own and manage a small or medium company, so the use of the term 'individual' is not as misleading as it may seem. A recent case in point is the purchase and now infamous misuse of IBJ discount debentures by restaurant owner and proprietress Nui Onoue.

While financial institutions were the principal purchasers of coupon debentures during the high growth era, individual investors were being courted as purchasers of one-year discount bonds. Discount bonds can be traced back to a 1920 financial crisis when issuance was allowed to IBJ to assist in the undertaking of emergency financing to distressed companies (IBJ, 1982, p. 38). The importance of discount bonds during the high growth era should not be underestimated. Constituting between 20 and 30 per cent of the outstanding volume of all financial debentures, as shown in Table 5.4, they served the role of a buffer to changes in demand for coupon debentures, and stabilized the overall quantity of funds that could be raised by the long-term credit banks. In times of monetary tight-

TABLE 5.4 Distribution of Outstanding Financial Debentures by Type
(per cent)

1952	1955	1965	1975	1985	1991	Type
88.2	82.4	73.8	69.9	65.2	71.9	Coupon Debentures
11.8	17.6	26.2	30.1	34.8	28.1	Discount Bonds

Source: Bank of Japan, *Economic Statistics Annual*, various years.

ening, when city banks would cut back on their purchases of coupon debentures, the long-term credit banks would meet funding needs by increasing the sales of discount bonds (Shimura, 1980, pp. 227–29).

The rate on discount bonds was set at exactly the same level as one-year time deposits. What made them even more attractive in 1955 was the introduction of a system in which securities companies were allowed to borrow for a fee the discount bonds of their customers, which they would then use as collateral in the call money market to finance stock purchases (*unyo azukari*, or 'use trusts'). In 1965, nearly 85 per cent of all outstanding discount bonds had been sold through securities houses, as shown in Table 5.5. Inflation also gradually increased the attractiveness of the discount bonds, by bringing the 10,000 yen unit within the reach of individual investors.

However, the *unyo azukari* system was abolished in 1965 when it became clear that Yamaichi Securities had become insolvent and an industry crisis was precipitated in no small part through abuse of the system (Adams and Hoshii, 1972, pp. 170–72). New measures were needed to increase the marketability of discount bonds. In 1967, the rate on discount bonds was lifted to a few basis points above the one-year time deposit rate. The same year, a new tax system was introduced whereby taxes on coupon bonds were limited to a 5 per cent withholding tax upon issuance, which compared favourably with the withholding tax rate on interest income and dividends of 15 to 20 per cent.

TABLE 5.5 Distribution of Discount Bonds by
Distributor
(per cent)

1965	1975	1985	Distributor
15.6	36.6	54.5	Issuing Banks
84.6	63.4	45.5	Securities Firms

Includes only bonds issued by long-term credit banks.
Source: Kinyu Seido Chosakai (1987) statistical appendix
p. 70.

Another important transition in the discount bond market followed the gradual expansion of the long-term credit banks' own retailing efforts. The long-term credit banks, which distributed only 15 per cent of their own discount bonds in 1965, had raised that proportion to more than 50 per cent in 1985. By 1985, the proportion of discount bonds among outstanding financial debentures had increased to more than 35 per cent (Tables 5.4 and 5.5).

While individual investors have consistently accounted for more than 95 per cent of the purchases of the discount bond market, a more recent development is their occupation of the principal investor category for coupon debentures (Table 5.3). The decline in the role of city banks in this market was set off by the issuance of government bonds in 1966. City banks dramatically slowed down their purchases of new bank debentures, both because of the burden placed on them to underwrite government bonds, and because the BOJ removed financial debentures from their open market intervention account. The attractiveness of coupon bond purchases having been drastically reduced, in 1967 city banks started actively selling large quantities of their holdings of outstanding bank debentures (IBJ, 1982, pp. 732–34). The decline in their relative holdings has been steady since the mid-1960s, and now approaches only 5 per cent of outstanding issues. Another factor behind the city banks' withdrawal from the bank debenture market since the early 1970s has been the active pursuit and use of funds for new lending opportunities in the small- and medium-sized business sector.

On the other hand, local banks and other financial institutions, which never were as dependent on BOJ financing as the city banks, and unlike the city banks have generally had more funds than lending opportunities, maintained their relative proportion of financial debenture purchases even after the end of the high growth era.

The decline in sales to city banks has been made up through large increases in the sale of coupon debentures to individuals. Some factors behind these increases have been tax-related: most recently the search by savers for alternative instruments in the wake of the elimination of the *maruyu* system. Also, in 1974, the maximum amount of debenture holdings whose interest could be exempt from income taxation was raised from 15 million to 30 million yen. Marketing efforts have also intensified: in 1981 a new and very popular type of coupon debenture was introduced by the long-term credit banks, which effectively was a zero-coupon debenture. Called 'wides', the interest on these instruments is compounded semi-annually, and one complete payment is made upon maturity. One IBJ strategy has been to go after the savings of workers of their large corporate clients such as Hitachi and Kansai Electric (IBJ, 1982, pp. 1076–79).

An important feature of discount and coupon bonds for some individual investors has been that they are in bearer form, and can be purchased anonymously. This facilitates the evasion of estate and income taxes— around 10 per cent of the 221 billion yen in concealed income identified in tax-evasion cases filed by the National Tax Administration Agency between 1989 and 1991 was accounted for by financial debentures (*Nikkei Weekly*, 15 March 1993). In addition, the purchase of financial debentures can be used as a means of laundering illicit income.

In response to public concern, measures have been recently taken to curb the abuse of the anonymity feature of financial debentures. The MOF issued a directive in 1990 to financial institutions which required that they confirm the identities of clients involved in transactions of more than 30 million yen. The Kanemaru case, in which at least a few billion yen of undeclared political donations were used to buy discount bonds, suggests that further reform may be necessary. Kanemaru had been able to circumvent the new identification rule through the cooperation of a securities company which divided his purchasing orders into small lots bought from different bank branches.

The maintenance of a steadily growing demand for financial debentures has been a significant achievement for the long-term credit banks, particularly since the decline in city bank purchases and the emergence of significant competition in the form of government debt. Though they now share the spotlight with government bonds, financial debentures retain a dominant share of the Japanese bond market (Table 5.6). This achievement has been the result of important tax and regulatory changes at critical moments of transition in the market, intensified marketing efforts by the institutions themselves, and the full exploitation of those advantages originally given to financial debentures in the 1952 law, as well as the continued repression of competitive instruments such as longer-term deposits or five-year corporate bonds.

Will this form of financing persist as an effective source of funds for long-term credit banks as more competitive instruments emerge as part of efforts to deregulate the financial system? Developments in the secondary market may lead to differing costs of capital among the long-term credit banks in line with their credit ratings. Throughout the post-war era, the long-term credit banks have issued their financial debentures at identical coupon rates, a process supported in the secondary market by identical yields. However in June 1992, there emerged significant gaps in the market yields of the five-year debentures of the three long-term credit banks, reflecting in particular worsening news about the condition of Nippon Credit Bank's non-bank affiliates. Given common coupon rates, future subscription to NCB issues by major investors such as insurance companies are likely to occur at discounts from par, implying a higher cost of capital. Whether this condition is temporary or not depends for the most part on the rehabilitation of NCB.

TABLE 5.6 Distribution of Bonds by Type
(per cent)

1955	1965	1975	1985	1989	Type
25.4	12.6	8.9	4.3	11.7	Corporate
6.2	7.1	10.9	3.8	3.0	Municipal
8.8	24.4	13.2	10.2	8.3	Public corporation
1.5	10.0	38.3	37.2	32.7	Government
58.1	45.8	38.5	42.6	43.1	Financial debentures
–	–	0.2	1.9	1.2	Foreign

Source: Shimura (1980) Appendix pp. 38–47; *Koshasai Yoran* (1990).

The history of Japanese regulatory practice suggests that any systemic damage done to the fund-raising capabilities of long-term credit banks by liberalization measures will be gradual, and compensated for by relaxed restrictions of their own activities in other areas. This includes, for example, their right since November 1991 to issue two-year debentures. The case of the government bond market suggests new entry into the bond markets can be managed in such a way as to increase the overall market rather than cut into the debenture issues of the long-term credit banks. As for the loss of borrowers that further development of the corporate bond market may entail, long-term credit banks may well be compensated by an increased growth in their fees from bond underwriting and trading of straight bonds, privileges granted in 1993.

The next section of this paper shifts focus to the asset side of the long-term credit banks' balance sheet. How has their steady growth translated into patterns in the financing of corporate clients? And what role have they come to play within the Japanese main bank system, either as participants, or as lead banks themselves?

COOPERATIVE FINANCING BY THE LONG-TERM CREDIT BANKS

To a greater degree than the other large banks in the Japanese financial system, the long-term credit banks have been involved in two types of joint, cooperative financing. First, they have worked with government financial institutions, particularly the Japan Development Bank, in policy-oriented financing projects. Second, they have provided supplementary long-term finance to leading companies in all of the enterprise groups, as well as those few not so affiliated.

Cooperative Financing with the Japan Development Bank

During the period when the Trust Fund Bureau was the principal purchaser of financial debentures, most of the funds supplied by the long-term credit banks were targeted to the designated priority industries of coal mining, steel, electric power, and shipping. The principal partner of the long-term credit banks in this activity was the Japan Development Bank (JDB). Of the nearly 300 billion yen in loans supplied by the JDB to industry between 1951 and 1956, nearly 85 per cent went to the priority sectors (JDB, 1993, p. 167). In 1956, of the outstanding plant and equipment loans to these sectors by city banks, long-term credit banks, trust accounts, and JDB, the JDB accounted for nearly 45 per cent, as compared to 30 per cent for the long-term credit banks (IBJ, 1982, pp. 203–8). Among the priority sectors, funding from the long-term credit banks was greater only in steel (Table 5.7).

However, even during its early history, the role of the JDB in determining the direction of Japan's credit flows should not be over-estimated. Unlike its predecessor, the Reconstruction Finance Bank (RFB), the JDB was not allowed to provide working capital loans, which often made loans in coordination with private banks a necessity. The Japan Development Bank Law explicitly prohibits the JDB from competing with banks and other financial institutions (Article 22). Rather, the JDB's legal mandate actively encouraged cooperation with the private banking system. An internal memo dated April 1952, states that since JDB credit was intended to supplement private bank funding, it should 'actively undertake cooperative financing' with the private banks (JDB, 1976, p. 55).

Another relevant point is that in its early years as a nascent institution, JDB relied heavily on the expertise in credit analysis of staff and directors seconded from other financial institutions, particularly the Industrial Bank of Japan. The Reconstruction Finance Bank had been founded as a division within the IBJ in August 1946, and a total of 127 people were seconded from IBJ during its brief lifetime (MOF, 1978, pp. 627–31; IBJ, 1982, p. 106). In addition to some personnel carried over from the RFB, upon its formation the JDB depended upon the expertise of staff and directors seconded from the IBJ, as well as the Kangyo Bank and the Bank of Japan. In all, nine individuals including two division chiefs and one section chief were seconded from IBJ to the Japan Development Bank upon its formation. A tenth, Sohei Nakayama, a future president of IBJ, served as a director. Combined with secondments from the Kangyo Bank and the BOJ, 27 out of the 46 male employees (not including directors but including 11 division and section chiefs) of the newly established JDB were appointed from outside institutions (Takasugi, 1987, vol. 3, p. 50; IBJ, 1982, p. 139; JDB, 1976, p. 44; JDB, 1993, p. 154).

In addition to steel, the long-term credit banks were the principal

TABLE 5.7 Share of Outstanding Loans for Plant and Equipment Investment in Selected Industries by Bank Category

(per cent)

	1956			1966			1974			1988		
	Long-Term Credit Banks	JDB	City Banks	Long-Term Credit Banks	JDB	City Banks	Long-Term Credit Banks	JDB	City Banks	Long-Term Credit Banks	JDB	City Banks
Machinery	64.7	14.5	6.8	42.9	5.9	5.0	36.7	5.5	18.4	12.0	5.6	28.6
Chemicals	56.2	14.9	10.7	41.5	10.3	14.4	38.0	7.3	18.6	26.2	14.1	26.7
Textiles	47.8	14.9	21.2	46.7	5.6	7.6	35.1	7.1	18.1	7.7	3.1	25.8
Mining	42.1	49.6	1.4	20.0	71.4	2.0	26.7	34.5	12.9	12.1	8.5	13.1
Steel and Iron	63.7	22.5	4.2	43.9	2.6	9.5	39.7	3.4	15.8	28.6	10.5	15.2
Shipping	22.5	47.6	24.7	3.5	70.8	9.8	17.7	59.7	12.9	9.8	39.2	14.5
Electric Power	29.2	46.3	12.2	28.1	44.7	6.1	32.1	28.2	11.1	25.6	35.3	10.4
All Loans for P&E Investment	37.5	33.1	16.8	36.1	17.4	15.2	29.1	11.3	30.2	8.9	6.0	32.9

Note: The category of machinery includes general industrial machinery, electric machine tools, transportation machinery (including automobiles and ships), and precision machinery. Totals do not add to 100% because trust accounts comprise the remainder.
Source: Industrial Bank of Japan (1982, pp. 208, 211, 540, 946) for 1956, 1968, 1974; *Nikkei Telecom Data Service* for 1988; Bank of Japan, *Economic Statistics Annual* (1989), for JDB.

lenders for investment in the other important manufacturing industries such as machinery, chemicals, textiles, cement and ceramics. In fact, the establishment of the long-term credit banks was a principal reason why the financing to industries other than the priority industries fell from 20 per cent of JDB loans in the early 1950s to 10 per cent in the mid-1950s. According to JDB historians, there was a reduction in the number of industries targeted for funding by the JDB starting in 1953 'because the enactment of the Long-Term Credit Bank Law had resulted in the inauguration of private long-term financial institutions which could devote themselves to the long-term financing of the remaining industries' (JDB, 1993, pp. 163, 167). Long-term credit banks provided more than twice the funds of JDB in those non-priority manufacturing industries in 1956, and nearly five times as much 10 years later. Although JDB loans to other industries began to increase again in the late 1950s (JDB, 1993, pp. 180–81), its concentration in the priority sectors in relation to other banks did not change. The significant proportions of JDB funding which went into relatively declining industries such as coal mining and shipping in the 1960s and 70s parallel those proportions for all government funding discussed in Hamada and Horiuchi (1987, p. 243).

The company-specific loan data presented in Table 5.8 yield similar implications. We see a strong correlation of JDB activity with that of the long-term credit banks: of the 161 listed companies that had a long-term credit bank in 1967 as the largest private lender, nearly half were also obtaining loans from the Japan Development Bank. (To avoid overestimating the importance of the long-term credit banks, the company's 'lead lender' is determined by aggregating the loans of all financial institutions in the group. Thus, a long-term credit bank can be a lead or primary lender only if its loan share exceeds that of each keiretsu's aggregate loan share.) An additional 20 per cent of the Table 5.8 sample had no JDB loans but financing from other government institutions such as the Export-Import Bank.

In terms of both numbers of firms and the average loan shares, JDB loans were concentrated more heavily than those of other banks in three areas: mining, electric power, and shipping. In the latter two industries, JDB lending averaged more than three times that of the leading long-term credit bank, and JDB was the lead lender in 16 out of 18 cases. But in other manufacturing industries, the JDB share averaged one-third to one-fourth that of the leading long-term credit bank.

Divergence was further accelerated in the mid-1960s when JDB expanded its lending for social welfare projects such as regional infrastructure (JDB, 1976, pp. 285–86; JDB, 1993, pp. 198–99). The two principal areas of JDB and long-term credit bank cooperation remain shipping and electric power. The JDB is also the largest lender to a number of companies in other industries, such as All Nippon Airways.

TABLE 5.8 Industry Breakdown of Cooperative Financing among the Long-Term Credit Banks and JDB: Companies Listed on the Tokyo Stock Exchange, 1967.

	Number of Companies for which Long-Term Credit Banks are Lead Private Lender (A)	Average Lead Long-Term Credit Bank Loan Share Among A per cent	Number of A to which JDB has Outstanding Loans (B)	Average JDB Loan Share Among B (per cent)	(B)/(A) (per cent)	Cases where JDB share Exceeds that of Long-Term Credit Bank
Mining	7	21	5	28	71	3
Steel	25	33	12	5	48	0
Machinery	35	40	17	11	49	1
Chemical	21	32	10	8	48	1
Textiles	8	35	4	14	50	1
Shipping	9	12	7	53	78	6
Electric Power	9	13	9	45	100	9
All Industries	161	31	78	21	48	21

Source: Keiretsu no Kenkyu, First Section Listed Company Volume (1968, pp. 233–78) and Section Listed Company Volume (1968, pp. 31–105).

Given that the largest lender to a number of the companies in these two industries is JDB rather than the long-term credit bank, some might interpret JDB as the main bank. However, they would be mistaken, for by all the remaining criteria by which the main bank relationship was defined in Chapter 1 of this volume, the JDB-firm relationship is either non-existent or weak. By statute, JDB is not allowed to own firm shares, provide bond-issue related services, or maintain corporate deposit accounts. Finally, though personnel are occasionally seconded to client companies, a leadership role in corporate rescues is absent from its history, in all likelihood ruled out by the above-mentioned inability to provide working capital finance.

The above limitations are hardly flaws; in fact, the rather narrow role of JDB can be considered part of a successful development bank design based on the precautionary desire to avoid the political and inflationary aspects of the RFB experience.[2]

Although JDB loans usually have the longest term and are thus junior in the sense of maturity, they often appear to be treated on a senior basis compared to private bank credit in times of financial trouble (JDB, 1993, p. 134; see further discussion in The Importance of Ties with Vertical Groups, below). In the 1950s and early 60s, JDB maintained write-off ratios of bad loans less than both IBJ and ordinary banks (JDB, 1993, p. 135). Although superior abilities in credit analysis is one possible reason, part of the performance of JDB loans may also be related to their status in terms of collateral: JDB has often been given the first rank of priority on hypothecs in cooperative financing ventures.[3]

Cooperative Financing with the Group Banks

Corporations, both in Japan and elsewhere, particularly when they exceed a certain size, tend to spread their borrowings among a number of banks. Statutory regulations limit the provision of loans by a bank to single large customers, although in Japan only since 1974. This is hardly

---

[2] For an informative table comparing differences of the RFB and JDB across a variety of characteristics, see JDB (1993, p. 156), for a history of JDB's establishment see the same source (pp. 154–60), and MOF (1983, pp. 95–159). For a detailed historical examination and comparative analysis of the performance and roles of development banks in Japan (including IBJ), see Yasuda (1993).

[3] In their book on credit and security in Japan, the two cases that Tanikawa and others cite (1973, pp. 113, 115) that involve the JDB both had the JDB's claim being of the first rank among the loan claims. JDB historians also imply that it was not unusual for JDB to 'demand a superior mortgage ranking in light of the collateral value' (see JDB, 1993, p. 267). In general, securing loans with collateral is a practice encouraged by the Japan Development Bank Law, which states that all granting of credit 'be deemed to be reliable' (Article 18.1.2), and the Statement of Business Methods, Article 6 of which states that all loans should be secured by real estate, floating mortgages, or other collateral whenever possible (JDB, 1976, App. p. 36).

inconsistent with the existence of a main bank with specialized monitoring capabilities: there are many reasons, not mutually exclusive, and many have been discussed elsewhere in this volume. A reason particularly relevant to the US system, where the securitization of loans has advanced, is differing costs of capital among banks (Gorton and Pennachi, 1990). (For recent theoretical analyses of the choice between single and multiple creditors, see Bolton and Scharfstein, 1994, and Berglöf and von Thadden, 1994.)

In the case of Japan, another clear motivation for the division of loans to specific companies was set in place by the Long-Term Credit Bank Law. Based upon the principle of specialization of long-term finance, it encouraged companies, regardless of group affiliation, to depend on the long-term credit banks for much of their long-term funding needs. And through the preferential treatment of financial debentures outlined in the first section, it encouraged group banks to participate actively in this arrangement. As an example, Horiuchi (1990) has looked into the breakdown of long- and short-term loans by both company and bank for specific companies in his study of bank-firm relationships in the synthetic fibre industry. Out of nine companies in 1989, only one had IBJ as an overall lead lender. However, six had IBJ as a principal long-term lender, indicating the particular importance of IBJ's supplementary role in the synthetic fibre industry.

The role of long-term credit banks as an independent and supplementary source of long-term funds to the leading firms across bank groups grew in importance during the period corresponding to the city banks' pre-eminence as debenture purchasers. From 1956 to 1960, the long-term credit banks went from providing 34.4 per cent of new term loans for plant and equipment investment to 40.6 per cent (from 6.7 to 11.4 per cent of all new loans). Meanwhile city banks dropped from providing 29.5 per cent of new loans for investment to 17.6 per cent (IBJ, 1982, p. 334). In fact, during this period, the net increase in city banks' coupon debenture purchases was nearly three-quarters the increase in city banks' own lending for plant and equipment investment. Especially in the heavy manufacturing industries, city banks were increasingly allowing the plant and equipment investment needs of their largest customers to be met by the long-term credit banks (IBJ, 1982, pp. 341–43).

More direct evidence of this phenomenon can be found in the specific loan details concerning bank and company loan quantities provided by *Keiretsu no Kenkyu*. Table 5.9 outlines the distribution of outstanding loans to firms listed on the first section of the Tokyo Stock Exchange in 1965 by the financial institutions of each of the six major keiretsu and the two largest long-term credit banks. While 46 per cent of IBJ's loans and over 58 per cent of LTCB's loans were directed to firms of one of the major six keiretsu, the percentage of loans of keiretsu financial institutions to firms of other keiretsu tended to be much lower. For the older ex-zaibatsu groups of Mitsui, Mitsubishi, and Sumitomo, the proportion varied between 18 and 28 per cent; for the newer bank groups of Fuyo, Sanwa, and Dai-Tchi, between 30 and 43 per cent.

The same distinctions are to be found in sharper relief in Table 5.10: IBJ was the second lender for 78 of the companies listed on the first section of Tokyo Stock Exchange in 1967, in comparison with an average of 44 for the six group banks. The Long-Term Credit Bank of Japan, which in terms of loan quantity and companies to which it was the lead lender was, and remains, at a second tier below the group banks, was still the second lender in more cases than all but IBJ. Even the Nippon Credit Bank, with only 4 companies to which it was the lead lender, was the second largest lender for more than 28 companies.

Not only did the long-term credit banks lend across city bank groups, but they did so in a more even fashion. For instance, while the lowest percentage of lending by IBJ to the companies of any one group was 5.8 per cent, Sanwa financial institutions lent only 3 per cent of their funds to Sumitomo group firms, Sumitomo financial institutions lent only 1.2 per cent of their funds to Dai-Ichi group firms, and Mitsui financial institutions lent only 2.7 per cent of their funds to Mitsubishi companies (Shimura, 1978, p. 161).

TABLE 5.9 Distribution of Loans from Major Bank Groups in 1965 (per cent)

Loans are to:

Firms Within Own Group	Firms in Other City Bank Group	Firms in Other Long-Term Credit Bank Group	Lending bank group
50.5	46.0	0.6	Industrial Bank of Japan
5.4	58.6	27.6	Long-Term Credit Bank
70.3	18.3	8.5	Mitsui
57.2	27.8	10.0	Mitsubishi
63.5	24.8	9.3	Sumitomo
41.8	35.0	15.3	Fuyo
49.4	30.5	14.0	Sanwa
39.7	43.1	11.9	Dai-Ichi

Totals for each bank group do not add to 100 because of lending that does not fit in any of these three categories. IBJ and LTCB constitute the only lending institutions of their 'groups'. A firm's group is identified as that group whose financial institutions in aggregate provide the most loans to the firm.

Source: Shimura (1978, p. 161) using data from *Keiretsu no Kenkyu* (1966).

TABLE 5.10 Second Largest Lender to Major Firms
(number of firms)

Year	IBJ	LTCB	NCB	Group Banks[1]	Other City[2]
1967	78	59	28	44	12
1990	91	53	21	60	23

This table shows the number of firms listed on the First Section of the Tokyo Stock Exchange having one of the three long-term credit banks, a group bank, or other city bank as the second largest lender in the year shown.

[1] The loans of group city and trust banks, insurance and trading companies are aggregated in calculating the position of group bank. The entry is the average for the six group banks.

[2] Average for the other city banks.

Source: *Keiretsu no Kenkyu* (1968, 1991).

According to rough estimates, the average period on outstanding loans in 1965 for the long-term credit banks was 4.8 years, compared to 2.9 years for the city banks, and 11.3 years for JDB (JDB, 1993, p. 132). Just as JDB loans appear to be compensated for their longer and more favourable credit terms with seniority in terms of collateral, loans provided by the long-term credit banks appear to have been compensated for their additional maturity risk with a greater proportion of security on real estate and floating mortgages. Table 5.11 compares the fraction of IBJ loans secured by real estate and floating mortgages with the similar proportion of all bank loans published in the aggregate figures of the Bank of Japan *Economic Statistics Annual*. Throughout the 1960s the IBJ percentage remained in the 60–70 per cent range, two to three times the national average.

This is likely to be related to the fact that a high proportion of IBJ loans were fixed loans for plant and equipment, which naturally served as the collateral. The difference remains, though at a somewhat lower level, if we include loans secured by stocks and bonds and the 'other security' category (for example, 69.8 versus 45.7 per cent in 1970). In contrast, long-term credit bank loans depend much less on third-party guarantees than average (for example, 23.0 versus 9.4 per cent in 1970). Although some institutions regard guarantees as more valuable than mortgages (Corbett, 1987, p. 43), the value of any guarantee will vary greatly depending on the quality of the guarantor. Since guarantors can vary in quality from being the main bank to being a related company or important shareholder—in 1975, 7.7 per cent of corporate bankruptcies in Japan were caused by allied business failures (Ballon and Tomita, 1988, p. 72)—the relative value of a guarantee versus a mortgage differs from

TABLE 5.11 Percentage of Loans Secured by Real Estate
or Mortgages. IBJ Compared with All Banks

1955	1965	1975	1979	
63.5	67.0	55.5	45.8	IBJ
25.2	25.4	31.2	30.0	All banks

Source: Bank of Japan, *Economic Statistics Annual*, various
years; IBJ (1982), supplementary volume.

case to case. In the account of Tanikawa and others (1973) the use of
guarantees usually involves directors or major shareholders. Often there is
little examination of the credit-worthiness of the guarantor, and a guarantor's role is 'frequently seen as providing merely another source of
pressure on the debtor to honor his obligations' (pp. 51–52).

The use of collateral to secure loans is common among all financial
institutions in Japan, and has served to protect against both risk and
morally hazardous actions on the part of the borrower. The 'collateral
principle' became an important feature of the Japanese financial system in
the twentieth century, and its development has been described in Suzuki
(1987, pp. 43–44). Along with main bank relationships, it has been called
by JDB historians a 'systemic characteristic' of the Japanese financial system, and has been expressed as follows: 'With the goal of safe transactions in mind, in principle important financial transactions, such as
corporate bond issues, bank loans and interbank transactions, will be
secured with collateral' (1993, p. 137).

The relatively more common practice of securing credit by long-term
credit banks may be in part responsible for write-off ratios of bad loans
consistently lower than those of ordinary and trust banks (JDB, 1993,
p. 135). As with JDB, superior capabilities in credit analysis may also be
a factor behind the lower write-off ratios. In addition, in the case of a
group firm with outstanding debt of mixed maturity, the greater security
puts the long-term credit bank in a stronger bargaining position *vis-à-vis*
main bank lenders if the firm runs into trouble. This contrasts with the
situation in the United States, where long-term debt is generally provided
by a bond market consisting of atomistic investors. Though recent model-
ling of the debt maturity choice based on the US environment has
explained this structure by motivating the power of better informed
banks both to make the refinancing decision and dilute the value of the
public's long-term debt claim (Diamond, 1991), the case of Japan's long-
term credit banks suggests that limitations on the ability to dilute long-
term claims have been viewed as desirable in the high growth
environment of post-war Japan.

Any reorganization plan involving the disposition of those secured firm assets either must pay the secured creditors back at least the value of the assets, or obtain the approval of those with senior claims on the assets. And in cases where the main bank chooses to let the firm go under, the long-term credit banks, by virtue of their senior claim to collateralized assets, are likely to recover the most from the disposal of the firm assets. Secured claims are generally treated favourably by Japanese bankruptcy law (Packer and Ryser, 1992). Especially in the mid-1960s, a time of a number of large corporate bankruptcies, IBJ played a major role in the handling of bankrupt corporations to which they were not the principal lender, most notably Sanyo Special Steel (IBJ, 1982, pp. 531–32). The existence of secured claims by long-term credit banks may provide a complementary explanation to implicit contracting models discussed in this volume in which the main banks are motivated to act 'as if' they were junior to other lenders in times of distress.

By 1979, the proportion of long-term credit bank loans secured by real estate and floating mortgages had declined to 1.5 times the national average. This was related to a growing convergence of city and long-term credit bank loan composition by both term and purpose. As investment demand declined after the high growth era, the long-term banks began to lend more on a short-term basis. And city banks, spurred by both the gradual (though incomplete) lengthening in the term of their deposits, and a drive to supply the investment needs of small and medium customers, started to direct longer-term loans toward plant and equipment investment (Figures 5.1 and 5.2).

With regard to loans for investment financing, the convergence of proportions of the two classes of banks is now complete. However, as Table 5.10 shows, this convergence does not appear to have resulted in the sharp decline of the long-term credit banks (IBJ in particular) as secondary lenders. Although, in the high growth period, city banks acted in concert with the long-term credit banks, in part because they had to, the provision of loans to the same customers by the city and long-term banks appears to have outlived its original motivation.

Cooperative Financing with Smaller Financial Institutions

As financial institutions other than the city banks were important purchasers of debentures, it follows that cooperative relationships on the lending side also emerged, in part to compensate these institutions for their purchases.

One mechanism was the common use of what were known as agency loans, which constituted 12 per cent of all outstanding long-term credit bank loans in 1969 (IBJ, 1982, p. 861). Long-term credit banks had the right to make long-term loans to regional customers through the

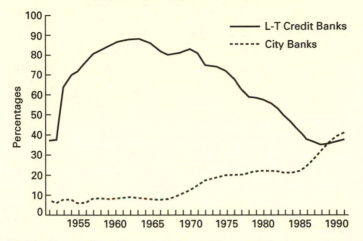

FIG. 5.1 The Percentage of Loans Going to Plant and Equipment Investment
Source: *Bank of Japan Economic Statistics Annual*, various years.

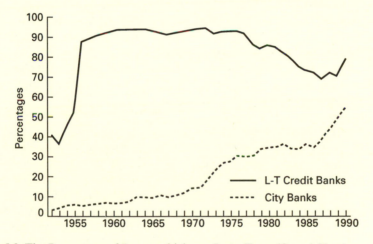

FIG. 5.2 The Percentage of Loans which are Long Term (Over 1 Year)
Source: *Bank of Japan Economic Statistics Annual*, various years.

incentive for the smaller banks was both to obtain long-term financing for their preferred customers, and to collect the fixed rate commissions as the agent for a long-term credit bank loan. Although the system gave the long-term credit banks the incentive to supply long-term funds to smaller firms in outlying areas, despite their relative lack of branch offices, the well-known links to debenture purchases have been at times a concern among policy-makers. (For a critical MOF overview from 1968 and IBJ rebuttal, see IBJ, 1982, pp. 861, 864.)

Another indirect benefit to debenture purchases was that the long-term credit banks would give preferred regional banks highly sought-after invitations to participate in large loans to prestigious customers. For instance, a large part of a syndicated loan to Hitachi was dispersed by IBJ to more than 20 local banks in the late 1950s (IBJ, 1982, p. 336).

THE LONG-TERM CREDIT BANK AS A MAIN BANK

Despite the importance of their role as secondary lenders to firms belonging to the groups of other banks, the long-term credit banks, especially the largest and most prestigious of them, the Industrial Bank of Japan, have maintained a large number of relationships with corporations in which there is little doubt that they are the main bank. In fact, a subset of these firms is so heavily influenced by IBJ loans and personnel appointments that a minor keiretsu group is often considered to have grown up around IBJ (Table 5.12).

In addition, IBJ has very close relationships with a number of the largest vertical groups that are either independent or only loosely affiliated with the six bank groups: Nippon Steel, Nissan Motor, Hitachi. IBJ has consistently been the largest single lender to the apex of these vertical groups and, as discussed later, to an exceptionally large proportion of the listed firms within those groups. The three companies heading these groups are the fourth, fifth, and sixth largest shareholders of IBJ (Meiji, Nippon, and Dai-Ichi Life Insurance are the lead shareholders). These ties pre-date World War II, when IBJ developed close relationships with the new zaibatsu (*shinko zaibatsu*) such as Nissan (the nuclei of which were Nissan Motor and Hitachi), Nippon Chisso, and Mori (IBJ, 1982, p. 50). The relationship with Japan Steel goes far back as well: IBJ headed syndicates for distributing and absorbing issues of Japan Iron and Steel Company, which was established in 1934 by the consolidation of the government's Yawata works and six private firms (Cohen, 1949, pp. 17, 26). The firm was broken up into two separate entities during the Occupation, but re-established with the Yawata-Fuji merger of 1968 (Hadley, 1970, pp. 297–98).

Bank Loans (δ)

In Chapter 1 of this volume, a number of aspects of the relations between a firm and its main bank were introduced. Other roles of Japanese banks, both in firm bankruptcy choice and in the certification of initial public offerings, are explored in Packer (1993). Table 5.13 compares the three

TABLE 5.12 The IBJ Group

Fisheries	Taiyo Fishery, Nippon Suisan
Construction	Aoki Construction, Toyoko
Textiles	Nitto Boseki, Kuraray
Paper and Pulp	Daishowa Paper, Tomoku, Superbag
Oil	Cosmo Oil
Iron and Steel	Nippon Steel, Godo Steel, Taiheiyo Metals
Specialty Steel	Daido Steel, Nippon Yakin Kogyo
Non-ferrous Metals	Nippon Mining, Dowa Mining
Chemicals and Glass	Tosoh, Nippon Soda, Chisso Corporation, Nippon Steel Chemical, Rasa Industries, Nissan Chemical Industry, Hodogaya Chemical, Central Glass
Industrial Machinery	Zexel, Ikegai, Riken
Shipbuilding	Nitchitsu
Automobiles	Nissan Motors, Nissan Diesel Motor, Fuji Heavy Industry
Household Electronics	SMK
Precision Machinery	Aichi Tokei Denki, Riken Keiki, Copal
Banks/Securities Companies	Tokyo Tomin Bank, Japan Securities Finance, New Japan Securities, Wako Securities, Toyo Securities
Restaurants/Leisure	Royal, Tokyo Disneyland, Yomiuri Land
Railways	Keisel Electric Railway, Nishi Nippon Railroad
Shipping	Navix (formerly Japan Line), Shinwa Kaiun
Airlines	Japan Airlines

Some of these companies are also considered members of other groups.

Source: Dodwell Marketing Consultants, *Industrial Groupings in Japan*, 8th ed. (1988/89, p. 134); Osano (1991, pp. 52–53).

long-term credit banks with the city banks across three of these aspects for the purposes of roughly comparing the relative number of main bank relationships among the banks at two widely separated points in time: 1967 and 1990.

One characteristic of these data is that there is a clear differentiation among the long-term credit banks in the number of lead lending relationships with listed companies, including second section companies. (The lead lender is determined by aggregating the loans of all financial institutions in the group.) For instance, while IBJ was the lead lender to 41 companies listed on the second section of the Tokyo Stock Exchange in 1967 (keiretsu group average: 43 firms), the LTCB was the lead lender to 14 firms and NCB to 12. There has also been a consistent difference in

TABLE 5.13 Main Bank Indicators: The Long-Term Credit Banks Compared with Other Banks

	1967 (1st Section Tokyo)			1990 (1st Section Tokyo)			1990 (1st and 2nd Section Tokyo)	
	Companies to which Lead Lender	Companies to which Seconded Director	of which President/or Chairman	Companies to which Lead Lender	Companies to which Seconded Director	of which President/or Chairman	Companies for which Leading Bank Share-Holder (Over 3%)	Companies for which Second Bank Share-Holder (Over 3%)
Mitsubishi	87	61	4	134	91	8	83	129
Sumitomo	78	42	4	113	50	7	77	106
Mitsui	78	31	2	102	40	0	48	89
Fuji	73	55	10	126	87	6	116	137
IBJ	70	48	8	70	75	17	85	106
DKB	61	58	11	95	103	10	127	127
Sanwa	52	34	3	62	56	4	102	132
LTCB	20	4	0	18	22	6	22	69
Tokai	17	13	1	29	30	2	88	102
Daiwa	9	16	1	16	25	2	47	82
Saitama	8	0	0	11	13	2	27	31
Kyowa	6	12	0	12	19	0	24	56
Taiyo-Kobe	5	7	1	15	26	3	49	80
JCB	4	3	0	5	6	0	5	36
BOT	2	7	1	8	27	3	8	12
Hokkaido	1	8	0	5	10	1	16	21

Note:
Following the conventions of *Keiretsu no Kenkyu*, the loans of all financial institutions in the six major bank groups (and the Tokai group) have been aggregated to determine the largest lender. Companies that have been seconded directors are calculated for the city banks individually. Dai-Ichi Kangyo and Taiyo-Kobe figures for 1967 are the sum of the pairs of pre-merger banks. Shareholdings for Mitsui and Taiyo-Kobe are from 1989.

DKB = Dai-Ichi Kangyo. BOT = Bank of Tokyo. Hokkaido = Hokkaido Takushoku.

Source: Keiretsu no Kenkyu. First Sected Listed Company Volumes (1968, pp. 75–91, 230–78; 1991, sections on loans and personnel); *Kigyo Keiretsu Soran* (1991, p. 74; 1992, p. 78).

the size of the bank firms affiliated with each long-term credit bank, with net sales approximately four times as large on average for IBJ-affiliated firms (*Keiretsu no Kenkyu*, 1991).

IBJ in 1967 was the lead lender to 70 companies listed on the first section of the Tokyo Stock Exchange, which was a number comparable with the average of 71 for the six major keiretsu groups. Meanwhile, LTCB and NCB lagged far behind with 20 and 4 companies, respectively, to which they were the lead lenders, numbers more similar in scale to the second tier of city banks.

Although the distinction between the long-term credit banks in the number of lead lending relationships remained evident in 1990, the number of lead lending relationships relative to other banks had slipped for IBJ, the number of which was lower than five of the six major groups (though still far above any of the other city banks). The numbers for LTCB and NCB remained comparable to those of the second tier of city banks though, as with IBJ, somewhat lower on a relative scale than 23 years previously. The decline in relative position could be interpreted as suggesting that a number of companies to which the long-term credit banks were leading lenders in 1967 had returned to the keiretsu group fold by 1990. However, a re-examination of the data used in Horiuchi, Packer, and Fukuda (1988) of a sample of companies continuously listed from 1963 to 1987 has unearthed no such general trend. A more likely explanation is that there is today a greater proportion of listed firms from industries in which the long-term credit banks have a relatively low representation, for example, services.

The Supply of Management Information and Resources (ϵ)

In the area of transfers of employees to director positions at related companies, a commonly used indicator of close firm-bank relationships in Japan, IBJ was, and has remained, a peer of the six group banks, while the numbers for LTCB and NCB are at a lower level comparable with the second tier of city banks. In contrast to the lead lender indicator, the relative position of this indicator has not changed greatly for IBJ, while it has grown greatly for LTCB.

Not all director positions are the same. In general, managerial authority in Japanese companies is concentrated in either the president (*shacho*) or chairman (*kaicho*) position. In terms of placement to these positions, IBJ does much better than its city bank counterparts, with 17 companies compared to 10 for the nearest city bank. Similarly, LTCB placements significantly exceed those of the second tier of city banks. This suggests IBJ has had an exceptional pool of employees from which to supply managerial resources, and lends some credibility to one of IBJ's many nicknames,

'The President-Export Bank' (*shacho yushutsu ginko*) (Osono, 1991, p. 52). IBJ's role in mediating mergers (discussed below) may also be responsible. In the case of Japan Line, an IBJ man was appointed president in part to smooth over factional disputes resulting from a 1964 merger.

Shareholding (β)

As is evident in Table 5.13, in terms of share ownership by banks looked at in isolation, IBJ is again a peer of the six group banks, being a principal financial institution shareholder at a level comparable to those of the major city banks. On the other hand, LTCB and NCB lag in stock ownership relative to the second tier of city banks. However, as the IBJ group of closely affiliated companies is not only far smaller but also does not include any of two classes of major shareholders in Japan, insurance companies and trust banks, there can be no significant comparison with the aggregate cross-shareholding proportions of the keiretsu groups. One estimate of the percentage of group company shares held by group firms ranges from 25 per cent for the Mitsubishi group to 11 per cent for the Sanwa group (*Keiretsu no Kenkyu*, 1991).

In contrast to its roles of principal lender and supplier of director personnel to related companies, the emergence of IBJ as a major bank shareholder in the Japanese economy is a relatively recent phenomenon. In the early 1960s, despite having a large number of customers, IBJ used most of its funds on lending and invested relatively little in the equity of many of its clients. Out of the 70 first section firms for which it was the lead lender in 1967, it was not a top ten shareholder for nearly one-quarter; further, it held less than 2 per cent in another fifth of the cases (*Keiretsu no Kenkyu*, 1968).

However, the shareholding role of the long-term credit banks has increased substantially to the point where IBJ overall share ownership now exceeds that of any of the city banks. By 1990, IBJ owned an average of 4.3 per cent of the first-section listed companies to which it was a top lender. In comparison with 1967, for only 4 per cent of the companies to which it is the lead lender did it not own stock, and only in another 6 per cent of the cases did it own less than 2 per cent of the company's shares.

In common with the other city banks, large shareholding stakes are not limited to companies to which it is the lead lender, but extend across a wide range of companies, many of which are owned in larger proportion by other banks.

Payment Settlement Accounts and Bond-Issue Related Services (α, τ)

A critical feature of Japan's long-term credit bank law is that while it prohibits the practice of consumer banking, it does not prohibit any of the standard banking practices which are essential to the establishment of close firm-bank ties in Japan, and constitute the different dimensions of the main bank relationship introduced in Chapter 1. We have already discussed the provision of loans, shareholding, and the supply of management information and resources. But allowed activities also include the taking of corporate deposits to facilitate payment settlement (α), bond-issue related services (τ), the two remaining aspects of the paradigmatic main bank relationship.

With regard to payment settlement (α), when required to do so, long-term credit banks are fully capable of providing the services of their city bank counterparts. Since long-term credit banks are limited to accepting deposits from corporate clients and government institutions, one rough indication of their activity in this area is the amount of deposits held: in 1960, deposits amounted to 17.7 per cent of outstanding loans by IBJ; by 1978, that percentage had increased to 33.3 per cent (IBJ, 1982, supl. vol. pp. 26–31). Another more recent and precise indication of their activity in this area can be found by looking at the identity of the paying bank of bills cleared in clearing-house data. In 1989, about 127 trillion yen of bills were presented at the Tokyo Clearing-house to be drawn on IBJ accounts, and 60 and 47 trillion yen of bills to be drawn on LTCB and NCB accounts, respectively. This compared with an average of 232 trillion for the six major city banks and 104 trillion for the other city banks (Zenginko Kyokai, 1990).[4]

Bond-issue related services (τ) are another aspect in which long-term credit banks are equally capable of solidifying the main bank relationship. Documentation concerning this point is provided by Hamao and Campbell in Chapter 10. With regard to the guarantees of straight and warrant attached bonds, as well as trustee administration for straight, convertible, and warrant bonds, IBJ, just like the six major city banks, is far more likely to be involved if it is the lead lender to the company.

---

[4] Whether the somewhat lesser importance of long-term credit banks along this dimension compared to others reflects the larger sample (bills of companies regardless of listing status), the fact that their clients may rely less on inter-firm transactions or, in fact, a weaker main bank relationship along this dimension cannot be answered without firm-specific data. What the clearing-house data do tell us, however, is that the long-term credit banks are very active as paying and collection banks in the nationwide promissory note markets.

The Importance of Ties with Vertical Groups

IBJ has a number of close relationships with the heads of large vertical groups which are either independent or only loosely affiliated with one of the six bank groups. Of course, there are many other vertical groups which lie firmly within the bank group axis as well (for example, the Mitsubishi Electric Group, the Sumitomo Metal Industries Group). Undoubtedly, firms of a vertical group whose head has a strong bank group affiliation will be more likely to have a bank from that group as its principal lender. But to what extent does membership in certain vertical groups affect the probability of having IBJ as the main bank?

In the interest of abstracting from the biases of industry specialization and size, for each company listed on the First or Second Section of the Tokyo Stock Exchange to which IBJ was identified as the principal lender in 1990, a company from the same industry (using the stock exchange's classification) was chosen which was closest to the original company in terms of net sales, but did not have a long-term credit bank as its lead lender. If no companion could be found within a factor of two, the original (IBJ-affiliated) company was dropped from the sample. Company pairs were the most difficult to construct in the electric power industry, where seven firms to which IBJ was the lead private lender were dropped from the sample.

Characteristics of the resulting sample are given in Table 5.14. Predictably, the large majority of the non-IBJ-affiliated firms have group financial institutions as their lead lender. While there do not appear to be significant differences between IBJ and non-IBJ affiliated firms in terms of financial statistics, such as the debt-equity ratio, the ratio of loans to debt, or the ratio of bonds issued to long-term liabilities, IBJ firms do have a significantly higher ratio of long-term loans to all loans. Even after controlling for size and industry, the term composition of borrowing by firms affiliated with IBJ remains distinct.

The lending shares are also of interest. While the average of IBJ loan shares to main bank clients significantly exceeds that of the individual group banks by more than 6 per cent, differences in the share figures are insignificantly different from zero when we compare them to the lending of all financial institutions in the relevant bank group. The data related to JDB lending suggest that IBJ-affiliated firms have neither an advantage nor a disadvantage when it comes to receiving JDB loans. After industry and size factors are controlled for, financing from JDB is no greater than average for IBJ-affiliated firms, particularly when compared to group bank affiliated firms. However, firms that are affiliated with a smaller city bank are less likely to have JDB funding, and firms that are independent are more likely to have JDB funding. The latter result is consistent with those of a recent paper on the impact of JDB loans, which found that the

TABLE 5.14 Comparison of IBJ Clients and Paired Sample, 31 March 1990

	Entire Sample	IBJ is Main Bank	Rest of Paired Sample	Main Bank is: Major Keiretsu Bank	Other City Bank	Unclear
Number of firms	146	73 —	73 —	54	13	6
Net sales (billion yen)	192.4	202.7 (60.3)	182.1 (52.7)	222.7	35.2	134.9
Outstanding loans (billion yen)	68.56	63.93 (24.43)	73.20 (31.08)	90.50	11.82	50.48
Loans from group as percentage of total	31.7	31.6 (2.0)	31.8 (1.9)	33.2	32.5	17.6
Loans from group bank as percentage of total	27.8	*31.4 (2.0)	24.3 (1.7)	23.1	32.5	17.0
Firms with loans from JDB	51	28 —	23 —	19	1	3
JDB loans as percentage of total (if any JDB loans)	11.9	12.0 (2.7)	11.9 (2.9)	11.0	1.3	21.1
Debt as percentage of debt + equity	69.0	67.4 (1.9)	70.6 (2.0)	70.6	73.3	64.8
Loans as percentage of debt	36.2	35.6 (2.5)	36.7 (2.5)	37.3	38.0	29.0
Long-term loans as percentage of loans	45.4	*51.5 (3.0)	39.4 (3.4)	37.4	39.8	56.6
Bonds as percentage of long-term liabilities	28.4	28.8 (3.3)	27.9 (3.6)	28.8	26.7	22.1
Number of firms affiliated with vertical group	51	26 —	25 —	21	2	2
of which lead firm in vertical group has IBJ as main bank	20	*14 —	6 —	5	0	1

See discussion in the text.

All data except number of firms are arithmetic averages of sample values.

Standard error of the mean is in parentheses.

* Difference between means of IBJ sample and rest of paired sample is statistically significant at the 5 per cent level.

Source: Nikkei data tapes. Columbia University; Keiretsu no Kenkyu (1990), section on loans, Kigyo Keiretsu Soran (1990, 1991), section on loans; Nihon no Kigyo Grupu (1991).

impact of a JDB loan on borrowing and investment is greater if the firm does not have a main bank (Horiuchi and Sui, 1993).

Turning to the importance of ties with vertical groups, the next to last column of Table 5.14 gives the number of companies that either have 20 per cent or more of their shares owned by another listed company, or are listed as belonging to the vertical group of another listed firm in *Nihon no Kigyo Grupu*, 1991. In general, the two categories are the same, though *Kigyo Grupu* does make a few important omissions as well as including a few firms that hold less than 20 per cent. The number of group affiliates differs little between IBJ and non-IBJ firms. The final column lists the number of vertical-group affiliated firms for which the group head has IBJ as the lead lender. This number is significantly larger—almost three times—for the IBJ-affiliated companies than for affiliates of the six bank keiretsu. Thus, the linkage between vertical group membership and the identity of the main bank extends to IBJ.

Aspects of the IBJ Record for Borrowing Firms in Financial Distress

Much of the main bank literature relates to the role that main banks take when a firm falls into financial distress. In particular, the next chapter explicitly addresses this issue in detail. The following provides further evidence that IBJ has acted as a main bank in this respect for a number of important cases of financial distress. We also document certain aspects of the IBJ-led resolution of financial distress that reflect its status as a bank neutral of keiretsu affiliation and with special government connections.

Active Managerial Intervention

As early in the post-war era as May 1953, Nippon Yakin Kogyo, a specialty steel manufacturer, averted bankruptcy through the support of the BOJ and a syndicate of private banks led by IBJ. In what became a case of considerable controversy, IBJ forced the president and five other directors to resign after agreeing not only that an IBJ employee be made vice president, but also that IBJ's choice—a president of a competing company in the same industry—take over as president.

Later in 1953, the Fair Trade Commission heard a suit from a Nippon Yakin Kogyo director, who charged that the management shake-up was a breach of the new anti-monopoly law. The case gained further notoriety when the *Asahi* newspaper reported charges by this same director of 'financial intimidation'. Although the FTC did not follow up on the case, it did issue a warning to IBJ that certain actions taken had been inappropriate, and minor adjustments were made in the make-up of the board (IBJ, 1982, pp. 216–18).

More than 20 years later, with an IBJ man as president, IBJ led a syndicate of banks in providing further financial assistance to this same company, mandating internal cost-cutting measures as well as organizing tie-ups and assistance from Showa Denko and Nippon Steel (Sheard, 1989, pp. 415, 419).

Nittoku Metal Industry is another renowned case. A manufacturer of small bulldozers and other industrial machinery, it was listed on the first section of the Tokyo Stock Exchange and had around 1,600 employees. In November 1964, its parent company, Nihon Special Steel, went bankrupt after its lead banks, Mitsubishi and Dai-Ichi, had rejected IBJ requests to rescue the company. In contrast, after sending a team of four employees to investigate its condition, IBJ decided to rescue the subsidiary to which it was the lead lender, supplying the necessary amounts of emergency financing, and convincing other banks to refrain from forcing default. By the next year, IBJ had located a willing partner for a joint venture, Sumitomo Machinery, which put the company back on its feet (IBJ, 1982, p. 532; for a dramatized account of the rescue, see Takasugi, 1987, vol. 2, pp. 69–107).

Another case of active intervention is machine-tool maker Ikegai Tekko in 1984. A president sent in by IBJ oversaw rationalization measures including asset disposals, and a joint venture was mediated with another firm in the industry, Tsugami (Sheard, 1989, p. 420). Both this and the previous case suggest an important supplement to IBJ managerial intervention has been the search for industrial partners to assist in the rehabilitation of the company, a feature to be examined in greater detail below.

The Search for Merger or Joint Venture Partners

Studies of the keiretsu groups often emphasize how intra-group coordination facilitates restructuring and mergers within the group (Gerlach, 1992). The main bank leadership role in this regard can be seen as substituting for an external take-over market (Sheard, 1989). While IBJ's active intervention is consistent with this interpretation, all three of the cases described above illustrate an additional element to IBJ's role: the ability to find merger or joint venture partners and negotiate with the banks and companies *of other groups*. Showa Denko's main bank was Fuji, Sumitomo Machinery's was Sumitomo, and Tsugami's was Mitsui.

IBJ's position of group neutrality in the mediation of mergers has given it an especially prominent role in periods of government-encouraged industry rationalization. In the automobile industry in the mid-1960s, IBJ played an important mediator role in the merger of Nissan and Prince, negotiating with Sumitomo Bank, the main bank of Prince (IBJ, 1982, pp. 679–81). In the drastic rationalization of the shipping industry in 1964, IBJ actively mediated two of the six mergers. One involved a firm in the Mitsubishi group; the merged firms became Japan Line, the IBJ main bank client discussed below.

Another merger involved close cooperation with Dai-Ichi Bank (*Keiretsu no Kenkyu*, 1961; IBJ, 1982, pp. 470–78). In contrast, major merger cases involving different companies of the six bank keiretsu are almost unknown. In a study of 63 major merger cases in Japan between 1953 and 1973, Iwasaki (1988, p. 503) found that only one occurred between companies of different *kigyo shudan*.

Of course, the range of IBJ main bank clients is large enough that there are often mergers and tie-ups of companies that both have IBJ as their main bank. Shortly after the Yakin Kogyo incident in 1955, IBJ assisted another specialty steel client, Daido Special Steel, in the midst of a credit crunch and mediated a merger with Shin Riken (IBJ, 1982, pp. 203–4). Though not an outright merger, after the Nissan-Prince merger IBJ later put together a significant capital alliance between Nissan and another company for which IBJ acted as the main bank, Fuji Heavy Industries (IBJ, 1982, p. 684). In the early 1970s, IBJ helped to mediate a merger between two of the largest companies in the paper and pulp business—Sanyo and Kokusaku Pulp (IBJ, 1982, p. 933).

IBJ also played a major role in the single most significant industrial merger of the post-war era, that of Yawata and Fuji Steel, to form New Japan Steel in 1969. Working in cooperation with MITI, they not only acted as an intermediator in the corporate negotiations, but also proposed the necessary spin-offs and technological agreements to satisfy the FTC, including the sale of a segment of the business to NKK, a firm to which they were a major, though not lead, lender. Throughout the highly public debate that surrounded the merger of the two largest firms in the Japanese steel industry, IBJ made a strong case for its benefits (IBJ, 1982, p. 688–705).

The Securities Industry Crisis

IBJ's special relationship with the government has also meant it is often called on to represent the private financial sector in industry crises of national significance. IBJ's central role in the Japanese economy was never more evident than during the financial crisis of the securities industry in 1964–65, which surfaced dramatically in the insolvency of Yamaichi Securities. IBJ men were brought in as presidents for all of the Big Four securities companies except Nomura. When Yamaichi's situation worsened, IBJ negotiated a rehabilitation plan which involved employee lay-offs as well as the suspension and reduction of interest payments, together with the two other lead banks of Mitsubishi and Fuji. When it became apparent that investor confidence was beyond repair without government assistance, IBJ successfully lobbied for special relief financing from the BOJ. A smaller securities firm Oi (now Wako) was saved in similar fashion, and IBJ played a further intermediary role in the merger of three troubled securities firms to form Shin Nihon Shoken. (A dramatized account of IBJ's role in the securities industry crisis is in Takasugi, 1987, vol. 4, pp. 262–98; IBJ, 1982, pp. 780–83, is its official account.)

The Case of Japan Line

The record of IBJ interventions, of course, is far longer than the few major cases briefly discussed above. Neither have large and important cases been limited to the high growth era, as the case of Japan Line, discussed by Sheard in Chapter 6, illustrates. A few aspects of this case are worthy of additional mention here.

First, the characteristic IBJ search across groups for a merger partner for Japan Line was part of the end game. The IBJ-selected merger partner was Yamashita-Shin Nihon, for which IBJ was the second largest lender and bank shareholder after Sanwa Bank. A merger followed intense negotiations with Sanwa Bank, where IBJ agreed to further write-offs of its outstanding loans as a condition of the merger.

Second, even though JDB consistently had more loans on an absolute basis than IBJ, there appears to have been little question that IBJ was the bank primarily responsible for managing the crisis, and all indications are that IBJ took the leadership role and bore a greatly disproportionate share of the losses. Outstanding JDB loans may have lent a political aspect to the case and IBJ probably was able to take advantage of this. Both during the many years of restructuring which preceded the merger, and after the merger, IBJ lobbied hard with the MOF, including personal meetings with then Finance Minister Miyazawa, to obtain permission for most of the debt write-offs to be taken as deductions from taxable income.

CONCLUSION

By providing a counterbalance to inward-looking aspects of the city bank groups, the long-term credit banks have been an important component of the main bank system. Acting at times in the capacity of independent development banks and at times in the capacity of main banks, the long-term credit banks have been heavily involved in both the financing of growing sectors and the restructuring of troubled ones. In particular, as befits its size and history, the role of IBJ has been central.

Nonetheless, it should be kept in mind that a major reason why the long-term credit banks have maintained a prominent position in the Japanese financial system—for all their ability in credit analysis and the provision of long-term funds—has been the result of law and public policy. Demand for their financial debentures has been maintained not only by the marketing efforts of the long-term credit banks, but also by limitations on the availability of competing instruments. As of the early 1990s, financial policy-makers in Japan had chosen not to present the long-term credit banks with the challenges of an unregulated domestic bond market.

The costs of these arrangements may have lain in the exclusion of certain companies from the long-term credit market, particularly in the high growth era. But the principal providers of short-term credit have been able to work with a set of institutions both knowledgeable in the valuation of the firm's prospects and familiar with the role of main banks themselves (if not in fact the company's main bank). In that the long-term credit banks allowed the major keiretsu banks to limit their own risks while retaining an ability to work closely with the principal holders of long-term claims, their role in the main bank system has been indispensable.

REFERENCES

ADAMS, T. F. M., and IWAO HOSHII. 1972. *A Financial History of the New Japan*. Tokyo: Kodansha.

AOKI, MASAHIKO, and PAUL SHEARD. 1992. 'The Role of the Main Bank in the Corporate Governance Structure in Japan.' Stanford University.

BALLON, ROBERT J. and IWAO TOMITA. 1988. *The Financial Behavior of Japanese Corporations*. New York: Kodansha.

Bank of Japan, Institute for Monetary and Economic Studies. 1986. *Wagi Kuni no Kinyu Seido*. Tokyo.

——. Various years. *Economics Statistics Annual*. Tokyo.

BERGLÖF, ERIK, and ERNST-LUDWIG VON THADDEN. 1994. 'Capital Structure with Multiple Investors.' *Quarterly Journal of Economics*.

BOLTON, PATRICK, and DAVID SCHARFSTEIN. 1994. 'A Theory of Secured Debt: Contracting with Multiple Creditors.' *Journal of Political Economy*.

BRONTE, STEPHEN. 1982. *Japanese Finance: Markets and Institutions*. London: Euromoney Publications.

COHEN, JEROME B. 1949. *Japan's Economy in War and Reconstruction*. Minneapolis: University of Minnesota Press.

CORBETT, JENNY. 1987. 'International Perspective on Financing: Evidence from Japan.' *Oxford Review of Economic Policy* 3(4).

DIAMOND, DOUGLAS. 1991. 'Debt Maturity Structure and Liquidity Risk.' *Quarterly Journal of Economics* 106(3): 709–37.

——. 1991. 'Monitoring and Reputation: The Choice between Bank Loans and Directly Placed Debt.' *Journal of Political Economy*, 99(4): 689–721.

DOI, SATOSHI. 1990. 'The Bank Debenture Market.' In Frank Fabozzi, ed., *The Japanese Bond Markets: An Overview and Analysis*. Chicago: Probus.

FELDMAN, ROBERT, YUZO HARADA, and EISUKE SAKAKIBARA. 1982. Testimony, 12 March. In Joint Economic Committee, Congress of the United States, *The Japanese Financial System in Comparative Perspective*. Washington DC.

FLANNERY, MARK J. 1986. 'Asymmetric Information and Risky Debt Maturity Choice.' *Journal of Finance* 41: 19–38.

FUKUZAWA, TOSHIHIKO. 1987. 'Deregulation of Financial Market Segmentation, Part I: The Reforms which are needed in Long- and Short-Term Segmentation.' *Fair Fact Series: Japan's Financial Markets*, vol. 13.

GERLACH, MICHAEL. 1992. *Keiretsu: A Primer.* New York: Japan Society.

GORTON, GARY, and G. PENNACHI. 1990. 'Banking and Loan Sales: Marketing Non-Marketable Assets.' Working Paper, National Bureau of Economic Research, Cambridge, MA. December.

HADLEY, ELEANOR. 1970. *Antitrust in Japan.* Princeton University Press.

HAMADA, KOICHI, and AKIYOSHI HORIUCHI. 1987. 'The Political Economy of the Financial Market.' In Kozo Yamamura and Yasukichi Yasuba, eds., *The Political Economy of Japan*, vol. 1: *The Domestic Transformation.* Stanford: Stanford University Press.

HAZAWA, OTOHIKO. 1975. *Nihon no Ruishinban: Nakayama Sohei.* Tokyo: Gekkanpensha.

HIGANO, MIKINARI. 1986. *Kinyu Kikan no Shinsa Noryoku.* Tokyo: Tokyo University Press.

HORIUCHI, AKIYOSHI, FRANK PACKER and SHIN'ICHI FUKUDA. 1988. 'What Role Has the "Main Bank" Played in Japan?' *Journal of Japanese and International Economies* 2(2): 159–80.

HORIUCHI, AKIYOSHI and QING-YUAN SUI. Forthcoming. 'Influence of Japan Development Banks Loans on Corporate Investment Behavior.' *Journal of Japanese and International Economies.*

HORIUCHI, TOSHIHIRO. 1988. *Mein Banku Kyoso to Kashidashi Shijo.* Tokyo: Toyo Keizai Shimposha.

——. 1990. 'The Adjustment and Restructuring of Japan's Synthetic Fiber Industry—Real and Financial Interdependence.' JCER-RAND paper, April.

HOSHI, TAKEO. March 1993. 'Evolution of the Main Bank System in Japan.' University of California, San Diego.

HOSHI, TAKEO, ANIL KASHYAP, and DAVID SCHARFSTEIN. 1990. 'The Role of Banks in Reducing the Costs of Financial Distress in Japan.' *Journal of Financial Economics* 27: 67–88.

Industrial Bank of Japan. 1957. *Nihon Kogyo Ginko: Goju Nenshi.* Tokyo.

——. 1982. *Nihon Kogyo Ginko: Shichijugo Nenshi.* Includes supl. vol. Tokyo.

ITOH, YOSHIAKI. 1993. 'Cracking Down on Tax Evasion.' *The Nikkei Weekly*, 15 March.

IWASAKI, AKIRA. 1988. 'Mergers and Reorganizations.' In Ryutaro Komiya, Masahiro Okuno, and Kotaro Suzumura, eds., *Industrial Policy of Japan.* San Diego: Academic Press.

Japan Company Handbook, First Section. 1991 summer ed. Tokyo: Toyo Keizai Shimposha.

Japan Development Bank. 1976. *Nihon Kaihatsu Ginko: Nijugo Nen Shi.* Tokyo.

Japan Development Bank and Japan Economic Research Institute. 1993. *Policy Based Finance: The Experience of Postwar Japan.* Tokyo. January.

Keiretsu no Kenkyo. 1968, 1991. Tokyo: Keizai Chosa Kyoka.

Kigyo Keiretsu Soran. 1990, 1991, 1992. Tokyo: Toyo Keizai Shimposha.

KIM, SUN BAE. 1991. 'Lenders cum Shareholders: How Japanese Banks Financed Rapid Growth.' PhD dissertation, University of Toronto.

KINYU SEIDO CHOSAKAI. 1987. *Senmon Kinyu Kikan Seido no Arikatani Tsuite.* Senmon Iinkai Hokoku, Tokyo.

Ministry of Finance. 1976. *Showa Zaisei-shi: Shusen kara Kowa made,* vol 12. Tokyo: Toyo Keizai Shinposha.

——. 1983. *Showa Zaisei-shi: Shusen kara Kowa made,* vol. 13. Tokyo: Toyo Keizai Shinposha.

Nihon no Kigyo Grupu. 1991. Tokyo: Toyo Keizai Shimposha.

OSONO, TOMOKAZU. 1991. *Kigyo Keiretsu to Gyokai Chizu.* Tokyo: Nihon Jitsugyo Shuppansha.

PACKER, FRANK. 1993. 'Three Essays on Banking and Corporate Finance in Japan.' PhD dissertation, Columbia University, New York.

PACKER, FRANK, and MARC RYSER. 1992. 'The Governance of Failure: An Anatomy of Corporate Bankruptcy in Japan.' Working Paper 62, Center on Japanese Economy and Business, Graduate School of Business, Columbia University, New York.

PATRICK, HUGH. 1967. 'Japan: 1868–1914.' In Rondo Cameron with others, *Banking and the Early Stages of Industrialization.* New York: Oxford University Press.

——. 1972. 'Finance, Capital Markets and Economic Growth in Japan.' In Arnold Sametz, ed., *Financial Development and Economic Growth.* New York: New York University Press.

PRESSNEL, L. S., ed. 1973. *Money and Banking in Japan.* New York: The Bank of Japan Research Department.

RAMSEYER, J. MARK. 1991. 'Legal Rules in Repeated Deals: Banking in the Shadow of Defection in Japan.' *Journal of Legal Studies* 20: 91–117.

SCHLEIFER, ANDREI, and ROBERT VISHNY. 1991. 'Asset Sales and Debt Capacity.' Working Paper 3618, National Bureau of Economic Research, Cambridge MA.

SHEARD, PAUL. 1989. 'The Main Bank System and Corporate Monitoring and Control in Japan.' *Journal of Economic Behavior and Organization* 11: 399–422.

——. 1991. 'Delegated Monitoring Among Delegated Monitors: Principal-Agent Aspects of the Japanese Main Bank System.' Center for Economic Policy Research Publication 274, Stanford University, Stanford CA, November.

SHIMURA, KIICHI. 1978. *Gendai Nihon Koshasairon.* Tokyo: Tokyo University Press.

——. 1980. *Nihon Koshasai Shijoshi.* Tokyo: Tokyo University Press.

SUZUKI, SADAHIKO, and RICHARD WRIGHT. 1985. 'Financial Structure and Bankruptcy Risk in Japan.' *Journal of International Business Studies* 16: 97–110.

SUZUKI, YOSHIO, ed. 1987. *The Japanese Financial System.* Oxford: Clarendon Press.

TACHIBANAKI, TOSHIAKI, and ATSUHIRO TAKI. 1991. 'Shareholding and Lending Activity of Financial Institutions in Japan.' *Monetary and Economic Studies,* vol 9. Tokyo: Bank of Japan, Institute for Monetary and Economic Studies.

TAKASUGI, RYO. 1987. *Shosetsu: Nihon Kogyo Ginko.* 5 vols. Tokyo: Kodansha.

TAKENAKA, ICHIRO. 1968. *Choki Kinyu Kiko no Bunseki.* Tokyo: Toyo Keizai.

TANIKAWA, HIROSHI, DAVID ALLAN, MARY HISCOCK, and DEREK ROEBUCK. 1973. *Credit and Security in Japan: The Legal Problems of Development Finance.* New York: Crane, Russak.

TERANISHI, JURO. 1982. *Nihon no Keizai Hatten to Kinyu*. Tokyo: Iwaba Shoten.

YASUDA, AYAKO. 1993. *The Performance and Roles of Japanese Development Banks*. Seniors Honors Thesis, Department of Economics, Stanford University.

ZENGINKO KYOKAI RENGOKAI. 1990. *Tegata Kokan Tokei Nenpo*. Tokyo: Tokyo Ginko Kyokai.

6

Main Banks and the Governance of Financial Distress

PAUL SHEARD

Perhaps the most striking aspect of the main bank system is the role that the main bank plays when client firms encounter financial adversity. In such cases, the actions of the main bank take on their most direct, intense, and arguably important form, going beyond the kinds of arm's-length information-gathering activities normally connoted by the term 'monitoring'. Sometimes the banks launch so-called 'rescue' operations, as in the famous Mazda case, in other cases they put together refinancing packages similar to a workout specialist in the United States, and in some cases they engineer a major restructuring or liquidation, akin to a privatized version of Chapter 11 or Chapter 7 bankruptcy in the United States. On occasion, a major listed firm will file for bankruptcy under the Corporate Reorganization Law (Kaisha koseiho), but usually this follows a period of close involvement by the main bank in its restructuring effort and is triggered by the bank's decision to curtail its activist role and rising financial exposure.

A number of interesting questions can be asked about the main bank's role in the governance of financial distress. Why does the main bank take on the role that it does? Does its behaviour merely reflect its incentives as a creditor and equity holder with a large financial exposure, or does it reflect a form of implicit contract between the bank and the firm—or indirectly, managers and employees who may be locked into long-term relations with the firm—or between the main bank and other lenders to

This chapter is based on work undertaken as Visiting Scholar at the Institute for Monetary and Economic Studies, the Bank of Japan; the Institute of Social and Economic Research, Osaka University; and the Foundation for Advanced Information Research, Japan. The research was supported by the Economic Development Institute at the World Bank; the Program on the Economy of Japan at the Center for Economic Policy Research, Stanford University; the International Cooperation (Osaka Gas) research fund at Osaka University; and by a grant from the Daiwa Bank Foundation for Asia and Oceania. The author would like to thank these organizations for their generous research support, and the many Japanese businessmen and officials who kindly provided their time and assistance in interviews, particularly Keiichi Ebisawa and Ken'ichi Iriyama. The author also benefited greatly from the comments of Koichi Hamada, Takeo Hoshi, Kensuke Hotta, Kazuo Matsui, Frank Packer, Mark Ramseyer, Minoru Sawai, Satoshi Sunamura, Dimitri Vittas, other participants in the project workshops and seminars at the Australian National University, the Bank of Japan, Chuo University, and the University of Tokyo, and especially Masahiko Aoki and Hugh Patrick. Any deficiencies, however, are the author's sole responsibility.

provide a form of capital market public good? Does the main bank system provide a less costly and more effective way of handling the problems of financial distress than other more market-oriented (take-over) or administrative (formal bankruptcy) processes? If the main bank 'rescues' its corporate borrowers when they fail, does this imply that it gives the firm a 'soft budget constraint' that weakens the incentives of managers (Kornai, 1980)? If not, how does the main bank system counteract such a tendency? This chapter assembles evidence from the high growth period in the 1960s to the present on the role of the main bank in the governance of financial distress, with the aim of casting light on these and related questions.

ECONOMICS OF FINANCIAL DISTRESS

It is useful to distinguish among five different aspects of financial distress.[1] One is how existing claims on the firm are settled. Financial distress occurs when a firm cannot meet its contracted obligations, meaning that decisions need to be made about who will receive the available returns. (In empirical studies—for example, Asquith, Gertner, and Scharfstein (1991) and Hoshi, Kashyap, and Scharfstein (1990b)—it is defined in terms of operating income being insufficient to cover interest income over a given period.) A second issue is what happens to the firm as a collection of physical, human, and intangible assets. The firm may continue as a going concern, usually after some restructuring, or it may be liquidated, with the assets of the firm being reallocated elsewhere through various secondary markets. A third aspect is what happens to the existing management of the firm. If the firm is liquidated, they lose their jobs, but if it is restructured, whether to replace the existing management becomes an important issue. A fourth aspect concerns how the firm raises new funds either for bridging purposes or for new investments. Even though the firm cannot meet current obligations, it may nonetheless have profitable investment opportunities or it may need bridging finance in order to remain in operation while it undertakes the time-consuming task of liquidating its assets. The fifth important aspect of financial distress concerns the choice of governance regime, between some form of

---

[1] A seminal paper in the literature on financial distress is Bulow and Shoven (1978) and recent contributions are Aghion and Bolton (1992), Bolton and Scharfstein (1990), Diamond (1990, 1991), Gertner and Scharfstein (1991), Hart and Moore (1989, 1990, 1991), and Shleifer and Vishny (1991); recent empirical work includes Asquith, Gertner, and Scharfstein (1991), Franks and Torous (1989), Gilson, Kose, and Lang (1990), Gilson (1990), Weiss (1990), and Wruck (1990). There has also been recently an active debate among legal scholars about appropriate legal institutions for dealing with financial distress; see, for example, Baird (1986), Jackson (1986), and Korobkin (1991), and for an economic analysis Aghion, Hart, and Moore (1992).

court-based bankruptcy or resolution on the one hand and an informal process of negotiation and settlement on the other.

The distinction between the *governance* aspect of corporate failure and the *asset reorganization* aspect is a critical one. The issue of how the process of financial distress is governed is distinct analytically and in practice from the issue of what happens to the firm as a collection of assets, as a legal entity, and as an economic organization, although the two clearly interact. The assets of a firm may be sold off piece-meal or together, or not at all, and this can happen under formal bankruptcy or in an informal resolution of claims. Liquidation can occur without formal bankruptcy proceedings, and a bankrupt firm or firm undergoing reorganization need not dispose of assets on a large scale. There is though some presumption of correlation; for instance, Chapter 7 bankruptcy in the United States is designed for liquidation of bankrupt enterprises, and Chapter 11 is meant for continuation.

A feature of the main bank system is that, unlike formal bankruptcy, the process is handled informally without recourse to the courts and without a change in the legal standing of the firm: in effect, the main bank replaces the judge and the court-appointed receiver; but like bankruptcy a range of asset reorganization outcomes is possible, not just restructuring of the enterprise and continuation as a going concern—as the popular term 'bank rescues' connotes—but also varying degrees of liquidation.

Stiglitz (1985) has pointed out that monitoring, take-overs, and other activities that improve the performance of the firm are a kind of local public good in that the benefits accrue to all the firm's security-holders. Financial distress and corporate reorganization, even fully fledged liquidation, are events where the public good aspects of monitoring, control, and management are probably most pronounced. An issue is who should provide the public good of sorting the affairs of the firm out, or overseeing the process, and what incentives they should be given. Legal bankruptcy, involving the oversight of a court or appointment of a receiver, can be viewed as one response to the problem, the main bank system as it operates in Japan as another.

Two important issues relate to information and incentives. Information plays a critical role in the process of financial distress. The capital market, observing the firm's failure, faces a 'signal extraction' problem, both with respect to the quality of the firm's management and the value of its assets. A firm may suffer financial distress as a result of the failure of its ventures, business failure, or because it is suffering a temporary set-back, a cash flow crisis. Even if financial distress reflects past failure, the firm may face good prospects. Two key issues for the capital market are: should the firm be refinanced, and possibly reorganized, to continue as an operating unit, or should its operations be wound up and its assets sold off, the liquidation option? If the former option is preferred, should the incumbent management remain or be replaced by a new management team? These decisions rest on the inferences that the capital market is able to draw from the available information, including that presented to it—perhaps in strategic, self-interested form—by incumbent management itself.

It is desirable that the party overseeing the process, the supplier of the public good in Stiglitz's terms, has good information about the firm's situation and prospects in order to make the right decisions: for instance, which assets to sell and which to keep, which operations to cut back and which to expand, which ideas coming from within the organization are of value and which are not, and so on. A feature of the main bank system is that the bank has already accumulated a significant stock of information as a key financier and *ex ante* monitor of the firm. A drawback of the legal solution is that the judge or receiver in general could not be expected to have good information, particularly of a firm-specific kind, which in general is the most valuable kind for making value-enhancing decisions.

A key idea in the literature is that conflicts of interest are acute and may lead to inefficiencies in the reorganization process. Conflicts of interest are likely to exist between different classes of security holder, usually debt and equity holders, between security holders and incumbent management, and between security holders and the general work force. One merit of the legal solution is that the supplier of the public good is, ostensibly at least, neutral in the bargaining and settlement process. The main bank is not neutral—it is one of the main parties affected by the whole process—but, as argued below, it appears to have good incentives to manage the process well.

An important aspect of financial distress is that existing claims cannot be met; some form of renegotiation needs to take place in order to bring the claims of security holders into line with economic values. Interestingly, such renegotiations are not necessary for 'soft claims' (Hart and Moore, 1990, p. 2) such as equity because the commitment by the firm is to pay a residual. Unless firms can renegotiate their claims, they may be unable to finance profitable investments because the suppliers of new funds are not able to internalize the full return; instead part may accrue to holders of senior claims as a 'beneficial externality' (Myers, 1977). (Of course, a trivial solution is for the investment to be financed by holders of existing senior claims, thereby internalizing the externality, but for various reasons this may not be feasible in particular real-world cases of interest.) One way to remove the debt overhang and realize the efficiencies is for the existing holders of fixed obligations to write down their claims.

Although it may be efficient to renegotiate *ex post*, it may not be so viewed *ex ante*. In a world of managerial moral hazard, achieving *ex ante* efficiency may call for harsh actions to be imposed *ex post*, such as cutting off finance to a failing firm or penalizing senior managers. *Ex post*, however, it may be efficient to 'let bygones be bygones' and refinance the firm or let the existing management stay in control, particularly if they have valuable firm-specific skills.

The security structure of the firm has an influence on whether financial distress is likely to occur, and if it does, how affected parties react. An important issue is the extent of dispersion or concentration in the security structure. In general, the greater the number of different security classes and the more dispersed the security holdings, the harder it will be to effect efficient renegotiation, unless there is a well-developed market in which the securities, or the votes which attach to them, can be traded and so concentration of holdings can be achieved *ex post*. However, such a market may not operate well for financially distressed firms if information asymmetries are severe (see Mailath and Postlewaite, 1990). On the other hand, a more dispersed security structure, to the extent that it makes *ex post* renegotiation difficult, may have desirable *ex ante* incentive properties; for a concentrated structure the reverse is true.

The maturity structure of claims (short-term versus long-term debt) and the priority structure (senior versus junior claims) also influence events. This insight comes from the literature on the endogenous design of securities—Grossman and Hart (1988), Harris and Raviv (1989), Zender (1991)—and from Diamond (1990, 1991). If the firm has a lot of short-term debt, it is more likely to fall into the technical condition of financial distress for a given maturity of investment. As Diamond (1990) analyses, the seniority of the short-term security can influence what happens in financial distress through its effect on the incentives of the security holders to liquidate the firm or allow it to be refinanced. In particular, when junior in priority, there is less incentive to force liquidation, given that a junior claim is less likely to be repaid, and its option value—which is positive only under continuation—is relatively more valuable.

Three features of the main bank system are particularly relevant in the light of these analytical insights. First, banks straddle the various security classes, holding both equities and loans in significant blocks, and also bonds when these are involved. Second, the security structure is relatively concentrated with the main bank and a small number of banks holding a significant block of the securities, but more importantly, with the main bank acting as a kind of delegated agent for security holders as a whole. Third, Japanese firms traditionally relied heavily on short-term borrowing, and the prominent main banks have specialized more in short-term lending and, at least according to convention, being main bank implies accepting a more junior status in loan priority.[2]

─────────────

[2] In 1975, 45.2 per cent of outstanding loans and discounts of city banks were of three months or shorter duration, compared to 4.5 per cent for long-term credit banks; 92.3 per

THE MAIN BANK'S ROLE IN FINANCIAL DISTRESS

Evidence on the main bank's role when client firms are in financial distress is presented in the Appendix, which contains details of 42 cases covering a 30-year period. Of these, 19 are from the high growth period and are associated with the 'recession' and stock market downturn in the mid-1960s; 9 cases are from the period of slow-down in economic growth and adjustment to the oil-price hikes from the mid-1970s, and 14 cases are recent ones in the wake of the bursting of the asset bubble since the late 1980s. More examples for the 1970s can be found in Sheard (1985, 1989a) and for non-listed firms in the recent period in Sheard (1992).

The characteristics of the corporate failures and the nature of the main bank's role differ from period to period, but the commonalities outweigh the differences. Although the details differ, and not all aspects are necessarily found in a particular case, the overall picture is one of the main bank coordinating, overseeing, and, in some cases, taking charge of an informal reorganization of the firm. In a typical case, existing debt is refinanced (principal repayments deferred and interest payments shelved or exempted) and some bridging finance may be provided; directors, and in major cases a team of middle-manager trouble-shooters who work closely with promising managers in the firm, will be sent in; senior incumbent managers—typically key individuals such as a long-time president and/or owner-founder figure—will be demoted or displaced; a large-scale rationalization plan will be drawn up and implemented, usually featuring a programme of asset disposals, repayment of bank borrowings, and organizational restructuring, ranging from changes in the internal decision-making process to merger or absorption by another firm. These aspects are examined in detail below.

Main banks provide a flexible, informal alternative to bankruptcy proceedings for managing the problems of financial distress and asset reorganization. Bankruptcies *do* occur in Japan, however. In 1990, 6,468 firms with liabilities of 10 million yen or more went into some form of bankruptcy, most commonly due to bank transactions being suspended after successive defaulting on trade bills; in 1984, the figure reached 20,841 bankrupt firms (Packer and Ryser, 1992, p. 57). However, most bankruptcies in Japan involve small unlisted firms. In 1990, 73 per cent of corporate bankruptcies involved firms with 50 million yen or less in paid-in

---

cent of long-term credit bank loans were of one year or longer duration, compared to 26.5 per cent for city banks (Bank of Japan, 1983, pp. 125–26). This specialization according to loan terms has weakened in recent years with changes in corporate financing patterns and loosening of regulations: in 1991, 9.9 per cent of city bank loans were of three months or shorter duration, compared to 7.7 per cent for long-term credit banks, whereas 79.7 per cent of long-term credit bank loans were of one year or longer duration, compared to 57.2 per cent for city banks (Bank of Japan, 1992, pp. 129–30).

capital and a further 25 per cent were unincorporated enterprises; only 27 firms with more than 100 million yen in paid-in capital (0.4 per cent of the total) went bankrupt (Packer and Ryser, 1992, p. 59).

In particular, the Corporate Reorganization Law, roughly the equivalent of US Chapter 11 proceedings, is not extensively employed in Japan: in 1990 there were 6 cases, and in high years some 20 to 40 (Packer and Ryser, 1992, p. 57). Bankruptcies among firms listed on the stock exchange are even more unusual, although not unknown. In the 12 years 1971–82, 31 listed firms went bankrupt, most of them filing under the Corporate Reorganization Law (there were about 1,600 listed firms in 1972, and 1,755 in 1982). Usually, these were less prominent firms and those seen as having weak or non-existent main bank ties or poor relations with their main bank. For example, the failure of pulp and paper manufacturer Kojin in 1975 appears to fall into the latter category, while trading company J. Osawa & Co., and sewing-machine maker Riccar in 1984 are in the former (Sheard, 1985).

As the Appendix shows, there have been a few cases where large listed firms with identifiable main banks have gone bankrupt: Nihon Special Steel and Sanyo Special Steel among the early cases, Eidai Industries and Sanko Steamship among others in the 1970s and 80s, and Daiichibo among recent cases. Informal reorganization with main bank oversight or intervention, however, seems to be the common way of handling the failure of large listed firms in Japan.

Renegotiation of Claims

Because a financially distressed firm cannot meet its contracted obligations, some renegotiation is necessary, assuming unilateral action is not taken by either creditors or the firm (such as suing or filing for bankruptcy). Such renegotiation of debt claims takes place in Japan under the guise of the lending financial institutions providing financial assistance (*kin'yu shien* or *kin'yu enjo*) to the distressed firm.

The renegotiation can take many forms, ranging from refinancing or rolling over of existing debt as it becomes due, even though the collateral backing of the debt has deteriorated, to the much more drastic option of forgiving principal repayments. There are two kinds of debt renegotiation: deferral, either of principal repayments or interest payments, and forgiveness, either a reduction in the required interest rate or, in extreme cases, forgiving of loans. The latter usually happens in cases of bankruptcy, either of a legal kind or following suspension of bank transactions, but it sometimes occurs in cases of informal main bank-led reorganization.

A common measure is for the principal repayments to be frozen, and deferrals or partial exemptions of interest payments to be granted for a specified period. Frequently there is a temporal progression through the various forms of assistance as the firm's plight goes from bad to worse. This might begin with a rolling over of debt, progress to the freezing of principal repayments and the granting of interest rate reductions, and end up with the banks having to write off loans as bad debts.

There is evidence of some form of financial assistance being given in 14 of the 19 cases from the 1960s, 5 of the 9 cases from the 1970s and 80s, and all of the 14 recent cases. Examples of bank loan write-offs occurring out of bankruptcy include Sumitomo and Kyowa's write-offs when Ataka failed, and Sumitomo's write-off due to Itoman, IBJ's write-off in the Japan Line case, Tokyo's write-off on loans to Fuji Kosan (see Appendix), and for a non-listed firm Nippon Credit's write-off in the Kurujima Dockyard case (Sheard, 1992, p. 58).

The main bank plays a pivotal role in debt renegotiations in two ways. First, it arranges the package. It is the bank that does most of the direct dealing with the firm, and in turn liaises with, and tries to extract agreement from, other lenders. Second, the main bank typically provides a higher degree of financial assistance than other lenders, for example by giving a larger interest rate exemption than other banks or by assuming a larger share of any write-offs; in some cases it is the only one to do so.

The details of financial relief vary from case to case, but a kind of pecking order is often in evidence corresponding roughly to status in the segmented banking system. Other city banks and long-term credit banks with large loan shares often give concessions similar to those of the main bank; banks further down the hierarchy with smaller loan shares, such as regional and shinkin banks or those with special regulatory status such as insurance companies or agricultural cooperatives, may resist giving interest reductions, but be persuaded to maintain their loans balances. The main bank thus is able to prevent a run on the firm's loan balances, but often at the cost of providing big concessions itself.

As an example, in the Nihon Housing Loan case, in early 1993 the Norin Chukin agricultural bank and various agricultural cooperative financial institutions with a combined loan share of 38.5 per cent in the company's 2,315.2 million yen borrowings agreed only to an interest concession—a reduction to 4.5 per cent—after many months of protracted negotiation. They were reported to have done so on the condition that they would not suffer any losses on principal and would receive priority on repayments, and only after Sanwa, Sakura and the seven other banks agreed to forgo interest completely on their loans (*Nikkei*, 29 January 1993, p. 1; 19 February 1993, p. 7).

Some further aspects of renegotiation of debt claims are as follows: renegotiation takes place among institutions not individuals, there being no equivalent of the public exchange offer; renegotiations are often renegotiated, with updating, revision, and fine-tuning of debt-repayment plans, including the interest rate; the renegotiation process is largely informal, taking place at meetings of loan officers at the main bank head-quarters or by telephone or in person in informal settings, although occasionally, in cases involving major corporations, the main bank holds an explanatory meeting for other financial institutions in a hotel conference room; there is minimal involvement of outside legal specialists but, in major cases, close communication between the main bank and the financial authorities (Ministry of Finance and Bank of Japan).

It might be asked what the reason is for having 'hard' claims like bank borrowings with contractually fixed repayments and interest payments to begin with if debts are going to be renegotiated in times of financial distress? (This is really part of a much bigger question—what determines capital structure—which is one of the key research agendas and organizing themes in financial economics (see Myers, 1989).) One answer is that such renegotiations, in the 'shadow of bankruptcy', bring the providers of capital face to face with management and give them the opportunity and means to mandate changes that they would not necessarily have under other 'softer' security structures (Jensen, 1986). The renegotiation of claims alone may not be as important as the opportunity this gives the capital market, through the intervention of the main bank, to effect changes in the firm's operations, management, and make-up.

Supply of New Capital

The main bank often plays a major role in arranging new capital for a firm by supplying emergency funds itself or by organizing cooperative finance with a small group of banks. Case study evidence suggests lower-level financial institutions seldom participate in new funding to a distressed firm. In particular, foreign banks operating in Japan and credit associations and second-tier regional banks frequently bow out at the time of debt restructuring. There are two interpretations: that the principal players are better off reducing the number of creditors and getting marginal minor players out of the action, on the grounds that they are more trouble than they are worth; or that the latter are more spot-market oriented and less prone to longer-term commitment-based banking relations (Mayer, 1988); that is, is their departure a case of being pushed or being pulled? In any case, the most the main bank can expect from them is to maintain their loan balances and give some interest rate relief.

There is some basic economic logic that suggests this outcome. Incremental finance to a distressed company is perhaps the riskiest kind of bank financing because there is little prospect of securing collateral, and the lending is presumably the most junior claim on the firm. (This provides one of the attractive features of some forms of legal bankruptcy, the ability to attract new finance by the granting of senior priority status.) A creditor with many claims sunk in the firm, like the main bank, may have the incentive to supply additional finance because it is able to circumvent the debt overhang problem. A creditor with superior information about the firm, like the main bank, may have incentives to supply additional funds, compared to less well-informed creditors. Of course, its better information may warn that refinancing is not a good idea, in which case it may decide to arrange for a winding-up of the firm in its current form (examples are Ataka, Eidai Industries, and Sanko Steamship, in the Appendix). In either case, for the adverse selection kind of reason discussed below, it may be that the main bank is trapped by its superior information.

One possibility is that when the main bank supplies new finance it does not necessarily do so as the most junior claim. Mark Ramseyer (personal communication) has suggested that, because it is managing the process as an insider, the main bank may be able to arrange for its junior claims to rise in the implicit seniority ranking, because it arranges the way repayments are made. Sheard (1994a) argues that the danger of this kind of agency problem gives rise to institutional arrangements and conventions that effectively subordinate the main bank's claims; there is extensive anecdotal and case study evidence consistent with this interpretation.

Dispatch of Managers

The main bank does more than supervise the firm as an arm's-length monitor in the capital market. Frequently, the main bank dispatches executives into senior managerial positions in the firm, often into decision-making posts such as president, vice-president, or senior executive director in charge of finance or corporate planning.[3] There is evidence of such director dispatches in 16 of the 19 cases for the 1960s, all of the 9 for the 1970s and 80s, and for 9 of the recent 14 cases listed in the Appendix. In 4 of the 5 recent cases where a new dispatch did not occur, there was already one or more senior executive director from the bank in the firm.

By placing its own executives in senior management positions in the firm, the main bank is better able to audit the firm's financial position and monitor the progress of restructuring than it can as an arm's-length monitor. In this way the main bank can become an active participant in the corporate reorganization process, able to direct and implement various measures. As suggested by Aoki (1990, pp. 16–17), this aspect of the main bank's role is reminiscent of Aghion and Bolton's (1992) characterization of bankruptcy through the debt contract as shifting control from

---

[3] Morck and Nakamura (1992), Kaplan and Minton (1994), and Sheard (1994c) are interesting quantitative studies; also see Sheard (1985, 1989a) for earlier discussion and evidence.

the inside manager to the outside investor—in this case, the main bank. As the discussion below shows, the main bank, when in control of the company under reorganization in this way, seems to implement measures that the incumbent management was either unwilling or unable to do.

In some cases, the bank has existing former officers in the firm, who entered at earlier points in time. However, the auditing and monitoring capacity they provide is not a perfect substitute for that provided by the new dispatchees. Two reasons are: they may have quite different capacities, having entered the firm earlier in a different context, for a different purpose; second, as several recent cases—notably the Itoman scandal— show, the incumbent former bank directors themselves are part of the management team that is now subject to potential monitoring, disciplining, and overhaul.

It is often claimed that the dispatch of a director by the main bank to a troubled firm signals other lenders that the main bank is prepared to support the firm. One way to interpret this is that the main bank tries to send a signal, in the sense of communicating some piece of information, to the other banks. Of itself, this is not very convincing, as the bank can communicate directly, presumably at lower cost and with more precision. Indeed, it is common for the main bank to organize a meeting of major creditors at its head office, or in some cases, to hold a briefing at a major hotel.

The more plausible argument is that the dispatch of directors gives *commitment* value to whatever signal (information) the bank is trying to convey. If the signal is 'as long as you [other lenders] cooperate, we—as main bank—will not abandon the firm, or if we do, we will not do it at your *undue* cost', the sending of the director can be viewed as making that implicit commitment a more credible one. Just why dispatching a director has such commitment value is a subtle issue, a detailed analysis of which is not attempted here. One possibility is that by dispatching directors the bank makes it more prone to administrative suasion by the regulatory authorities to honour various implicit codes of behaviour as a main bank, as some recent examples involving finance companies seem to indicate.

If the main bank was contemplating pulling the plug on the company, it is unlikely that it would dispatch a director just before doing so. This is what happened, however, to Nihon Special Steel, Maruko, and eventually in the Eidai Industries and Sanko Steamship. In these cases, it is plausible to believe that, rather than being driven by strategic considerations, the decision to cut off finance occurred as a result of information uncovered by the dispatch.

Another possibility is that even if signalling is not the principal purpose, the main bank's intervention might imply the firm's prospects have improved and other lenders may be less likely to withdraw their finance as a result. It might be argued that if the main bank is aware that the other lenders will infer something from its actions, then it may have an incentive to manipulate these beliefs to its advantage, that is, to engage in some form of strategic behaviour. This seems far-fetched in this case as the dispatch of the director has a substantive purpose, as detailed below and in the Appendix, suggesting that any signalling effect is complementary to that.

Formulation of a Recovery Plan

Whenever financial institutions allow a firm to renegotiate its borrowings, they require it to present a recovery plan (*saiken keikaku*). The plan usually sets out the measures the firm intends to take in order to recover from its financial problems: rationalization of problem assets; organizational changes; and often reducing the work force. It contains estimates of future cash flows, timing and size of borrowing repayments, as well as details of any requests for debt concessions and interest relief.

The main bank plays a central role in the formulation and approval of this plan. In some cases, its role is more arm's-length, scrutinizing and improving the firm's plan before giving its approval and seeking that of other lenders. In other cases, the bank plays a more pro-active role in formulating and implementing the plan through the directors and trouble-shooter team it dispatched to the firm.

There are two plausible economic interpretations of the main bank's role. One is the delegated monitoring argument, noted earlier, that the bank's input is a form of (local) public good: the main bank system ensures that it is supplied, but avoids unnecessary duplication (Sheard, 1994a). The second is that by delegating the task of negotiation to a single bank, creditors as a whole are better able to commit to certain actions. (There is an analogy to the industrial organization literature where competitors can channel their interaction through a common agent (marketing agent) in order to enhance credibility of their commitments (facilitate collusion); Bernheim and Whinston, 1985.) Even if the main bank is prone to bailing out or soft budgeting, it can argue that other lenders will not provide assistance unless certain measures are taken. Creditors can resist being picked off in one-on-one negotiations by insisting on negotiating indirectly through the main bank. It should be noted, however, that although the main bank tries to obtain widespread agreement from other creditor financial institutions, because the process is informal there is no requirement that agreement be unanimous.

Financial assistance, or renegotiation of debts, is made contingent on approval of the plan. Frequently, this involves hard negotiations, both between the main bank and the firm, and the main bank and other creditors. The main bank often requires that certain restructuring measures be taken as a condition of its approving the plan. It is not unusual for agreement on wider assistance to a firm to be delayed by non-main banks arguing that more drastic measures be taken or that the main bank carry a larger share of the burden. The main bank runs the risk that if it does not accede to other creditors' pressures to extract further concessions from the firm, it may be left to shoulder an increased financial burden itself as other banks withdraw their finance or refuse to provide interest reductions, or being seen as a main bank that forced a client into bankruptcy. This pressure in turn makes its own bargaining power over the firm even stronger. The fact that the main bank has to carry other creditors with it increases its incentives to extract tough concessions from the firm; and the fact that failure to secure agreement from other creditors will greatly increase its own burden may make credible its threat to abandon (not refinance) a firm that resists the measures. This, in turn, induces most firms to cooperate.

Although there is a sense in which the main bank acts on behalf of other creditors, there is always concealed tension in the relationship. There is a tendency for creditors to be exigent with the main bank, appealing to the higher level of responsibility that being main bank implies. Frequently, such disputes between the main bank and creditors are arbitrated in behind-the-scenes negotiations involving the banking authorities (as with the interest concessions and debt rescheduling of the housing finance companies).

Trade creditors are an important category, with bank and institutional lenders, in Japan. A firm's major direct trade creditors are usually one or more of the general trading companies (*sogo shosha*) (Sheard, 1989b). Extensions of credit by trade creditors are generally short term (although, like bank loans, they may be rolled over); they tend to be unsecured or, if secured, it is by inventory. Trade creditors are on the one hand vulnerable in cases of bankruptcy, but on the other can recover their credits relatively easily. An attempt to recover their credit would either precipitate the firm's bankruptcy or result in the main bank having to provide the shortfall. An important concern of the main bank, therefore, is to maintain the flow of trade credit to the firm, which is presumably why main banks often express support for distressed firms.

Trading companies are generally happy to see the firm stay out of bankruptcy as this secures their own claims. For example, senior executives of Mitsui & Co., Mitsubishi Corporation, and C. Itoh, with claims of 6.6 billion yen, were reported to have visited the banks three days after Sanyo Special Steel filed for bankruptcy, and strongly urged them to restructure the company informally (*Nikkei*, 10 March 1965, p. 7). Trading companies often provide assistance in tandem with the main bank and other creditors (examples in the Appendix include Osaka Iron & Steel, Fuji Car, Mamiya Camera, Mazda, and Itoman). Sometimes they play a somewhat similar role to main banks in restructuring affiliated companies (Sheard, 1986), and some of the notable cases of main bank interventions and rescues have involved trading companies (Gosho and, later, Kanematsu-Gosho, Tsusho, Ataka, and Itoman).

Some level of work force reduction is a central component of many restructuring plans, and sometimes it is quite drastic in scale. Permanent employment does not mean that Japanese firms can avoid having to reduce the work force when their business is under threat, although it does place constraints on how they do so. In some cases a concern for employment security—or managerial reluctance to bite the retrenchment bullet—may be a factor accelerating the advent of financial distress. Main bank rescues do not generally preserve jobs that are no longer economically viable, although the higher degree of protection of workers' rights to jobs, or contingent claim on adjustment assistance, implicit in Japanese management and employment practices, may increase the costs of liquidation to the firm and to its creditors. Aoki (1994) provides an interesting theoretical analysis of the relationship between main bank intervention and the employment system.

In formulating a rationalization plan that involves work force reductions, negotiations with the company union will be necessary and its agreement and cooperation secured. As might be expected, unions sometimes resist, but full-blown labour disputes are rare; this may reflect the cooperative ethos of management-labour relations in contemporary Japan, but it is just as likely due to the weak bargaining position a union finds itself in when its employer faces imminent failure.

The union did take a stand in the Japan Line case; this is instructive as this is the only major industry in Japan with an industry-craft union. The Japan Seamans' Union opposed the plan that Japan Line devised in tandem with its major assisting banks in early 1986—which included a further reduction of 850 in the work force—by lodging a restraining order against the company in the Tokyo District Court. In response, Japan Line president Kataoka Seishiro held a press conference stating his fears that if the union continued its opposition the banks would not provide the 100 billion yen in bridging finance required to complete the company's restructuring; the union appears then to have backed down. (See *Nikkei*, 5 March 1986 evening edition, p. 3; 6 March 1986, p. 11; 29 August 1986, p. 11.) Kataoka was well qualified to offer a view on the banks' likely reaction as he had been dispatched to Japan Line as vice-president in 1980 by the company's main bank, the Industrial Bank of Japan, where he was senior managing director.

Another case is Ataka & Co., a massive corporate failure that prompted a large-scale intervention by Sumitomo Bank, leading to liquidation of assets and partial absorption of one-third of the company by C. Itoh and other parts by Itoman, Okura & Co., and Sumitomo

Forestry. The Ataka company union opposed Sumitomo's intervention and the merger with C. Itoh, demanding that Sumitomo and Kyowa pull out the 16 advisors they had dispatched to the company and calling on the Ministers of Labour, Finance, and International Trade and Industry to intervene. Later the union dropped its opposition to the merger, focusing its efforts on securing employment and re-employment assistance guarantees. (*Nikkei*, 23 January 1976, p. 7; 30 January 1976, p. 7; 2 February 1976, p. 7; 13 February 1976, p. 7; 14 February 1976, p. 6; 23 February 1976, p. 2.)

Removal of Top Management

A common feature of main bank intervention is the removal of incumbent managers, such as the president, chairman or senior directors. In some cases, such managers are forced out of the company, in other cases they may remain on the board but be removed from front-line decision making.

The top executive often is an owner-founder or associated figure, who has long exerted control over decision-making; Sheard (1994c) found that the president was an inside-owner (a founder or founding family figure) in 25 per cent of all listed firms in Japan in 1991. In the Daishowa Paper case in 1982, the main bank, Sumitomo, succeeded in replacing Saito Ryoei, eldest son of the founder and president of the company since 1961, with his brother (then a member of the Diet) (Sheard, 1985), although after the company's recovery, in an unusual turn of events, Saito Ryoei reasserted control and the company broke off its main bank relation with Sumitomo (Sentaku, 1986). In a further twist, not directly related, but instructive about the issues of corporate monitoring and governance nonetheless, Saito Ryoei, by this time honorary chairman of Daishowa, was arrested in 1993 on charges of having paid a 100 million yen bribe to the (previously arrested) governor of Miyagi prefecture to relax a planning control and expedite a development request (*Nikkei*, 11 November 1993 evening edition, p. 1).

In the Mazda case in 1975, Matsuda Kohei, the founder's grandson who succeeded his father as president in 1970, remained president (until the tie-up with Ford in 1978) in a nominal role, while control rested with the vice-president and other managers sent in from Sumitomo (for details see Pascale and Rohlen, 1983; Sheard, 1985). In the Itoman case, Sumitomo forced the resignation of the president who, ironically, was a former Sumitomo executive director dispatched as president in 1975 in an earlier phase of financial distress.

Asset Sales and Recovery of Debts

A key part of reorganization under main bank supervision or management is the implementation of a plan of asset sales with proceeds typically used to recover bank loans. A programme of asset disposals is usually the centre-piece of the recovery plan. It can take on many different forms depending on the circumstances, industry, type of assets, and so on. Two kinds of asset disposal can be identified: disposal of assets at the core of the corporate failure, such as excess capacity to be scrapped or depreciated real estate (common in the recent financial failures); and disposal of assets aimed at generating cash-flow to pay down debts (a typical example being shareholdings of related firms and transaction partners, including the main bank and other lenders).

A common procedure in the former case of asset disposal is for organizational restructuring which removes the problem assets to an off-balance sheet liquidation company. This procedure has a number of dimensions closely related to the renegotiation of debt. Often, the main bank, either by itself or with a small number of key lenders, usually including at least one long-term credit bank, will finance the transfer of assets. This results in a deterioration in the quality of loans held by cooperating lenders. Often the restructurings in stylized form look like the following: suppose the debtor has $100 in debts and 10 per cent of the associated assets are non-performing, and lender A has a 20 per cent loan share. The problem assets are hived off to a liquidation company with the associated $10 of borrowings financed by lender A, who ends up with a 100 per cent loan share in the liquidation company and an 11.1 per cent loan share in the parent company. The overall loan share and amount of loans is unchanged, but the composition has shifted to lender A's detriment. Lender A's portfolio of claims changes from being 20 per cent problem assets and 80 per cent good assets to being 50 per cent of each.

Examples abound, including the shedding of problem real estate assets by Tobishima, Daikyo, Itoman, and Daiichi Housing Loan in the early 1990s. Among cases in the 1970s and 80s are the disposal of surplus tankers by Japan Line and by Sanko Steamship, of problem real estate assets by Kanematsu-Gosho, of problem assets by Ataka, and of aluminium operations by Sumitomo Chemical, Mitsubishi Chemical, and Showa Denko (Sheard, 1987, 1991c). Examples from the 1960s were the effective disposal by Yamaichi Securities and Oi Securities (now Wako) of problem assets by transferring only viable operations to new companies.

Merger and Acquisition

As well as taking the short- to medium-term measures described above, the main bank, in attempting to secure the longer-term viability of the firm, often arranges a tie-up or combination with another, usually larger, firm. This can take many forms: a loose association involving production sharing, or technical or marketing assistance, as in the Osaka Seiko, Mamiya Koki, and Janome cases; a partial acquisition, with the firm becoming an affiliate in the acquiring firm's group, as in the Fuji Heavy Industries, Fuji Car, Nitto Chemical, Toyo Linoleum, Mazda, and Cosmo Securities cases; or even full-fledged merger, as in the Uraga Heavy Industries, Gosho, Ataka, Itoman, and Japan Line cases. Of the cases in the Appendix, there were 10 tie-ups or mergers in the 1960s, 3 in the 1970s and 80s, and 5 among the recent cases.

It is worth noting that the direct intervention of main banks achieves the same outcome that economists have traditionally attributed to the take-over mechanism, namely the displacement or punishment of ineffective managers, the shake-up of failing corporations, and the transfer of corporate assets from lower- to higher-yielding uses. Increasingly, however, economists are less sanguine about this role of take-overs. For a succinct survey, see Holmstrom and Tirole (1989, pp. 98–101).

An interesting contrast can be made. Take-overs work through an indirect mechanism that relies on 'exit' in Hirschman's (1970) terms: existing shareholders sell their shares to an agent who, after gaining enough shares, is able to exercise control. In contrast, main bank intervention involves the exercise of 'voice' which may itself be facilitated by the difficulty of 'exit'. (For a fuller discussion of this perspective, see Black, 1992; Coffee, 1991; and Sheard, 1991b, 1994b. For some empirical results consistent with the argument on top management turnover in large Japanese firms in comparison with the United States, see Kaplan, 1994.)

Although the roles of the main bank have been discussed separately, they are closely related and complementary to one another. The main bank is prepared to provide financial assistance because the ability to dispatch executives as top managers gives it both access to information not available to the wider capital market and the ability to exert considerable leverage over the firm's management. The company union cooperates because the restructuring, painful as it may be, is necessary for the ongoing viability of the firm. The banks provide bridging funds to finance voluntary retirements and retrenchments; they do so because asset sales are in the offing, facilitating recovery of their debts.

MAIN BANK INCENTIVES

What are the incentives for the main bank to behave as it does? There are two levels at which this question can be posed. One is the narrower issue of what incentives the main bank has once it is faced with a client firm in financial distress. The second, larger issue is what incentives a bank has to become a main bank. Put another way, how does the main bank earn a sufficient return to compensate for the seemingly onerous responsibilities and risks (or losses) that it assumes when dealing with client firms in financial distress?

Incentives in Financial Distress

It is worth considering the options a main bank faces, given that it shoulders some special obligations when a client firm suffers financial distress. In general, the main bank's response might depend on the level of its explicit or implicit exposure, the history of its relationship with the firm, what caused the firm's financial distress, and the firm's future prospects. The attitudes of relevant regulatory authorities, concerns for its reputation as a sound main bank, and for its corporate image at large, may also be relevant factors, particularly when a large-scale corporate bankruptcy could result.

It is possible to distinguish four options in principle: (1) the main bank gives up its position and withdraws its credits to the firm; (2) the main bank refuses to refinance the firm, and is replaced by another lender or group of lenders; (3) the main bank refuses to refinance and the firm fails (goes bankrupt) as a result; and (4) the main bank refinances the firm and participates in its reorganization, without causing bankruptcy in a legal sense.

The first option is suggested by the familiar argument that the main bank, as the capital market's delegated monitor, is particularly well informed about the firm's condition and prospects. If any capital market player is capable of doing so, the main bank should be able to predict the fact that the firm is heading into financial distress. In that situation a rational—albeit, in the context, opportunistic—response might be to recover as much finance as possible, leaving other creditors with the bad debts. Participants in the Japanese capital market have a name for this, *baba o nuku* (to draw the joker).

Theoretical, as well as practical, institutional considerations, suggest in most cases this may not be a feasible option, or at least is not equilibrium behaviour for the main bank. Even if it would like to use its superior information, the other creditors are well aware of the main bank's incentives. An 'adverse selection' argument would suggest that other lenders will be particularly wary of attempts by the main bank to abandon its clients in adverse times. Institutional arrangements seem to operate to minimize the chances of main bank opportunism. In particular, it is difficult in practice for a main bank, which generally has the largest absolute share of loans, to withdraw or decrease the amount substantially without drawing the attention of other lenders.

A main bank can only withdraw if other lenders agree to increase their financing to make up the deficit (holding other operating policies of the firm constant). According to interviews with a former loan manager of a major city bank, the normal practice in bank lending is for the firm twice yearly to present a borrowing plan to all of its lenders with a detailed breakdown of how much is proposed to be borrowed from each bank. Lenders may agree to this or may seek a revision, but decisions are made based on symmetric information among lenders. It is not possible in general for a lender to be caught by surprise, although this conceivably could happen as a result of unethical behaviour or behaviour that verged on being fraudulent.

One possibility is that the bank and the firm collude against other creditors, for example, by having the firm dispose of assets to generate the cash flow to repay the main bank's borrowings; this would allow the main bank to have its loans repaid without other banks having to increase their loans to finance the repayment. In practice, though, it is unlikely this could happen except in isolated cases. First of all, the creditors will eventually find out what happened, and it is these creditors whom the firm will have to deal with in financial distress; it is not clear why the firm would want to help the main bank to flee, when it will have to bear the consequences—confrontation with angry creditors—later on. Putting this point aside, it is unlikely that the firm will be able to dispose of assets—in many cases a time-consuming process—on a large enough scale to repay the largest creditor's claims (or a significant fraction of them) without this coming to the attention of the other lenders. One important reason is that the assets in question are most likely to be pledged as security against the firm's borrowings, including those of other creditors. Again, size seems to be an important factor: such behaviour is more likely to be possible for smaller unlisted firms than for larger public ones.

Although main bank-firm ties are relatively stable, there is competition in the long run for the main bank position. Main bank relations are probably most flexible, and therefore competition for the main bank slot most active, in the case of smaller, rapidly growing firms, rather than for large established listed firms. For a main bank to capture its information rent, it would probably need to imply it had lost the competition for main bank position, rather than withdrawing to minimize its losses. This puts a constraint on the way it reduces its exposure, namely gradually over time, rather than in a discrete jump. Another way is for the main bank to make it appear that it has fallen out with the firm for other reasons, unrelated to the increased prospects of corporate failure.

In summary, for opportunistic withdrawal to be feasible, there must be a long enough time lag between when the main bank makes its decision and when evidence of imminent failure comes to the attention of the other creditors, otherwise they will halt the main bank's withdrawal. This suggests that opportunistic withdrawal by the main bank, leaving other creditors with what will later be revealed as bad loans, is likely only in the case of smaller unlisted firms, and even then only in rather special circumstances.

The second option is similar to the first, in terms of the main bank's motivation, but for adverse selection reasons again, it does not appear to be important in practice. The theoretical argument runs as follows. The main bank, by definition, is better informed than any other lender. If the main bank refuses to refinance the firm, it must be because its information tells it that it is not profitable to do so. But if it is not profitable for the main bank, which already has prior claims that must be senior to any new finance coming into the firm, then it cannot be profitable for the supplier of incremental funds. The only time that a main bank would want to cut off finance would be when the firm is a bad prospect; inferring this, no other lender will extend finance.[4]

This suggests the decision on whether a client firm that needs an injection of finance to remain afloat obtains the required funds or not rests with the main bank. In practice, also, this appears to be the case. Most corporate failures in Japan occur as a result of suspension of bank transactions following successive default on promissory notes within a six-month period, under an arrangement of all banks operating through the bill clearing house system. A firm dishonours a bill when there are not sufficient funds in its settlement account (*toza yokin*) for payment on the due date. But this is tantamount to an inability to obtain short-term funds to place in the settlement account. (See Aoki and Sheard, 1992, for more details on the main bank's role in settlement accounts and the relationship to the trade credit bill system.)

Whether the firm defaults or not is effectively a decision variable of its main bank, which must decide whether or not to extend the finance necessary to meet the obligation or not. According to interviews, bank loan officers worried about the possibility of default on bills whose settlement they are asked to finance may contact the loan officer of the main bank to ask whether the firm will be able to meet payments at the main bank (where settlements tend to be concentrated). This is an example where the main bank could opportunistically withdraw from the firm by suggesting it will meet settlement, leading other banks to provide finance for settlement of bills at their branches, but in fact not do so. However, the main bank will only be able to recover an incremental flow of funds, rather than its total, or even a significant fraction of its exposure. The attendant

[4] Another possibility in theory is that the bank uses its asymmetric advantage (over other lenders) to extract some organizational rents from the firm by threatening to behave as if it is going to desert the firm. If other lenders interpret the main bank's withdrawal as a signal that the firm is a bad prospect, then the main bank may be able to use this threat to its advantage. However, by construction, the main bank must also be worse off under the bankrupting scenario (even though it does not occur in equilibrium) so the Nash equilibrium (bank extracts rent and firm accedes) is not sub-game perfect.

loss in reputation is easily likely to outweigh that short-term rather small gain.

There is something to be said, in theory, for structuring institutions in such a way that the main bank (the informed party) controls the decision on whether a failing firm is refinanced or forced into some form of bankruptcy. (See the excellent survey by Packer and Ryser, 1992, regarding the many forms this can take on in Japan.) The analogy here is to Diamond's (1990) analysis: borrowers prefer that a more informed lender make decisions about continued credit-worthiness.

The main bank, in most cases, is faced with a choice between option three and option four: to refuse finance and force into bankruptcy or to refinance and participate in the ensuing process in an active way. As Diamond (1990) argues, there is a difference between having the *right* to force bankruptcy (liquidation in his model) and having the *incentive* to do so. As noted earlier, there are two issues: whether the financially distressed firm continues in operation or is partially or fully liquidated, and how the process is managed. The choice that creditors make between a legal process of reorganization with bankruptcy and an informal process ('workout') is, largely an issue of governance: creditors must decide whether they want to control the process themselves or delegate to a third party—the bankruptcy court or corporate receiver.

The corporate failure rate in Japan is in fact quite high, as Ramseyer (1991) and others have pointed out, although concentrated among smaller, particularly unlisted, firms. Combined with the apparent fact that many small and medium firms operate under a kind of 'main bank system' (Horiuchi and Murakami, 1991), this suggests that main banks do not always either refinance or supply the public good involved in restructuring managements. In most cases involving larger firms, however, creditors in Japan renegotiate the debt of the firm, rather than force it into bankruptcy; they decide to manage the process themselves with the main bank taking the lead role. As seen above, doing so does not preclude major changes being made in the firm's organization and asset base.

What is to stop the main bank from acting opportunistically by abusing its position when it intervenes? How are problems of conflict of interest between the main bank and other creditors, or possible collusion between the main bank and the firm, minimized? It may well be that in the process of intervention the main bank is able to extract information or control rents of some kind, but these might just be compensatory for the costs that it also has to incur. Conflicts are also limited by the fact that, because the firm is not legally bankrupt, other creditors, including trade creditors as well as lenders, still have legal claims unless they have explicitly agreed to a concession or roll-over. The main bank is constrained by the fact that its actions are closely monitored by other lenders and in varying degrees by the banking authorities, and by a convention resembling the US equitable subordination doctrine, as well as having its own reputation to consider.

One possible form of main bank opportunism involves a combination of options three and four: the main bank will intervene but then force the firm into bankruptcy after having secured its own claims. Sometimes main banks have forced firms into bankruptcy after a period of intervention. However, the case evidence suggests this is most likely to occur when one or more of the following factors are in evidence: the bank's intervention and audit of the firm's affairs reveals that the management of the firm has been concealing information and engaging in fraudulent behaviour; the incumbent management is resisting the measures being requested by the banks; or the prospects for recovery of the firm are poor. Withdrawal of support by the main bank in such cases corresponds to the bank implementing its credible threats and appears to reflect a rational calculation of commercial benefits and costs, rather than strategic opportunistic behaviour based on inside information or control. The fact that in such cases the main banks typically write off large amounts of loans as bad debts, in some cases not even waiting for a judgement under the bankruptcy proceedings (for example, Eidai Industries, Sanko Steamship), is consistent with that interpretation.

Even when the firm goes bankrupt under the Corporate Reorganization Law, the main bank may continue to play an important role, although in a more arm's-length capacity. For example, in the Sanyo Special Steel case, Kobe Bank's advising attorney was appointed receiver, in the Nihon Special Steel case the banks arranged for reorganization specialist Hayakawa Tanezo to become receiver, and in the Eidai Industries case Daiwa Bank supplied an executive as president after filing for bankruptcy took place.

Incentives to Become Main Bank

To the extent that the main bank assumes special responsibilities when a client firm is in financial distress, it must be adequately compensated for the additional costs and risks involved. The main reason banks are willing to take on this burden is that when the firm is in normal or prosperous times, the main bank enjoys special benefits not available to other lenders. In particular, it is widely believed that the main bank is able to garner a disproportionately large share of various banking-related business, such as placement of corporate bank deposits, operation of settlement accounts, involvement in bond issues as trustee administrator (domestically) and co-underwriter (internationally), handling of foreign exchange transactions, and access to banking business of related firms. More discussion and supporting evidence is presented in Chapter 1 by Aoki, Patrick, and Sheard, and in Aoki and Sheard (1992).

A kind of implicit social contract appears to operate among financial and corporate participants in the capital market. Ordinary lenders assume that the firm, if it has a main bank, is being monitored and if it runs into trouble that the main bank will intervene. This lowers the risk to lenders and they can economize on monitoring costs. On the other hand, as low-risk, low-cost lenders, they do not expect to garner much lucrative fee-based service business. For the main bank, the situation is reversed: by accepting the responsibility of monitoring, it indirectly certifies the credit-worthiness of the firm (though not as explicitly as a ratings agency), and at the same time is in a position to maximize its commercial advantage as a banking service intermediary.

The firm is also part of this complicated bargain. By maintaining a good main bank relationship, providing the main bank with necessary access to information and preferential commercial benefits, it obtains a form of insurance against corporate adversity (and against hostile take-over in normal times; see Sheard, 1994b) but importantly *not* it appears against managerial incompetence. It can resist extensive intrusion by the capital market by pointing to the fact that it has a main bank, with all that that fact implies.

EVALUATION

It seems beyond dispute that main banks have played, and continue to play, a central role in the corporate governance of large firms in Japan. More contentious are the questions whether the main bank system per-forms well and whether, and in what ways, it might have applicability elsewhere, particularly in developing and transforming socialist economies still in the process of crafting systems of capital market monitoring and control.

A qualitative assessment suggests that the main bank system performs rather well in handling the problems of firms in financial distress as an alternative to more market-oriented processes of corporate control on the one hand and the more administrative process of reorganization or liqui-dation under legal bankruptcy on the other. Quantitative studies that bear on this issue include the series of papers by Hoshi, Kashyap, and Sharfstein (1990a, 1990b, 1991), and earlier work by Nakatani (1984) and Suzuki and Wright (1985). Usually, when main banks intervene, they do so quickly and effectively. Their intervention is targeted, selective, and (in many cases) appropriate. It is generally clear to participants (although not necessarily to outsiders) who has responsibility for what, what the rules are, and what needs to be done. Protracted disruptive creditor dis-putes are rare, main bank backing helps to maintain the intangible asset base of the firm, and management and the creditors are able to focus on the substantive issues of restructuring and management. In short, the main bank system seems to minimize the costs associated with coordination problems, conflicts of interest, and strategic behaviour that loom so large in discussions of bankruptcy reform in the United States and elsewhere.

One argument, however, is that because they are prone to renegotiate financial commitments and rescue failing firms, main banks may give firms soft budgeting constraints, and thereby dull managerial incentives. This is a relevant policy issue in developing economies and, particularly, in economies emerging from the shackles of centrally planned systems. There is some theoretical support for the view that the main bank system will suffer from a soft budgeting tendency, but the implications are not necessarily negative ones (Dewatripont and Maskin, 1990).[5]

The soft budgeting argument is usually framed in terms of the enterprise being refinanced or liquidated. Debt, coupled with the threat of bankruptcy, is seen as a positive incentive for managers and workers to work harder and make better decisions (Grossman and Hart, 1982; Harris and Raviv, 1990; Jensen, 1986). If the main bank's role was merely to loosen the otherwise hard debt constraints by rescuing failing firms, the soft budgeting view would apply.

The point that emerges strongly from the analysis in this chapter is that the main bank does not passively provide funds *ex post* to finance losses; it actively intervenes, punishes and displaces managers, and sometimes the general work force, and oversees or engineers organizational and asset reorganizations. The firm that emerges from a period of main bank intervention is usually different, both managerially and organizationally, from the way it began. An important point is that the main bank is able to fine-tune its actions and punishments, and engage in what can be termed *selective intervention* (Kester, 1991, pp. 69–75; Sheard, 1991b). It also has, or can acquire, the necessary information to do so. In contrast, debt, combined with the threat of bankruptcy, appears to be a blunt instrument for providing incentives to such a complex collection of cooperating actors as a large corporation.

The effectiveness of a system of capital market incentives and controls, however, has to be judged from an *ex ante* as well as *ex post* perspective. Main banks may be good at intervening in adverse times, but as monitors are they good at preventing the actions that lead to failure from occurring in the first place? Are they part of the cause, as well as the cure?

If there is a soft budgeting problem with main banks, it is more an *ex*

---

[5] Note that in the context of the debate about whether main banks provide an insurance function to firms or not, soft budgeting can be thought of as a form of insurance. In particular, whereas soft budgeting connotes distorted *ex ante* incentives—moral hazard—the emphasis in the main bank insurance literature has been more on provision of incentives for various forms of intertemporal investments in human and organizational capital. See also von Thadden's (1990) interesting notion of banks' providing information insurance.

ante than an *ex post* form. Main banks engage in *ex ante* and interim monitoring, but their capacity to check managerial excesses or take remedial action before the effects of poor investments become blatantly manifest may be limited. The extent to which the main bank can exercise leverage *ex ante* depends on its bargaining power and its credible threats, and the incentives that its own managers face. If a main bank feels that a firm's management is on the wrong course, it can advise and push for changes, but its ultimate sanction is to refuse finance. In the high growth period, the banks' leverage over firms *ex ante* was probably quite strong. With funds in short supply, the financial system highly regulated, and investment opportunities abundant, a main bank's threat to refuse finance was probably more credible and costly to a firm than in more recent times.

If alternative sources of finance are abundant, as has been the case in recent years, and the firm's current position is sound, refusing to provide finance may have limited effect. To refuse to finance *incremental* projects is tantamount to taking the *discrete* step of giving up its position as main bank, if the firm can find funds elsewhere. By virtue of its desire to hold on to the main bank position, the bank may find itself acceding to requests for financing that it would have denied, or at least modified, had it been able to provide credible hard budget constraints *ex ante*. The extent and scale of recent failures and managerial excesses in the finance and real estate sectors suggest that at least in recent years the main bank system has suffered from an *ex ante* soft budgeting tendency, although its *ex post* intervention function remained operable.[6]

In a second-best world, any system of capital market controls has to balance trade-offs between competing goals. The market for corporate control provides high-powered incentives (Williamson, 1985, p. 132) but, it can be argued, at the cost of inducing short-term horizons and diverting scarce managerial and investor resources into socially unproductive activities (Bresnahan, Milgrom and Paul, 1990; Shleifer and Summers, 1988). Where the main bank is concerned, vesting incumbent managers with secure control rights in normal times may go hand in hand with their switching to the main bank when things go wrong; if so, tolerating a higher level of managerial discretion and risk of decision errors *ex ante* may be the cost of having a system that governs the process of financial distress in a predictable and effective way.

---

[6] The reported non-performing loans (loans to bankrupt firms or loans on which interest payments are six months or more in arrears) of the 21 city, long-term credit, and trust banks totalled 13,400 billion yen as of the 31 March 1993 end of fiscal 1992 (*Nikkei*, 5 May 1993, p. 1). This represented 4.7 per cent of their total outstanding loans and discounts as calculated from Bank of Japan (1993).

APPENDIX

Examples of Main Bank Involvement in Restructuring of Listed Firms

This Appendix is divided into three periods: the mid-1960s, from the mid-1970s to mid-1980s, and more recent restructurings. The firms are grouped by industry, more or less in the order one finds them (or would have found them, since many no longer trade) in a Japanese stock listing. The code number for the stock of traded companies is in parentheses after the industry (square brackets if the company is no longer traded).

The figures in parentheses after the name of a main bank are the percentage of the firm's shares held by the bank, and the bank's share of loans to the firm, both at the time restructuring measures were begun.

na = not available

Sources appear at the end of each listing. Additional sources are various editions of Keizai Chosa Kyokai, *Nenpo keiretsu no kenkyu: daiichibu jojo kigyohen (Annual Research on Corporate Affiliations: First-Section Listed Firm Edition)*, Tokyo: Keizai Chosa Kyokai; and Toyo Keizai Shinposha, *Kigyo keiretsu soran (Corporate Affiliation Directory)*, Tokyo: Toyo Keizai Shinposha.

Mid-1960s

Mitsui Chemical

Industry: chemicals (4001)

Main bank: Mitsui (1.8%, 23%)

Background: na

Restructuring: Toyo Koatsu (Mitsui group) chairman entered as president in Nov. 1966. Merged with Toyo Koatsu in Oct. 1968.

Bank Involvement: Mitsui dispatched executive director as vice president in Nov. 1966 and brokered merger.

Source: *Nikkei*, 7 Oct. 1966, p. 5.

Nitto Chemical

Industry: chemicals (4002)

Main bank: Dai-Ichi (5.0%, 26%)

Background: Rolled-over losses of 5 billion yen from deficit operations.

Restructuring: Two-thirds write-down of capital; Mitsubishi Rayon took equity holding in subsequent doubling of capital issue, took over most (45%) of Nitto's 50% holding in joint venture subsidiary with Union Carbide, and supplied vice president as concurrently serving president.

Bank Involvement: Dai-Ichi dispatched auditor as auditor in Nov. 1966, brokered Mitsubishi Rayon's take-over of Nitto, financed its share purchase, and took over part of Nitto's joint venture holding (5%); with IBJ and Kangyo Bank gave interest exemption on 12 billion yen of loans for three years.

Source: *Nikkei*, 15 Apr. 1965, p. 5; 3 Aug. 1965, p. 5; 10 Oct. 1965, p. 5; 28 Nov. 1965, p. 5.

Maruzen Oil

Industry: petroleum refining (5003)

Main bank: Sanwa (3.4%, 22%)

Background: Accumulated losses from deficit operations.

Restructuring: Rationalization plan involving overhaul of top management and reduction in directors' salaries, simplification of administration and transfer of head office functions to Tokyo, reduction of work-force by 500, absorption of sales subsidiary and eight regional sales companies and construction of 100 new gas stations, expansion of affiliate operations with outside capital, and negotiations with shipping companies to reduce high tanker rates (1963).

Bank Involvement: Sanwa dispatched branch manager as executive director (Feb. 1963), a senior officer as managing director (Jun. 1963), and a vice president as president (Nov. 1964), at which time IBJ dispatched an auditor as executive director. Maruzen presented to Sanwa a rationalization plan and request for 3 billion in cooperative financing and reduction of 1 billion yen in 5 billion yen annual interest bill; Sanwa reported to have required tougher measures, including more drastic work-force reduction.

Source: *Nikkei*, 19 Apr. 1963, p. 5; 17 Feb. 1963, p. 4; 27 Oct. 1964, p. 5; 29 Oct. 1964, p. 4.

Onoda Cement

Industry: cement (5233)

Main banks: Industrial Bank of Japan (1.8%, 15%); Mitsui (1.5%, 11%)

Background: Suffered losses from downturn in cement industry and failed to pay dividend in second half of fiscal 1964; excess capacity.

Restructuring: Rationalization plan involving overhaul of top management, asset sales to repay borrowings, transfer of offices to central research building, 15% reduction in directors' salaries, 20% reduction in work-force, application of cost-saving technologies at seven plants, and rationalization of unprofitable subsidiary operations.

Bank Involvement: Mitsui dispatched executive director as executive director and IBJ dispatched branch manager as executive director in May 1965 and supplied 2 billion yen in necessary investment funds; Kyowa dispatched an auditor as auditor in Nov.

Source: *Nikkei*, 16 Dec. 1964, p. 5; 5 May 1965, p. 5.

Chubu Steel Plate

Industry: steel (5461)

Main bank: Tokai (na, na)

Background: Managerial weaknesses exposed by recession in steel industry.

Restructuring: Overhaul of senior management including replacement of president and demotion of key directors; rationalization of output and reduction of work-force by 650 to 850; 60% capital write-down and new share issue.

Bank Involvement: Tokai formed 'reconstruction committee' with Yawata Steel and seven trading companies; Yawata bought up block of shares from market and dispatched manager as vice president; vice president of Yawata affiliate entered as Chubu president. Recovery plan announced involving freezing of Tokai and trading company claims for two years and exemption of interest in first year and half of interest in second year, and Tokai's providing up to 200 million yen in bridging finance.

Source: *Nikkei*, 13 Apr. 1965, p. 4; 24 Apr. 1965, p. 4; 9 Feb. 1966, p. 4; 11 Feb. 1966, p. 5; 18 Mar. 1966, p. 5; 1 Apr. 1966, p. 6.

Nihon Special Steel

Industry: steel

Main bank: Dai-Ichi (6.2%, 26%)

Background: Internal management power struggles, prolonged labour strife, and failed investments in affiliates; failure triggered by recession in steel industry.

Restructuring: Filed for bankruptcy under Corporate Reorganization Law in Nov. 1964 with 21 billion yen in liabilities. Completed reorganization in 1970.

Bank Involvement: Dai-Ichi attempted to arrange merger with Mitsubishi Seiko but preparations aborted when Dai-Ichi and Mitsubishi bank inspection revealed hidden liabilities; Dai-Ichi dispatched senior officer as executive director prior to bankruptcy and, with other main creditors, informally arranged for reorganization specialist Hayakawa Tanezo to become receiver.

Source: *Nikkei*, 1 Dec. 1964, p. 4; 2 Dec. 1964, p. 4; Hayakawa, 1975, pp. 114–71.

Osaka Iron & Steel

Industry: steel (5410; now trades OTC)

Main bank: Industrial Bank of Japan (na, 18%)

Background: High input costs, capital equipment old and small scale, poor labour-management relations. Large operating losses triggered by recession in steel industry.

Restructuring: Rationalization plan implemented involving closure of open-hearth furnace and reduction of work-force by 500; president and chairman resigned. Entered into tie-up with Yawata Steel involving technical assistance, raw materials supply, and marketing of output through Yawata's distribution channels.

Bank Involvement: IBJ reported to have been making financial assistance conditional on formulation of rationalization plan and removal of owner-chairman from frontline management. IBJ provided new long-term loan of 1.2 billion yen on guarantee from large creditors (Mitsubishi Corp., Mitsui & Co., Mitsubishi Chemical).

Source: *Nikkei*, 1 Dec. 1965, p. 4; 23 Oct. 1965, p. 5; 13 Jan. 1966, p. 4; 7 May 1966, evening, p. 2; 6 Nov. 1966, p. 4.

Sanyo Special Steel

Industry: steel

Main banks: Kobe (4.0%, 15%), Mitsubishi (na, 8%)

Background: Financial crisis triggered by recession in steel industry; falsification of accounts (13 billion yen) and of monthly bank reports prior to failure; two senior executive directors and an executive director misappropriated 6 million yen as interest-free loans from the company.

Restructuring: Filed for bankruptcy in Mar. 1965 under Corporate Reorganization Law (largest post-war bankruptcy at the time).

Bank Involvement: Kobe dispatched auditor as executive director and Mitsubishi dispatched department chief as vice president in Nov. 1963. Asahi Life Insurance (4% loan share) president entered as auditor in Nov. 1964. Five banks in cooperative financing group (Kobe, Mitsubishi, Fuji, Mitsui, IBJ) carried out investigation of Sanyo's finances and prospects in Feb. 1965 with view to securing Fuji Steel's (4.4% shareholder) cooperation; refused to finance settlement of 1.8 billion yen bill due on 10 Mar. Kobe advising-attorney appointed receiver. Kobe and Mitsubishi, under pressure from MOF, made early repayment of US$1.1 million of Sanyo's borrowings from three foreign banks that they had guaranteed.

Source: *Nikkei*, 11 Feb. 1965, p. 4; 25 Feb. 1965, p. 5; 28 Mar. 1965, p. 4; 8 Apr. 1965, p. 3; 17 Jun. 1965, p. 7; *Asahi Shinbun*, 6 Mar. 1965, evening, p. 1; 11 Mar. 1965, p. 7; 25 Mar. 1965, p. 14.

Nachi-Fujikoshi Corp.

Industry: industrial machinery (6474)

Main bank: Tokai (1.0%, 16%)

Background: Unprofitable steel operations.

Restructuring: Rationalization plan announced involving sale of office space at Tokyo head office and sale of land to cover 920 million yen rolled-over loss, spin-off of steel operations as joint venture with Daido Seiko, sale of machine tool plant to Nippon Denso and consolidation of production at Toyama plant, and reduction of work-force to 6,500 after lay-off of 880.

Bank Involvement: Tokai dispatched manager from loans-screening department as senior executive director in 1964; 3.7 billion yen in cooperative financing provided.

Source: *Nikkei*, 13 Jan. 1965, p. 4; 12 Feb. 1966, p. 4; 16 Oct. 1966, p. 5.

Hachio Electrical

Industry: electrical machinery

Main banks: Dai-Ichi (na, 28%), Saitama (2.5%, 32%)

Background: Financial losses; failure to pay a dividend in fiscal 1964.

Restructuring: President (founder and 8.8% owner) resigned (initially to new position of chairman, three months later as director); organizational restructuring of three departments and 18 sections under new president involving simplification of organizational structure, centralization of administration, and establishment of independent budgeting.

Bank Involvement: Dai-Ichi dispatched executive director as president in Apr. 1965 and, with Saitama, provided financial assistance.

Source: *Nikkei*, 14 Apr. 1965, p. 4; 17 Apr. 1965, p. 5; 7 Aug. 1965, p. 5.

Uraga Heavy Industries

Industry: shipbuilding

Main banks: Dai-Ichi (na, 12%), Sumitomo (na, 12%)

Background: Downturn in business and cash-flow crisis.

Restructuring: Eight directors resigned and two demoted in wake of 25% cut in directors' salaries; Sumitomo Machinery and Kawasaki Heavy Industries formed reconstruction committee with Sumitomo and Dai-Ichi and took over 16 million Uraga shares held by the two banks as collateral, Kawasaki sending in a senior executive director as president, Sumitomo Machinery an auditor as vice president (1963). Sumitomo group took over Kawasaki Heavy Industries' (KHI) shareholding and Sumitomo

Machinery dispatched senior executive director (entered from Sumitomo Bank in 1960) as vice president (1965); replaced president in Jan. 1967. Capital written down 50%. Strengthened tie-up with Sumitomo Machinery (1967), with whom it merged in Jun. 1969.

Bank Involvement: Sumitomo and Dai-Ichi brokered tie-up with Sumitomo Machinery and KHI and provided necessary finance to Uraga in equal amounts. Sumitomo dispatched senior executive director as chairman in Jan. 1967.

Source: *Nikkei*, 14 Feb. 1963, p. 4; 8 Mar. 1963, p. 5; 26 Mar. 1963, p. 4; 13 Apr. 1963, evening, p. 2; 24 Apr. 1963, p. 4; 10 Jan. 1965, p. 1; 23 Jan. 1965, p. 4; 23 Apr. 1965, p. 4; 28 Jan. 1967, p. 4; 28 Feb. 1967, p. 5.

Fuji Car Manufacturing

Industry: rolling stock (7104)

Main bank: Sanwa (1.9%, 33%)

Background: Continued to pay dividends while accumulating losses and falsifying accounts for ten years; accumulated losses of 3.3 billion yen (1964 FY).

Restructuring: Replacement of top management; Ube Kosan purchased block of Fuji Car Mfg stock to become largest (effective) shareholder at Sanwa's request and sent in vice president as president, who also became chairman of reconstruction committee formed with Sanwa, Ube, Nichimen, Nichido Marine, and Daisuegumi; asset sales and 60% capital write-down.

Bank Involvement: Sanwa refused financing after discovering loss cover-up and demanded removal of top management; arranged for Ube Kosan

to take lead role in rescue after similar approach to Hitachi Shipbuilding failed. Sanwa dispatched senior officer as executive director and executive director as auditor in Feb. 1965. Shelving of interest on loans.

Source: *Nikkei*, 12 Dec. 1964, p. 4; 18 Dec. 1964, p. 5; 9 Jan. 1966, p. 4; 25 Feb. 1965, evening, p. 2.

Fuji Heavy Industries

Industry: automobiles (7270)

Main bank: Industrial Bank of Japan (9.4%, 39%)

Background: Management weaknesses; small scale (4.5% domestic market share).

Restructuring: Overhaul of top management with head of NTT brought in as president (1963); tie-up with Nissan involving Nissan sub-contracting production and increasing shareholding in Fuji H.I. from 2.1% (1969) to 8.5% (1972).

Bank Involvement: IBJ dispatched executive director as vice president in May 1963, branch manager as executive director in May 1964, and head of president's office as director in Nov. 1965; brokered tie-up with Nissan (president of Nissan was former IBJ branch manager who entered as director in 1947).

Source: *Nikkei*, 20 Apr. 1963, p. 4; 20 Oct. 1968, p. 2; 21 Oct. 1968, p. 5; 22 Oct. 1968, p. 6.

Mamiya Camera

Industry: optical equipment

Main banks: Fuji (6.2%, 8%); Industrial Bank of Japan (2.3%, 32%)

Background: Deficit operations.

Restructuring: Rationalization plan involving all output being marketed through J. Osawa & Co. and restricting production of 35 mm cameras to orders issued by it; spin-off of sales division as separate company and contraction of administrative operations; transfer of 200 workers to main Urawa plant and reduction of workforce through natural attrition.

Bank Involvement: Fuji and IBJ agreed to shelve 150 million yen of loans for two years.

Source: *Nikkei*, 12 Jun. 1965, p. 5.

Toyo Linoleum Mfg.

Industry: chemicals [7971]

Main bank: Sanwa (10.0%, 24%)

Background: Deficit operations.

Restructuring: Tokuyama Soda (Sanwa group affiliate) purchased 1 million shares (number three shareholder) and president became managing director.

Bank Involvement: Sanwa dispatched auditor as president in Jul. 1966 and brokered Tokuyama's involvement.

Source: *Nikkei*, 9 Oct. 1966, p. 4.

Gosho

Industry: trading company

Main bank: Tokyo (6.7%, 43%)

Background: Unprofitable operations.

Restructuring: Formulated five-year rationalization plan involving rationalization of unprofitable operations, spin-offs, and work-force reduction, and asked Tokyo for interest reductions (Jan. 1966). Merged with Kanematsu (5 Gosho shares for 1 Kanematsu) (Apr. 1967) after seeking reduction in work-force of 700 and capital write-down.

Bank Involvement: Tokyo dispatched deputy head of loans-screening department as managing director in May 1965 and brokered merger.

Source: *Nikkei*, 20 Jan. 1966, p. 5; 26 Nov. 1966, p. 1; 8 Jan. 1967, p. 4; 1 Feb. 1967, p. 5.

Totsu

Industry: trading company

Main bank: Tokyo (10.0%, 49%)

Background: Suffered losses from recession in steel industry, including 1.56 billion yen claim on failed Sanyo Special Steels, and attempt to diversify trading base.

Restructuring: Sought assistance from Tokyo and Nippon Kokan (largest trading partner; one-third of turnover) and implemented rationalization plan including reduction of more than 100 in work-force. Nippon Kokan dispatched two executives to head finance operations and former executive as president and provided 2 billion yen of finance. Merged with Marubeni (4 Totsu shares for 1 Marubeni) (April 1966). Six Totsu directors accepted by Marubeni, but not chairman and president.

Bank Involvement: Tokyo dispatched branch deputy manager as managing director in 1963; together with seven other banks agreed to finance 1.56 billion yen Sanyo bad claims for five years. Nippon Kokan, Fuji Bank and Tokyo brokered merger after earlier attempt by Tokyo and Nippon Kokan to arrange merger with C. Itoh failed (Nippon Kokan and Marubeni both Fuji affiliated).

Source: *Nikkei*, 10 Feb. 1965, p. 5; 1 May 1965, p. 5; 9 Nov. 1965, p. 1; 13 Nov. 1965, p. 5; 15 Jan. 1966, p. 4; 16 Mar. 1966, p. 5.

Oi Securities

Industry: securities company (8608)

Main banks: Mitsubishi Trust (na, na); Industrial Bank of Japan (na, na)

Background: Hit by 1964 downturn in stock market; cash-flow crisis resulting from early redemptions of custodian contracts.

Restructuring: Viable operations transferred to new company, with problem assets and liabilities managed by old company for gradual liquidation; top management replaced.

Bank Involvement: Mitsubishi Trust and IBJ gave interest reductions and requested BOJ to supply special rescue finance. BOJ provided 5.3 billion yen in special finance (in same way as for Yamaichi) through two banks, which was repaid fully in four years.

Source: Nihon Ginko hyakunenshi henshu iinkai, 1986, pp. 151–65.

Yamaichi Securities

Industry: securities company (8602)

Main banks: Fuji (na, na); Mitsubishi (na, na); Industrial Bank of Japan (na, na)

Background: Hit by 1964 stock market downturn, accumulated losses reached 26.2 billion by the end of Mar. 1965 (against 8 billion capital level); cash flow crisis resulting from early redemptions of custodian contracts.

Restructuring: Viable operations transferred to new company, with problem assets and liabilities managed by old company for gradual liquidation.

Bank Involvement: Fuji and Mitsubishi dispatched managers as senior executive directors in 1962 and IBJ supplied manager as president in 1964. Three banks shelved interest on their loans and negotiated with 15 other lenders to do likewise; requested BOJ supply special rescue finance to meet Yamaichi's cash needs as customers redeemed custodian contracts. BOJ provided 28.2 billion yen in special finance (outside normal window guidance limits and effectively without collateral) through three banks, which was repaid fully in four years.

Source: Nihon Ginko hyakunenshi henshu iinkai, 1986, pp. 151–65.

Mid-1970s to mid-1980s

Daishowa Paper Mfg.

Industry: paper (3871)

Main Bank: Sumitomo (3.2%, 10%)

Background: Owner-dominated firm suffered financial failure after business downturn and diversification into real estate.

Restructuring: Owner-president forced to resign and internal decision-making procedures overhauled; 260 billion yen asset sale and borrowing reductions plan implemented and complicated affiliate structure overhauled.

Bank Involvement: Sumitomo dispatched directors as vice president and managing director and set up internal trouble-shooting team to oversee the reorganization; after Daishowa recovered, family re-asserted control and broke off main bank relation with Sumitomo; Daishowa turned to Industrial Bank of Japan for assistance when further failure was suffered in 1991.

Source: Sheard, 1985, pp. 69–74; *Nikkei*, 8 Jul. 1992, p. 1.

Chisso Corp.

Industry: petro-chemicals

Main Bank: Industrial Bank of Japan (5.0%, 27%)

Background: Responsible for pollution causing Minamata sickness (46.7 billion yen compensation paid to victims, 1973–80); explosion at main plant in 1973; financial viability of business deteriorated due to 1973 oil price hike (losses since 1971).

Restructuring: Sale of securities and land-holdings; sale of silicon business to Mitsubishi Metal; delisted from stock exchange in 1978.

Bank Involvement: IBJ and other financial institutions implemented three-year assistance plan in 1973 involving suspension of long-term loan repayments (IBJ loan share 32.5%) and annual interest exemptions of 1 billion yen (IBJ share 50%) and deferrals of 1.3 billion (IBJ share 35.4%), maintenance of short-term loan balances at prime rate, and provision of shortfalls in working capital. IBJ dispatched manager as vice president in 1974. Financial assistance extended for further three years in 1976. IBJ approached government in 1977 and rescue package agreed upon involving issuing of 30-year prefectural bonds (60% to national government, 40% to financial institutions) to finance prefectural loans on same terms to Chisso (12.7 billion yen by 1981) and financial institutions extending their assistance measures until public loans fully repaid.

Source: Nihon Kogyo Ginko hyakunenshi henshu iinkai, 1982, pp. 1049–61.

Hitachi Zosen Corp.

Industry: shipbuilding (7004)

Main Bank: Sanwa (4.9%, 20%)

Background: Badly affected by shipbuilding recession from 1970s.

Restructuring: Asset sales, closure of problem operations, and reduction of work-force by 5,300.

Bank Involvement: Sanwa led six other lenders in providing bridging finance of 160 billion yen in fiscal 1986 to finance retrenchments and asset sales, and in 1986–88 dispatched vice chairman as president, senior executive director as vice president, executive director as senior executive director in charge of finance and related firm operations, executive director as executive director in charge of sales, branch manager as director in charge of president's office, and 14 department and section heads to finance, sales, planning, and personnel areas.

Source: Nikkei, 14 Nov. 1985, p. 8; 13 Dec. 1985, p. 8; 20 Dec. 1986, p. 1; 28 Dec. 1986, p. 4; Sekigami, 1992, p. 41; Toyo Keizai Shinposha, 1991, pp. 931–932.

Mazda Motor Corp.

Industry: automobiles (7261)

Main Bank: Sumitomo (4.0%, 14%)

Background: Managerial weaknesses exposed by plummet in sales following first oil crisis.

Restructuring: Asset sales, revamping of internal decision-making structures, overhaul of production, sales, and sub-contracting systems, work-force reductions and redeployment, cost-cutting drive; Ford took 25% capital stake in 1978.

Bank Involvement: Sumitomo dispatched nine-member trouble-shooting team in 1975 including Tokyo head-office chief as vice president and, with Sumitomo Trust, provided 24 billion of 34 billion yen in emergency financing to avert collapse, mobilized sales and input supply support from Sumitomo group firms, and arranged tie-up with Ford.

Source: Pascale and Rohlen, 1983; Sheard, 1985, pp. 62–69.

Eidai Industries

Industry: housing construction

Main Bank: Daiwa (7.7%, 28%)

Background: Suffered financial failure after recession and sudden death of owner-chairman brought serious business weaknesses to light (1974–78).

Restructuring: Successive rationalization plans implemented involving asset sales, closure of problem operations, and reductions in work-force, but losses continued at rate of several billion yen per month and Eidai filed for bankruptcy under Corporate Reorganization Law in 1978.

Bank Involvement: Daiwa formed consortium with four other assisting banks, arranged for replacement president to be brought in, and dispatched 11 officers to Eidai including a director to oversee restructuring. After bankruptcy, Daiwa bought up Eidai bonds at face value (with two other banks), took several measures to minimize related bankruptcies, and arranged for former bank executive to become Eidai president.

Source: Daiwa Ginko hyakunenshi henshu iinkai, 1988, pp. 193–200.

Ataka & Co.

Industry: trading company

Main Bank: Sumitomo (8.5%, 15%)

Background: 300–400 billion yen in losses from failed investments in Canadian refinery and domestic operations (1975–77).

Restructuring: 17 directors replaced, and US$336 million Canadian losses and 299 billion yen of domestic problem assets hived off to new liquidation companies set up by banks led by Sumitomo; assets sales followed by viable remaining operations being taken over by C. Itoh and other companies.

Bank Involvement: Sumitomo dispatched senior managing director as president and set up internal trouble-shooting department to manage the reorganization and liquidation of assets, including engineering mergers; absorbed 57% share of residual losses against initial 15% loan share.

Source: Sheard, 1985, pp. 53–62.

Kanematsu-Gosho

Industry: trading company (8020)

Main Bank: Tokyo (10.0%, 16%)

Background: Suffered losses in mid-1970s from investments in depressed industries and real estate.

Restructuring: Problem real estate assets hived off to separate company; asset sales implemented, including sale and lease-back of head office.

Bank Involvement: Tokyo dispatched chairman as vice president in 1977 and with Dai-Ichi Kangyo provided interest reductions or exemptions on 35 billion yen of steel industry and real estate investments.

Source: *Nikkei*, 28 Apr. 1977, p. 1; Sheard, 1985, pp. 43–44.

Japan Line

Industry: overseas shipping (9105)

Main Bank: Industrial Bank of Japan (9.3%, 7%)

Background: With largest tanker division in world, badly hit by world-wide tanker recession in 1970s.

Restructuring: Successive rationalization plans involved overhaul of senior management, asset disposals, hiving off of surplus tankers to liquidation companies, restructuring of leasing arrangements, and large-scale workforce reductions; merged with Yamashita Shinnihon Steamship in 1989 after capital write-down.

Bank Involvement: IBJ dispatched executive directors as president in 1978 and as vice president in 1980, led bank financing of asset hive-offs, provided bridging finance and funds for scrapping of surplus tankers, implemented with other major lenders loan rollovers and interest rate deferrals and reductions, arranged merger, and wrote off 50 billion yen of 160 billion yen loans in 1989.

Source: Sheard, 1985, pp. 74–78; *Nikkei*, 20 Dec. 1985, p. 1; 12 Sep. 1986, p. 11; 16 Dec. 1986, p. 1; 23 Dec. 1988, p. 1; 20 Jan. 1989, evening, p. 1; 26 May 1989, p. 6; 30 May 1989, p. 7.

Sanko Steamship

Industry: overseas shipping

Main Bank: Daiwa (6.7%, 16%)

Background: Suffered financial failure after tanker recession and over-expansion of fleet.

Restructuring: Hive-off of 16 tankers and 70 billion yen of borrowings to separate company for liquidation; continued to make losses and filed for bankruptcy in 1985 after government refused to provide financial rescue.

Bank Involvement: Daiwa dispatched executive director as vice president

and a further four managers in 1982 and formed assistance consortium with two other major lenders in 1987, providing loan rollovers, interest rate reductions, and new loans to cover monthly recurrent losses. Daiwa wrote off 79.3 billion yen in 1985 and a further 4.5 billion yen in 1988.

Source: Daiwa Ginko hyakunenshi henshu iinkai, 1988, pp. 201–209.

Recent cases

Ishihara Construction

Industry: construction (1825, 2nd §)

Main Bank: Mitsubishi Trust (4.7%, 8%)

Background: Losses on real estate investments including 21 billion yen loan guarantee to failed steel fabricator Kyowa.

Restructuring: Sale of owner-president's 26% shareholding to Misawa Homes and 12 billion yen share issue to Dai-Ichi Corporation, Mitsubishi Trust and 19 other firms. Plan put to banks involving asset sales to reduce group liabilities from 100 to 40 billion yen over five years and financial assistance; head office sold for 5.2 billion yen, with proceeds used to repay bank borrowings.

Bank Involvement: Mitsubishi Trust arranged initial restructuring plan including deferral of principal repayments and reduction of interest rate on borrowings to 5%; reported to be making further request for freezing of principal repayments and reduction of interest rate from 5% to 3% for three to five years contingent on tougher measures.

Source: *Nikkei*, 18 Feb. 1992, p. 12; 8 May 1993, p. 9.

Tobishima Corp.

Industry: construction (1805)

Main Bank: Fuji (4.8%, 11%)

Background: 123.4 billion yen loan exposure to failed developer Nanatomi.

Restructuring: President forced to resign; three-year plan to reduce borrowings from 950 to 410 billion yen by hiving off real estate to subsidiaries and selling securities; reduction of 20% in administrative staff.

Bank Involvement: Fuji dispatched director as senior executive director and vice president as chairman, arranged for 80 lenders to reduce interest rate from 6.5% to 3% (1% for subsidiary), and arranged for Taisei Construction to subcontract 10–20% of Fuji Bank group construction work to Tobishima.

Source: *Nikkei*, 23 Jan. 1991, p. 17; 27 Feb. 1991, p. 10; 27 Apr. 1991, p. 27; 13 May 1991, p. 525; 24 Jun. 1991, p. 1; 3 Apr. 1992, p. 11; 24 Jul. 1992, p. 1; 23 May 1993, p. 7.

Daiichibo Co.

Industry: textiles (3119)

Main Bank: Sakura (5.0%, 28%)

Background: Increased import competition; financial failure of subsidiary; accumulated losses exceeded capital by 62.3 billion yen (Feb. 1993).

Restructuring: Plan to consolidate production, rationalize affiliate operations, sell off plant and real estate assets, and assume 18.1 billion yen of losses from an affiliate put to banks with request for 2 billion yen in interest deferrals (Jul. 1992).

Bank Involvement: Sakura provided bridging finance but refused to make

further loans after other banks refused to increase loans and San'in Godo Bank (non top-10 lender) placed a temporary seizure order on Daiichibo land; Daiichibo filed for bankruptcy under Corporate Reorganization Law (Oct. 1992).

Source: *Nikkei*, 23 Jul. 1992, p. 15; 10 Oct. 1992, p. 9; 16 Oct. 1992, p. 1, 11; 29 May 1993, p. 9.

Fuji Kosan

Industry: petroleum refining (5009)

Main Bank: Tokyo (5.0%, 28%)

Background: Unprofitable operations.

Restructuring: Refining division spun off as joint venture with Mitsubishi Petroleum, which became top shareholder (10.6%) through new share issue.

Bank Involvement: Tokyo dispatched senior executive director as president in 1988; 40 billion yen of loans written off by 4 of 17 lending banks, 36.5 billion by Tokyo.

Source: *Nikkei*, 17 Dec. 1991, p. 1; 1 Oct. 1992, p. 7; 20 Feb. 1993, p. 11.

Janome Sewing Machine

Industry: sewing machine maker (6445)

Main Bank: Saitama (4.4%, 64%)

Background: Involved in complicated financial manoeuvrings with share-cornering group Koshin and failed developer Nanatomi, including having to assume 235.5 billion yen of Koshin's debt obligations.

Restructuring: Asset sales of 43.5 billion yen planned and business tie-up with machinery maker Amada.

Bank Involvement: Saitama dispatched adviser as vice president, provided bridging finance, increasing its loans from 4.3 to 36.8 billion yen between 1990 and 1991, and arranged the tie-up; reduced interest rate below discount rate from 1992.

Source: *Nikkei*, 13 Mar. 1991, p. 1; 16 Mar. 1991, p. 14; 18 Apr. 1991, p. 15; 20 Jun. 1991, p. 11; 19 Mar. 1992, p. 13; 8 Jul. 1993, p. 17.

Crown Corp.

Industry: electrical goods (6766)

Main Bank: Sanwa (1.4%, 14%)

Background: Increase in bad loans associated with dubious financial dealings with group finance company and owner-president's companies.

Restructuring: President forced to resign and 23.2 billion yen of bad loan guarantees hived off to new company.

Bank Involvement: Sanwa led bank financing of hive-off and made financial assistance contingent on restructuring.

Source: *Nikkei*, 10 Mar. 1992, p. 17; 25 Apr. 1992, p. 10; 28 May 1992, p. 11, 16.

Itoman & Co.

Industry: trading company (8009)

Main Bank: Sumitomo (3.4%, 8%)

Background: Failed real estate investments and top-level management fraud.

Restructuring: President and senior directors forced to resign and asset and borrowing reduction plan implemented based on hive-off of 500 billion yen of real estate assets to liquidation companies; merged with Sumitomo group trading company Sumikin Bussan in Apr. 1993.

Bank Involvement: Sumitomo dispatched five managers as troubleshooters including executive director as vice president, took over loans of other banks, increasing its loan share from 8% to 35% between 1990 and 1991, implemented interest rate reductions, wrote off 300 billion yen in losses in 1993, and arranged the merger.

Source: *Nikkei*, various issues (see Sheard, 1991a, pp. 47–52); 29 Sep. 1992, p. 11; *Yomiuri Shinbun*, 7 Apr. 1993.

Daiichi Housing Loan

Industry: housing finance (8578, 2nd §)

Main Bank: Long-Term Credit (5.0%, 11%)

Background: Increase in bad real estate loans following market collapse (50% of 1,600 billion yen loans non-performing in May 1993).

Restructuring: five-year plan to reduce loans and assets by 40% and withdraw from large corporate lending; hiving off of 85 billion yen of problem assets to new subsidiary.

Bank Involvement: Long-Term Credit initially provided 3 percentage point interest rate reduction on 213 billion yen of loans and requested other lenders to maintain loan balances; later agreed to exempt interest for ten years and ask other lenders to implement same interest reductions as for Nihon Housing Finance, and agreed with Nomura Securities (5% shareholder) to take up third-party share issue of 10 billion yen each.

Source: *Nikkei*, 1 Apr. 1992, p. 1; 14 May 1992, p. 1; 15 May 1992, p. 7; 14 Feb. 1993, p. 1; 13 Apr. 1993, p. 1; 13 May 1993, p. 7; 27 May 1993, p. 18; 29 May 1993, p. 14.

Nichiboshin

Industry: finance company (8582)

Main Bank: Dai-Ichi Kangyo (4.6%, na); Daiwa (5.0%, na); Hokkaido Takushoku (4.0%, na); Yasuda Trust (1.9%, na); Mitsubishi Trust (3.1%, na); Sumitomo Trust (3.7%, na)

Background: Increase in bad real estate loans following market collapse (500 billion of 1,100 billion yen loans non-performing in Mar. 1993).

Restructuring: Asset sales and borrowing reductions of 350 billion yen planned and president replaced by ex-MOF official.

Bank Involvement: Plan involved six banks reducing interest rate on 450 billion yen of loans (38% of total) from 7% to 2.5% and providing 2 billion yen in new loans; Dai-Ichi Kangyo and Daiwa dispatching branch managers as directors.

Source: *Nikkei*, 1 Mar. 1992, p. 1; 20 Mar. 1992, p. 4; 27 Mar. 1992, p. 7; 13 May 1992, evening, p. 1; 4 Sep. 1992, p. 17; 3 Nov. 1992, p. 15; 19 Jun. 1993, p. 13.

Central Finance

Industry: finance company (8588)

Main Bank: Tokai (4.9%, 8%)

Background: Increase in bad real estate loans following market collapse.

Restructuring: 110 billion yen of bad loans hived off to new subsidiary for liquidation. Cost-cutting plan involving reduction of offices from 110 to 53 and reduction of work-force by 700 over three years.

Bank Involvement: Tokai financed loan hive-off, dispatched seven managers to oversee asset disposals, and took over 12.7 billion yen bad loan.

Source: *Nikkei*, 6 Feb. 1992, p. 7; 28 Feb. 1992, p. 7; 15 Sep. 1992, p. 7; 4 Feb. 1993, p. 11.

Nihon Housing Loan

Industry: housing finance (8581)

Main Bank: Sanwa (5.0%, 7%)

Background: Increase in bad real estate loans following market collapse (58% of 2,240 billion yen loans non-performing at end of fiscal 1992).

Restructuring: Overhaul of board including forced resignation of president and plan to reduce borrowings by 700 billion yen over five years by recovering loans and selling assets and securities.

Bank Involvement: Sanwa dispatched officers to assess financial position and arranged initial assistance package involving interest rate reductions by nine banks from 6.5% to 3.25% and the provision of 60 billion yen in new loans; later extended to reduction of interest rate to zero on nine banks' loans, to 4.5% on loans by Norin Chukin and other agricultural cooperative loans, and to 2.5% on loans by other financial institutions for ten years on 2,315 billion yen of loans, giving rise to 84.2 billion yen annual interest relief.

Source: *Nikkei*, 1 Apr. 1992, p. 1; 21 Apr. 1992, evening, p. 2; 22 Apr. 1992, p. 7; 29 Apr. 1992, p. 15; 14 May 1992, p. 7; 25 May 1992, p. 4; 13 Jun. 1992, p. 13; 3 Jul. 1992, p. 19; 11 Jul. 1992, p. 4; 23 Jul. 1992, p. 7; 18 Aug. 1992, p. 7; 15 Oct. 1992, p. 7; 3 Nov. 1992, p. 15; 26 Jan. 1993, p. 1; 29 Jan. 1993, p. 1; 11 Feb. 1993, p. 1; 20 Feb. 1993, p. 4; 18 Mar. 1993, p. 7.

Cosmo Securities

Industry: securities company (8611)

Main Bank: Daiwa (5.0%, 16%)

Background: 120 billion yen losses from share-trading scandals including 70 billion yen loss precipitating collapse in Aug. 1993.

Restructuring: Ten executives involved in scandal resigned, including chairman, president, and vice president; 10–30% reduction in directors' salaries for three months; work-force reduction and rationalization of branches.

Bank Involvement: Daiwa dispatched Daiwa Bank Card president as vice president, replacing president soon after; injected 78 billion yen in emergency third-party share issue on special exemption from MOF to give it a 59.6% shareholding (reported to have previously provided 77 billion yen through overseas branch to finance purchase of shares involved in share trading loss).

Source: *Nikkei*, 9 May 1992, evening, p. 1; 16 Feb. 1993, p. 7; 14 Aug. 1993, p. 1; 15 Aug. 1993, p. 2; 18 Aug. 1993, p. 7, 17; 20 Aug. 1993, p. 7; 24 Aug. 1993, p. 15; 26 Aug. 1993, evening, p. 2.

Daikyo Inc.

Industry: real estate developer (8840)

Main Bank: Sanwa (3.8%, 11%)

Background: Rapid increase in unsold apartments.

Restructuring: Plan to reduce real estate assets and borrowings by 200 billion yen, and reduce work-force by 20% over four years; and hive off 50 billion yen of problem assets to new subsidiaries.

Bank Involvement: Sanwa led bank financing of hive-off and dispatched senior executive director as vice president.

Source: *Nikkei*, 16 Jul. 1992, p. 13; 1 Oct. 1992, p. 1.

Seacom

Industry: shipping (9125, 2nd §)

Main Bank: Long-Term Credit (1.1%, 21%)

Background: Increase in bad real estate loans following market collapse.

Restructuring: Plan to sell 10 billion yen of overseas assets.

Bank Involvement: Long-Term Credit provided new working capital and, with four other banks, shelved interest payments on loans.

Source: *Nikkei*, 18 Jul. 1992, p. 13.

REFERENCES

AGHION, PATRICK and PATRICK BOLTON. 1992. 'An Incomplete Contracts Approach to Financial Contracting.' *Review of Economic Studies* 59(3): 473–94.

AGHION, PHILIPPE, OLIVER HART, and JOHN MOORE. 1992. 'The Economics of Bankruptcy Reform.' *Journal of Law, Economics, and Organization* 8(3): 523–46.

AOKI, MASAHIKO. 1990. 'Toward an Economic Model of the Japanese Firm.' *Journal of Economic Literature* 28: 1–27.

——. 1994. 'The Contingent Governance Structure of Team Production: An Analysis of Systematic Effects.' *International Economic Review*.

AOKI, MASAHIKO and PAUL SHEARD. 1992. 'The Main Bank System and Corporate Governance Structure in Japan.' mimeo, Stanford University.

ASQUITH, PAUL, ROBERT GERTNER, and DAVID SCHARFSTEIN. 1991. 'Anatomy of Financial Distress: An Examination of Junk-Bond Issuers.' National Bureau of Economic Research Working Paper 3942.

BAIRD, DOUGLAS G. 1986. 'The Uneasy Case for Corporate Reorganization.' *Journal of Legal Studies* 15: 127–47.

BANK OF JAPAN. Various issues. *Economic Statistics Annual.* Tokyo, Bank of Japan.

——. 1993. *Economic Statistics Monthly*, July.

BERNHEIM, B. D. and M. D. WHINSTON. 1985. 'Common Marketing Agency as a Device for Facilitating Collusion.' *Rand Journal of Economics* 16: 269–81.

BLACK, BERNARD S. 1992. 'Agents Watching Agents: The Promise of Institutional Investor Voice.' *UCLA Law Review* 39(4): 811–93.

BOLTON, PATRICK and DAVID S. SCHARFSTEIN. 1990. 'A Theory of Predation Based on Agency Problems in Financial Contracting.' *American Economic Review* 80: 93–106.

BRESNAHAN, TIMOTHY, PAUL MILGROM and JOHNATHON PAUL. 1990. 'The Real Output of the Stock Exchange.' CEPR Publication 215, Center for Economic Policy Research, Stanford University.

BULOW, JEREMY and JOHN SHOVEN. 1978. 'The Bankruptcy Decision.' *Bell Journal of Economics* 9: 436–45.

COFFEE, JR., JOHN C. 1991. 'Liquidity Versus Control: The Institutional Investor as Corporate Monitor.' *Columbia Law Review* 91(6): 1277–368.

DAIWA GINKO NANAJUNENSHI HENSHU IINKAI. 1988. *Daiwa Ginko nanjunenshi* (*Seventy Year History of Daiwa Bank*). Osaka: Daiwa Ginko.

DEWATRIPONT, M. and E. MASKIN. 1990. 'Credit and Efficiency in Centralized and Decentralized Economies.' Discussion Paper 1512, Harvard Institute of Economic Research.

DIAMOND, DOUGLAS W. 1990. 'Seniority and Maturity Structure of Bank Loans and Publicly Traded Debt.' Working paper, Graduate School of Business, University of Chicago.

——. 1991. 'Debt Maturity Structure and Liquidity Structure.' *Quarterly Journal of Economics* 1066(3): 709–37.

FRANKS, JULIAN R. and WALTER N. TOROUS. 1989. 'An Empirical Investigation of U.S. Firms in Reorganization.' *Journal of Finance* 44(3): 747–69.

GERTNER, ROBERT and DAVID SCHARFSTEIN. 1991. 'A Theory of Workouts and the Effects of Reorganization Law.' *Journal of Finance* 46(4): 1189–222.

GILSON, STUART C. 1990. 'Bankruptcy, Boards, Banks, and Blockholders: Evidence on Changes in Corporate Ownership and Control When Firms Default.' *Journal of Financial Economics* 27(2): 355–87.

GILSON, STUART C., JOHN KOSE and LARRY H. P. LANG. 1990. 'Troubled Debt Restructurings: An Empirical Study of Private Reorganization of Firms in Default.' *Journal of Financial Economics* 27(2): 315–53.

GROSSMAN, SANFORD J. and OLIVER D. HART. 1982. 'Corporate Financial Structure and Managerial Incentives.' In J. McCall, ed., *The Economics of Information and Uncertainty*. Chicago: University of Chicago Press.

——. 1988. 'One Share-One Vote and the Market for Corporate Control.' *Journal of Financial Economics* 20: 175–202.

HARRIS, MILTON and ARTUR RAVIV. 1989. 'The Design of Securities.' *Journal of Financial Economics* 24: 255–87.

——. 1990. 'Capital Structure and the Informational Role of Debt.' *Journal of Finance* 45(2): 321–49.

HART, OLIVER and JOHN MOORE. 1989. 'Default and Renegotiation: A Dynamic Model of Debt.' Massachusetts Institute of Technology, Department of Economics, working paper.

——. 1990. 'A Theory of Corporate Financial Structure Based on the Seniority of Claims.' National Bureau of Economic Research Working Paper 3431.

——. 1991. 'A Theory of Debt Based on the Inalienability of Human Capital.' National Bureau of Economic Research Working Paper 3906.

HAYAKAWA, TANEZO. 1975. *Kaisha saiken no ki* (*A Record of Corporate Reconstructions*). Tokyo: Nihon Jitsugyo Shuppansha.

HIRSCHMAN, ALBERT O. 1970. *Exit, Voice and Loyalty*. Cambridge MA: Harvard University Press.

HOLMSTROM, BENGT R. and JEAN TIROLE. 1989. 'The Theory of the Firm.' In Richard Schmalensee and Robert D. Willig, eds., *Handbook of Industrial Organization, vol. I.* Amsterdam: North Holland.

HORIUCHI, TOSHIHIRO and EIJI MURAKAMI. 1991. 'Wagakuni ni okeru mein banku torihiki jittai: anketo kekka kara mita kigyo kin'yu no sugata' ('The State of Main Bank Transactions in Japan: the Shape of Corporate Finance as Seen from Questionnaire Results'). In Toshihiro Horiuchi, ed., *Jiyuka kokusaika jidai no kigyo kin'yu no henbo: mein banku no kino to hensei* (*Transformation of Corporate Finance in the Era of Liberalization and Internationalization: the Function and Transformation of the Main Bank*). Nihon Keizai Kenkyu Senta kenkyu hokoku 75.

HOSHI, TAKEO, ANIL KASHYAP, and DAVID SCHARFSTEIN. 1990a. 'Bank Monitoring and Investment: Evidence from the Changing Structure of Japanese Corporate Banking Relationships.' In R. Glenn Hubbard, ed., *Asymmetric Information, Corporate Finance and Investment*. Chicago: University of Chicago Press.

——. 1990b. 'The Role of Banks in Reducing the Costs of Financial Distress in Japan.' *Journal of Financial Economics* 27(1): 67–88.

——. 1991. 'Corporate Structure, Liquidity, and Investment: Evidence from Japanese Industrial Groups.' *Quarterly Journal of Economics* 106: 33–60.

JACKSON, THOMAS H. 1986. *The Logic and Limits of Bankruptcy Law*. Cambridge: Harvard University Press.

JENSEN, MICHAEL C. 1986. 'Agency Costs of Free Cash Flow, Corporate Finance, and Takeovers.' *American Economic Review* 76: 323–29.

KAPLAN, STEVEN N. 1994. 'Top Executive Rewards and Firm Performance: A Comparison of Japan and the U.S.' *Journal of Political Economy*. (Previously published as National Bureau of Economic Research Working Paper 4065, 1992.)

KAPLAN, STEVEN N. and BERNADETTE ALCAMO MINTON. 1994. 'Appointments of Outsiders to Japanese Boards.' *Journal of Financial Economics* 34.

KESTER, W. CARL. 1991. *Japanese Takeovers: The Global Contest for Corporate Control*. Boston: Harvard Business School Press.

KORNAI, JANUS. 1980. *The Economics of Shortage*. Amsterdam: North Holland.

KOROBKIN, DONALD R. 1991. 'Rehabilitating Values: A Jurisprudence of Bankruptcy.' *Columbia Law Review* 91(4): 717–89.

MAILATH, GEORGE and ANDREW POSTLEWAITE. 1990. 'Asymmetric Bargaining Problems with Many Agents.' *Review of Economic Studies* 57: 351–67.

MAYER, COLIN. 1988. 'New Issues in Corporate Finance.' *European Economic Review* 32: 1167–89.

MORCK, RANDALL and MASAO NAKAMURA. 1992. 'Banks and Corporate Control in Japan.' mimeo, University of Alberta.

MYERS, STEWART C. 1977. 'Determinants of Corporate Borrowing.' *Journal of Finance* 5: 147–75.

——. 1989. 'Still Searching for Optimal Capital Structure.' In Richard W. Kopcke and Eric S. Rosengren, eds., *Are the Distinctions between Debt and Equity Disappearing?* Federal Reserve Bank of Boston.

NAKATANI, IWAO. 1984. 'The Economics of Financial Corporate Grouping,' In Masahiko Aoki, ed., *The Economic Analysis of the Japanese Firm*. Amsterdam: North Holland.

NIHON GINKO HYAKUNENSHI HENSHU IINKAI. 1986. *Nihon Ginko hyakunenshi dairokkan* (*A Hundred Year History of the Bank of Japan*) *vol. 6*. Tokyo: Nihon Ginko.

NIHON KEIZAI SHINBUNSHA. Various editions. *Kaisha nenkan jojo kigyohen* (*The Company Annual: Listed Firm Edition*). Tokyo: Nihon Keizai Shinbunsha.

NIHON KOGYO GINKO NENSHI HENSHU IINKAI. 1982. *Nihon Kogyo Ginko nanjugo-nenshi* (*A Seventy-Five Year History of the Industrial Bank of Japan*). Tokyo: Nihon Kogyo Ginko.

Nikkei (*Nihon Keizai Shinbun*). Various issues. Tokyo, Nihon Keizai Shinbunsha.

PACKER, FRANK and MARC RYSER. 1992. 'The Governance of Failure: An Anatomy of Corporate Bankruptcy in Japan.' Working Paper 62, Center on Japanese Economy and Business, Graduate School of Business, Columbia University, New York.

PASCALE, RICHARD and THOMAS P. ROHLEN. 1983. 'The Mazda Turnaround.' *Journal of Japanese Studies* 9: 219–63.

RAMSEYER, J. MARK. 1991. 'Legal Rules in Repeated Deals: Banking in the Shadow of Defection in Japan.' *Journal of Legal Studies* 20: 91–117.

SEKIGAMI, SO. 1992. 'Fujii Hitachi Zosen fukuhai naru! mein banku no saimu hatashita Sanwa Ginko' ('Fujii's Hitachi Zosen Declaring Dividend Again! Sanwa Bank Discharges Responsibility as Main Bank'). *Ginko jihyo*, September, pp. 40–43.

SENTAKU. 1986. 'Daishowa shuryoku ginko fuzai no 'hoigaku keiei'' ('Daishowa's Management Shifting Direction Without a Main Bank'). *Sentaku*, July, pp. 90–3.

SHEARD, PAUL. 1985. 'Main Banks and Structural Adjustment in Japan.' Pacific Economic Papers 129, Australian National University, Canberra.

——. 1986. 'General Trading Companies and Structural Adjustment in Japan.' Pacific Economic Papers 132, Australian National University, Canberra.

——. 1987. 'How Japanese Firms Manage Industrial Adjustment: a Case Study of Aluminium.' Pacific Economic Papers 151, Australian National University, Canberra.

——. 1989a. 'The Main Bank System and Corporate Monitoring and Control in Japan.' *Journal of Economic Behavior and Organization* 11: 399–422.

——. 1989b. 'The Japanese General Trading Company as an Aspect of Interfirm Risk-sharing.' *Journal of the Japanese and International Economies* 3(3): 308–22.

SHEARD, PAUL. 1991a. 'Delegated Monitoring Among Delegated Monitors: Principal-Agent Aspects of the Japanese Main Bank System.' CEPR Publication 274, Center for Economic Policy Research, Stanford University.

——. 1991b. 'The Economics of Interlocking Shareholding in Japan.' *Ricerche Economiche* 45(2–3): 421–48.

——. 1991c. 'The Role of Firm Organization in the Adjustment of a Declining Industry in Japan: the Aluminum Case.' *Journal of the Japanese and International Economies* 5(1): 14–40.

——. 1992. 'The Role of the Japanese Main Bank When Borrowing Firms are in Financial Distress.' CEPR Publication 330, Center for Economic Policy Research, Stanford University.

——. 1994a. 'Reciprocal Delegated Monitoring in the Japanese Main Bank System.' *Journal of the Japanese and International Economies* 8(1), pp. 1–21.

——. 1994b. 'Interlocking Shareholdings and Corporate Governance.' In Masahiko Aoki and Ronald Dore, eds., *The Japanese Firm: Sources of Competitive Strength*. New York: Oxford University Press.

——. 1994c. 'Bank Executives on Japanese Corporate Boards.' *Bank of Japan Monetary and Economic Studies*.

SHLEIFER, ANDREI and LAWRENCE H. SUMMERS. 1988. 'Breach of Trust in Hostile Takeovers.' In Alan Auerbach, ed., *Corporate Takeovers: Causes and Consequences*. Chicago: University of Chicago Press.

SHLEIFER, ANDREI and ROBERT W. VISHNY. 1991. 'Asset Sales and Debt Capacity.' National Bureau of Economic Research Working Paper 3618.

STIGLITZ, JOSEPH E. 1985. 'Credit Markets and the Control of Capital.' *Journal of Money, Credit, and Banking* 17: 133–52.

SUZUKI, SADAHIKO and RICHARD WRIGHT. 1985. 'Financial Structure and Bankruptcy Risk in Japan.' *Journal of International Business Studies* 16: 97–110.

TOKYO SHOKEN TORIHIKISHO CHOSABU. Various editions. *Tosho yoran* (*Fact Book on the Tokyo Stock Exchange*). Tokyo: Tokyo Shoken Torihikisho Chosabu.

TOYO KEIZAI SHINPOSHA. 1991. *Yakuin shikiho <jojo gaishaban> 1992-nenban* (*Directors' Annual [Listed Firm Edition], 1992 Edition*). Tokyo: Toyo Keizai Shinposha.

VON THADDEN, ERNST-LUDWIG. 1990. 'Bank Finance and Long Term Investment.' WWZ Discussion Paper 9010, University of Basel.

WEISS, LAWRENCE A. 1990. 'Bankruptcy Resolution: Direct Costs and Violation of Priority of Claims.' *Journal of Financial Economics* 27(2): 285–314.

WILLIAMSON, OLIVER E. 1985. *The Economic Institutions of Capitalism: Firms, Markets, Relational Contracting*. New York: Free Press.

WRUCK, KAREN HOPPER. 1990. 'Financial Distress, Reorganization, and Organizational Efficiency.' *Journal of Financial Economics* 27(2): 419–44.

ZENDER, JAMES F. 1991. 'Optimal Financial Instruments.' *Journal of Finance* 46(5): 1645–63.

7

Explicit Reasons for Implicit Contracts: The Legal Logic to the Japanese Main Bank System

J. MARK RAMSEYER

If the firm is a nexus of contracts, the stylized Japanese main bank system is a nexus of implicit contracts—or, as Aoki, Patrick and Sheard nicely put it in Chapter 1, 'a nexus of relationships'. Of the many characteristics commentators often ascribe to it, take four:

I The main bank monitors its debtors more intensively than the amount of its loans would suggest.
II It insures its clients against business failure.
III It lends its clients large sums, both long and short term.
IV Arrangements I and II it makes implicitly.[1]

These characteristics raise two quite different inquiries. Characteristics I through III lead readers to ask *why* these phenomena occur; IV should lead them to ask *whether* I and II occur.

Implicit main bank contracts are not promises that chain-smoking CEOs make in ornate conference rooms. Neither are they promises they make in dimly lit Akasaka restaurants while sipping Scotch and flirting with hostesses. Instead, implicit contracts are promises they never made—for had they made them, they would not be implicit. Make no mistake. It may be a simple definitional matter, but it is a basic one. An agreement is not 'implicit' just because it may be unwritten or incomplete. Even if oral and incompletely specified, it will still be an explicit and (generally) court-enforceable contract. (Japanese law has no general requirement that contracts be written (Suekawa, 1975, pp. 1–6).) Judges may prefer written and complete agreements, but they know how to handle swearing

The author acknowledges with gratitude the careful comments and generous suggestions of Masahiko Aoki, Douglas Baird, Theodor Baums, Ronald Gilson, John Haley, Koichi Hamada, Shinsaku Iwahara, Howell Jackson, Hideki Kanda, William Klein, Geoffrey Miller, Frank Packer, Hugh Patrick, Eric Rasmusen, Mark Roe, Frances Rosenbluth, Arthur Rosett, Richard Sander, Ulrike Schaede, and Paul Sheard; as well as workshop participants, and the participants in the Columbia University conference on Relational Investing. He received generous financial support for this research from the World Bank, the Lynde and Harry Bradley Foundation, and the John M. Olin Foundation.

[1] Many discussions add a further characteristic: the main bank buys stock in its clients. For an explanation of this phenomenon based on insider trading, see Ramseyer (1993).

contests over who promised what to whom. Instead, in most cases a contract is implicit if, but only if, no one explicitly made it. That Japanese main bank contracts are implicit thus implies that few Akasaka hostesses have ever seen a bank officer agree either to monitor debtors disproportionately or to insure them against failure. With a few notable exceptions—including Miwa (1990, 1991, 1993), Horiuchi, Packer and Fukuda (1988), and Horiuchi (1987)—most scholars of Japanese main banks, whether in this volume or elsewhere, ask why banks and debtors tacitly cut these bizarrely unspoken deals. This chapter examines whether they cut them at all.

In comparing the American and Japanese legal regimes, I suggest three discrete hypotheses. First, Japanese firms borrow more heavily from banks than American firms, in part because of regulatory structures (first section). During the late 1970s and early 80s, regulated interest rates more closely tracked market rates in Japan than in the United States; during most of the post-World War II decades, regulation made the bond market a less cost-effective source of funds in Japan than in the United States. For both reasons, firms in Japan had less incentive to avoid the bank loan market.

Second, given the size and character of banking transactions, rational bankers and borrowers will generally negotiate their contracts explicitly (second section). If they do not draft contracts about issue x explicitly, one should not conclude they draft them implicitly. One should conclude they draft no contracts about x at all.

Third, Japanese banks may rescue borrowers when they do because the legal system keeps them from committing themselves to jettisoning them (third section). By punishing banks that intervene in their borrowers' affairs, perhaps American judges enable banks more credibly to commit to letting troubled firms die. Because Japanese judges do not punish such banks, perhaps they do not let them commit. Even though Japanese banks would prefer to commit to jettisoning troubled borrowers, perhaps they cannot.

THE HEAVY JAPANESE RELIANCE ON BANK DEBT

Differential Reliance

Most scholars claim Japanese firms rely more heavily on bank debt than American firms do. Although they find idiosyncratic ways of measuring the reliance and although much depends on accounting definitions, they usually conclude the same: Japanese firms borrow from banks a bigger share of the money they need than American firms do. The Bank of Japan, for example, found that in 1982 American firms borrowed 85 cents from banks for every dollar they borrowed on the securities markets. French firms showed a ratio of 2.65, British firms of 4.08, German firms of 4.20, and Japanese firms of 5.33. During the three preceding years, American firms borrowed 1.69 times as much from banks as through securities, and Japanese firms borrowed 5.33 times as much (Kitahara, 1970, pp. 17, 115). Whether in the United States or Japan, most small firms cannot issue bonds. Were one to examine the debt patterns only of the bigger firms, the cross-national differences would loom larger still.

Much of this difference stems from two sources. First, some of it stems from the heavy disintermediation that occurred in the United States in the late 1970s and early 80s. Accordingly, the next part of this section outlines the interest rate regulations that contributed to that phenomenon. Second, some of it stems from aspects of the Japanese securities market that raised the costs of securitized finance. The third part of the section traces the source of those costs.

Interest Rate Policy

American Policy

During the half-century before the mid-1980s, American bureaucrats limited the interest banks could pay their depositors. In the late 1970s, however, they let inflation drive market interest rates high. While the prime rate neared 20 per cent, individual savings accounts paid 6 per cent interest or less, and corporate and checking accounts paid 0. By early 1980, the difference between the treasury bill yield and the regulated rate on one-year time deposits (pegged at 6 per cent) reached 7.46 per cent. By mid-1981, it topped 9 per cent (see Table 7.1). The difference between the T-bill rate and the pass-book savings rate (pegged at various rates from 5 per cent to 5.5 per cent) hit 9.84 per cent.

Effectively, the divergence between the market and regulated rates created a rent. To be sure, the banks may have competed some of it away. If they did not, however, depositors and borrowers could avoid it by circumventing the banks and transacting directly. Increasingly, they did. While market rates stayed low, corporate treasurers could cite convenience to justify keeping cash in zero-interest demand accounts. When market rates rose, so did the opportunity cost to keeping their cash there. Increasingly, they chose not to incur that cost.

American banks did offer market returns to their largest customers. Since 1961, they had sold negotiable CDs. Although the Federal Reserve Board had initially applied Regulation Q to the certificates, by 1973 it exempted them entirely (Loring and Brundy, 1985, p. 349). Hence, during the late 1970s American corporate treasurers could earn market rates by buying these CDs. Because they could always liquidate their investment

TABLE 7.1 The Interest-Rate Gap

Date[1]	Japan			United States		
	Market[2]	Guided[3]	Difference[4]	Market[5]	Guided[6]	Difference[4]
1978–1	6.12	5.25	0.87	6.41	6.0	0.41
1978–2	6.01	4.50	1.51	6.48	6.0	0.48
1978–3	6.15	4.50	1.65	7.32	6.0	1.32
1978–4	6.08	4.50	1.58	8.68	6.0	3.68
1979–1	6.48	4.50	1.98	9.36	6.0	3.36
1979–2	7.83	5.25	2.58	9.38	6.0	3.38
1979–3	7.84	6.00	1.84	9.63	6.0	3.63
1979–4	8.60	6.00	2.60	11.80	6.0	5.80
1980–1	9.27	7.00	2.27	13.46	6.0	7.46
1980–2	9.22	7.75	1.47	10.05	6.0	4.05
1980–3	9.06	7.75	1.31	9.24	6.0	3.24
1980–4	9.31	7.00	2.31	13.71	6.0	7.71
1981–1	8.63	7.00	1.63	14.37	6.0	8.37
1981–2	8.67	6.25	2.42	14.83	6.0	8.83
1981–3	9.03	6.25	2.78	15.09	6.0	9.09
1981–4	8.31	6.25	2.06	12.02	6.0	6.02
1983–1	7.76	5.75	2.01	12.89	6.0	6.89
1982–2	8.05	5.75	2.30	12.36	6.0	6.36
1982–3	8.38	5.75	2.63	9.71	6.0	3.71
1982–4	8.02	5.75	2.27	7.93	6.0	1.93
1983–1	7.61	5.75	1.86	8.08	6.0	2.08
1983–2	7.52	5.75	1.77	8.42	6.0	2.42
1983–3	7.47	5.75	1.72	9.19	6.0	3.19
1983–4	7.08	5.75	1.33	8.79	—	0
1984–1	6.83	5.50	1.33	9.13	—	0
1984–2	7.02	5.50	1.52	9.84	—	0
1984–3	6.95	5.50	1.45	10.34	—	0
1984–4	6.42	5.50	0.92	8.97	—	0

Notes and sources

[1] Year and quarter.

[2] The government bond yield, as given in various monthly issues of International Monetary Fund, *International Financial Statistics.*

[3] The Bank of Japan 'guideline' interest rate applicable to 1-year time deposits, in effect at the end of each quarter, as given in various issues of Nihon ginko chosa tokei kyoku, *Keizai tokei geppo (Economic Statistics Monthly)*, table 60.

[4] The difference between the market rate and the guided or regulated rate.

[5] The 3-month treasury bill yield, as given in International Monetary Fund, *International Financial Statistics.*

[6] The maximum legal interest rate applicable to 1-year time deposits, in effect at the end of each quarter. From 1983–84 there has been no limit. Board of Governors of the Federal Reserve System, *Federal Reserve Bulletin*, table 1.16.

at the discounted present value of the certificate pay-out, the CDs gave them both market returns and liquidity. Most treasurers with money to park, however, placed their money in the commercial paper (CP) market, the market for short-term unsecured corporate obligations. Other treasurers turned to the market to borrow. In 1959, firms had raised $3.7 billion in the CP market. By 1976, they raised $52.6 billion, and by 1989 $493 billion.[2]

Individual depositors abandoned banks too. Securities firms had offered mutual funds for decades: now they offered open-end funds investing in the money market. There, depositors found a close substitute for checking accounts, and earned 10 to 20 per cent interest to boot. Faced with these options, depositors fled the banks. Faced with their flight, regulators abandoned the restrictions on almost all rates. By 1989, however, investors had already moved $338 billion to money market funds.

Japanese Policy

Although Japanese bureaucrats fixed interest rates too, they more effectively limited inflation and more closely let those rates track market rates. Granted, they banned interest on corporate demand deposits. Yet they allowed near-market rates on a variety of savings accounts. Precisely because they let those rates track market rates so closely (see Table 7.1), Japanese investors had less reason to avoid banks. Indeed, Hugh Patrick notes that the treasury bill rate is a short-term rate while the Japanese government bond rate is a long-term rate, and suggests that under most theories the long-term rate will be higher than the short-term rates. If so, this table may *under*state the contrast between Japan and the United States.

For most of the time between 1978 and 1984, Japanese bureaucrats kept the difference between the market rate and the regulated rate on one-year time deposits under 2 per cent; they never let it exceed 3 per cent. They did let the difference between the market rate and the passbook savings rate (pegged at various rates from 1.75 per cent to 4.0 per cent) hit 6.03 per cent in the third quarter of 1981. Otherwise, they kept it under 6 per cent.

Japanese bureaucrats gave the largest depositors significant market-rate options. For example, in 1979, Japanese bureaucrats let banks sell negotiable certificates of deposit (CDs). Initially, they set a 500 million yen minimum to the accounts. In 1984, they lowered that amount to 300

---

[2] Note that much of what is thought to be disintermediation in the United States is instead intermediated finance through the non-bank sector. Although the amount of commercial paper outstanding (generally cited as an index of disintermediation) in the American market in 1987 was $353 billion, $275 billion of that amount was issued by such financial intermediaries as finance companies (for example, GMAC).

million yen, in 1985 to 100 million, and in 1988 to 50 million. Second, in 1985, bureaucrats let banks offer floating interest money-market certificates. Initially, they set a 50 million yen deposit minimum, and let banks pay a rate that floated at 0.75 per cent under the weekly Bank of Japan rate for CDs. Soon, they lowered the minimum—to 30 million yen in 1986, and 20 million, and then 10 million yen in 1987. By 1989, they let banks offer a new small deposit money-market certificate. They originally required a 3 million yen deposit, but then lowered that floor to 1 million yen, to 500,000 yen, and by 1992 eliminated the floor entirely. Third, in 1985 bureaucrats let banks pay market interest on deposits of at least 1 billion yen. Again, they have since lowered the minimum—in steps (as with the other accounts) but by 1991 to 3 million.

In 1985, 9.8 per cent of the deposited amount at the city banks paid unregulated interest; by 1990, that amount was 57.9 per cent, and in the early 1990s it seems to have stabilized around the 60 per cent level.

Although Japanese investors still earned positive rents by avoiding regulated bank accounts, they earned lower rents than in the United States. And because they earned lower rents, so did the entrepreneurs who created the institutions necessary to let them avoid the banks. Institutions are not free. With smaller incentives to create the institutions that would facilitate disintermediation, those entrepreneurs did less to facilitate disintermediation in Japan than in the United States.

The Securitized Loan Market

Not only did Japanese investors and borrowers find bank terms more advantageous than their American peers, they also had fewer options. American corporate borrowers could raise funds in the bond and CP markets. American investors could obligingly park their money there. Before the mid-1980s, however, most Japanese firms had almost no cost-effective non-bank sources for funds, and most Japanese investors had no cost-effective non-bank places to park their savings.

American Bond Markets

Large American borrowers have long been able to obtain funds through the bond market. Although the Securities and Exchange Commission (SEC) has regulated most sectors of that market, it has not (except with junk bonds) killed any sector. In several ways, it has even relaxed the regulatory framework. Through some of these changes, it has significantly cut the cost of securitized finance. As but one example, take shelf registration. Beginning in 1982, the SEC offered it as an alternative to the traditional registration procedure. Borrowers must usually file elaborate disclosure statements to issue long-term (over nine months) public debt. Under the shelf-registration regime, they can reduce the cost of the process by filing a blanket statement covering future issues. Rather than register each time they need extra cash, they can now issue their bonds 'off the shelf.' On a typical $90 million issue of 15-year 12 per cent coupon bonds in the early 1980s, they saved $2.3 million (present-valued aggregate savings) (Kidwell, Marr and Thompson, 1984, p. 192; Bhagat, Marr and Thompson, 1985). Although Japanese regulators now permit shelf-registration too, they have done so only since the fall of 1988 (Yamakawa, 1988a, 1988b).

Japanese Bond Markets

Until the late 1980s, most Japanese issuers—even many of the safest firms—found the bond markets either closed or prohibitively expensive. The reason lay in part in the political power of the banks. In order to protect the spread they earned on the difference between the rates they paid on deposits and earned on loans, the banks had to control the securitized loan market (bonds and CP). They also, of course, had to limit access to the equity market—a subject beyond the scope of this chapter. After all, if large firms could freely turn to a securitized market, they could easily circumvent the bank-loan cartel. Corporate treasurers and individual investors could transact directly or through mutual funds; corporate borrowers could issue bonds or CP. Together, they could split the regulatory rents banks would otherwise sometimes earn.[3]

The banks did not disable the bond market entirely: instead, they levied a toll charge on firms that used it. Any rational monopolist would have done the same. Although bank loans often do economize on transactional and informational costs (Horiuchi and Okazaki, 1992; Hoshi, Kashyap and Scharfstein, 1991), they do not always do so. Sometimes, securitized loans are cheaper. When they are, a borrowing firm and a monopolistic lender can both gain if the firm (a) borrows its funds in the securitized market and (b) pays the monopolist an access charge. That access charge the lenders will set approximately equal to the difference between (1) the (effectively unregulated) rates they can charge their borrowers and (2) the (artificially low) rates they pay their depositors.

Granted, no given bank would directly have lost monopoly rents if one of its borrowers had issued bonds and used the proceeds to repay its bank loan. After all, the banks loaned their funds at market rates. Collectively, however, the banks would have lost money. Necessarily, whenever a bank borrower moved to the securitized market, it took with it depositors who would otherwise have invested at the artificially low

---

[3] The spread between loan and deposit rates was smaller in Japan than in the United States, but larger than a market spread. The banks did not maximize the spread between the rates. Rather, they maximized the *politically maintainable* spread. The much larger American spread quickly disintegrated as Americans developed alternatives to banks. Note that legally CP is not a security in Japan. For a sophisticated analysis of the regulation of mutual funds in Japan, see Miwa (1993, pp. 277–89).

interest rates. Necessarily, every time a firm issued bonds, the banks collectively lost low-interest deposits (though they may not have lost quite as much as it appears, since the banks themselves bought many of the bonds).

The banks collected their toll charge by managing the collateral to the bond issues. The story begins in 1933 when the major banks (who were then also underwriters) collectively agreed to underwrite only secured bonds (Kuroda, 1987, p. 112). When the Americans bifurcated Japanese commercial and investment banking in the 1940s, the banks expanded their group (eventually known as the Bond Committee, the *kisaikai*) to include the securities firms. The ban on unsecured bonds, however, they retained. (On the lack of a legal basis or antitrust exemption for the Committee, see Negishi, 1992, pp. 28–29; Takeuchi, 1987, p. 6.)

By law, only banks could manage collateral. By requiring bond issuers to post collateral, the Bond Committee thus could force them to pay banks a fee for using the securities markets (Horiuchi and Sakurai, 1989, p. 106). By pricing those collateral-management fees strategically, it then could preserve the banks' monopoly pricing scheme. By all odds, it did set the price high. According to one survey (of Tokyo Stock Exchange listed firms that had recently issued bonds abroad or made large private placements domestically), 85.7 per cent of the firms gave Japanese bank commissions as a reason for selling bonds abroad (Miwa, 1992, p. 313). On a typical 10 billion yen bond in the Euromarket, banks earned commission fees of 3.5 million yen. In Japan they earned 53 million.[4]

In exchange for cooperating with the banking cartel, the securities firms shared the regulatory rents. In order to obtain their acquiescence, the banks priced their collateral management services strategically: they priced them in ways that shared with the securities firms (who collectively set underwriting fees) the monopoly rents they as banks earned (Miwa, 1992, pp. 324–27). Obviously, in any given industry (like the financial services industry) there can only be one monopoly rent. Having cartels among both collateral management firms (banks) and underwriting firms (securities firms) thus would not have increased the total monopoly rent extracted. The contest between the banks and securities firms instead would have been over the distribution of that rent.

All this occurred with Ministry of Finance (MOF) approval. A telling example of MOF's role occurred in mid-1991. As underwriters to the issuing firms, the securities firms had been selling at a discount the bonds

---

[4] Frankel and Morgan, 1992, p. 587. The 'collateral management' services may have been largely a sham. If so, then the collateralization requirement itself may have been largely a wealth transfer from issuers to banks. Evidence of the sham nature of the arrangement appears in the security interests themselves. Many of the bonds were secured by a 'mortgage' on the firm itself under the Enterprise Security Law (Kigyo tampo ho), Law 106 of 1958. Such a 'security interest' is not a security interest at all, but simply an unsecured priority claim.

they had just underwritten. They were reselling bonds from new issues, in short, at prices below those they had paid the issuer. Effectively, they were cheating on their own cartel. Having quoted supra-competitive underwriting fees, they were then discounting those fees by underwriting the bonds themselves at above-market prices. Once it noticed the practice, the MOF—acting as 'cartel cop'—intervened. Using its general police powers under §54 of the Securities Exchange Act, it ordered the firms immediately to stop their price competition (Miwa, 1992, pp. 324–27; 1993, pp. 71–74; Anon., 1992, p. 87).

In effect, the firms in the financial services industry (the banks *and* the securities firms) had together cartelized the entire industry. Whether a borrower tried to raise its money in the bank-loan market or on the securities market, they collected a monopoly rent. Precisely because they controlled both markets, a borrower could not avoid the monopoly rents in one market by raising funds in the other.

Recent Changes

Only recently did Japanese firms begin to borrow significant funds in the domestic bond market. Although for decades they operated a market in government bond repurchase contracts (known as *gensaki*), that market was small for many years and never gave banks much competition. In it, those firms that needed short-term working capital sold their portfolio of government bonds, together with a promise to repurchase them (at a price reflecting an implicit interest charge) within a few months (generally one or two). Those with excess cash then earned market returns by buying those bonds with the repurchase agreements attached. Essentially, the bond constituted collateral for what was a short-term loan. Because one could not profitably sell government bonds that one did not own, the market worked as a fund-raising device only for firms that already owned them.

As Table 7.2 shows, the domestic industrial bond market stayed small at least until the mid-1970s. By the MOF's own calculations, in the first half of that decade the largest firms—those with 1 billion yen or more in paid-in capital—raised 6 per cent of their total funding through bonds, and 10.3 per cent of their borrowed funds through bonds. For the smaller firms, the market was simply not an option (Kamochi, 1987, p. 63).

Japanese firms did eventually develop a large bond market, but only because of events overseas. Primarily for reasons exogenous to the banking industry, the Japanese government eased foreign exchange controls in the early 1980s. European firms had maintained an active market in foreign-currency corporate bonds, and these new foreign exchange rules now let large Japanese firms tap that market. In it, they could issue unsecured bonds. Effectively, they could avoid the banks' toll charge and a host of regulatory requirements besides. When the government revised the foreign

TABLE 7.2 Bond Issues by Japanese Industrial Companies

(billion yen)

Year	Domestic	Overseas	Year	Domestic	Overseas
1965	391		1980	1,091	683
1970	723	16	1981	1,815	1,118
			1982	1,513	1,374
1975	1,835	475	1983	1,561	1,919
1976	1,222	368	1984	2,335	2,795
1977	1,403	368			
1978	1,590	555	1985	2,585	3,253
1979	1,652	735	1986	4,552	4,117
			1987	5,970	5,340
			1988	7,744	6,892
			1989	9,284	11,129

Note: Includes convertible issues and issues with warrants attached.

Source: Okura sho shoken kyoku, *Okura sho shoken kyoku nempo (Annual Report of the Ministry of Finance Securities Bureau)*, various years; Koshasai hikiuke kyokai, *Koshasai nenkan (Bond Annual)*, various years.

exchange rules effective late 1980, Japanese firms increased the money they raised abroad from 680 billion yen in 1980 to 1.1 trillion yen in 1981. When it liberalized those rules further in early 1984, they increased the amount raised abroad from 1.9 trillion yen in 1983 to 2.7 trillion yen in 1984. By 1989, Japanese firms borrowed 11 trillion yen abroad. (Due to the domestic recession, bond issues have fallen since 1989.)

Once the large firms could issue bonds in the Euromarket, Japanese banks had little choice but to ease the terms they offered those firms. First, the banks let firms issue unsecured bonds within Japan. Given that the large firms would raise their funds overseas unless the banks let them avoid the toll charge, they let them avoid it (Kuroda, 1987, pp. 136–37). Firms issued their first unsecured domestic bonds in the 1970s, and by 1984, the Bond Committee had lowered its standards to the point where 16 firms qualified. By 1991 400 companies qualified, and the banks cut their collateral management fees even on issues that remained secured. The Japanese Fair Trade Commission has also pressured the Bond Committee to abandon its uniform pricing schedule. Henceforth, the issuer and its bank are to negotiate their own collateral management fees.

Second, the banks acquiesced to a CP market. Because of the gap between market and regulated interest rates, American firms had been paying banks regulatory rents that they could avoid if they could learn to borrow from investors directly; they did just that through the CP market. Japanese firms had not turned to a CP market because they did not have one; they had not created a CP market because of the political power of the banks. Although the law did not explicitly ban CP (Takeuchi, 1987, p. 7), it did not clearly permit it either. Because of the ambiguous status of CP, banks could threaten to use their power within the MOF, power that stemmed from their ties to the ruling Liberal Democratic Party, the LDP.[5]

Given that risk, Japanese firms bargained first. Because of the competitive pressure from the Euromarket, they did eventually negotiate a CP market. Their politically charged negotiations took time, however, and they did not obtain their CP market until late 1987 (Tsujimura, 1989, p. 21). Once they obtained it, they used it. Within a year, the market passed the Euro-CP market. By December 1990, it hit 15.7 trillion yen.

EXPLICIT AND IMPLICIT DEALS

Legally Enforceable Claims

Basic to *any* banking system is a legal regime that lets people enforce and transfer rights to assets. The ordinary bank loan is itself no more than one such set of (explicit) contracts. One party (the lender) transfers to another party (the borrower) assets to which it has a legally enforceable claim (cash). The borrower agrees to return the cash after a stated time, together with a fee for using it (the interest). The lender makes at least the risk-adjusted return it would earn on the cash elsewhere; the borrower pays no more than the risk-adjusted return it will earn on the cash. Such are the usual gains from trade.

Many of these gains disappear in the absence of enforceable claims. Most lenders will not lend unless the borrower gives them the right to sue if it does not return the cash. Many lenders will not lend unless the borrower also agrees to repay them before it pays anyone else. Often, such agreements lower the price a lender would otherwise charge for the funds. Usually, they increase the supply of funds a lender will provide. Either way, they increase social welfare.

Alternative Enforcement Schemes

Not that the banking industry would collapse without courts. Lenders and borrowers can usually protect their claims in other ways. For

---

[5] See Ramseyer and Rosenbluth (1993). For nice summaries of the politics and ambiguities involved, see Litt, Macey, Miller and Rubin (1990) and Schaede (1990).

instance, they can hire private armies. Whether in New York or Tokyo, they sometimes do—and whether here or there, the problems are obvious. Private debt-collection work may have made the Corleone family thrice a box-office smash; it imposes large externalities on everyone else.

Lenders and debtors sometimes also keep their word just because they hope to repeat the transaction. Assume a firm earns a higher return on some kinds of deals than on others. The firm will try hard to repeat such deals. If it must keep its word to ensure repetition, then it may even keep its word. The key, however, is the assumption: that it expects to earn supra-market returns by repeating these deals in the future. Without those future rents from repetition, rational firms may renege (Klein and Leffler, 1981; Ramseyer, 1991; Shapiro, 1983; Telser, 1980).[6]

Enforcement Schemes in Japan

Although many differences in Japanese and American banking patterns derive from differences in the legal regimes, consider first some basic commonalities. Both countries have capitalist economies and both countries maintain sophisticated courts. In both countries, those courts protect most rights to private property, and enforce most consensual bargains.

That Japanese courts do all this suggests Japanese firms may not use implicit agreements as often as usually argued. If courts will indeed enforce explicit contracts, rational parties will seldom leave large deals to implicit terms. By definition, implicit contracts are not contracts: courts will not enforce them. Because they are not enforceable, rational parties will keep them only if they expect to earn supra-competitive rents by continuing the relationship into the future. Parties will comply with implicit contractual terms, in other words, only if the future repeated transactions earn them an expected return larger than that they can expect to earn elsewhere.

In deciding whether to negotiate the terms of a deal explicitly, rational parties thus face a trade-off. They will use implicit rather than explicit contracts if, but only if, (1) the future rents (present valued, of course) necessary to induce compliance voluntarily (the minimum compliance-inducing rents) are less than (2) the costs of drafting the contract explicitly and enforcing it in court (the contracting costs). Whenever the compliance-inducing rents exceed the contracting costs, they will draft contracts. Note that the calculus does not change if rephrased in terms of the effect that reneging has on the bank's reputational capital and ability

---

[6] Some observers may suggest that hostage mechanisms (Williamson, 1983) could support self-enforcement in Japan. Although possible in theory, the point is unlikely to apply to Japanese bank-borrower relations in practice. The most likely hostage would be the cross-shareholdings, but because stock does not have relationship-specific value, it does not work as a hostage. (See Ramseyer, 1993.)

to deal implicitly with other borrowers. Whether the bank earns a return of z on one contract or a return of nz on n contracts, the calculus is the same.[7]

In the banking industry, the trade-off overwhelmingly militates against implicit contracts. The reason: the minimum compliance-inducing rents vary with the size of the transaction, while contracting costs are largely independent of it. In the financial services industry, a firm that reneges on a deal will generally pocket the cash advanced it. Accordingly, for it not to renege it must anticipate rents with a discounted present value greater than the cash advanced. The bigger the deal, the bigger will be the minimum compliance-inducing rents.

By contrast, legal fees are largely independent of the size of the deal. There are obvious exceptions: for example, the larger the deal, the greater the incentive to find higher-priced lawyers. Yet the costs of negotiating and drafting a contract depend primarily on attorney hours, which in turn depend on the complexities and idiosyncrasies of the deal. They depend only tangentially on the money at stake. Typically, therefore, once the size of a deal reaches a certain threshold, the compliance-inducing rent will exceed contracting costs. At that point, rational firms will negotiate all contracts explicitly.

Recall the contexts where scholars first developed the theories of implicit self-enforcing contracts. First, many scholars found the theories helpful in understanding labour markets. Where factory workers could easily shirk and managers could not cheaply monitor, employers could save resources by paying workers a supra-market wage (that is, efficiency wages) (Shapiro and Stiglitz, 1984). Second, scholars found that the theories helped explain how markets worked where buyers could not cheaply confirm product quality *ex ante*. Where buyers could not check quality before buying, they saved money by paying a higher price to an established seller. Rather than risk a fake from a peddler outside Ueno station, they bought their Rolexes from Ginza jewellers (Klein and Leffler, 1981). Last, scholars used the models where courts could not reach the parties involved. Unable to use courts, medieval international traders relied on

---

[7] Readers will note that some rents will accrue simply from the mutual investments in relationship-specific information. Unless these exceed the one-shot gains from reneging, however, these rents will not suffice to make the deal self-enforcing. Moreover, readers should note that the same rents accrue to the parties even if they draft explicit contracts—the parties do not abandon the relationship-specific rents by drafting court-enforceable agreements.

Those who complain that court enforcement is expensive largely miss the fact that most rational parties settle out of court *by reference to* the expected legal outcome (Ramseyer and Nakazato, 1989). Because the vast majority of contract disputes in both the United States and Japan are settled out of court, the relevant enforcement costs for explicit contracts are not (the relatively high) litigation costs, but rather (the much lower) settlement costs. Note, however, that the higher the costs of litigation, (a) the more likely the parties are to settle, and (b) the greater the variance in settlements.

reputations and trading clubs (Greif, 1992; Milgrom, North and Weingast, 1990).

None of these situations remotely resembles the Japanese banking industry. First, and most obviously, courts exist and work. The parties involved are not peripatetic medieval merchants, wandering from jurisdiction to jurisdiction. Second, the stakes are high. Explicit contracts may not efficiently prevent factory workers from shirking or street vendors from peddling fake watches. But these are not factory workers earning $30 an hour or street vendors selling $3,000 watches. These are firms with legally trained staffs, law firms within easy reach, and millions of dollars at stake. Modern scholars use implicit contracts to explain why these firms behave as they do on million-dollar deals. They need first to explain why the firms reject straightforward court-enforceable contracts.

In response to this, some fans of implicit contract theory may cite problems of verification: parties will prefer implicit contracts, they will argue, where the deal depends on information courts cannot verify. Although hard to verify promises exist (for example, to cherish and obey till death do us part), the putative main bank contracts (such as, to insure against business failure) are not among them. Creative lawyers can easily suggest a wide variety of verifiable indices of business trouble, and can easily list just as many verifiable bank responses. They regularly (and explicitly) draft contracts that insure fashion models' legs, football players' arms, and singers' voices. Writing an insurance contract against business failure they will find boringly mundane. *If* verification by a court is problematic, reliance on the bank's reputational capital will not solve the problem either, since verification by the bank's *other* partners will be equally problematic. And if third parties cannot verify a bank's performance, the bank's reputational capital will not accurately reflect its performance.

If insurance agreements seem unlikely candidates for implicit contracts, consider whether disproportionate monitoring agreements are any more likely. (Sheard, 1991, discusses the model with particular insight.) Implicit contract theorists argue that in Japan the main bank implicitly agrees with other banks both (1) to monitor the debtor disproportionately and (2) to bear losses disproportionately. The Mitsubishi Bank, for example, may *explicitly* agree to lend Iroha Sushi 30 per cent of the bank loans Iroha needs. At the time it does so, it may also *implicitly* agree to bear 80 per cent of the costs of monitoring Iroha and to absorb 80 per cent of any losses should Iroha fail.

It is hard to imagine a less-likely implicit contract than this Mitsubishi-Iroha arrangement, for it is hard to imagine a more needlessly complicated agreement. If Iroha's creditors collectively find it efficient for Mitsubishi to bear 80 per cent of the monitoring costs, the straightforward way to reach that result is to have Mitsubishi lend 80 per cent of the money. It will then have a greater incentive to monitor (even if not precisely 80 per cent), and will absorb exactly 80 per cent of any resulting losses (provided all loans have equal priority). Because the total loans outstanding will not change, this explicit alternative will not raise any bank's capital requirements. And because Mitsubishi bears 80 per cent of Iroha's default risk under either scheme, neither does it reduce Mitsubishi's diversification.

INSURANCE CONTRACTS

Initial Doubts

According to the traditional stylized facts, Japanese main banks more often rescue ailing borrowers than American banks do. When times are bad, the main bank cuts the interest rate it charges. When firms start to fail, it decides whether they have any future prospects. If they do, it lends them extra money and gives them extra expertise. Through such moves, it insures its borrowers against business failure. Many observers consider all this an implicit insurance contract.[8]

Over the past decade, scholars have written several brilliant studies exploring the phenomenon. They include several more within this volume. Nonetheless, it is clear neither that Japanese firms would want this insurance, nor that they buy it. Consider each point in turn.

Would Firms Want It?

If a bank offered insurance against firm failure, it would invite classic problems of adverse selection. Unless the bank had perfect information, the least credit-worthy firms would disproportionately apply for the insurance. Because the bank cannot distinguish risk levels perfectly, the higher risk level in the pool would cause the bank to raise the insurance premium it charged. The safest firms in the pool would then decline the insurance contract, and the average risk-level would rise further. The bank would raise the premium still higher, still more firms would decline the contract, and so forth. The process would continue relentlessly—until the market for the insurance disappeared (Akerlof, 1970).

The bank would face equally severe problems of moral hazard. Just as

---

[8] This is a fundamentally different theory from Hoshi, Kashyap and Sharfstein's (1991) argument that the main bank lowers the cost of financial distress. They do not argue that the main bank necessarily offers an implicit insurance contract. Rather, they argue that its presence reduces the transactions costs of reorganizing distressed firms.

Some observers describe the implicit insurance contract as something close to a mixed strategy: the main bank agrees to rescue the firm with probability x, where x is positive but less than 1. Despite some suggestions to the contrary, it is not clear why this would eliminate either moral hazard or adverse selection, as long as the main bank has less than perfect information about the debtor's strategy.

Barbara Stanwyck (sort of) played a nice kid before buying her husband accident insurance with a double indemnity clause, rational firms would pretend to invest in low-risk projects in order to buy their implicit insurance against failure more cheaply. Just as Stanwyck then (sort of) tossed her husband off the train, rational firms would then hike the risk level of the projects they undertook.

Some implicit insurance theorists argue that main banks can prevent this moral hazard by punishing the incumbent managers in the firms they rescue. Unfortunately, the gain to the firm's shareholders from the moral hazard will often exceed the loss to the few fired managers. (Note that the main bank will own no more than 5 per cent of the firm's stock; see Ramseyer, 1993.) As a result, rational shareholders can compensate their managers *ex ante* for any punishment the managers will incur if the bank later intervenes and punishes them. To do so, they need simply to pay the managers a supra-market salary. As long as they pay them wages that include a premium equal to the risk-adjusted loss the managers suffer if the firm fails and the main bank intervenes, both the shareholders and the managers gain.

Do Banks Sell It?

Whatever the logic to implicit contracts, to date no one has shown that banks actually offer them. Indeed, no one has shown that Japanese banks more regularly rescue debtors than American banks. Consider some of the evidence. First, large numbers of Japanese firms fail regularly. From 1981 to 1985, an average of 18,700 firms with debt of over 10 million yen went out of business every year. Granted, most of the failing firms were small. Yet that fact itself suggests the first caveat: banks do not insure small firms. In turn, the caveat suggests the first problem: why not insure small firms? Banks should find it no harder to monitor small firms than large. Small firms should want the insurance as badly as large. If (as seems likely) small firms generally run less diversified operations than large, they may even want the insurance more. If banks and large firms can negotiate mutually advantageous implicit insurance, so should banks and small firms. And if banks and small firms do not find implicit insurance mutually advantageous, perhaps something else better explains the apparent bank rescues of large firms.[9]

Second, several scholars who have tried to locate empirical evidence of the insurance have not found it. Horiuchi, Packer and Fukuda (1988), for example, used data from the chemical industry to ask whether main

---

[9] Note (a) that the per-asset-value premium on the insurance could be higher for small firms if they systematically have inferior management, (b) that the premium could also be higher for small firms if there are economies of scale to monitoring, and (c) that the insurance might be unavailable entirely if owner-managers presented more serious moral-hazard problems.

banks lowered interest charges to troubled firms. They found no evidence that they did. Miwa (1990, chapter 6) asked whether main banks increased their percentage of a firm's loans when the firm fell into distress. He, too, found no evidence.

Last, no one has ever found any evidence that firms pay for this insurance (Miwa, 1991, p. 16), and without that payment one would not expect banks to offer insurance. Some scholars suggest that those firms that want the insurance pay a higher interest rate on loans from their main bank than on loans from other banks. No one has found any evidence that this occurs. Others suggest, more promisingly, that those firms that want the insurance direct a greater share of their fee-based business to their main bank. Since all firms need the fee-based services, however, this effectively suggests *all* firms might receive the insurance. To be sure, some firms use more such services than others. Given a single industry, large firms will typically buy more foreign exchange than small; given a single firm size, export-oriented firms will buy more foreign exchange than others. Nonetheless, the firm's need for these fee-based services will seldom correlate with its riskiness. If so, the bank cannot be pricing its insurance very efficiently. And if banks are not pricing it carefully, the best conclusion about the implicit insurance contracts may be that banks do not sell them.

Equitable Subordination and Bank Rescues

Consider, however, another possibility: perhaps Japanese banks do rehabilitate large borrowers more than American banks, but do so because they cannot credibly threaten to let them fail. Given that Japanese courts will let a bank rescue a borrower without jeopardizing its rights in bankruptcy, perhaps Japanese banks find some rescues profitable *ex post*. By contrast, perhaps American banks abandon borrowers because they cannot cheaply save them. Given that American courts sometimes punish a bank for intervening in its debtors' affairs, perhaps American banks find rescues more often unprofitable even *ex post*.

The Ex Post *Incentive*

All else equal, creditors sometimes (not always) have an incentive *ex post* to intervene and rescue debtors who threaten default (see Bulow and Shoven, 1978). Explicit contracts are unlikely to help much here. Even if the bank explicitly stated *ex ante* that it would not help a debtor in distress, it might still have an incentive to break that statement and defer repayment. Obviously, the borrower will not complain if the bank does so.

Many firms find themselves in trouble at least partly because they lack adequate cash—they find themselves illiquid even when not insolvent. A bank that has lent such a firm large amounts will sometimes find that lending it extra funds, even short term, pays. If it refuses to lend those funds, the firm will fail. If it has secured its past loans, it may then receive a share of the liquidation proceeds, but its share is likely to fall short of its outstanding claim. If it lent its money unsecured, it will receive even less. Simply by advancing such a firm cash, the bank can sometimes recover its principal and interest in full. As a result, all else equal, American and Japanese banks will sometimes be tempted *ex post* to save their failing debtors.

The Ex Ante *Logic*

If a bank would find it profitable to rescue a troubled firm *ex post*, it faces serious problems *ex ante*. Most basically, it will find it hard credibly to threaten to punish a borrower who defaults. As the punishment will be unprofitable *ex post*, the threat to punish will be incredible *ex ante*. Unable to threaten *ex ante*, the bank can now sell only bundled credit-insurance contracts. In turn, to the extent it cannot constrain its debtors, those debtors will exploit the bundled contract by increasing the risk level of their projects. The bank will anticipate this, of course, and raise the price it charges. The inability to commit *ex ante*, in other words, will create incentives *ex post* that in turn will generate adverse selection and moral hazard *ex ante*. Disintermediation will ensue: firms that would prefer to undertake lower-risk projects will leave the bank-loan market entirely.

With small borrowers, a bank may yet be able to make its threat credible by combining pre-commitment strategies with a concern for its reputation. BCCI notwithstanding, for most banks the credit business is an iterated game. Precisely because of the moral-hazard and adverse-selection problems that bundled credit-insurance contracts aggravate, a bank may hope to cultivate a ruthless reputation for *not* insuring its borrowers. If it lends money often enough and discounts the future at a rate low enough, with small borrowers such a reputation-based strategy may work (Kreps and others, 1982; Rasmusen, 1989, 5.4).

With large debtors, a bank will find it harder to make such reputational strategies work. Even banks that can jettison small borrowers find it hard to bully firms to whom they have lent enormous amounts. College professors with southern Californian mortgages may find their finances dominated by their local savings and loan. But insolvent third-world strong-men with multi-billion dollar loans seem sometimes to dictate terms to the great money-centre banks. Models of repeated games and pre-commitment may explain why banks adopt strategies that otherwise do not seem credible, but they work only if the bank's one-shot loss from punishing a firm is small compared to its future reputational rents. When a firm's debt is large enough, the bank's *ex post* unprofitable strategy will make the bank's *ex ante* threat less credible. When a large enough debtor threatens to fail, even a ruthless bank may try to rescue it.

The American Law of Firm Rescues

In effect, Japanese banks may be selling the largest firms implicit insurance contracts that the firms do not want. When a large firm borrows from a Japanese bank, perhaps it knows that, should it find itself in trouble, the bank may save it. Even if the firm does not want the insurance, the bank cannot credibly sell it unbundled credit. Unable credibly to threaten to let failing large debtors fail, the bank has no choice but to include insurance with its credit.

Even if American banks less often rescue their borrowers than Japanese banks do (a proposition no one has proved), that fact would not necessarily show that willing Japanese banks sell implicit insurance to willing Japanese borrowers. American banks instead may be jettisoning their clients because US bankruptcy law more readily lets them commit to doing so. The hypothesis follows.

By tradition, American judges have looked sceptically at creditors who intervene in a debtor's business. Those who do so, they reason, may try to restructure the debtor to their private advantage. Should a bank intervene, therefore, American judges sometimes subordinate its claims. Interventionist creditors have also been required to pay various debtor liabilities out of their own pockets (Douglas-Hamilton, 1975).[10]

At stake is the doctrine of 'equitable subordination': for the sake of 'fairness', a judge may subordinate the claims of a creditor who intervenes before Chapter 11 in its debtor's affairs. '[A]s a court of equity,' Chaitman (1984, p. 1561) explained, a bankruptcy court 'has the power to subordinate the claims of one creditor to those of other creditors where the claimant has engaged in some type of inequitable conduct which has resulted in an unfair advantage to the claimant or an injury to the other creditors.' Hence, a bank can lose its priority whenever 'the bank has taken control of the debtor, thus assuming the fiduciary duties of a controlling shareholder, and then breached those duties to the injury of general creditors' (Chaitman, 1984, p. 1562).

At trial, banks argue that the doctrine prevents them from saving troubled clients. Nonetheless, many judges remain sceptical:

While defendant [i.e., the bank] argues that subordination will cause members of the financial community to feel they cannot give financial assistance to failing companies, but must instead foreclose on their security interests and collect debts swiftly, not leaving any chance for survival, the Court is singularly unimpressed. (*In re* American Lumber Co., 5 B.R. 470 at 478 D.C. D. Minn. 1980.)

[10] Absent collective action problems among creditors (but *only* absent such problems), creditors could vitiate the effect of the equitable subordination doctrine by unanimously agreeing *ex ante* not to argue the theory in court.

The bank in the case had restructured a troubled debtor and advanced it extra funds. When the debtor started to fail anyway, it tried to ensure that the debtor repaid its debts to the bank. The unsecured creditors complained, and the court took their side. Once in control of the debtor, the bank could not use its control to its private advantage. Having tried, it now stood last in line.

American bankers have not missed this risk of subordination. The problem 'has generated much debate and fear among members of the financial community', DeNatale and Abram (1985, p. 417) noted. Of course, courts do not necessarily subordinate creditors who intervene: they do so only when they think creditors intervened and misbehaved. According to the usual judicial formula, they subordinate a creditor's claim only when: the creditor 'engaged in some type of inequitable conduct', the creditor obtained 'an unfair advantage' over other creditors, and equitable subordination is not 'inconsistent with the provisions of the Bankruptcy Act' (*In re* Mobile Steel Co., 563 F.2d 692, 700 (5th Cir. 1977)). Unfortunately, the formula does not much help. Judges subordinate claims whenever 'equity' demands it and equity, like pornography, lies in the eye of the beholder. Ultimately, American creditors restructure their debtors at their peril.

Equitable subordination does not make bank rescues impossible; it makes them more costly. When a firm hits bad times, creditors will seldom lend more money without controlling the way it uses it. Under American law, they can do so before a Chapter 11 filing only by gambling all: if the firm succeeds, the bank recovers its claim; if the firm fails and the other creditors convince the judge that the bank indulged its private biases, it potentially loses all. For the sake of making credible threats, perhaps that risk often suffices. Precisely because of this *ex post* risk to intervention, perhaps American banks can more credibly threaten to jettison defaulting debtors *ex ante*. Often, of course, there will be public debt subordinate to the bank's loan. Because the indenture trustee cannot legally waive the default, rescues often can be made only by the bank.

The Japanese Law of Firm Rescues

Japanese judges use no doctrine analogous to equitable subordination. The proposition, understandably, is impossible to prove, risky even to advance. Few things in comparative legal work are harder than proving a categorical negative, and doubly so when the issue involves a matter so entrusted to judicial whimsy. Whether in the United States or Japan, in bankruptcy cases judges wield enormous discretion. They can disallow sales, payments, and security interests, for example, sometimes even when the parties complete the transaction before anyone files for bankruptcy.

Moreover, even though they may phrase it differently, Japanese judges do exercise their discretion in ways that often resemble the American judicial concern for 'equity'. If a bankrupt firm repays a debt to benefit one specific creditor, the judge may void the payment. If it repays a debt knowing that it thereby harms other creditors and the payee knows that too, the judge may void the payment. If it sells real estate (even at fair market value) and might squander the cash, the judge may void the sale. And if a debtor grants a security interest after it has started to default on its notes, a judge may void the security interest.

What one does *not* see in these cases, however, is any equivalent of equitable subordination—any series of decisions where judges voided security interests to punish a major secured creditor who intervened in the debtor's affairs. Without such a doctrine, a creditor will more often find such intervention profitable *ex post*. Profitable *ex post*, its threats will be less credible *ex ante*.

The Absent Evidence

The question, then, is whether the absence of an equitable subordination doctrine in Japan increases the incidence of firm rescues. To answer it, we need several pieces of evidence we do not yet have. First and most basically, if the proposition is true, then (all else equal) Japanese banks should more readily rescue troubled firms than American banks. We do not know this. We know only that both Japanese and American banks rescue a few large troubled firms, and jettison most.

Second, large Japanese debtors should be at a greater disadvantage in the loan market than large American debtors. According to the hypothesis, (x) the absence of equitable subordination prevents Japanese banks from committing to jettisoning borrowers with large debts to the bank, (y) the presence of the doctrine allows American banks to make that commitment, and (z) reputational considerations enable both Japanese and American banks to commit to jettisoning borrowers with small debts. If so, then large American debtors should do better in the credit market relative to small American debtors, than large Japanese debtors do relative to small Japanese debtors. On this too we have no evidence.

Third, Japanese debtors should try to keep their debts at any one bank small. If the hypothesis is true, then Japanese debtors will try harder than American firms do to avoid borrowing large amounts from any one bank. We do know that Japanese firms diversify their borrowings (Ramseyer, 1991). Unfortunately, we do not know whether, all else equal, they do so *more* than American firms.

Last, the absence of equitable subordination in Japan should promote disintermediation. If the absence of equitable subordination prevents Japanese banks from credibly committing to jettisoning troubled clients, it necessarily forces them to bundle 'implicit insurance contracts' with the credit they sell. Because moral hazard and adverse selection will raise the price banks must charge for these bundled credit-insurance contracts, low-risk firms will try to avoid the bundled package. The best way to do that is to leave the bank-loan market entirely.

Japanese firms *have* started to leave the bank-loan market. From 1985 to 1989, firms increased the amounts they raised through bond issues nearly four-fold. According to Hoshi, Kashyap and Scharfstein (1991), from 1983 to 1990, firms listed on the Tokyo Stock Exchange reduced their ratio of bank debt to total debt by a third. Those able to issue bonds not guaranteed by a bank reduced it by over 40 per cent. The safest firms, it seems, deserted the banks *en masse*. As Hoshi, Kashyap and Scharfstein (1991) put it, firms with 'good performance, valuable investment opportunities, or valuable assets' turned to the bond market. Only those with significant 'scope for inefficient behavior' remained.

Ultimately, equitable subordination remains a tenuous hypothesis. Most obviously, the only evidence we have on the point is that of disintermediation—and that, of course, is a phenomenon subject to an enormous variety of explanations. We also do not know the aggregate effect of bankruptcy law, for equitable subordination is but a small part of the picture. Although all American courts in theory apply the doctrine, more is at stake. Some American courts treat the doctrine sceptically. Some American courts punish banks for *not* rescuing a firm (on the grounds that the bank refused the additional credit in 'bad faith'). And most American courts let a bank safely 'rescue' firms as long as it waits until after they file Chapter 11 petitions. In the end, a basic empirical vacuum remains: although Japanese banks help some troubled borrowers, they jettison most; although American banks jettison most troubled borrowers, they help some. Beyond that, we cannot say.

CONCLUSION

As part of the institutional structure of an economy, legal rules shape the deals firms cut. By altering the costs of alternative forms of economic exchange, they alter the transactions firms enter. The differences between American and Japanese commercial practice form a case in point: some of the most puzzling differences may largely be artefacts of the different legal regimes in place.

The Japanese main bank system (to the extent a distinctive system exists) may be one such idiosyncratic result. Recent observers use the system to explain the large bank debts Japanese firms use and to posit aesthetically appealing models of implicit contractual arrangements: agreements where one bank agrees with the other banks to act as their delegated monitor, and agrees with the firm to insure it against business failure. It is not that these models are theoretically impossible. At stake are indefinitely repeated transactions, and we know from the game-theoretic folk theorem that in such worlds anything can be an equilibrium. It is rather that they are realistically implausible.

Any differences between the Japanese and American banking systems may derive from far more mundane reasons. Consider why Japanese firms borrow so much of their money from banks. First, during the late 1970s and early 1980s, Japanese bureaucrats caused regulated rates to track market rates more closely than in the United States. As a result, investors and firms faced smaller incentives to devise ways of avoiding the banks. Second, for most of the post-war period Japanese banks levied a large toll charge (in the form of collateral management fees) on anyone who used the bond market. Firms thus could avoid the banks through the bond market only if they repaid much of their savings to their bank.

If Japanese banks rescue large failing clients more often than American banks rescue them (an unproven proposition), consider why they might do so. The discussion above suggests one obvious reason— Japanese banks rescue firms more frequently (and monitor more extensively) than do American banks because they have lent more funds. For regulatory reasons, Japanese firms borrow more heavily from banks than do American firms. If so, banks in Japan have more money at stake in the client firms and, all else equal, should monitor more heavily and rescue more frequently for that reason alone. Japanese banks do not lend heavily, in other words, because they monitor or rescue extensively; they monitor and rescue extensively (if indeed they do) because they lend so heavily.

But there may be another reason Japanese banks rescue firms. Japanese banks may rescue their clients because they cannot credibly threaten to abandon them; American banks may abandon their clients because they cannot cheaply save them. American law sometimes punishes creditors who intervene in a debtor's business; perhaps Japanese law does not. Hence, perhaps American banks can more credibly threaten to let troubled firms fail. In doing so, they avoid the moral-hazard and adverse-selection problems they might otherwise face. Because Japanese law does not penalize banks that intervene, perhaps Japanese banks often cannot credibly threaten to punish defaulting clients. Unable to threaten *ex ante*, perhaps they involuntarily sell their clients bundled credit-insurance packages. Unfortunately, we do not yet have the data to test the hypothesis.

For all their analytic elegance and mathematical sophistication (and they *are* both elegant and sophisticated), the recent models of implicit contracts raise a more basic problem besides: if banks and firms want these arrangements so badly, why do they not negotiate them explicitly and draft court-enforceable agreements? If they did draft an agreement insuring a firm against specified business problems, the firms could rely on the courts. Although complicated contracts seldom come cheap, for transactions this large they should come cheaper than the rents a firm would need to pay a bank to make an agreement self-enforcing. Notwithstanding those potential savings, the firms do not draft such agreements. Perhaps the reason is simple. Perhaps they do not make them at all.

REFERENCES

AKANE, RYUJI. 1985. *Kin'yukai (The Financial World)*. Tokyo: Kyoiku kai.
AKERLOF, GEORGE A. 1970. 'The Market for "Lemons": Quality Uncertainty and the Market Mechanism.' *Quarterly Journal of Economics*, 84: 488.
ANONYMOUS. 1987. Note, 'Equitable Subordination and Analogous Theories of Lender Liability: Toward a New Model of "Control".' *Texas Law Review* 65: 801.
——. 1987. 'Zoshi hakusho' ('Capital Increase White Paper'). *Shoji homu* 1115: 1.
——. 1988. 'Zoshi hakusho' ('Capital Increase White Paper'). *Shoji homu* 1150: 1.
——. 1991. 'Zoshi hakusho' ('Capital Increase White Paper'). *Shoji homu* 1254: 1.
——. 1992. 'Zoshi hakusho' ('Capital Increase White Paper'). *Shoji homu* 1290: 1.
BHAGAT, SANJAI, M. WAYNE MARR and G. RODNEY THOMPSON. 1985. 'The Rule 415 Experiment: Equity Markets.' *Journal of Finance*, 40: 1385.
BOARD OF GOVERNORS OF THE FEDERAL RESERVE SYSTEM. Various months. *Federal Reserve Bulletin*. Washington DC: Federal Reserve Board.
BULOW, JEREMY I., and JOHN B. SHOVEN. 1978. 'The Bankruptcy Decision.' *Bell Journal of Economics* 9: 437.
CHAITMAN, HELEN DAVIS. 1984. 'The Equitable Subordination of Bank Claims.' *Business Lawyer* 39: 1561.
Chusho kigyo kin'yu koko geppo (Small and Medium-Sized Company Finance Corporation Monthly). Various years.
CLARK, ROBERT CHARLES. 1986. *Corporate Law*. Boston: Little, Brown and Co.
——. 1981. 'The Interdisciplinary Study of Legal Evolution.' *Yale Law Journal* 90: 1238.
——. 1977. 'The Duties of the Corporate Debtor to its Creditors.' *Harvard Law Review* 90: 505.
Collier on Bankruptcy, 15th ed. New York: Matthew Bender.
DENATALE, ANDREW, and PRUDENCE B. ABRAM. 1985. 'The Doctrine of Equitable Estoppel as Applied to Nonmanagement Creditors.' *Business Lawyer* 40: 417.
DOUGLAS-HAMILTON, MARGARET HAMBRECHT. 1975. 'Creditor Liabilities Resulting from Improper Interference with the Management of a Financially Troubled Debtor.' *Business Lawyer* 31: 343.
EGASHIRA, KENJIRO. 1982. *Sho torihiki, ge (Commercial Transactions: II)*. Tokyo: Kobundo.
FRANKEL, ALLEN B., and PAUL B. MORGAN. 1992. 'Deregulation and Competition in Japanese Banking.' *Federal Reserve Bulletin*, August.
GREIF, AVNER. 1992. 'Institutions and International Trade: Lessons from the Commercial Revolution.' *American Economic Review* 82(2): 128 (Papers and Proceedings).

HERZOG, ASA S., and JOEL B. ZWEIDEL. 1961. 'The Equitable Subordination of Claims in Bankruptcy.' *Vanderbilt Law Review* 15: 83.

HORIUCHI, AKIYOSHI. 1987. 'Kin'yu kikan no kino (The Function of Financial Institutions).' In Ryuichiro Tachi and Shoichi Royama, eds., *Nihon no kin'yu (Japanese Finance)*. Tokyo: University of Tokyo Press.

HORIUCHI, AKIYOSHI and RYOKO OKAZAKI. 1992. 'Capital Markets and the Banking Sector: The Efficiency of Japanese Banks in Reducing Agency Costs.' University of Tokyo Faculty of Economics Discussion Paper 92-F-6.

HORIUCHI, AKIYOSHI, FRANK PACKER and SHIN'ICHI FUKUDA. 1988. 'What Role Has the "Main Bank" Played in Japan?' *Journal of Japanese and International Economies* 2: 159.

HORIUCHI, AKIYOSHI, and HIROJIRO SAKURAI. 1989. 'Kinyu, shihon shijo no tenkai (The Development of Financial and Capital Markets).' In Hirofumi Uzawa, ed., *Nihonkeizai (The Japanese Economy)*. Tokyo: University of Tokyo Press.

HOSHI, TAKEO, ANIL KASHYAP and DAVID SCHARFSTEIN. 1990. 'The Role of Banks in Reducing the Costs of Financial Distress in Japan.' *Journal of Financial Economics* 27: 67.

——. 1991. 'On the Choice Between Public and Private Debt: An Examination of Post-Deregulation Corporate Financing in Japan.' November.

ISHIKAWA, HIROSHI. 1987. 'Shoken shijo no gorika to kigyo kin'yu' ('The Rationalization of the Securities Market and Corporate Finance'). In Sogo kenkyu kaihatsu kiko, ed., *21 seiki no Nihon no kigyo kin'yu (Japanese Corporate Finance in the 21st Century)*. Tokyo: Toyo keizai shimposha.

KAIZUKA, KEIMEI, KAICHI SHIMURA and SHOICHI ROYAMA, eds. 1981. *Kin'yu-shoken koza (Lectures in Finance and Securities)*, vol. 5. Tokyo: Toyo keizai shimposha.

KAMOCHI, OSAMU. 1987. 'Mein banku shisutemu no shorai (The Future of the Main Bank System).' In Sogo kenkyu kaihatsu kiko, ed., *21 seiki no Nihon no kigyo kin'yu (Japanese Corporate Finance in the 21st Century)*. Tokyo: Toyo keizai shimposha.

KIDWELL, DAVID S., M. WAYNE MARR and G. RODNEY THOMPSON. 1984. 'SEC Rule 415: The Ultimate Competitive Bid.' *Journal of Financial and Quantitative Analysis* 19: 183.

KITAHARA, MICHINUKI. 1970. *Nihon no kin'yu (Japanese Finance)*. Tokyo: Zaikei shoho sha.

KLEIN, BENJAMIN and KEITH B. LEFFLER. 1981. 'The Role of Market Forces in Assuring Contractual Performance.' *Journal of Political Economy* 89: 615.

KOHN, MEIR. 1990. *Money, Banking, and Financial Markets*. Chicago: The Dryden Press.

KREPS, DAVID, PAUL MILGROM, JOHN ROBERTS and ROBERT WILSON. 1982. 'Rational Cooperation in the Finitely Repeated Prisoners' Dilemma.' *Journal of Economic Theory* 27: 245.

KURODA, AKIO. 1987. 'Kaigai shihon chotatsu no zoka to kokunai shasai shijo kaikakuno hitsuyo sei' ('The Increase in Overseas Capital Issues and the Necessity of Reform in the Domestic Bond Market'). In Sogo kenkyu kaihatsu kiko, ed., *21 seiki no Nihon no kigyo kin'yu (Japanese Corporate Finance in the 21st Century)*. Tokyo: Toyo keizai shimposha.

LITT, DAVID G., JONATHAN R. MACEY, GEOFFREY P. MILLER and EDWARD L. RUBIN. 1990. 'Politics, Bureaucracies, and Financial Markets: Bank Entry into Commercial Paper Underwriting in the United States and Japan.' *University of Pennsylvania Law Review* 139: 369.

LORING, H. HELMUT, and JAMES M. BRUNDY. 1985. 'The Deregulation of Banks.' *Washington and Lee Law Review* 42: 347.

MATSUSHITA, JUN'ICHI. 1993. 'Ketsugo kigyo no tosanho teki kisei' ('The Legal Regulation Under the Bankruptcy Law of Affiliated Firms'). *Hogaku kyokai zasshi.*

MILGROM, PAUL R., DOUGLASS C. NORTH and BARRY R. WEINGAST. 1990. 'The Role of Institutions in the Revival of Trade: The Law Merchant, Private Judges, and the Champaign Fairs.' *Economics and Politics* 5: 97.

MINAGUCHI, KOICHI. 1987. 'Shasai seido no kaikaku no tameni' ('Toward the Reform of the Bond System'). *Bessatsu shoji homu* 95: 52.

MIWA, YOSHIRO. 1990. *Nihon no kigyo to sangyo soshiki (Japanese Firms and Industrial Organization).* Tokyo: Tokyo University Press.

——. 1991. 'Mein banku to Nihon no shihon shijo' ('Main Banks and Japanese Capital Markets'). *Kin'yu*, August, p. 11.

——. 1992. 'Kin'yu seido kaikaku no seiji keizaigaku' ('The Political Economy of Financial System Reform'). In Keimei Kaizuka and Kazuhito Ikeo, eds., *Kin'yu riron to seido kaikaku (Finance Theory and Institutional Reform).* Tokyo: Yuhikaku.

——. 1993. *Kin'yu gyosei kaikaku (Financial Administration Reform).* Tokyo: Nihon keizai shimbunsha.

NEGISHI, AKIRA. 1992. 'Kin'yu shihon shijo ni okeru Dokusen kinshi ho no tekiyo mondai' ('Issues Regarding the Applicability of the Antimonopoly Act to the Financial Capital Market'). *Kosei torihiki* 497: 24.

OKURA SHO KOKUSAI KIN'YU KYOKU. 1988. *Dai 12-kai Okura sho kokusai kin'yu kyoku nempo (12th Annual Ministry of Finance International Finance Bureau Report).* Tokyo: Kin'yu zaisei jijo kenkyu kai.

PRIEST, GEORGE L. and BENJAMIN KLEIN. 1984. 'The Selection of Disputes for Litigation.' *Journal of Legal Studies* 13: 1.

PROWSE, S. D. 1990. 'Institutional Investment Patterns and Corporate Financial Behavior in the United States and Japan.' *Journal of Financial Economics* 27: 43.

RAMSEYER, J. MARK. 1991. 'Legal Rules in Repeated Deals: Banking in the Shadow of Defection in Japan.' *Journal of Legal Studies* 20: 91.

——. 1993. 'Columbian Cartel Launches Bid for Japanese Firms.' *Yale Law Journal* 102: 2005.

RAMSEYER, J. MARK and MINORU NAKAZATO. 1989. 'The Rational Litigant: Settlement Amounts and Verdict Rates in Japan.' *Journal of Legal Studies* 18: 263.

RAMSEYER, J. MARK and FRANCES McCALL ROSENBLUTH. 1993. *Japan's Political Marketplace.* Cambridge: Harvard University Press.

RASMUSEN, ERIC. 1989. *Games and Information.* Oxford: Basil Blackwell.

ROE, MARK. 1987. 'The Voting Prohibition in Bond Workouts.' *Yale Law Journal* 97: 232.

ROSENBLUTH, FRANCES McCALL. 1989. *Financial Politics in Contemporary Japan.* Ithaca: Cornell University Press.

ROYAMA, SHOICHI. 1981. 'Kin'yu-shoken seisaku no yukosei' (The Effectiveness of

Financial and Securities Policy)'. In Keimei Kaizuka, Kaichi Shimura and Shoichi Royama, eds., *Kin'yu-shoken koza (Lectures in Finance and Securities)*, vol. 5. Tokyo: Toyo keizai shimposha.

SADAKI, NOBUO, SHUICHI KOMURA, TAKAYOSHI KITAOKA and KEN'YA FUJIWARA. 1992. *Gendai kin'yu ron nyumon (Introduction to Modern Finance Theory)*. Tokyo: Keiso shobo.

SCHAEDE, ULRIKE. 1990. 'The Introduction of Commercial Paper—A Case Study in the Liberalisation of Japanese Financial Markets.' *Japan Forum* 2: 215.

SHAPIRO, CARL. 1983. 'Premiums for High Quality Products as Returns to Reputations.' *Quarterly Journal of Economics* 98: 659.

SHAPIRO, CARL and JOSEPH E. STIGLITZ. 1984. 'Equilibrium Unemployment as a Worker Discipline Device.' *American Economic Review* 74: 433.

SHEARD, PAUL. 1989. 'The Main Bank System and Corporate Monitoring and Control in Japan.' *Journal of Economic Behavior and Organization* 11: 399.

——. 1991. 'Delegated Monitoring Among Delegated Monitors: Principal-Agent Aspects of the Japanese Main Bank System.' CEPR Publication 274, Center for Economic Policy Research, Stanford University, November.

SHIMOJIMA, KOICHI. 1990. *Tosan ho taikei (Overview of the Law of Firm Failures)*. Tokyo: Keiso shobo.

STIGUM, MARCIA. 1990. *The Money Market, 3d ed.* Homewood IL: Business One Irwin.

SUEKAWA, HIROSHI. 1975. *Keiyaku ho, ge (Contract Law: II)*. Tokyo: Iwanami shoten.

SUZUKI, YOSHIO. 1987. *The Japanese Financial System*. New York: Oxford University Press.

TAKEUCHI, AKIO. 1987. 'Shasai hakko shijo no arikata' ('The Proper Shape of the Bond Issue Market'). *Shoji homu* 1100: 4.

TELSER, L. G. 1980. 'A Theory of Self-Enforcing Agreements.' *Journal of Business* 53: 27.

TERANISHI, JURO. 1991. *Kogyoka to kin'yu shisutemu (Industrialization and the Financial System)*. Tokyo: Tokyo University Press.

TSUJIMURA, KAZUSUKI. 1989. *Nihon no kin'yu, shoken, kawase shijo (Japan's Finance, Securities, and Currency Markets)*. Tokyo: Toyo keizai shimposha.

WILLIAMSON, OLIVER E. 1983. 'Credible Commitments: Using Hostages to Support Exchange.' *American Economic Review* 73: 519.

YAMAKAWA, HIROKI. 1988a. 'Sansho hoshiki no don'yu' ('The Introduction of the Reference System'). *Shoji homu* 1160: 36.

——. 1988b. 'Hakko toroku seido no don'yu' ('The Introduction of Shelf-Registration'). *Shoji homu* 1161: 20.

8

The Effect of Firm Status on Banking Relationships and Loan Syndication

The relationship between banks and firms varies significantly in degree of breadth and intensity depending on the status of both the firm and the bank. Further, it is dynamic and flexible, as both banks and firms seek more benefits. This chapter looks at specific aspects of these general observations using empirical research collected and analysed by the author since the early 1980s. The status of a firm is determined by a number of factors; here we are concerned primarily with aspects of size.

The existence of segmented loan markets—Japan created a number of financial institutions to deal with smaller firms, while historically the large (city) banks serviced large firms—is well known. Going beyond this, the first part of this paper analyses how and why smaller firms have banking relationships different from larger ones. The second part looks at an activity reserved for large firms—loan syndication—and traces its evolution from before World War II to the present.

Categories of Banks

The banks a firm does business with can be divided into four groups like concentric circles or, from a Japanese perspective, a hierarchy: main, core, clearance, and other banks. Core banks (*shuryoku ginko gun*) include the main bank and those banks the firm has 'almost as important a relationship with as with the main bank'. As the name implies, clearing banks handle daily cash transactions, and usually include core banks. In general, the larger the firm, the larger the number of banks in each group that a firm does business with, but the ranges are quite wide for each category of firm. Data are in Table 8.1.[1]

The author would like to thank Kazuo Ueda, Akiyoshi Horiuchi, Paul Sheard, Ryoko Okazaki, Hugh Patrick, Masahiko Aoki, and other participants of the workshops for helpful comments on an earlier version of the chapter.

[1] The results here draw on a survey of corporations made by the author with the help of the Japan Center for Economic Research (JCER), further details of which are covered in Horiuchi (1991) and Horiuchi and Murakami (1991). In October 1990, 1271 firms were sent questionnaires. This includes all 118 companies in the electric machinery industry of the Tokyo Stock Exchange (first and second sections), all 364 firms traded in the over-the-counter market, plus random selections of other listed and unlisted firms (301), as well as an

TABLE 8.1 Number of Banks Used by Different Categories of Firms

Smaller, Non-Traded (70)	Smaller, Traded (56)	Larger, Non-Traded (33)	Larger, Traded (276)	Bank Type
3.0 (2.6)	5.0 (2.9)	5.3 (4.3)	6.4 (5.0)	Core[1]
3.0 (2.2)	4.1 (2.2)	6.3 (6.7)	7.9 (9.1)	Clearing
5.7 (3.9)	9.7 (6.3)	19.6 (18.7)	20.8 (21.8)	Total

The number of firms in each category is in parentheses in column headings. Entries are the average (and standard deviation) number of banks of each bank type for the category of firm given in the column heading. Larger firms have over 300 employees. Traded means the company is listed on a stock exchange or traded over-the-counter.

[1] Core banks. Clearing banks include core banks.

Source: Compiled by the author from a 1990 survey he conducted with Japan Center for Economic Research.

In our 1990 survey, firms were asked to indicate up to three main banks, which they considered the most important of all the banks they dealt with. Although the idea of a main bank would inherently seem to mean there is just one, in fact many companies have multiple main banks; 28 per cent of large firms, and 25 per cent of smaller firms in the sample had two or three (the maximum number they could list). Statistical tests do not reveal any significant difference among firms having one, two, or three main banks as regards the number of employees, profits or borrowing (the last two are measured as a percentage of assets). Interestingly, 18 respondents (almost 4 per cent) could not identify any bank as their main bank. Of these, 11 were larger traded firms and 5 were smaller non-traded—representing under 4 per cent and just over 7 per cent of their respective groups. Data are in Table 8.2.

City banks—because they have had larger domestic and international branch networks than other kinds of banks, and have been able to offer a wider array of services—are the most common main banks for all but smaller non-traded firms. Both of these reasons are legacies of the earlier market segmentation. Although the long-term credit banks are as big as some of the city banks, they were restricted in their activities. So were the trust banks, which, in any case, are mostly smaller than any city bank and are all either members of one of the Big Six financial keiretsu or otherwise closely identified with a city bank.

A city bank is a main bank for 80 per cent of all sample firms and for 77 per cent of those with only one main bank. For larger traded firms

additional random selection of firms investing overseas (71), and all 113 JCER members not already included. There were 457 responding firms, 273 of which were in manufacturing. Of these, 435 could be used for the analysis in Tables 8.1 and 8.2.

TABLE 8.2 Type and Number of Main Banks, Distributed by Client Firm Size

Type of Bank Serving as Main Bank	Smaller, Non-Traded			Smaller, Traded			Larger, Non-Traded			Larger, Traded		
Number of Main Banks	1	2	3	1	2	3	1	2	3	1	2	3
City Bank	25	5	3	31	11	4	18	6	2	179	37	28
Long-term Credit Bank	1	0	1	2	4	1	0	2	2	10	21	25
Trust Bank	0	1	1	1	2	2	1	1	1	1	9	12
Other[1]	32	12	4	7	5	5	4	7	1	17	15	19
Number of Firms	58	9	3	41	11	4	23	8	2	207	41	28

No criteria were given for what constituted a main bank, each respondent used its own definition. Larger firms have over 300 employees. Traded means the company is listed on a stock exchange or traded over-the-counter.

[1] Other includes regional banks, second regional banks, and credit associations.

Source: Compiled by the author from a 1990 survey he conducted with Japan Center for Economic Research.

these numbers rise to 88 per cent and 86 per cent. Generally speaking, for firms with multiple main banks, one is a city bank and any other is a long-term credit bank or a trust bank. In these cases, the non-city bank is called a sub-main bank (*heiko mein*) or L-main (*choki mein*: the L is for long-term credit bank, although a trust bank will also be called L-main). Core banks also tend to be city banks.

Within the sample of large traded firms, Dai-Ichi Kangyo (the largest bank in Japan from the time of its creation by merger in 1971) was a main bank for 50 firms, Fuji for 38, Sakura (formed by a 1990 merger that included Mitsui Bank) for 35, Mitsubishi 32, and Sumitomo 29. These are the five largest city banks. The Industrial Bank of Japan (IBJ) is an exceptional case, serving as a main bank for 43 firms, including 4 for which it is the sole main bank (see Chapter 5 by Packer).

THE SIZE FACTOR IN MAIN BANK RELATIONSHIPS

We examine here the reality of main bank relationships of smaller firms. Within MITI there is a Small and Medium Enterprise Agency, and we are interested in that Agency's constituency, which includes firms with fewer than 300 employees *or* less than 100 million yen of paid-in capital (except in wholesale trade, where the cut-off is 100 employees or 30 million yen, and retail trade and services with 50 employees or 10 million yen). Unincorporated enterprises are also included. (Before April 1988 only paid-in capital was used as a criterion. The paid-in capital levels have been raised as the economy has grown, as detailed in the notes to Table 8.4; the current levels have been in effect from October 1973.)

For convenience, 'small and medium enterprises'—and there are a lot of them—are referred to simply as smaller firms; in some statistical sources they are 'small enterprise'. Non-financial corporations with less than 100 million yen of paid-in capital were 98.8 per cent of the total of 2.1 million firms in March 1993; firms with less than 50 million yen were 95 per cent, and those with less than 2 million were 26 per cent.

Having defined the research target, what things can we say about it? Smaller firms seldom have cross shareholdings with a bank. Indeed, while large firms tend to be mainly owned by other corporations (financial and non-financial), a small firm is almost always owned by its managers, often the top manager and his family.

For a majority of these firms, a key factor for their survival is to have a special, long-term relationship with at least one bank, which they call their main bank. At the same time, firms seek to have as wide a network as possible of sources for funding and other financial services. In many ways this is like the main bank relationship of large corporations, and it is thus sometimes assumed that main bank relations are similar, regardless of firm size. However, this is not the case. We know such firms have different banking relationships than large corporations, if only because small firms do less banking business and generally have higher default risks than large firms. (For a more detailed comparison of size-related differences, see Horiuchi, 1993.)

Smaller firms are considered to be generally more flexible than large ones; this usually means they are more likely to have to adapt to circumstances (and can do so more easily) than to impose circumstances. There is another aspect of this flexibility: smaller firms are more ambivalent about their relationships—particularly banking relationships. Empirical research shows that smaller firms are always eager to switch to a higher quality main bank and to diversify their lenders. One reason for this is that smaller firms tend to face oligopolistic lenders in each region (Patrick and Rohlen, 1987, p. 362). The degree of concentration in the loan market (defined as a prefecture) has a significant effect on loan rates for smaller firms (Horiuchi, 1988a).

Overview of Small Firms

Japanese start businesses for a wide range of reasons. These include not just to obtain a job or generate income and wealth, but also to be one's own boss, or to utilize and develop personal talents, skills, experience, assets, contacts, etc. Small-scale family enterprises are generally rational in the classic economic sense: they have a sense of their own self-interest and they try to maximize it.

As Table 8.3 shows, the number of firms has been increasing steadily. There were almost six times as many non-financial incorporated enterprises in 1991 as in 1956, a period in which the population increased by less than 40 per cent. The distribution of firms is affected by long-run inflation when the thresholds between groups remain fixed; thus, there has been a shifting toward larger-size categories. If one applies the consumer price index to the thresholds, the 50 million yen level in fiscal 1991 is equivalent to 9.2 million yen in 1956. For comparative purposes, the smallest, small and middle categories in 1991, and the smallest and (most of the) small categories in 1956 should be combined. This suggests a fairly stable inflation-adjusted size distribution for the number of firms.

Looking at employment in Table 8.3—and again combining the smallest, small and middle categories in 1991, and the smallest and (most of the) small categories in 1956—smaller firms have increased their share of employment by some 9 percentage points. Smaller firms have always been a policy target for stabilizing labour demand in Japan. (For an overview, see issues of the annual White Paper prepared by the Small and Medium Enterprise Agency.) Although in adjusted terms they have represented a declining share of 'executive' positions, the absolute increase in the number of firms suggests there is a strong desire in Japan to be one's own boss.

Economic dualism is apparent in the table's data. Although paid-in capital is an imperfect proxy for working capital, the table is consistent with the fact that smaller firms have considerably lower capital-labour ratios than large ones. A good deal of this difference is explained by the fact that certain very capital-intensive activities are, and often can be, undertaken only by large firms, while the smallest firms tend to be in services. Smaller firms earn more on their paid-in capital than do larger ones, as a direct result of being more labour-intensive. Thus, they have significantly lower profitability per employee.

Loan Market Segmentation

The aggregate loan market before the mid-1980s can be divided into a small-medium firm, local-area market and a large firm, metro-area market. However, it should be remembered that the reasons small and medium firms, as loan demanders, have mostly dealt with smaller banks and financial institutions, as loan suppliers, are not simply geographic. Geography is important to the extent that city banks, while called national, were allowed few if any branches outside the major cities. But even the many small and medium firms in major metro areas dealt primarily with regional banks, mutual savings (*sogo*) banks, and credit associations (*shinken*). Segmentation was a well-understood government policy adhered to by the banks. From February 1989 sogo banks mostly became classified as second-tier regional banks (members of the Second Association of Regional Banks) within the general category of ordinary banks.

Although exceptional firms with excellent wealth characteristics exist in the smaller-firm universe, it is generally not profitable for banks to identify them—either by searching for them or even (for larger banks) by careful examination of those firms presenting themselves as potential borrowers. Indeed, smaller firms historically have had relatively less bargaining power than larger firms, in part reflecting their lower reputation. In consequence, most smaller firms will usually have a relationship with banks located close to them. At the same time, smaller firms that are subcontractors of larger firms will sometimes establish a relationship with the larger firm's bank.

Segmentation was created by bank regulators, geography, and the costs of collecting information about (monitoring) one's borrowers. By encouraging each category of banks to concentrate on a different type of client, the expectation was that the banks would develop specialized skills in servicing their niche, to the mutual benefit of both banks and customers. Segmentation assumed market failure in the allocation of loans and sought to mitigate it. Mitigation for the banks meant those designated to

TABLE 8.3 Distribution of Incorporated Firms in Japan by Amount of Paid-in Capital

(per cents, except Totals)

paid-in capital in million yen		1956	1961	1966	1971	1976	1981	1986	1991
Number of Firms									
< 5	(smallest)	96.6	94.1	88.3	84.3	76.0	68.8	63.9	58.9
5–10	(small)	1.6	3.2	5.7	7.8	11.6	15.1	17.8	20.5
10–50	(middle)	1.4	2.0	4.3	6.3	10.7	14.0	15.9	18.0
50–100	(upper middle)	0.2	0.3	0.8	0.8	0.9	1.1	1.4	1.5
> 100	(large)	0.3	0.4	0.9	0.8	1.0	1.0	1.0	1.2
Total in thousands		336	497	516	875	1,209	1,568	1,831	1,937
Number of Employees									
< 5	(smallest)	49.3	51.8	36.5	34.6	28.7	26.0	21.9	18.7
5–10	(small)	4.7	8.9	8.3	9.0	11.0	11.7	11.6	11.7
10–50	(middle)	10.5	10.3	13.9	18.4	24.2	27.7	29.9	32.2
50–100	(upper middle)	4.0	3.0	6.5	5.8	5.2	6.3	8.0	7.2
> 100	(large)	31.6	26.0	34.8	32.2	30.9	28.3	28.5	29.5
Total in thousands		7,893	14,216	15,831	22,087	25,281	27,962	31,447	34,261
Number of Executives									
< 5	(smallest)	92.6	88.4	79.5	74.2	64.8	59.1	53.6	49.1
5–10	(small)	2.7	5.0	7.7	9.9	13.6	16.1	18.9	20.7
10–50	(middle)	3.0	4.4	7.9	10.8	16.4	19.7	21.8	24.0

Category								
50–100 (upper middle)	0.6	0.7	2.0	2.0	2.0	2.3	2.7	2.8
> 100 (large)	1.1	1.6	3.0	3.2	3.2	2.9	3.0	3.4
Total in thousands	1,069	1,466	1,487	1,905	2,939	3,872	4,425	4,644

Paid-in Capital

Category								
< 5 (smallest)	24.1	15.3	7.6	8.6	8.0	7.5	6.0	4.0
5–10 (small)	2.9	3.5	2.8	3.9	4.8	5.7	5.7	4.5
10–50 (middle)	7.6	6.3	6.3	9.5	13.7	16.3	15.6	13.7
50–100 (upper middle)	4.2	2.6	3.9	3.9	3.7	4.6	4.8	3.6
> 100 (large)	61.2	72.4	79.5	74.1	39.8	65.8	67.9	74.1
Total in billion yen	1,067	3,041	6,756	10,935	17,922	24,921	34,319	52,630

Current Profit Before Taxes

Category								
< 5 (smallest)	26.5	23.7	16.3	16.1	16.3	8.5	3.3	6.6
5–10 (small)	3.1	6.2	5.1	6.4	8.0	5.8	5.2	5.4
10–50 (middle)	8.0	9.5	12.2	15.4	26.5	19.5	18.7	22.3
50–100 (upper middle)	4.0	2.9	5.4	4.9	3.0	6.3	7.7	6.8
> 100 (large)	58.5	57.7	60.9	57.1	46.2	59.9	65.1	58.9
Total in billion yen	688	1,296	1,916	6,578	5,956	19,703	21,480	38,915

Data are for 31 March of the year shown (fiscal year end). Excludes financial institutions.

Source: Ministry of Finance. *Annual Statistics of Financial Statements of Incorporated Enterprises*, various issues.

borrow from them had few places to turn to, enhancing the banks' bargaining position relative to their borrowers. (See Sharp, 1990, on the monopolistic power bestowed on banks by segmentation. Reaction of firms to this power is discussed later.)

For firms, mitigation meant government policies directed funds to smaller borrowers through a number of public financial institutions. To a minor extent, local governments also channelled money through private banks. The Small Business Finance Corporation (SBFC) and People's Finance Corporation (PFC) have been the principal government institutions. Others include the Small Business Credit Insurance Corporation, as the central organization for a Credit Guarantee Association in each prefecture. Serving corporations regardless of size are the Hokkaido and Tohoku Development Corporation (covering the northern part of the country), and Norinchukin (the central bank for agriculture, forestry and fisheries cooperatives).

Table 8.4 gives data on loans outstanding to smaller firms for 1956–91. The share of smaller firms in total lending has been quite stable, and while the split between private and public sources of these loans has fluctuated, it ended the period where it began.

During the high growth era, city banks mostly supplied funds to large corporations. This is reflected in the second panel of Table 8.4, which shows the share of city bank loans going to smaller firms declining from the 1950s through the 1960s by some 8 percentage points and then stabilizing during the 1970s (although the huge expansion of outstanding loans meant a significant increase in the absolute amount of loans). As the liberalization of financial markets progressed in the 1980s, lending to smaller firms in the middle and upper-middle classes (10–100 million yen of paid-in capital) increased as a share of city banking lending, in part as they responded to reduced loan demand by large corporations.[2]

Data on lending to new firms are limited. According to a survey conducted by the author in 1991, private banks of all types supplied 58 per cent, and public financial institutions supplied 17 per cent. The rest came from the savings of participants in the business and other sources. The survey covered a sample of prefectures throughout Japan (Kyoto, Hyogo (Kobe), Toyama, Kanagawa (Yokohama), Shizuoka, and Nagano) that should be representative of the country as a whole.

Changes in Lending Sources

There have been major changes in the shares of lenders to smaller firms, as the third panel in Table 8.4 shows. The city bank share decreased

---

[2] Note that a broad definition of total lending is used in the table's series. When only domestic lending to private businesses is considered, the fall in share is smaller and short lived; by 1970 smaller firms had gained share compared to 1955 and their share has continued to increase.

TABLE 8.4 Smaller Firms in the Loan Market

	1956	1961	1966	1971	1976	1981	1986	1991
Smaller Firm Share of Total Lending Outstanding[1]								
Share (%)[2]	34.0	33.0	33.5	34.7	31.1	33.0	32.8	34.1
Total in trillion yen	5.9	15.3	38.6	86.5	208	351	547	802
Smaller Firm Share of City Bank Lending Outstanding								
Share (%)	31.8	26.2	23.6	25.2	26.6	35.2	40.1	41.5
Total in trillion yen[3]	1.9	4.9	11.1	22.6	48.0	71.5	124	213
Distribution of Lending to Smaller Firms By Source of Funds (per cents)								
City Banks	30.3	25.5	20.2	19.0	19.7	21.7	27.7	32.3
Regional Banks	27.2	25.2	23.0	21.9	20.3	20.1	21.7	21.9
Long-term & Trust	2.7	4.5	3.6	4.9	4.6	7.9	7.3	8.9
Mutual Banks	18.7	19.7	20.7	17.5	16.9	15.2	13.4	9.9
Credit Associations	11.0	14.3	18.5	21.1	20.1	17.4	15.5	14.1
Shokochukin	3.0	3.4	3.9	4.0	5.3	4.6	4.6	3.6
SBFC	2.4	3.0	2.8	3.0	3.7	3.8	2.9	2.4
Other	4.7	4.4	7.3	8.6	9.4	9.3	6.9	6.9
Total in trillion yen[4]	2.0	5.1	12.9	30.0	64.8	116	180	274

Data are for 31 March of the year shown (fiscal year end). Excludes financial institutions.

The definition of a small enterprise has changed through the years. From January 1953 to December 1964 it was 10 million yen of paid-in capital; January 1965 to September 1973, 50 million (10 million for trade and services); current thresholds are given in the text.

[1] Based on flow of funds data. The total is for all lending net of lending between financial institutions.

[2] Total lending to smaller firms (panel 3) as a percentage of total lending in this panel. See note 4.

[3] Total lending by city banks as reported by the Small Business Finance Corp (SBFC). Includes lending by foreign branches and to public institutions and individuals.

[4] Total lending to smaller firms as compiled by SBFC.

Sources: Various issues of Bank of Japan, *Economic Statistics Annual*, Economic Planning Agency, *1991–92 Economic Survey of Japan*, and SBFC *Annual Report.*

during the 1950s and 60s by some 11 percentage points and then stabilized during the 1970s. During the 1980s it rose as city banks sought smaller firms as clients.

An important structural change is the disappearance of cyclical movements in the share of smaller firms in total lending. Before the 1980s these firms garnered more of the increase in city bank lending during periods of easy money (that is, their share of loans increased), and their borrowing was cut back more in periods of tight money (that is, their share of loans decreased). One explanation for this is that, as stable providers of funds to large corporations, the city banks made most of their cyclic adjustments in their lending to smaller firms. In easy times, marginal money went to marginal customers; in tight times, such borrowers were cut back first. (See Teranishi, 1974; Kaizuka, 1976.)

Borrowing Diversification

Smaller firms borrow from a variety of sources. This section looks at public financial institutions, main banks, and sub-main banks. The advance of city banks into the smaller firm loan market is taken up later.

Several public financial institutions were created to have small firms as their client base. The People's Finance Corporation (PFC) aims to lend long-term money to very small firms, such as unincorporated enterprises, those with a few workers, and start-ups. In particular, the PFC has a special loan programme that does not require any collateral. Applicants for PFC loans need a formal recommendation from the Chamber of Commerce and Industry in their region. In March 1992 (the end of fiscal 1991) the PFC had 7,522 billion yen of loans outstanding to 337,000 firms. Of this, only some 8.5 per cent (642 billion yen) was uncollateralized.

The Small Business Finance Corporation (SBFC) aims to lend long-term money to firms in the small to upper-middle classes (5–100 million yen of paid-in capital) that have been unable to secure adequate private financing. This lending is generally provided against collateral. Compared to private banks, SBFC loans are at lower nominal rates and do not require compensating balances. This means firms that can borrow from private banks will borrow from SBFC when possible.

Although various types of firms borrow from SBFC, the smaller the size of a firm, the more it depends on SBFC as a source of loans. This is, in fact, quite pronounced. In 1984 firms with an annual turnover of less than 100 million yen depended on the SBFC for 46.6 per cent of their financing, while for firms in the 2–5 billion range the level was only about 15.1 per cent. Consistent with the SBFC's mission, the more long-term borrowing a firm does as a percentage of total borrowing, the greater the percentage of its loans from the SBFC, although by only a few points. (These data are from Horiuchi, 1988a.)

The Credit Guarantee Association (CGA) helps firms with insufficient collateral to borrow from private banks. Its guarantees stood at 23,810 billion yen in March 1992, equal to 8.3 per cent of bank lending to smaller firms. Distribution of guarantees by lender in March 1990 was: city banks 45 per cent, regional banks 26 per cent, credit associations 14 per cent, other private financial institutions 14 per cent, public financial institutions 2 per cent.

Most smaller firms do business with what can be called a sub-main bank as well as with a main bank. They do this to increase the availability of funds and to gain bargaining power. (See Horiuchi, 1988a, and Ramseyer, 1990, for detailed discussions.) Loans from both banks carry a similar rate of interest, not only in terms of nominal rate, but also effective rate, which takes into account compensating balances. Table 8.5 compares the terms of loans for a variety of firm characteristics in 1984.

City Bank Lending to Smaller Firms

As the financial market has been liberalized since the early 1980s, city banks have raised the percentage of their lending going to small firms. Their entry into this market has meant new fund-raising channels. Impact loans and privately placed bonds are the two most important of these.

Impact Loans

Impact loans are 'untied' foreign loans, that is, they are not tied to a specific purpose as, for example, are World Bank development project loans. The funds originate as foreign currency (usually Eurodollars) borrowed by the bank. However, the loan is made in yen at an interest rate comparable to a conventional yen loan, and is typically done at a fixed spread between what the borrowing firm pays the bank and the funds' cost to the bank. Typically, the borrower enters a forward contract for the foreign exchange necessary for repayment. Obviously only a bank with the ability to borrow overseas and deal in foreign exchange transactions can make such loans.

While impact loans developed in the 1960s for large firms, as deregulation increased competition among banks, city banks expanded the market for them to smaller firms. A survey of small firms covering 1982–84 found that about 60 per cent of impact loans were made on the initiative of the main bank. That is, having agreed there would be a loan, the bank offered to make it an impact loan without being specifically asked. For firms without a city bank as a main bank, city banks made the impact loans and promoted their availability to credit-worthy smaller firms. This has been an important factor in making the loan market for smaller firms more competitive, and helped erode the main bank status of small banks.

TABLE 8.5 Terms of Loans from Main Banks and Sub-Main Banks by Firm Characteristics, 1984

| Compensating Balance[1] | | Effective Interest Rate (%)[2] | | | | Characteristic |
| Main | Sub-Main | Short-term | | Long-term | | |
		Main	Sub-Main	Main	Sub-Main	
40	39	6.40	6.34	7.62	7.58	All firms
						Annual Turnover in million yen
—	37	7.32	7.34	7.96	7.80	Less than 100
39	40	6.91	7.05	7.72	7.80	100–500
41	39	6.51	6.59	7.67	7.59	500–1000
40	37	6.26	6.30	7.56	7.59	1000–2000
40	37	5.98	6.03	7.54	7.50	2000–5000
41		5.71	5.73	7.45	7.36	Over 5000
						Pretax Profit Margin
35	34	6.64	6.66	7.76	7.62	Negative
38	37	6.45	6.42	7.59	7.61	Less than 1%
39	37	6.35	6.37	7.62	7.59	1–2
42	40	6.32	6.39	7.60	7.44	2–3
45	41	6.29	6.23	7.52	7.48	3–5
45	43	6.22	6.20	7.54	7.45	Over 5

Net Worth/Assets					
Less than 3%	32	6.77	6.80	7.78	7.80
3–10	37	6.57	6.58	7.64	7.60
10–20	41	6.27	6.27	7.56	7.64
20–30	44	6.16	6.16	7.53	7.34
Over 30	50	6.14	6.14	7.44	7.35
Type of Main Bank					
City Bank	44	6.09	6.06	7.49	7.43
Regional Banks	38	6.43	6.34	7.63	7.55
Sogo Mutual Banks	37	6.72	6.50	7.86	7.57
Credit Associations	41	7.11	6.86	7.92	7.89

[1] As a percentage of the loan.
[2] Nominal interest rate adjusted for effects of compensating balances.

Source: Horiuchi (1988a).

Privately Placed Bonds

City banks, either as main bank or as a sub-main bank, have promoted the extension of privately placed bonds, especially to firms with 10–50 million yen of paid-in capital. The capacity to issue bonds is an important indicator of a firm's credit-worthiness and thus enhances its reputation. Private placements by firms of all sizes went from 863 in 1989, and 830 in 1990, to 1,650 in just the first nine months of 1991, and in the six months through March 1991, 46 per cent of placements were by smaller firms. Banks can expect explicit fees for arranging these placements; bond buyers bear the credit risk; and institutional investors, such as life insurance companies, are the major purchasers.

Information on bond market conditions comes to smaller firms through various channels, such as their banks, accountants, security companies or even the mass media. However, the main bank has been the most important source in 93 per cent of cases for firms placing bonds. Bond placement is one area where the main bank has shown more power than the sub-main bank.

Smaller firms with a city bank as main bank generally use it as the manager of their bond placement. However, city banks are often used as the manager by firms with some other type of bank as a main bank, as Table 8.6 shows. This again illustrates the willingness of smaller firms to go to whoever can provide them with a service they want, even if it means forsaking their main bank if it is a smaller institution. It is important to smaller firms to diversify and be flexible in their bank relationships.

The Reality of the Main Bank Relationship

This section empirically analyses the main bank relationships of smaller firms in the 1990s. It draws on a telephone survey conducted by a consulting firm in June 1992 in a prefecture just outside Tokyo. The companies contacted were clients of a former sogo bank (now a second-tier regional bank). The response rate was 12 per cent (367 of 2,994 firms), and respondents mostly belonged to the smallest category (paid-in capital of less than 5 million yen). The average number of employees per respondent was 20, but over half (192) had fewer than 10.

The bank that commissioned the survey was the main bank for 58 per cent (214 firms) of the sample and the sub-main bank for 16 per cent (58); 13 per cent (47) of respondents did not identify a main bank, though that does not necessarily mean they did not have one. Despite the small size of the firms, the average number of banks used was three. For the sample as a whole, 88 per cent (319) had more than one bank. Even for firms with fewer than 10 employees, 86 per cent (163 of 189) had more than one bank. Table 8.7 provides additional data.

TABLE 8.6 Distribution of Type of Bank Managing Private Bond Placements by Type of Main Bank (per cent)

City Bank	LTCB[1]	Trust Bank	Regional Bank	SRB[2]	NB[3]	Number of Firms	Type of Main Bank
98.0	1.1	0.4	0.4	0.1	0	760	City Bank
0	100.0	0	0	0	0	13	LTCB \1
14.3	14.3	71.4	0	0	0	7	Trust Bank
15.8	6.7	0.6	74.5	2.4	0	165	Regional Bank
17.6	5.9	0	0	76.5	0	17	SRB \2
79.9	3.7	0.9	13.1	1.9	0.4	982	Total

[1] Long-Term Credit Bank
[2] Second Regional Bank
[3] Norinchukin

Source: Small and Medium Enterprise Agency *Report on the Private Bond Issuing of Small and Medium Firms and Others* (1992).

TABLE 8.7 Distribution of Very Small Firms by the Number of Banks They Use (per cent)

	Number of Banks Used				Number of Employees (and
1	2	3	4	5	number of firms responding)
11.4	24.0	24.6	16.0	24.0	10 or more (175)
13.8	23.3	37.6	6.3	19.0	Fewer than 10 (189)

Source: A 1992 consulting firm telephone survey (see text).

The survey asked firms to choose as many factors as applied from a list of 10 that might have been used in selecting their main bank. Interestingly, most firms chose only one. The length of relationship (over 45 per cent) and convenience of location (30 per cent) were the most frequent choices. The next most common, both at 6 per cent, were the recommendation of others and 'the banker's good personality'. One implication of these responses is that the number of branches affects the number of firms a bank serves as main bank.

Data in Table 8.8 reinforce the importance of location in being a main bank. Asked to pick statements that formed part of their image of their main bank, some 86 per cent of responding firms said accessibility for consultation. Contribution to the local economy as a whole was also considered important to a positive image. A wide branch network in an area is an indispensable element in doing this. Branch regulation policy in the past kept city banks out of many areas; small banks may lose some of their previous advantage when city banks enter metropolitan suburbs.

TABLE 8.8 Very Small Firms' Image of Their Main Bank

Percentage of firms selecting response				Response
Group 1	Group 2	Group 3	Total sample	(characteristic of the bank)
86.4	84.9	83.0	85.6	Easy accessibility for any consultation
64.0	64.2	63.8	64.0	Reliability in troubled circumstances
59.4	61.3	63.8	60.5	Contribution to the local economy
25.2	30.2	25.5	26.7	Opportunistic policy
44.4	55.7	51.1	48.5	Profit-oriented business policy
214	106	47	367	Number of firms

Group 1: Firms identifying surveying bank as their main bank.
Group 2: Firms identifying some other bank as their main bank.
Group 3: Firms not identifying a main bank.

Source: A 1992 consulting firm telephone survey (see text).

The choices included some negative characteristics, and over a quarter of respondents felt their main bank was opportunistic. For firms with fewer than 10 employees, this rose to a third. It is thus not surprising that firms seek to diversify their borrowing relationships. Indeed, 20 per cent of the firms said they would change main banks if they had the chance to establish a main bank relationship with another bank. At the same time, over three-fifths of the firms believe their main bank will be a reliable supporter in troubled times. This, together with the expectation of easy consultation, imply diffusion of an ex-post monitoring role even to small main banks serving small firms.

LOAN SYNDICATION

Although the main bank and loan syndication are much discussed topics, at the present level of empirical research we do not have sufficient data to characterize what these terms represent in actual operation at the micro level. This analysis seeks to fill the gap regarding loan syndication in Japan: what it is, how it pertains to the main bank relationship of large corporations, and how it has evolved in the post-war period. A major source of material is a 1990 survey of large corporations conducted by the author with the Japan Center for Economic Research (JCER) (see footnote 1).

The term 'loan syndication' has been applied in a number of ways in Japan, and should be defined. Logical reasoning from that definition demonstrates that syndication represents a synergistic division of labour in the corporate loan market: every player—the manager bank, other banks, and the corporation—is better off with syndication. There are a few micro studies on syndication that have been concerned primarily with firms in distress, such as Chapter 6 by Sheard. However, it is important to know the nature and extent of the incentives a firm will give to a manager bank or a main bank in normal times to ensure the bank's willingness to play a rescue role should the need arise.

As far as academic works are concerned, there are a few interesting studies, including Chapter 2 by Teranishi. Wilson (1968), Gandhi, Hausmann and Sanders (1985), and Kato, Packer and Horiuchi (1992) are quite theoretical. Sachs (1984) discusses empirically the impossibility of international syndication arrangements in the absence of strong leadership by a manager bank because of the cautious attitudes among member banks. His discussion is related directly to the main bank relationship in Japan. Horiuchi (1988b) discusses the application of this relationship for the world economy through the internationalization of large Japanese banks, which have extensive experience and know-how in this field.[3]

[3] Campbell and Kracaw (1980), Diamond (1984) and Leland and Pyle (1977) are other

In the next section, after defining loan syndication, the incentive relationships among the firm, its manager bank and other banks are discussed. This is followed by an overview of the historical evolution of syndication, which has been in six stages so far. An example of an actual syndication in the late 1980s is given, and the organization of *de facto* loan syndications during the mid to late 1980s, the sixth stage, is analysed using my 1990 survey data.

The Nature of Loan Syndication

The borrowing needs of large firms are typically too large to be satisfied by one bank's lending capacity, and banks often prefer not to lend all the money a firm needs. At the same time, firms prefer to diversify their sources of funds. Being dependent on one or a few lenders can be as risky to the firm as being over-extended to one firm can be for a bank. Information asymmetry between a borrowing firm and the banks brings about this situation. Under these conditions, syndication is preferable for both a firm and the banks. Loan syndication is an example of group action among a manager bank, other banks, and a firm in the corporate loan market. One bank, the manager bank, is responsible for managing loan evaluation, implementation, and follow-up on behalf of all participating lenders.

The incentives of the participants can be summarized as follows. The borrowing firm reduces its costs. This is because banks avoid duplication of monitoring and administration when syndicating, and some of these savings can be captured by the borrower. Further, the corporation can expect stable funding because of the long-run monitoring role of the manager bank. The manager bank can expect preferential profit opportunities in direct fees, as well as from deposit absorption and other fee business. Other member banks obtain lending opportunities without incurring the costs of gathering information or monitoring, or without acquiring the skills to do so.

Relative resource endowment affects the bargaining power of the participants and thus the actual division of labour and the distribution of costs and benefits. When few banks have the skills to be a manager bank, banks that have them can command rents from those banks that merely

major theoretical works on the role of syndication in financial intermediation. A common definition of a syndicate is a group of individuals who must make a common decision under conditions of uncertainty that will result in a pay-off to be shared jointly. Wilson (1968) shows that only under very narrow circumstances is the group's behaviour consistent with optimal sharing (the Savage axioms). As an extension, Gandhi and others (1985) presented a concept of group certainty equivalent, which can lead to optimal sharing rules for a broader class of syndicate member preferences or utility functions. In the case of loan syndication, the group certainty equivalent is revealed in stable sharing under normal circumstances. Assuming risk aversion by banks, Kato and others (1992) discuss a theoretical model of *de facto* syndication organized by the main bank.

have money to lend, as well as from the corporation wishing to borrow. When many banks have syndication skills, banks that do not, as well as borrowing firms, are in a better bargaining position. When money is tight, a bank with loanable funds is in an improved bargaining position relative to the borrowing firm and a managing bank seeking participants.

We can conclude that loan syndication is a spontaneous and endogenous response (as distinguished from one requiring policy direction by regulatory authority) to the problem of information asymmetry and the need of both banks and borrowers to diversify their loans.

However, public institutions may directly or indirectly perform the manager role by providing the information necessary to induce involvement by private banks, and by participating in making the loan. This is a type of 'cowbell' effect, which was very important in Japan before the early 1970s (see Higano, 1986). As Japanese markets have grown and liberalized, the value of policy-directed investment allocation through such mechanisms as the 'cowbell' have been called into question.

Syndicates tend to have the same members participating at more or less the same shares from one loan to the next. (Such historical determination may work as a group certainty equivalent, as analysed by Gandhi and others, 1985.) Either or both the manager bank and the borrower are principally involved in determining shares. In this way, all participants acquire syndicate-specific information; that is, data about each other (borrower and lending banks) that are specific to ongoing syndications for the borrowing firm.

The Manager Bank and the Main Bank

A manager bank serves as both the *ex ante* monitor and arranger of the loan's conditions. This role involves the following:

1. Investigating the borrower's business and financial condition (*ex ante* monitoring).
2. Negotiating with the borrower on the terms (loan amount, interest rate, maturity date, amortization rate, and collateral).
3. Communicating and intermediating among syndicate members.
4. Exchanging information with the financial authorities if required, explicitly or implicitly.
5. Interim monitoring of how the loan is used, if necessary.

The manager bank has sufficient management resources to undertake this role and is expected both to perform it efficiently and to cover its costs directly from manager fees or indirectly through related business. Other banks have the money to lend, but are unable or unwilling to commit the resources to perform these functions (basically, gathering and analysing information) in all cases. Horiuchi's optimal management model of Japanese banks (1990) proves that comparative management resource endowment is a determinant of how a bank allocates between lending as a main bank and lending as a non-main bank.

In practice, which bank manages which firm's loans is determined more by factors such as the historical relationships between banks and firms than by more open competition for the role of manager. Thus, when a firm has substantial relationships with a number of banks, as most large firms do, its regular main bank usually manages most of its syndications. Nevertheless, if some other financial institution is especially adept at the type of syndication being arranged or has more analytical and management capability available to devote to it, then it will serve as manager.

The manager bank usually maintains its leading position over time because this allows it to accumulate greater firm-specific information, and thus to be able to monitor the firm more efficiently. In the usual case of a stable relationship between the manager and the firm, there does not need to be much additional information gathering in each syndication. The position of a manager bank is very much like that of a main bank, with one important exception: while there may be interim monitoring on how the loan is used, a manager bank is not expected to be involved in any rescue (*ex post* monitoring). In its role as *ex post* monitor, a main bank does all three types of monitoring because it can expect more profit opportunities in its dealings with the firm in normal times (see Chapter 4 by Aoki). These dealings typically cover all areas of financial services: deposits, disbursements, short- and long-term lending, foreign exchange, and bond issue.

A main bank's *ex ante* monitoring signal is seen as more credible by other banks than a signal from a specialist manager in long-term lending. In other words, a main bank captures economies of scope in its monitoring, and thus can perform the role of syndication manager even in the case discussed by Sachs (1984). Accumulated information is the key to these economies of scope. Horiuchi (1988b) discusses the application of this mechanism for the world economy.

EVOLUTIONARY CHANGES IN LOAN SYNDICATION

Changes in the nature of loan syndications in Japan since the late 1930s, particularly shifts in relative power among the participants, are analysed in this section. The period is divided into six parts to reflect these shifts of power. The breaks come in the late 1940s, mid-1950s, late 1960s, at the first oil crisis (1973), and the Plaza Accord (1985).

Before 1947

During the war period (which began in July 1937), the Japanese economy and financial system came under strict regulation and control by the government. At the same time, large zaibatsu firms and banks had a powerful influence on the government. Loan syndication emerged spontaneously among the zaibatsu banks to meet the requirements of credit rationing in the wake of the Temporary Fund Adjustment Law of September 1937 and the compulsory lending system implemented by the Industrial Bank of Japan (IBJ) in March 1939. Syndications were led primarily by the IBJ and the zaibatsu banks. In August 1941 the 10 largest commercial banks and IBJ established an organization to intermediate syndications. A newly established regulatory board succeeded to this role in May 1942.

In January 1944 the Ministry of Finance assigned specific financial institutions to finance specific munitions companies; each company was assigned one or two banks, one of them a manager bank. If necessary, and it was, other financial institutions, including life insurance companies, were to form cooperation associations (syndicates) to provide the required financing. The designated bank handled negotiations on behalf of all the other lenders, making them little more than sub-contractors.

However, in March 1945, syndication was eliminated by a law extending the pairing of specific financial institutions to specific firms in addition to munitions companies. Some 2,550 firms received funds under this system, each having a relationship with just one bank, which took care of every financing need of the company. (Chapter 2 by Teranishi covers this period in more detail.)

January 1947 to February 1954: Bank of Japan Guided Loans

Like most of the economy, the banking system ended the war in disarray. The zaibatsu and their banks were targets for dissolution by the Occupation and there was hyperinflation. As the situation stabilized, the Bank of Japan (BOJ) began to perform the role of manager in loan syndications. This system, called BOJ-guided loans, started in 1947 and lasted for seven years. Although there were strong incentives to perform the role, the private banks were too weak in both funds and managerial skills to undertake it on their own.

The system was consistent with the desire to allocate funds to key industries as part of the Target Production Policy. Principal recipients were steel, textiles, machinery, and chemicals; together they received over two-thirds of the funds. Most of the cumulative total of almost 6,000 loans were for working capital and were made during 1948–49.

The BOJ in its official history gives three reasons for the rapid expansion of guided loans in the late 1940s. (1) Banks faced decreased lending potential to industrial firms because there was a ceiling on the increase in total lending. (2) Firms sought to increase the number of banks they borrowed from, as many firms wished to borrow more than one bank could lend to a single firm. (3) Banks could expect preferential lending by BOJ when they participated in guided loans. The BOJ also felt that even large banks depended significantly on it, not only for funds to lend, but also for monitoring. However, the banks showed a willingness to monitor and otherwise take the initiative in lending when they were given the chance.

As early as the middle of 1948, the BOJ was reducing its own role in syndications and diffusing the principles of syndications to other banks. In July it organized the Yushi Assen Iinkai (loan guidance committee) with a majority of its members (19 of 24) from large banks. In August the BOJ division responsible for loan guidance was made independent.

The Zenkoku Ginko Kyokai (Association of All Banks, AAB) organized the voluntary loan restraint committee in July 1951 to adjust the lending activities of its members in the face of demand that far exceeded supply. (Interest rates were regulated and set at below a market-clearing rate.)

New guided loans decreased sharply from May 1950, but the BOJ resorted to them again in 1950 for Korean War special demand loans, in 1951 to finance imports, and in 1952 to aid trading companies. The guided loan division was abolished in February 1954.

High Growth Era: the Mid-1950s to the Late 1960s

The government continued to exercise considerable influence over allocation of loans during this period. However, the channel for intervention underwent an important change, shifting to administrative guidance and the use of the bankers' association (AAB). Although the banks had more flexibility, firms were subject to MITI's control of technology imports. New foreign technology was an important factor in investment in new plants and equipment, and thus on loan demand. The government restricted international capital inflows, as well as outflows, which meant there was a balance of payments determined ceiling on investments by large firms.

The AAB presidency was rotated among the presidents of the city banks and long-term credit banks during this period. The AAB's president's bank was expected to be particularly responsive to government guidance, as an example to other AAB members. Because the major banks take turns in this position, an incumbent president and his bank could expect support from the others.

To coordinate plans among the government, firms and banks—and thus increase the effectiveness of government intervention—a number of institutions were established by the government and, later, by the private sector. The MOF created a council in 1956, which was superseded in February 1958 by MITI's Council on Industrial Rationalization, to report guidelines on the investment and finance of large firms. In October and December 1965, AAB set up committees where banks and firms could exchange information and negotiate with each other and the government to establish guidelines for investment and fund raising.

Government-established councils included not only representatives of groups directly involved, but also academics, journalists and other members of the public who were presumed neutral. Horiuchi (1985) examines the cooperation in the synthetic fibre industry to reduce capacity after the 1974 oil shock. This industry exemplifies the role of the Rationalization Council and the cooperation among the council and various committees established by firms in the search for consensus. MITI had targeted that industry because it had been both a major exporter and a heavy user of imported technology in this period.

What conflicts did these groups seek to resolve? With the recovery of the economy in the 1950s, firms that had been members of pre-war zaibatsu began to coalesce into groups that included a bank. These groups, commonly referred to as the Big Six financial keiretsu, expected substantial growth in heavy and chemical industries, and thus had strong motives to invest in them. MITI sought to pace the build-up of capacity in these areas. When a bank's client was prevented from investing in plant and equipment, the bank was prevented from making a loan. Loan syndications were a way of mitigating this limit on a bank's business. This is all related to the 'overloan' issue, and thus to credit rationing; how all these fit together is an empirical issue requiring further research. (For related issues, see Komiya and others, 1988.)

Table 8.9 provides data on the extent to which MITI was able to induce firms to reduce their investment plans, and thus their need to raise funds. In every year from 1958 to 1964, except 1961, members of the AAB provided a smaller share of the funding for the adjusted plans than they would have provided for the original investment plans. The last column of the table shows how much the banks' actual lending was reduced from what they would have lent had the plans not been adjusted.

The three long-term credit banks were not members of a financial keiretsu and they—particularly the IBJ—worked as agents of the government. The IBJ was often the implicit manager of government-ordained syndicates. Their share of long-term lending decreased through the period as the private commercial banks were allowed—and were more able—to make further plant and equipment loans. However, they were allowed to enter the short-term and small and medium firm markets, which more than offset the lost long-term business. (See Chapter 5 by Packer.)

TABLE 8.9 MITI-Instigated Adjustments to Investment Fund Raising and AAB's Share, 1958–64

Fiscal Year	Original Fund-Raising Plan		Fund Raising after Adjustments		Reduction of	
	total in billion yen	AAB's share[1]	total in billion yen	AAB's share[1]	total fund raising[2]	AAB lending[3]
1958	852	17.9	672	13.1	21.1	42.3
1959	843	17.5	772	10.4	8.4	45.6
1960	1284	18.3	1134	11.6	11.7	44.0
1961	1755	11.5	1620	11.7	7.7	6.1
1962	1952	12.4	1586	7.9	18.7	48.2
1963	1690	13.2	1561	10.2	7.6	28.6
1964	1895	10.9	1614	8.1	14.8	36.7

[1] AAB's lending as a percentage of total fund raising.
[2] As a percentage of the original fund-raising plan.
[3] As a percentage of what AAB would have loaned under the original plan.

Source: Zenkoku Ginko Kyokai (1965).

Loan syndications were used for a variety of purposes, as the following examples illustrate. Overall credit rationing and directed investment were primary elements.

In autumn 1955 the MOF announced expected decreases in Japan Development Bank (JDB) lending, and persuaded the AAB to increase member lending to cover the gap. The banks agreed to lend 13 billion yen, 6 billion of which went to electric power companies by syndication. The AAB also intermediated syndicated loans to other industries. In other words, the AAB assumed a role that had earlier been played more directly by the BOJ.

In December 1957 the BOJ asked banks to organize loan syndicates to reduce the growth of lending and tighten the loan market. The BOJ expected this would decrease competition among banks and prevent them from funding duplicate ('excess') investment by large firms. The banks, the AAB, and representatives from (most importantly) steel, chemical and electric utilities negotiated consensus limits on lending.

Also in December 1957 the government asked the AAB to arrange a syndicate loan for nine (privately owned) electric power companies, and this was done. City banks took 5 billion yen, while long-term credit banks and trust banks handled 1 billion yen each. The loan syndicate then became a bond consortium, placing 9.8 billion yen of bonds into member banks. At the government's direction, the AAB itself, acting through the bank of the AAB's president, served as manager, supported by the other major AAB member banks.

In April 1960 the AAB explicitly announced its commitment to loan syndication as a means of rationing credit 'because any independent loan adjustment by each bank will not bring successful results'. Further, 'AAB takes the initiative in the adjustment among banks as well as between banks and firms in order to strengthen the loan adjustment.' To many readers, these examples will strongly suggest the presence of a cartel. I have emphasized the desirable effects and neglected the distortions. What the net effect was remains an open question, difficult to identify or measure.

During the high growth period most firms started to have special relationships with several banks, with one of them taking the leading position as the firm's main bank. Although the role of delegated monitor was beginning to appear, the main bank did not manage loan syndications, as the AAB performed that function itself. The banks, with this experience of AAB-initiated loan syndication, began to spread the use of syndicates among large corporations.

Late 1960s to the First Oil Crisis

Membership in loan syndicates expanded to more banks and other financial institutions during this period. As main banks began to manage syndications, so the AAB's role faded. While the bank could not seek an explicit manager fee, it could be compensated indirectly through provision of other fee-based services and through absorbing deposits with regulated, low rates of interest.

In the late 1960s preparatory steps were taken to open Japan's capital markets. The government encouraged banks and firms to increase the cross holdings of stock to make it difficult for foreign investors to acquire controlling interests in existing large companies (see Okumura, 1991). Banks could hold 10 per cent of a corporation's stock, so several banks and other financial institutions together could hold a block large enough to thwart anyone else. It is in this period that the IBJ became a major stockholder in a variety of companies (see Chapter 5 by Packer).

A firm's major shareholding banks—its core banks—were the principal, sometimes the only, participants in its loan syndications. The main bank, as one of the largest stockholders (though not necessarily the largest), had even more incentive to monitor than before, and was in a better position to do so. From the firm's standpoint, having several large financial institutions as major shareholders gave it some diversity in where it could borrow or obtain other financial services. Still, firms tended to keep the distribution of their business fairly stable among its core banks. Because their largest creditors and largest shareholders generally were the same, firm managers not only could feel secure from challenges to their control of the company under normal circumstances, they could expect some rescue effort in times of financial distress.

Adjustment Period After the First Oil Crisis

Two important trends emerged in the mid-1970s regarding main bank relationships and loan syndications, both as part of firms' adjustment to the first oil crisis. First, large corporations gained relative power and shifted to *de facto* syndications (discussed later). Second, they still depended on banks for any rescue help.

Even before the oil price hikes beginning in October 1973, inflation had started to be a concern in Japan. Combined with revaluations of the yen, there was a serious disruption of relative prices during the 1970s that changed the competitiveness of entire industries, particularly the heavy and chemical companies that had been the principal beneficiaries of MITI industrial policy. Firms seeking to exit declining markets and enter new ones needed funding. From the standpoint of the banks, lending for restructuring and for new ventures was riskier in the new environment of slower growth and greater uncertainty than in the heady, high growth days of the 1960s.

Firms nonetheless turned to their banks for a stable supply of funds. It was in this period that the presumed commitment of main bank as an *ex post* monitor, playing an active role in restructuring, was put to the test. Japan's success in adjusting during the 1970s, compared to other developed countries, was due in part to the existence of long-term main bank relationships. (This is not to denigrate the role of sub-contracting, labour market practices, relatively competent government involvement, and other factors in Japan's superior performance.)

Many suffering firms in declining industries, such as steel, chemicals, textiles and raw materials, sold their shareholdings in their banks and used the proceeds to reduce debt (mostly) or fund operations. A list of major shareholders in banks in the early 1970s, particularly the long-term credit banks, includes a number of major industrial firms that a few years later had much reduced shareholdings. The principal example is Nippon Steel: in March 1974 it was one of the five largest shareholders in two long-term credit banks, four city banks, and three trust banks. By 1981 it was merely the sixth largest holder of one city bank (Fuji), and among the five largest at two trust banks. Firms also sold some land to reduce debt.

As firms adjusted to slower growth, they reduced their rates of plant and equipment investment and, accordingly, their borrowing. At the same time, firms in the electrical and machinery industries, which became the major exporters during the 1970s, had lower levels of borrowing. In part, this reflected relatively lower levels of capital intensity. Another factor is that they were not industries targeted by MITI—although they were helped indirectly by MITI's support of semi-conductor research and other high technology research—and thus they did not have as ready access to loans. Offsetting this is the fact that credit was generally available in the 1970s.

By the early 1980s the large banks found themselves facing a shrunken lending business; they had lost bargaining power with their traditional customers, large firms, in setting terms for loans. So, they looked to small and medium firms as new clients.

Since the 1985 Plaza Accord

In this period, 'implicit' syndications came to be used by most firms to allocate their borrowing from major banks. A large firm decides the relative shares of a loan it expects each participating bank to fund: there is no formal syndication, and thus no manager and no fee. This situation is called *de facto* syndication. However, there is an assumed stable hierarchical ranking, with the main bank at the top, which gives the main bank and a few other major banks preferential treatment in the firm's procurement of financial services. Because of the monitoring role of the main bank, other lenders are willing to participate, and the firm has an incentive to compensate its main bank for this monitoring.

With the bursting of the speculative bubble in the 1990s, risks have become larger and banks weaker. The role of rescuer often cannot be played by just one bank, as tradition had it; there is thus a shift by firms to having a group of core banks, as was discussed earlier.

An Example of a Syndication

For this illustration of the formal elements of a syndication during the financial liberalization period, we use stylized facts for a major electric power company, with the pseudonym Denryoku. Denryoku has one city bank as its main bank and two core banks—a trust bank in the same financial keiretsu as the main bank and a long-term credit bank. With its huge appetite for loans, several trillion yen, the company of course seeks to diversify its borrowing as much as possible. For Denryoku commercial banks are the principal syndicate members only for short-term funds. It is typical for insurance companies and trust banks to supply most of the syndicated long-term funds.

Denryoku has one consortium for short-term borrowing, four for long-term borrowing, and one for trade financing. Together this represents 51 per cent of total borrowing, including 44 per cent of long term and 92 per cent of short term (the trade finance is long term). Two of the consortia are made up of insurance companies—one each for life and non-life insurers—one of which acts as manager in each case. A core bank has been the manager for the four consortia involving banks. One of these involves all seven trust banks and another involves the seven trust banks and the trust department of a city bank. City banks are involved in only two consortia, a small one with the Export-Import Bank and the short-term one. Table 8.10 gives details of the consortium members.

The manager plays largely a passive role regarding how much of the

TABLE 8.10 The Structure of a Large Electric Power Company's Syndication, 31 March 1991

Distribution of Lending among Six Consortia and within Each (per cents)

15.5	Life Insurance Companies	1.9	Casualty Insurance Companies
	21.1 *Dai-ichi*		15.1 *Yasuda Fire & Marine*
	18.8 Nippon		15.0 Tokyo Fire & Marine
	8.3 Asahi		15.0 Mitsui Fire & Marine
	51.8 15 others		54.9 9 others
15.5	Trust Banks (all 7 participate)	1.3	Export-Import Bank of Japan
	21.4 *Mitsui Trust*		32.0 *Sakura Bank*
	20.3 *Mitsubishi Trust*		22.1 *IBJ*
	13.7 *Toyo Trust*		45.9 4 other city banks
	44.6 4 others	13.5	Short-Term Borrowing
3.7	Pension Trusts		23.5 *Sakura Bank*
	16.0 *Mitsui Trust*		11.7 Dai-ichi Kangyo Bank
	16.0 Mitsubishi Trust		11.7 Mitsubishi Bank
	16.0 Daiwa Bank		11.7 Fuji Bank
	52.0 5 other trust banks		41.4 18 other banks

Manager bank in italics.

loan each participant will take down and what the terms will be; Denryoku does the negotiating itself, generally separately with each bank or insurance company. Each year there is a ceremonial meeting at which the company informs the managers and the major lenders of its borrowing plans in the year ahead. The participants might give advice on timing, and the core banks will support the company in negotiations with other lenders. With such a limited role, the managing bank does not receive any fees directly, but of course benefits indirectly from other business with the company.

As Chapter 1 by Aoki, Patrick and Sheard indicates, the details of loan syndication will vary depending on a firm's status, including its wealth condition. Many firms in Japan use a framework similar to Denryoku, but dispense with the ceremonial meeting to announce the relative shares to lenders.

In these *de facto* syndications there is a generally stable relative share among banks. This means firms do not need to negotiate with each bank; negotiations are with the core banks, particularly the main bank. The long-term relationship between banks and firms has become the foundation of *de facto* syndication.

MAIN BANK RELATIONSHIP POLICY

Firms seek to maintain stable relative shares in their syndications and other borrowings. Changes would only take time and incur the costs of negotiation, particularly as if one bank's share is changed, then at least one other's must change as well. Firms seek to increase their bargaining power by adjusting the distribution of their use of the services banks offer. In other words, they have an incentive to control the distribution of profit opportunities among banks. The firm's chief concern is the extent to which it should give these opportunities to its main bank.

Table 8.11 illustrates the distribution of firms by their degree of dependence on their main bank for three types of borrowing and three types of services. Firms were asked to indicate in which quintile their dependence fell. One of the most significant results is that main banks have relatively higher shares in foreign exchange transactions and liquid deposits, which are generally the two most profitable of the six activities for a bank.

The relationship between dependence and size, profitability, and ratio of borrowing to total assets was also investigated using full factorial analysis of variances for each of the three characteristics. The F ratios are given in Table 8.11. The distribution is influenced by the number of either all banks or of main banks by firm size. A natural consequence is the lower dependence of larger firms than of smaller firms. Firms in the highest dependence quintile are indeed smaller, and those in the lowest quintile, larger, than the average.

The more a firm depends on bank borrowing, the greater its dependence on its main bank, although the effect is not as great as for firm size. The profit rate has no significant effect on the level of main bank dependence.

The Stability of Shares and Project Financing

The stable hierarchy policy of keeping the relative shares of each core bank more or less the same in various areas of bank services is reflected in Table 8.12. This stability is a natural consequence of long-term relationships with core banks, and thus becomes a key for analysing firms' main bank policies. In a long-term relationship, both banks and firms can save total transaction costs.

TABLE 8.11 Distribution of Firms by Their Dependence on Their Main Bank

Firm Characteristics			Per cent of Firms	Banking Service and Level of Dependence on Main Bank[4]
Size[1]	Profit[2]	Debt[3]		
(2.455)	(1.041)	(3.681)		Long-Term Borrowing
5.8	5.7	16.2	45.9	0–20
3.6	5.7	25.5	25.2	20–40
1.7	5.1	19.5	17.4	40–60
1.5	3.4	20.8	4.6	60–80
1.6	7.1	19.4	6.9	80–100
(2.436)	(1.163)	(0.904)		Fixed Investment Borrowing
5.2	5.8	18.0	43.3	0–20
3.4	6.1	22.3	26.1	20–40
1.8	4.6	18.8	16.7	40–60
1.0	4.0	16.9	5.1	60–80
2.0	6.7	21.4	8.8	80–100
(2.971)	(0.932)	(0.446)		Short-Term Borrowing
4.8	5.9	18.7	17.9	0–20
5.3	5.6	17.7	42.0	20–40
2.3	5.4	15.6	21.0	40–60
1.5	5.7	15.8	11.1	60–80
1.4	7.5	19.3	8.0	80–100
(0.370)	(0.370)	(3.261)		Liquid Deposits
3.9	5.7	23.3	16.2	0–20
3.5	5.9	15.4	33.1	20–40
3.8	6.1	13.6	24.3	40–60
2.4	5.9	15.6	15.8	60–80
3.6	7.0	16.4	10.7	80–100
(2.515)	(0.944)	(2.817)		Time Deposits
5.1	5.2	18.5	37.7	0–20
3.4	6.4	19.0	27.1	20–40
2.3	6.4	11.9	17.6	40–60
0.8	5.5	13.8	9.4	60–80
1.8	6.7	22.9	8.2	80–100
(4.997)	(1.216)	(0.436)		Foreign Exchange
3.1	6.3	17.7	19.9	0–20
8.2	4.8	15.6	25.5	20–40
4.1	5.6	16.3	22.1	40–60
1.7	5.9	13.2	12.1	60–80
2.4	6.0	16.5	20.4	80–100

Numbers in parentheses are F-ratios from full factorial analysis of variances for each of the characteristics.

[1] Size is number of employees in thousands.
[2] Profit is pretax current profit as a per cent of total assets.
[3] Debt is borrowing as a per cent of total assets.
[4] Dependence is measured by the percentage of a service a firm receives from its main bank.

TABLE 8.12 Adherence to a Stable Relative Shares Policy

Firm Characteristics			Distribution of Responses		Banking Service and Response
Size[1]	Profit[2]	Debt[3]	Total Firms	Per cent	
(0.588)	(2.683)	(1.687)			Fixed Investment Borrowing
3.8	7.0	20.2	142	60.9	Usually
4.5	6.9	16.3	63	27.0	Case by Case
2.6	7.7	17.2	28	12.0	Never
(4.461)	(1.030)	(0.244)			New Project Borrowing
3.4	5.9	18.7	52	23.5	Usually
7.3	5.4	17.0	98	44.3	Case by Case
3.0	6.4	17.8	71	32.1	Never
(5.078)	(6.910)	(8.465)			Working Capital Borrowing
2.4	5.6	15.5	203	74.9	Usually
6.1	5.0	23.3	48	17.7	Case by Case
4.2	9.2	25.2	20	7.4	Never
(1.859)	(0.338)	(0.110)			New Stock Issue Allocation
4.3	6.0	15.6	111	43.2	Usually
6.0	5.7	16.3	98	38.1	Case by Case
2.4	6.3	16.7	48	18.7	Never
(1.500)	(2.510)	(0.056)			Corporate Bond Guarantee
2.4	5.3	16.3	123	51.0	Usually
3.7	6.1	16.8	90	37.3	Case by Case
4.9	7.3	17.3	28	11.6	Never

Numbers in parentheses are F-ratios from full factorial analysis of variances for each of the characteristics.
[1] Size is number of employees in thousands.
[2] Profit is pretax current profit as a per cent of total assets.
[3] Debt is borrowing as a per cent of total assets.

New project financing and allocation of new equity issues were the only areas where a majority of firms said they did not usually follow a stable relative share policy, and for new equity issues, only 43 per cent of firms said they kept stable shares. These areas both presumably require more negotiation and information exchange, as well as monitoring, than routine transactions.

The three characteristics—employment size, profits and borrowing (the last two measured as a percentage of total assets)—show little relationship to the propensity to maintain relative shares. For working capital borrowing, which is the service with the highest adherence to stable relationships, the firms departing from the policy tend to be those with the highest profit ratios. Firms with higher borrowing ratios are particularly likely to maintain the policy. Both of these results are intuitively logical.

As shown in Table 8.13, there are differences in when banks are informed of investment plans between new project and routine project financing. Twice as many firms bring their banks in at an early stage of planning new projects than for routine projects, and fewer firms simply inform their banks of decisions already taken on new projects than with routine projects.[4]

When negotiating new project finance, firms are more willing to deviate from a stable-share policy. This suggests that they see enough negative effects from a stable share policy (with its implicit reduction of competition among funding sources) to justify the possibility of tapping into

TABLE 8.13 When Firms Inform Their Banks of Investment Plans

Firm Characteristics			Distribution of Responses		Type of Project and When
Size[1]	Profit[2]	Debt[3]	Total Firms	Per cent	Bank Informed, Relative to When Plans Made
(4.37)	(1.42)	(4.72)			Routine Projects
1.6	4.3	24.5	27	10.5	Before
3.7	5.9	17.7	149	58.0	At Time
4.2	5.8	14.5	81	31.5	After
(2.53)	(0.207)	(3.49)			New Projects
2.2	6.1	23.1	54	21.8	Before
3.4	5.7	16.7	129	52.0	At Time
5.0	5.6	15.5	65	26.2	After

Numbers in parentheses are F-ratios from full factorial analysis of variances for each of the characteristics.

[1] Size is number of employees in thousands.

[2] Profit is pretax current profit as a per cent of total assets.

[3] Debt is borrowing as a per cent of total assets.

[4] The interaction between when-inform policy and stable-share policy has a significant statistical effect for routine investing, but for new project financing there appears to be no interaction. A chi square test of the null hypothesis of interaction using a two-way frequency table yields 7.395 and 0.015, respectively.

other sources of funds and expertise. From these results, I would say that the widespread adherence to a stable relative share policy for working capital makes it the most important single policy within the main bank relationship as a whole.

Ex Post *Monitoring and the Stable Shares Policy*

A main bank is assumed to be willing to take a leading role in assisting a company in the event of financial distress, a role termed *ex post* monitoring (see Chapter 8 by Sheard). A firm must pay for this in some way, but such payments are implicit, as there is no explicit rescue insurance market. There are economies of scope between the rescue function and the normal financial business between firm and bank; the information exchanged during the latter gives the bank an understanding of the firm and its industry that is useful in the event of a rescue.

It would seem logical for a firm to use its main bank as a loan syndicate manager for a fee that in effect subsumed some part of the premium for the *ex post* monitoring function. But many large firms are in a sufficiently strong bargaining position to keep that premium very low; there being little likelihood the bank will be called on to lead a rescue. However, even if the actual rescue premium is small, the main bank has to be making money somewhere in its relationship with the company if it is to assist in time of need.

Thus, although a large firm can avoid paying explicit syndication fees and much of a premium for potential rescue, it directs a large portion of its other banking business to its main bank—it has to do business somewhere—and tends to maintain a stable share policy for the financial services it obtains from its core banks. In effect, much of the premium and syndication 'fees' are the assuredness of future business. That is an incentive for a firm to maintain stable relationships.

CONCLUSION

The bargaining power of smaller firms *vis-à-vis* lending institutions has increased since the 1980s because the large banks have moved down-market to serve them. Thus, for small firms and small banks, the most important structural change since liberalization of the financial system began has been the strategic emergence of city banks in the smaller-firm market. Credit-worthy small firms could borrow from innovative city banks through new financial channels, such as impact loans and privately placed bonds. Smaller firms have shown a good deal of flexibility in taking advantage of their new opportunities, seeking to reduce costs by diversifying sources of funding and services while maintaining a relationship with smaller banks and public financial institutions.

The surplus of savings over investment and the ability of large firms to tap directly into capital markets have been the primary forces driving this change, both directly and through their impact on the financial liberalization process. Smaller firms will always be treated differently from large ones for good business reasons, and in that sense there is not a full convergence in the credit markets. Nonetheless, city banks for some time have been working to encourage firms of all sizes to use them for their credit and other financial services needs.

Changing economic conditions have also meant the evolution of loan syndication in Japan. Since the late 1940s, the major participants—the main bank, other core banks, the bankers' association (AAB), government authorities (BOJ, MOF, MITI), and the borrowing firms—have shown dynamic flexibility as power has shifted among them. In each period, syndication was made effective by the leadership with the highest bargaining power at the time. Initially, this was the BOJ. As the high growth era got underway in the 1950s, the IBJ and AAB performed the leadership role for major industrial firms and the capital-hungry electric power companies. MITI also emerged as a major champion of large heavy and chemical industry firms. It should be noted that active organization and management of a syndication by a single financial institution for an explicit fee has been the exception rather than the rule throughout most of the post-war period.

By the early 1980s, the initiative had passed from lenders to borrowers, and syndication became endogenous for many large firms; they acted as their own *de facto* managers, although a financial institution was nominally identified as manager. The syndicates thus formed have been quite stable over time, a reflection of a stable relative share policy generally followed by firms and financial institutions alike. This policy, in turn, reflects a hierarchical relationship among the banks—main, core, peripheral—doing business with the firm.

Many large firms have, in a sense, been more or less able to take their banks' willingness to lend to them for granted, as indicated by the substantial number who simply inform their banks of their investment plans after company managers have decided them. This is much more common for routine investment than for new project investment.

The results of this survey suggest the role of a main bank in Japan is so general that it is not going to disappear. However, the power of main banks relative to their firms will further erode, and the system will evolve into something different. Part of this is a broadening of a firm's banking relationships to close relationships with several core banks. In losing banking business to core banks, the main bank also reduces some of its responsibility for *ex post* monitoring. This system has already begun to diffuse among the largest firms. The Japanese banking system has displayed dynamic flexibility, and will continue to do so.

REFERENCES

CAMPBELL, T. S., and M. KRACKAW. 1980. 'Information Production, Market Signalling, and the Theory of Financial Intermediation.' *Journal of Finance* 54.

DIAMOND, DOUGLAS W. 1984. 'Financial Intermediation and Delegated Monitoring.' *Review of Economic Studies* 51: 393–414.

GHANDI, D. K., R. HAUSMANN Jr, and ANTHONY SAUNDERS. 1985. 'On Syndicate Sharing Rules for Unanimous Project Ranking.' *Journal of Banking and Finance* 9: 517–34.

HIGANO, M. 1986. *Kin'yu-kikan no Shinsa-nouryoku* (*Monitoring Ability of Financial Institutions*). Tokyo: Tokyo University Press.

HORIUCHI, TOSHIHIRO. 1985. 'Gosen Sangyo ni okeru Setubi Shori to Kyodo Koi' ('Capacity Reduction and Cooperation in the Synthetic Fibre Industry'). *Journal of Japan Economic Research* 14: 22–46.

——. 1988a. *Mein Banku Kyoso to Kashidashi Shijyo – Kin'yu Kikan no Keiei Senryaku* (*The Relationship Between Main Bank Competition and Loan Markets: Operating Strategies of Financial Institutions*). Tokyo: Toyo Keizai Shinposha. (Chapter 9 is translated as 'Main Bank Competition and the Loan Market: The Case of Small Financial Institutions' in *Japanese Economic Studies* 18: 3–29.)

——. 1988b. 'Sekai Keizai o do kaeruka – Kin'yu Kikan no Kokusai Kin'yu Senryaku' ('What Impacts on Japanese Main Bank: Its International Financial Strategy'). TBS Britannica, Tokyo.

——. 1990. 'Management Structure of Japanese Banks and Their Optimal Relationship with Firms as "Main Banks".' Discussion Paper 309, Kyoto Institute of Economic Research, Kyoto University, Kyoto.

——. 1993. 'An Empirical Overview of the Japanese Main Bank Relationship in Relation to Firm Size (Based on the Results of a Survey Performed in 1990).' Forthcoming in *Revista Internazionale di Scienze Economiche e Commerciali* 40: 977–1018.

HORIUCHI, TOSHIHIRO and EIJI MURAKAMI. 1991. 'Wagakuni ni okeru mein banku torihiki jittai: anketo kekka kara mita kigyo kin'yu no sugata' ('The state of main bank transactions in Japan: the shape of corporate finance as seen from questionnaire results'). In Toshihiro Horiuchi, ed.

——, ed. 1991. *Jiyu-ka Kokusai-ka Jidai no Kigyo-kin'yu no Henbo* (*Changing Corporate Finance in the Period of Liberalization and Globalization*). Japan Center for Economic Research Report 75, Tokyo.

KAIZUKA, KEIMEI. 1976. 'Shinyo-Wariateron: Teranishi ronbun ni yosete' ('Comment on Teranishi's paper on Credit Rationing'). *Keizai Kenkyu* 27.

KATO, M., FRANK PACKER, and AKIYOSHI HORIUCHI. 1992. 'Mein Banku to Kyochoteki Yushi' ('Main Bank and Syndication Loan') *Keizai-gaku Ronshuu* 58: 2–22.

KOMIYA, RYUTARO, MASAHIRO OKUNO, and KOTARO SUZUMURA, eds. 1988. *Industrial Policy of Japan*. San Diego: Academic Press. Translation of *Nihon no Sangyo Seisaku*. Tokyo: Todai Shuppankai, 1984.

LELAND, H. E., and D. H. PYLE. 1977. 'Information Asymmetries, Financial Structure, and Financial Intermediation.' *Journal of Finance* 52: 371–87.

OKUMURA, H. 1991. 'Corporate Relations in Japan.' Paper presented at the Workshop of Italian and Japanese Economies in the '80s: A Comparative View, Siena University, September 1991.

PATRICK, HUGH T., and THOMAS P. ROHLEN. 1987. 'Small-Scale Family Enterprises.' In Kozo Yamamura and Yasukichi Yasuba, eds., *The Political Economy of Japan* vol 1: *The Domestic Transformation*. Stanford CA: Stanford University Press.

RAMSEYER, MARK. 1990. *Ho to Keizai-gaku: Nippon Ho no Keizai-bunseki* (Law and Economics: Economic Analysis of Japanese Law). Tokyo: Kobundo.

SACHS, JEFFREY D. 1984. 'Theoretical Issues in International Borrowings.' *Princeton Studies in International Finance* 54 (July).

SHARPE, STEVEN A. 1990. 'Asymmetric Information, Bank Lending, and Implicit Contracts: A Stylized Model of Customer Relationships.' *Journal of Finance* 55: 1069–87.

TERANISHI, JURO. 1974. 'Sengo Kashidashi-Shijyo no Seikaku ni tsuite (Characteristics of the Postwar Loan Market).' *Keizai Kenkyu* 25.

WILSON, R. 1968. 'The Theory of Syndicates.' *Econometrica* 36: 119–32.

ZENKOKU GINKO KYOKAI. 1965. *Zenkoku Ginko Kyokai 20-nen Rekishi* (*20 Years of the Association of All Banks*). Tokyo: Zenkoku Ginko Kyokai.

9

The Development of Main Bank Managerial Capacity

SATOSHI SUNAMURA

Omne tulit punctum, qui miscuit utile dulci—Quintus Horatius Flaccus[1]

This chapter examines the way in which a Japanese main bank develops its managerial capacity, from a practitioner's point of view. The author hopes this will help the reader to understand how bankers endeavour to enhance the quality of staff in their management of credit-risk control and business growth, and their long-term relationship with clients.

A commercial bank, as a licensed financial intermediary, receives deposits from the general public and lends money to credit-worthy corporate borrowers at a profit. The bank is, therefore, dealing with multiple tiers of clients, and its credibility and standing with the public needs an appropriate infrastructure, both 'hard' and 'soft', for effective operation. The establishment of a branch network and a computerized accounting system may be the 'hard' aspects of banking infrastructure; the collection of information as well as the application of technology, know-how, credit appraisal and consulting are the 'soft' elements. All these resources—credibility, money, hard and soft features—need to be organized by bank management to meet the requirements of all clients and changes in the business environment. Banking is primarily a service industry and ultimately its resources or strengths depend solely on its employees. Indeed, accountability, quality, profitability and diversity in banking can be achieved and facilitated only by building up the competitive managerial capacity of bank staff.

Banking, as a licensed enterprise, must also comply with economic and social objectives on three dimensions. At the micro level, its business must be sustainable and competitive while maximizing profits, protecting depositors and fostering firms with good prospects. At the system level, its operational structure must ensure accountability in its functions, improve efficiency in resource allocation, minimize risks in its implementation, and promote credibility in its information services. At the macro level, it must be able to respond flexibly to changes of economic climate within professional rules, fulfilling social expectations, and conforming to economic policy targets.

---

[1] 'He has gained every vote who has mingled profit with pleasure.'

The Japanese main bank system defined as a well-established form of relationship management which successfully developed in the post-war growth period 1955–73, may be seen as an effective mechanism for achieving the objectives listed above, and for facilitating industrial and corporate growth by allocating scarce investment funds and monitoring corporate governance under conditions of uncertainty and acute shortage of capital. Those conditions are more or less similar to circumstances prevailing in developing and transforming economies.

The essential factors for running a banking concern as a service industry can be narrowed down to managerial capacity or, in other words, the quality of staff involved in the main bank operation. Banking management must ensure that managerial capacity is constantly reviewed, improved and tested at all levels of an organization if it is to fulfil its primary functions—to assist the sound growth of corporate clients and to comply with social expectations.

This chapter is organized as follows. The first section examines the interlocking nature of the major functions and attributes of main banks, explicit as well as implicit, through which managerial capacity can be most effectively employed. The second section describes the normal course of career development which enables staff to acquire basic skills, to build up managerial capacity in specialized areas according to individual aptitude or preference, and ultimately to enhance the ability to deal with different corporate clients. The third section examines the implicit aspects of corporate monitoring and restructuring procedures through credit risk appraisal in response to changes in individual corporate performance. The fourth section provides an overview of the explicit aspects of business growth and corporate relationship management through an overall review of the way banks manage their portfolios in response to changes in the economic environment. The fifth section reviews those features of managerial capacity at micro, system and policy levels that may be indispensable to improving general accountability, productivity, restructuring ability, and relationship management in developing and transitional economies moving toward more market-oriented systems. Banking principles and functions may be universal, but differences in the organization of resources, as well as management style or emphasis, appear to affect overall managerial capacity in terms of accountability and the other objectives listed. For this reason the Japanese model described here may be useful in other countries in the developing or transforming process.

MAJOR ATTRIBUTES AND FUNCTIONS OF MAIN BANKS

Prima facie, the honour of main bank status is normally given to the largest lending bank which not only keeps a relatively high share of equity holding on its own account, but also influences corporate governance because of the *de facto* equity cross-holding among group companies and often through the bank's representation on the corporate board. Whether such main bank status would be confirmed by borrowers is often another story, particularly in recent years with so much availability and diversity of market instruments. In fact, the real qualification for main bank status depends on the bank's ability to undertake restructuring or to bear the ultimate credit risk of clients. Such an undertaking is only possible if it is based upon extensive credit appraisal as well as careful monitoring of corporate performance. For this reason, the major qualifications of a main bank must be endorsed by practical managerial capacity in the *ex ante*, interim, and *ex post* relationships with clients.

The main bank plays the role of syndication arranger or trustee for raising funds by explicitly committing the largest share of loans to corporate clients itself in order to signal its positive attitude to other participating lenders.[2] Specific services, such as the provision of credit information and arranging or advising modalities of syndication, are extended to obtain the overall benefits of foreign exchange business, trustee fees, large deposit balances, or to keep the cash flow between major clients within the bank's branch network. In fact, other participating lenders can generally save the cost of information gathering, credit analysis (periodic or *ad hoc*) by relying principally on the main bank's monitoring capacity whenever necessary. The larger the loan and number of syndicate members, the greater is the detailed analysis and the more extensive the counter checking. The real qualification of the main bank is whether it is ready to act as the lender of last resort when a borrower faces difficulty, even though it has not been formally contracted to do so.[3] If borrowers are unable to respond in time or to comply with requests from core bankers, they might risk losing an *ex post* back-up normally expected from their main bank. The timely disclosure, as well as the reliability, of information and the ethics of corporate management are the critical questions.

The managerial capacity to act as main bank can be identified through six main attributes which, although interlocking, are each independent. Three of them may be explicit, while three others are often implicit, as shown in Figure 9.1.

---

[2] This includes long-term loans on a roll-over basis, or bonds with mortgages on land and machinery. Other lenders may join the syndication for differing motives: to keep up the relationship with credit-worthy and growing borrowers, to look for more lucrative business opportunities, to diversify their portfolio, to get detailed information on specific projects, or to learn some technicalities. On agreement with borrowers, the main bank may take only a 10 per cent share of a loan in popular deals, but is prepared to take 25–50 per cent in cases of vital importance or confidential projects.

[3] Recent issues involving large loans provided to real estate and non-bank finance companies have amply illustrated the vagueness in such qualifications. In reality, there must have been prior inquiries, consultation, or warning by their main bank or core bankers as to

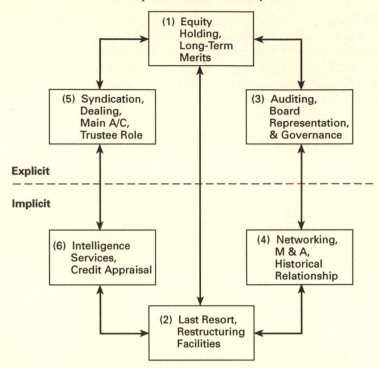

FIG. 9.1 Major Attributes of Main Banks

Where all six elements exist and both bank and firm are satisfied with each other, the position of the main bank may be secure on a long-term basis, as, for example, is often the case with banks serving the six major *keiretsu*. However, not all of these functions are necessarily fulfilled in all cases; in many cases the relationship continues with only two or three elements. Each case depends on how the relationship began and how satisfied each has been with the performance of the other over the years.

The closeness of the relationship can differ from case to case because the bank's commitment to the firm and the firm's mandate to the bank do not necessarily contain all the six elements. Where availability of information on the firm is limited, the bank's managerial capacity may also be limited. A loose relationship with a bank may often be identified with a new, rapidly growing firm or at a time of a serious credit squeeze. Changes in a relationship may develop, depending on the strength of the six elements and particularly when there are substantial changes in the credit system or capital markets. Sometimes the reasons are complicated

the current valuation of assets, limit of commitments, availability of collateral or future cash flow. It is not always the case that the largest lender is the main bank.

and fairly specific, as with Eidai and Daiwa Bank in 1975 and Daishowa Pulp and Sumitomo Bank in 1989. The time to review the role and function of the main bank is often when deals in merger and acquisition, or restructuring, are negotiated. Ultimately, a bank's commitment to act as the lender of last resort, and the need for this support on the part of a firm, are the determining factors of the degree of closeness between bank and firm.

As firms grow larger and more successful, whilst financial markets are further deregulated and globalized, some credit-worthy corporate borrowers may opt for diversification in their funding sources, rather than relying only on borrowing. They will go directly to the capital markets to issue public bonds or equity for which a credit-rating agency and securities underwriters may be approached. Neither, however, can ultimately replace the role of lender of last resort. They normally may not be as dependable as management advisors, since neither of them can undertake credit risk on their own account, nor be as well endowed with extensive credit or market information as the main banks. It might therefore be recognized that the role of the main bank is useful and effective, particularly at times of capital shortage, uncertain conditions, or a credit crunch, and that, typically, when corporate borrowers grow out to seek credit ratings directly in capital markets on their own, the requirement for lending from the main bank might become weakened. Historically, however, a main bank account is rarely moved to another bank unless both managements seriously distrust each other. From the main bank's point of view, there may be merely a change in composition of profit and loss items.

While equity holding and last-resort facilities are the backbone of a main bank position, qualifying a bank to exercise leadership in syndication or corporate governance, competition with other banks may often change the degree of a bank's relationship to particular firms, especially when those firms are disappointed with the quality of services or the level of commitment in credit undertaking. While equity holding, last-resort facilities, and board representation need to be resolved by top management, routine business relationships (items (4), (5) and (6) in Figure 9.1) are functions best developed at working levels. These routine matters can be the channels for changing the relative position of the banks assisting a firm. In essence, a long-term relationship is vital for main banks.

Whether the last-resort facility is really available, or whether any special understanding that historically associated them really exists, is not always altogether clear (unless a firm clearly belongs to one of the six major keiretsu), nor is the quality of intelligence services offered to the firms. Typical successful cases from among small or medium firms at the early stage of venture capital were Matsushita, Sony and Honda of 40 years ago. Those firms were fostered at a time of capital shortage by their main or core banks; their associations have never been loosened, even after the firms have virtually outgrown their banks in terms of return on investment or manageability of international business. In other words, these implicit elements could often be instrumental in paving the way for becoming main bank or core bank to certain firms, depending on their requirements at the time of their business development; the extent of the relationship depends on the bank's qualifications and functions. The opportunities to use the wider ranges of banking services are open to Japanese firms in a more global setting.[4]

Usually equity holding is connected with restructuring or last-resort facilities, board representation and syndication or trustee roles. Fund raising is closely associated with intelligence services and credit appraisal; it may be considered the most important function at a time of capital shortage, as in the case of Japan during the period 1955–73. Involvement in governance, including auditing and board representation, normally flow from long-standing historical relationships, equity holding, or involvement in a merger or acquisition deal.

As deregulation advanced after 1964, when Japan became an adherent to Article 8 of the IMF, and the market environment by the early 1970s enabled Japanese banks to engage more heavily in international transactions, typically in Euro markets, corporate demand for diversified or sophisticated fund-raising activities substantially increased. New ideas and innovative instruments are welcomed most by firms that have become international in their operations and want more than stereotypical Japanese banking services. New and widespread opportunities arose for banks established firmly in their particular business.

Japanese financial markets, groomed under regulated rules of the game over the decades of the high growth period, were assumed to have achieved by the end of the period a competitive, efficient and effective commercial banking system, which had not yet been sufficiently tested in world markets. Intelligence services in, say, overseas bond or equity issues, a combination of various forms of credit for overseas project finance, hedging devices for long-term exchange risk, cost-effective arbitrage deals, and, in the 1980s, swaps, options and derivatives as well as investment management, are the sorts of deals that turn corporate treasurers' eyes to banks other than traditional main banks. Quality in intelligence services may now be the basis for changing the banks' pecking order in specific deals.[5] Commercial banks in Japan have survived long

---

[4] For example, US investment bankers and British merchant bankers may excel in identifying and arranging attractive overseas packages of mergers and acquisitions or lucrative capital market deals, whilst Japanese main banks will be helpful in further consultation or appraisal of credit-worthiness, or scrutinizing the hidden loss (or profit) of targeted firms, or identifying problems in information memorandum as a matter of due-diligence, and can afford to stand-by or fund the deals, short or long term, to enable their clients to choose the right timing.

[5] Although the role of syndication for long-term fund raising in the domestic arena is

enough in fierce domestic competition where the professional rules of the game are relatively simple and effectively strict.[6] Japanese banks have now developed the managerial capacity, as well as the sophisticated techniques in undertaking corporate clients' overseas deals, normally associated with Anglo-American investment bankers.

Board representation may be possible for major shareholders of good reputation if the bank and firm have collaborated in the past on certain symbolic or breakthrough projects. Equity holdings as well as availability of last-resort facilities may be essential elements for fostering young firms and those with good prospects. If these are backed by a main bank, a small firm like Sony or Honda in the 1950s could concentrate on the development of its own technology on a long-term basis.

In short, main banks have played a significant role as agents for corporate growth in the development process. In a deregulated and more competitive global setting, main banks must endeavour to upgrade their managerial capacity and credibility. Main banks are constantly required to review the composition of their portfolios and to monitor their relationships with their clients, *ex ante*, interim, and *ex post*.

BUILDING MANAGERIAL CAPACITY IN AN ORGANIZATION

In the eyes of corporate borrowers, the position of main bank can only be fulfilled by qualified banks. Borrowers particularly require banks that are dependable at the time of a credit shortage, that will provide reliable management consultation (often needed in the case of restructuring) and that have managerial expertise to deal with any type of financial issue. Bank management capacity must therefore be developed and practised in line with sound banking principles, but must also be able to meet these specific requirements of corporate clients.

primarily derived directly from a bank's status of large lending or equity holding, quality in intelligence services, for example rendered in overseas deals, seems to have challenged such main bank positions under the more liberalized banking environment. Further deregulation, for instance, of Article 65 of the Securities Act, will permit bank subsidiaries to engage broadly in securities business; steps towards this were taken in 1993. Japanese banks' motivation to opt for universal banking is now not only high, but their capacity to place new issues or to manage more diversified financial instruments may be sufficiently mature to enable them to compete in more global markets.

[6] The scope of operation of licensed banks in Japan has been strictly confined to pure commercial banking. Neither equity underwriting nor brokering has been permitted under Article 65 of the Securities Act. Ceiling rates on deposits are effectively imposed. A foreign exchange control system was maintained until 1980, when virtually every control was removed. However, no prime underwriters' positions, even in overseas issues of corporate bonds, were given to bank affiliates operating in the Euro market, where universal banking prevails. It is generally argued that this kind of over-extended protection for securities companies might have created the oligopolistic privileged position for securities houses which led to the latest scandals.

A study of the history of banking, which may be traced back a few centuries, would teach bankers what are sound banking principles: (1) accountability in operation, (2) quality in service, (3) steadiness in profit-making, and (4) diversification or sophistication in portfolio (refer to Table 9.1).[7]

These principles must be widely recognized, learned through experience, by discipline and practice at all levels, from top management, mid-level managers, down to young working-level officers. Any bank's overall credibility, management quality and business performance will be judged by these principles, where human resources, the quality and availability of information, and an efficient computerized system are the primary assets. Ultimately, the quality of staff is the vital component in banking.

Let us look at the general career development of bank staff in the typical case of a Japanese bank and at what sorts of skills they are expected to acquire, how conscientiously they serve their clients, and how they are expected to comply with the banking principles at different levels of responsibility.

Banks compete to recruit potentially capable, personable, robust and well-educated students directly from university.[8] When they join individual banks, new staff typically are put into intensive training programmes, organized by the personnel division, for about four weeks; then they are sent to branches or divisions where their on-the-job training starts. There is not much difference in the treatment of staff at this level because of, say, their academic career or sex, and salaries are fairly similar. The primary objective is to provide basic knowledge, training and discipline to be a good banker. Deposit taking, accounting or some research work may be their initial task. They learn these skills before they are moved to work with a specific team of foreign exchange, bond-dealing or credit-appraisal experts where junior officers learn directly from their individual superiors. New staff must be well trained, disciplined and sincere while they are 'fresh'.

---

[7] Table 9.1 illustrates the major assignments for bank staff broadly at three levels, in line with the old banking principles. The description here mainly follows major categories in managerial capacity expected from a main bank. These principles may sound like rules of thumb, but with experience, each clearly corresponds to different management categories requiring specific managerial capacity: for example, (1) accountability is qualitative as well as quantitative, involving credibility and control, or soft and hard infrastructure, in the system; (2) quality of service is the most competitive way to maintain a relationship; (3) steadiness in making profits indicates long-term and effective business progress (rather than, for example, high volatility in dividend distribution) and, besides, an unusually large margin on lending or fee charges may be criticized for not assisting corporate growth or eroding good relationships; (4) diversification in business is required not only to avoid risk, but more to expand multifold relationships and cultivate firms with good prospects for long-term growth.

[8] Competition is such that the Federation of Bankers Associations set a rule for banks not to solicit before the summer of a student's final year. In 1954 university graduates in a major city bank accounted for only a quarter to a third of the total recruited, in 1964 they occupied about half, and by 1974 almost all new male staff were graduates.

TABLE 9.1 Managerial Capacity to be Developed for Different Discretion Levels

Banking Principles	Discretion Levels		
	Working Officer *(on-the-job training and discipline)*	Mid-Level *(strategy and effectiveness)*	Management *(leadership and judgement)*
Accountability in operation	Cash flow analysis; precise accounting; asset valuation; secondment to client	Appraising credit standing, collateral and investment projects; auditing; provisioning; computerization update	Personnel assignment; sanctions on restructuring; equity holding, board representation; monitoring overall performance
Quality in services	Visiting clients; efficiency in services; effective information gathering; offering swaps and options	Good communication; industrial and technical survey; advising ALM; providing innovative menu	Overall management consultancy; financial information services; visiting major shareholders and clients; reconciliation and restructuring
Steadiness in profitability	Deposit and foreign exchange taking; prospectus preparation for bond issues and syndications	Pursuing overall benefits; proposing specifics for deals; handling investment management; controlling expenses	Networking overall business; developing joint ventures and overseas projects; budget control; overall strategy
Diversification in business portfolio	Offering useful research work on industries; visiting potential clients; providing intelligence service	Proactive consulting; restructuring proposals; identifying and analysing venture capital deals; long-term business plan	Cultivating prospective clients; offering merger and acquisition services; taking new 'relationship' equity positions

Until their early thirties, all staff will be trained to be generalists, but will be encouraged to become specialists in at least two or three fields by their mid-forties. The exceptions to this are traders in foreign exchange and money markets, specialists in capital market operations, and research staff, who may be groomed as specialists from the beginning of their career under a separate wage scale that is in line with external labour markets for these skills.

On-the-job training includes a study of the following components which form the basis for individual career development: (a) precise accounting practice, asset valuation, and cash flow analysis, (b) efficiency in services to clients, effective and relevant information gathering, soliciting deposit and foreign exchange business, as well as identifying new clients, (c) extensive research on industries or capital markets, increasing skills gradually to deal with a report on, say, the production system at a client's factories or on a specific money market, and (d) preparing a credit appraisal or a prospectus for a bond issue or large syndication. Developing skills in credit appraisal, money market dealing or research work may be the major tasks for staff at this level: they are expected to learn at least (a), (b) and (c), and, if possible, (d) in five years. Staff are expected to acquire in three to five years, while working full time, the basic skills that may be taught at an MBA course in an American university. There will be few differences in training programmes or rotation at this stage for all personnel, including women, on the management track.

Each section is equipped with manuals compiled over the years by previous staff: these manuals serve not only as text books, but also as a significant accumulation of case studies of a variety of deals, valuable information and know-how. Each member of staff is expected to contribute new ideas to enrich the contents of the manuals.

Senior officers are responsible for educating juniors by guiding them properly: it is important to inspire them to advance according to their individual aptitudes and talents. After assessment of performance, disposition, potentials and interests, some may be picked out for overseas training, or to study for an MBA, or training at a merchant bank. Others may be put on secondment for a few years to the treasury office of corporate clients or a research institution or government agency in order to broaden their basic knowledge and to carry out studies in depth from different perspectives.

Allocation of staff on secondment is determined by the clients' requirements. Some require accounting work, others, foreign exchange dealing or credit appraisal or money market research. Assistance is found useful and is much appreciated by small and medium firms or institutions. On return to the bank such staff are normally put in their preferred areas (usually not in charge of those same clients). Clients' requirements vary according to prevailing economic conditions. Their capacity to absorb and to learn from these secondments is normally much greater for younger, rather than older, people, and the experience will enhance their management capability later in their career.

At about this point in their training some talented staff may wish to leave the bank to pursue an academic or other professional career if they are disappointed with the people, quality or policy of their bank. About 10 per cent of trainee staff in their twenties might be lost at this stage.

Periodic, formal, or private counselling is therefore indispensable at this level. However, it should be emphasized that whatever different assignment a trainee is given after five years, there still will be a variety of courses in store for them. Normally, they will be rotated around different divisions during the first 10 years. In fact, many incumbent board members of banks were not necessarily on elite courses at the early stage of their career. Assessments of career development need to look at periods of 10 to 20 years.

In approximately 10 years' time young prospective officers become section managers. Their assignment should now be specialized and upgraded, but diversified to include budget control, personnel affairs and general matters. Their responsibilities usually cover (1) assessment of business performance, merits and credit-worthiness of individual clients, specific investment projects, medium- to long-term business plans and restructuring proposals, (2) surveys on industry and new technology, (3) money and capital market dealing, producing innovative financial instruments through specific engineering (swap, option, derivatives), offering asset and liability management or investment management services, (4) proposals for structured finance, mergers and acquisitions or other devices to expand overall benefits, (5) pro-active consultation with clients' management on policies or issues, or identifying and appraising the potential of new business or venture capital, and (6) personnel allocation.

At this mid-level career stage section managers are given actual responsibilities, for example, for a major work-out of business strategy, for developing effectiveness in operation and efficiency in management and for training young bank staff. The accumulation of knowledge, hard work, building of skills, team work and strategic thinking, in addition to a good personality, are essential attributes for good bankers. New ideas or creative proposals to promote business will be positively assessed, while any business failure, if repeated, may be fatal for further promotion. It is, in fact, the quality of these complex services offered by mid-level management that leads directly to an assessment of a bank's qualification to act as a main bank.

It is around this period of 10 to 18 years' experience that a comprehensive and objective personnel assessment file is completed for each individual, based upon accumulated information on their past performance, behavioural pattern, specialization, aptitude and personality, and this will be reflected in their salary scale and help determine future assignments. All bank staff by then may be broadly categorized into special fields or divisions for future career development: corporate finance and relationship building (mainly in branches), credit or project appraisal, money and capital market operations, accounting and treasury, computerization and systems control, overseas business strategy, research work, personnel affairs, and central planning.

Every member of staff may be given a chance at least annually to express any preference as to which career path to pursue. Female staff who wish to pursue a professional career will be required to accept reassignment or transfer to other positions, either domestic or overseas, on the same basis as male staff. Any staff member with proven ability would then be upgraded to the level of assistant general manager. This is also about the time when some of the most able staff may be requested by the bank's clients, often medium and small firms, to assist their management with the tacit assurance of a senior post in those firms in due course. Those staff have to consider their future careers in terms of leaving or staying with the bank. They are often transferred on secondment to firms and, if this move proves satisfactory for both parties, may change their status to be the client's, not the bank's, executive. In the early 1990s, for example, nearly 40 per cent of staff recruited in the same year might have left for other firms or professions by their mid-forties, as against 20 per cent of them in the early 1970s. This kind of secondment into client firms will assist good long-term relationships and the transfer of management know-how to corporate clients in Japan.

After 17 to 25 years of service, some bank staff reach the level of general manager at branches or headquarters, with full discretion in their field of responsibility. The primary task for them is decision making as general managers, occupied with continuing the dialogue with the top management of firms, attending meetings (with shareholders, bankers associations, local authorities, Bank of Japan, Ministry of Finance, and others).

Such a hierarchical career-development system is a rational *modus operandi* in the banking industry where staff are on the whole trained to be generalists. Bank staff trained in this way for more than 20 years could be useful in assisting, say, accounting or treasury divisions of corporate clients, as well as improving their management control system. In fact, some staff in their mid-forties or early fifties may be willing to leave the bank and join a client firm where they will be general managers or the equivalent, with the assurance of reasonable remuneration until they are 60 or 65 years old.

Bank staff regularly move to different jobs, learn multiple skills, cultivate the habits of improvement, whatever their current assignment may be, and of coordination with colleagues on other teams. In such an organization, new information, ideas and suggestions for improvement in quality and for productivity gains, come from the bottom level of management to the top. Indeed, those skills acquired at different levels—decision making, imposing sanctions, and the like, as shown in Table 9.1—are the essential managerial capacities necessary to act as a main bank. They are acquired only through learning by doing and working in teams. Main bank credentials can only be acquired by quality in corporate governance and a high degree of managerial capacity in line with the traditional banking principles.

Some general managers with outstanding performance records of many years' standing will be selected as board members after 24 to 28 years' service if they are not opposed by an incumbent board member. Some might argue that this form of banking career development was shaped typically under the Japanese corporate climate, characterized in particular by three elements: permanent employment, promotion from within, and a strong seniority element in promotion.[9]

These may, however, no longer be *absolute* pre-requisites for career development. Training of, say, 15 to 20 years may be sufficient to reach a certain level of management capability; after that time, some may wish to leave the bank of their own accord. Often they are employed by corporate clients in need of capable treasurers or senior managers who can contribute to enhancing the quality of the firms' administrative and control processes. These clients are not necessarily within a bank's *keiretsu*. They are more often firms with good growth prospects, generally mid-size or venture capital start-ups. Some companies undergoing restructuring also want the skills of capable and experienced ex-bank staff. A loss of, say, 30 to 40 per cent of staff at this stage would not really undermine the management structure of the bank. Rather, a reduction in the number of senior staff helps to shape an effective hierarchy in overall management.

These three elements may not be culture specific to Japan; they may be more or less common to any established or developing organization in the world. Moreover, they possibly provide an effective framework for organizing corporate order and improving staff quality in the development process, considering the enormous energy, cost and other management inputs required for enhancing personal motivation, teamwork and productivity, as well as for tackling lay-offs, moral hazard, reorganization, court disputes and similar pitfalls. Bank management is assumed to deal with such shortcomings in a pre-emptive manner with discretion and responsibility.

[9] Admittedly, there may be a risk or short-coming in such a long-term career system; for example, (a) young graduates have to decide their life-time profession at an early stage, whilst banks have to be selective about the potential human resources at the time of employment, (b) much time and initial cost may be incurred in giving appropriate training, education and motivation until each member can really contribute to the bank's business development, (c) there may be inequities in treating a bright young generation in terms of salary scale, academic career and specific posting, (d) there may be a tendency to produce stereotyped staff, irresponsive to the needs of customers, changes in the system, or the environment in a broader sense. However, it must be noted that bank staff are not bound by any life-time contract and that they are free to leave at any time. There is some mobility now developing in the Japanese labour market, specifically for the young generation in their twenties (say, dealers) and those over mid-forty, like professionals generally in service industries (securities brokers, accountants, consultants, lawyers, academics, and so on). In the future, Japanese corporations will include board members from outside to diversify their business relationships and to bring in innovative ideas.

Ozaki (1991, pp. 26–28) notes:

conventional economics assumes that labour mobility generally enhances productivity. . . . [However,] the external labour market both inhibits firm-specific skill formation, and discourages cooperative efforts between workers. . . . In the internalized market, workers operate as members of a team. They compete for promotions and higher pay, and are evaluated on the basis both of their individual productivity and of their ability to cooperate with other members of the team in enhancing group productivity. Job rotation is the norm; each worker cultivates a sense of interrelatedness of different functions and holistic perception of the entire production process.

Issues of corporate culture or management style can be further assessed in relation to their objectives, principles and philosophy. Japanese bankers emphasize quality of service (without fees) and long-term relationship management. They know how best to train young staff, and how to motivate them to improve their overall productivity and fulfil their responsibilities in society as part of a going concern as well as professionals. Main banks always endeavour to build up a long-term and trustworthy relationship with good corporate clients; main bank staff study hard to acquire specific skills. Their experience as generalists at a working level helps enhance their specialist expertise at mid-level, leading eventually towards overall leadership in corporate governance at the top level. A successful banker is experienced, mature and quick in decision-making, and willing to work in a team. The quality of a main bank may be judged by whether its relationship with clients is well maintained at all levels. These means of enhancing managerial capacity are not at all culture specific, as will be proved by their long-term competitiveness in the global market.

CREDIT RISK MANAGEMENT

The six functions of a main bank can be fully carried out in a coordinated manner only by well-trained and experienced bankers, who are usually shrewd, sensitive, tough, and sympathetic. Managerial capacity can be measured against traditional banking principles, but the standing of main banks can be examined more specifically in respect of credit risk control systems, profitability growth and relationship management. Main bank credit risk may be assessed by their larger lending share. Whilst maximum benefits may be pursued by absorbing associated business, every effort is made to reduce the lending share by way of wider syndication. The lending limit to an individual firm is imposed by prudential regulation against a bank's own capital, and the bank's aggregate assets are controlled by Bank for International Settlements (BIS) convention, despite the differences in taxation systems and accounting practices in each country. Therefore, the crucial issue here is the quality or substance of those assets.

Credit risk management may be evaluated broadly in terms of credit quality, market exposure, system control and environmental changes. Apart from credit risk, other areas of risk management may be more or less similar to any bank operation. Market risk is mainly due to volatility in rates and should be controlled by the system against primary capital, unrealized profit (loss) of equity assets, and subordinated debt (refer to the latest Basle convention). System controls relate to hard and software infrastructure. Changes in environment affect every bank. In this section, major features of credit risk management and the quality of loan assets at a main bank are examined.

Let us look into credit risk management. Loan officers in charge of particular firms are responsible for updating credit information files which contain periodic reports, specific analysis and *ad hoc* information on corporate performance. This might include a brief history of the company, full descriptions of the career and characters of board members, reports on the quality of major products, detailed analysis of balance sheet and profit and loss statements, debt structure, cash flow features, cost and productivity analysis, assessment on unrealized profit or hidden loss and real net worth, latest project evaluations and, more importantly, reviews of profitability and strategy on relationship management. Any member of staff can have access to the files through their chief officers. A loan officer usually looks after 10 to 50 firms, depending on the modes and degrees of business relationships.[10] Each credit file has to be scrutinized at least by his chief and branch management, as well as specialist credit officers at head office (*shinsa-bu*). A loan officer's abilities and talents must be fully demonstrated to all other colleagues in order to be a general manager in the future.

Abundant recent data are available on any listed firm from specialized credit information companies. The reliability of information can be more properly assessed or confirmed, however, only by direct dialogue with treasurers of firms, interviews with their suppliers and buyers, and scrutiny of detailed financial statements or back-up data not necessarily appearing in an auditor's report (for example, off balance sheet transactions). Any major problems or related issues will then be checked or reconfirmed by their chief, managers, seconded staff and, if necessary, at the level of general managers, as well as board members or auditors, over lunches, by visits, or at weekend recreation clubs.

---

[10] Perhaps a Japanese loan officer's productivity (in ratio of revenue against expenses) as well as performance (in terms of time and dedication to the bank) are higher than those for foreign banks. For example, see Sakura Sogo (1992), which is based upon the annual report of 36 major banks operating internationally over six countries despite differences in domestic taxation systems and regulatory frameworks.

Each firm may be classified, for example, into Super, Good, Ordinary, Watch, and Hospital Care, in order of credit-worthiness. Whilst such classification is necessary to monitor performance and to review or determine the extent of the bank's involvement or credit commitments, other categorizations of clients may be applied as part of a relationship strategy to expand overall business (see the next section). Both are integral parts of exercises in main bank managerial capacity.

Any sign of change in the performance of Watch and Hospital Care categories of companies will be reflected *ex ante* in changes in revenues, terms of bills in receivables and payables, cash flow in the main account, style of activities, morale of employees, and rumours among suppliers and buyers, as well as the company's competitors. These are easily detected by loan officers or managers if they keep in daily or frequent contact with the right people. Enquiries into the condition of those companies can be made at different levels on learning about potential problems. If the issue is critical, further detailed investigations will be made of their factories, accounting or marketing divisions, clients or employees' union.

The chief officer then will be made aware of the latest credit appraisal report and investigation. Normally, he can obtain an acceptable explanation for changes in performance, and can suggest measures to be taken by the firm, as officers are usually well versed in the problems of firms in the Watch or Hospital Care category. If not, he is expected to work out programmes for restructuring which need to be sanctioned by the manager, by loan specialists at headquarters and, ultimately, by the general manager, as they might often need to meet the firm's request for bridge financing. Daily cash flows on accounts will be scrutinized by both loan and chief officers. Reassessment of collateral or security may be carried out confidentially.

In serious cases, a confidential meeting is organized at the general manager's level to discuss comprehensive measures. The main bank may have to make a judgement on whether: (a) a quick intermediate rescue package or bridge financing is to be organized with core banks, (b) a special stand-by arrangement or curtailment of the credit commitment may be required to match available security or collateral, or (c) more fundamental restructuring is imperative. The case of (a) applies usually to firms of long-term relationship which are normally in a position to recover by increasing their revenue. Case (b) may apply when the market share of a firm's major products has been substantially eroded due to a basic cost increase or the emergence of competitive products, or the firm's failure to expand. If the firm has kept in regular consultation with the main bank in advance of any potential problem, or its operation is reasonably diversified, or new products are expected based on R&D work, or a new overseas market can be cultivated, the main bank would normally stand by as the lender of last resort with support from core banks.

The real question is option (c), which may be divided further into three cases: (i) fundamental changes in revenue due to the emergence of substitute products or technological advance which compel firms to close down their principal product lines, there being no scope for diversification into related industries; (ii) substantial losses incurred through speculation in non-principal business, such as in securities, real estate or commodities, affecting normal operation of the principal lines of business; or (iii) business failure involving fraud, management ethics and labour disputes.

These three cases could usually have been identified by core banks well in advance of public knowledge (as, for example, the current real estate issue). The main bank would usually have had consultations with management of firms some time before any real difficulty was envisaged. The announcement of liquidation is normally just a matter of confirmation after long consultation, or reconciliation, or required procedures. If problems are discovered too late for restructuring by the parties concerned, all members in charge of the loan commitment will be either demoted or dismissed. The main bank policy procedure is then simple.

If the problem is identified at the earliest stage as in case (i), a special rescue team is organized with the head of the task force chosen from the main bank's top management. The utmost effort is made first to maintain business as usual so as to keep existing employees instead of immediately laying them off. Part-time work or wage cuts will normally be proposed. Obvious lines of unprofitable operation will immediately be closed. Relocation of the work force may be suggested with related companies or their suppliers or buyers. The primary objective is to minimize the ultimate size of the loss the main bank may be obliged to carry. All legal procedures will be taken to seize any possible collateral under the banking agreements, as the main bank normally holds first mortgages. The main bank will not, however, use its priority claims simply for its own loan recovery.

Depending on the history of the business relationship, lending share, equity holding, relationship with major shareholders and other creditors, each case will be carefully evaluated by main bank top management taking into consideration reputation and specific costs required for reconstruction, in close consultation with core banks on its undertaking a share of the final loss. The main bank would normally take the largest share of a write-off to demonstrate its primary responsibility. The most common style of rescue operation may be first to mitigate the debtor's interest payment burden in accordance with lending shares among core banks, and at worst to write off some unrecoverable portion of loans. The firm may then be sold to other firms that can afford to take on the remaining resources or workable assets, including staff, franchise rights, technology patents or R&D institutions. Ultimately, merger with other firms may be the best option in normal cases.

In the case of (ii), the obvious procedure is to separate non-principal business operations and transfer or sell those to other reliable firms engaged in the same lines of business. Case (ii) coupled with (iii) could be the very worst for the main bank. Whilst the main bank rescue or restructuring strategy is simple, team members have to go through long and difficult work. After liquidation has been effected, all members have to be fully compensated in terms of a special bonus or a move to other more enjoyable posts. The real reputation of a main bank may hang on the way in which matters are handled in such cases, and in the manner of dealing with creditors and debtors in the liquidation process. It should also be noted that the primary functions of a main bank lie in seeking and fostering new clients with good prospects (*ex ante*), expanding and diversifying existing business (interim) and organizing the monitoring team to act as the lender of last resort in case of need (*ex post*).

The skills normally applied in restructuring proposals may also be more actively used for merger and acquisition deals, those popular and lucrative games enjoyed largely by Anglo-American bankers during the 1980s. In fact, Japanese main banks that are experienced as managers or lead-arrangers in project finance or syndication in global markets are fully equipped to undertake M&A deals. A problem often associated with such deals involving overseas firms is the depth and coverage of corporate information provided in the prospectus or memorandum by overseas bankers, which does not normally evaluate the quality of assets and management attributes of targeted firms. (Consider the cases of Fuji Bank's take-over of Walter Heller and Mitsubishi Bank's take-over of Bank of California.) Similar issues may be raised in real estate business and the like. Due diligence is the main point in question. These lacunae may be only discovered at a later stage of take-over, as often identified in the major deals Japanese firms were invited to bid for in the past. As Japanese bankers highly esteem their long-term relationship with clients, they are usually very sensitive to the quality of products they might offer and would not consider M&A as once-and-for-all deals. Main banks expect to look after firms and to build up more routine business even after such deals.

The quality of managerial capacity in the main bank rests in well-trained human resources and practical credit appraisal, organized in teams broadly at three levels of experience as bankers. It may be worthwhile to note that corporate information on Japanese firms is so widely available and, in many cases, so evident, and the main bank's research is so extensive in evaluating potential assets as well as technology, that it is effectively a good climate for venture capital. More than 90 per cent of corporate accounts held with city banks are those of small and medium firms.

A caveat may be in the current crisis in real estate as is widely acknowledged to be due to the nature of information available in Japan, caused by the easy money environment of 1985–89, as well as a firm belief in the myth that Japanese land prices never decline seriously. Such a crisis is a direct consequence of the poor management of non-bank finance companies and their main banks, none of which took account of changes in the climate, and particularly the effects of interest rate liberalization. However, assuming that the total of bad loans at city banks is 14 to 20 trillion yen and that about 30 per cent discounting of collateral may be inevitable, the amount may be yet reasonably manageable in the current market when matched against unrealized profits on other assets. At worst, some financial institutions may have to be taken over by others. This is a good lesson for such institutions at this phase of financial development.

BUSINESS GROWTH AND RELATIONSHIP MANAGEMENT

In addition to individual credit risk control, main bank managements are concerned with the prospect, over a five-year span, for the aggregate growth, quality and profit structure of bank business, as well as the style of corporate relationships as clients' positions change with the economic environment. A bank's business structure may be analysed in terms of volume (loans, deposits, trading, and so on) or time and cost spent or, even more, by margins, commissions and profits from trading both with clients and on own account.

A bank's planning division (*kikaku-shitsu*) or industrial research division (*sangyo chosa shitsu*) is normally put in charge of a rolling three-year business plan. Growth patterns of corporate business may be broadly categorized into several industrial groups which may be analysed in terms of growth in turnover, cumulative amount of fixed investment, average age of employees, and the increase in the number of accounts. These groups are, in the order they probably appear in a bank's 1992 portfolio: (a) regional development projects (for example, real estate, construction); (b) financial institutions (securities firms, leasing, insurance); (c) major export industries (electronics, automobiles, new materials, software); (d) overseas projects; (e) equipment industries (electrical machinery, petrochemicals, pharmaceutical); (f) steady ordinary business (trade, services); and (g) long-established industries based on traditional technology facing obvious structural problems or innovation (agriculture, mining, textiles, pulp makers, shipbuilders).

An incumbent main bank management would probably like to see its portfolio composed more or less in the order of (c), (e), (b), (d), (a), (f) and (g), to maximize overall profits and to make sure of the comfortable expansion of business ahead. It is obvious under the current economic conditions that not only real estate and non-bank finance companies are required to transform their business styles, but also banking itself needs to restructure its overall portfolio as well as profit structure. Generally speaking, major main banks have been the institutions most tied up with the aftermath of the 'bubble' after long-term credit banks and trust banks, because of their traditional relationship with clients in real estate; though a part of that business through their affiliated non-bank finance companies mushroomed during the easy-money period from 1986 to 1990, together with deregulation measures.

Each item of the bank's profit and loss accounts as well as the composition of its assets and liabilities will be analysed during examination of its profit structure. The accounting division scrutinizes movements in every account, and makes regular enquiries of the divisions in charge as to their business progress based upon the budget plan or specific policy framework authorized by the management at the beginning of each fiscal year. Bank revenue can be generated from (a) interest income on loans, (b) fees and commissions (for guarantees, syndications and custodial arrangements, mergers and acquisitions, and so forth), (c) trading profits (in foreign exchange, bonds, swaps, options, derivatives, and the like), and (d) capital gains (in equity, real estate, and the like).

In the case of Japanese banking, (a) is still the largest source of income, but (c) as well as (b) are increasing fairly rapidly. Publicly available data clearly indicate that per capita assets, revenue, income, number of deposit accounts, and number of corporate clients of major Japanese banks—that is, various measures of productivity—are high against overhead cost (Sakura Sogo, *Kenkyusho* 1992). This may be mainly because of larger loan assets per capita. Increase in off balance sheet revenue (mainly through (b) and (c)) is conspicuous since the 1980s, due to the proliferation of deals in swaps and options initiated by US, and followed by European and Japanese banks. Off balance sheet transactions of US money centre banks in 1990 reached a larger amount than on balance sheet transactions, whereas for German and Japanese banks these items were around 14 per cent of total assets. As a result, BIS now argues for recognizing the market risk of off balance sheet transactions due to the volatility of interest and exchange rates. This might involve Tier 3 capital, which includes subordinated debt of two to five years at surface value; however, in early 1994 details had yet to be worked out.

A survey for the Federal Reserve Bank of New York by Hertle (1991, p. 40) suggests that competitive success in the swap markets largely relates to size and market share, dealers' access to market orders, information flows as well as credit standing (rating) of institutions. Perhaps the depth of corporate relationship may be added here to get a fairer picture.

The main bank's strategy is obviously to build a quality portfolio and to raise profitability in the long term. The best way to achieve this is: to increase the number of main accounts and secure repeated transactions, to diversify (interim) trading of new financial instruments with existing growing firms and expand dealings (arbitrage) in markets on their own account, to explore (*ex ante*) new firms in growing industries and foster young, small and medium firms with good prospects, and to reappraise (*ex post*) total performance and merits of maturing or matured firms. Analysing these items in more detail we see that:

- The performance or profitability of a bank as a financial intermediary can be evaluated by the volume of transactions channelled through it. The greater the number of accounts (both of depositors and firms) a bank looks after, the greater the benefits and profits that can be expected, particularly on those large or main accounts held by existing firms. (Interim benefits will be usually very large.)
- As deregulation, securitization, globalization and computerization progress, financial instruments will continue to be diversified, and ever-more sophisticated combinations of interest rates, maturities, and spot and forward currencies are designed.

  Control systems over the exposure positions (commitment structure) and volatility (market risk) have been devised. Netting agreements may be required to reduce gross aggregate exposures. The more diversified a bank is in handling various instruments, the more arbitrage is possible. The more volatility and risk emerges in markets, the more profitable deals or hedging chances arise. Highly trained teams of engineers and dealers work full time designing unusual structures of various instruments. Young engineers and specialists have been specifically brought in since 1985 and have become increasingly competitive in dollar to yen and yen to yen swaps. Banks with a large presence in the market and good access to information on money flows are better positioned for making up varieties of deals (*ex ante* as well as interim opportunities exist).
- One of the main social roles expected of main banks is to foster small and medium firms with good prospects. Association with new, promising firms or venture capital using new technology or innovative ideas brings potential for a long-lasting relationship and good profits. The most competitive and qualified banks, in terms of managerial capacity, concentrate their relationship strategy on identifying and associating with emerging firms with innovative products. Emerging firms normally require start-up funds both in equity and loans, as well as management consultancy (*ex ante*). Banks' appraisal of potential firms covers a survey of their technology, quality of products, entrepreneurial skills, management structure, required size of new investment, potential suppliers and buyers, as well as competitors. Real competition in current Japanese banking lies in the search for firms of good potential (domestic as well as overseas). This is assumed to be the major feature of a

main bank as equity holder and lender of last resort in the development process. This effort may be initially costly, requiring time and patience, but can turn out to be lucrative once new firms successfully take off in their business with main bank support.

• A main bank takes good care of old clients, particularly maturing or matured firms. It would be happy to second someone appropriate to assist a firm's management and to bring in new proposals, not only on market deals or instruments or investment management, but also on useful merger and acquisition proposals for further business development (*ex post* operation).

In a bank's portfolio, some firms are growing steadily while others may be declining in terms of both volume and quality. The portfolio of clients may be regrouped into: growing and with future prospects (*ex ante*), steady and secure (interim), and maturing or matured (*ex post*). If you denote these three respectively as A, I, and P, you see an interesting trend in main bank portfolios. For example:

x A > I > P   Expansive portfolio for the future (circa 1950–73)
y A < I > P   Steady and safe in operation (circa 1973–90)
z A > I < P   In need of structural changes (current situation)

This grouping is primarily based on prospective business growth (in revenue turnover or foreign trade), taking into consideration a company's history, management, shareholders, technology, market potential, employees, and so forth. For example, the annual revenue growth rate for **A** may be larger than 12 per cent, **I** may be 5 to 12 per cent, and **P** may be below 5 per cent, with the actual numbers depending upon the bank's current position. A, I, and P can be combined in six ways, but bank managers tend to assess the bank's portfolio primarily in terms of the position of **I** (interim group) clients, so it is useful to rank portfolio positions in terms of the relative position of **I** firms, hence the format of *x, y* and *z*.

Incumbent bank management might opt for steady and safe I > A > P. A well-performing main bank generally wishes to maintain a position of A > P for credit risk control. Positions where A < P may pose problems and suggest a need for the bank to reshuffle its portfolio. Certainly the worst situation is A < I < P; every pre-emptive effort is made to avoid this case.

A qualified main bank would always aim for position (*x*) A > I > P by employing all its managerial capacity. Normally, the main bank would exercise the most positive effort to explore and foster new and young firms with good prospects (A), for which equity holding, credit information, cash flow analysis and assessment of hidden assets (goodwill, new technology, or unrealized profit) may be the key areas of interest. Steadily growing firms (I) contribute to the core portion of repeated business.

Networking services and funding or transactional market deals will be important in relationship management for enjoying more stable profits with this group (see Table 9.2). Regular monitoring or consultation may be desirable for maturing or matured firms (P), which might welcome management advice, restructuring proposals, merger and acquisition deals, or networking services. In any event, the main bank constantly reviews its portfolio in terms of the growth pattern of different groups, as well as its corporate relationship, and works out a specific strategy for each group.

TABLE 9.2 Ranking of Main Bank Strategies in Relationship Management by Type of Firm

Type of Firm			
A Young with good prospects	I Steady and growing	P Maturing or matured	Main Bank Functions (see Figure 9.1)
1	5	6	Equity holding
3	6	3	Last-resort facility
6	4	2	Auditing and monitoring
5	2	1	Networking services
2	1	5	Funding syndication and market deals
4	3	4	Appraisal and intelligence services

The number indicates the order of importance to the bank the function has in the relationship for each of the three types of firms. All six functions are not necessarily being undertaken, but the first three will be key elements for firms. In terms of routine, *absolute* levels of activity, networking services and funding are the most important aspects of relationship management.

Managerial capacity built up in an organization and exercised through the six functions listed above has been the basis of strength, achievements and reputation of main banks. It was most effective during the period of capital shortage, economic uncertainty and regulated rules of the game in markets. However, as higher economic growth has been achieved, further changes in terms of deregulation, securitization, globalization and computerization forced Japanese banks to transform their *modus operandi* during the 1980s.

By 1990, the managerial capacity of main banks, affected by recent events, faced five main areas of adjustment: (a) two of the six functions— equity holding[11] and last-resort facilities (the backbone of the main bank

[11] Kurosawa (1992) points out that main banks' long-term equity holding was possible, not only because of profitability expected from dividends and capital gains, but also because

functions)[12]—may have to be reviewed in the light of the cost of equity holding and social reputation in restructuring measures, (b) major companies now tend to switch their funding methods from domestic bank borrowing to bond issues or overseas equity related issues largely because of cost effectiveness, (c) banks' lending ability is curtailed due to prudential regulation (the ceiling on lending to individual borrowers and the overall lending limit on weighted risk assets under the BIS convention are defined relative to their Tier 1 capital, while the substantial fall in stock prices during 1990–92 also decreased the Tier 2 capital of Japanese banks), (d) off balance sheet transactions bring new business opportunities for banks to achieve better returns on equity (for example, yen-dollar swaps for medium-term note issues or yen-yen swaps between fixed and floating rates are popular arrangements), (e) banks will now be permitted to move effectively into universal banking through their securities subsidiaries and trust banks.

Before 1973 competition among Japanese banks was specifically in collecting more individual deposits (for scale economy) and offering intelligence services, rather than in terms of interest rates. However, with liberalization of interest rates, globalization and computerization, competition in interest rates, coupled with ideas and intelligence, became fierce. Whilst unqualified or unsophisticated banks may be doomed to merge with others, top quality banks are now comfortably prepared to compete with both universal banking and investment bankers once new regulations are enacted and use of the yen becomes more prevalent. It appears to be a world trend for bankers to shift the weight of their business from *ad hoc* transactions to long-term relationship banking sooner or later.

of good interest income gained through continuous lending opportunities during the high growth period. However, he stresses that with the general increase in business risk (as reflected in declining return on assets before taxes) rises in rates of interest, as well as rapid increases in companies' own capital (net worth) after 1975, the leveraged debt ratio (that is, borrowing) has gradually declined. Particularly during 1986–89 many firms easily raised cheap equity capital. The general decline in share prices during 1990–92 triggered by tight money policy, which has put securities and real estate markets in distress, might have put traditional cross-share holding relationships in a more fragile setting, possibly for future review.

[12] A main bank loan officer normally enquires in advance into the cause and possible remedy borrowing firms can take if they run continuous losses on current accounts, say for two years, triggering the danger of negative net worth. If no measures are taken by management, despite prior consultative advice or warning, within the prescribed time, a main bank may gradually decrease its exposure, which may trigger the withdrawals of other banks. Under normal circumstances, however, actions that initiate bankruptcy are unlikely, as Japanese are very conscious of public criticism and their reputation in society. But, increasingly, some main banks may find difficulty in consultation or negotiation with some clients wanting to organize substantial restructuring plans. The main bank may want to get out of that relationship. Some clients are in fact slow, lenient, and undetermined. Some main banks feel it is too costly to deal with poor managements. An implicit aspect of main bank functions may be identified. Certainly, there is an economic rationale, even in the Japanese system, to eliminate inefficiency.

In such a globally competitive environment, disparity in performance will be reflected in a major change in ranking of world banks, unless relationship banking or niche marketing is fully recognized by their managements.

Managerial capacity acquired through practice of the traditional credit risk control system and restructuring management can also be used for merger and acquisitions deals. Experience acquired during the period of rapid internationalization of banking (1974–89) through overseas subsidiaries could be used in corporate equity or medium-term note issues. Competition for swaps and derivatives is increasingly fierce among Japanese market makers.

Main banks are re-organizing their strategy through subsidiaries to cope with the new economic environment of deregulation to be in a position to perform the functions that clients expect of them. This kind of response to a changing market is only possible because of the quality of manpower which is trained, organized, experienced, and sophisticated. There may be a growing number of cases where banks are dissatisfied with firms' poor management or clients decide to manage their own finances; banks may in the future become more selective and less committed to act as main bank for the categories of Watch and Hospital Care, or at least remain implicit in their role of lender of last resort. To judge a main bank's commitment only from its lending amount or explicit elements may be misleading: a main bank's primary role is still to foster new firms. Once firms grow beyond the need for the main bank's back-up facilities, their relationship will be judged on its merits, although main bank accounts would normally continue. Main banks should be able to compete in rates and ideas on the same footing as other banks specifically for market deals. If main banks continue to train their staff properly, as well as review their relationships and portfolios constantly, they should be able to manage any difficulty.

Ultimately, it is human ability and managerial capacity that enables banks or firms to manage their own problems in a new environment. Any well-qualified management should be able to anticipate and cope with any difficulty or crisis.

IMPLICATIONS FOR DEVELOPING MANAGERIAL CAPACITY

Managerial capacity in main bank qualifications can be exercised through six functions (Figure 9.1). The implementation of training assignments (Table 9.1) may not be superficially different from ordinary commercial banking or the investment banking business. The difference in practice in bank management may arise from the way individual staff are trained, organized and given authority, and the philosophy, principles and emphases that lie behind management development programmes.

There may be four distinct features in the Japanese case that are in contrast to Anglo-American management styles. First, the multiplicity of stakeholders in banks: client firms; employees; shareholders; the community; the central bank; and the Ministry of Finance. It is not only shareholders who exercise corporate governance: employees and client firms with a long-term relationship in bank transactions (often with only small shareholdings) may be the most vocal stakeholders; neither can you ignore the strong influence of the central bank, the Ministry of Finance and society, who highly value equitable roles as well as effective systems. A typical example may be employment policy. Japanese management would not opt for straightforward lay offs, but would choose wage cuts, part-time work or diversification in other jobs, if necessary. Second, the career development programme is designed for the long term in line with traditional banking principles, training generalists in order to cope with fierce competition in the quality of services (rather than simply price competition).

Third, the ultimate rationale or motivation for banking may be to maximize profits, but Japanese are prepared to pay the cost of training, employment and staff welfare on a long-term basis (permanent employment system) whereas the Anglo-American system is said to pay its staff to perform specific tasks. The Japanese also believe a banker's social responsibility is to foster firms with good prospects, appropriate technology, or new ideas, but which lack funding, management skills, or information. Fourth, although career development may include the acquisition of all-round experience in most financial institutions, equity holding and last-resort restructuring facilities—the backbone of main bank functions—may not be the normal practice in the case of Anglo-American styles of business.

The four features listed are not at all culture-specific; they can be implemented in any organization in any country, depending on management philosophy or, in particular, investment cost per employee. Life employment and the seniority system are not essential conditions: it is a question of initial training or discipline for about four years, then rotation for 10 to 14 years thereafter to acquire the qualities needed for main bank functions.

Training and experience for managerial capacity at a main bank has three levels: micro-management, institutional setting, and macro policy implementation. At the micro level, emphasis is placed on developing talents from within on a long-term basis at each of three broad levels of experience, as shown earlier in Table 9.1. Each member of the staff must gain experience in building up deposits, promoting business and evaluating the credit-worthiness of clients, while other talents and more specialized skills are pursued on their own initiative. Every effort is made to maximize the mutual benefits in building relationships with prospective client firms on a long-term basis. Staff will be rotated through different sections and branches every two to four years and will not be put in charge of the same clients again for a period of about 10 years.

To aid in determining future assignments, personnel files may be compiled over 10 to 15 years, recording the ability, aptitude, personality and behavioural pattern of staff as evaluated by various managers. Fostering enterprises with good prospects by holding equity, providing credit and last-resort facilities as well as management advice, is a key role of main banks. The main areas of management responsibility are to ensure good communication, sound motivation, credible relationships, effective allocation of resources and a flexible response to changes in environment.

In the institutional setting, main banks are expected to supply corporate information and advice. Banks in Japan compete with each other to offer seminars or training programmes for basic skills. Cross-checking management information and practice may be possible amongst members of loan syndicates through main banks or specialist banks in the field.[13] Banking rules or new practices, once they have been discussed in detail among representatives of the banks, can be implemented in a cooperative and competitive manner. Asymmetric information can be rectified through multilateral dialogue or channels in an institutional setting, and agency costs will be reduced substantially.

Efficiency and credibility in the payment mechanism is the primary function and responsibility of all licensed banks, although its cost is shared. Consensus on system building, adjustment or organized action may be taken by the incumbent chair of the Federation of Bankers Associations of Japan (FBAJ). Close dialogue and representation of

---

[13] In the post-war period, some specialized banks played unique pilot roles in their own special fields. They helped in delivering useful information on projects, know-how in arrangements, and in enhancing the managerial capacity of participating banks, particularly at the early stage of development when foreign banks were not at all helpful in domestic banking. They might justly have been called main banks in their special fields and roles. For example, the Industrial Bank of Japan took the lead in credit appraisal of priority projects for heavy industries in line with the Ministry of International Trade and Industry's guidelines on priority industries. The Bank of Tokyo was instrumental in providing intelligence services on overseas markets and set up efficient competitive practices in the foreign exchange market in Tokyo. During 1982–90 it took the lead in organizing a consensus among all Japanese institutions in dealing with developing-country debt through individual Bank Advisory Committees (on 17 countries) for each sovereign government. Although the task was complex, tough and costly, almost 100 per cent participation was achieved by the Japanese banks in every deal, whereas coordination by American counterparts was always divided although the issue itself was recognized in global banking circles as virtually American. Obviously, managerial capacity at an institutional level involving many parties may be assessed in terms of accountability, effectiveness, efficiency and equity. These may be the most crucial elements in developing or transforming economies. Specialized banks, however, are now obliged to choose whether to diversify their business or to concentrate on traditional niche areas, in the face of complete interest rate liberalization and rapid globalization. Nevertheless, their professional functions and equitable contributions in their fields have been significant in the development process, and highly regarded by current competitors.

banks' group interests will be made to the regulatory bodies through FBAJ on professional rules of the game, guidelines, practices, system support, legal considerations, taxation, rates, advertisement and compliance.

At the macro level, an equitable control system or guidance for credit allocation may be organized by the central bank through dialogue with each main bank. Effective market operations can be implemented by identifying the positions of major banks. Accountability in policy implementation is much improved as every bank can have open access to information on markets and policy guidelines.[14] Managerial capacity developed in such a main bank system will be instrumental in improving accountability, effectiveness, efficiency and fairness at these three levels.

There may therefore be a significant case for considering developing such managerial capacity in banking in the developing or transitional economies on four fronts.

• Bank credit may be the major source of corporate finance because of a shortage of funds (against potential investment demand) and the lack of a local capital market. Central bank rediscount facilities for qualified trade bills or short-term government bonds, even under a low rate-of-interest policy, may not be sufficient. Syndication efforts by main banks, initially for about two to five years, on a short-term roll-over basis based upon cash flow analysis, may be an appropriate way to support prospective corporate finance and encourage participation of various other financiers.

• Basic skills on prudent banking can be more easily acquired under the simple rules of commercial banking, rather than a universal banking system, at least until the basic market mechanism or growth of financial assets of various maturities is in place. An active inter-bank money market, competitive (narrow-margin) foreign exchange dealing and some kind of medium-term notes or minimum number of equity issues may need to be in place before full deregulation or interest rate liberalization can take place. A standard model of operation could be demonstrated by major banks or by their securities subsidiaries, perhaps initially with technical assistance from professional teams of bankers, accountants and consultants.

• Accountability and effectiveness at the micro- and system-management level may be the crucial objective of major banks, not only in twinning programmes but in long-term career development and in competition for enhancing managerial capacity. The participation of many institutions for financing new projects under the initiative of main (or state)

---

[14] For example, Klitgaard (1991, p. 75) presents the equation *corruption = monopoly + discretion − accountability*. There may be adequate proof of his equation. In fact, an effective, efficient and equitable banking system enhances accountability in developing and transforming economies. The main bank system would be useful for transitional economies.

banks would help establish market practices, competition, transparency and accountability.

- Interlocking relationships between state enterprises and state banks, due to their inherited debt, may best be rectified by prudential regulation over the licensed commercial banks. Portfolio clean-up efforts can be openly implemented by main (or state) banks, even in the presence of principal-agent problems. Major state enterprises will have to be split into several corporations, perhaps in line with specific technology or production lines, because of limits on bank lending to one borrower. Some debt must be replaced with equity or government bonds which may be sold in markets. Other units may have to be liquidated. Main (or state) banks' managerial capacity can be instrumental in restructuring or privatizing state enterprises. Technical assistance may initially be indispensable.

CONCLUSION

As an economic system may be largely determined by non-economic factors such as history, community values and international relations, so management styles in banking will be determined not only by the relevant stakeholders, but by awareness of social responsibility, long- or short-term costs of career development and the price or quality of competition. Under the prevailing circumstances in developing or transforming economies, realistic decisions must be made on whether growth is preferred to stability, or whether bank credits or securities issues can be the major sources of funding for new investment. As examined above, the managerial capacity of main banks, the multiple functions they exercise, the training of their human resources, the corporate growth fostered through relationship management and inter-bank competition which conforms to government guidelines, are the salient features of the main bank system. The main banks' know-how may be adopted universally if managerial capacity, human resources, quality in services, and long-term productivity are considered to be major elements in competitive banking in the development process. The effectiveness of managerial capacity can best be proved in a global market which transcends differences in languages, currencies and management styles.

As one banker puts it: 'Money is our business. In so far as our clients trust us and they are clean in business ethics, we will stand by as the lender of last resort. We wish to grow together with our clients. Together we aspire, together we achieve our goals as well as prosperity in society for long years to come, as going concerns. Our duty and responsibility rests together with our society.'

REFERENCES

HERTLE, BEVERLY. 1991. 'Factors Affecting the Competitiveness of Internationally Active Financial Institutions.' *Federal Reserve Bank of New York Quarterly Review* 16(1): 38–51 (Spring).

KLITGAARD, ROBERT E. 1991. *Controlling Corruption*. University of California Press.

KOIKE, KAZUO. 1991. *Daisotsu white collar Nojinzai Kaihatsu*. Tokyo: Toyo Keizi Shinposha.

KUROSAWA, YOSHITAKA. 1992. 'Business Risk to Shihon-Kosei.' *Sangyo Keiei Kenkyu* 13.

LONG, MILLARD and SILVIA B. SAGARI. 1991. 'Financial Reform in Socialist Economy in Transition.' Working Paper Series 711. World Bank, CED, Washington DC.

OZAKI, ROBERT. 1991. *Human Capitalism*. New York: Penguin.

SAKURA SOGO KENKYUSHO. 1992. 'Saikin no Shuyoskuku Ginko no Keiyei Shihyo (Major Bank Competitiveness).' *Economic Report* April 15.

SHENG, ANDREW. 1990. 'Bank Restructuring in Transitional Economies.' World Bank, CECFP, Washington DC.

SUNAMURA, SATOSHI. 1991. 'Some Notes on External Debt Management.' Speech at British Council Seminar, Oxford, England, 4 November. Subsequently, a paper for World Bank, CFS, Washington DC.

——. 1992. 'The Role of Banking System in Transitional Economies.' World Bank, CFS, mimeo Washington DC.

TERANISHI, JURO. 1982. *Nihon no Keizaihatten to Kin'yu*. Tokyo: Iwanami Shoten.

——. 1991. *Kogyo-ka to Kin'yu System*. Tokyo: Iwanami Shoten.

10

Changing Patterns of Corporate Financing and the Main Bank System in Japan

JOHN Y. CAMPBELL AND YASUSHI HAMAO

For most of the post-war period, the United States and Japan have had polar opposite corporate financial structures. The US system has featured *low leverage and low monitoring* of corporate management by investors, while the Japanese system has featured *high leverage and high monitoring*. One of the standard stories is that high leverage in Japan is justified by low bankruptcy costs. These in turn come from two important features of the main bank system: there is a high probability of bank rescues for large firms with main banks, and main banks often hold equity in firms as well as providing loans, thereby reducing conflicts of interest.

During the last 15 years, however, the two systems have begun to converge. Leverage has increased in the United States, particularly when measured by interest expense ratios, and the increase has been concentrated in certain firms (see Bernanke and Campbell, 1988). In Japan, leverage has decreased across the board. In the US, debt-holders' interests may now be represented more effectively; Jensen (1989) argues that leveraged buy-out (LBO) partners are a new organizational form which can monitor corporations more effectively. In Japan, while the role of a main bank as a delegated monitor is similar to the LBO partners in the US, the growing use of public debt held by outsiders rather than main banks suggests the opposite trend.

This paper uses cross-sectional data to reveal more clearly the changing capital structure of Japanese corporations. We first classify firms into two groups based on their outstanding bank loans in fiscal 1983/4. We call a firm a 'main bank firm' if the largest quantity of loans to it is made by one of 19 major banks; we call a firm 'unaffiliated' if it has no outstanding bank loans in 1983/4, or if the largest quantity of loans is made by a smaller regional bank. This definition of a main bank firm is narrower than that proposed by Aoki, Patrick, and Sheard in Chapter 1. Almost all

The authors thank Masahiko Aoki, Kenneth Singleton, Takeo Hoshi, Kensuke Hotta, Anil Kashyap, Junichi Nishiwaki, Hugh Patrick, Paul Sheard, and other participants at the workshops for useful comments, and Kei Ichiki and Il-Pyung Park for research assistance. Hamao gratefully acknowledges support from the Batterymarch Fellowship and the Mitsubishi Trust and Banking Professorship.

Japanese firms are main bank firms in Aoki, Patrick, and Sheard's sense, whereas we identify numerous firms that are unaffiliated in our sense.

We next show that the trends in capital structure are very different for our two classes of firms. Main bank firms show only modest changes in capital structure, whereas unaffiliated firms have dramatically reduced their reliance on bank debt in favour of equity and equity-related debt instruments (warrant and convertible bonds). Thus unaffiliated firms have moved more decisively towards American patterns than have main bank firms.

We also study the bond issuance services provided by main banks. As described by Aoki, Patrick and Sheard in Chapter 1, these services include guaranteeing, trustee administration and underwriting. Fees generated by these activities are said to have become a significant part of revenue for large banks. We find that when main bank firms do use the bond markets, they often turn to their main banks to facilitate bond issuance. Unaffiliated firms have also used bank guarantees, but increasingly these firms have been able to issue non-guaranteed bonds.

The paper is organized as follows. The next two sections describe our data and briefly summarize the deregulation that has taken place in the corporate financial market. The third section examines corporate capital structure using firm-level data. We document the differences in the capital structure of firms with and without main banks by analysing ratios such as debt to assets, bonds to total debt, and short-term debt to total debt. The fourth section presents further evidence on the role of main banks using data on individual bond issues.

DATA DESCRIPTION

We concentrate on large, public corporations listed on the first and second sections of the Tokyo Stock Exchange (excluding banks, insurance companies, and securities companies) during the period 1970–91. The number of observations ranges from about 1,100 companies in 1970 to 1,400 in 1991. Our data come from four separate sources.

First, we measure the market value of equity (price per share times the number of shares outstanding) using a data-base described in Hamao (1991). This series starts in January 1970.

Second, we take accounting data from the Nikkei NEEDS Corporate Financial Data tape (unconsolidated). This tape contains balance sheet information for all listed companies except for banks and securities companies from 1965–91. Since our capitalization data start in 1970, our observation period is from 1970–91. Delisted firms are included in the sample. The items extracted are: (1) short-term borrowings (including overdraft on bills due in one year); (2) current position of long-term debt due within one year; (3) bonds and debentures maturing within one year;

(4) bonds and convertible bonds (debentures); and (5) long-term borrow-ings. Since the majority of companies choose March as their fiscal year end, we take March every year as the observation point and used the most recent available information if a company adopts a month other than March as their fiscal year end.

The definition of the quantities are as follows:

Debt = (1) + (2) + (3) + (4) + (5);
Short-term debt = (1) + (2) + (3);
Bonds = (3) + (4);
Market value of equity = number of shares outstanding × price; and
Total assets = debt + market value of equity.

We use the book value of debt rather than trying to calculate market value; this calculation is indirect and cumbersome and has a relatively minor effect in US data in the 1980s (see Bernanke and Campbell, 1988).

Third, we use a data-set containing information on newly issued securi-ties for all listed companies since 1970. The original data were taken from Nikkei Corporate Action Data tapes. For each firm, we extracted infor-mation (including issuing market, yen equivalent amount raised, maturity, and names of guarantors and trustees; because the names of guarantors and trustees are only in 16-bit non-ASCII kanji characters, they were translated to corresponding numerical codes) for new issues of straight bonds, convertible bonds, and bonds with detachable warrants from 1970 to 1991. The new issues data captures flow numbers measured at the time of each new issue, as opposed to the balance sheet figures, which are stock numbers at the end of a fiscal year. This could make a difference because a new issue of a convertible bond can be converted to equity before it is recorded as an outstanding balance in the balance sheet. In order to be consistent in our analysis, we use stock figures when we com-pute ratios—such as debt to asset, bond to total debt—and flow figures are denoted as 'new issues' to make the distinction.

The fourth data-set contains information on the main bank for each firm and is taken from the 1987 and 1992 editions of *Kigyo Keiretsu Soran*. We are particularly interested in whether a firm has a main bank or not. The definition of a main bank, however, is not immediately trans-parent. For example, while firms with no bank loan may be considered independent of banks, most of those firms have some banks as their largest shareholders, and sometimes even have directors or auditors on their staff who have been despatched from banks. In our paper, we deter-mine a firm's main bank in terms only of its borrowing. Thus if a firm has no bank loans, it is considered as 'unaffiliated'.

One might argue that there are firms with no bank loans outstanding that still claim to have a main bank. We do not suggest that there are not. However, our empirical work cannot extend the definition of main bank too far. If one includes personnel exchanges and shareholdings as measures of a main bank relationship, almost all Japanese firms have main banks. The following empirical analysis indicates that there are significant differences in the behaviour of firms based on our definition.

For each firm, we find the bank with the largest outstanding loan balance in 1983/4. Our set of banks includes 19 major city, trust, and long-term credit banks.[1] Only these were capable of functioning as guarantors or trustees of bond issues of corporations. If the bank with the largest loan share is not one of our 19 banks, we record the firm as unaffiliated. If this bank is one of our 19 banks, we consider it to be the firm's main bank. If there is a tie (or approximate tie) between two of our banks in their loans outstanding to a firm, we record both banks as the firm's main bank.

We do not include regional banks in our set of main banks. Our assumption here is that for the firms in our sample (large, listed firms), it is a firm's (not a lender's) decision not to have one of the large 19 banks as its main bank. Thus we assume that a firm with the largest loan share from a regional bank has chosen to be independent of the main banking relationship with major banks. We note also that those firms with regional banks as top lenders often have a tie in the outstanding loan amount with one of the 19 large banks. We classify such a firm as having a large bank as its main bank.

In order to check the robustness of our results, we have also used two alternative ways to classify firms. First, we have used the classification scheme proposed by Aoki, Patrick, and Sheard (1993, Appendix Table 1). Their definition drops trust banks and adds regional banks. They also pay attention to stability by examining the continuity of the main bank relationship over three recent years (1989–91). Their data, however, cover only three industries (507 firms). Despite these differences, our main results are essentially unchanged when we use their approach.

Second, we have used outstanding bank loans in 1991 to classify firms. This is theoretically less satisfactory because it raises the possibility that firms' financing decisions in the 1983–91 period drive our classification. For example, suppose a firm with bank loans in 1983 reduced its loans and issued bonds over the following eight years. To identify this firm as unaffiliated would be to overstate the changes undertaken by unaffiliated firms. This is a much less serious problem for our 1983 classification scheme because the Japanese bond market was then still highly regulated. In any case, despite the theoretical problem with the 1991 classification scheme, we find it gives essentially the same results as our 1983 classification scheme.

---

[1] They are Asahi Bank, Bank of Tokyo, Dai-Ichi Kangyo Bank, Daiwa Bank, Fuji Bank, Hokkaido-Takushoku Bank, Industrial Bank of Japan, Long-Term Credit Bank of Japan, Mitsubishi Bank, Mitsubishi Trust and Banking, Mitsui Trust Bank, Nippon Credit Bank, Sakura Bank, Sanwa Bank, Sumitomo Bank, Sumitomo Trust and Banking, Tokai Bank, Toyo Trust Bank, and Yasuda Trust Bank.

One might guess that our procedure for classifying firms would separate them by size; large, more established firms would tend to have closer relations with our 19 main banks than smaller firms. On the contrary, mean (median) capitalization in 1983 is ¥57.8 billion (¥15.6 billion) for firms with large main banks (N = 1,067), whereas it is ¥65.7 billion (¥11.9 billion) for firms without main banks (N = 314). There is some variation across industries in the proportion of main bank firms, as shown in Table 10.1, but every industry has some firms in each category.

A BRIEF HISTORY OF POST-WAR JAPANESE
CORPORATE FINANCING

The reconstruction of post-war Japan was mainly financed by bank loans. The Industrial Bank of Japan as well as major city banks played a critical

TABLE 10.1 Proportion of Firms with Main Bank, by Industry (per cents)

Fishing, Mining	87
Construction	83
Food	70
Textile	79
Paper, Pulp	83
Pharmaceutical	57
Oil, Rubber	93
Ceramics, Glass	82
Steel	88
Non-Ferrous Metal	79
Machinery	66
Electric	64
Shipbuilding	100
Auto	72
Precision Machinery	72
Printing; Office Machine	88
Trading	80
Retail	94
Non-Bank Financial	88
Real Estate	90
Land Transport	94
Air, Sea Transport	97
Warehouse, Communication	83
Electricity, Gas	87
Service	64
Mean of full sample	77

role in financing industrial projects and firms (see Chapter 5 by Packer). The corporate bond market was tightly regulated until the beginning of the 1980s. There was a ceiling on bond interest rates which inhibited the development of the market. The issuance of bond instruments required government permission and a large amount of collateral, and only a small number of large industrial firms, regulated utilities and long-term credit banks issued corporate bonds. Firms had to satisfy various accounting conditions to establish their eligibility to issue even secured bonds. The Secured Corporate Bond Trustee Law required trustees (of collateral) to assume major responsibilities in establishing and administering pledged properties on behalf of all bondholders. These and other restrictions on corporate bond issues are discussed in more detail in Nihon Keizai Shimbun Sha (1987) and in Chapter 7 by Ramseyer.

The issue of unsecured bonds was a relatively new phenomenon which required clearance of a different set of bond eligibility criteria introduced in 1979. These conditions were so rigid that only Matsushita Electric and Toyota Motors were qualified to issue unsecured convertible or straight bonds in 1979. The criteria for both secured and unsecured bonds were relaxed gradually in the 1980s, and by 1989 approximately 300 firms were eligible to issue unsecured straight or warrant-attached bond issues, and 500 firms were eligible to issue unsecured convertible bonds. Hoshi, Kashyap and Scharfstein (1993) summarize three changes in the eligibility conditions for secured convertible bonds in the 1980s.

In 1990, eligibility criteria based on accounting information were replaced by a single bond rating criterion. The quantity of straight bonds actually issued, however, did not grow as fast as the quantity of equity-related bonds, perhaps because of the overwhelming appeal of warrant and convertible bonds during the stock price 'boom' period of the late 1980s.

The removal of restrictions on overseas financial activities by the amendment of the Foreign Exchange Law of 1980 enabled firms to issue bonds in overseas markets. The Ministry of Finance used essentially the same eligibility criteria for overseas bond issues as for domestic bond issues, so that there was virtually no case of a Euro issue of a corporate bond by a domestically ineligible firm. Euro issues did, however, offer several advantages: (1) even after eliminating exchange risk with a currency swap, it was often possible to realize a lower yen interest rate for dollar-denominated issues and the domestic issue of foreign currency denominated bonds was not permitted; (2) exporting firms were able to match dollar-denominated liabilities with dollar-denominated accounts receivable to reduce or eliminate exposure to exchange risk; (3) in contrast with the domestic market where collateral is normally required, the Euro market did not require collateral; and therefore (4) bond trustee administration fees for Euro issues were much lower than for domestic issues.

To take advantage of the stock market boom of the late 1980s, many firms issued equity-related bond instruments. These too were issued mainly in the Euro market. In 1981, bonds with equity warrants (originally undetachable) were legalized, and in 1986 the detached warrant components were allowed to be traded in Japan. Warrants typically had strike prices 20–25 per cent above the stock price at the time of issue. Convertible bonds were also popular; the conversion price for such bonds was mostly set to be only 5–10 per cent above the stock price at the time of issue.

Although we do not have detailed data on the buyers of corporate bonds, Nihon Keizai Shimbun Sha (1987) provides a breakdown of investors for the new issues in 1985. The largest share was purchased by individuals (49.1 per cent) and financial institutions bought 28.5 per cent.

Table 2 shows new issue quantities for various types of bonds in both domestic and overseas markets during the periods 1984–87 and 1988–91. We note that there are large increases in convertible and warrant attached bond issues. Warrant attached bonds became especially popular in the overseas market. Each category is further divided into bank guaranteed and non-guaranteed issues. Convertible bonds were rarely guaranteed, perhaps because the option of conversion to equity makes the amount to be guaranteed uncertain *ex ante*. We will discuss this point in more detail in the next two sections.

Fig. 10.1 Debt to Asset Ratio, Value-Weighted

TRENDS IN CAPITAL STRUCTURE AND THE MAIN BANK RELATIONSHIP

In this section, we compute several measures of corporate leverage and relate these to the issuers' relationship with their main banks.

Figure 10.1 shows the ratio of debt to total assets for the full sample, computed as $\Sigma(\text{Debt})/\Sigma(\text{Asset})$ where the summation is taken across firms.

TABLE 10.2 Amount of Newly Issued Bonds
Panel A. Straight Bonds

Issuing Market	Amount Issued		Bank Guarantees	
	In Billion Yen	As % of Total	In Billion Yen	As % of Total
1984–87				
Japan	3,142.5	43.0	0.0	0.0
Overseas	4,202.4	57.0	1,607.0	38.2
Total	7,344.9	100	1,607.0	21.9
1988–91				
Japan	5,119.0	60.9	3.0	0.1
Overseas	3,282.4	39.1	339.0	10.3
Total	8,401.4		342.0	4.1

TABLE 10.2 Panel B. Convertible Bonds

Issuing Market	Amount Issued		Bank Guarantees●	
	In Billion Yen	As % of Total	In Billion Yen	As % of Total
1984–87				
Japan	6,929.5	67.7	0.0	0.0
Overseas	3,309.4	32.3	21.3	0.6
Total	10,238.9	100	21.3	0.2
1988–91				
Japan	16,139.0	88.1	0.0	0.0
Overseas	2,188.3	11.9	2.8	0.1
Total	18,327.3	100	2.8	0.02

TABLE 10.2 Panel C. Warrant Attached Bonds

Issuing Market	Amount Issued		Bank Guarantees	
	In Billion Yen	As % of Total	In Billion Yen	As % of Total
1984–87				
Japan	142.0	4.0	0.0	0.0
Overseas	3,452.2	96.0	2,662.4	77.1
Total	3,594.2	100	2,662.4	74.1
1988–91				
Japan	1,180.0	6.1	0.0	0.0
Overseas	18,269.8	93.9	6,159.1	33.7 ·
Total	19,449.8	100	6,159.1	31.7

For the universe of 1,471 firms listed on the Tokyo Stock Exchange, excluding banks, insurance and securities firms.

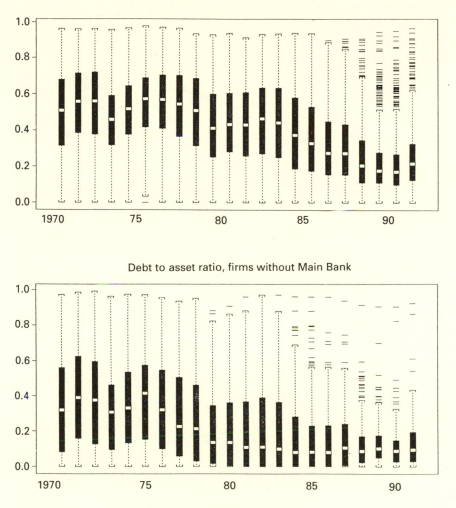

Debt to asset ratio, firms with Main Bank

Debt to asset ratio, firms without Main Bank

Fig. 10.2

This aggregate ratio can be thought of as the value-weighted average for the sample. The aggregate debt to asset ratio has declined from 0.60 to 0.25 over the sample period, increasing slightly in the last two years, because of the decline in stock prices.

There is an important caveat. Table 10.2 shows a large increase in equity-related bond issues in the late 1980s. Taking the whole amount raised by those instruments as debt overstates total debt since warrant and convertible bonds contain equity components. For example, the present value of a warrant attached bond (the amount raised by the issuer) is the sum of the present value of the warrant component and that of the coupon bond. Many warrant bonds were issued at an effective yen interest rate close to zero (Chang, 1992); that is, the promise to pay 100 yen five years in the future, together with the attached warrant, fetched 100 yen at issue. With a Japanese government five-year interest rate of 5 per cent, a promise to pay 100 yen five years in the future should be worth no more than 78 yen today, suggesting that only 78 per cent of the value of the warrant bond is straight debt. We do not pursue this further, but simply take care to distinguish warrant and convertible bonds from straight bonds and bank loans.

We next divide the sample into firms with and without main banks. We present the comparison using boxplots (Figure 10.2), which show the time series of the median and the quartiles around the median. Isolated bars represent outliers. These plots show that within each group, firms have become more homogeneous in their debt to asset ratios, especially during the late 1980s. However, the two groups have diverged in that unaffiliated firms show a stronger decline in their debt to asset ratios.

A second measure of corporate capital structure is the ratio of bonds to total debt. In the face of deregulation, corporations have tended to shift their source of debt financing from bank loans to bond issues. The choice between bonds and bank loans is discussed in detail by Hoshi, Kashyap and Scharfstein (1993), who find that profitability (as measured by Tobin's q) is positively related to the ratio of bonds to total debt. Here we focus instead on the relation between main bank affiliation and bond issuance.

In aggregate, bonds have become increasingly important. However, treating all bond issues as 'public debt' is misleading since some bonds are guaranteed by banks. Bank guarantees, which make bonds virtually a securitized version of bank loans, apply to some Euro issues of straight bonds and warrant attached bonds. The issuing firms benefit from lower interest rates when their bonds are guaranteed by banks with a high credit rating, while the banks get fees for their guarantees. Figure 10.3 shows two measures of the bond to total debt ratio; the first one uses a conventional definition of bonds without distinguishing the issues that are guaranteed by banks, and the second one excludes bank guaranteed issues. The 'conventional' one is essentially the same as figure 2a of Hoshi, Kashyap and Scharfstein (1993). There is a remarkable growth in the share of bonds in total debt, but the bank guarantee correction proves to be a sizeable 5 percentage points in 1991.

We again divide the sample into firms with and without large main banks, excluding bank guaranteed issues (Figure 10.4A). The difference between the two groups is striking. Although some firms with main bank alliances increased their use of bonds, the median bond to debt ratio

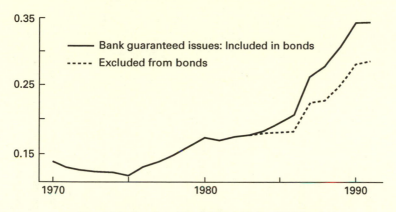

Fig. 10.3 Bond to Total Debt, Value-Weighted

remains very close to zero. On the other hand, firms without main banks increased their use of bonds dramatically after 1985 and the median bond to debt ratio for this group is close to 20 per cent in 1991. We also note that the distribution of the ratio is much more dispersed for the unaffiliated firms, indicating greater variation of financing strategies among these firms.

When we repeat the same exercise including bank guaranteed issues in bonds, the difference between main bank and unaffiliated firms becomes even larger (Figure 10.4B). This suggests that unaffiliated firms were willing to use bank guarantees as they moved aggressively to exploit newly available bond instruments. Qualified unaffiliated firms did not seek the traditional main bank relationship of increasing bank loans, but rather obtained bank guarantees.

Bank loans from city banks are typically short term whereas bond issues (straight, convertible or warrant attached) have maturities of more than one year. Thus the ratio of short-term (less than one year) debt to total debt can also reveal a shift between bank loan and bond issues. Figure 10.5 displays the aggregate series, and Figure 10.6 shows the breakdown between main bank and unaffiliated firms. Just as one would expect from looking at the bond to total debt ratio, the short-term debt ratios of the two types of firms diverge around 1985, with unaffiliated firms using substantially less short-term debt. The yield spread between Japanese five and six year government bond and the short rate narrowed over 1980–85 and the yield curve stayed relatively flat in 1985–90 (see Campbell and Hamao, 1993). Furthermore, as mentioned earlier, issuing equity-related bonds in the Euro market gave issuing firms access to even cheaper funds. Unaffiliated firms appear to have reacted more swiftly to this opportunity than main bank firms. In part, this may have been

Bond to total debt ratio, firms with Main Bank

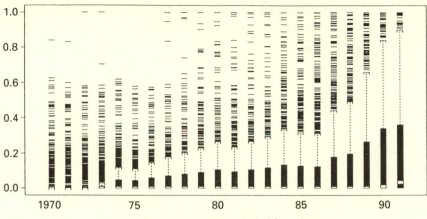

Bank guaranteed issues excluded from bonds

Bond to total debt ratio, firms without Main Bank

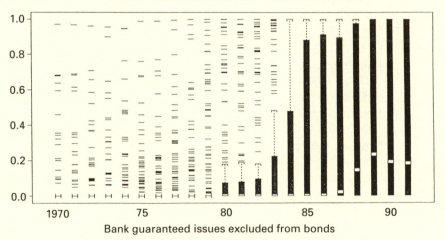

Bank guaranteed issues excluded from bonds

FIG. 10.4a

because firms affiliated with main banks were able to roll over short-term borrowing quite readily, thereby using them for longer-term finance purposes.

Finally, Figures 10.7 and 10.8 show that for unaffiliated firms, equity-related bonds substituted for short-term bank loans in the late 1980s. Main bank firms made considerably less use of these instruments. Again, it should be noted that the distribution of the ratios for unaffiliated firms

Bond to total debt ratio, firms with Main Bank

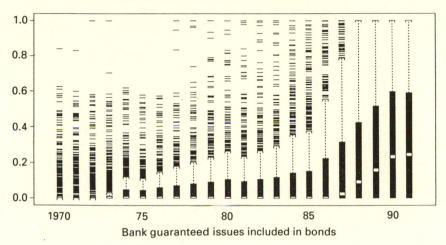

Bank guaranteed issues included in bonds

Bond to total debt ratio, firms without Main Bank

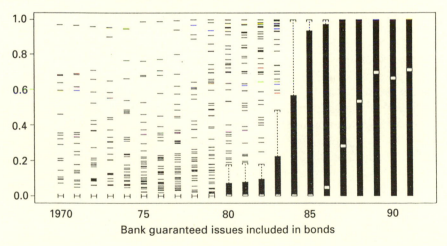

Bank guaranteed issues included in bonds

FIG. 10.4b

are much more dispersed, indicating that the change did not occur uniformly among unaffiliated firms.

To highlight these findings, we report some summary statistics in Table 10.3. We compute the ratios of warrant, convertible, and straight bonds to total debt. Here the numerators are cumulative new issues of those bonds during 1988–91 and the denominator is total debt in 1988. The sample is then divided into groups above and below the median for these

Fig. 10.5 Short-Term Debt to Total Debt Ratio (Value Weighted)

ratios. For each group we compute the means of capitalization, the debt
to asset ratio, the loan to debt ratio, and the score of (1 = main bank
firm, 0 = unaffiliated firm). There is a clear distinction between the
equity-related bonds and straight bonds. For convertible and warrant
bonds, the firms above median are smaller in capitalization, lower in
existing debt to asset and loan to total debt ratios, and weaker in main
bank relations than the firms below median. For straight bond to total
debt ratio, larger firms tend to issue more, but existing debt to asset and
loan to total loan ratios, as well as main bank relations, do not seem to
be strongly related to the firms propensity to issue straight bonds.

There is an apparent contrast between these results and those of Hoshi,
Kashyap and Scharfstein (1993). They investigate the effect of industrial
groups (keiretsu) and present weak evidence that non-group firms with
attractive investment opportunities rely more heavily on bank financing.
These findings are not in fact contradictory because the distinction between
group and non-group firms is not the same as the distinction between main
bank and unaffiliated firms under the definition used here. Unaffiliated
firms may belong to a group (for example, Shiseido, which is a member of
the Dai-ichi Kangyo Bank group, but has no bank loan) while non-group
firms may still have main banks (for example, many family controlled businesses). In fact, of the 52 firms they classify as group firms, 44 (85 per
cent) are main bank firms in our sense; of the 60 firms they classify as non-
group firms, 46 (77 per cent) are main bank firms. Thus there is only a
weak correlation between the two classification systems.

The study of Hoshi, Kashyap and Scharfstein is relevant in another
way. One possible objection to our analysis is that we ignore the bond
eligibility conditions that restricted companies' ability to issue bonds during much of our sample period. It could be argued that unaffiliated firms
are simply those which meet the bond eligibility conditions, and this is
why they have behaved differently from main bank firms. They consider
112 firms that were continuously eligible to issue convertible bonds from

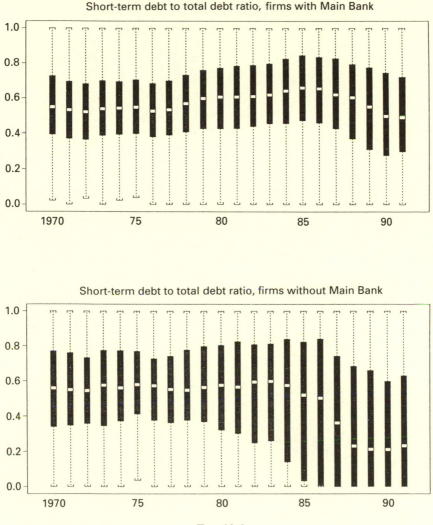

FIG. 10.6

1982 to 1989. By discarding all firms which did not continuously satisfy the bond eligibility conditions, they eliminate any spurious effects of bond eligibility. The cost of this strategy is of course that they work with a much smaller sample of firms.

We reproduced our analysis represented in Figures 10.2, 10.4 and 10.6 for the 112 firms considered by Hoshi, Kashyap and Scharfstein. (We thank Takeo Hoshi for providing the data. The results in figure form are available upon request from the authors.) The 90 main bank firms in this sample shifted their financing more toward bonds and equity-related

Warrant bond to total debt, firms with Main Bank

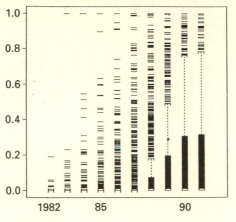

Warrant bond to total debt, firms without Main Bank

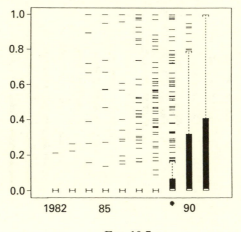

FIG. 10.7

instruments than did the larger group of main bank firms considered earlier; but it is nonetheless the case that the 22 unaffiliated firms moved towards these financing strategies even more decisively than the 90 main bank firms. Thus the distinction between main bank firms and unaffiliated firms appears to be important even when one controls for bond eligibility.

Putting these results together, we reach the following conclusions about changing corporate finance patterns in Japan. Firms with main bank relations rely more heavily on debt than unaffiliated firms; in addition these firms shift less toward newly deregulated equity-related bond instruments

Convertible bond to total debt, firms with Main Bank

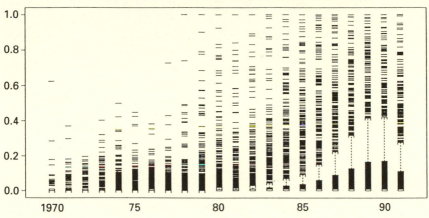

Convertible bond to total debt, firms without Main Bank

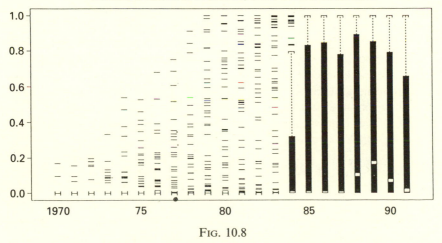

FIG. 10.8

and stay with traditional bank loans. Thus the major changes in corporate finance have occurred among unaffiliated firms, not main bank firms.

ANALYSIS OF INDIVIDUAL BOND DATA: BANK GUARANTEES

In this section, we analyse data on individual bond issues and investigate the relations between bond issuers and their main banks. Of particular interest are the cases where banks become guarantors or trustees of bond issues (see Chapter 1 by Aoki, Patrick and Sheard). As discussed earlier, bank guarantees on straight and warrant attached bonds can be considered as an extended form of bank loans. Facing financial deregulation (including the gradual removal of the Japanese version of Glass-Steagall restrictions) and increasing demand for bond issuance, it is likely that banks have intended to become major players in the securities industry by building up their corporate bond-issuing related business. Bank guarantees were especially necessary in the earlier stages of the introduction of Euro bonds when most issuers were unfamiliar to foreign investors. The knowledge of issuing firms obtained through traditional monitoring enabled main banks to screen bond issues for guaranteeing. The market for bond guaranteeing was said to have been as competitive as the loan market, and several banks offered guarantee fees as low as 0.1 (usually 0.15–0.2)per cent.[2]

Another bond issuance service is to provide trustee administration. The responsibilities of a trustee bank often go beyond straightforward administration, especially in the case of secured bonds. Traditionally, domestic corporate bonds have been collateralized by specified plant and equipment. Trustee banks are then responsible for examining the collateral and securing the payments on behalf of general bondholders. In fact, from 1945 to 1990 there were 11 corporate bond defaults. Of these firms, 10 went through the legal process of corporate reorganization, 9 of those 10 issues had collateral (or a bank guarantee), and all were bought back by trustee banks even though they were not legally obligated to do so. Thus the role of a trustee bank is similar to that of a guaranteeing bank. We document the relationship between bond guarantors (and trustees) and the main bank alliance by examining six large city banks and the Industrial Bank of Japan.

First, from Table 10.2 we note some changes in bank guarantees in straight and warrant bond issues between the 1984–87 and 1988–91 periods. For straight bonds the total amount of new issues did not grow substantially, but the guaranteed portion of overseas issues decreased from 38 per cent to 10 per cent. For warrant bonds there was dramatic growth of the total amount issued; the percentage guaranteed for overseas issues dropped from 77 per cent to 34 per cent, although the quantity guaranteed increased from ¥2.6 trillion to ¥6.2 trillion.

---

[2] Guaranteed bonds are carried on the books as a risk asset. BIS (Bank for International Settlement) regulation on capital adequacy, however, was not a binding restriction, especially for our first sub-period (1984–87), since the condition was established in 1988 to be accomplished by 1993, and the Japanese stock market stayed at a high level until the end of 1989.

Underwriting of Eurobonds is also an important business for main banks through their overseas subsidiaries. Unfortunately, we are unable to extend our analysis to this since our data-base does not provide names of underwriters if they are overseas subsidiaries of Japanese banks or securities houses.

TABLE 10.3 New Bond Issues and Firm Characteristics

	No. of firms	mean capitalization (billion yen)	mean Debt/Asset ratio	mean Loan/Debt ratio	mean MB score
CB/DEBT					
Above median	277	186.97	0.153	0.647	0.635
Below median	277	336.99	0.358	0.768	0.866
WB/DEBT					
Above median	237	176.17	0.193	0.672	0.684
Below median	237	351.98	0.376	0.776	0.886
SB/DEBT					
Above median	130	615.18	0.229	0.724	0.846
Below median	130	266.60	0.391	0.813	0.885

CB/DEBT, WB/DEBT, SB/DEBT ratios are computed using the following definitions. CB (WB, SB) = amount of new convertible (warrant attached, straight) bond issues during 1988–1991; DEBT = total debt in 1988. For firms with non-zero ratios, summary statistics are computed for above and below median of those ratios. Means are taken cross-sectionally. Loan in Loan/Debt ratio includes bank-guaranteed bonds. 'MB score' is computed using (1 = have large city, trust or long-term credit bank as main bank, 0 = do not).

We sort firms by the proportion of guarantees in new issues and take summary statistics for them. For each firm in the 1984–87 and 1988–91 periods, cumulative total and guaranteed amounts of new issues of warrant and straight bonds are computed, and the ratios of guaranteed to total are calculated. The distributions of the ratios are in all cases bimodal with 0 per cent and 100 per cent most frequently observed. Thus the samples in the two time-periods are divided into two; one with all new issues guaranteed and the other with none guaranteed. For these two categories the mean of capitalization, the debt to asset ratio, the loan to debt ratio, and the main bank 'score' (as of 1987 and 1991 respectively) are computed. Table 10.4, Panel A shows the results. In all cases, capitalization again shows a clear distinction between the two groups. Firms that issued guaranteed bonds are smaller than those that were able to issue bonds without guarantees. The loan to total debt ratio also exhibits a consistent pattern. A higher loan ratio is observed for the firms that have a higher guarantee ratio. There is no clear pattern with respect to main bank relations.

Given the significant change in the proportion of guaranteed warrant bond issues over the two sub-periods, it is interesting to examine what types of firms have moved away from bank guarantees when they issue new bond instruments. We take the difference of the guarantee ratio

TABLE 10.4 Panel A. Bank Guaranteed Bond Ratio and Firm Characteristics

	No. of firms	mean capitalization (billion yen)	mean Debt/Asset ratio	mean Loan/Debt ratio	mean MB score
1987					
WB 100% guaranteed	215	160.72	0.309	0.839	0.850
WB 0% guaranteed	30	798.67	0.276	0.512	0.833
SB 100% guaranteed	102	203.00	0.396	0.851	0.870
SB 0% guaranteed	95	101.22	0.328	0.650	0.882
1991					
WB 100% guaranteed	280	133.61	0.268	0.896	0.831
WB 0% guaranteed	165	745.11	0.244	0.351	0.761
SB 100% guaranteed	32	159.63	0.282	0.874	0.864
SB 0% guaranteed	226	419.78	0.280	0.610	0.841

Ratios of guaranteed amount of total new issue for straight and warrant attached bonds are computed for each firm in two periods (1984–87 and 1988–91). Then statistics as of 1987 and 1991 are obtained for firms that have 100% or 0% guaranteed bonds. Means are taken cross-sectionally. Loan in Loan/Debt ratio includes bank-guaranteed bonds. MB score is computed using (1 = have large city, trust or long-term credit bank as main bank, 0 = do not).

•

TABLE 10.4 Panel B. Change in Bond Guarantees and Firm Characteristics

	No. of firms	mean capitalization (billion yen)	mean Debt/Asset ratio	mean Loan/Debt ratio	mean MB score
SB guarantee ratio					
Increased	5	155.11	0.239	0.781	1.000
Decreased	44	401.51	0.420	0.820	0.831
WB guarantee ratio					
Increased	9	143.60	0.363	0.867	0.889
Decreased	77	352.45	0.298	0.788	0.793

Summary statistics are computed for the firms that changed from 100% guaranteed to 0% guaranteed (and vice versa) between two periods (1984–87 and 1988–91). Means are taken cross-sectionally. Loan in Loan/Debt ratio includes bank-guaranteed bonds. MB score is computed using (1 = have large city, trust or long-term credit bank as main bank, 0 = do not).

between the two sub-periods and again calculate the attributes of the firms that increased or decreased their reliance on bank guarantees. The results are tabulated in Table 10.4, Panel B, which show that the firms with decreased dependence are larger in size and weaker in their main bank alliances.

This point can be examined more directly by inspecting individual bond issue data. We ask two questions, one from the viewpoint of the main banks, the other from the viewpoint of the issuing firms. (1) Out of the bond issues guaranteed by bank A, what proportion is for firms that have bank A as their main bank? (2) Out of the guaranteed bonds issued by a firm with bank A as its main bank, what proportion is guaranteed by bank A? These questions can be asked not only for guarantees, but also for trustee administration. We investigate this point for the Industrial Bank of Japan and six major city banks (Dai-Ichi Kangyo, Fuji, Mitsubishi, Sakura, Sanwa, and Sumitomo).

Table 10.5 summarizes the results. In general, the correlation between the main bank and the guarantor-trustee bank is high for major keiretsu banks. Except in a few cases, the bonds banks guarantee are more than 60 per cent for their main bank clients, and firms also turn more than 70 per cent of the time to their main bank for bond guarantees. We can confirm similar strong correlations for trustee banks as well. It is customary to have three trustee banks for each issue of bonds. Since the first-listed trustee bank (*shujutaku ginko*) plays a major role in trustee administration, we take only the first bank as the trustee.

Another point to note is that for guaranteed or trusteed issues, the percentages described above do not change very much between the two sub-periods. In other words, the guarantee or trustee role of the main bank alliance is not disturbed by the secular movement toward more non-guaranteed issues. Banks remain likely to guarantee the bonds issued by their main bank clients, and if a bond is guaranteed it is likely to be done by the issuer's main bank, rather than other banks.

To complement this point, we also computed the ratio of bank guarantees for unaffiliated firms in the same two sub-periods. For unaffiliated firms, the ratios of guaranteed bonds to total bond issues have declined sharply, from 66 per cent to 10 per cent for straight bonds, and from 72 per cent to 20 per cent for warrant attached bonds. These figures indicate a much more distinctive decline in the proportion of bank guarantees compared to the general data for the whole sample shown in Table 10.2, suggesting more willingness for the unaffiliated firms to cut any dependence on banks.

In summary, there is a growing tendency not to utilize bond issue guarantees, but the decision to have a guarantee or not seems to be made before the decision about which bank to use. Firms with main banks tend not to disturb that relationship by breaking the tie with their banks when a bank guarantee is needed. Rather, most qualified firms have chosen an altogether different route and issued bonds without any bank guarantee at all.

CONCLUSION

We have argued that the main bank system continues to have an important role in Japanese corporate finance. There appear to be two types of Japanese firms with rather different behaviour: firms with main banks continue to rely heavily on bank debt and guaranteed bond issues, while

TABLE 10.5 Main Bank and Bond Issue-Related Services
Panel A. Bond Guarantees

	Straight Bonds		Warrant Attached Bonds	
	1984–87	1988–91	1984–87	1988–91
Industrial Bank of Japan	58	46	88	72
Dai-Ichi Kangyo Bank	89	59	69	76
Sakura Bank	43	64	69	85
Mitsubishi Bank	51	60	60	71
Fuji Bank	50	59	72	72
Sumitomo Bank	68	70	60	82
Sanwa Bank	78	42	72	75

This table gives the answer to the question: Out of the bond issues guaranteed by bank A, what percentage (of total amount) is for firms that have bank A as their main bank?

	Straight Bonds		Warrant Attached Bonds	
	1984–87	1988–91	1984–87	1988–91
Industrial Bank of Japan	61	100	79	79
Dai-Ichi Kangyo Bank	71	96	72	100
Sakura Bank	52	100	83	98
Mitsubishi Bank	77	71	99	97
Fuji Bank	97	71	82	70
Sumitomo Bank	74	61	82	94
Sanwa Bank	78	100	73	70

This table gives the answer to the question: Out of the guaranteed bonds issued by a firm having bank A as its main bank, what percentage (of total amount) is guaranteed by bank A?

TABLE 10.5 Panel B. Bond Trustee Administration (continued)

	Straight Bonds					Convertible Bonds					Warrant Attached Bonds	
	1970–75	1976–79	1980–83	1984–87	1988–91	1970–75	1976–79	1980–83	1984–87	1988–91	1984–87	1988–91
Industrial Bank of Japan	60	54	61	44	47	79	89	91	95	75	100	100
Dai-Ichi Kangyo Bank	70	83	100	95	0	53	92	60	50	64	80	100
Sakura Bank	95	97	98	100	100	97	50	49	75	67	100	100
Mitsubishi Bank	72	80	73	100	100	98	100	99	93	75	100	100
Fuji Bank	60	79	100	94	100	63	92	74	56	61	0	100
Sumitomo Bank	96	97	98	95	0	91	76	83	85	94	0	76
Sanwa Bank	53	74	66	69	0	60	94	80	37	53	100	100

This table gives the answer to the question: Out of the trusteed bonds issued by a firm that has bank A as its main bank, what percentage (of total amount) is trusteed (as the first trustee) by bank A?

TABLE 10.5 Panel B. Bond Trustee Administration (continued)

	Straight Bonds					Convertible Bonds					Warrant Attached Bonds	
	1970–75	1976–79	1980–83	1984–87	1988–91	1970–75	1976–79	1980–83	1984–87	1988–91	1984–87	1988–91
Industrial Bank of Japan	93	94	96	96	96	65	65	71	71	73	58	77
Dai-Ichi Kangyo Bank	98	91	98	6	0	88	100	87	73	83	100	100
Sakura Bank	96	97	98	100	100	72	49	42	50	47	100	100
Mitsubishi Bank	75	77	82	51	100	66	63	71	57	63	58	25
Fuji Bank	40	26	45	100	100	61	73	47	65	60	0	75
Sumitomo Bank	73	79	71	100	0	77	69	56	62	53	0	100
Sanwa Bank	92	94	98	97	0	81	96	70	49	76	100	61

This table gives the answer to the question: Out of the bond issues trusteed by bank A (as the first trustee), what percentage (of total amount) is for firms that have bank A as their main bank?

during the last 10 years unaffiliated firms have turned to non-guaranteed bond issues and innovative debt instruments, such as warrant and convertible bonds. The difference between the two groups of firms is apparent even when we confine our attention to a smaller sample of the 112 firms (used by Hoshi, Kashyap and Scharfstein, 1993) that were eligible to issue bonds over the whole period 1982–89.

In the United States and United Kingdom it is often argued that the future of commercial banking lies with fee-generating services, over-the-counter derivative products, and sophisticated risk management, as opposed to the traditional provision of bank loans. To a limited extent this trend is apparent in Japan, as large banks have substituted bond guarantees for some direct lending. Nonetheless, main banks continue to have an important role in traditional lending to those firms affiliated with them.

REFERENCES

BERNANKE, BEN S. and JOHN Y. CAMPBELL. 1988. 'Is there a Corporate Debt Crisis?' *Brookings Papers on Economic Activity* 1: 83–125.

CAMPBELL, JOHN Y. and YASUSHI HAMAO. 1993. 'The Interest Rate Process and the Term Structure of Interest Rates.' In Kenneth J. Singleton, ed., *Japanese Monetary Policy*. Chicago: University of Chicago Press.

CHANG, P. H. KEVIN. 1992. 'Pricing Inefficiencies in Japanese Equity Warrant Markets.' Working Paper, New York University.

HOSHI, TAKEO, ANIL KASHYAP, and DAVID SCHARFSTEIN. 1993. 'The Choice Between Public and Private Debt: An Analysis of Post-Deregulation Corporate Financing in Japan.' Working Paper, University of California, San Diego.

HAMAO, YASUSHI. 1991. 'A Standard Data Base for the Analysis of the Japanese Security Markets.' *Journal of Business* 64: 87–102.

JENSEN, MICHAEL C. 1989. 'Eclipse of the Public Corporation.' *Harvard Business Review* 89: 61–74.

NIHON KEIZAI SHIMBUN-SHA, ed. 1987. *Koshasai Hakko Shijo* (*Bond Primary Markets*). Tokyo.

TOYO KEIZAI SHIMPO-SHA, ed. 1987 and 1992. *Kigyo Keiretsu Soran* (*Almanac of Firm Affiliations*). Tokyo.

PART II

THE COMPARATIVE CONTEXT: RELEVANCE FOR DEVELOPING AND TRANSFORMING ECONOMIES

11

The Relevance of Japanese Finance and its Main Bank System

HUGH PATRICK

What lessons can be learned from the Japanese experience with its main bank system and, more broadly, its financial system? How relevant is that experience for developing market economies and for transforming socialist economies? These are the central themes of this chapter, which explores a range of key generic issues in the design of good financial systems for developing market and transforming socialist economies in the light of Japanese experience. A major focus of this chapter is on the main bank system in its heyday, namely the rapid growth era from the early 1950s to the early 1970s; and on placing the main bank system within the overall architecture of the Japanese financial system, its structure and the government's financial policies.

A comparative analysis from the perspective of the banking systems of other countries is provided in Part II. The next chapter, in providing an analysis of the relationships among large German banks and large industrial corporations, makes clear that while Japanese and German banking are broadly similar (hence the 'Japanese-German model' of banking-based finance), they differ significantly in certain details, especially with regard to corporate governance. The remaining five chapters illuminate the issues of finance and banking from the perspectives and experiences of three major developing market economies—Korea, India, and Mexico—and two transforming socialist economies—China and Poland. These country studies utilize and build upon the detailed studies of the Japanese main bank system in Part I.

The next section of this chapter addresses general analytic concerns. The basic objectives of any nation's financial system are to provide a stable, reliable, safe means of payment; to encourage and facilitate real saving; to mobilize those savings in financial form; and to allocate them

This essay is based upon the chapters in this book and upon a wider body of research on the Japanese financial system. The author is especially indebted to the other authors and participants in the project workshops for their substantive comments. He acknowledges in particular the writings over the years of Juro Teranishi; the recently completed project on the financial development of Japan, Korea, and Taiwan (Patrick and Park, 1994); and the World Bank *World Development Report 1989* and its various more recent Working Papers. Nonetheless, this essay is his assessment and evaluation, and no others are responsible for the judgements presented here.

efficiently and effectively to finance the most productive investment projects. A hierarchy of issues must be considered in the creation of a good financial system. They can be classified at three levels of analysis, while recognizing that interactions among issues are pervasive and important. At the most fundamental, systemic level are issues about the basic nature of the economy and of macroeconomic policy. At an intermediate level are issues concerning the architecture of the financial system and financial policies. At the micro level are issues concerning the nature of the banking system and the effective operation of banks. How Japan has dealt with these, and in particular how the main bank system fits in, are discussed in the following three sections. The relevance, lessons, and transferability of the Japanese financial system, in particular the main bank system, to developing market and transforming socialist economies are addressed in the final sections of the chapter.

ANALYTICAL ISSUES

The approach in this chapter is to consider key generic elements in the creation of a good financial system and how Japanese policy-makers, financiers, and markets have dealt with them, rather than arguing that the Japanese financial system, especially its main bank system, should (much less could) simply be replicated in other countries. Each developing market economy or transforming socialist economy (TSE) has its own specific circumstances, experiences, institutions and history. Given national differences, there is no single optimal financial system model for all countries at all levels of development.

Unlike Part I, where most of the discussion focuses on the Japanese main bank system in the context of the Japanese financial system and its evolution, this chapter appraises the Japanese experience in light of the basic structural, institutional, and policy problems of finance that most developing market and TSEs currently face. To a greater or lesser degree, the problems have been: inflation and macroeconomic instability; weak legal, economic and financial infrastructure; inadequate economic and financial information and its asymmetric distribution among economic actors; weak banking systems and capital markets; the short supply of human resources with finance skills, including credit analysis; financial repression; soft budgeting; and corruption.

Financial systems, like economies, evolve over time in response to changing economic circumstances and opportunities, as well as sociopolitical conditions and objectives. The broad contours of the long-run historical pattern of financial evolution are common across countries. At the earliest stage of development saving is done by investors; finance is internal. Indeed, internal finance continues to be the dominant source of industrial finance even in the most advanced economies. However, its overwhelming role is attenuated over time as savers and investors increasingly become different entities and as entrepreneurs and firms develop new profitable investment projects larger than can be financed internally.

In all economies banks have been, and continue to be, the dominant external source of business finance, certainly for the entire sector of smaller enterprises and even for many large companies. At some point— and timing differs significantly among countries and financial instruments—large companies obtain financing through the issuance of equity, bonds, and commercial paper in capital markets. Whether first to create institutions and pursue policies favouring bank-loan finance or securities market finance, or to do both simultaneously, is a key issue in designing financial systems. If priority is given to banking, as has been the historical experience of financial development for many countries, when and how is such preferential treatment brought to an end? We have two historical models. In the Anglo-American experience, securities markets developed early. Post-war Japan and Germany are major examples of the banking-based model; securities markets have developed only recently.

Wise policy-makers consider a range of alternative systems and institutional arrangements, and learn from the successes and failures in the actual experiences of other countries, as well as from theory. To narrow one's scope and perspective can lead to making wrong policy choices: there is always the danger of giving excessive weight to the comparative experience one knows best. To what extent are East European economies heavily influenced by continental Western European models, or by advisers intellectually grounded in the Anglo-American model? Are Korea, Taiwan, China, or Southeast Asian nations seeking guidance predominantly from the Japanese experience?

What Periods of Japanese Financial Development are Relevant, and for Whom?

Is the Japanese economic and financial development experience so distinctive that it should be considered unique? The answer is certainly no. The differences in the Japanese financial system are ones of degree, not of kind. Japanese policy-makers have had to deal with the same major issues in developing the architecture and operations of their financial system as have policy-makers in all market economies.

The different stages of Japan's evolutionary financial development offer different insights—lessons—and hence are differentially relevant for countries at various stages of market development. (See, particularly, the chapters by Teranishi and Aoki.) Japanese policy-makers and financiers in the late nineteenth century established a modern financial system by adopting and adapting Western models and institutions. Initially, entry was very easy, with low minimum capital requirements and virtually no prudential regulation or protection of deposits. By the first decade of the twentieth century, some 2,300 banks were in operation, mostly small, local, unit banks established by industrialists seeking to finance their enterprises. The successful growth of the banking system was marred by occasional bank runs and financial panics, culminating in the dramatic banking crisis of 1927. Greater government regulation, higher minimum capital requirements, consolidation, and the increasing size and market share of a few large banks resulted.

World War II brought further regulation, consolidation, and control. That experience, especially coupled with the immediate post-war disloca-tion, high inflation, conversion from munitions to civilian goods produc-tion, the huge overhang of bad debts for both companies and banks, and efforts to create a democratic society, is particularly relevant for the cur-rently transforming European socialist economies. Insights, even lessons, can be derived from the way Japanese policy-makers dealt with the same sorts of problems as those currently facing the TSEs. (See Chapter 17 on Poland by Hoshi, Kashyap and Loveman.) Nonetheless there are impor-tant differences as well. Perhaps most important is that post-war Japan had several generations of pre-war experience in a free market, private enterprise system in which financial institutions became well developed and considerable human resource skills were accumulated. Moreover, Japan was under Allied occupation, and institutional and other changes could be more readily imposed, subject of course to the willingness of the Japanese to accept and maintain those changes, especially once indepen-dence was restored in 1952.

The subsequent high growth era was the heyday of banking and of the main bank system. It was the period of exceptionally rapid real GNP growth, averaging close to 10 per cent annually, as private business investment and private saving increased dramatically absolutely and as a share of GNP. Corporations needed ever-increasing amounts and propor-tions of external finance, and banks provided the great bulk of it. It was an era of modest financial repression in which real interest rates were positive, but low, and of relatively limited programmes of directed credit for government-defined key activities and sectors. In many respects, the main banks came to epitomize, or symbolize, Japan's economic system in the high growth era. And it is this era that probably is most immediately relevant for developing market economies and, as their transitions pro-ceed, for TSEs as well.

By the late stages of the high growth era—the early 1970s—both the real economy and the financial system had grown, evolved, deepened in structure, and become institutionally stronger. The balance of payments constraint on growth had been lifted. Inflationary pressures had been suc-cessfully contained for more than two decades. Japan's export capacity had increased rapidly and the yen, initially over-valued, had become under-valued. Loan interest rates had been positive throughout, financial markets had come to work increasingly well, and the proportion of directed credit for developmental purposes, never high in aggregate, had declined substantially. Financial institutions and their management capabilities—and the associated accounting, auditing, and reporting infrastructure—had become quite well developed. The system was more than ready for further financial reform: deregulation, liberalization, a widening range of financial instruments and markets, the final termination of foreign exchange controls over capital outflows and inflows—in other words, the transition (some would say overdue) to a competitive financial system (World Bank, 1989, p. 127). This took place gradually and piecemeal from the mid-1970s, and in some respects is yet to be completed.

Japan's subsequent experience as an advanced industrial economy in the sustained good growth era from the mid-1970s to the early 1990s is also of considerable relevance. Economic growth slowed, though to rates still above the OECD average. For the first time *ex ante* private saving exceeded *ex ante* private investment, and the financial system was flush with funds. In the second half of the 1970s the government resorted to fiscal stimulus through budget deficits and large government bonds issue, thereby bringing about the development of a secondary bond market. In the 1980s Japan developed a huge current account surplus, thanks in part to the over-valued US dollar. The government during this period implemented a gradual, piecemeal programme of financial deregulation. Financial repression ended and greater competition ensued in most financial markets, with new stresses on, and opportunities for, individual financial institutions. Securities markets burgeoned as many large listed firms found bond and equity issue a less-expensive source of external funds than bank loans. While the domestic corporate bond issue market remained relatively underdeveloped and restricted, Euro-market bond issues thrived. During this period the main bank system evolved and became embedded in market-based finance.

These trends were seriously exacerbated by the asset bubble, the great boom in the stock and land market prices, between 1985 and 1990. In retrospect, this was a period of system-wide failure. The speculative mania was fed by the mistaken, but widespread, belief, shared even by conservative banks and government regulators, that asset prices would not decline seriously or for any sustained period of time. During 1985–90 banks and other financial institutions lent on ever-easier terms for purchase of ever-higher-priced land and for real estate development projects. The bursting of the bubble from 1990 has left in its wake the difficult problems of a serious bad debt overhang for the entire banking system, the first since the late 1940s.

Japan's long historical experience as a successful developing market economy clearly is directly relevant for other developing market economies which, after all, have gone through their own banking and financial market development. The TSEs, however, have to create the full panoply of private ownership, capitalist market institutions, incentives, and behaviour virtually from the ground up. While they face tremendous difficulties and obstacles in virtually creating a new financial system, rather than modifying an existing one, the TSEs can learn much from the Japanese model and experience, both in determining their basic financial architecture and policies and in dealing with their important immediate problems of inflation, overhang of bad debts and bank insolvency, soft budgeting, and lack of human resources.

At the same time, several cautionary notes about the Japanese experience should be sounded for those seeking lessons. First, the fact that a particular set of policies and institutional arrangements worked well in Japan does not mean they were optimal. Second, Japan's extraordinarily successful economic performance does not mean that everything was done right. Third, the Japanese model cannot simply be applied directly or simply; it must be adapted to each country's own requirements. Fourth, what counts is substance, not form; mere adoption of institutions or policies without appropriate incentives and regulatory arrangements will not succeed.

Fundamental Characteristics of the Japanese Main Bank System

The nature, operations, effectiveness, and evolution of the Japanese main bank system are described and analysed in rich, nuanced detail in Chapter 1 and the other chapters of Part I. However, it is useful to repeat here its key features, although stylized, as an introduction to, and reference point for, what follows. The discussion focuses on the high growth era of the early 1950s to the early 1970s. The main bank system is based on the special relationships that developed between Japanese large banks (predominantly the twenty-odd city banks, trust banks, and long-term credit banks) and large industrial corporations, notably the 1,000 or so then listed on the stock exchanges. While the main bank system is conceptually different from the six financial keiretsu business groups (Mitsubishi, Mitsui, Sumitomo, Dai-ichi, Fuyo, and Sanwa), in practice most of the main bank relationships are with their banks or with the Industrial Bank of Japan, the largest of the three private long-term credit banks.

Relationships between bank and borrower are a general characteristic of banking in all countries, since repeated transactions and accumulated knowledge of borrower credit-worthiness are always important. The Japanese main bank system is a highly developed, more intensive, closer and, in certain other respects, distinctive form. It can be regarded as the epitome of relationship banking. The system was not a deliberate creation of special government policy; it was an institution which developed and evolved as an effective response to the costs of monitoring in an environment of highly imperfect information and to the overall institutional framework and set of government financial policies.

The main bank-corporate client relationship is multidimensional. In stereotype, the main bank typically is the largest single lender to its corporate client (15–25 per cent of loans) and its largest shareholder among banks (close to the then 10 per cent ceiling). Further, it is the main clearing bank for payment settlement accounts, trustee for collateral for any bonds issued, major beneficiary of foreign exchange and other fee-based business, and provider of (financial) management human resources. It is the major monitor of the client firm's management and performance. It takes the lead in arranging *de facto* lending syndicates with other banks and financial institutions for its clients. Most important, it takes special responsibility for rescuing and restructuring a client firm in distress, taking on costs greater than its formal exposure; this is the most distinctive feature of main bank functions. Unless the situation appears to be virtually hopeless, the presumption—of the main bank, of the client, and of the business, financial, and public policy communities—is that the main bank will rescue the firm through restructuring or merger rather than liquidating it. These relationships, arrangements, and commitments are based, not on legal contracts, but on a history of understandings and expectations, the accumulation and investment in trust and reputational effects.

The essence of the main bank system has lain in its strong information collecting, related monitoring capabilities, and management consulting. To that end, banks have established systems and built up human resources, both in their personnel system of permanent employment, on-the-job training, and rotation in assignments, and in the development of special teams dedicated to manage the relationship with each major corporate client. Monitoring is of course costly, but the main bank did not directly charge to cover the costs. Neither did it receive higher interest rates. Rather, it has been compensated by preferential access to the client's transactions deposits and to the deposits of its employees, subsidiaries and subcontractors, and preferential provision of fee services and the handling of foreign exchange transactions in less price-competitive markets.

From the perspective of the borrowing firm, the main bank has been a secure source of loans when credit was tight, as it was most of the time during the high growth era, even for large firms; a source of financial information and expertise; and a friend in times of distress. The firm was prepared to provide its main bank with considerably more information about its ongoing and proposed activities and plans, and subject itself to ongoing monitoring, than it was to other potential monitors. At the same time it maintained good relations with several other competitor city banks as a hedge against opportunistic behaviour by its main bank. It held a modest proportion, up to 1 per cent or so, of the equity of its main bank; stable cross-shareholding solidified the relationship and turned out to be a good long-run financial investment, despite very low dividend rates, as share prices have appreciated substantially, despite the decline since 1990. In the high growth era large firms grew extraordinarily rapidly, 10–15 per cent a year on average. They increased their direct investment even more rapidly, far beyond their capacity to finance internally despite very low dividend pay-out ratios. They invested a lot, saved a lot, borrowed a lot, and increased financial assets (compensating deposit balances, trade credit, cross-shareholding) a lot.

The stylized facts, as well as theory, suggest the main bank system was quite efficient in two major respects. First, through investment in monitoring, main banks were able to increase information and improve credit evaluation, thereby reducing loan risk premia; and they probably improved corporate management performance by providing incentives not to shirk. The main bank system accordingly reduced the agency costs of external finance, overcame problems of imperfect information and its asymmetric distribution, and made it possible for firms to overcome the liquidity constraints of reliance on internal financing. The system enabled banks to diversify portfolios by being main banks for some large corporations, and participants in a syndicate of lenders to others.

Second, the system reduced the costs of reorganizing and restructuring firms in distress; there is considerable case study evidence of this. Rescued firms were able to produce, sell, and invest more than similarly distressed firms without a close main bank relationship. Japanese costs of restructuring large firms were significantly lower than for distressed American firms using the bankruptcy procedures of the United States. Japanese bankruptcy laws are credible and relatively strong, including removal of top management; the possibility of bankruptcy certainly acted as a deterrent, encouraging quick settlement on terms negotiated with the main bank. In the high growth era there were only a few clear-cut instances of firms that should have been liquidated but were bailed out—referred to as soft budgeting problems or Type 2 errors.

There is much less evidence on the effectiveness of (interim) monitoring of firms in the ordinary course of business. Some practitioners indicate it was quite effective; others say it was frequently pro forma and routine, increasingly so as time passed, relationships were established, and firms prospered. Yet there have been a number of cases of quiet restructurings in less-extreme situations, on terms not made public. The post-bubble era of serious bad loan problems is imposing high costs on many banks; the speculative myopia of the late 1980s overwhelmed what previously had been effective main bank monitoring systems.

The Japanese main bank system is not a panacea. It has weaknesses as well as strengths. The main bank relationship is private, and, not surprisingly, participants are secretive about the specifics. The regulatory authorities have used administrative guidance and informal communication with banks; the degree of public disclosure has been limited. The cosy relationships between regulators and banks were based on preferential access to information and mutual trust, not to be shared with outsiders. The entire financial system is appropriately characterized as opaque. Thus, there are few careful, detailed empirical studies of the costs and benefits of the main bank system.

A serious problem has been the potential collusive exercise of oligopolistic market power by the large banks, both as main banks and more generally as financiers of big business. The evidence is mixed, but it appears there was a substantial degree of competition among the dozen or so city banks. Relationship banking provides insider access to information for lenders; the main bank system increased that degree of access and hence the possibilities of exploitation for institutional or personal benefit. Corrupt behaviour in lending or other decisions by bankers or the regulating officials has been the exception. Despite some notable, indeed flamboyantly scandalous exceptions, there is little evidence that this was a serious problem overall. The system was basically honest.

SYSTEMIC ISSUES AND MACROECONOMIC PERFORMANCE

The most fundamental question is what kind of economic system a country wants. The assumption here is that policy-makers in developing market and transforming socialist economies, like the Japanese, are committed to a predominantly private enterprise, free and competitive market economic system for goods, services, labour, land, and capital, including finance. Yet many economies are reluctant to give up state ownership, particularly of 'strategic' sectors however defined, but often including the banking system (see the chapters on India by Bhatt and China by Qian). This is a key issue for TSEs, but has been important in many developing market economies as well (see the chapter on Korea by Nam and Kim and on Mexico by Reynolds).

What is a country's development strategy: export oriented versus import substituting? What are the respective roles of domestic saving and foreign borrowing? What is the nature and degree of industrial policy, however defined? An open economy—the free international flow of goods, services, and capital—may be an ultimate objective, but it is typically far from current reality. How quickly should an economy be opened, and in what sequence? An autarchic Japan benefited from being forcibly opened to free trade in 1859. It also probably benefited from import protection and capital outflow restrictions in the early phases of the post-war high growth era of rapid domestic market expansion and government-encouraged strong competition among Japanese firms, many of them new entrants.

Two further policy issues are of systemic importance. First, macroeconomic stability—especially reasonable price stability—is essential for the effective and efficient functioning of a financial system and, while the evidence is mixed, for overall economic performance as well. Second, the establishment of institutions to support the market economy—particularly the legal system and information systems of accounting, auditing, disclosure, and transparency—is essential. Who monitors companies, banks, and other economic players? How, and how well do they monitor? A central theme of this book is that the main bank system of monitoring well met the needs for information prior to the establishment of adequate information systems. Efforts to achieve macroeconomic stability, build the institutional support structure, and create financial institutions are likely to be going on simultaneously, particularly in TSEs. They are all requisites for a good financial system.

Japan's Economy and Finance in the High Growth Era

Japanese economic growth in the two decades beginning in the early 1950s was extraordinary, averaging close to 10 per cent annually. But it was not a miracle. It can be well understood and explained in terms of standard economic factors, supportive government policies, and an improving and expanding international environment. Control over inflation, price stability, and a fixed exchange rate were fully accepted as the macroeconomic requisites for successful economic and financial growth. In the early to mid-1950s Japan succeeded in overcoming the overwhelming economic problems of the early post-war period: high inflation, the shift to civilian goods production, war-damage bottlenecks, reconstruction. Moreover, it established or solidified its political, social, and economic institutional structure. These, especially macroeconomic stability, were the foundations for the sustained spurt of rapid growth, which no one anticipated and in the early years no one believed could be sustained. Given Japan's negligible natural resource base, growth was founded on rapid industrialization, and the development of manufacturing firms in virtually every (civilian goods) industry as the industrial structure deepened. (Standard analyses in English of Japan's economy and economic performance in the high growth era include Patrick and Rosovsky (1976), Nakamura (1981), Kosai (1986), and Yamamura and Yasuba (1987).)

As surprising as it seems today, Japan in the mid-1950s was classified as a less-developed country because of its low income per capita; it graduated to developed country status only in 1964. However, Japan differed from other low-income countries in that it had a labour force at least equivalent in education to Western Europe's, a sustained pre-war experience of successful economic development, and considerable numbers of managers, engineers, and technicians capable of absorbing foreign technology. Its technological gap behind best-known practices was substantial. Sustained very rapid growth was achieved by firms effectively utilizing the increasingly educated and skilled labour force, importing huge amounts of foreign technology, and engaging in unprecedentedly rapid plant and equipment investment in new, more productive capacity.

Two related issues in interpreting Japanese experience remain controversial even among specialists: whether growth was state-led or led by private enterprise; and whether industrial policy was successful or not. My judgement is that while the state played a significantly constructive role, the engine of Japan's successful industrialization was private business entrepreneurship and investment; without this, government support and intervention would have been ineffective, if not counterproductive. The results of industrial policy were mixed: some industries were promoted and became globally competitive, others did not; the success of many winner industries was due primarily to business leadership and the evolution of comparative advantage—from labour intensive products such as textiles to medium-skill, medium-tech industries such as automobiles and consumer electronics—not to a differentially supportive industrial policy. For general discussions of industrial policy see Johnson (1982), Patrick (1986), Dore (1986), Komiya and others (1988), and Okimoto (1989); for industry-specific studies see Samuels (1987), Friedman (1988), Anchordoguy (1989), and Genther (1990).

Certainly, the government role was important. It pursued an investment-encouraging macroeconomic policy mix of restrictive fiscal policy and expansive monetary policy. The government budget was essentially balanced; there was virtually no new net government debt issue until the mid-1970s. Inflation had wiped out the war-time government debt, and during the high growth era government debt as a share of GNP was low. One by-product was no secondary market in Treasury bills or longer-term government debt.

The government provided a supportive environment for private business industrial entrepreneurship, including the necessary physical infrastructure of utilities, transportation, and communications. There were no state enterprises in manufacturing aside from cigarettes and other tobacco products, a monopoly for revenue purposes. Importantly, following post-war reconstruction the government gave highest, indeed almost sole, priority to economic growth as the solution to almost all problems. It did not compete with private business for resources, the government sector was small, and social costs of rapid industrialization (air and water pollution, urban congestion, lagging improvements in housing) were allowed to accumulate until the early 1970s. The development strategy was to encourage broad-based industrialization in competitive domestic markets. It encouraged new domestic entry, but continued the early post-war protection of industry against import competition or direct investment in Japan by foreign multinationals.

'Export and Save' was the slogan on a huge banner across the entrance to the Bank of Japan in the 1950s and 60s. Even so, like the United States but unlike most rapidly growing economies, Japanese post-war economic growth has been predominantly driven by domestic market demand. Exports have never been more than 10–15 per cent of GNP. This reflected the size of the potential domestic market in a country whose population was twice that of any Western European country. At the same time, in the high growth era imports of machinery, equipment, and raw materials were essential and the balance of payments became the operative constraint. In that respect, exports were vital to pay for essential imports, rather than representing an export-led growth strategy. In the world capital market conditions of the 1950s and 60s, Japan was not able to finance a current account deficit by heavy foreign borrowing, unlike Korea and other countries in the 1970s.

One feature worth noting in Japan's successful growth performance was the tremendous increase in household saving as a share of family income and of GNP, peaking in the mid-1970s before declining gradually since then. Nonetheless, while burgeoning investment demand was almost always straining against domestic saving constraints, this showed up from time to time as a current account deficit rather than high inflation. The fixed exchange rate, taken by policy-makers as a given until 1971, and the persisting allergy against inflation engendered by the early post-war traumas made macroeconomic control of inflation essential.

Rapid economic growth was, and is, a virtuous circle. It justified, by making profitable, the rapid expansion of productive capacity by firms and generated demand for new projects and products. It increased the value of new projects and investment in them. It meant that even marginal projects were not outright failures; the instances of large firm bankruptcy or restructuring were relatively few and the costs limited. Many small firms were created and many of them failed, most sooner rather than later; both entry and exit rates for small firms in Japan have been high relative to the United States and other industrial countries. Rapid growth generated high saving rates by households and corporations. It generated rapid increases in real wages and consumption, thereby providing a social rationale for low interest rates on saving deposits. However, the slowdown in growth rates since 1973 has had the opposite effects. Over time, firms prospered, grew more powerful and competitive, and became increasingly independent of government influence. Japan's export success, commensurate with its domestic growth, made it possible to reduce import barriers gradually, although primarily in manufactures and, to a significant degree, in response to foreign pressures.

Some Important Institutional Features

Japan, like other countries, has a private enterprise, private ownership, market economy; it also has its own specific features of capitalism. We briefly consider several as of particular relevance for understanding the Japanese financial system. These include: reliance on business relationships; various types of business groups (to which the term 'keiretsu' is typically loosely applied); and the high quality of the central government bureaucracy, especially those encouraging, supervising, and regulating the financial system.

One important feature of the Japanese economy is that many markets are not impersonal, arm's-length, spot markets. They are moderated by relationships among market participants founded upon the building and maintenance of trust through repeated transactions and honourable (non-opportunistic) handling of unanticipated situations. In the Japanese ideal, institutional relationships are expected to continue for a very long time— for practical purposes the game is usually assumed to go on forever. Relationships are multidimensional, complex, and subtly nuanced. Although built upon personalistic relationships, they transcend their implementation by specific individuals representing the partners.

Relationships are reflected in labour markets, subcontracting, buyers and suppliers, brand loyalty, and in banking, epitomized in the main bank system, as well as other financial services. Such relationships are characteristic of business in all economies, so the matter is one of degree not of kind. It is commonly assumed, though solid empirical evidence is limited, that business based on relationship arrangements and networks is more extensive and intensive in Japan than in the United States.

A system of economic transactions in which relationships are important has both efficiencies and inefficiencies. Japanese seem to have maximized those efficiencies while limiting the inefficiencies. Relationships enhance the degree and reduce the cost of access to information and monitoring. Relationships require an investment of resources into what become relationship-specific sunk costs. They are created over time, as they have to be built upon trust engendered by repeated experience; trust is conditional upon the behaviour and performance of the partners. The pay-off is that relationships increase the return on relationship-specific investments (such as subcontractors designing an auto part for a particular model, or a main bank loan) by enhancing confidence that the partner will not behave opportunistically. Relationships overcome some of the inefficiencies in a spot market arising from imperfect, asymmetric information, such as underinvestment in specific assets due to failure to safeguard against opportunism, or overinvestment due to multiple sourcing or duplication of monitoring effects. It is also argued that supplier-buyer relationship systems overcome bureaucratic diseconomies within vertically integrated firms. Relationships provide an effective mechanism for dealing with uncertainty and unanticipated changes of circumstances (states of nature), since it is impossible to write, much less implement, a perfectly complete contract.

Relationship systems can also result in serious inefficiencies and social costs. They are essentially exclusive insider systems; entry by outsiders is difficult. They are murky and opaque, not transparent; they create opportunities for fraud and abuse of power. A relationship system is subject to personalistic objectives such as nepotism, disproportionate benefits to particular cliques, and other non-efficiency-based corrupt behaviour. Firms in the same industry can establish relationships, often through industry associations, to engage in oligopolistic or cartel-type behaviour. It is difficult to terminate relationships; reciprocal obligations built up over time may result in Type 2 errors (continuation of support well beyond rational assessments).

In many societies the social costs of relationship systems far outweigh their efficiency gains. Yet it appears this has not been the case in Japan. Why? The sanctions against and penalties for abusing trust are high. The most important sanction is the competitive market-place. If a relationship becomes persistently less efficient than any alternative, eventually it will wither away. The discipline of the market-place is reinforced by the competitive, ambitious drive of many Japanese individuals and institutions. The incentive system rewards good performance and makes poor performance embarrassing and shameful, as well as economically costly. Those perceived as not living up to the obligations of existing relationships suffer tremendous loss of reputation, making them less reliable partners for any future business. Reputational costs are reinforced by the high value placed upon status.

Many Japanese apparently approach relationships conditionally, with a healthy degree of scepticism and latent mistrust. It is not accidental that companies simultaneously seek a main bank relationship and, in aggregate, borrow most of their loans from other, frequently competitor, financial institutions. And it is not accidental that main banks monitor their major clients, and indeed that partners in all relationship arrangements engage in some degree of ongoing monitoring of each other. Nonetheless, to develop good, strong relations participants must regard each other as trustworthy, and to be willing to rely upon informal agreements rather than formal contracts for much of the conduct of business. It is typically assumed that whoever one does repeated business with is trustworthy. And the elite central government bureaucracy has been deeply trusted, at least until recently.

The various types of keiretsu business groups (financial, vertical, enterprise, distribution) embody relationship arrangements among independent but affiliated companies. There is an extensive literature on keiretsu; see, for example, Aoki (1988) and Gerlach (1992). The six city banks with the largest number of main bank relationships are core members of the Big Six financial keiretsu: Mitsubishi, Mitsui, and Sumitomo, formed out of pre-war zaibatsu; and Dai-ichi, Fuyo, and Sanwa. However, the main bank system is not the same as the Big Six keiretsu; other large banks also have main bank relationships. In particular, the Industrial Bank of Japan, the largest long-term credit bank, has had as many main bank relationships with listed companies as the average Big Six city banks; with its own business group of affiliated companies, it must be included as a major player in the main bank system (see Chapter 5 by Packer).

While all core members of a particular financial business group have the member bank as their main bank, the bank also has a main bank relationship with other large firms and, through the syndication process, the firms often borrow less from their keiretsu financial institutions (the main bank, trust bank, insurance companies) than they do from non-members. While there may be benefits for the main banks in having a keiretsu system, certainly the application of the main bank model in other countries does not require the formation of affiliated, autonomously managed, groups of business firms.

Three further aspects of Japanese industrial organization have some relevance for the operation of the main bank system. First, stock ownership in almost all large industrial corporations and financial institutions is widely dispersed; ownership is separated from control which, in normal circumstances, is exercised by a self-perpetuating autonomous professional management. Management's stated goals are to benefit all its stakeholders, including importantly its workers, not simply to maximize shareholder value. Corporate governance is exercised through the main bank system, and control can shift from management to the main bank in times of distress. Second, take-over of companies has not been a major instrument of corporate governance or of company diversification into unrelated product lines. Mergers have been of weak firms into stronger, usually mediated by the main banks. Third, particularly in the rapid growth era but even subsequently, firms tended to stay within their own narrowly defined industry; American-style conglomerates did not emerge. A major reason was that rapid growth—first of domestic markets and then the ability to compete in foreign markets—absorbed the management capabilities of enterprises, and kept them in the industries they knew best.

Japan has an excellent system of sound central government administration. Over time it developed an elite bureaucracy that is generally respected, trusted, and in whom politicians have vested great power because of their presumed capability, honesty, and identification with the national interest (or at least each ministry's avowed perception of the national interest). Those on the fast track in the ministries are able, recruited from the few elite universities, and promoted from within; only the minister and parliamentary vice-minister are outsider, political appointments.[1]

At the apex is the Ministry of Finance which, among other responsibilities (such as making the budget and designing and implementing the tax system), oversees, promotes, guides, and supervises, and otherwise establishes and monitors the rules of the game for the financial system, and especially the banking system. Trust and confidence in the Ministry of Finance and other economic ministry bureaucrats have had important implications for the financial system, especially in the high growth era when bureaucratic power was greatest. Everyone believed that the Ministry of Finance and Bank of Japan guaranteed bank safety. Close supervision (monitoring) would prevent mismanagement, excessive risk-taking, fraud. The system was believed in, even though it was opaque and government officials have relied on administrative guidance rather than law in composing and implementing rules and affecting behaviour. The sanctions against poor performance, much less corrupt behaviour, by government officials were severe: loss in the promotion game, reduced post-retirement job opportunities, at the extreme, disgrace—all in an imperfect labour market for senior managers and government officials.

The process allocating bank credit to specific firms in Japan has been based on objective criteria, without serious problems of direct bureaucratic intervention. Known instances of direct bribery and corruption of government officials to influence specific loan decisions are few. While some undoubtedly were not discovered, and others hidden from public view, corruption has not been a serious problem for government administration of the financial system. It has been basically honest and effective, especially in comparison with many developing market economies and TSEs.

In practice, the Ministry of Finance and Bank of Japan have been insulated from the direct corruption more pervasive in politics.[2] This is

---

[1] See the papers prepared for the World Bank Workshop on the Roles of the Civil Service in Japanese Economic Growth (1993). For a rational choice approach see Rosenbluth (1989) and Ramseyer and Rosenbluth (1993).

[2] To be elected and stay in office, politicians have had to maintain and somehow pay for a large staff, and are expected to make gifts of US$75–150 to the families of constituents on the occasion of each birth, death, or marriage. They raise much of these funds through business contributions which are frequently related to regulatory restrictions (such as the Sagawa trucking licence scandal), government purchases (notably the system of rigged government construction contracts, termed *dango*), lax tax enforcement (such as small business evasion of income taxes), or stock market scandals (the Recruit case). That these arrangements are generally tolerated as long as they stay within limits suggests a series of implicit social compacts which can only be addressed through comprehensive political reform.

not to say they have complete autonomy. They certainly were responsive to the electoral and other needs of the Liberal Democratic Party politicians in power; the 'iron triangle' of cosy, mutually supportive, and beneficial big business (including finance), LDP politicians, and government bureaucracy relationships has been an important reality. As in every country, Japanese banks have had a strong vested interest in shaping the regulatory system and government financial policies to their benefit. Their relationships were based on general support of the system, not on specific favours. The city banks were among the largest legal contributors to the Liberal Democratic Party, and they undoubtedly made contributions directly to individual political leaders as well.

Public confidence in the regulatory authorities and in the banking system and the securities industry was shaken in the early 1990s when a series of financial scandals surfaced in the aftermath of the bursting of the stock and land price bubbles. These demonstrated not corruption but the apparent lack of competence of government officials in supervision, and their tolerance of sleazy if not outright illegal practices as interim measures in the process of financial institution adjustment to new market realities. In mid-1993, belief that the regulatory authorities would continue to protect the safety of the banking system, and especially depositors, remained strong but was more conditional than before; a few small banks thought to be in particular difficulty even had considerable deposit withdrawals.

FINANCIAL SYSTEM ARCHITECTURE AND THE JAPANESE EXPERIENCE

The government designs the architecture of the financial system; the market gives it substance, fills its halls, and even alters the design itself. Government policy establishes the framework whereby system stability is maintained, and determines whether competition in financial markets flourishes or is emasculated. To the extent that market forces predominate, they bring about changes in structure as new financial markets, instruments, and institutions develop in response to market demand for them. Governmental authorities—the Ministry of Finance, central bank, financial institution supervisors—play a major role. At the micro level, they oversee banks and other financial institutions with prudential regulation and supervision. But they do far more than that. They build and modify the institutional structure and hence the industrial organization of finance; they set and enforce the rules of the game.

Japanese policy-makers in the early 1950s had to address the same issues of financial system structure and policy facing developing market economies and TSEs today. Once independence was restored in April

1952, Japanese policy-makers had the freedom to alter, amend, or accept the existing structure, to create new institutions, and in particular to implement their own financial policies. This section addresses important issues of financial structure and policy for developing market economies and TSEs, and discusses how Japanese policy-makers and decision-makers, public and private, have dealt with them. These include banking-based financial systems; universal versus commercial bank systems; bank safety; interest rate policy and financial repression; and long-term and directed credit policies.

Banking and Securities Markets

A securities market-based system and a banking-based system can develop simultaneously while being of vastly differing significance in different time periods and for different players. Both require a set of prudential and administrative rules and regulations, in other words, an appropriate institutional structure and administrative framework in order to function effectively and efficiently. The important issue is thus whether the institutional structure, the incentives structure, and the rules of the game should discriminate substantially in favour either of banks or of securities markets; or whether they should be more neutral in order to let market forces determine the relative importance of each over time.

As a practical matter, until a late stage of economic development, securities markets will not be the dominant source of business external finance for the corporate sector as a whole or probably even for large firms. A key point is which financial institutions can most effectively and efficiently monitor borrowers. The economics of information collection and monitoring, and the reluctance of firms to subject themselves to significant disclosure, limit the demand for public securities issue. Equally important, there is a term mismatch between savers and investors. In relatively low-income countries, few individual savers are willing to take on the risks of impersonal securities investments or to make long-term commitments in financial assets. The risks are correctly perceived as higher in countries with recent experiences of inflation or substantial degrees of socio-political as well as economic uncertainty.

Many TSEs are seeking to privatize their mammoth state enterprises, often by widespread distribution of equity to individuals at low prices. Such programmes will almost inevitably, and desirably, lead to the creation of stock markets to facilitate changes in ownership of the outstanding shares. That can have important advantages, such as increasing pressure to create adequate information systems and transparency, and providing market-determined price information (signals) about yields and valuations. However, in the absence of overwhelming (and costly) incentives, it is unlikely that securities markets in TSEs will become a major source of *new* funds for listed companies in the foreseeable future. And it remains to be seen whether institutional investors (such as mutual funds) that do emerge will be more efficient and effective monitors than government bureaucrats (probably so) or bank managers (unclear).

The post-war Japanese financial system owed much to its early post-war, war-time, and pre-war institutional heritage. The Ministry of Finance opted for a system of bank loan-based finance for industrial corporations. It used regulatory restrictions and economic disincentives to severely inhibit corporate bond issue and the development of a secondary market (see Chapter 7 by Ramseyer). Essentially, only public utilities and long-term credit banks could issue bonds in any quantity, and this was done mainly through non-arm's length placements. Equity issue was expensive for management-controlled firms, both because dividends were paid out of after-tax profits while interest payments were a deductible expense, and because the pre-war custom of new stock issue at par rather than market prevailed well into the 1970s. The issuance of commercial paper for short-term finance was not allowed until 1987. Business, growing rapidly and always in need of new loans for working capital and fixed investment, had no choice but to borrow from banks.

The basic rationale for Japanese policy-makers' discrimination in favour of bank finance over corporate bond or equity issue lay in their perception that savers in the early post-war period wanted safe, liquid, short-term financial assets. The inflationary experience was too traumatic and recent; financial and real wealth was low and relatively equally distributed; the stock market had difficulty absorbing the shares released through the zaibatsu dissolution programme. Moreover, only banks had bond underwriting experience and expertise from before the war, and the Occupation-imposed Article 65 of the Securities and Exchange Law of 1948, based on the American Glass-Steagall Act, separated banking and underwriting or dealing in securities. Only in the 1970s and 80s were the restrictions on corporate bond issue substantially eased, considerably later than was desirable. Nonetheless, these policies were an essential component of building a strong banking system during the rapid growth era.

Banking System Structure

Because universal banking was prohibited under Article 65, the operative issue for Japan was what banking system structure would be most appropriate. What are the respective benefits and costs of a system founded primarily on nationwide branch banks or on larger numbers of local and regional banks? Nationwide banks may generate economies of scale, scope, and portfolio diversification, but local banks may be better able to monitor local borrowers than local branches of nationwide banks. Moreover, should commercial banks be expected to lend for all categories of borrowers, or is it desirable to have specialized financial institutions for agriculture and small business to overcome harmful market imperfections? In substantial part as a consequence of its historical evolution, Japan's banking structure was functionally specialized.

The Japanese financial authorities ratified and, where necessary, created a system of specialized financial institutions and segmented financial markets.[3] The dozen or so nationwide city banks, including the subset of six major main banks, were to provide short-term and, to some extent, longer-term loans to big business. Local banks, mutual savings banks, and credit associations were to lend to medium and small firms. Agricultural cooperatives lent to farmers. The seven trust banks financed commercial real estate and industrial projects with longer-term loans; the long-term credit banks made term loans to finance large enterprise fixed investment. The government established and owned financial institutions to finance priority activities. The largest and most important in the high growth era were the Japan Development Bank and the Export-Import Bank of Japan.

The Fair Trade Act of 1947 set a 5 per cent limit on Japanese bank ownership of a company's shares, in contrast to the prohibition of ownership in US law and UK custom. However, once independence was restored, the authorities amended the law in July 1953 to allow Japanese banks to purchase up to 10 per cent of a company's equity; one purpose was to make bank-client relationships closer and stronger (Teranishi, 1993, p. 22). Institutionally and legally, these relationships were even closer in the German system where, in addition to unlimited equity ownership, control over proxies and representation on the supervisory board have given German banks what are conventionally viewed as substantially greater powers. Baums argues such powers were limited to a relatively small number of firms and were not really exercised (Chapter 7).

The predominant source of funds for the financial system was deposits, particularly the saving deposits of households, as their saving rates rose dramatically and there were few safe alternative financial assets. Even government financial institutions were financed primarily by private saving through their borrowing of post office savings deposits. Central bank credit, sufficient to support money-supply growth while maintaining price stability, was provided through cheap loans and discounts to the city banks—more or less in proportion to their size—which in turn lent to large businesses or to finance exports, and purchased—on an allocated basis—bonds issued by the long-term credit banks, electric power compa-

---

[3] The most comprehensive description in English of the Japanese financial system—institutions, markets, assets and liabilities, interest rate system, monetary policy—has been prepared by the Bank of Japan and appears in Suzuki (1987). There are a number of good analyses available of the high growth era and of the subsequent period of deregulation, including the chapter by Hamada and Horiuchi in Yamamura and Yasuba (1987), chapters by Teranishi, and Kurosawa and Kitagawa, in Patrick and Park (1994), Cargill and Royama (1988), and Suzuki (1980 and 1986).

nies and other utilities, and the small number of qualified corporate clients. Establishment of new bank branches was profitable, since deposit interest rates were kept artificially low while the demand for loans was high. The Ministry of Finance controlled the number and allocation of branches, and used that as an incentive device to ensure bank compliance with its guidance. Saving was more widely dispersed geographically than large enterprise fixed investment, and the inter-bank call market, in which city banks borrowed substantially and persistently, reduced disequilibria in the segmented deposit and loan markets.

Banking System Safety and Stability

A basic issue, which has significantly shaped Japanese policy-makers' thinking, is how to maintain the safety and stability of the banking system. To what extent and how should depositors be protected? Should individual banks be allowed to fail? How can the moral hazard of excessive risk-taking by banks be overcome? To what extent do measures to promote safety conflict with the objective of enhancing financial market competition? Can high minimum capital adequacy ratios substitute for government guarantees in protecting depositors? These are major questions under debate in the finance literature. In my view, high capital adequacy requirements, prudential regulation, pro-active supervision, and transparency are collectively the appropriate policies. Government guarantees, explicit or *de facto*, not only raise moral hazard problems but increase the likelihood the government both will intrude excessively in loan decisions and other aspects of bank behaviour, and will find itself committed, or unable to refuse to commit, to further loans to refinance failing banks or industrial companies (the soft budgeting problem).

The reality, however, is that, like early post-war Japan, banks in almost all developing market economies and TSEs are undercapitalized, have limited prospects for raising additional capital, and have serious bad loan problems, disclosed or undisclosed. The overhang of huge and still rising bad loans to state enterprises means that banks in some TSEs are insolvent. A solution of these problems through sustained growth sounds good, but is only ameliorative. More likely, they will be resolved, as in early post-war Japan, through a combination of *de facto* bankruptcies and restructuring, and inflation (which reduces the real value of loans and deposits); sequestering of existing ('old') bank deposits and loans in order to start fresh with 'new' deposit and loan accounts; cleaning up the bad debt overhang over time by writing off equity and 'old' deposits to the extent necessary; and the revaluation of corporate real assets once inflation ends (or as it proceeds).

The hand of history has been heavy on Japanese financial policy-makers, as it has for Germany, the United States, and indeed most countries. For its first 50 years Japan's modern banking system was highly competitive and lightly regulated, with easy entry and scant supervision. However, recurring bank failures and financial panics, culminating in the Banking Crisis of 1927, generated a strong regulatory commitment to banking system stability, safety, and orderliness that has persisted to the present. The post-war authorities conservatively created a system and pursued policies which, in practice, not only fully protected all deposits and depositors, but prevented any bank from failing. Deposit insurance was not a factor; indeed a government compulsory deposit system was not established until 1971.

While serving as the lender of last resort, the monetary authorities did not want to create moral hazard disincentives or condone mismanagement. The policy approach was two-fold: to enact prudential regulation and carefully supervise banks, intervening in bank management when necessary; and to impose ceiling interest rates on deposits and loans with a sufficiently wide spread that even the most marginal bank, reasonably managed, would be profitable, since investment demand, and hence demand for loanable funds, was high (see Chapter 3 by Ueda). The entry of new banks was prohibited. While relatively high minimum capital-asset ratios (10 per cent) were required in principle, in practice, they were very low, on the order of 2 to 4 per cent; the other policies were sufficient to guarantee bank safety. Capital-asset ratios became an issue only as banking was deregulated and especially after major Japanese banks became significant international players, leading to the 1988 BIS capital-adequacy ratio arrangements.

The banking system was indeed stable and safe throughout the high growth era. No bank failed; a few merged. Realized loan losses were very low, in part because loans were generally well collateralized, but also because rapid growth resulted in few outright business failures of any significance. There were modest economic losses borne by banks as they rescued and restructured firms in distress, typically by reducing interest rates on loans and extending repayment schedules. Perhaps the most significant cost of the otherwise effective policies promoting stability was that bank management, especially in small banks, became complacent, and was ill-equipped to operate effectively in the more competitive financial environment deregulation has brought.

Low Interest Rates and Financial Repression

A key issue in financial development policy is whether interest rates should be determined by supply and demand in the market-place or be set at low ceiling rates through government policy. Low interest rate policies reduce the cost of funds to investors and the return to savers, thereby providing incentives to investment and disincentives to saving. Under a policy-man-dated low interest rate regime, demand exceeds the supply of funds and credit rationing becomes essential. Credit rents—the difference between ceiling interest rates and market interest rates—are created and allocated among direct and indirect participants. The credit allocation process accordingly becomes distorted by political factors, personalistic considerations, rent-seeking behaviour, and corruption. To maintain the system, entry has to be limited, competition among financial institutions and financial instruments constrained, and capital outflows to foreign countries restricted. This is the standard description of financial repression.

Low interest rate (financial repression) policies have long been criticized on both theoretical and empirical grounds.[4] For almost all economies the lack of saving is a more severe constraint than lack of investment demand. To the extent that savings are real interest rate elastic—the evidence is mixed on marginal changes, but positive where large changes occur, due to substantial reductions in inflation—then low interest rate policies are counter productive. On the investment side, low interest rates create credit rents and distort credit allocation away from the most productive investment projects. Corruption in the distribution of credit rents occurs at two levels: that of individual banks or bankers, their borrowers, or regulators; and, as political economists have pointed out, the institutionalized corruption of the political system whereby credit rents become a significant source of finance for the political leadership.

The *degree* of financial repression is important both as a policy matter and theoretically. There is no substantial theoretical case or empirical evidence that negative real interest rates enhance economic and financial development. Even with positive real rates the distortions can be large. As an illustration, assuming national credit outstanding amounts to 50 per cent of GDP and the gap between ceiling and market interest rates is 10 percentage points, then the annual credit rents amount to 5 per cent of GDP. These rents are redistributed from savers and taxpayers to those who obtain them. These static costs of credit rents rationing are surely smaller than the dynamic consequences of inefficient resource allocation.

A recent theme in the 'new institutional economics' analytical approach is that a small degree of financial repression may, on net balance, be beneficial or even required, in order to build financial institutions needed for economic growth. The analysis begins with the proposition, certainly well recognized by all practical policy-makers, that institutions matter. In the real world of imperfect markets and imperfect and asymmetrically distributed information, it is sometimes necessary to provide incentives

---

[4] The classic treatments are Shaw (1973) and McKinnon (1973); more recent analysis is provided by Fry (1988) and McKinnon (1991). The World Bank, *World Development Report 1989*, especially chapters 3 and 4, is replete with discussion, examples, and data on financial repression and its costs. For a comparative evaluation of financial repression in Japan, Korea, and Taiwan, see Patrick in Patrick and Park (1994).

(direct or implicit subsidies) to create and manage effectively appropriate institutions. A strong, effective, and safe banking system is essential in an uncertain world to mobilize savings and to allocate credit to productive business uses.

Assuming that saving is interest-inelastic, few alternatives to savings deposits are available, and depositors have a high preference for safety over yield, then low interest rates on deposits are an effective way to subsidize banks. Ceiling loan interest rates are designed in principle so that banks retain part of this subsidy through a wide spread and pass on part of it to borrowers. Such a banking system should be autonomous, objective, and rational in its loan decisions, subject to prudential regulation and supervisory overview. The degree of credit rent that borrowers obtain is based upon objective performance criteria (output growth, cost reductions, exports) determined by industrial policy. In this view, business credit rent seeking induces growth-seeking outcomes (performance-indexed rent-seeking behaviour). In this view, the degree of financial repression should equate at the margin its institution-building and allocative benefits and its saving disincentive and rent-seeking costs, and should be decreased as institutions become stronger.

The early post-war development of the Japanese banking system is held up as an outstanding example of the success of a modest degree of financial repression (see most chapters in Part I, though Ramseyer takes exception). The argument is that the early post-war banks were fragile and required the implicit subsidies of low interest rates and wide spreads to build up internal reserves and become strong, and the entire system had been made safe by restrictions on entry and other means of implicit subsidy. Credit rents were used for institution-building and to provide incentives to appropriate corporate performance and, in this sense, were desirable.

Bank interest rate ceilings were operative mainly on the deposit side. Nominal ceiling loan rates set by law or agreement were neither comprehensive in coverage nor, more important, binding where they did apply. Banks required compensating balances and fee business against loans to raise stated interest rates above the ceilings, if not up to market-clearing levels.[5]

Aoki, among others, has argued plausibly that some credit rents were captured by 'well-performing' industrial firms, since there was some variance in loan terms even among credit-worthy borrowers; the micro evidence to test this proposition is, not surprisingly, limited.

A considerable portion of the credit rents of regulation in the era of

---

[5] Suzuki (1987) estimates the effective loan interest rate during 1964–73 was 8–10 per cent for city banks, and 9–13 per cent for local banks. The GNP deflator rose at an annual average rate of about 2 per cent prior to the 1973 inflation; while the consumer price index rose more rapidly (reflecting price increases in services), wholesale and export prices were very stable. Ceiling rates on savings deposits in real terms ranged between slightly positive and slightly negative.

high business demand for funds accrued to banks. How did the banks allocate those rents? Certainly not to loan officers; borrowers were not able to obtain preferential access to loans by bribing them. Part went into bank profits (shared with the government as taxes and otherwise mostly retained as additions to capital); part went into higher salaries for managers of banks than for industrial enterprises; part funded management inefficiencies; and some modest portion went to very large depositors who also were able to evade ceiling interest rates (Patrick, 1966).

The rents created in the high growth era by low interest rate policies were relatively small, estimated to be 1.7 per cent of GNP in 1966–70 and 2.4 per cent in 1971–75 by Teranishi (1993, p. 29) and somewhat less by Ueda (Chapter 3). While the main beneficiaries were large firms and the banks themselves, the costs of financial repression were borne by depositors who received low real returns and by small businesses which paid oligopolistically determined high interest rates.

Rent-seeking and corruption, individual or institutional, have not been a pervasive characteristic of the Japanese financial system, so distortion of credit allocation criteria were minimized. This is not because Japanese were necessarily morally superior, although the perception that Japanese banks, bankers, and regulatory bureaucrats in general are honest and responsible seems valid. Rather, credit rents from financial repression were not large, while the sanctions—regulatory, economic, and reputational—were severe.

For comparative 'lessons', the important fact about Japan's policy of financial repression is that it was so modest and circumscribed in comparison with the experience of many developing market and transforming socialist economies. Official ceiling interest rates were perhaps several percentage points below market-clearing rates; however, in real terms, ceiling loan interest rates were positive and nominal rates were above those in world markets. More important, since banks circumvented ceiling loan rates the policies were effective mainly on the deposit side. The dramatic increase in savings nonetheless flowed into saving deposits both because of liquidity and preferential tax treatment and the lack of alternative low-risk financial or real assets. The greatest cost was that the cosy system of regulated, low interest rates and other components of financial repression persisted too long. Inertia is a powerful force, and it was not until fundamental structural changes in Japan's macro economy occurred in the mid-1970s that the shift to deregulation and liberalization brought financial repression to an end.

Directed Credit and Long-Term Financing of Business Investment

Related to financial repression, but analytically and empirically separable, are policy issues of directed credit and the long-term financing of business investment. Should government policy make possible the provision of credit to selected activities or industries at below-market rates and with easy availability? If so, how should this be achieved—through government or private financial institutions? Who should bear the costs of such credit subsidies? What activities should receive the benefit? Certainly, a system of market-based interest rates without financial repression, but together with subsidized rates for certain activities is feasible, as American experiences in subsidizing credit for housing and student loans demonstrate.

A case can be made that relatively cheap credit is an efficient way to support an export-oriented development strategy, particularly where other policies or market distortions make for disincentives to exporting. Similarly, a case can be made for relatively cheap credit for infrastructure investment—public utilities, transportation, communications—where external economies are significant. The most controversial component of directed credit policies is toward selected 'strategic' winner industries (or smoothing the adjustment of declining industries)—that is, industrial policy. Cheap credit is an important instrument for industrial policy, in part because this form of subsidy is politically attractive since it is not readily transparent.

The Japanese government had a clear, straightforward, and relatively simple economic development and growth strategy as a follower nation behind Western Europe and the United States. Achieving this meant deepening industrialization as the basis of evolving comparative advantage and productivity growth; exports as the means to pay for essential imports, the balance of payments being the operative constraint on rapid growth; development of infrastructure to support industrial activity; and basic reliance on private enterprises and market mechanisms to carry out the strategy. Japan was to climb the development ladder by moving into ever more skill-intensive, higher technology, and capital-intensive industries in which entry of new firms was encouraged in order to create competition in domestic markets protected from imports. An important policy instrument was the directed use of credit.

Policies to provide preferential financing for exports had several dimensions. The Bank of Japan rediscounted short-term export trade bills at a low rate based on the New York market. The city banks played the major role by lending to their exporting industrial clients and especially to general and other trading companies that handled so much of the exports. The Export-Import Bank made longer-term loans (the functional equivalent of supplier credits) on preferential terms to foreign purchasers of Japanese exports, especially of ships, as well as machinery and other capital goods. The Japan Development Bank was created to support the development of targeted industries, and some of them were involved in export production. Overall, the subsidy involved in export credits was not large, and exports had to meet the competitiveness tests of international markets. The disciplinary role of the export strategy was important. Firms were judged on their readily observable export performance, so monitoring of performance was easy.

Industrial policy in the late 1940s and 50s targeted traditional basic industries: steel, coal, fertilizer, electric power, transport. This subsequently shifted to prospective winner industries (identified by the demand and industry structures of the United States and Western Europe), such as petrochemicals, aluminium, shipbuilding, commercial aircraft and, later on, computers and semi-conductors. The basic approach was to rely on large private firms to carry out the investment necessary to create a new, more sophisticated and more competitive set of industries, and for government policy to provide substantial incentives for key, targeted industries. A wide panoply of incentives were utilized; especially important were import protection, tax benefits, and preferential access to credit at below-average interest rates.

As in other countries, the Japanese government had two ways to shape the allocation of credit: it could lend funds under its direct control, and it could influence how private financial institutions lent theirs. Government lending was limited, but of some significance; government influence over private lending was indirect, relying on the financial and incentive structures created, rather than directly controlling the allocation of credit to specific industries, much less specific firms. The contrast with Korea is worth noting, as discussed by Nam and Kim in Chapter 13; see also chapters by Park, and Park and Kim in Patrick and Park (1994).

Certainly, the banks and other financial institutions funding large enterprises were well aware of the government's industry priorities; lending by the Japan Development Bank (JDB) and Export-Import Bank provided signals regarding government policy. However, Ministry of Finance directives to banks about which industries to lend to ended in the mid-1950s. The industrial patterns of bank lending were broadly congruent with government industrial priorities, but this was because such loans were viewed as profitable and safe. Bank lending was much lower to those few sectors deemed high priority by the government, but judged by the banks as being less safe and profitable, notably ocean shipping. Indeed Teranishi (in Patrick and Park, 1994) and others (see JDB, 1993) stress that even in the high growth era, in practice, a significant proportion of government funding went to facilitate the structural adjustment process of industries in trouble or decline, to which banks were much less willing to lend, such as coal mining once oil became a cheaper energy source.

Most subsidized directed credit programmes were carried out directly through government financial institutions. Theoretically, the government could have generated its loanable funds in a number of ways. In practice, it relied predominantly and increasingly on the allocation of postal savings deposits through the Ministry of Finance Trust Fund Bureau to government financial institutions. Financing by loans directly from the central bank, or indirectly through fiscal deficits, were adamantly rejected as that had been the major cause of the post-war inflation. Financing by running a government budget surplus, theoretically possible, was not feasible politically (in that respect the Taiwan experience may be virtually unique). The government and its financial institutions (most notably the Japan Development Bank) did borrow from abroad and serve as a *de facto* conduit for substantial World Bank loans for specific projects in the late 1950s and early 60s, but, in aggregate, the amounts were relatively low compared to total business fixed investment.

Reliance on, and utilization of, postal savings to finance directed credit programmes were important. It created the general perception that postal savings were being used productively, and that lending by government financial institutions was not inflationary. Significantly, it set a *de facto* floor on the interest rates at which government financial institutions could lend as they were required to cover the interest cost of postal savings deposits, any loan losses, and be profitable.

Perhaps most importantly, the specific loan decisions of government financial institutions were not subject to political or government bureaucratic interference; they were rather well insulated from the sorts of direct personalistic, corrupt, or politically motivated pressures that have plagued lending practices in so many other countries. Once broad policy parameters were established (export credits and the financing of fixed investment for infrastructure and the priority industrial sectors), credit was allocated by loan officers applying objective credit-worthiness criteria. They evaluated the quality and risk of projects, they required specific collateral, and they were tough on potential defaulting borrowers. Actual lending practices were conservative, and were extraordinarily successful: there were virtually no cases of outright borrower failure, loan losses were very low, and the government institutions did not lose money.

Japanese policy-makers recognized the central role of business fixed investment, and established an institutional structure and a set of policies to provide preferential access to long-term financing at relatively low cost for large firms, especially those in targeted sectors. The general theoretical rationales were market failure and term mismatch. On the one hand, uncertainty of success of investment projects and inadequate information to evaluate project feasibility and firm credit-worthiness made the long-term commitment of funds appear even more risky than in fact was the case. On the other hand, savers preferred safe, relatively short-term financial assets, especially since secondary markets were undeveloped and inflationary fears persisted.

Long-term funding was supplied primarily by term loans made by government financial institutions, the three long-term credit banks, city banks, trust banks, and life insurance companies (see Chapter 5 by Packer; and JDB, 1993). This was typically in the form of *de facto* syndication of project loans involving all these types of institutions. The private long-term credit banks, particularly the Industrial Bank of Japan (IBJ), played the central role, especially in project evaluation. Over time, the main bank developed a greater capability and took a larger role in project evaluation of its clients. Project loan syndication typically was organized by a long-term credit bank in close consultation with, or co-organization by, the borrowing firm's main bank. A close, symbiotic relationship developed between the main bank and the long-term credit banks, though the latter were careful to work with the full range of main banks, and not to identify particularly with any single Big Six keiretsu.

A significant source of long-term funding, in practice, not recorded in the data, was the rolling-over of short-term credits by the commercial banks, in particular by the main banks to their clients as an integral component of their long-term relationship. A main bank commitment to its relationship implied a promise to roll over short-term credits, and this was an important signal to the other lenders to its client.

By law and practice, the Japan Development Bank played a significant but more narrow role, complementary to private financial institutions. In 1961, 90 per cent of its outstanding loans for plant and equipment investment were to four industries—electric power, ocean shipping, coal mining, and iron and steel—while those of the long-term credit and other private sector banks were distributed over a far wider range of industries. The JDB's main broader role was as an information producer for borrowing firms, thereby reducing agency costs. Through its close relationship with the Ministry of International Trade and Industry (MITI) it could make firms aware of investment opportunities and government policies towards industry, especially those without stable long-term main bank relationships (Horiuchi and Sui, forthcoming).

The JDB has been a successful exception to the sad history in most developing market economies of government-owned development banks, precisely because it was constrained to be conservative in loan decisions. It had to require collateral, which it seized and sold upon default; syndicate its loans; and be profit-making. The JDB floor lending rate was at its cost of funds (6.5 per cent), while the nominal long-term interest rate for private financial institutions was 8.7–9.1 per cent (JDB, 1993, p. 131, table III–10); as a hypothetical market-clearing rate was somewhat higher, the JDB loan subsidy was on the order of 3 to 6 percentage points, substantial, but far less than in many developing market economies or TSEs.

Credit rationing was more significant in long-term finance than in the short-term loan market. Small firms were strongly discriminated against;

their demand far exceeded the supply made available to them. Even among large firms it mattered to some degree whether they were in priority industries or not. Access to credit, once project profitability, firm credit-worthiness and specific collateral requirements were met, was probably more important in promoting targeted industries than was the favourable interest rate on loans. The main point is that there were many potentially profitable projects, so lenders could behave conservatively; credit rationing directed funds to targeted rather than other uses. The relatively low long-term interest rates benefited companies both in cost terms and in providing a favourable numeraire for project evaluation.

The effective interest rate on long-term loans was positive, higher than for short-term loans, and yet lower than (implicit) market long-term rates. The average effective rate was reduced by the blending of rates on different components of the syndicated loan: lowest from government financial institutions, higher on the private long-term credit bank portion, and (probably) highest on the main bank, other city bank, and trust bank portions. The private financial institutions offset, at least partially, their low nominal long-term rate by requiring compensating balances and high fees for other financial services. Long-term credit banks required borrowing firms to purchase their financial debentures (their main source of funds) as a compensatory offset.

Policy support for relatively low long-term interest rates came from two sources: the flow-through of cheap postal savings deposits, and the provision of cheap credit by the Bank of Japan. The Bank of Japan provided for stable growth of the money supply primarily by lending to the city banks (and only the city banks), which chronically borrowed a substantial portion of their total funds from it. This policy was not inflationary because the government maintained a balanced budget, the increase over time in foreign exchange reserves was modest, and open market operations did not exist. Central bank loans and discounts were at low rates, and hence very profitable. Not only were they rationed (essentially by bank size as long as the banks followed the guidance of the authorities), but collateral was required. The city banks could use as collateral their holdings of financial debentures, the main source of funds for the private long-term credit banks. In this way, relatively low-cost funds flowed from the central bank through the city banks to the long-term credit banks.

The financing of fixed investment for targeted infrastructure projects relied on the same ultimate sources of inexpensive funds—postal savings and central bank credit—but through somewhat different mechanisms. The central government directly owned the national railroad and telecommunications systems, and local governments owned some utilities. They were financed by postal savings through the Fiscal Investment and Loan Program (FILP) of the Ministry of Finance. Privately owned utilities, most notably the nine regional electric power companies that service most of Japan, issued substantial amounts of bonds as well as engaged in long-term borrowing from the JDB and private institutions. Their bonds were also issued at relatively low interest rates and served as collateral for Bank of Japan loans to the city banks. Bond issue by industrial corporations was severely restricted; they were purchased disproportionately by the main bank. Secondary markets were discouraged for all bonds: government, financial, utilities, or corporate.[6]

BANKING SYSTEM ISSUES

The issues addressed above on financial system architecture and government financial policy impinge directly on the policies and behaviour of banks. Three issues at this more micro level are considered here: corporate governance; credit analysis, requisite human resources, and use of collateral; and the financing of small business.

The Governance of Banks

Who owns the banks, who controls them—in normal circumstances, and in times of bank distress? Governance involves control over management and determination of basic business strategy, while leaving day-to-day operations to the bank management. However, depending on the ownership structure and government policy, those who own or control may be much more intrusive, going as far as to shape specific loan decisions. Governance is particularly important in situations where financial markets are far from fully competitive; information is imperfect, asymmetrically distributed, costly, and monitoring is important; and management is a relatively autonomous agent. Under these circumstances—typical in almost all developing market economies and TSEs—banks inevitably will have a certain degree of market power.

A central issue, especially relevant in the context of developing economies and TSEs, is the potential for misuse of power—particularly intrusion of non-objective criteria into specific loan decisions—by owners, by the government, or by autonomous bank managers themselves. State-owned banks are directly subject to the policies and pressures of government bureaucrats, and at least indirectly to the political leadership, with all the potential for the infusion of political, rent-seeking, turf-maximizing

---

[6] Secondary markets for long-term financial instruments were very thin. The best indicator of market long-term interest rates was the secondary market yield on *den-densai*, the small-denomination bonds issued by the government-owned Nippon Telephone and Telegraph Company that had to be purchased by new telephone subscribers and which they often immediately sold over the counter. Those yields were typically substantially above nominal ceiling long-term rates and several percentage points above effective short-term bank loan rates.

or other non-objective criteria (see the chapters by Qian, Bhatt, and Hoshi, Kashyap and Loveman). At the other extreme is the situation where ownership is in the hands of an industrial family or business group. (Chapter 15 by Reynolds on Mexico describes the shift from private to state ownership and back again to business group ownership.) The danger there is that the business group will preferentially concentrate bank loans to its own enterprises, at the expense of potentially better loans, or minority shareholders, or depositor protection. Where stock ownership is widely dispersed, as in the case of large Japanese financial institutions, then ownership and control are separated with great power vested in autonomous management.

A basic objective of government prudential regulation and supervision, and disclosure requirements to enhance transparency, is to prevent the misuse of power by owners or managers. But, even when substantial ownership is private, in some countries the government exercises substantial control over bank lending and related policies and practices, not just to specific industries or for specific activities, but even to specified firms. (Korea, following its privatization of the commercial banks in the early 1980s, is a good example.) The presumption is that, even aside from questions of personal or institutional corruption, credit allocations and loan decisions by government bureaucrats are usually less efficient and effective than those made by bankers.

The managers of Japanese city banks and other large financial institutions have had great autonomy from shareholders. Stock is held predominantly by friendly industrial corporations to which the banks lend (and in turn hold shares), but in a highly dispersed fashion in which typically no single company holds much more than 1 per cent. Hostile take-over bids are unknown. The president and the board of directors (selected by the president) in almost all instances have been promoted from within, having risen over 25 years or longer through management ranks. The Ministry of Finance and Bank of Japan set the rules, supervise, and provide administrative guidance, but they do not intervene in bank decision-making or in personnel matters. The rules of the game of good behaviour were specific and precise, monitoring by the authorities was presumably intensive and informed, and the incentives for playing the game—greater growth of bank size and profits by obtaining branch licences and cheap central bank credit—were substantial.

In normal times, governance was subtle and indirect. The corporate ethos valued firm size; the status of a bank and its management depended more on its ranking in terms of assets than its return on assets or equity. Reputation and peer group pressure were important, reinforced by the system of delegated monitoring among the main banks. Despite substantial variance in profitability, banks moved along in a 'convoy' of relatively stable growth and ranking.

What happens when a bank falls into difficulty or distress? In the high growth era that was never really an issue, given the policy and structure; it occurred for only a few small banks, and then the Ministry of Finance intervened, reducing dividend rates, changing management, dispatching a Ministry of Finance official to take over. In the worst case, the economically failed small bank was easily merged into a larger bank as it had the valuable asset of deposit-collecting branch offices. All this was done quietly, discreetly, with little disclosure. With separation of ownership and managerial control, stockholders have had little power. Depositors, by far the largest creditors, had the power to exit at little cost, but they virtually never did so because they believed the safety of their deposits, and indeed of the bank, was guaranteed by the government.

It may well be that serious governance problems for Japan's banks will emerge in the 1990s. The overhang of bad loans seems to have put several large banks as well as many small ones, into serious difficulty. Merger will not be as easy a solution as earlier since deregulation has sharply eroded the franchise value of branch offices. Under these new circumstances, it will nonetheless be the Ministry of Finance, assisted by the Bank of Japan, that will exercise control, providing credit and fiscal incentives behind the scene. Hostile mergers through the stock market are very unlikely.

Credit Analysis and Human Resource Requirements

Providing finance requires that creditors have the capability to evaluate potential projects and corporate clients, and to carry out the provision and management of financial services. The single most important bank lending problem is how to assess the credit-worthiness of borrowers. Risk assessment is not easy under the best of circumstances as information is imperfect, asymmetric, and costly to obtain, and the future is uncertain; some possible states of nature create losses beyond the control of the enterprise or bank. The essence of credit analysis is monitoring, but monitoring under the main bank system is more than that. It includes evaluation of new projects, evaluation and some influence on the performance and behaviour of the enterprise's ongoing activities, and rescue or liquidation of a firm in acute distress.

Banking and finance skills are particularly important where the information infrastructure of accounting, auditing, economic intelligence, and disclosure are underdeveloped. The shortage of human resources is a serious problem, particularly in transforming socialist economies which have little history of such skill formation. One approach is initially to concentrate skilled staff at a few institutions—banks, development banks, institutional investment funds—and, over the longer run, build up the human resource base through training and on-the-job learning and spread it through a wider number of institutions.

A complementary approach is to require specific collateral against loans. Collateral reduces the need for costly credit analysis, particularly where information about the borrower or a project's prospects are limited. The key credit decision then depends on the ability to determine the market value of the asset used as collateral, in effect substituting knowledge about the collateral for knowledge about the borrower. The problem is that owners of assets are not necessarily the best entrepreneurs, developers of projects, and managers.

Japan's pre-war and war-time experience in operating and managing banks produced a fairly large number of commercial bank managers with substantial human skills. The IBJ provided an important reservoir of talent skilled in project appraisal and long-term financing; some were transferred to the JDB directly, which also received skilled staff from the Bank of Japan and other long-term financial institutions. All banks have made considerable effort recruiting outstanding university graduates and developing staff capabilities, reinforced by the systems of permanent employment, job rotation, and competition for promotion based also on seniority within a hierarchical system (see Chapter 9 by Sunamura). In particular, the main banks developed strong monitoring capabilities regarding their major corporate clients, especially for ongoing activities and in situations of trouble and difficulty. However, the immobile permanent employment system, especially the policy not to hire mid-career managers from other institutions, seriously inhibited the transfer of human skills from one bank to another.

Japanese financial institutions have a long history of requiring specific collateral, especially against long-term loans and bonds. Yet this has been regarded as one component of a bank-client relationship, not as a substitute for developing that relationship. Plant and equipment has typically been sequestered as collateral; since the scrap value was relatively low, project evaluation required cash flow analysis as well. In the high growth era there were enough entrepreneurs with good projects and with collateral (including third-party guarantees) that credit allocation worked effectively. The main bank system has always combined the use of collateral with intensive monitoring to ascertain a firm's future prospects, seeking to distinguish between potential borrowers with excellent growth prospects, but little collateral, and those simply with sufficient assets.

The Financing of Small Relative to Large Business

Japan's industrial development strategy was based on the assumption large firms were the engines of growth and should receive credit on preferential terms relative to everybody else. Accordingly, city banks were at the core of the financial system, and the regional banks, and particularly the smaller local financial institutions, were at the periphery. Because the function of the main bank system was to finance large industrial enterprises, it discriminated against smaller borrowers.

The financial institutions' behaviour was fundamentally rather conservative. They could afford to be conservative because, with such rapid growth of output and so many profitable investment opportunities, business demand for loans—short term as well as long term—was persistently strong and growing rapidly. Banks wanted to lend to safe companies, and they typically required collateral. Large enterprises were generally regarded as safer borrowers than small ones.

Yet small enterprises produced most of the industrial output and employed most of the industrial labour force. Most had access to short-term credit, but at relatively high cost; they were rationed out of substantial access to long-term funds. The government was little help: the JDB lent almost entirely to large firms; and the Small Business Finance Corporation came to play a significant role only from the 1970s (Calder, 1988). Smaller firms faced an oligopolistic loan market, reinforced by market segmentation rules and practices. They had to pay substantially higher effective interest rates, even after adjusting for transaction costs and risk; their compensating balances were much higher than those of large firms.

In fact, default risk was low because lenders required full collateral from small borrowers. When borrowers defaulted their collateral was seized and sold, so the actual loan losses by financial institutions lending to small business were small during the high growth era, less than 1 per cent. During this period, reflecting their respective degree of market power, in terms of return on equity, credit associations were the most profitable, then mutual savings banks (*sogo ginko*, which in 1987 were transformed into second-tier regional banks), regional banks and, least profitable of all, city banks. Market segmentation apparently resulted in less than optimal allocation of loans by firm size, despite an active inter-bank call market.

The main bank system, as defined throughout this book, was essentially only for large industrial firms, even though small enterprises typically claim some form of main bank relationship with their primary lending institution (see Chapter 8 by Horiuchi). Most fundamentally, there was no bank commitment to rescue or restructure a small firm in distress. The nature of the banking relationship was narrow; small firms did not issue bonds, have foreign exchange transactions, or generate other fee business, and banks did not own any of their equity. Much of the problem in lending to small business was the lack of information, the cost of obtaining it, and hence the difficulty in evaluating the credit-worthiness of small business borrowers and their collateral. Monitoring of company performance accordingly was far less thorough; the costs outweighed any benefits.

There were other important sources of small business credit, notably the huge amounts of trade credit. Large manufacturing firms and large trading companies became *de facto* financial intermediaries, borrowing from their main bank syndicate and providing credit to related subsidiaries, subcontractors, and wholesalers, since in the normal course of business they developed superior access to information about their creditworthiness.

Venture capital institutions to provide risk capital for new, small entrepreneurial start-ups did not exist in the high growth era, and have been slow to develop subsequently. New small firms had to finance themselves just like new firms everywhere: the owner's savings, borrowing against the owner's real assets, and credit guarantees by relatives and friends. Yet the entrepreneurial drive to set up one's own firm, to be one's own boss, is strong in Japan; every year more new small firms were established than in the United States, and every year more failed or otherwise exited. And some grew to become large and well known, such as Sony, Honda, and Kyocera.

LESSONS FROM JAPANESE FINANCIAL DEVELOPMENT

The main bank system was at the apex of the Japanese financial system in the high growth era and arguably still maintains that position. In important respects it has epitomized Japan's financial structure and policies. In the economic and financial environment of the high growth era the main bank system matured and flourished. It represented a successful solution to a key developmental problem: how to finance large industrial enterprises efficiently and effectively. Directly and indirectly, notably in cooperation with the long-term credit banks, the main banks were typically the single most important source of external finance, long term as well as short term, for most of Japan's large industrial enterprises. The specific merits of the main bank system as a model for other countries are discussed in more detail later in this section.

Even broader lessons can also be derived from the Japanese case of financial development, particularly in the post-war high growth era. The main bank system cannot be evaluated in isolation; it is a subset of the banking system which has constituted the core of the Japanese financial system. The acknowledged effectiveness of the Japanese financial system depended upon its institutional structure (financial architecture), government financial policy, and the macroeconomic policy environment, as already discussed. This does not mean that another country should aim to replicate the Japanese financial system in toto. It is necessary to identify the key issues and the relevance of the Japanese experience, or model, for dealing with them.

The lessons for financial institution development and for appropriate policies are essentially structural and longer run. Policy-makers must have some long-term (10 to 20 year) vision of what the financial system should be, and an understanding of the process by which these long-term objectives can be achieved. As stressed at the beginning of this chapter, the most effective institutional arrangements and policies depend critically on each country's own goals, its own history, and its current situation. It is important to remember that even in the economically most advanced countries, as recent finance theory has stressed, markets are incomplete, information is imperfect and costly to obtain, and it is not possible to write complete contracts covering all contingencies; the conditions in developing market economies and TSEs are much further removed from the neo-classical, perfectly competitive model.

A sceptical view of the stylized facts of the prototypical developing market economy is that it has a host of problems: macroeconomic instability; a limited institutional and physical infrastructure; low levels of economic, business, and financial information; quite imperfect markets with considerable market power and profound information asymmetries; weak banks and capital markets; and lack of human capital skills in finance and other areas. Typically, its government pursues low interest rate policies, restrictions on competition among financial institutions, and credit rationing; in other words, financial repression is moderate to severe. Accountability, in terms of sanctions and rewards for decisions, is not high; corruption, both personal and institutional, is a problem of some seriousness; and soft-budgeting practices, especially for large, state-controlled or 'strategic' enterprises, tend to misallocate resources and undermine macroeconomic stability. These difficulties are more extreme in the typical transforming socialist economy, which has a much more limited historical heritage of a market economy and its institutions, and a profound lack of requisite human skills. It is from this perspective that transferability of the Japanese experience should be considered.

General Lessons

Macroeconomic Stability

The most important general lesson, and not just from the Japanese experience, is that macroeconomic stability is essential to achieve rapid, sustained economic and financial development and, over time, a more open and competitive economic system with strong financial institutions. Control over inflation is essential for the development and effective functioning of the financial system. Most savers mainly demand safe, liquid financial assets (deposits) whose real value is not eroded by inflation; only as their wealth accumulates are they willing to diversify into longer-term and riskier assets.

Following the Occupation stabilization policy of 1949, Japan pursued a fiscal-monetary policy mix of fiscal tightness and rapid money-supply growth commensurate with price stability. The government budget was balanced, government debt issue was negligible, and the ratio of government debt to GNP was very low. This macroeconomic policy mix supported the modest role of the government in domestic demand and the central role of private sector finance, particularly bank loans, in funding business growth.

It is important in any country that there be enough political stability to reduce to reasonable levels both any uncertainties about major economic and social policies and the likelihood of disruption of ordinary economic activities. The Japanese experience was extraordinary in the degree of political stability achieved in 1955 by the alliance of moderate parties to form the Liberal Democratic Party, which was in power continuously until 1993. Perhaps equally important in the high growth era was the widespread consensus that government policy should focus on economic growth, a consequence in part of the dramatic loss of World War II.

Economic policy on the whole promoted the development of a competitive environment, particularly in product markets. Initially, producers were protected from imports; easy entry nonetheless resulted in quite competitive domestic markets, reinforced by the very size and rapid growth of the economy. There were less competitive sectors, and some became increasingly so as the economy grew: most notably, agriculture and wholesale and retail trade. Labour markets were, in principle, free, but the ever-growing demand of large firms for labour trained to their specific needs made the development of a permanent employment system efficient. The land and stock markets were, on the whole, competitive. Finance is most effective when ensconced in a competitive economy; it can respond to the right price signals. At the same time, finance itself was the slowest sector to develop competitive markets. However, at least initially, the regulatory restrictions on competition were strongly supportive of, and many would argue essential for, the development of a strong banking system (see the discussion below).

One consequence was the development of a producer-oriented society, but consumers and savers also benefited enormously, if indirectly. Japan's fast growth from the early 1950s to the mid-1970s generated rapid increases in wages, household incomes, and consumption. Japan's standard of living, despite many problems, rose far more rapidly than it ever had before and more rapidly than any other country in the world during that time period. There was an implicit social contract until late in the period whereby households accepted low yields on savings deposits and poor housing quality in exchange for a system that generated rapid growth in GNP and household incomes.

The Structure of the Financial System

The Japanese experience, and indeed that of all market economies, is that banks play a predominant role in business finance. Securities markets became a significant source of large enterprise finance only in the 1980s. The policy issue was whether large enterprise finance, particularly for plant and equipment investment, can be achieved effectively through a banking-based system. The Japanese main bank system, involving close coordination between city banks and long-term credit banks, has demonstrated that it can. Moreover, it suggests Japanese policy-makers were correct in rejecting US Occupation proposals to develop a corporate bond market as a major source of corporate finance.

There are several strands in the analysis. First, the demand for industrial long-term finance was particularly strong. As a consequence of both the destruction in World War II and their technology absorptive capabilities, firms in large-scale, capital-intensive (heavy and chemical) industries were in a good position to develop profitable projects. Second, there was a term mismatch. Savers were not prepared to purchase corporate bonds since their assets were limited; they well remembered the all-too-recent disastrous effects of inflation on bond portfolios, and they were risk averse, wanting to hold safe, short-term, liquid financial assets. Third, information about corporations was limited and it was difficult to assess risk. Institutions such as accounting, auditing, securities analysis, and credit rating agencies which support monitoring through a corporate bond market were under-developed or non-existent. Fourth, the human resource skills to evaluate the credit-worthiness of large corporations and their projects—to monitor—were in very scarce supply. It made sense to concentrate them in a relatively small number of institutions, namely the long-term credit banks and the city banks. Fifth, the Occupation induced the legal separation of commercial and investment banking. Because pre-war banks had underwritten corporate bond issues, they still had the human capital skills, while the securities companies (investment banks) had neither the experience nor the trained personnel. Even if the bond issue market had not been repressed, it is likely that the financial debentures of long-term credit banks would have been preferred to corporate bonds, so that the flow of funds, at least in the early years, would not have been so different.

Formally, Japan established a system of commercial banking, unlike Germany's universal banking. Yet Japanese banking incorporated several of the attributes of universal banking: establishment of a close long-term relationship with large industrial clients; arrangement of long-term as well as short-term finance; close monitoring of firms, from new project evaluation to ongoing performance to rescue restructuring in times of distress; and direct investment in the company's equity.

There is no definitive answer to the question whether the Japanese main bank model or the German universal bank model is more appropriate for developing market economies and TSEs. My view is that the Japanese model has the edge. (The lack of experience in underwriting securities issue is not a major practical problem where securities markets have not yet developed into a significant source of finance.) It has been argued that the German system involves cosier, more self-serving, oligopolistic relationships among a small number of banks and large firms. One aspect to which many attach considerable significance is the degree of bank ownership of a company's equity. Ownership certainly has symbolic value in Japan; the main bank is typically the largest bank shareholder of a firm. The power to exercise control directly is much less clear since ownership was limited first to 10 per cent and then reduced to 5 per cent in 1987. The lesson is that allowing banks to own non-controlling shares in companies is desirable where it is an important element in developing and maintaining the close bank-corporation relationship.

The Japanese banking system incorporated specialized financial institutions and segmented financial markets. The former may be appropriate for other economies; the latter may not. The system discriminated in favour of large industrial enterprises; city banks were presumed to provide them short-term and, increasingly, long-term loans, while long-term credit banks, trust banks, and insurance companies provided longer-term loans. Regional banks, mutual banks and credit associations financed medium and small enterprises, and agricultural cooperatives financed farmers. In both cases effective interest rates were substantially higher even when adjusted for risk (which was low because collateral requirements were high). The regulators and the ethos of bankers perpetuated this dynamic disequilibrium in segmented financial markets throughout the high growth era.

Market equilibrium analysis implies that small business enterprise investment was too low relative to large firms. The counter argument is that large firms were key agents of growth as the importers and improvers of technology, and as they diffused technology to smaller firms. My presumption is that most policy-makers in developing market economies and TSEs perceive large firms to be the engine of growth and their financing to be essential. Even if this is true, they should be aware of the need not to distort financial flows excessively away from smaller enterprises. Special attention needs to be given to creating and providing incentives for financial institutions to finance small business activities.

The three Japanese private long-term credit banks, especially the Industrial Bank of Japan, played a crucial role in financing large firm plant and equipment investment, not only in providing funds, but especially in examining credit-worthiness during project evaluation. They worked closely with the city banks in syndicating term loans for main bank clients. This was an effective division of labour until their respective capabilities and business strategies increasingly converged, especially in the deregulation and easy money environment from the 1970s, when private saving outstripped private investment. The Japanese experience suggests that a system of commercial banks and long-term credit banks working together is effective.

The respective roles of privately owned banks and other financial institutions, and of government financial institutions must also be examined. In many countries the government owns the major banks and long-term development finance institutions. In the long term, that is usually a mistake. It is difficult to insulate government-owned (or controlled) institutions from the political process, and decision-making is bureaucratic rather than market-oriented.

The Japanese experience demonstrates that an effective role can be found for government financial institutions, where their lending activities are focused, limited, and complementary to private financial institutions. Two factors were important to their success: they had to be profit-making institutions, and they had autonomy from government bureaucrats and politicians in loan decisions, which they based on objective credit-worthiness criteria of projected cash flow and specific collateral. In this respect the Japanese lesson is cautionary. It is not an accident that the Japanese Development Bank is one of the few cases of successful government development financial institutions.

An important reason for the success of Japanese government financial institutions is that they had access to cheap funds through the government's postal savings system, where deposit interest rates, as in private financial institutions, were subject to low ceilings. Postal savings, utilizing ubiquitous post office branches, are a cheap, convenient and effective way for a government to mobilize private saving. One danger of this access, which Japan avoided, is that postal savings become an easy way for the government to finance fiscal current expenditure rather than channelling the funds to productive private business investment. Another danger is that postal savings deposits directly compete, often on more favourable terms, with bank saving deposits, thereby channelling savings away from private financial sector intermediation. This did happen in Japan, in large part because the Postal and Telecommunications Ministry, rather than the Ministry of Finance, has had authority over postal savings.

Financial Public Policy Issues

Deposit Safety, Bank Safety, and Prudential Regulation

Public confidence in the banking system, and the financial system more broadly, is essential for successful financial development. Deposit safety is a high priority, particularly for household savers, who often are ill-informed about the conditions and trade-offs among risk, yield, and liquidity of various financial assets. Deposit insurance, or government guarantees that banks will not be allowed to go bankrupt, can ensure depositor protection.

The Japanese government pursued a conservative policy of guaranteeing banks against formal failure. While the guarantee was implicit, depositors and indeed all financial market participants fully believed that the regulatory authorities would not allow a bank to fail, much less let depositors take any default losses. When a problem bank emerged, the regulatory authorities would intervene and, where necessary, merge it into a stronger institution. Any bank was 'too big to fail'. In the turmoil of the early post-war period, this guarantee was essential and highly effective; an additional guarantee of deposit insurance was of marginal significance.

One dilemma of such strong bank safety guarantees is that they increase the moral hazard of banks taking excessive risks. To prevent this, and to reduce the government's financial exposure, the regulatory authorities have a range of policy options. They can require high minimum capital-asset ratios, exercise strong prudential regulation and effective supervision, or ensure bank profitability through constraints on competition. There is a danger that measures taken to restrict competition will result in rent-seeking behaviour and credit misallocation.

Japan legislated, but did not enforce, high capital adequacy rules, and actual ratios were low. A basic problem was that equity capital was short and the only effective way to increase bank capital was through retained earnings, achieved by making banks profitable and restricting dividend pay-out. Japanese policy-makers did constrain the terms of bank competition by restricting entry, segmenting markets, and setting a ceiling rate on deposits low enough to make deposit-based lending very profitable (but sufficiently high, combined with favourable tax treatment, to prevent potential depositors from fleeing to real assets).

Prudential regulation and effective supervision are essential in any banking system to prevent fraud, excessive risk-taking or other forms of bank mismanagement, and to enforce rules designed to enhance bank safety. Japanese regulatory controls and supervision were effective in the high growth era in ensuring bank safety and good performance. They were enforced both by valuable incentives (cheap central bank loans, new branch office licences) and potentially severe sanctions (dividend pay-out reduction, replacement of management, merger), in an environment in which bankers were willing to play the regulatory game with the Ministry of Finance. The regulatory authorities knew the actual conditions of every city, regional, trust and long-term credit bank (there were fewer than 90 in the high growth era), worked quietly to solve any problems through guidance, and seldom disclosed those problems to avoid undermining public confidence.

The Japanese public trusted the power, authority, and honesty of the Ministry of Finance and the regulatory framework and its administration. One cost was that it reinforced a non-transparent system of regulation by administrative guidance and informal negotiations between the banks and the Ministry of Finance, in what became cosy, non-arm's-length relationships. In countries where the public may be more sceptical of government bureaucrats, and as a long-run objective even for Japan, a transparent regulatory system is highly desirable, even necessary.

Low Interest Rate Policies and Financial Repression

Japanese experience provides two important lessons concerning financial repression. First, in comparison to many developing market economies and TSEs, the degree of Japanese financial repression was limited and modest. Ceiling interest rates were positive in real terms. Banks were able to adjust loan rates closer to market rates by requiring compensating balances, thereby reducing the likelihood of credit misallocation and rent-seeking behaviour. Despite restrictions on entry there were a significant number of banks, especially in the large enterprise loan market, so that a reasonably competitive environment apparently emerged. Banks were insulated from political and bureaucratic pressures in making specific loan decisions. In sum, Japanese policy and behaviour apparently kept the adverse effects of even the modest degree of financial repression to a minimum.

Second, low interest rates, the wide interest rate spread, and the restrictions on competition effectively subsidized the strengthening of what, in the early 1950s, was a fragile Japanese bank system. In this respect, the rents from limited financial repression were used beneficially for institutional development. Many, though by no means all, experts on Japanese banking and financial markets deem this support to have been essential for the building of a strong banking system and, by extension, a strong main bank system. It also has been argued that the (modest) credit rents some categories of borrowers obtained were constructively indexed to objective, performance-enhancing indicators.

If the present situation in a developing market economy is that the degree of financial repression is moderate to severe—real interest rates are very low or negative, competition is limited, and credit rationing is substantial—then the lesson from the Japanese experience is that less financial repression is better. The trade-off between the benefits of institutional development and the costs of credit misallocation and rent-seeking behaviour have to be weighed carefully, and the tendency to excessive financial repression resisted. Moreover, as the banks become stronger, the need to subsidize institutional support decreases and the degree of financial repression should be reduced accordingly. To some extent this occurs through market forces as financial market participants find loopholes. In addition, the government will find it desirable to pursue policies of financial deregulation and liberalization. One danger, as was the case in Japan, is that deregulation will be delayed because of bureaucratic inertia and desire to retain power, and the creation of vested interests in the regulated system.

Directed Credit

It is assumed that the government's development strategy will place priority on certain activities which will be subsidized in various ways, including preferential allocation of credit at lower interest rates. The issues involve the type of activity, the degree of subsidy, the nature of the credit allocation mechanism and process, and the potential inflationary consequences of the funding process.

The Japanese government directed credit to promote exports, build physical infrastructure essential for industrial growth, and develop certain strategic or targeted industries. In comparison with similar programmes in most developing market economies and TSEs, these Japanese subsidies were relatively low. Moreover, the credit allocation process was objective, and successful performance was a requisite for continued support. Export trade credit and loans for export production were not differentially subsidized by sector, with the exception of Export-Import Bank term loans for sales of ships and machinery. Infrastructure investment was financed directly through government budgets, by government financial institutions, and to some extent by private financial institutions (notably for the private electric power companies). Interest rates were below long-term credit bank rates, but were positive; government financial institutions were not allowed to lose money and they relied on postal savings, which set a floor on their lending rates.

The role of industrial policy in the development process is more controversial. So too is detailed evaluation of Japan's experience. The most significant facts of the Japanese experience are that while some of the winner industries of the high growth era obtained directed credit, others did not, and there were some cases of failure in target selection. Lending by government financial institutions was the major form of subsidized, directed credit and was initially important, but became much less so from the 1960s. Government influence over private bank lending was indirect, relying on the financial structure and its incentives rather than on direct control of credit allocation. While industries were targeted, specific firms within them were subject to standard credit evaluation and project analysis. A major proportion of directed credit for plant and equipment investment in the 1950s went to four industries, iron and steel, electric power, marine shipping and coal mining. Two of these, shipping and coal, became inefficient, declining industries from the 1960s, and absorbed a large proportion of Japan Development Bank loans because private banks judged them unattractive. In the 1960s, the proportion of targeted loans in total plant and equipment investment finance decreased substantially, and was not significant thereafter.

The basic features of Japan's directed credit policy determined its success, and are directly relevant for other countries. They included: a relatively broad targeting concept (industries not firms); credit allocation by bankers using objective credit-worthiness criteria; little interference by government officials or politicians; positive real interest rates, with relatively modest degrees of subsidy; implementation primarily through government financial institutions; reliance on private savings mobilized through the postal savings system; and utilization of the private institutional structure of long-term credit banks, city banks (especially to their main bank clients), and trust banks for the provision of long-term finance. A further important lesson is that government financial institutions and their management must be held accountable. In Japan they were not allowed to be unprofitable, and had to be severe in requiring collateral and taking it in instances of loan default. They worked with, and were supplementary to, private financial institutions, rather than being little more than the agents of government bureaucrats who determined specific allocations of 'policy loans'.

Avoidance of Rent-Seeking and Corruption

Policy-makers must confront the reality that in some economies corruption is a serious problem. In the financial sphere, opportunities for rent-seeking and corruption are endemic when loan interest rates are set far below market-clearing rates, credit is rationed, and the regulatory environment is weak. There are two levels of problem: individual and institutional.

The finance literature emphasizes the importance of prudential supervision and of transparency to prevent individual banks, firms, or persons from engaging in excessive risk-taking, favouritism, insider exploitation of asymmetric information, or fraud and payment of bribes to obtain rationed credit on favourable terms. Institutionalized corruption is more systemic in nature; it involves the financing of politics and the political leadership through illegal payments in exchange for official decisions to have credit allocated on preferential terms to favoured firms. In effect, credit rents are created by government policy and used in part to support the government leadership. This is the central political economy issue of finance; it has not been subject to extensive empirical research for obvious reasons.

The most effective way to deal with corruption is to eliminate credit (and other regulatory) rents by promoting a high degree of market competition supported by an appropriate legal and institutional framework. This sharply reduces the opportunity for rent-seeking behaviour. However, achievement of a highly competitive market economy is an ideal, and certainly will not be achieved overnight. In finance, the degree of corruption is directly related to the degree of financial repression, which creates the regulatory credit rents.

Financial repression in Japan was modest and limited. Credit rents were relatively low. Specific credit allocation decisions were insulated from political pressure or bureaucratic interference, and were made by bankers using objective criteria of collateral and cash flow. With the exception of government financial institutions, effective interest rates on loans were only modestly below market-clearing rates. Legal, economic, and social sanctions against various forms of morally hazardous behaviour were severe, prudential regulation was strong, and bank supervision was effective. These are the lessons for other nations.

Thus, despite a few notable scandals, the Japanese financial system, by and large, has not been subject to individual corruption. The degree of institutional corruption, hidden illegal donations to politicians and political parties by financial institutions, has not been perceived by most Japanese to have been an intolerable problem. However, this is a murky area. The nature of the relationships between Japanese banks, large and small, and politicians, national and local, is apparently close and particularly opaque, yet to be subject to substantive investigative reporting. It is worth noting that none of the scandals of recent years regarding the transfer of regulatory rents by businesses to politicians and bureaucrats (government procurement, trucking route licences, terms of IPO issue) have involved banks.

The Main Bank System as a Model for Financing Large Industrial Enterprises

In any market-based financial system banks play a major role, certainly in the financing of small and medium firms and, except for the United States, in the financing of large industrial enterprises as well. The Japanese main bank system epitomizes, in many respects, the success of the Japanese banking system in mobilizing savings and allocating them effectively through loans to business, particularly large enterprises. It is an especially appropriate model for bank financing of large enterprises in many developing market and transforming socialist economies.

The essential features of the main bank model are micro. It is a low-cost, efficient and effective institutional solution to the problems of costly, imperfect, and asymmetric information about borrower credit-worthiness, given the reality that markets are not, and cannot be, perfectly competitive and complete (Stiglitz, 1991). In a market-based credit-rationing model, lenders classify borrowers—albeit imperfectly—into categories by degree of risk (credit-worthiness) in order to overcome adverse selection and incentive problems (Stiglitz and Weiss, 1981). The least risky categories are preferred customers; the most risky simply do not get loans. The degree of rationing in intermediate categories depends on the supply of loanable funds, the quality of information for credit analysis and, to some degree, on the effective interest rate it is possible to charge.

In a regulatory model of credit rationing, government influence on the effective interest rate has some significance on the terms of bank loans; and its policies or signals indicating which activities or industries are of high or low priority influence bank thinking as to which categories firms should be assigned. A regulatory credit rationing framework enhances the power of the bank *vis-à-vis* the borrower by widening the gap between demand and supply, and makes the establishment of a main bank relationship even more valuable to both bank and firm.

This book emphasizes that the essence of the main bank system is the ability of the bank to monitor effectively and to arrange for funding for those large industrial clients with which it has a particularly close and sustained main bank relationship. The city banks worked closely with the long-term credit banks in new project evaluation and provision of long-term funding through the main bank relationship. The main bank took responsibility both for gathering and producing information on the ongoing activities of its client, and for providing the client information and advice (in effect, management consulting services) to enhance enterprise performance. It also took responsibility for, and a disproportionate share of the cost of, rescuing, restructuring or liquidating a firm in distress. These monitoring functions are essential in any financial system. They constitute the core of what can, and in many cases should, be transferred to other countries as they develop their own banking systems.

The most distinctive feature of the Japanese main bank system is its central role in the restructuring of large firms in distress, at considerable cost to the bank. This has proved to be a cheap and effective restructuring mechanism. Rescue is by no means automatic: the main bank makes a rational calculation as to whether the firm is worth more by liquidating its assets or by restructuring its activities and financial position and continuing in operation. Liquidation is a complex and gradual process, ultimately involving merger into a stronger firm without going through formal bankruptcy. The bank requires a detailed financial and business plan, into which its own staff provide significant input; it has the power to replace management; and it is able to determine (through negotiation with other creditors) the firm's new financial structure. Inevitably, there is considerable uncertainty in estimating a firm's potential future prospects; the presumption is that a close main bank relationship ensures the firm will be treated more generously than severely within that range. The great danger is that of soft budgeting, of providing new funds for the continued operation of firms that are not economically viable and should be liquidated. Japanese banks in the high growth era avoided the problems of soft budgeting, with only a few mistakes. The lessons are that a commitment to rescue and restructure should be conditional upon economic feasibility, the restructuring should be carefully planned and implemented, and the main bank should be tough in exercising its leadership both *vis-à-vis* the firm and other creditors.

There were three direct incentives for Japanese banks to seek out main bank relationships. The most important was the rent (or return) derived from investing in information about the borrower, and hence the reduction in risk premium for good borrowers. The need to recoup monitoring costs even in a relatively competitive short-term loan market was eased by the system of delegated monitoring among banks. Second, the main bank received preference in providing various lucrative financial services to the borrower, including transactions deposits, foreign exchange business, trustee and other fee business, and the business of subsidiaries and affiliated companies. These financial services markets were not completely competitive; relatively high prices were set by regulation or oligopolistic behaviour. Third, main bank ownership of corporate enterprise equity, even in the relatively limited amounts allowed, provided incentives to and benefits from monitoring (Kim, 1991), and signalled the closeness of the relationship. Further, it can be argued that the regulatory framework and the modest degree of financial repression effectively subsidized the institutional strengthening of banks in general, and made them more willing and able to develop main bank relationships. Certainly, the main bank system, which evolved in response to the economic and regulatory environment rather than as a consequence of direct government policies, well met the interests of the government in promoting large enterprises as the engine of growth.

Issues in Transferring the Main Bank System

The relevance, usefulness and transferability of the Japanese main bank model has to be placed in the context of a broader range of issues of finance and banking development. Moreover, an effective main bank system cannot be created overnight. As with other types of institutional development, it takes time for learning, development of skills, creation of knowledge, and growth.

The governance of the large banks that will be engaged in main bank relationships raises issues of bank ownership, and control of bank policy towards both basic business strategy and specific loan decisions. Concentrated ownership makes for shareholder control. The new privatization of Mexican banks places ownership and control in the hands of business groups; it is not yet known whether prudential regulation will be effective in preventing the owners from manipulating bank lending for their own benefit. In India, commercial banks and development banks are owned by the government; they are bureaucratic and far from efficient. In China and Poland, the banking systems are government owned and nascent. In Korea, bank equity ownership is dispersed, while control has been vested in the government to a considerable degree, and this has had a dominant influence on bank policies, even at the level of certain specific enterprise and business group loan decisions. In Japan, bank ownership is widely dispersed (except for a few small banks) and, in normal circumstances, management has great autonomy within the general parameters and guidelines set by the Ministry of Finance.

Management autonomy, a feature also of most large Japanese industrial enterprises, has worked well in Japanese banking. Their incentives and sanctions, and insulation from politically motivated government pressures or self-serving pressures of concentrated stockholders, have enabled them to allocate credit effectively. Yet it is by no means clear that management autonomy in bank governance will operate nearly as effectively in different institutional and policy environments. There are dangers that a self-serving management may expropriate rents for its own benefit. Perhaps the most significant lesson is that bank governance is an important matter since the efficient operation and effective credit allocation of banks is at stake.

Related both to corporate governance and the structure of the financial system is the issue of where scarce human capital in banking skills should be concentrated initially, and how they should be expanded and diffused over time. In early post-war Japan, project evaluation skills were initially concentrated by virtue of history in the long-term credit banks, especially the Industrial Bank of Japan. Over time, city banks, particularly those with strong and extensive main bank relationships, developed project evaluation skills. City bank staff had some skill in monitoring the ongoing operations of their clients; over time, particularly through the requirements of the main bank relationship, they built up those skills. Those with a substantial number and range of main bank relationships also developed skills in restructuring clients in distress, accumulating learning by doing and documenting. The lessons suggested by Japanese experience are that scarce human skills might initially be concentrated in a relatively small number of institutions, that skilled personnel should be trained up, and that over time they should be diffused among a sufficiently large number of non-governmental institutions so that information quasi-rents and oligopoly market power are reduced.

The main bank system is effective in overcoming problems of project evaluation and lack of information about a client's credit-worthiness. Nonetheless, where the basic information is weak or where banking skills are lacking, asset-based lending is a conservative complement to—rather than substitute for—cash flow and other techniques of performance analyses. During the asset price boom of the late 1980s, asset-based lending dominated cash flow analysis for many real estate projects; the expectation was that prices would only go up, which has proved to be an incorrect and costly assumption.

The Japanese banking system since its modern beginning in the 19th century has had a history of requiring specific collateral for loans, particularly longer-term loans, and of selling that collateral when loans were defaulted. Despite potential inefficiencies, in that entrepreneurs with excellent projects but inadequate collateral are rationed out of the credit market, requiring collateral enhances bank safety and reduces borrower (and lender) moral hazard. In many developing market economies and TSEs, these benefits probably outweigh the costs. An even more conservative approach given high risks, especially in TSEs, is initially to limit corporate finance to equity ownership, then non-bank lending, and eventually limited fully collateralized, self-liquidating short-term loans (McKinnon, 1991).

The main bank system is a particularly intensive and close form of relationship banking. The relationship in Japan is multidimensional and comprehensive. It includes equity ownership, is based on substantial trust by both sides, and involves careful bank monitoring. The main bank leadership role in rescue and restructuring of a firm in distress is an important distinctive feature. As so defined, the main bank system applies in Japan only to the financing of large industrial corporations listed on a stock exchange. Smaller companies have a less intensive form of relationship banking, which they also refer to as having a main bank, but the bank *ex ante* commitment to rescue and restructure is limited, if it exists at all. But this does not mean that the financing of small business is unimportant: quite the contrary. In the high growth era, and even at present, smaller non-listed firms produce most manufacturing output and other industrial value added, and are the predominant source of employment. One way or another, their growth has been financed. The lesson is that policy-makers must recognize the role of smaller enterprises and ensure that the financial structure provides funds to them.

The main bank system can and does work well in a deregulated, competitive financial environment, as shown by the Japanese experience since the mid-1970s. It was the major main banks that pressured the Ministry of Finance to deregulate. Under changed domestic and international market conditions they saw new opportunities and believed (correctly) in their superior abilities to compete. They had to adjust to the shifting of some major clients from bank loans to securities market issue, and the main bank relationship with some of them loosened and changed form.

Does the main bank system represent an intermediate stage of large enterprise finance, in place only until economies grow and mature, and securities markets become the more efficient mechanism? The development of a more competitive environment and the rise of an effective securities issue market will not result in the demise of the main bank system, but will transform it somewhat. A subset of very large, successful, Japanese companies no longer need a deep, substantive relationship with a main bank; they are able and willing to finance internally or to utilize less expensive securities finance. Although they will become increasingly independent, many large industrial companies will want to continue their well-established main bank relationship for its mutual shareholding and financial service features. Smaller listed enterprises, without high credit agency ratings, have relied upon main bank guarantees for their bond issues; the main bank continues to monitor, but for fees rather than income from loans. As the 1990s progress, some banks may well end their main bank relationship with certain smaller, weaker, less-attractive listed enterprises, selling off their equity holdings in the process. However, these are the companies for which main bank monitoring services create the most value, so the main bank relationship is likely to be shifted from one bank to another. Only those companies where the risks, and costs, of potential distress are high will be excluded from (rationed out of) the main bank system altogether. They will then be potential candidates in an emergent take-over market. On the other hand, banks are likely to seek out new main bank relationships, including equity holdings, with unlisted, smaller companies with good growth prospects that are candidates for public listing (Packer, 1993). Thus, the main bank monitoring function will continue to be important for all but a relatively small proportion of large companies.

Special Problems of the Transforming Socialist Economies

The transforming socialist economies can learn much from the Japanese historical, institutional, and policy experience of financial development and growth. As they succeed in making the transition to market economies, Japan's high growth era will be particularly relevant. In their process of transition, the TSEs face many problems similar to those of Japan in the early post-war period of dislocation and transition to democracy and a market economy. Japan had to deal with severe problems of shifting from armaments to civilian goods production, rampant inflation, very limited trade and stringent exchange controls, a virtually insolvent banking system, and many insolvent large enterprises due to a bad (government-repudiated) debt overhang. How Japan solved these problems offers insight into good macroeconomic policies and to the resolution of soft budgeting and debt overhang difficulties (see Teranishi, 1993). There are major differences to keep in mind, however. Japan had long experience as a private market economy and a quite well-developed institutional infrastructure, only briefly interrupted by war-time controls and economic planning. It had a reasonable supply of human capital skilled in commercial and development banking. The early post-war

Allied Occupation was an external force which could impose pro-market, pro-democracy changes in institutions, policies, and practices, though to be successful they ultimately had to be acceptable to Japanese policy-makers and the general public, as in fact almost all were.

The important questions are: what can the TSEs learn from the architecture and policies of the Japanese financial system and, congruent with the purposes of this study, from the main bank system? The answers depend on the particular problems policy-makers face in each TSE, as are well reflected in the chapters on China and Poland. There is a burgeoning literature on the appropriate financial architecture and policies for TSEs, much of it generated by the World Bank (see for example Caprio and Levine, 1992, as well as McKinnon, 1991). It is not the purpose of this chapter to review and assess that literature, or to judge what might be the best model of financial structure and policy for TSEs.

We can say that the Japanese experience represents a good model for the TSEs in several essential respects. It is a banking-based system, and at this stage of TSE development, banking is a more efficient mechanism for industrial finance for large enterprises than the securities market (Corbett and Mayer, 1992). Active stock markets apparently will develop relatively early in many TSEs as a result of the privatization process of large state enterprises. These are likely to be trading markets, useful for stockholder liquidity and for the function of price discovery. However, they will not be markets for substantial new fund-raising through enterprise stock or bond issue; the uncertainties are too great, the information too poor, the risks too high.

Bank monitoring, as based on the Japanese main bank model, will more efficiently and effectively overcome information problems for lenders and, in the process, instruct enterprises in the basics of cash flow analysis, cost accounting, and other internal information-generating systems essential for creating viable firms. The creation of securities markets will facilitate the effectiveness of a main bank system by more readily providing the opportunity for bank ownership of enterprise equity, thereby strengthening the incentives for deep monitoring and for commitment to take the leadership in rescue (or liquidation) of firms in distress.

TSEs have two particularly important problems: the overhang of state enterprise accumulated bad debt, a problem compounded when the debt is held by financial institutions rather than the government; and continued financing of economically non-viable large enterprises (soft budgeting) for political, social or other reasons. The banking system, or a main bank system, cannot solve these problems; they are essentially political in nature. Most of the costs of accumulated past bad debts will have to be absorbed by the government (society). If non-viable enterprises are to continue to receive financial or other subsidies, it should be done directly through the government budget rather than indirectly, and often in hidden ways, through financial institutions. If banks, or any financial institutions, are to be effective monitors and allocators of credit, they have to be prepared and able to deny funding to poorly performing enterprises, whether state or privately owned. This may well be the greatest impediment to developing an effective banking system in TSEs. A further dilemma is the lack of human skills; many financial officers in TSEs have experienced only soft, not hard, budgeting.

How much control over large industrial enterprises should banks have? There is no easy answer; the financial architects for each TSE will have to take into account the particular country's circumstances. In the early stages there is probably some danger of too little control, of relatively limited relationships and monitoring. At the other extreme there is very much the danger of too great control, either by the banks themselves or, more likely, as instruments of the government (for example, Korea and India). In between the extremes are the Japanese main bank and German universal bank models.

The choice between Japanese and German models of very close relationship banking will depend on a country's specifics of history, institutions, and values. What can be said is that the German and Japanese types of bank-based finance are similar, and each has performed well in its own context.

The main bank system is not a panacea: form without substance is usually a recipe for disaster. To be successful it must be buttressed by appropriate policies and behaviour: good prudential regulation and effective supervision; competitive financial as well as goods markets; and strong sanctions against poor performance. A very real problem is to devise a structure and policies that minimize opportunities for rent-seeking and corruption. Even aside from information asymmetries, the transition process in TSEs has been creating huge rents in the arbitrage between regulated and market prices, allocations by licensing and rationing (especially credit rationing), and the privatization process of state enterprises and assets.

Given the reality of information imperfections, costs, and asymmetries, institutional mechanisms for monitoring within, and in support of, a generally competitive environment are essential. The Japanese structure of a dozen or so nationwide city banks and three long-term credit banks as the major financiers of large enterprises led to workable competition, despite some constraints and distorted incentives. Fewer institutions would have resulted in greater oligopolistic behaviour. A further lesson is the importance of the constraint that *all* financial institutions, government owned as well as private, be profitable.

CONCLUSION

'What has worked for Japan is what works everywhere: thrift, honesty, hard work, education, property rights, a willingness to sacrifice for tomorrow, and strong families that take good care of children.' (Rauch, 1992, p. 110.)

There is no magic to Japan's economic and financial success. The Japanese financial system and its main bank system have evolved over more than 40 years and more in response to economic development and growth, occasional profound shocks, and the deepening of financial markets and financial intermediation. The systems also reflect basic government decisions about the appropriate financial structure and policies to achieve broader developmental objectives and to support the financial system. For the developing market economies and the transforming socialist economies, Japanese experiences of early post-war and the high growth era to the early 1970s are particularly relevant and useful.

The problems and difficulties the Japanese financial system and its banks face in the 1990s, in the aftermath of the bursting of the speculative asset boom bubble of 1986–90, do not undermine the fundamental lessons of the Japanese case. What that experience demonstrates is that even strong systems and institutions, not only banks but their regulators, can fall prey to collective myopia, and that greed in periods of speculative mania can outweigh rational, conservative calculation of project viability, borrower credit-worthiness, and collateral value.

For policy purposes in other countries, understanding of Japanese finance should be at three levels: how the Japanese system operated; how the banking system operated; and how the main bank system of close and special relationships with large industrial enterprises operated. The lessons are both positive and cautionary.

While the minimal package of institutions and policies necessary for an effective transfer of the Japanese main bank system cannot be precisely specified, as a practical policy matter that may not be necessary. A great deal depends on the financial architecture and policies being pursued in the transferring country. Very few are now pursuing policies whereby interest rates are market-determined, entry is relatively easy, a bond issue market is encouraged, and financial market competition is vigorous. There is a debate, in principle, over the benefits and costs of Japanese policies of low interest rates, repression of the bond market, and restrictions on competition. From the perspective of developing market economies and the TSEs, the important points are that the Japanese degree of financial repression was modest, real interest rates and other incentives were positive, there was considerable competition, credit allocation was based on objective, efficiency-based criteria without substantial outside interference, and corruption was low.

The most important lesson from this study is that the Japanese main bank system is not only a relevant and useful model for large industrial enterprise finance, it may well be better for developing market economies and transforming socialist economies than other models.

REFERENCES

ANCHORDOGUY, MARIE. 1989. *Computers, Inc.: Japan's Challenge to IBM*. Cambridge MA: Harvard University Press.

AOKI, MASAHIKO. 1988. *Information, Incentives, and Bargaining in the Japanese Economy*. Cambridge: Cambridge University Press.

CALDER, KENT E. 1988. *Crisis and Compensation: Public Policy and Political Stability in Japan, 1949–1986*. Princeton: Princeton University Press.

CAPRIO, GERARD JR. and ROSS LEVINE. 1992. 'Reforming Finance in Transitional Socialist Economies.' Working Paper 898, Country Studies Department, World Bank, Washington DC, April.

CARGILL, THOMAS F. and SHOICHI ROYAMA. 1988. *The Transition of Finance in Japan and the United States: A Comparative Perspective*. Stanford: Hoover Institution Press, Stanford CA.

CORBETT, JENNY and COLIN MAYER. 1992. 'Financial Reform in Eastern Europe: Progress with the Wrong Model.' *Oxford Review of Economic Policy* 7(4).

DORE, RONALD P. 1986. *Flexible Rigidities: Industrial Policy and Structural Adjustment in the Japanese Economy 1970–80*. Stanford CA: Stanford University Press.

FRIEDMAN, DAVID. 1988. *The Misunderstood Miracle: Industrial Development and Political Change in Japan*. Ithaca NY: Cornell University Press.

FRY, MAXWELL J. 1988. *Money, Interest, and Banking in Economic Development*. Baltimore MD: Johns Hopkins University Press.

GENTHER, PHYLLIS. 1990. 'A History of Japan's Government–Business Relationship: The Passenger Car Industry.' Ann Arbor MI: Center for Japanese Studies, University of Michigan.

GERLACH, MICHAEL. 1992. *Alliance Capitalism: The Social Organization of Japanese Business*. Berkeley: University of California Press.

HORIUCHI, AKIYOSHI and QING-YUAN SUI. 1993. 'The Influence of the Japan Development Bank Loans on Corporate Investment Behavior.' *Journal of the Japanese and International Economics* 7(4).

Japan Development Bank, Japan Economic Research Institute. 1993. *Policy-Based Finance: The Experience of Postwar Japan*. Tokyo, January.

KIM, SUN BAE. 1991. 'Lenders cum Shareholders: How Japanese Banks Financed Rapid Growth.' PhD diss., University of Toronto.

KOMIYA, RYUTARO, and others, eds. 1988. *The Industrial Policy of Japan*. San Diego CA: Academic Press.

KOSAI, YUTAKA. 1986. *The Era of High-Speed Growth—Notes on the Postwar Economy*. Tokyo: University of Tokyo Press.

MCKINNON, RONALD I. 1973. *Money and Capital in Economic Development*. Washington DC: The Brookings Institution.

NAKAMURA, TAKAFUSA. 1981. *The Postwar Japanese Economy—Its Development and Structure*. Tokyo: University of Tokyo Press.

OKIMOTO, DANIEL I. 1989. *Between MITI and the Market*. Stanford CA: Stanford University Press.

PACKER, FRANK. 1993. 'Venture Capital, Bank Shareholding, and the Certification of Initial Public Offering Evidenced from the OTC Market in Japan.' PhD diss, Columbia University, New York.

PATRICK, HUGH. 1966. 'Interest Rates and the Grey Financial Market in Japan.' *Pacific Affairs*, Winter 1965–66.

——, ed. 1986. *Japanese High Technology Industries: Lessons and Limitations of Industrial Policy*. Seattle: University of Washington Press.

PATRICK, HUGH and HENRY ROSOVSKY, eds. 1976. *Asia's New Giant: How the Japanese Economy Works*. Washington DC: The Brookings Institution.

PATRICK, HUGH and YUNG-CHUL PARK, eds. 1994. *The Financial Development of Japan, Korea and Taiwan: Growth, Repression and Liberalization*. New York: Oxford University Press.

RAMSEYER, J. MARK and FRANCES MCCALL ROSENBLUTH. 1993. *Japan's Political Marketplace*. Cambridge MA: Harvard University Press.

RAUCH, JONATHAN. 1992. *The Outnation: A Search for the Soul of Japan*. Boston: Harvard Business School Press.

ROSENBLUTH, FRANCES. 1989. *Financial Politics in Contemporary Japan*. Ithaca NY: Cornell University Press.

SAMUELS, RICHARD J. 1987. *The Business of the Japanese State: Energy Markets in Comparative and Historical Perspective*. Ithaca NY: Cornell University Press.

SHAW, EDWARD S. 1973. *Financial Deepening in Economic Development*. New York: Oxford University Press.

STIGLITZ, JOSEPH E. 1991. 'Government, Financial Markets, and Economic Development.' National Bureau of Economic Research Working Paper 3669, April.

STIGLITZ, JOSEPH and ANDREW WEISS. 1981. 'Credit Rationing in Markets with Imperfect Information.' *American Economic Review* 71:393–410 (June).

SUZUKI, YOSHIO. 1980. *Money and Banking in Contemporary Japan*. New Haven CT: Yale University Press.

——. 1986. *Money, Finance and Macroeconomic Performance in Japan*. New Haven CT: Yale University Press.

——, ed. 1987. *The Japanese Financial System*. Oxford: Oxford University Press.

TERANISHI, JURO. 1990. 'Financial System and Industrialization of Japan: 1900–70.' *Banco Nazionale del Lavoro Quarterly Review* 174:309–42 (September).

——. 1993. 'Emergence and Establishment of the Financial System in Postwar Japan—Government Intervention, Indirect Financing and the Corporate Monitoring System.' Paper presented at a Seminar on Public Policy during Japan's Rapid Growth, World Bank, Tokyo, 25 January.

YAMAMURA, KOZO and YASUKICHI YASUBA, eds. 1987. *The Political Economy of Japan*, vol. 1: *The Domestic Transformation*. Stanford CA: Stanford University Press.

12

The German Banking System and its Impact on Corporate Finance and Governance

THEODOR BAUMS

The task of this chapter as originally described in the outline of the current project was to compare the German banking system, as one type of 'relationship banking', with the Japanese main bank system. This was, of course, not simply meant in the sense of a mere description and comparison of different institutions. A meaningful contribution has to look instead at the functions of a given banking system as a provider of capital or other financial services to their client firms, to ask in what respect one or the other system might be superior or less efficient, and to analyse the reasons for this. A thorough analysis would have to answer questions such as, for instance: to what extent investment is financed by long- or short-term bank loans; whether German banks—because of specific institutional arrangements like owning equity, having seats on company boards or having other links with their borrowers—have informational or other advantages that make bank finance cheaper or more easily available; how such banks behave with respect to financial distress and bankruptcy of their client firms; and what their exact role is in corporate governance.

Banking systems and bank-firm relationships concern corporate governance as well as corporate finance. After a brief analysis of the structure of the German banking system and its special traits, we turn to the question of whether, and to what extent, equity holdings of banks, their position as proxy-holders, and their role on the boards of firms—issues normally analysed from the perspective of corporate governance—also help corporate finance. Subsequent sections look at corporate governance from the standpoint of corporate finance, including the role of German banks as delegated monitors in widely held firms. The various links between firms and banks, including the instruments of control available to banks, are explored and an assessment is made of their impact on firms and their managements. The advantages and disadvantages of the

The author wishes to express his gratitude for helpful comments that have been given by Masahiko Aoki, George J. Benston, Jeremy S. Edwards, Koichi Hamada, Christian Harm, Larry Meissner, Hugh Patrick, Martin Peltzer, and Ernst-Ludwig von Thadden.

German corporate governance structure is also analysed. Finally, a comparison is made between the monitoring potential of a system that relies on a market for corporate control and a bank- (institution-) oriented corporate governance system. The interesting issue of the historical development of the German system is not discussed.[1]

Universal Banking and Group Banking

German banks can be divided into universal banks and special purpose banks. The latter, which includes mortgage banks and the like, are not covered here. Universal banks offer a large palette of financial services under one roof. This includes classical banking business as well as investment and securities business (floating and trading stock; depository or custodial services for shares, proxy services; owning stock on own account; setting up and owning investment funds), dealing in real estate, organizing rescue operations for firms in financial distress, doing mergers and acquisitions, and the like. Table 12.1 lists the German banks, their numbers and balance sheet totals as of April 1991.

Universal banks can be divided into three sub-groups: commercial banks (*Geschäftsbanken*) which, because of their much broader powers, should not be confused with their US counterparts, savings banks (*Sparkassen*) and cooperative banks (*Kreditgenossenschaften*). Competition is more vigorous among the groups than within them. Indeed, the savings banks and cooperative banks cooperate among themselves to a large extent (group banking). The most important group by numbers of banks as well as by balance sheet total is the savings banks. The cooperative sector is formed by a large number of small banks.

Commercial banks are the most inhomogeneous of the universal banks. There are the *Großbanken*—Deutsche Bank, Dresdner Bank, and Commerzbank plus their Berlin subsidiaries—which, with a market share of about 11 per cent of the universal bank sector, are the three largest; a large number of more regionally centred private credit banks; and banks run by a partnership or a sole proprietor. The core of this group's business traditionally is in credit and securities. Credits of all commercial banks to non-bank firms make up about 65 per cent of their balance sheet total (long-term loans are 30 per cent). Large German firms formerly had *Hausbanken* (house banks) from this group, and there are still close relationships between large firms and the top commercial banks.

Savings banks are almost all owned by local municipalities and hence

---

[1] There is a large literature in English on German banking that readers can refer to: for the historical development of the system, see Gerschenkron (1962), Harm (1992), Neuburger and Stokes (1974), Schmitz (1992), Tilly (1966) and (1986), Tilly and Fremdling (1976). The section on universal and group banking is extracted from the more detailed discussion of Baums and Gruson (1993); also see Benston (1994).

TABLE 12.1 Structure of the German Banking System, April 1991

Number of banks	Balance sheet		Category
	Total[1]	Share[2]	
4526	5246		All banks
4457	4038	77.0	Universal
69	1208	23.0	Special purpose
			Universal
340	1400	26.5	Commercial
771	1853	35.4	Savings
3346	785	15.0	Cooperatives
			Commercial
5	481	9.1	Großbanken[3]
192	770	14.7	Regional and others
60	82	1.5	Foreign[4]
83	67	1.2	Private[5]
			Special purpose
28	446	8.9	Private mortgage
8	152	2.9	Public mortgage
16	72	1.4	Postal[6]
17	518	9.9	Other[7]

[1] In billion deutschmarks. Excludes foreign branches.

[2] Category's share of balance sheet total for all banks.

[3] The three largest banks: Deutsche, Dresdner, Commerz and two Berlin subsidiaries.

[4] Branches. In addition, there were 80 banking entities with foreign majority ownership in other categories. The 140 total foreign banks had 4.1% of total assets (DM 218 billion).

[5] Owned by partnerships or a sole proprietor.

[6] Postal giro and postal savings bank offices.

[7] Banks with special tasks, such as the Reconstruction Loan Corp, Landwirtschaftliche Rentenbank, and AKA Ausfuhrkredit.

Source: Data are from Statistische Beihefte zu den Monatsberichten der Deutschen Bundesbank, Reihe 1, Bankenstatistik nach Bankengruppen, June (1991).

are restricted to their immediate area. They are important to small and medium firms and can, as sole financier, even play the role of a house bank of such a firm. Traditionally, these banks finance themselves primarily with savings deposits of private households. Long-term loans (to households and municipalities as well as to private non-bank firms) make up more than half of their assets. Regional or central institutions address common tasks such as clearing giros (Deutsche Girozentrale-Deutsche Kommunalbank).

Whether and under what conditions savings banks hold equity in non-bank firms depends on state as well as federal laws. The regional *Landesbanken* are less restricted in their powers and activities than local savings banks. They can and do acquire shares in firms, including large ones, and provide financing and financial services that exceed the resources or powers of a savings bank. Savings bank personnel serving on the boards of client firms seem to be less common than for commercial banks.

Industrial structure in Germany can be compared to a wood: a few big trees, many medium ones (*Mittelstand*), and a lot of underbrush (handicrafts, shopkeepers, small farms). As the providers of start-up capital and finance to small firms, especially in rural areas, cooperative banks historically have been extremely important for the development of the undergrowth of industry. At one time credit could only be granted to members, but this restriction has been repealed. These small banks generally are intimately familiar with the local conditions, characteristics and riskiness of their clients, which gives them an informational advantage. As with the savings banks, certain functions are taken on by central institutions. (Bonus, 1987, is an interesting study of the economics of cooperative banks. Also see Bonus and Schmidt, 1990.)

Categorizing Systems of Finance and Corporate Governance

The German systems of investment finance and corporate governance are often described as bank based, as opposed to market oriented like the United States and United Kingdom. This structure is said—interestingly, often by observers from these countries—to lead to considerable benefits, especially in two respects: the availability of cheaper and longer-term bank (mainly loan) finance for firms, and better corporate governance in terms of fewer agency problems. Classifying existing financial systems into broad categories, such as bank oriented and market oriented (as does, for example, Rybczynski, 1984, pp. 275, 277–80) does not exhaust the possible characterizations. One task of this chapter is to check whether the German corporate finance and governance system fits into this scheme. The distinction between bank-oriented and market-oriented or market-based and credit-based systems disregards the role of internal finance as well as alternative corporate governance systems and control devices. Firms within a given system, for example, might rely to much greater extent on internal finance than on either bank loans or securities finance. It seems improper to describe this system as bank oriented simply because credit finance plays a comparatively more important role than securities finance. The same is true for corporate governance, where simple dichotomy excludes devices that do not rely exclusively on either markets or on banks as institutional monitors.

To prove there are advantages to a specific structure of bank-firm relationships, we should first look at the underlying theoretical arguments, then ask whether there is empirical evidence for the assumptions made and the alleged advantages. This is done in the sections that follow.

THEORY

Usually the advantages claimed for a bank-oriented system are derived from the number and nature of close links between a universal bank as financier and its client firm. German banks are seen as being much more closely involved with the firms they supply funds to than banks are in market-oriented systems. The links include: ownership of equity in a borrowing firm; bank personnel serving on a client's board; voting custodial shares; and serving as exclusive provider of funds and other financial services to a firm (house bank). This section looks at those links

Debt-Equity Finance

Universal banks may and do acquire equity in industrial firms. There have been several propositions put forward in the literature concerning the benefits of a combination of debt and equity finance. For instance, financiers typically have less information about firms than the entrepreneurs or managers, and they are subject to various types of moral hazard after the conclusion of a credit contract. How does combined debt-equity finance reduce these problems? Are there clear advantages compared to mere debt (credit) finance?

Moral Hazards

Financiers are subject to various moral hazards: the riskiness of the borrowing firm's strategies, managerial effort, distribution of assets to shareholders irrespective of the position and interests of its creditors, and reported return realizations. These cause difficulties for the provision of finance to industry. (See Jensen and Meckling, 1976, pp. 305–60.)

By providing debt as well as equity finance to a borrower at the same time, a bank might exclude or lessen these problems. Two propositions have been made in this respect. First, the position as a stockholder (equity owner) can give the bank the means to control the behaviour of a borrower and its management more effectively than is possible as a mere creditor. Second, when a bank holds equity it directly shares in the successful outcome of risky behaviour by the borrowing firm. The obverse of this is that there is less for the managers and other shareholders, and this reduces their incentive to take excessive risk.[2]

[2] On the first proposition, see Berglöf (1990, pp. 237–38), Cable (1985, pp. 118, 121), Charkham (1989, pp. 8–9), Frankel and Montgomery (1991, p. 293), McCauley and Zimmer

Incentives for risky behaviour at a borrowing firm are particularly strong in two cases. (1) The firm has a low ratio of equity to debt and limited liability of the owners. In the case of a failure, any financial losses in excess of equity are borne by creditors, whereas gains accrue to the owners, 'heads I win, tails you lose'. (2) The firm is in financial distress, and management fears losing their jobs when the firm goes bankrupt.

These incentives could be lessened if a bank grants equity rather than debt finance or splits up its funds into a debt and an equity position ('strip finance') under certain conditions: if the bank's equity stake is large enough to get better information about the projects and behaviour of the firm than when it is a mere creditor, and if it can, as an equity owner, influence the behaviour and projects of the firm, or, if the bank's equity position is large enough so that the outcome of projects has to be shared to a sufficient extent with the bank.

Whether a bank gets better information as a strip financier or shareholder than as a mere creditor with the same amount of funds extended to the firm is doubtful, as long as the firm is run by a separate management. Even seats on supervisory boards do not seem to provide for better information than a large creditor has (Vogel, 1980). But there may still be, with additional costs, better means for a shareholder than for a creditor to control and avoid hazardous behaviour of the firm, depending on the size of the equity stake and on the legal form of the firm. (German corporate law, for example, grants much more influence on management to shareholders of companies with limited liability than to those of stock corporations.)

Similar considerations apply to moral hazard concerning the borrower's (or management's) effort. First, the equity stake has to be large enough to provide the necessary means to control the borrowing firm and its management effectively. Second, if the owners have to share the outcome of increased effort with the bank as a shareholder, the incentives to such increased effort are diminished accordingly. Third, the disciplining functions of debt finance (the claim of the creditor to fixed payments and the threat of a call of the loan or even bankruptcy) fade to the extent to which equity instead of debt finance is chosen.

The distribution of assets to the shareholders leads to a higher gearing of the firm and, in a corporation with limited liability, to two further risks for its creditors. First, the owners have an increased incentive to risky behaviour. Second, the funds available for distribution to creditors in the case of bankruptcy are diminished. An equity participation of a creditor may help if it is large enough to avoid distributions made irrespective of the interests of the creditors, and thus smooth out the interests of shareholders and creditors, especially in times of financial distress.

(1989, pp. 51–52), Pozdena (1987). On the second, see Pozdena (1990, pp. 9–11), Kim (1990, pp. 15, 24).

Inaccuracies in reported return realizations may make creditors believe there is no reason to call a loan, or to adjust its conditions to reflect a deteriorated situation (for instance, by asking for more collateral), or even file for bankruptcy. Splitting up the funds a bank is willing to extend into debt and equity only helps if this strip finance provides the financier with better information than a mere lender, which is doubtful.

After all, it seems safe to say that there are trade-offs and only under restrictive conditions might a combination of debt and equity finance be superior to mere debt finance for moral hazard problems. Further, a financier who plans to offer strip finance instead of debt has to take additional risks into account. The equity capital may not be reclaimed from the firm itself like a loan if the firm is in financial distress. That means the debt part also becomes locked in, either because the financier does not want to give a negative signal to the market by calling the firm's credits, or because it wants to avoid still more trouble for the firm before the share stake is sold. There is still another risk. If the firm goes bankrupt, not only the equity stake, but also the credit capital extended by the shareholder bank may be subordinated to other debt, even if the loan is secured. This depends, among other things, on the legal form of the firm. For stock corporations the rule normally applies only to a holder of 25 per cent or more of the stock. (Proxies voted by a bank as custodian are not counted as holdings.)

Hidden Information

Financiers typically have less information about firms than the entrepreneurs or managers. Despite careful evaluation, a bank still has imperfect information about the risk of a loan. In such a setting, the lender is unable to raise the contract interest rate to offset fully the expected risk of the contract without attracting risky projects (termed 'adverse selection', see Stiglitz and Weiss, 1981). There may be other kinds of information asymmetries as well (see Myers and Majluf, 1984).

Pozdena (1990, pp. 8, 9) has argued that strip finance permits the debt component to be priced at a smaller premium than the one required in a pure debt contract. This lower loan rate reduces the tendency for the lender to attract projects of greater risk. But why should a bank ask for a lower loan rate? Additional assumptions are needed for this to be the case. For instance, the willingness to acquire equity in the firm could provide the bank with better information about the risk of a project because the entrepreneur or managers are more willing to disclose information to a future shareholder than to a creditor. That might happen under special conditions (which depend on the size of the equity stake and the legal form of the firm).

Debt-Equity Finance as a Commitment Device

Debt-equity finance could serve as a commitment device (Fischer, 1990). An equity participation of a bank can exclude competition by other suppliers of financial services in two ways. As a shareholder, the bank could threaten management with punishment if it switches to another financier. Competitors believe the house bank has better information about the firm and, hence, are cautious or even reluctant if asked to finance a certain project that the house bank does not finance. This reduction of competition could lead to a commitment by the firm to the bank and, in turn, allow the bank to finance projects at comparatively lower costs because it can be sure it will be compensated at later stages for the risks that it took initially. This can be especially important in cases of venture finance or in rescue operations. Again, conditions have to be satisfied—the equity must be relatively large enough, and company law must give the financier effective means to bind management. There might be drawbacks with such a structure. Normally we think of competition as a mechanism of protection, so any lessening of competition from other financiers exposes the firm to the possibility of an abuse of power by the strip financier. Why shouldn't the bank raise the interest rate it demands and thus exploit its position? (See Hellwig, 1991, pp. 35, 56.)

Banks and Board Membership

Widespread membership of bankers on their clients' boards is another of the specific arrangements widely believed to contribute to advantageous finance conditions for German firms. These personal links are said to provide the financier with better information and better means to control the behaviour of the borrowing firm's management. (See Cable, 1985, pp. 119–21; McCauley and Zimmer, 1989, pp. 50–52.)

Informational advantages

All stock corporations and all companies with limited liability to which the codetermination laws apply are required by law to have a management board and a separate supervisory board. Management has to report to the supervisory board periodically; if a bank's representative holds the board's chair, there is steady contact with the firm's management and a continuous flow of information. This can give the bank better information about the plans and prospects of the firm, the risk of its projects, and the abilities of its management. The bank can become an inside rather than an outside financier, better able to assess risks and adjust the conditions of finance to the specific structure of the firm.

This argument is not without doubts. Let us compare the structure of the German two-tier board system to a US or UK style one-board system. The flow of information to a separate supervisory board might be much smaller than to the directors of a firm in a one-board system, especially if employee representatives sit on the board, as is obligatory if codetermination laws apply to the firm. Further, supervisory board members have to keep the information they get in that capacity confidential. They are normally well aware of this, because a breach is a criminal offence.

On the other hand, if we define 'information' in a broader, more general sense—familiarity with the firm and its people—then a financing bank may well have influence, may create or strengthen personal relationships with the owners or managers, including gaining knowledge of the ability and skills of the management, and may improve the understanding of any problems at the firm. All of these help the bank assess risks and adjust the conditions of finance.

Influence on Management Behaviour

The knowledge of being observed may influence behaviour and prevent risk and hazardous action. Does supervisory board membership give a bank additional means if risky and hazardous behaviour against its interests are observed? A majority of the board can vote to recall incumbent management or—more practically—not renew their contracts (usually a five-year term). The influence of the bank's representative depends on the size and composition of the board, the size of the bank's equity stake, its importance as a creditor, and the position its representative holds—being chair, for instance. Personal links may indeed help mitigate conflicts between the firm and its managers or owners on one side and its creditor on the other, and the advantages might exceed the costs of board representation.

The House Bank as Sole Financier

Debt-equity combinations and personal links combine as elements of a structure that was, historically, typical for bank-firm relationships in Germany, house banks (*Hausbanken*) of firms. This relationship has some special traits (Fischer, 1990, pp. 3–4).

- It is a long-term relationship between a bank and a firm. This conveys thorough information about the firm to the bank.
- The house bank has the largest share of the financial business of the firm, including credit extensions, and may be the sole financier.
- The bank has a special responsibility for the firm in times of financial distress, especially regarding rescue and reorganization.
- The bank is represented on the firm's supervisory or advisory board.

House bank relationships are fading and are of only limited relevance today, although they still exist between smaller firms and banks.

Interestingly, the economics of these relationships have been analysed only recently. One can think of explanations such as scale economies in monitoring or the advantage there is in not having to reveal confidential information to more than one institution, let alone to the open capital market.

Mayer (1988) suggests that Japanese banks are more willing to engage in corporate rescues than financiers elsewhere because the bank-firm relationship in Japan involves a mutual long-term commitment. This has been further developed by Fischer (1990), who asks whether this notion of a long-term bank-firm relationship as a mutual commitment is the rationale that underlies and explains the house-bank structure in Germany.

Fischer observes that a serious threat to long-term investment finance by a bank is competition from other financiers at the stage where it is clear that a venture or rescue operation is successful, but the returns have not yet been fully reaped. This is true even when there are contracts. Competition at this stage might drive the profits from future business, which the existing financier expects as part of its compensation for start-up support, to zero. That is, all surplus from later periods stays with the firm. According to Fischer, a house bank relationship in which a bank serves as the sole financier provides for this decreased competition and the commitment of a firm to a bank necessary for a long-term investment that has low returns in its early periods. The sole financier in the early period gains better information about the firm, including the quality of its management and the riskiness of its projects. This informational advantage tempers the competition from outside financiers in later periods, as they are afraid of a 'winner's curse'. The initial financier continues to extend loans and provide other financial services in future periods and is thus able to appropriate some of the surplus of the project. This supports its willingness to supply start-up capital or to support a rescue.

Note that Fischer addresses only one threat to (long-term) credit finance. He does not deal explicitly with the moral hazard problems and informational asymmetries discussed earlier. If the house bank structure brings the advantages Fischer describes, why hasn't it emerged in other economies? There could be regulatory or other impediments, but that does not explain why house banking is fading in Germany, too.

EVIDENCE REGARDING CORPORATE FINANCE AND BANKS

This section explores the evidence regarding the various hypotheses discussed in the previous section.

Debt-Equity Finance

Is there evidence for a widespread use of debt-equity finance (strip finance) instead of debt finance, and if so, is it used because of its alleged advantages (lessening of moral hazard; improvement of information; commitment of the borrowing firm to the creditor)?

Figure 12.1 shows the sources of net external funding of non-financial businesses for the United States, United Kingdom, Germany and Japan (flow of funds data). These data support the frequent characterization of the German system as being bank oriented. If we look only at external sources of funds, banks provide about twice the amount as direct securities markets (stocks and bonds). However, things look different if we include internal sources of funds. Table 12.2 presents estimates for the sources of gross financing for the period 1983–87 for the United Kingdom, Japan and Germany.

Retentions (retained earnings) were the most important source of funds in all three countries. German firms raised the smallest share in securities markets. Although bank finance was the largest single source of external

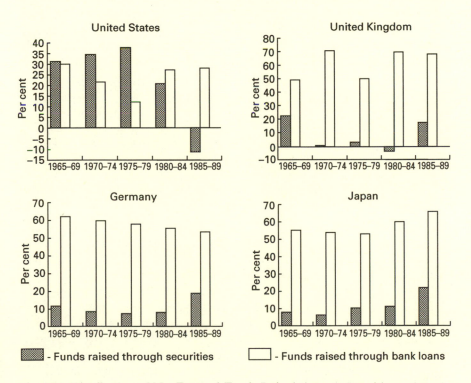

Fig. 12.1 Distribution of Net External Funds Raised through Securities and Bank Loans, 1965–89

TABLE 12.2 Distribution of Sources of Funds, 1983–87
(per cent)

United Kingdom	Japan	Germany	Source
66	53	72[a]	Retained earnings
10	3	3	Share issue
1	0	0	Direct investment
22	44	22	Debt
–	–	3	Residual
Distribution of Debt as Percentage of All Sources			
18	40	14	Credit institutions
4	5	2	Securities
0	4	0	Trade credits
0	–	6	Other

[a] Includes transfers equal to 7% of total sources.

Source: Bario (1990, p. 13).

finance in all three cases, it represents a quite small part of German corporate financing, especially compared to Japan.

The data reveal there was at best only limited use of debt-equity finance during 1983–87. Roggenbuck (1992, pp. 154–62) has analysed equity holding by banks in firms (partnerships as well as corporations) with a capital of DM 1 million or more. For 1985 he found 160 instances of banks acquiring 5 per cent or more of the equity, excluding firms in bank-related businesses. Firms with capital of less than DM 10 million made up 38 per cent of the total, while firms with more than DM 100 million were 15 per cent.

Deutsche Bundesbank data for 1989 show that all banks together held 4.69 per cent of the shares issued by stock corporations and 7.8 per cent of shares in limited liability companies. These numbers include shares banks own through their subsidiaries, but exclude holdings of bank-owned investment funds. Edwards and Fischer (1991, p. 24) estimate bank equity holdings including the investment funds at 10.3 per cent in 1984 and 11.6 per cent in 1988. (Also see Roggenbuck, 1992, p. 357.)

A clear picture emerges from these data: equity finance plays a negligible role compared to credit finance, and the amount of equity participation of all banks together in firms is, although important in individual cases, well below 10 per cent on average. It follows that the use of debt-equity finance by German banks is at best limited, although our data do not indicate exactly the amount of equity they own in companies to which they lend.

One might argue that in addition to directly owned stock, shares the bank votes (quasi-participations) also should be taken into consideration. Banks act as custodians of client shareholdings and are rarely given instructions on how to vote. This position as a proxy-holder is applicable only to stock corporations, and then mainly to firms with scattered small shareholdings. These tend to be large corporations, and they raise much less from bank finance than the corporate sector as a whole. That does not square well with the hypothesis that equity participation should lead to a higher degree of bank finance because of the alleged advantages of such a financing technique.

What then are the reasons for bank acquisitions of equity positions? Roggenbuck (1992) has analysed the acquisition by banks of stakes of 25 per cent or more in non-bank firms from 1976 to 1989. In about half of the 21 cases the bank acquired equity from the founding family or the sole proprietor, who apparently could not find a buyer at the moment they would have liked to, and the bank undertook to act as an interim holder, although sometimes shares were kept to deepen the existing business relationships or as profitable source of income. Another 6 were part of placements (banks took over and held stock until it could be floated). In 3 cases a bank acquired equity in a borrowing firm that was in financial distress. These last cases are certainly interesting from our perspective and deserve further research (see Fischer, 1990, pp. 124–41, with further references). From this evidence, however, it seems safe to say that acquiring equity in non-bank firms normally is not done simply to support the finance (credit) business with a borrowing firm. Firms in financial distress might be an exception.

An interesting case, on which we simply lack thorough studies, is the provision to new firms of both credit and equity finance (the latter provided by a bank subsidiary that acts as a venture finance company (*Unternehmensbeteiligungsgesellschaft*)). (See Roggenbuck, 1992, pp. 386–404.)

Banks and Board Membership

Is there evidence that bank representation on the boards of their client firms improves the bank's information, excludes or lessens risky or hazardous behaviour by the borrower, and that this leads to better (cheaper, more easily available) credit finance for those firms?

Edwards and Fischer (1991) have tested this hypothesis by comparing the extent of loan finance of firms with a supervisory board to that of all firms. The obligatory supervisory board system applies only to stock corporations (*Aktiengesellschaft*) and companies with limited liability (*Gesellschaft mit beschränkter Haftung*) and more than 500 employees. Limited liability companies with fewer than 500 employees and partnerships are not obliged to have two-tier boards.

Edwards and Fischer examined the question whether stock corporations with an obligatory supervisory board (which is likely to have at least one banker on it) use relatively more bank borrowing than other forms of enterprise. They found that such enterprises relied hardly at all on bank borrowing during 1971–85, and instead were largely internally financed. Bank loans were more important as a source of finance for the producing enterprises sector as a whole than for stock corporations with a supervisory board, from which it seems reasonable to deduce that enterprises in Germany without supervisory boards made more use of bank borrowing than did enterprises with supervisory boards.

However, this does not say much about whether or not bank representation on supervisory boards reduces problems of asymmetric information between borrowers and lenders. First note that although there are no supervisory boards in smaller firms, they often have advisory boards (*Beirat*) with a representative of one or more banks (data on this are not available). Hence it is not clear to what extent large and small firms differ with respect to representation by creditor bank on their boards.

Second, the fact that large firms rely more on internal, rather than on bank, finance need not contradict the view that bank representation on a firm's board reduces problems of asymmetric information. It is possible that these large firms have better, more efficient ways to finance investments (internal finance; easier access to immediate market finance) than bank loans, even if bank finance to a large firm is less fraught with informational problems because of bank membership on the firm's board. Because bank finance puts a tighter rein on them, management in large firms may prefer other finance techniques (also see Hellwig, 1991, pp. 57–61). Similarly, international comparisons show that large German firms with bank representatives on their boards rely less on credit finance than their foreign counterparts without bank representation (for example, the United Kingdom). This does not answer the question either, however, as foreign firms might have less chance to rely on internal finance than German firms. The question remains open to further research.

House Banks

What is the evidence regarding house banks? There have been only a few empirical studies, the most thorough of which is Fischer (1990), who used interviews. He found that for all but the smallest companies, exclusive financing by a single bank (house bank) is the exception rather than the rule. Large, publicly traded companies can use organized markets for their securities and even give short-term credits to each other without the intermediation of a bank. They have a deliberate policy of maintaining relations with 5 to 10 principal or main banks and also use other banks. The market for credits, especially to good borrowers, is highly competitive. The same applies to firms with a turnover of more than DM 500 million. For smaller firms the large commercial banks tend to become the sole financier if the borrower is a good risk. In such cases, firms prefer relations with a handful of competing banks in order not to endanger their independence. Apart from the large commercial banks, other types of banking institutions act as sole financier to a much lesser extent, except for very small firms.

Further, there is—according to Fischer's study—no evidence that banks have informational advantages that enable them to avoid bankruptcy risks. A main bank relationship does not seem to be considered a binding commitment to support a firm in financial distress. As to the reorganization and restructuring of firms in financial distress or bankrupt, evidence indicates a wide variety between different sized banks' behaviour. (For an empirical study of the role and behaviour of credit institutions in cases of financial distress or insolvency of client firms, see Gessner and others, 1978, pp. 232–67).

What are the reasons for the increasing emancipation of firms from close banking relationships, including the reliance, especially by large firms, on internal finance and direct market finance? Hellwig (1991) offers some explanations:

- A risk-averse intermediary may have a diversification incentive to share the risks of the firms it finances.
- Reliance on outside finance decreases as more internal finance is available.
- Management in large firms may have a bias to excessive retentions.

These remarks should show that the description of the German corporate finance system as bank oriented as opposed to market oriented is one-sided, as the distinction is based on only two sources of finance. Furthermore, some of the widespread assumptions about specific features of the German corporate finance system (the role of equity finance by banks; the role of bankers on firms' boards; the role of house banks) and their benefits seem doubtful. This is in part because empirically these features are not as important as assumed (debt-equity finance) or are fading (house bank relationships). In addition, some of the underlying hypotheses concerning the benefits of this structure are theoretically unconvincing.

BANKS AND CORPORATE GOVERNANCE IN LARGE FIRMS

The specific features of the German banking system and the bank-firm relationship concern corporate finance as well as corporate governance. The previous section examined whether, and to what extent, equity holdings of banks, their position as proxy-holders and their role on the boards of firms—features normally analysed from the perspective of corporate governance—help corporate finance, too. If we discuss the role of banks in corporate governance, we could put the question the other way round and examine the role of debt finance in corporate governance, such as scrutinizing the borrowing firm before granting or extending credit, monitoring during the credit relationship, pressing claims to fixed payments irrespective of the unsteady flow of returns to the borrowing firm, and threatening forcing a firm into bankruptcy. These means available to a bank as a creditor, however, are not characteristics of corporate governance specific to German firms. Nevertheless, we must consider to what extent the banks' role in corporate governance, especially when acting as proxies, is reinforced or hampered by the role as creditor.[3]

German corporate governance, like the corporate finance system, is often described as bank oriented, as opposed to market oriented, as it is in the United States and United Kingdom. This is true only in a limited sense. Banks play a particular role in corporate governance only in stock corporations that have small scattered shareholders. In the following, we deal only with this small number of firms. To be sure, banks may and do hold equity in firms with other legal forms. In such cases, they exercise their rights like any other shareholder. Another channel to influence managements of non-stock corporations may be advisory or supervisory board positions. Although we lack recent studies, it seems safe to say this influence is mostly restricted to an advising rather than a monitoring or controlling function. The distribution of ownership, and hence the composition and tasks of the supervisory or advisory board, normally do not allow for influence similar to that exerted on a large stock corporation with scattered shareholders.

A market for corporate control in terms of public hostile take-over bids does not exist in Germany, but that does not mean that there are no hostile take-overs. The management of Hoesch AG, taken over in 1992 by Krupp, would probably have liked to hinder this shift of control if there had been a chance to do so. Resistance to a hostile take-over is not always possible (Baums, 1993b), and becomes particularly difficult for a management if it loses the support of several, or even one, custodial banks (banks voting proxies on behalf of shareholders). This means that the large custodial banks, in particular, play an important, if not decisive role, in the market for corporate control.

---

[3] The relevant literature on the relationship between corporate governance and corporate finance includes Aghion and Bolton (1989), Allen (1989, a survey article), Mathis (1992, p. 108–13), Mayer (1990), and Williamson (1988). Parts of this section are updated from parts of Baums (1993a).

Corporate Structure

In Germany firms can be a sole proprietorship, a partnership or a corporation, as shown in Table 12.3. This chapter deals only with publicly held stock corporations (*Aktiengesellschaft*) with widely held stock—that is, there is no controlling individual or institutional shareholder. Although this is a small number of firms, only some 80, most are among the 100 largest in Germany. Understanding corporate governance in large stock corporations and the role of the banks in it requires mention of some special features of German corporate law. (A detailed description is Conard, 1984; also see Meier-Schatz, 1980.)

TABLE 12.3 Legal Forms of German Firms

Number[1]	Abbreviation	German	English
–	OHG	offene Handelsgesellschaft	Unlimited partnership
–	KG	Kommanditgesellschaft	Limited partnership
434	GmbH	Gesellschaft mit beschränkter Haftung	Private limited company
2.7[a]	AG	Aktiengesellschaft	Public limited company (stock corporation)

[1] In 1990, in thousands. The numbers increased substantially after reunification. In May 1992 there were 510,000 GmbH and 3,100 AG.

[a] Of these, 665 trade on a stock exchange.

A key feature is the two-tier or dual boards system, which was established in 1870. It consists of a management board and a separate supervisory board (*Aufsichtsrat*). Supervisory boards, which have between 3 and 21 members, appoint managers—mostly for five-year terms—and can recall them, but only for good cause. Management runs the day-to-day business of the firm. Complete power rests with neither management nor the board; rather, there is a complex balance of powers. Shareholders are limited to basic decisions such as changes of the statutes, approval of the annual statements of accounts, distribution of half of the annual balance sheet profits, election of half the members of the supervisory board, and consent to structural changes such as mergers, issuance of new stock and the like.

Under the codetermination system, at firms with more than 2,000 employees, half the members of the supervisory board are elected by employees—blue and white collar, as well as lower-ranking management—and labour unions. Although the present codetermination laws came into force after 1945, there is an older tradition of obligatory representation of employees on supervisory boards. (See Wiedemann, 1980.)

Members of both the supervisory board and the management board are considered to be agents of all stakeholders in the firm, not just of the shareholders. German employees are stakeholders not only in the usual sense of labour contracts and the like, but also because their pension capital is—unlike the practice in Anglo-American countries—to a large extent kept within the employing firm and serves as an important source of capital.

Unlike Anglo-American firms, the board or management does not solicit proxies. Instead, shares are either voted by the shareholders themselves or—in the case of smaller shareholdings—by institutions, mainly banks, which act as custodians for the shares. This voting power of a few banks—for many firms, sometimes not more than three or four, each with a large block of votes—gets bank representatives on the supervisory boards. This has important consequences, which are discussed later.

The Proxy System

The typical large German firm with dispersed shareholders finds its shares in voting blocks controlled by a few banks which, if aggregated, comprise 30 per cent or more of all votes, as shown in Table 12.4. This voting power, which helps place representatives of the banks on the supervisory board, comes from different sources: from directly owned stock, from investment companies controlled by banks, and from shares held by banks as custodians.

Publicly held German corporations predominantly issue bearer shares; smaller shareholdings are mostly part of a single global document. A shareholder wishing to hold actual certificates has to pay additionally for them. This drives stock into institutions, and, for a fee, banks offer the requisite custodial services, including collecting dividends and the like. To vote deposited shares, a bank needs a special written power of authority—a proxy. Proxies are revocable at any time, and by law cannot be given for more than 15 months, though they are renewable. Before a shareholder meeting, custodial institutions must ask their clients how they want their shares voted; the cost of doing this is borne by the bank, not by the firm. The banks can and do recommend how to vote. Holders of only 2–3 per cent of shares provide voting instructions. For the others, the bank votes according to its recommendations. Generally, banks can vote custodial stock on any matter, and there is no ceiling limiting the exercise of voting rights by banks to a certain percentage of a firm's shares. (Investment companies may not own more than 10 per cent of a firm's shares.)

Most banks have widely held stock. At its own shareholder meeting, a bank may vote custodial holdings only if it receives explicit instructions. As the data in Table 12.4 show, in contrast to the 2–3 per cent response for non-banks, holders of a large percentage of bank shares provide instructions. I have been unable to get an explanation for this.

There were several empirical studies on banks as proxy-holders in the 1970s. A government commission found that in 1974–75 for 74 large stock-exchange listed companies, 52.5 per cent of the shares were voted by banks or investment companies as proxies and another 10.2 per cent as owners (BdS, 1979, p. 111). More recent are Gottschalk (1988) and Böhm (1992).

From the list of the 100 largest firms in 1984, Gottschalk selected those with more than 50 per cent of their stock either widely held or owned by banks. These 32 companies, with a (nominal) equity capital of DM 29.5 billion, represented about a quarter of the nominal capital of all German stock corporations. Included were 7 of the country's 10 largest firms, measured by *Wertschöpfung* (surplus, adjusted for certain items), collectively representing about 8 per cent of the economy's *Wertschöpfung* in 1986.

Gottschalk aggregates the voting power of the banks' own shares, their custodial shares, and shares held by investment companies that are bank subsidiaries. He found that, on average, banks represented more than four-fifths (82.67 per cent) of all votes present at meetings. With one exception, they represented at least a majority (more than half) of the votes present. Consequently, banks were able to elect the members of the supervisory board chosen by shareholders and changes in the corporate statutes could not be effected against their votes. In 22 or two-thirds of the firms, the banks voted more than three-fourths of the stock present and thereby could change the statutes. No other shareholder could block these decisions. Note that most of these corporations (by the votes of the banks) have provisions in their statutes that no one shareholder may vote more than (typically) 5 per cent of all shares of the company. This rule does not apply to banks voting proxies for clients.

Gottschalk shows that voting power is highly concentrated in the three largest private banks (Deutsche Bank, Dresdner Bank, and Commerzbank). Together they voted on average approximately 45 per cent of the stock represented at the general meetings of the 32 companies. In almost half the cases (15 firms), they held the majority; in a further third (10 firms) they had a blocking minority. In individual cases, one or another of the big banks dominates. In most cases the votes are distributed roughly equally among them, or two banks together have about the same number of votes as the third alone.

The extent to which banks coordinate behaviour in their voting has not been empirically determined. A government commission noted that 'the banks mostly vote in the same sense' (Monopolkommission, 1978).

TABLE 12.4 Percentage of Shares Voted by Banks at 1986 Shareholder Meetings of Widely Held Companies

Size Rank[1]	Company	Shares Present[2]	Deutsche Bank	Dresdner Bank	Commerz Bank	Big 3 Banks	All Banks
27	Allianz-Holding	66.20	9.91	11.14	2.35	23.41	60.08
6	BASF	55.40	28.07	17.43	6.18	51.68	96.64
5	Bayer	53.18	30.82	16.91	6.77	54.50	95.78
52	Bayr. Vereinsbank	62.40	11.42	2.71	3.59	17.72	68.69
57	Bayr. Hypobank	67.90	5.86	7.05	1.20	14.11	92.09
96	Bergmann	99.12	36.89	0	0	36.89	62.15
34	Commerzbank	50.50	16.30	9.92	34.58	60.81	96.77
56	Continental	35.29	22.77	9.99	6.04	38.81	95.55
2	Daimler Benz	81.02	41.80	18.78	1.07	61.66	69.34
51	Degussa	70.94	6.86	33.03	1.89	41.79	67.09
12	Deutsche Bank	55.10	47.17	9.15	4.04	60.36	97.23
59	Deutsche Babcock	67.13	7.58	9.67	5.29	22.54	97.01
21	Dresdner Bank	56.79	13.39	47.08	3.57	64.04	98.16
98	Hapag-Lloyd	84.50	48.15	47.82	0.39	96.36	99.50
7	Hoechst	57.73	14.97	16.92	31.60	63.48	98.34
29	Hoesch	45.39	15.31	15.63	16.73	47.67	92.39
28	Karstadt	77.60	37.03	8.81	33.02	78.86	87.27
35	Kaufhof	66.70	6.29	13.33	37.18	56.80	98.45

37	KHD	72.40	44.22	3.82	1.50	49.54	85.29
36	Klöckner-Werke	69.13	17.30	3.78	3.55	24.63	53.00
68	Linde	52.99	22.76	15.73	21.36	59.87	90.37
18	M.A.N. (GHH)	64.10	6.97	9.48	13.72	30.17	52.85
13	Mannesmann	50.63	20.49	20.33	9.71	50.53	95.40
	Mercedes-Holding	67.20	11.85	13.66	12.24	37.75	57.35
41	Metallg'schaft	90.55	16.42	48.85	0.35	65.62	75.95
73	Ph. Holzmann	82.18	55.42	0.91	6.49	62.82	74.81
44	Preussag	69.58	11.15	5.60	2.59	19.34	99.68
67	Schering	46.60	23.86	17.46	10.17	51.50	99.08
1	Siemens	60.64	17.84	10.74	4.14	32.52	79.83
94	Strabag	83.02	6.80	19.15	1.37	27.32	95.24
11	Thyssen	68.48	9.24	11.45	11.93	32.62	53.11
9	VEBA	50.24	19.99	23.08	5.85	47.92	98.18
3	Volkswagen	50.13	2.94	3.70	1.33	7.98	19.53
	Average	64.49	21.09	15.30	9.05	45.44	82.67

'Widely held' corporations are those having no single non-bank shareholder with a stake larger than 5 per cent. Entries include the shares held by banks on their own account and by investment companies that are bank subsidiaries, as well as proxies for custodial holdings.
Data for Siemens, Veba and Continental are 1987.

[1] Ranking is by 1984 *Wertschöpfung* (surplus adjusted for certain items).
[2] Percentage of all shares outstanding present at the meeting.

Source: Gottschalk (1988 p. 298).

Banks as Shareholders

A second source of bank influence in corporate affairs is their position as stockholders. German credit institutions can hold stock in non-bank firms for their own account, and there are no rules limiting such holdings to some percentage of the firm's capital. There are limits with respect to the bank's capital to protect depositors and creditors: participation in one firm may not exceed 15 per cent, and all holdings together 60 per cent, of the bank's capital.

By the end of 1989 German credit institutions held 4.69 per cent of all shares of domestic stock corporations. This number alone is not very informative in discussing banks and corporate control. It does not tell us to what extent, and in which banks, holdings are concentrated; in how many cases holdings are portfolio investments rather than controlling blocks; whether they are acquired for short-term, placement or trading purposes, or as long-term investments; or whether the remaining shares are widely dispersed or concentrated.

Data on bank shareholdings in the 100 largest industrial firms (measured by turnover) are in Table 12.5. Böhm (1992, pp. 231–38) analysed the holdings and found that in 1986, 12 credit institutions held equity in 22 of these firms, with holdings ranging from 5 per cent (all banks in one firm) to more than 50 per cent (a single bank in one firm). Holdings on own account have little relation to the number of shares voted by banks as proxies. Holdings are rather stable over time, an impression confirmed when recent data are compared to older data.

Interlocking Directorates

Influence on management, its decisions, its appointment and dismissal, is not exercised directly by the shareholders but by the supervisory board. Seats on the board are crucial for every shareholder or institution that wants to have a say in corporate governance, obtain relevant information, and the like. For board membership at other firms, banks support not only their own top managers and supervisory board members, but also professional board members—people who serve on multiple boards. (Although an individual cannot be on more than 10 boards at the same time, an institution can place representatives on as many boards as it can.) The 'informal' relationship between a bank and a professional board member does not need to be disclosed, although affiliation of board members with a bank must be.

Members of the managing board or the supervisory board of a bank can be members of the supervisory board of a firm, whether as a consequence of the equity participation of the bank, its position as proxy-holder, or its business relationship with the firm, especially a long-term

TABLE 12.5 Bank Stockholdings in Large Industrial Firms, 1986, as a Percentage of Nominal Capital

Size Rank[1]	Company	Nominal Capital[2]	Deutsche Bank	Dresdner Bank	Commerzbank	Other Banks	All Banks
26	AEG	931	16	0.9	0.9	1.8	20
54	AGIV	80	0	0	0	44	44
83	Bilf u Berger	70	0	>25	0	0	>25
14	BMW	750	0	5–10	0	0	5–10
49	Continental	312	>10	0	0	0	>10
1	Daimler Benz	2116	28.5	1.6	1.6	3.2	35
27	Degussa	284	0	>10	0	0	>10
47	Dt Babcock	250	0	0	0	>5	>5
99	Dyckerhoff u Widmann	57	6.7	0	1.4	13	21
91	Fichtel u Sachs	128	0	0	35	0	35
46	Hochtief	200	0	0	>16.2	>25	>41
12	Klöckner Werke	469	7.2	3.2	3.2	16.4	30
58	Linde	238	0	0	>10	0	>10
21	MAN	674	0	0	>8.2	0	>8
43	MBB	600	0	5–10	>0.3	5.0	10–15
19	Metallges	280	11.2	16.5	0	0.6	28
37	Ph Holzmann	90	35	0	7.6	0	43
32	Preussag	402	0	0	0	43	43
81	PWA	200	0	0	0	44	44
80	Strabag	55	0	0	0	>50	>50
8	Thyssen	1565	0	0	>5	0	>5
41	VEW	1000	6.3	0	0	10.5	17

[1] Ranked by revenue (turnover).

[2] In million deutschmark. Nominal capital is the equivalent of the total par value of shares issued in US financial accounting terminology.

Source: Böhm (1992, pp. 225, 226).

credit relationship. That does not mean a firm's management does not try to influence the selection of its supervisors.

Nothing in German law prohibits service on boards of competing firms, but direct cross-links (a member of A's supervisory board sitting on B's management board, and vice versa) are forbidden by law. However, the rule does not apply to advisory boards (*Beiräte*). The large commercial banks have such boards (regionally and nationwide) made up of leading managers of their client firms (see Roggenbuck, 1992, p. 424).

The supervisory board appoints the managing board and may dismiss its members, though only for good cause. It is responsible for monitoring, although in practice it acts more as an advisory committee than as a monitoring panel, except in times of financial distress. To perform its duties, the board has the right to receive comprehensive information. Management must report to it periodically on all important questions, and the board may always ask for reports. The board reviews the annual reports and balance sheets. It may require management to obtain prior approval before entering into certain transactions, such as obtaining (or granting) loans above a specific amount. Board members must treat company information confidentially.

The chair has a particularly influential position, convening the meetings—which are held three or four times a year, less frequent than, for example, in the United States—and proposing the agenda. There is steady contact with management, as it has to brief the chair immediately on all important events. If there is a tie vote under a codetermination regime (a rare event), the chair breaks the tie.

Comprehensive data on the personal links between firms and banks in Germany do not exist. Various studies have been done at different times in different sectors (most recently by Roggenbuck, 1992, p. 424; in English see Edwards and Fischer, 1991, pp. 28–32).

Of the 100 largest firms surveyed by Böhm (1992, pp. 194–96, 257–63), 92 had a supervisory board in 1986. Banks were represented on 75 (81 per cent) of them, holding more than 10 per cent of all seats and more than 20 per cent of seats selected by shareholders. On average they had more than two representatives on each board. The three Großbanken held more than 61 per cent of all bank seats, with Deutsche Bank having 54 seats at 44 firms. The key position of chair of the supervisory board was held by a bank representative at 20 of the 92 firms.

Although these numbers, which refer only to direct personal links between a bank and the large firms, do not give us the whole picture of the potential influence which can be exerted by banks through the supervisory boards, it is safe to say that there is a significant potential for banks to get information, give advice and monitor management in most of these large firms. But do banks really exert their influence and, if so, to what extent and with what results? If these questions cannot be answered satisfactorily, can we at least say something about the incentives and dis-incentives to monitor or behave in a way which might be advantageous for the bank, but disadvantageous for the other shareholders, including bank custodial clients?

CONTROL, INCENTIVES AND DISINCENTIVES TO MONITOR

How does a bank exercise the influence and control it has? What are the incentives and disincentives for its using its power, and are there draw-backs to banks having the power they do? These issues are analysed in this section. Aspects of how banks exercise control include (1) control by means of better access to information; (2) influence by giving advice to management on an ongoing basis; (3) influence by appointing the members of the management board; and (4) interim and *ex post* monitoring.

The knowledge of being observed may influence behaviour. The management board must report to the supervisory board on a continuing basis. Hence information about the firm and its management, as far as it is given to the supervisory board at all, is available to any bank representative on the board. Thus, information about the plans and the quality of the firm's management, which the banks perhaps would not otherwise get, is available privately. However, it is doubtful whether this is of prac-tical consequence because of the board's infrequent meetings (three or four times per year). Indeed, Fischer (1990, p. 80) found that banks do not expect to get any better or more complete information from board representatives than they do as creditors. Moreover, board members must keep the information they get in that capacity confidential; a breach of this duty is a criminal offence. In all, it does not seem likely the informa-tion a bank gets from its position on the supervisory board puts a tighter rein on management than is the case without board membership.

Bank representatives on supervisory boards have specialized know-ledge, particularly in the field of finance. Often they have an office at their bank with special facilities, such as the help of an assistant, to sup-port them as a board member. Large banks have departments specialized in corporate finance, analysing financial markets as well as the financial needs of their client firms. This information is also available to the repre-sentatives. Thus, they can provide firms with specialized advice, financial knowledge and information. In addition, banks can, by exercise of their stock voting power, place other professionals on the board, who in turn can provide management with information and experience. (For data on the composition of supervisory boards, see Gerum, Steinmann and Fees, 1987.)

A poll by Bleicher (1987, p. 57) found 9 out of 10 board members in his sample believe that the actual influence of their advice on management is 'strong'. This does not mean this is in fact the case, especially given the rather infrequent sessions of the supervisory board, although there is some evidence there are informal contacts between the board and management between formal meetings. One also must make a distinction between the board chair and members of certain sub-committees on the one hand and regular members on the other.

Where advice cannot be given because of institutional impediments (infrequent meetings, for instance), and where the supervisory board cannot monitor management, the more important question is whether the board is capable of sorting out managers who from the beginning are capable of doing a good job. This seems to be the most important task of the board, and banks seem to play a role in this respect. In our sample, all banks together determine who sits on the shareholders' side of the board, even if there are no personal links. Furthermore, if there is an open conflict between shareholder and employee representatives, the shareholders can push their management candidates through, because of the tie-breaking vote of the chair. Thus banks have a decisive influence on who gets into the management boardroom, even though members of the supervisory board are legally independent and may—should a conflict arise—act independently. To the extent that one bank dominates the shareholder meeting, is represented on the nominating committee of the supervisory board, or holds the position of chair, its influence will be greater accordingly.

In their role as creditors, shareholders, proxy-holders and with representation on many supervisory boards, banks should know the market for managers well. Nevertheless, banker influence on the appointment of managers could be detrimental if only one institution, with limited knowledge about the firm's industry, had to decide. But that seems not to be the case. If we keep in mind that the three big banks often have similar voting holdings or that two of them can outweigh the other, that board members are not bound to follow the instructions of the shareholders, and that the shareholder representatives would think long and hard before pushing a candidate through against the vote of the employees, then it becomes clear that a candidate for the management board has to clear several hurdles, and is not simply appointed by one dominating institution. In this context it would also be interesting to know the extent to which managers are selected from within rather than from outside the firm. That would be a measure of the relative influence of the supervisory board and of incumbent management on the nomination process for top managers. Here we lack, to my knowledge, empirical studies.

Selection of managers is an aspect of *ex ante* monitoring. Interim monitoring occurs in situations where management must ask the board for its consent, as, for instance, in shutting down a plant, entering a loan agreement and so forth. The board is likely to be more involved when the firm is in financial distress. Apart from these cases, interim monitoring seems to be limited.

The supervisory board may be able to measure management performance by results at the end of certain periods. If so, there may be an incentive for management to perform well even if it is not monitored continuously, if it can be recalled in the case of disappointing results. At first sight, *ex post* monitoring in this sense does not seem to be directly related to the role banks in particular have in corporate governance, and could theoretically occur without them. There is, however, a link between the *ex post* monitoring role of the supervisory board and the existence of custodial institutions. It becomes evident when one considers the difference between a system with outside directors who are there because of the influence of the managing directors, the chair, or the CEO and a two-tier system where outside board members are appointed by large influential institutions. The readiness of the supervisory board members to act and, if necessary, even to dismiss or not prolong the contracts of the members of the management board should be stronger because of the independence guaranteed through the existence and role of influential institutions.

How does the supervisory board measure the performance of the incumbent management? Under German law, management must prepare and publish the firm's balance sheet and profit and loss statement annually. Both are reviewed by independent public accountants who are responsible to the supervisory board and report to it. There are additional obligatory interim reports that are provided only to the supervisory board. The board can put questions to management and compare the firm's current and past results, as well as to those of the firm's competitors (to the extent such information is available). The fact that internal monitoring relies heavily on comparisons with the previous results and the performance of competitors reveals a limitation of the system that will be examined later.

A potential outside bidder may have information about, say, a new technology the board of a specific firm does not have. Is outside governance by a (hostile) take-over that forces a firm to react to technological change sooner than it otherwise might, a necessary supplement to an internal monitoring system that fails in such cases?

Can boards react, and do they really react, if they observe bad performance? If so, this can be anticipated by management, which gives it an incentive to try harder. Terminating the employment of an incumbent manager generally occurs only in cases of criminal offences, and because of attendant bad publicity, even these are usually handled as discreetly as possible. There is, however, the more subtle threat of not renewing employment contracts, which expire in five years or less.

Poensgen and Lukas (1982, pp. 281–82) have collected data that show a significant involuntary fluctuation of management board members, not only in cases of serious problems or financial distress, but also in situations in which the board was not content with the performance of individual managers or with the management board as a whole. These observations do not by themselves say anything about the monitoring performance of the supervisory boards. Did they react too late? Did they dismiss the right people? To what signals did they react? Does the incentive structure drive management in certain directions? Kaplan (1993) has tested for differences in the relationship between management board turnover and performance at firms controlled by large shareholders and firms where voting rights are controlled primarily by banks. He did not find any systematic difference. To answer these questions better, we also need to take into account the incentives and disincentives for institutions like banks to exercise corporate control.

Incentives

Why do banks get involved in corporate governance, act as proxy-holders, and hold positions on supervisory boards?

Banks receive fees for being custodians. But that alone does not explain why banks vote custodial and their own stock, appoint their managers to supervisory boards of other firms, and spend money to support their monitoring work. Banks could (as owners of stock) free-ride, and other shareholders could deposit their stock with institutions that promised no monitoring but also no expenses (except such services are not offered). Further, investment companies that are subsidiaries of banks will not try to dilute the position of their parent banks.

There may be other incentives or advantages that accrue to banks from their governance activities. First, they can try to protect their own equity investment. The ability to vote custodial stock (at low additional costs) gives a bank leverage to protect or strengthen its own investment position without making a capital infusion. For instance, a bank with an equity position of 12 per cent of a firm's stock cannot prevent the issuance of new stock or the elimination of shareholders' pre-emptive rights. But, if it commands another 15 per cent through custodial shares, it can block such actions. Of course, this incentive has to be ruled out in all cases in which banks vote proxies without holdings of their own. For such cases, we have to look for other incentives for banks to act in the interests of shareholders.

Creditors face the problem of asymmetric information, both before and after conclusion of a loan contract. It is often argued that an equity stake by a bank in a borrowing firm improves information for the bank, and reduces the problem of asymmetric information. That is doubtful. A shareholder typically does not receive earlier or better information than a creditor bank—although a small creditor and a majority shareholder with immediate access to the management should not be compared. Even if represented on the firm's board, a bank will normally not receive better or earlier information than it does as a creditor.

If these positions do not provide the bank with better information, they may nonetheless help exclude or minimize risks for the bank during the course of a credit relationship, and thus lower the agency costs associated with debt.

There is no doubt that a bank can improve its position as creditor in certain aspects if it is also an equity owner or votes custodial stock of the firm. A creditor commanding over half the votes at a shareholder meeting can choose who manages the firm. Perhaps the creditor is not capable of electing the best managers, but at least it will choose people who implicitly promise not to harm the interests of the creditor by engaging in risky projects, distributing assets to shareholders, and the like, without the bank's approval. Because the cost to a bank of itself owning a majority of the equity normally is too high, the addition of custodial shares seems to be a perfect arrangement to get the necessary leverage on a firm's management to protect the bank's own equity and credit investment. This power usually has to be shared with other banks, but as creditors they have, to a large extent, parallel interests in dealing with the firm's management.

If this is so, we can expect credit finance to play a more important role for these firms than it does for firms that do not have banks in a comparable position. However, large corporations raise significantly less bank finance than the German corporate sector as a whole. Indeed, Mayer and Alexander (1990) have shown that German stock corporations use less bank-loan finance than comparable large public limited companies in the United Kingdom, where banks have neither proxy voting power nor board seats. Although these findings do not completely rule out the possibility that banks take advantage of company and banking law to protect their investments if necessary, they do apparently prove that these regulatory advantages do not inevitably lead to higher bank finance.

Another incentive for a bank to take on the costs of voting stock on behalf of small shareholders and to place representatives on boards could be to try to capture all or a part of the firm's financial business. If banks use their position in this way, they have not been very successful, as Fischer's work and other evidence discussed earlier has shown. However, Fischer does not consider whether there are syndicates rather than exclusive business relationships with a single bank (as has always been contended in the literature), especially for fee-based business such as underwriting. Normally, a management board will think long and hard before it chooses to give all of its financial business to competitors of banks represented at its shareholder meeting and on its supervisory board if the latter offer the same services on roughly the same conditions.

Although there may be, apart from reputation effects, no clear incentive discernible for banks to act in their clients' interests as proxy-holders and representatives, it is also not obvious that banks successfully use their position as custodians to protect or promote their other finance business.

Disincentives

Are there disincentives for banks engaging in corporate control activities? Yes. Banks have reasons for not engaging in corporate control activities. Thus, a bank offering financial services to a firm might find it competitively advantageous to refrain from being a nuisance to management as long as things run reasonably well (Böhm, 1992, pp. 138–41). This depends on different questions in each case: what position do the offering banks and other banks take regarding management, and can management decide independently to choose a competitor or an outside bank?

Another disincentive can come from implicit management coalitions. The large banks are themselves generally corporations with widely distributed ownership. This leads to the same sympathetic understanding of how corporate governance should function, or even to certain arrangements. The simplest of these—having a manager of A sit on the supervisory board of company B and vice versa—is forbidden by law. Nonetheless, in the past, banks have helped managements of other large firms protect themselves against take-overs, usually by changing the target firm's corporate statutes to dilute the voting power of the challenger. Of course the bank may also have been protecting its own varied interests, not doing management a favour.

Banks can support or punish each other to a certain extent because they hold and vote roughly similar blocks of proxies as the other banks. This might be a strong disincentive to monitor and control the management of other banks. The three großbanken have no supervisory board members in common.

Drawbacks

When analysing institutions that represent small investors at shareholder meetings and on boards, and act as corporate monitors on shareholders' behalf, we should ask three questions. What are their incentives? Are there conflicts of interests or other drawbacks? How are the institutions themselves monitored? So far I have only described the role of banks in corporate governance—their instruments, incentives, and disincentives. This may be accepted as a substitute for more precise measurements of their performance, which economists still owe us. This section deals with whether there are drawbacks—disadvantages for shareholders as well as for the firms—connected with this governance system other than those already identified as possible disincentives.

Several large banks typically share a firm's business. There are no relationships between any large firms and a single banking institution that allow the bank to exploit the firm, although the literature says there is oligopolistic behaviour in fee-based underwriting (see Böhm, 1992, pp. 154–55, with further references). As to lending, exploitation through imposition of above-market interest rates seems highly unlikely. Financial dependence of the firm on a single bank thus does not seem to be a problem.

Institutional proxy-holders who are also creditors are sometimes alleged not to support innovative (and thus, perhaps, more risky) policies that might increase shareholder value. In other words, banks may influence investment decisions to protect an existing business relationship. They may prefer projects that need (higher) external (credit) finance to projects with a comparatively higher net present value for the firm and thus are of greater benefit to the shareholders. Banks may indeed have this preference if they are not shareholders themselves.

If the assertions of the managerialists are correct, corporate managers do not pursue profit maximization, but rather seek size or growth maximization. This means there is a common interest between managers and custodial banks at the expense of shareholders. On the other hand, debt is considered a device to discipline management. So why should management yield to its alleged incentives for growth maximization with the help of credit finance? Here we need a more systematic analysis of the relationship between the financing patterns of large firms and the underlying interests of those involved directly or as stakeholders.

A related issue is dividend policy. Management may prefer to retain earnings rather than distribute them, as this provides a way to conceal fluctuations in future reported earnings and thus reduces management's accountability for losses. Free cash flow and retained earnings give management the means to achieve growth maximization without being monitored by outside financiers, even at the expense of their own shareholders. Banks are said to support this restrictive dividend policy either because they want to get a share of the firm's transaction business or—and this seems to be the main argument—to protect their credit extensions. On the other hand, as the internal funds grow larger, managements become increasingly independent and emancipated from external finance. It is possible that banks tend to neglect this long-term development to protect their present interests. However, there are limits to the emancipation of managements because of the role banks play as proxies at shareholder meetings and on supervisory boards. Again one would like to see more theoretical and empirical studies, with reference to the tax and other cost issues affecting a firm's dividend policy. (Hort, 1984 is an empirical study. Also see Böhm, 1992, pp. 139–49 with further references; König, 1990.)

Even though there is no proof of abuse by interested parties, there is certainly a potential for it because of conflicts of interest. There is a long-standing discussion about how manipulation can be avoided without destroying the advantage of having an institutional arrangement that overcomes shareholders' passivity and serves as a professional monitor. It is not necessary to go into this discussion in detail; suffice it to say that the existing rules against abuse seem to be insufficient.

Another problem is how the performance of institutions that monitor managements on behalf of small investors can themselves be measured and controlled. By having an institution to solve the principal-agent problem at the level of the corporation, we get a principal-agent problem at the level of the intermediary. Do we have similar problems (that is, asymmetric information, collective action, and the like) at this second stage, too, and how can they be solved?

Although these questions concerning the monitoring performance of institutions as custodians for shareholders remain unanswered, in the next section an attempt is made to compare the institutional solution to a market solution, more specifically, to the threat of hostile take-over. This threat has often been claimed in the literature to align the interests of shareholders and managers adequately, and to address the problem of managerial inefficiency (see Baums, 1993c).

COMPARISON OF INSTITUTIONAL AND MARKET CONTROL

A comparison between market and institutional monitoring systems must start with a caveat. The comparison is narrowly focused in that it considers only one instrument—take-overs—from among several intended to complement each other within a given legal system in coping with managerial inefficiency, self-dealing, and related problems. If, for instance, the take-over market cannot deal with some types of management inefficiency, but the institutional control of managers can, there may be, in a system that relies on market rather than on institutional control of managers, other effective instruments available. The following comparison should be understood as theoretical rather than as a comparison of two different corporate governance systems.

Divergence of Interests

A good starting point is Eisenberg's list of how the interests of shareholders and managers can diverge. Eisenberg (1989) differentiates among shirking, traditional conflicts of interests, and positional conflicts.

Shirking—working at a slack pace and avoiding the effort and discomfort involved in adapting to changed circumstances—can arise when an agent cannot be observed, and performance cannot be controlled.

Traditional conflicts of interest involve diversion of the principal's assets to the agent's own use through unfair self-dealing. Positional conflicts arise from the interest of top managers in maintaining and enhancing their position even at the expense of shareholders. Examples include managers making it particularly difficult to monitor their performance, imposing high barriers to their own removal, and seeking to increase corporate size or free cash flow to enhance their power, prestige and salary rather than to increase the firm's value.

How do hostile take-overs and institutional monitoring through banks cope with these problems? To start with, neither is aimed at lessening shirking or self-dealing.

Because their self-esteem is tied to their work and accomplishment, most top managers refrain from shirking. Further, the selection process as well as the mutual control among agents tends to eliminate shirkers (Varian, 1990).

Most top managers probably will refrain from unfair self-dealing because they have internalized the rules of social morality. The take-over market probably has very little impact on traditional conflicts of interest like self-dealing. A hostile bid rarely succeeds unless it is significantly above the previous market price. In addition to this premium, a hostile bidder must pay large fees to investment bankers, lawyers, and others. Therefore, a take-over bid would not be economically justified if the bidder's only aim is to end unfair self-dealing by managers. That means other legal provisions must deal with this particular conflict of interest, and the same is true for a system relying on institutions such as banks rather than on take-overs as monitors. If a supervisory board finds unfair self-dealing by management, it is not just because banks have representatives on the board.

Much more interesting are the effects of take-overs and institutional control on positional conflicts. Take-over activity is motivated by the inefficiency of the target's management, as well as by factors such as synergy gains. The first question here is whether the outside bidder has information about the inefficiency of incumbent management. An inside monitor may have an information advantage. The next question is under what circumstances an outside bidder and an inside institutional monitor will react when they observe inefficiency. Unless management is extremely inefficient, it seems unlikely that a hostile bidder can procure sufficient gains simply from replacing the incumbent management. An inside monitor represented on the supervisory board can act without incurring these costs. A problem here, however, is that an institutional monitor has an incentive not to act in cases where the inefficiency is favourable to the monitor. It is unlikely that initiatives for restructuring, disposing of under-performing subsidiaries, or splitting up a conglomerate will come from bank representatives as long as the firm is not in financial distress.

(See Eisenberg, 1989; Jensen, 1988. A thorough overview of take-overs is Romano, 1992.)

Ex Ante, *Interim and* Ex Post *Monitoring*

Management replacement resulting from a take-over is *ex post* control, whereas institutional control is not. To be sure, control through the threat of replacement is thought to give management an incentive to try harder, but it works in a different way than monitoring by an inside institutional monitor. The threat of take-over will not affect the behaviour of managers who do not realize they are inefficient or think they are already doing all they can (Eisenberg, 1989, p. 1498). Ideally, the system should react before the firm has incurred considerable losses, not after. This means identifying competent managers from the beginning and gathering information continuously.

Turnover v. Relational Monitoring

The notion that the governance system we are examining is based on a long-term relationship between a few custodial institutions and firms is another contrast to a system with no intermediaries between management and shareholders. Few shareholders are active in corporate governance except by voting with their feet, especially in the case of a take-over. Shareholders, individual and institutional, may have short time horizons, if only because of liquidity needs. Short horizons and the resulting high turnover in a firm's shares can make it difficult for a company to establish meaningful relationships and two-way communications with its shareholders.

   Short-term investments in a firm's stock not only make it difficult for shareholders to influence a company's affairs, they leave the take-over mechanism as the major device to align the interests of management with those of constantly changing shareholders. They also raise the question of the extent to which shareholders who own stock only for a short period of time should be given influence in corporate affairs.

   In a system where proxies are given to professional institutions that remain the same over time, irrespective of the turnover in the underlying shares, long-term relationships and two-way communications between them and management can be established. There may be greater willingness to give more information and to concede more rights and influence to these institutions. Of course, such stable relationships do not inherently protect small shareholders because they have no control over the intermediary and because there may be conflicts of interests, as already discussed.

Long Term v. Short Term

Quarterly reports, interim dividends, and the investment policy of pension funds and other institutional investors are blamed for forcing managements to take short-term views. Hostile take-overs are said to contribute to this, too. The plans of the EC Commission to abolish caps on shareholder voting rights and dual class voting under the Fifth EC directive have been strongly opposed by German industry, especially on the grounds that the resulting (hostile) take-over activity would lead to short-termism and have a negative effect on resource allocation and the German economy as a whole.

How do managers behave in a system without stable, long-term relationships with their shareholders when there is a threat of a hostile take-over? Do they seek to keep the current stock price high by inflating current earnings through slashing expenditures that pay off only in the long term? This has frequently been contended in the literature as well as in the political debate.

Some economists say investors are short-sighted and behave myopically to sacrifice long-term benefits for immediate profits. As a consequence, firms that engage in long-term planning and make substantial investments in research and development are undervalued by the market and become take-over targets. Shleifer and Vishny (1990) argue that the short time horizon of arbitrageurs, who focus on short-term assets because they are relatively less expensive to arbitrage, may result in market underpricing of a corporation's equity. This phenomenon is said, in turn, to impose a short time horizon on managers. They supposedly react by avoiding long-term investments, which are said to depress share prices in the short term, and make the corporation vulnerable to a hostile take-over.

Stein (1988) has developed a formal model in which the threat of take-overs encourages myopic behaviour on the part of managers. A central prediction of this model is that firms that construct barriers to take-overs are able to increase profitable long-term investments such as research and development.

What is the empirical evidence? Firms actually *decrease* R&D intensity after the introduction of shark repellents and take-over impediments may even reduce incentives to engage in long-term investment in general (Meulbroek and others, 1990; also see Gordon and Pound, 1991; Romano, 1992, p. 145 with further references). Furthermore, there is evidence that the stock market responds positively to announcements of increases in R&D and other capital investment expenditures (Chan, Martin and Kensinger, 1990; also see Marsh, 1990, p. 19 with further references). This does not mean there are no informational asymmetries between the markets and firms regarding such expenditures, as management perhaps does not want to communicate commercially sensitive information to the market. It may well be that managers, in order to avoid undervalued stock which might lure hostile bidders, shift from profitable long-term investment to short-term projects—although this hardly seems to be a good defence against unwanted bids.

Is it possible at least to establish that the corporate governance structure of large German firms supports a long-term view by management? To my knowledge there is no evidence available on this. My guess is that management is encouraged to maintain a focus on the long term. First, top managers have secure long-term tenure, at least in the five-year increments of their election. Second, the equity holdings of banks as well as the proxies they hold have been stable over time, and this is likely to continue. This means the monitoring institutions have remained the same. Long-term projects can be discussed with them, and this discussion can be a dialogue rather than just a signal to an anonymous market. On the other hand, we must take into account the incentives of banks as creditors—they might prefer projects that are relatively less profitable to the firm.

In short, there is no clear-cut answer to our question as to whether the elements of the governance systems discussed here favour rather than discourage long-term investments with higher net present values.

Adaptability to Change

In order to assess management performance, an internal monitoring system must rely on comparisons between actual and plan results, current and previous results, and the firm's results and those of competitors. This suggests a limitation of internal monitoring that outside governance may overcome.

A potential outside bidder may have information about, say, a new technology that a firm's management and supervisory board do not have, in part because it is not yet in use within the industry. To the extent that outside governance by (hostile) take-overs forces a firm to adapt to technological changes, is it a necessary supplement to an internal system that fails in such cases? Here one must differentiate between the mere lack of information and reluctance to act. Hostile take-overs are not necessary to disseminate new information.

Management and the supervisory board may, however, be reluctant to make changes that raise the firm's market value. This includes situations where the required changes—layoffs, wage reductions, investment cutbacks, or divestitures—would harm the employees, who are considered more important to the organization than shareholders, or result in negative publicity or problems with local authorities. In such cases a hostile bidder could buy the firm and implement profit-increasing changes against the wishes of both the board and top management. More generally, take-overs play a role in changing a firm's policy and in replacing managers the supervisory board is unable or unwilling to force to take the necessary steps.

There is interesting empirical evidence for this role of hostile take-overs in the United States. Morck, Shleifer and Vishny (1989) examined the circumstances under which a company's poor performance leads to an internal governance response—the incumbent board replacing management—as opposed to the external governance response of a hostile take-over. Tracking a sample of 454 Fortune 500 companies over the period 1981–85, the authors conclude that an internal governance response is more likely when a company performs poorly compared to its competitors, while hostile take-overs are more common when it is the entire industry that shows poor performance. In the latter cases (airlines, steel, oil), boards apparently were reluctant to remove unresponsive managers. Instead, this function was accomplished by hostile take-overs.

CONCLUSION

The description of the German corporate finance system as bank oriented as opposed to market oriented is one-sided as this distinction is based on only two of many sources of finance. Furthermore, some of the widespread assumptions about specific features of the German corporate finance system—including the role of equity finance by banks, the role of bankers on firms' boards, the role of house bank—and their benefits for corporate finance seem doubtful. Empirical evidence shows that some of these features—for example, debt-equity finance—are not as important as assumed, and others are fading—for example, house bank relationships. In addition, some of the underlying hypotheses concerning the benefits of the bank-oriented structure are not convincing.

The description of the German corporate governance system as bank oriented is misleading. Only a small number of banks act as monitors of management on behalf of shareholders in a small number of firms, and even for this case, limited empirical work on the banks' role suggests great care in drawing conclusions. For all other firms, there is an even greater lack of data and thorough studies on the extent to which German banks play a role in corporate governance that differs markedly from the monitoring role of credit institutions in other countries.

REFERENCES

AGHION, PHILIPPE and PATRICK BOLTON. 1989. 'The Financial Structure of the Firm and the Problem of Control.' *European Economic Review* 33: 286–93.

ALLEN, F. 1989. 'The Changing Nature of Debt and Equity: A Financial Perspective.' In Richard W. Kopcke and Eric S. Rosengren, eds., *Are the Distinctions between Debt and Equity Disappearing?* Conference Series 33. Federal Reserve Bank of Boston.

BAUMS, THEODOR. 1993a. 'Takeovers vs. Institutions in Corporate Governance in Germany.' In D. D. Prentice and P. R. J. Holland, eds., *Contemporary Issues in Corporate Governance*. Oxford: Clarendon Press.

——. 1993b. 'Hostile Takeovers in Germany: A Case Study on Pirelli vs. Continental AG.' Arbeitspapiere 93–3. Universität Osnabrück, Institut für Handels- und Wirtschaftsrecht.

——. 1993c. 'Feindliche Übernahmen und Managementkontrolle—Anmerkungen aus deutscher Sicht.' Arbeitspapiere 93–1. Universität Osnabrück, Institut für Handels- und Wirtschaftsrecht.

BAUMS, THEODOR and MICHAEL GRUSON. 1993. 'The German Banking System—System of the Future?' *Brooklyn Journal of International Law* 19: 101–29.

BdS (Bericht der Studienkommission). 1979. 'Grundsatzfragen der Kreditwirtschaft.'

BENSTON, GEORGE J. 1994. 'Universal Banking.' *Journal of Economic Perspectives* 8(2) (Spring).

BERGLÖF, ERIK. 1990. 'Capital Structure as a Mechanism of Control: A Comparison of Financial Systems.' In Masahiko Aoki and others, eds., *The Firm as a Nexus of Treaties*. London: Sage Publications.

BLEICHER, KNUT. 1987. *Der Aufsichtsrat im Wandel*. Gütersloh: Verlag Bertelsmann-Stiftung.

BÖHM, JÜRGEN. 1992. *Der Einfluss der Banken auf Grossunternehmen*. Hamburg: S+W Steuer- und Wirtschaftsverlag.

BONUS, HOLGER. 1987. *Die Genossenschaft als modernes Unternehmenskonzept*. Genossenschaftswissenschaftliche Beiträge. Vorträge Heft 10, Institut für Genossenschaftswesen der Universität Münster.

BONUS, HOLGER and GEORG SCHMIDT. 1990. 'The Cooperative Banking Group in the Federal Republic of Germany: Aspects of Institutional Change.' *Journal of Institutional and Theoretical Economics* 146: 180–207.

BORIO, C. 1990. 'Leverage and Financing of Non-Financial Companies: An International Perspective.' Economic Paper 27. Basel: Bank for International Settlements.

CABLE, JOHN R. 1985. 'Capital Market Information and Industrial Performance: The Role of West German Banks.' *Economic Journal* 95(377): 118–32 (Mar).

CHAN, SU HAN, JOHN D. MARTIN, and JOHN W. KENSINGER. 1990. 'Corporate Research and Development Expenditures and Share Value.' *Journal of Financial Economics* 26(2): 255–76 (August).

CHARKHAM, JONATHAN. 1989. 'Corporate Governance and the Market for Control of Companies.' Panel Paper 25. Bank of England, London.

CONARD, A. 1984. 'Comparative Law: The Supervision of Corporate Management: A Comparison of Developments in European Community and United States Law.' *Michigan Law Review* 82: 1459.

EISENBERG, MELVIN ARON. 1989. 'The Structure of Corporate Law.' *Columbia Law Review* 89: 1471–74.

EDWARDS, JEREMY and KLAUS FISCHER. 1991. 'Banks, Finance and Investment in

West Germany since 1970.' CEPR London Discussion Paper Series 497. Cambridge MA: Cambridge University Press.

FISCHER, KLAUS. 1990. *Hausbankbeziehungen als Instrument der Bindung zwischen Banken und Unternehmen—Eine Theoretische und Empirische Analyse*. Diss. rer. oec. Bonn: Rechts- und Staatswissenschaftliche Fakultät der Universität.

FRANKEL, ALLEN B. and JOHN D. MONTGOMERY. 1991. 'Financial Structure: An International Perspective.' *Brookings Papers on Economic Activity* 1: 257–97.

GERSCHENKRON, ALEXANDER. 1962. *Economic Backwardness in Historical Perspective*. Cambridge MA: Harvard University Press.

GERUM, ELMAR, HORST STEINMANN, and WERNER FEES. 1987. *Der mitbestimmte Aufsichtsrat—Eine empirische Untersuchung*. Stuttgart: Verlag C. E. Poeschel.

GESSNER, VOLKMAR, BARBARA RHODE, GERHARD STRATE, and KLAUS A. ZIEGERT. 1978. *Die Praxis der Konkursabwicklung in der Bundesrepublik Deutschland*. Köln: Bundesanzeiger Verlagsges.

GORDON, LILLI A. and JOHN POUND. 1991. 'Governance Matters: An Empirical Study of the Relationship between Corporate Governance and Corporate Performance.' Corporate Research Project John F. Kennedy School of Government, Harvard University.

GOTTSCHALK, ARNO. 1988. 'Der Stimmrechtseinfluss der Banken in den Aktionärsversammlungen von Großunternehmen.' WSI-Mitteilungen.

HARM, CHRISTIAN. 1992. 'Historical Notes on the Development of the German Banking System.' Working paper. New York University.

HELLWIG, MARTIN. 1991. 'Banking, Financial Intermediation and Corporate Finance.' In Alberto Giovannini and Colin Mayer, eds., *European Financial Integration*. Cambridge, Mass.: Cambridge University Press.

HORT, H. 1984. 'Zur Dividendenpolitik der Aktiengesellschaften des verarbeitenden Gewerbes der Bundesrepublik Deutschland—Ein empirischer Beitrag.' Doctoral thesis, University of Saarbrücken.

IMMENGA, ULRICH. 1978. *Beteiligungen von Banken in anderen Wirtschaftszweigen* (Studien zum Bank- und Börsenrecht) 2nd ed. Baden-Baden: NOMOS Verlagsgesellschaft.

JENSEN, MICHAEL C. 1988. 'Takeovers: Their Causes and Consequences.' *Journal of Economic Perspectives* 2: 21–48.

——. 1989. 'Agency Costs of Free Cash Flow, Corporate Finance, and Takeovers.' In Clifford W. Smith, Jr., ed., *The Modern Theory of Corporate Finance* 2nd ed.

JENSEN, MICHAEL C. and WILLIAM H. MECKLING. 1976. 'Theory of the Firm: Managerial Behavior, Agency Costs and Ownership Structure.' *Journal of Financial Economics* 3(4): 305–60 (October).

KAPLAN, STEVEN N. 1993. 'Top Executives, Turnover and Firm Performance in Germany.' Working Paper. University of Chicago.

KIM, SUN BAI. 1990. 'Modus Operandi of Lender-cum-Shareholder Banks.' Working paper. Federal Reserve Bank of San Francisco.

KLEIN, WILLIAM A. and JOHN C. COFFEE, Jr. 1990. *Business Organization and Finance: Legal and Economic Principles* 4th ed. McGraw Hill.

KÖNIG, ROLF JÜRGEN. 1990. *Ausschüttungsverhalten von Aktiengesellschaften, Besteuerung und Kapitalmarktgleichgewicht*. Hamburg: S+W Steuer- und Wirtschaftsverlag.

MARSH, PAUL. 1990. *Short-Termism on Trial.* A report commissioned by the Institutional Fund Managers' Association (IFMA). London: IFMA.

MATHIS, PETER J. 1992. 'Mechanismen zur Kontrolle von Managern in großen Kapitalgesellschaften—Eine ökonomische Analyse.' Doctoral thesis, University of Saarbrücken.

MAYER, COLIN. 1988. 'New Issues in Corporate Finance.' *European Economic Review* 32: 1167–89.

——. 1990. 'Financial Systems, Corporate Finance, and Economic Development.' In R. Glenn Hubbard, ed., *Asymmetric Information, Corporate Finance, and Investment.* Chicago: University of Chicago Press.

MAYER, COLIN and IAN ALEXANDER. 1990. 'Banks and Securities Markets: Corporate Financing in Germany and the United Kingdom.' *Journal of Japanese and International Economies* 4(4): 450–75 (Dec).

MCCAULEY, ROBERN N. and STEVEN A. ZIMMER. 1989. 'Explaining International Differences in the Cost of Capital: The U.S. and U.K. vs. Japan and Germany.' Research Paper 8913. Federal Reserve Bank of New York.

MEIER-SCHATZ, CHRISTIAN J. 1980. 'Corporate Governance and Legal Rules: A Transnational Look at Concepts of International Management Control.' *Journal of Corporate Law* 13: 431–80.

MEULBROEK, LISA K. and others. 1990. 'Shark Repellents and Managerial Myopia: An Empirical Test.' *Journal of Political Economy* 98: 1108–17.

Monopolkommission. 1978. 'Zweites Hauptgutachten 1976/77, Fortschreitende Konzentration bei Großunternehmen.'

MORCK, RANDALL, ANDREI SHLEIFER, and ROBERT W. VISHNY. 1989. 'Alternative Mechanisms for Corporate Control.' *American Economic Review* 79: 842–52.

MYERS, STEWARD C. and NICHOLAS S. MAJLUF. 1984. 'Corporate Financing and Investment Decisions When Firms Have Information that Investors Do Not Have.' *Journal of Financial Economics* 13: 187–221.

NEUBURGER, HUGH M. and HOUSTON H. STOKES. 1974. 'German Banks and German Growth 1883–1913: An Empirical View.' *Journal of Economic History* 34: 710–31.

POENSGEN, OTTO H. and ANDREAS LUKAS. 1982. 'Fluktuation, Amtszeit und weitere Karriere von Vorstandsmitgliedern.' *Die Betriebswirtschaft* 42: 187.

POZDENA, RÅNDALL J. 1987. 'Commerce and Banking: The German Case.' *Federal Reserve Bank of San Francisco Weekly Letter* December 18.

——. 1990. 'Why Banks Need Securities Powers.' Working paper. Federal Reserve Bank of San Francisco.

ROGGENBUCK, HARALD E. 1992. *Begrenzung des Anteilsbesitzes von Kreditinstituten an Nichtbanken—Gesetzliche Regelungen, empirischer Befund sowie anlage- und geschäftspolitische Bedeutung.* Frankfurt am Main: Verlag Peter Lang.

ROMANO, ROBERTA. 1992. 'A Guide to Takeovers: Theory, Evidence, and Regulations.' *Yale Journal on Regulation* 9: 119–80.

RYBCZYNSKI, TAD M. 1984. 'Industrial Finance System in Europe, U.S. and Japan.' *Journal of Economic Behavior and Organization* 5(3–4): 275–86 (September–December).

SCHMITZ, CHRISTOPHER. 1992. 'Cooperative Managerial Capitalism: Recent Research in German Business History.' *German History* 10: 91–103.

SHLEIFER, ANDREI and ROBERT W. VISHNY. 1990. 'Equilibrium Short Horizons of Investors and Firms.' *American Economic Review* 80: 148–53.

STEIN, JEREMY C. 1988. 'Takeover Threats and Managerial Myopia.' *Journal of Political Economy* 96: 61–79.

STIGLITZ, JOSEPH E. and ANDREW WEISS. 1981. 'Credit Rationing in Markets with Imperfect Information.' *American Economic Review* 71(3): 393–410 (Jun).

TILLY, RICHARD H. 1966. *Financial Institutions and Industrialization in the Rhineland 1815–1870.* Madison WI: University of Wisconsin Press.

——. 1986. 'German Banking 1850–1914: Development Assistance to the Strong.' *Journal of European Economic History* 15: 113–52.

——. 1989. 'Banking Institutions in Historical and Comparative Perspective— Germany, Great Britain and the United States in the 19th and 20th Century.' *Zeitschrift für die gesamte Staatswissenschaft (Journal of Institutional and Theoretical Economics)* 145: 189–209.

TILLY, RICHARD H. and RAINER FREMDLING. 1976. 'German Banks, German Growth and Econometric History.' *Journal of Economic History* 36: 416–27.

VARIAN, HAL R. 1990. 'Monitoring Agents with Other Agents.' *Journal of Institutional and Theoretical Economics* 146: 153–74.

VOGEL, WOLFGANG. 1980. *Aktienrecht und Aktienwirklichkeit—Organisation und Aufgabenteilung von Vorstand und Aufsichtstrat.* Baden-Baden: NOMOS Verlagsgesellschaft.

WIEDEMANN, HERBERT. 1980. 'Codetermination by Workers in German Enterprises.' *American Journal of Comparative Law* 28: 79–82.

WILLIAMSON, OLIVER E. 1988. 'Corporate Finance and Corporate Governance.' *Journal of Finance* 43: 567–91.

13

The Principal Transactions Bank System in Korea

SANG-WOO NAM AND DONG-WON KIM

It has been widely recognized that the Korean government's intervention in the country's financial sector was a crucial element in the development policy that guided the process of Korean economic development. As recently as the early 1980s, nationwide commercial banks were owned by the government and allocated credit according to priorities set by governmental development policy. However, the government's policy of industrial support using financial intervention also produced serious side effects. Development efforts under high inflation and interest rate regulation resulted in weak corporate capital structure. As economically unjustified investments were undertaken, the efficiency of the Korean economy was hampered. At the same time, government financial intervention accelerated the concentration of economic power in large business groups (*chaebol*).[1]

A credit control system was introduced in the mid-1970s to correct these problems. Korea has a particular form of bank-enterprise relationship that links each large business group to a particular bank in the context of the credit control system. This 'principal transactions bank system' is distinguished from the Japanese main bank system in several aspects, as is discussed later, and it is hard to say that a 'main bank system' exists in Korea as a generalized form of bank-enterprise relationship. The Korean system regulates bank credit extended to large corporations through what are called their 'principal transactions banks'. The major functions of these banks include reporting to the government (the Office of Bank Supervision and Examination) to help it monitor the financial situation and investment activities of corporations, as well as implementing government credit control measures against the corporate sector. The role of principal transactions banks is played only in the context of the credit control system.

The nature of government control exerted on the corporate sector has

---

[1] A *chaebol* is a group of large corporations holding controlling shares in each other. They are different from Japanese keiretsu in that a chaebol is tightly controlled by a single owner and his family, while a keiretsu is a loosely connected group of corporations in a cooperative relationship without any single controlling shareholder. Because of the ownership concentration, concentration of economic power in chaebol represents a skewed distribution of wealth in the society. The terms chaebol, business group, and group are used interchangeably in this chapter. The word 'chaebol' is singular or plural as context dictates.

changed, reflecting the emerging challenges the Korean economy is facing. The system was first utilized to encourage large corporations to finance their growth through the stock market. In the 1980s it was used as a means to reduce the concentration of economic power to large business groups, while in the later years it was mainly aimed at curbing real estate acquisitions and encouraging R & D investments. Despite these changes of objectives, the credit control system remains as a regulatory framework ensuring government control of the corporate sector. It is far from being an autonomous bank-customer relationship. Consequently, as the credit control system assumed a more regulatory nature, so did the principal transactions bank system.

However, in the process of opening the domestic Korean economy to foreign competition, which calls for immense restructuring efforts on the part of corporations, there has been increasing concern that the credit control system poses a serious impediment to structural adjustment. As such, the principal transactions bank system is at a crossroads where it has to be reoriented to a normal bank-customer relationship rather than retain a regulatory role.

The focus of this chapter is to investigate the role of the principal transactions bank system in Korea as well as the costs that accompany such a system. For those wishing to know more about Korean financial development, Park and Kim (1994) and Park (1994) are concise analyses. Of course, our final objective is to draw lessons from the Korean experience on the desirability of a Korean-type system in developing economies.

The first section examines the evolution of the principal transactions bank system in accordance with shifts in the government's development objectives. The second section reviews the structure of the present principal transactions bank system, the role the banks play, and the nature of the controls the government imposed on the corporate sector through the banks. In the third and fourth sections we evaluate the performance of the system in mitigating the problems produced by government intervention in credit allocation, looking first at the system's performance and then at its problems. In the fifth section we examine the roles of the Korea Development Bank and the Korea Long-Term Credit Bank; both have been an important source of long-term capital for Korean companies and for this and other reasons have played different roles from the principal transactions banks. The sixth section compares Korea's principal transactions bank system with the Japanese main bank system, identifying the similarities and differences between them. Through this comparison, we explain why Korea's principal transactions bank system has developed in a markedly different manner from the Japanese system, and argue for the introduction of a main bank system in developing economies. The final section summarizes the lessons we feel can be learned from the Korean experience.

EVOLUTION OF THE PRINCIPAL TRANSACTIONS
BANK SYSTEM

The role of financial institutions as mobilizers of savings in Korea was recognized only after the interest rate reform in September 1965, which contributed significantly to the deepening of the financial market. The military coup in the early 1960s led to the nationalization of commercial banks, and a number of new financial institutions were established to perform specialized activities such as financing small and medium firms, housing, and foreign exchange business.

Throughout the 1970s, the Korean financial system was under increasing repression with rigid interest rate controls despite accelerated inflation and extensive government intervention in credit allocation. Consequently, financial development was rather slow. However, with the Presidential Emergency Decree in 1972 which froze the informal curb loan market, short-term finance, mutual savings, and finance companies were established, contributing to the diversification of Korea's financial markets. The capital market has also grown rapidly since 1972 due to strong promotional measures by the government.

Promotion of the heavy and chemical industries in the 1970s through the provision of subsidized bank loans resulted in a multiplicity of side effects: inefficient investment allocation, weak capital structure of large corporations, limited access of small and medium firms to bank credit, concentration of economic power, and managerial inefficiency of banks.

The serious consequences of excessive government intervention in resource allocation gave rise to the need for financial liberalization in the early 1980s. The liberalization effort started with the lifting of many restrictions on bank management and lowering entry barriers to various financial services in order to promote competition and efficiency. In addition, the government divested its equity shares in all of the nationwide commercial banks. Most preferential interest rates applied to various policy loans were abolished and, in the 1990s, there has been some deregulation of interest rates.[2]

Korea's principal transactions bank system started as a way of exerting credit control on the *chaebol*. The evolution of the credit control system must first be analysed in order to understand the principal transactions

---

[2] Policy loans are loosely defined as those provided with preferential interest rates or earmarked for specific sectors or industries. They include export financing; National Investment Fund (NIF) loans, supplied mainly to heavy and chemical industries; loans for small and medium firms, housing, agriculture and fisheries; loans in foreign currency; credit to the KDB and the Korea EXIM Bank; and special loans for facility investment. In recent years, export financing and loans to specific industries have been more or less phased out, even though credit of deposit money banks to the KDB and EXIM Bank as well as that for housing, agriculture and small and medium firms have expanded substantially.

bank system, since the role of the principal transactions banks and their relationship with the corporate sector were defined within the structure of the credit control system. The system has gone through many complicated revisions since its start in 1974, but for analytic convenience its evolution can be divided into four broad stages.

The Credit Control System

The credit control system was introduced with the May 29 Measure in 1974, which aimed at improving the capital structure of large corporations by encouraging direct financing through public offerings of equity while holding down borrowing from financial institutions. The highly leveraged capital structure and the insolvency of many companies were mainly due to the excessive business expansion during the course of rapid economic development in the latter half of the 1960s. Between 1965 and 1970, the equity ratio of manufacturing firms showed a significant decline, going from 51.6 per cent to 23.3 per cent.

The sharp increase in bank lending after the interest rate reform in 1965 and the full-scale introduction of foreign capital in 1966 resulted in excessive dependence on borrowing and insolvency of many corporations despite rapid economic growth. The government undertook restructuring of insolvent companies between 1969 and 1971 and carried out the August 3 Measure in 1972 in order fundamentally to address the problem of the worsening corporate capital structure and excessive financial burden (see Cole and Park, 1983). The government then adopted a credit control system as an institutional tool to promote the sound capital structure of corporations.

Credit Control of Business Groups (1974–78)

To implement the May 29 Measure more effectively, the Council of Banking Institutions agreed on credit control of business groups in July 1974. Understandably, this Agreement was prepared with the administrative guidance of the government. It was applied to all the member companies of any business group whose total credit from banking institutions exceeded 5 billion won (slightly over US$11 million at the time). It designated the bank with which the principal company of a *chaebol* had major business relationships as the principal transactions bank for all the companies belonging to that group. The main functions of a principal transactions bank were as follows:

- Examine clients' plans for improving their capital structure and evaluate the results.
- Set a ceiling on the credit used as operating capital by its clients.

- Promote the capital structure improvement and efficient management of its clients.
- When non-principal banks extend new credit to a corporation, they have to consult the corporation's principal transactions bank.

After the Agreement was put into effect it was discovered that a group's principal transactions bank could not carry out its role fully. Group members were not very dependent on the bank for their borrowings because they often had major business relationships with other banks. To deal with this, and to complement the existing Agreement on Credit Control over Business Groups, the Agreement on the Operation of the Principal Transactions Bank System was adopted in July 1976. The main contents of this Agreement were as follows:

- The principal transactions bank supervises the overall credit to large corporations above a certain size.
- The authority to set a credit ceiling for a client company is transferred to its principal transactions bank from the bank with whom the company has maintained major business relationships.
- The principal transactions banks' position in the overall corporate credit management of the group and its members is strengthened as the banks are allowed to set ceilings on operating capital, provide business information, and give management guidance to companies.

Consolidation and Tightening of Control (1978–84)

Even though the authority of the principal transactions banks was strengthened by the 1976 Agreement, the dualistic operation of the credit control system in which the 1976 Agreement coexisted with the Agreement on Credit Control over Business Groups of 1974 caused many problems. First, the dualistic operation proved to be inefficient, rather than mutually beneficial, in handling information about business groups and promoting improvement of their capital structure. Second, there was a limit to the effective implementation of credit control because both agreements could only impose weak sanctions against offending corporations, such as recommending voluntary management improvement.

To address these problems, the Council of Banking Institutions signed the Agreement on Credit Control by Principal Transactions Banks in 1978, combining the 1974 and 1976 agreements and expanding the role of principal transactions banks in enforcing them. Under the new Agreement, prior consultation with the borrowing corporation's principal bank became mandatory for non-principal banks when they lent more than a specified amount. In addition, a corporation had to consult its principal bank before closing its books for the year and deciding its dividend. The point worth noting is that even though the Agreement was voluntary among banks, it included official regulations of the Office of Bank Supervision and Examination (OBSE). The 1978 Agreement was revised 14 times to further tighten regulations until it was abolished in 1984. Consequently, the supervisory function of the principal transactions banks over their client companies was strengthened, particularly in the areas of real estate acquisitions and investment in other companies.

An interesting change in the credit control system during this period was that the objective shifted from improving the capital structure and efficiency of use of capital by *chaebol* to restricting real estate acquisitions and investment in other companies. This shift was introduced in order to support the September 27 Measure of 1980 which was undertaken to reinforce corporate competitiveness. In the early 1980s, Korean companies suffered from a severe recession caused by the second oil shock, as well as political and social unrest following the assassination of President Park. The government seems to have believed that weakening international competitiveness was fundamentally attributable to their imprudent investment behaviour in real estate acquisitions and ill-planned business expansion into new industries.

The September 27 Measure forced firms to repay borrowing from banking institutions by selling their non-operating real estate, as well as the real estate held by business owners and managers, while coercing 26 business groups with too many member companies or weak capital structures to dispose of some of their companies. As a result, 309.9 billion won of borrowing from banking institutions, equal to 2.7 per cent of the broadly defined money supply, was repaid by selling real estate and 166 member companies were disposed of by the end of 1984. Of the real estate sold, 56 per cent (in terms of value) was purchased by individuals and companies not subject to credit control, and the rest was sold to the Land Development Corporation, a government-invested corporation.

Institutionalization of the System and Tightening of Credit Control (1984–91)

With the start of the 1980s, the credit control system based on the 1978 Agreement among banking institutions faced two problems. Even though this system bound firms, in a practical sense, on the basis of assumed collusion among banking institutions, it lacked the legal foundation to become an official regulation. The discontent voiced by large corporations increased as credit control became tighter and, in particular, as the September 27 Measure forced sales of real estate and disposal of some of the groups' member companies.

Second, the Agreement, based on the assumed collusion among the banking institutions, was against the Monopoly Regulation and Fair Trade Act. For these reasons, the credit control system was reformed into an official regulatory system following the revision of the General Banking Act at the end of 1982. The revised General Banking Act provided the legal foundation for credit control of business groups. Article 30–2 states that (1) The Monetary Board may restrict, by fixing ceilings, the aggregate volume of outstanding loans, guarantees or assumptions of obligations of a banking institution for any individual business group. (2) The scope of corporations belonging to a business group as provided in Paragraph (1) shall be determined by the Monetary Board.

The Agreement on Credit Control by the Principal Transactions Banks was abolished simultaneously with the application of the Monopoly Regulation and Fair Trade Act to the banking sector in July 1984, and gave way to official administrative controls based on the Monetary Board's 'Regulation on Credit Operations of Banking Institutions'.

The credit control system has undergone significant changes in objective and characteristics since 1984, reflecting the progress in financial liberalization as well as political and social changes. These changes resulted in the concentration of credit control mainly on the 30 largest *chaebol* while control on other corporations eased (Table 13.1).

First, since so many business groups and companies were subject to credit control, restrictions on large chaebol tended to be lax while those

TABLE 13.1 Number of Corporations Subject to Credit Control

Dec 1984	Mar 1985	Dec 1987	Dec 1988	Oct 1989	
161	63	50	50	48	Business groups
1,459	696	807	845	913	Companies in group
280	–	–	–	–	Companies not in a group

Notes: Criteria for corporations subject to credit control:

Jul. 1984   * Corporations that have more than 5 billion won of total credit (loans + payment guarantees) and at the same time belong to business groups whose total credit exceeds 20 billion won.
* Corporations that have more than 10 billion won of total credit or more than 5 billion won of loans, even if they do not belong to a business group.

Mar. 1985 Corporations belonging to business groups that have more than 100 billion won of total credit.

Jan. 1987 Corporations belonging to business groups that have more than 150 billion won of total credit.

Jun. 1991 Corporations that are part of one of the 50 largest business groups selected on the basis of loans from banking institutions (excluding loans of major corporations).

Source: Unpublished data submitted to the National Assembly by the Office of Bank Supervision and Examination.

on other firms were very restrictive. Because the amount of credit available for a company was decided on the basis of its past requirement, small but fast-growing companies were always in dire need, but large and well-established companies had an ample supply of credit. The restrictions were so severe that they limited normal business activities. In order to correct such inefficiencies, the number of *chaebol* subject to credit control was reduced, and a 'basket credit control' was adopted which regulated the share of business groups in the total credit of banking institutions.

Second, the mode of allocating bank credit became rigid as the companies subjected to control accounted for 50 per cent of total bank loans and 63 per cent of total bank credit at the end of 1984. Furthermore, because credit control was applied uniformly to a broad range of activities, the credit evaluation capacity of banking institutions was hampered, and corporate activities were unduly limited. With the progress in financial liberalization in the 1980s, these excessive regulations needed to be relaxed. Accordingly, the credit control system was improved and major emphasis was placed on discouraging real estate acquisition and investment in other companies.

Third, the objectives of credit control shifted from improving the capital structure of corporations to suppressing the concentration of economic power (Table 13.2) and promoting access to bank credit. Two factors were mainly responsible for this shift. The government began to adopt the view that economic development that depended heavily on large business corporations was no longer desirable in terms of efficiency. At the same time, people's desire for better allocative equity increased after the democratic reform in 1987, and this contributed to a social atmosphere that was critical of large corporations. As a result, the credit control system assumed a rather complicated nature, reflecting these political and social considerations in addition to its original objectives. Consequently, a strong basket control system was adopted in 1988 which led to a steady reduction of the shares of the 5 largest and 30 largest business groups in total bank credit.

Finally, credit control also played an important role in monetary management, as the monetary expansion caused by the foreign sector was

TABLE 13.2 Share of the Largest Business Groups in Manufacturing Sales (per cent)

	1977	1982	1987	1989
5 largest	15.7	22.6	22.0	21.3
30 largest	34.1	40.7	37.3	35.4

Source: Jung and Yang (1992, p. 41); unpublished KDI survey data.

enormous due to the large current account surpluses between 1986 and 1989.

Relaxation of Credit Control Since 1991

As the current account returned to deficit in 1990, there was renewed concern over the growth potential of the Korean economy as well as the international competitiveness of the manufacturing sector. As a result, the tight credit regulations of the 1980s started to be relaxed in 1991. The criterion for selecting business groups subject to credit control was changed from those with total bank credit of more than 150 billion won to the 50 largest business groups in terms of borrowing from banking institutions. Credit guarantees provided by banks were excluded from the selection criteria.

To encourage specialization, each of the 30 largest *chaebol* was allowed to select up to three 'Major Corporations' from among its member companies; these were exempted from credit control. To ease the administrative difficulties stemming from duplicative regulations regarding the basket ceiling imposed on loans of each bank and the total basket ceiling on the aggregate loans of all banks, which had applied to the 5 largest and 30 largest *chaebol*, the rules are now applied only to the 5 largest.

STRUCTURE OF THE CURRENT SYSTEM

Credit control is imposed on the 50 largest business groups selected annually by the Office of Bank Supervision and Examination (OBSE) on the basis of the average end-of-month outstanding borrowings from banking institutions in the fourth quarter of the previous year. However, the degree of credit control applied to the 30 largest groups is quite different from that applied to the remaining 20. The 30 largest are subject to basket control (ceilings), need approval from their principal transactions banks for investment in new businesses, and have to fulfil the requirement of 'self-help effort' in financing their real estate acquisitions and investment in new businesses. Also, investment in new businesses by the group owner and persons with special relations with the owner should be reported to, and accepted by, the principal transactions bank.

The remaining 20 business groups need the approval of their principal transactions banks only in the case of real estate acquisitions and are exempted from basket control of credit as well as regulations on specialization and self-help financing efforts. They are under the general guidance of their principal transactions banks for capital structure improvement. As for the business groups which are not subject to credit control but have borrowed more than 50 billion won from banking institutions, banks have to submit a monthly report on their investment in new businesses to the OBSE. Business groups whose principal corporation is placed under the management control of a bank or a court are exempted. Also, loans extended by overseas bank branches and post-shipment export credit are not included in the basket credit control. Otherwise, listed corporations whose ownership is well dispersed—combined equity share below 8 per cent for the group owner and those with special relations with the owner—are not subject to credit control.

Basket Control of Credit

Control of bank credit in Korea basically starts from the M2 growth target that is set with a view to stabilizing prices. Until the late 1970s, the level of domestic credit consistent with the M2 target was set by the monetary authorities and allocated each month among banks. Even though this kind of strict credit allocation has been relaxed somewhat since the 1980s, the direct control of M2 to meet its growth target has continued.

By setting a ceiling on the share of large business groups in banks' total credit, the government tried to ensure credit availability for small and medium enterprises under a given M2 growth target. Article 6 of the Regulation on Credit Operations of Banking Institutions states that the OBSE can set a ceiling on the total share of *chaebol* subject to basket control in each banking institution's total loans. The Operational Bylaw on Credit Control over Business Groups also states that a bank should not let the collective shares of the 5 largest and 30 largest *chaebol* in its total loans exceed the levels set by the OBSE. For example, the credit ceilings for the groups in 1991 were 5.8 and 10.81 per cent, respectively. The actual shares at the end of 1991 were 5.44 per cent and 9.81 per cent. Loans from non-bank financial intermediaries and issuance of bank guaranteed corporate bonds are not subject to ceilings.

In extreme cases, the OBSE may even determine the amount of credit for each business group, although this has not been done. Not all borrowings of the 30 largest groups are subject to basket control; loans to Major Corporations (three companies within each group so designated by the group) and Corporations with Highly Dispersed Ownership (those with less than 8 per cent of equity held by the group owner and those with special relations with the owner) are exempted. Loans extended by overseas branches and post-shipment export financing are also exempted.

As ceilings were imposed on the groups subject to basket control as a whole, as well as on individual banks, imbalance in credit access among different business groups was frequently observed. Thus, during the 1988–90 period, ceilings of borrowing shares were imposed on not only the 30 largest groups as a whole, but also on individual groups. Under this regulation however, an individual bank could not know whether additional lending to corporations belonging to a business group, though not exceeding the ceiling on the bank, would exceed the ceiling on the business group. This difficulty led to the revision of the provision in April 1991, which imposed the ceiling on borrowing shares only on banks.

Selection of the Principal Transactions Banks

The principal transactions bank system is applied only to corporations subject to credit control as designated by the OBSE. The principal transactions bank is selected through a conference among banks that have business relations with the corporation. The principal transactions bank for the principal corporation of a business group usually becomes the principal transactions bank for all the corporations belonging to that group. The principal corporation is decided by the OBSE in consideration of the company's position in the group, and that depends on asset size and influence on other companies.

Even though any banking institution is eligible, only the five major nationwide commercial banks and the Korea Exchange Bank have been selected as the principal transactions bank of the 30 largest chaebol. Neither the Korea Development Bank nor any of the smaller commercial banks has been selected. Corporations try to meet their financing requirements through their principal transactions bank as much as possible before they go to other banks. Therefore, the principal banks are better positioned to earn fee income than other banks, as the corporations tend to give fee-generating business to banks from which they borrow the most. However, it is not unusual for a principal transactions bank to lend as much to the other business groups of comparable size as to its client business groups. When necessary, the OBSE can change a group's principal transactions bank, and groups can also ask to change their principal transactions bank. For example, a small business group changed from a regional to a nationwide commercial bank as it grew in size. However, a change of principal transactions bank has rarely happened.

Role of the Principal Transactions Banks

Handling Information

The principal transactions bank supervises the overall credit of its clients, including local financing by their overseas offices. Information about client corporations collected by non-principal banks is transmitted to the principal transactions bank. In reality, handling of credit information by principal banks does not seem to be effective. For example, contrary to the regulations, non-principal banks rarely notify the borrower's principal bank when they provide loans to corporations under credit control.

However, information concerning corporations with more than 2 billion won of bank loans is stored in the computer network linking banking institutions, with a separate code for each company. Since information about new bank loans to these corporations is entered into the network and is accessible to any bank, the principal transactions banks, and other banks, have a good picture of the bank borrowings of corporations. Information about non-bank loans is not entered into the network except by some of the short-term finance companies. Thus, a clearer picture of a client group's overall debt composition, including loans from non-bank financial institutions, is available only from reports of the group. Information on loans is not available to non-bank financial institutions or individuals, although data on bank loans to corporations under credit control are released to the press by the OBSE at the request of the National Assembly as part of the national audit.

Provision of Loans

The principal transactions bank sometimes takes the initiative, with or without a government intervention, to organize a loan consortium when large-scale loans and guarantees (such as those related to overseas construction projects) are to be provided to its client group. In this case, the principal transactions bank plays the role of monitoring overall performance of the project and corporation by handling the relevant information on behalf of other participating banks. However, due to the credit control system and usually tight monetary policy, principal transactions banks' credit supply to their client corporations is typically inadequate, which limits the influence the banks have.

Our interviews with bank loan officers involved in credit control of large business groups and financial managers of large corporations revealed the following facts about the roles of principal transactions banks:

- Each year principal transactions banks require firms to submit a report about their annual investment and financing plans.
- However, a principal transactions bank's evaluation of the plan does not influence the corporation significantly. A favourable evaluation does not necessarily lead to its financial support. Also, even if a principal bank objects to the plan, the corporation may still carry it out.
- The bank that exerts the most influence on corporations' investment plans in practice is the Korea Development Bank, as it provides most large long-term loans for facility investment.
- When corporations are experiencing a tight credit situation and are badly in need of working capital, the attitude of principal transactions banks has more impact on them.

Improvement of Corporate Capital Structure

The principal transactions bank provides guidance on external financing and its uses to client corporations. A client must consult its principal bank in advance concerning its annual plan for financing. The role of the bank is to urge business groups to improve their capital structure on the basis of the 'guided equity ratio' set by the OBSE for each industry. For those groups that have experienced noticeably decreased equity ratios or significantly increased borrowing from banks, their banks must take appropriate measures, such as restricting new credit and urging repayment of loans by selling securities or real estate. In particular, groups are put under special management guidance when their equity ratio, calculated semi-annually, declines over 30 per cent from the end of the previous year to below the guided ratio or when the equity ratio falls short of the 70 per cent level, which is the guided ratio. These measures are duties of the principal transactions banks specified in the Monetary Board's regulations; if they fail to fulfil them, they are reprimanded by the OBSE.

However, the banks have few means to put corporate management guidance into effect. Principal transactions banks send out official letters to client groups to urge capital structure improvement or notify them of the banks' evaluation of the planned investment projects. This inadequate leverage is due to the limited capacity of the banks to meet the credit demands of clients in the face of chronic excess demand. As shown in Table 13.3, only 227 (43 per cent) of the 523 companies under credit control satisfied the guided equity ratio at the end of 1991.

Apart from these measures, if the OBSE deems it necessary for the improvement of corporate capital structure, it can designate the method, scale, and deadline of self-help financing efforts of business groups and individual corporations. The corporations subject to these measures are not explicitly specified but are judged to be those groups put under special management guidance for the improvement of their capital structure. Therefore, in extreme cases, it is possible to dismantle a group when the OBSE orders the disposal of member corporations or the divestiture of equity shares of controlling stockholders on the grounds of improving the capital structure.

In reality, however, this has not happened. Restructuring of large corporations in Korea is not simply a matter of corporate finance. Restructuring or liquidation of large corporations could bring bankruptcy to companies that have business relationships with those corporations and, as a result, threaten the employment stability of the economy. In addition, bankruptcies of large corporations could have a serious impact on the credibility of Korean companies and banks in the international financial and export markets. Decisions concerning restructuring are, therefore, usually made at the government level (with the Industrial

Policy Deliberation Committee and Ministry of Finance playing a major role) and the principal transactions banks simply carry out the plan.

Restructuring Troubled Corporations, 1986–88

The following shows a clear picture of the roles played by the government, the OBSE and the principal transactions banks in the restructuring of problem corporations during 1986–88.

- The Ministry of Finance selected the corporations to be restructured.
- Among the 78 corporations restructured during this period, 21 were dealt with as a supplementary measure to the earlier restructuring of the shipping and overseas construction industries in 1984–85. Among the remaining 57 companies, 49 were formally designated as the target for rationalization by the Industrial Policy Deliberation Committee. When an industry was designated to be rationalized it received tax benefits such as an exemption from corporate income tax and the acquisition tax on sales of real estate or subsidiaries.
- The principal transactions bank selected candidate companies that might take over the problem corporation and, after investigating the assets and liabilities of the troubled corporation, discussed the terms of the take-over with the candidate companies.
- The OBSE examined and coordinated the terms of the financial support package agreed upon between the principal transactions bank and the acquiring company.
- After consultation with other ministries and agencies involved, the Ministry of Finance confirmed the final terms of the restructuring.
- In the restructuring process, financial support played a critical role and was given in the following fashion: (1) a grace period for principal repayment of 5 to 30 years with normal interest payment, (2) loans with subsidized interest rates (ranging from 2 per cent to 10 per cent per annum) payable over 5 to 30 years, (3) seed money: loans with interest rate of 10 per cent payable over 10 years following a ten-year grace period, extended to compensate for the estimated loss from acquisition of defaulting companies, (4) write-off of principal (Table 13.4).
- Special loans totalling 1,722 billion won at an annual interest rate of 3 per cent were offered by the Bank of Korea to banks to relieve them of the burden of financial support in the course of restructuring (300 billion won in December 1985, 684.4 billion won in May 1986, and 737.8 billion won in May 1987).

Restructuring the Kukje Group

The Kukje group, with 23 member corporations, was the sixth largest business group in terms of sales at the end of 1983. It was completely broken up in 1985. In January 1984, the government announced suspension

TABLE 13.3 Status of the 30 Largest Business Groups, 1991

	Sales (billion won)	Debt/ Equity (%)	Number of Corporations Subject to Credit Control	Number of Corporations Satisfying Guided Capital Ratio	Principal Transactions Bank	Equity Share in the Principal Transactions Bank
Samsung	21,169	323.6	49	27	Hanil	4.9[1]
Daewoo	9,938	298.1	19	9	Korea First	–
Hyundai	23,401	443.4	38	19	Exchange	–
Hanjin	3,838	1,411.3	17	7	Hanil	–
Lucky-Goldstar	12,196	355.1	53	17	Korea First	3.2[2]
Sunkyung	6,813	244.2	29	17	Korea First	–
Kia	4,144	328.7	8	3	Korea First	–
Hanil	759	529.3	12	5	Hanil	–
Ssangyoung	5,685	173.4	20	11	Chohung	1.7[3]
Kumho	1,402	238.6	25	12	Chohung	–
Korea Explosives	2,277	290.6	21	8	Hanil	–
Daelim	1,953	436.4	12	7	Hanil	3.7[4]
Doo san	1,839	260.8	23	10	Commercial	–
Hyosung	2,177	317.0	14	7	Hanil	–
Kukdong Oil Refining	–	–	4	1	Commercial	–

Dongkuk Steel Mill	1,447	158.6	11	4	Seoul Trust	1.5[5]
Lotte	1,384	330.9	29	12	Commercial	—
Halla	578	372.5	9	3	Exchange	—
Kohap	884	422.6	7	3	Hanil	—
Dongbu	1,749	288.5	7	0	Seoul Trust	—
Kukdong Eng. & Const.	330	267.5	6	4	Chohung	—
Dong-Ah Construction	1,609	1,044.7	13	5	Commercial	—
Kolon	1,876	252.6	20	11	Hanil	—
Sammi	1,223	280.4	15	6	Commercial	—
Byucksan	765	507.2	15	4	Commercial	—
Samyang Co.	753	217.5	5	3	Commercial	1.1[6]
Jinro	301	421.8	19	5	Commercial	—
Oriental Chemical	720	352.0	9	6	Hanil	—
Hatai	644	483.1	8	1	Chohung	—
Woosung Construction	720	539.6	6	0	Korea First	—

Notes:

[1] Holdings of Sumsung Insurance Co.
[2] Holdings of Lucky Securities and Lucky Insurance Co.
[3] Holdings of Ssangyoung Cement Co.
[4] Holdings of Daelim Industries.
[5] Holdings of Dongkuk Steel Mill.
[6] Holdings of Samyang Co.

Source: (Unpublished by the OBSE), data submitted to National Assembly.

TABLE 13.4 Financial Assistance to the 78 Restructured Corporations (trillion won)

	Shipping Industry Rationalization	Overseas Construction Rationalization	Others	Total
Grace period for principal repayment	0.8	0.5	0.4	1.7
Long-term loans with interest subsidy	–	–	4.2	4.2
Seed money: loans for loss compensation	–	–	0.5	0.5
Write-off of principal	–	–	1.0	1.0
Total assistance (principal)	0.8	0.5	6.0	7.3
Total credit from financial institutions	1.8	1.1	6.8	9.7

Source: Office of Bank Supervision and Examination.

of new bank credit for the 30 largest business groups and, in September, credit from short-term finance companies to these groups also became heavily regulated. In this difficult situation, the Kukje group relied heavily on informal financing similar to repurchase agreements. As the government strictly banned such deals in November, the group was faced with severe financial distress. Until February 1985, when the break up of the group was announced, Korea First Bank, Kukje's principal transactions bank, and five other banks provided 245.4 billion won of emergency credit.

The Kukje group was doomed to break up when Korea First Bank decided to stop providing emergency credit. The massive amount of emergency credit to a large business group could have a grave impact on the reserve management of the banks and on the monetary control of the government. Thus, the decision to provide or to stop emergency credit cannot be made solely by the principal transactions bank without consulting the monetary authorities. In addition, providing substantial emergency credit requires the formation of a loan consortium to relieve the principal bank of the burden. However, since a principal bank usually does not have leadership strong enough to organize the consortium, it needs the support, even if only tacit, of the government. When it made the decision to stop providing emergency credit, Korea First Bank formed an inspection team with other creditor banks to examine the financial situation of the group and to search for prospective buyers. Eventually, each corporation in the group was taken over.

The May 8 Measure (1990)

The May 8 Measure for Curbing Inflation and Real Estate Speculation (1990) urged voluntary disposal of excessive real estate holdings by large corporations and financial institutions. Large corporations were directed to sell their non-operating real estate, and were prohibited from acquiring real estate not directly used for productive activity. Financial institutions were prohibited from taking non-operating real estate as collateral. The purpose was to prevent the large *chaebol* from engaging in real estate speculation. This was part of efforts to hold real estate prices down and reduce the economic and financial power of *chaebol* by keeping them from garnering any gains from the run-up in land prices, which were rising at an annual average rate of 21.3 per cent during 1987–91, when inflation in terms of consumer prices recorded 6.7 per cent a year.

Under the May 8 Measure, corporations belonging to the 30 largest *chaebol* must obtain prior approval from their principal transactions bank when they want to invest in new business or acquire real estate. (Investment in new business does not include the expansion of an existing business into a new product line.) The restriction on investment in new business is designed to encourage business groups to specialize and to discourage debt-financed expansion of business areas. The intention of the restriction on real estate purchase is to prevent debt-financed acquisition of non-operating real estate. The 31st to 50th largest business groups need the approval of their principal transactions bank only in the case of real estate acquisitions.

If an investment requires over 500 million won or when a real estate purchase is larger than 10,000 square metres, it must be presented to a committee led by the OBSE and composed of bank directors in charge of credit operations before a principal transactions bank gives its approval. This applies even to investments or purchases financed entirely from the corporation's own capital. Due to cumbersome procedures and delays, approvals related to the acquisition and use of real estate frequently are issued *ex post facto*. The details concerning the restrictions on real estate acquisition and investment in new business are as follows:

- Non-major corporations belonging to business groups that are subject to credit controls cannot purchase real estate or invest in new businesses, including setting up a subsidiary, buying an existing company, equity participation, and merger. Purchase of factory buildings or annex facilities directly used for product manufacturing may be approved when deemed essential by the principal transactions bank.
- Investment in a non-major corporation or a non-major sub-industry

(product line) is prohibited. Non-major sub-industries include those declared as such by the owner of the group and those reserved by the government for small and medium firms for major operation or sub-contracting. Non-major corporations are defined as those with sales in non-major sub-industries exceeding 50 per cent of their total sales.[3]

- Corporations whose equity ratio is below the guided ratio are prohibited from investing in business firms, except for investment in member firms of their own business group.
- Corporations belonging to the 30 largest chaebol should make self-help efforts in financing their investments in new business or purchase of real estate, if such investment or purchase is to be approved by their principal transactions bank. More specifically, non-major corporations can invest in new business or real estate only when they finance through self-help effort, that is, through public offering of equity shares or real estate disposal. Self-help effort includes raising new capital from sales of real estate or security holdings, new stock issuance, and sales of equity holdings by large shareholders. It does not include using depreciation allowances and retained earnings. The requirement of financing through self-help varies depending on the purpose of financing and on whether the corporation and group as a whole achieved their guided-equity ratios.
- When a business group invests in new business or purchases real estate in order to enter into a new (allowed) sub-industry, non-major member corporations (or non-major business), worth at least double the required amount must be disposed of to satisfy the requirement of self-help financing effort.

PERFORMANCE OF THE CREDIT CONTROL SYSTEM

Since the role of the Korean principal transactions banks is defined within the credit control system imposed on business groups, it will be more relevant to evaluate the credit control system rather than the principal transactions bank system itself. As discussed in the first section, credit control of business groups began as an institutional mechanism designed to alleviate the side effects of strong government support for business groups through intervention in credit allocation. Thus, the evaluation of the credit control system should be based on its contribution to alleviating such side effects.

---

[3] Many sub-industries (products) have been reserved exclusively for small and medium firms in an effort to promote these firms. In early 1992, there were 237 such sub-industries designated by the Ministry of Trade and Industry, but 58 were scheduled for delisting that September. For the purpose of sub-contracting, 1,160 products in 42 sub-industries are also reserved for small and medium firms.

The primary side effect was that government's financial support induced large corporations to expand their businesses through excessive borrowing from financial institutions. As the economic environment worsened, this led to the insolvency of corporations and deterioration of bank asset portfolios. Many signs indicated that the growth potential of the Korean economy was hampered. Another effect was the concentration of economic power, accompanied by skewed allocation of bank credit. In the 1990s, the major objective of the credit control system shifted from alleviating the side effects of earlier development strategies to strengthening the competitiveness of the manufacturing sector. Thus, evaluation of the credit control system should be made on the basis of its effect on the improvement of the capital structure and solvency of large corporations, the reduction in the concentration of economic power, the correction of disproportionate credit allocation, and the strengthening of manufacturing industry's competitiveness.

Improvement of Capital Structure

It cannot be easily judged whether credit control has contributed to the improvement of the capital structure of large corporations. No separate data are available on the changes in capital structure of subject companies since the introduction of the credit control system in 1974. However, the capital structure of Korean companies in general worsened during the 1970s (Table 13.5), and many large corporations that invested heavily in heavy and chemical industries had difficulty repaying their debts in the early 1980s. In the light of these developments, the credit control system does not seem to have contributed to improving the capital structure of the large corporations in the 1970s in any significant way.

In the 1980s, the capital structure of Korean companies showed some improvement. The government implemented strong measures against large corporations with weak capital structures, urging them to repay their bank loans by raising money in the capital market during the 1987–89 period. In May 1987, the government designated 82 companies among those with more than 50 billion won of bank loans and made them repay 10 per cent of their loans with funds raised in the capital market by the end of that year. The government made the principal transactions banks of these companies check on the progress of repayment and penalize them by prohibiting extension of existing loans and suspending new loans, except for policy loans, if they did not fulfill the requirement.

The equity ratio of the 30 largest chaebol rose from 17.4 per cent to 20.8 per cent between 1986 and 1990. This improvement, however, was mainly attributable to the stock market boom between 1987 and 1989. Although the credit control system forced companies to repay their loans

TABLE 13.5 The Equity Ratio of Korean Corporations
(per cent)

	Manufacturing (total)	Manufacturing (large corporations)	Corporations subject to credit control
1974	24.0	23.7	–
1975	22.8	22.1	–
1976	21.5	21.2	–
1977	22.2	22.3	–
1978	21.4	21.6	–
1979	21.0	20.9	–
1980	17.0	16.5	–
1981	18.1	18.1	–
1982	20.6	20.9	–
1983	21.7	21.7	–
1984	22.6	22.7	–
1985	22.3	22.5	–
1986	22.2	21.9	17.4
1987	22.7	23.1	19.8
1988	25.3	26.0	24.7
1989	28.2	29.4	23.8
1990	25.9	26.7	20.8
1991	24.4	25.6	19.4

Source: Bank of Korea, *Financial Statements Analysis*, various issues.

with funds from the capital market, it does not seem to have contributed to the fundamental improvement of corporate capital structure. As corporations faced difficulties in direct financing due to the downturn of the stock market in the early 1990s, their capital structure worsened again with increased borrowing from banks. The fact that only 9 out of the 30 largest business groups met the guided-equity ratio in 1990 indicates that the stock market situation was the main reason for the improvement in the capital structure in the late 1980s.

Concentration and Credit Access

With respect to reducing the concentration of economic power and providing more equitable access to credit, the credit control system seems to have been successful. Since 1984, a credit ceiling (basket) has been imposed on the chaebol, and the government has steadily reduced their share of total bank credit.

As a result of this tight credit control, the share of the 30 largest groups' bank loans subject to credit control fell from 25.3 per cent of total bank loans in 1986 to 13.5 per cent in 1990 on a year-end basis. Including loans not subject to credit control, their share in total bank loans fell from 28.6 per cent in 1986 to 19.4 per cent at the end of 1990 (Table 13.6). It is worth noting that these groups' share in total bank loans fell from 26.3 per cent in 1987 to 20.7 per cent in 1989, while their share in GDP declined only marginally, from 14.6 to 14.1 per cent. The share of small and medium companies in the total loans of deposit money banks rose from 31.5 per cent in 1986 to 56.8 per cent in 1991.

TABLE 13.6 Share of the 30 Largest Business Groups in Bank Loans and GDP (per cents)

	1986	1987	1988	1989	1990	1991
Share in Bank Loans						
Loans subject to credit control	25.3	21.6	18.6	14.7	13.5	8.8 (1)
Total loans	28.6	26.3	24.2	20.7	19.4	18.9
Share in NBFI Credit	–	37.9	36.5	42.1	43.6	–
Share in GDP	–	14.6	13.5	14.1	–	–
Equity Ratio	17.4	19.8	24.7	23.8	20.8	19.4

Note: Excludes credit to Major Corporations, Corporations with Highly Dispersed Ownership, loans extended by overseas bank branches and post-shipment export financing.

Source: Korea Investors Service (1988, 1989, 1990); Management Efficiency Research Institute (1987); *Maeil Kyungje* (newspaper), 31 March 1992; Min (1991).

The largest business groups' share in total credit of non-bank financial institutions (NBFIs) such as short-term finance companies, merchant banking corporations and insurance companies, whose credit is not subject to control, has substantially increased. In other words, the groups have shifted to non-banks for much of their financing needs.

Another issue related to the concentration of economic power in Korea is the tendency of large business groups to diversify their activities. Thus, one of the major motivations behind the tight restrictions on investment in new businesses is to prevent their further diversification. However, the credit control system appears to have been unsuccessful at this: between 1986 and 1991, 20 of the 30 largest groups increased the number of their member corporations in spite of the burden of self-help financing (Table 13.7). However, their diversification activity might have been more pronounced without credit control or the addition of new firms which might have contributed to those groups' specialization. Thus, the increase in the number of member firms in itself does not provide definite evidence concerning the impact of the credit control system on diversification.

TABLE 13.7 Number of Member Companies of the 30 Largest Business Groups

	1981	1986(A)	1987	1988	April 1989	1991 (B)	(B) – (A)
Samsung	21	31	31	41	42	48	+17
Daewoo	25	25	28	28	30	24	-1
Hanjin	13	12	16	16	18	22	+10
Hyundai	30	43	30	36	37	42	-1
Lucky-Goldstart	30	43	30	36	37	42	-1
Sunkyong	16	13	16	21	22	26	+13
Hanil	6	10	11	12	14	13	+3
Ssangyong	13	16	21	21	21	22	+6
Kia	12	7	10	10	10	10	+3
Daelim	9	12	13	13	13	14	+2
Kumho	10	5	8	13	14	22	+17
Hyosung	27	19	12	12	14	14	-5
Doosan	14	19	–	20	21	23	+4
Korea Explosives	16	20	21	25	25	27	+7

Dongkuk Steel Mill	–	12	13	13	13	14	+2
Kukdong Oil	–	–	–	4	4	4	–
Kukdong Eng. & Const.	15	12	16	16	16	16	+4
Dong-Ah Construction	15	12	16	16	16	16	+4
Lotte	16	26	26	31	31	32	+6
Dongbu	7	11	12	13	14	11	0
Sam Yang	–	3	–	7	6	6	+3
Kolon	16	10	18	16	18	21	+11
Sammi	4	5	9	11	14	15	+10
Byuksan	–	6	–	14	20	21	+15
Woosung Const.	–	–	–	7	7	6	–
Kohap	5	4	5	7	7	7	+3
Halla	–	–	5	6	6	9	+4
Cho Yang Shipping	–	–	–	–	–	10	–
Jinro	–	–	–	–	18	20	–
Oriental Chemical	–	–	–	–	11	13	–

Source: Unpublished data submitted to the National Assembly by the Office of Bank Supervision and Examination; *Maeil Kyungje*, 7 May 1991.

Strengthening Competitiveness

In the 1990s, strengthening the competitiveness of manufacturing has emerged as one of the important objectives of the credit control system. For two reasons, the government exempted the Major Corporations from credit control. As a consequence, bank loans to 76 Major Corporations of the 30 largest chaebol rose by 38.1 per cent in 1991. This increase is, however, less than that of total bank loans, which expanded by 23.6 per cent in 1991, and bank loans to non-major corporations of these chaebol increased by only 8.6 per cent. However, there is still little evidence that the credit control system has contributed to the strengthening of manufacturing competitiveness. On the other hand, since the Major Corporations now have more flexibility in financing, the problem of credit diversion from them to the non-major corporations has emerged.

Effectiveness of the Controls

In evaluating the performance of the credit control system, we should examine its effectiveness in controlling business activities. At the end of March 1992, 25 companies, or 4.2 per cent of the 586 member corporations of the 30 largest chaebol, were under sanctions by the OBSE for violating credit control regulations. These companies invested in new business or purchased real estate without the prior approval of their principal transactions bank. However, these violations seem to be primarily the result of ignorance of the regulations and the lack of coordination among departments in a corporation, rather than to any intentional flouting. For instance, contact with banks is usually made by the finance department while decisions about the use of real estate are made by plant management.

PROBLEMS WITH THE CREDIT CONTROL SYSTEM

As we pointed out in the second section, the credit control system was helpful in correcting certain problems caused by earlier development policies which relied heavily on government intervention in credit allocation. On the other hand, the credit control system produced regulatory costs because it imposes substantial restrictions on banks as well as on corporations. Our interest here is to review the nature and magnitude of these costs.

Continuous Conflict

Since the credit control system was launched, continuous conflict between the government and the corporate sector has been its most noticeable aspect. The corporate sector's resistance was not apparent in the beginning because the system started as a mechanism to solve problems caused by government intervention to provide financial support for business. However, resistance grew stronger in the 1980s as credit control became, in essence, a mechanism for regulating business activities. This problem became more serious as government support for the corporate sector was reduced substantially. While those subject to credit controls keep asking for their abolition, the government still uses the system as an important tool for controlling large business groups.

Hampering of Bank Management

The credit control system seriously hampers autonomous bank management. The operation of principal transactions banks shows they are, in effect, supervisory institutions with the authority to issue prior approval for various corporate activities and penalize their client companies. They are positioned as a hand-maiden of the OBSE with the obligation to collect and report back information related to credit control. They also implement measures initiated by the OBSE and monitor the results. The principal transactions banks' status as mediators in the private sector was strengthened in the 1980s as credit control of chaebol tightened. In particular, when security issues by large corporations in overseas markets were placed under the control of the principal transactions banks by the 1991 reform of the credit control system, the banks began to oversee all aspects of the financing activities of large business groups. The securities authorities imposed restrictions for a certain period on the amount and timing of bond issuance for a company that was subject to disciplinary punishment by its principal transactions bank for violating credit control regulations.

However, the status of principal transactions banks as the overall supervisors of financial management is somewhat shallow, since their power is limited in practice. For example, the imposition of a severe penalty, such as suspending new bank loans to a corporation that violated credit regulations, could affect the corporation's export performance negatively and bring severe difficulties to its sub-contractors. For these and other reasons, the OBSE is very cautious about imposing sanctions on banks. As an example, in April 1992, Hyundai Electronics, one of the Major Corporations of the Hyundai group, transferred some of its bank loans to one of its major shareholders, which is a clear violation of the credit regulations. However, the Korea Exchange Bank, the group's principal transactions bank, did not apply any penalty measures, and the OBSE acquiesced. However, this does not mean large corporations can ignore the regulations. Repeated violations, though they may not result in direct penalties immediately, worsen the corporation's relationship with the government, which is detrimental in the long run.

The cost the banks have to pay has been substantial. Since the principal transactions banks carry out a supervisory role on behalf of the OBSE, they are subject to penalties, such as restriction of access to central bank credit and penalty interest rates, in the event of violating the Regulation on Credit Operations of Banking Institutions and its Operational Bylaw (Regulation, Article 10). In a normal bank-enterprise relationship, a bank can refuse to provide new loan or ask for early repayment of existing loans if it decides, through its own credit evaluation, that the intended use of a loan is not acceptable or if there is a danger of insolvency. Thus, as long as the bank is fully autonomous in making credit decisions, there is no real benefit in having the authority to issue prior approvals to control the behaviour of its clients. Also, there is no reason to undertake the cumbersome burden of reporting to the OBSE and to be subject to penalties in the course of implementing the credit control system.

In particular, the commercial banks' burden related to credit control is known to be substantial, occupying one-third of their loan officers' time, and the banks maintain a separate department for the credit control operation. There also seem to be difficulties in evaluating whether a real estate holding is non-operating or idle in the context of tax laws. Bank officers have serious complaints against the OBSE as, in effect, they are burdened with what should be the Board's responsibilities. In addition, there seem to be many unnecessary and trivial items which need the principal transactions bank's approval, and these are the cause of inefficiency and conflict between banks and their clients.

Autonomy in bank management is impaired as long as banks perform credit control functions on behalf of the government. For greater efficiency, banks with a more market-oriented management mentality are needed, but this is not expected under the current situation in which control of corporate clients constitutes a major part of the banks' business. The banks appear to be a subordinate organization to the OBSE. Improvements in bank credit operation, an urgent task in the new environment of financial liberalization, are not expected. For efficient credit operation, the current system of credit evaluation, which focuses on conformity to rules and regulations, should be changed to one stressing the positive prospects of the projects under review.

Pursuit of Conflicting Objectives

The current credit control system pursues two conflicting objectives: strengthening manufacturing competitiveness and reducing the concentration of economic power. These objectives make the government's policy choices challenging. By exempting the Major Corporations from controls, the government has put priority on strengthening international competitiveness at the cost of more equitable access to credit and a reduction of concentration of economic power.

The problem, however, is that the system has serious constraints to achieving its objective of strengthening competitiveness. There is a possibility that the relaxation of credit controls on Major Corporations will lead business groups to select firms with large financing requirements as their Major Corporations rather than those with a good prospect of achieving international competitiveness, which are more desirable for the long-term development of the economy. For example, all five of the largest business groups have chosen a petrochemical company as one of their Major Corporations and made huge investments since 1989. It is hard to imagine all of them growing to be internationally competitive.

Legal Ambiguities

The credit control system has had some serious legal problems. Article 1 of the Regulation on Credit Operations of Banking Institutions specifies that the Regulation is based on Articles 3, 72, 73, and 116 of the Bank of Korea Act and Article 30.2 of the General Banking Act. Article 3 of the Bank of Korea Act, however, merely declares the objectives of the Bank of Korea (BOK), such as stabilizing the value of money, promoting efficient use of national resources, and maintaining a sound banking and financial system. Therefore, it cannot serve as the basis for specific policy measures. Article 72 of the Bank of Korea Act prescribes the Monetary Board's control of the BOK's credit operation. Article 73 states that the BOK can choose to refuse credit to a banking institution even if the securities offered as collateral are satisfactory. Finally, Article 116 is on sanctions. In sum, Articles 72, 73, and 116 constitute the basis of Article 10 (sanctions) of the Regulation on Credit Operations of Banking Institutions. The basket control of credit against business groups is derived from Article 30.2 of the General Banking Act.

The Operational Bylaw on Credit Control over Business Groups, which is the subordinate regulation to the Regulation on Credit Operations of Banking Institutions, specifies that the principal transactions banks can issue prior approval for investment in new business (Articles 11 and 12) and real estate acquisition (Article 13). However, this authority is unrelated to the regulation on basket credit control. Moreover, the Operational Bylaw is, in fact, a much stronger regulation than Article 30.2 of the General Banking Act in that it exercises approval authority on corporate activities that are unrelated to a bank's credit operation. It is certainly inconsistent for a subordinate regulation to establish stronger rules than are prescribed in its superior law. Thus, the legal foundation of Articles 11 to 13 of the Operational Bylaw on Credit Control over Business Groups is very weak.

Disruption of Bank-Client Relationship

The bank-enterprise relationship in the framework of the credit control system is that of supervisor and supervised. However, since the principal transactions banks impose administrative supervision while they are unable to meet all the credit demand of their client companies, it is often natural for the corporations under credit control to have a less than satisfactory relationship with their principal banks. As a result, companies do not always give them fee-generating business; they often give it to whichever bank has helped them ease short-term financial difficulties. The stronger the capital structure and the less financial problem a company has, the more independently it acts; whereas a financially weak company shows a more favourable attitude towards its principal transactions bank.

Such relationships hamper the overall efficiency of the economy and sound economic growth that is driven by competition and the profit motive of the private sector. As the scope and magnitude of government support for industries are reduced, structural adjustment and other efforts of the private sector to enhance efficiency become all the more important as factors that determine industrial competitiveness. The government-bank-enterprise relationship constitutes a critical superstructure in determining competitiveness, and in Korea it has become a serious obstacle. The current bank-enterprise relationship is far from desirable, as the conflict between the government and business has been intensified by the credit control system.

Credit Diversion

Relaxation of credit control on Major Corporations may divert credit from major to non-major corporations to circumvent the controls. Loans to Major Corporations and corporations with highly dispersed ownership, which are not subject to credit control, accounted for 53.6 per cent of the total loans to the 30 largest business groups at the end of 1991 and, accordingly, the share of loans to the 30 largest groups subject to credit control declined to 8.8 per cent of total bank loans outstanding (Table 13.8). If groups mobilize all the required funds of their member companies through the two exempt groups, then the credit control system can no longer function as a measure to correct concentrated access to credit.

Under the Operational Bylaw on Credit Control over Business Groups (Article 9), principal transactions banks must submit quarterly reports to the OBSE on the results of *ex post* monitoring of loans to Major Corporations and revoke the designation if they diverted loans to other uses. Despite this severe penalty, the possibility that Major Corporations will divert loans always exists. Monitoring the use of bank loans is difficult, and the banks have to make judgements entirely on the basis of

TABLE 13.8 Share of Loans to Major Corporations and Corporations with Highly Dispersed Ownership, 1991
(billion won, per cents)

	Total Loans	Loans to Major Corporations and Corporations with Highly Dispersed Ownership	Loans Subject to Credit Control
Largest 5 Groups	13,437	6.768 (50.4)	6,669 (49.6)
Next Largest 25 Groups	12,500	7,138 (57.1)	5,362 (42.9)
Total	25,937	13,906 (53.6)	12,031 (46.4)
Share in Total bank Loans	18.9	10.1	8.8

Source: Bank of Korea, Bodo Jaryo (official information the press) 15 March 1992.

data presented by the companies. *Ex post* supervision of loans for operating capital is virtually impossible unless the bank traces all the cheques written by the company; loans for facilities investment are easier to track and fairly well supervised. In addition, since the Major Corporations typically hold guarantees for other member companies that are roughly equivalent to three times their equity capital, they cannot help but divert some of the loans from their principal transactions bank to help a member company.

As loans to Major Corporations increased much faster than total loans, administrative guidance was imposed so that their rate of increase is in line with the increase in total loans. The goal of strengthening industrial competitiveness by relaxing credit control on Major Corporations is in conflict with this guidance.

Expansion of Regulations

Even though the credit control system has held down the bank borrowing of large business groups, they have utilized cross-payment guarantees to borrow from non-bank financial institutions and issue bonds. They also increased the number of affiliated companies. At the end of June 1992, payment guarantees for corporations belonging to the 30 largest chaebol amounted to four times their equity capital (Table 13.9). To redress such problems, the government prohibited cross-payment guarantees at the end of June 1992 and revised the Monopoly Regulation and Fair Trade Act, forcing business groups to limit guarantees to a maximum 200 per cent of their equity capital by April 1996. With this revision, the issue of reducing economic concentration of business groups, one of the major

TABLE 13.9 Equity Capital and Payment Guarantees of the 30 Largest Business
Groups, June 1992
(billion won)

	Equity Capital	Outstanding Cross Payment Guarantees
Largest 5 groups	16,315	77,821
Next 25 groups	15,087	47,831
Total	31,402	125,652

Source: Unpublished data submitted to the National Assembly by the Office of Bank
Supervision and Examination.

objectives of the credit control system, has been passed to the domain of
the Monopoly Regulation and Fair Trade Act.

DEVELOPMENT INSTITUTIONS

The Korea Development Bank (KDB)

While the relationship between commercial banks and large corporations
has been dictated by the credit control system and limited mainly to that
of lender and borrower, the relationship between the Korea Development
Bank (KDB) and large corporations is much closer and more cooperative. Sharing risk and information, the KDB has played a role very similar to that of Japanese main banks in their relationship with large private
and public corporations. However, other roles and characteristics of the
KDB make it quite different from Japanese main banks.

The KDB was established in 1954 to finance major industrial projects
considered essential for Korea's economic development, with all the initial equity capital subscribed by the government. In this initial stage, the
KDB served as a channel through which government funds were distributed and managed for the development of basic industries and social
infrastructure. At the same time it brought in foreign loans on behalf of
the government (from the US Agency for International Development
starting in 1958, from the International Bank for Reconstruction and
Developoment in 1962, and from the Asian Development Bank in 1969).
In the 1970s, it started to raise long-term foreign capital through bond
issues in the international capital market. The main sources of KDB
loans were government funds during the 1960s, but during the 1970s and
early 80s, foreign loans and the National Investment Fund (NIF) became
the chief contributors. In recent years, domestic bond issues have played

the major role. KDB credit has mostly been provided to heavy and chemical industries and social infrastructure investments, frequently at subsidized interest rates. Data on KDB lending and clients are in Tables 13.10 to 13.12.

TABLE 13.10 Share of the KDB in the Financing of Plant and Equipment Investment
(per cents)

1960	1970	1980	1990	
69.1	56.6	48.9	33.7	Korea Development Bank
–	–	5.1	6.8	Long-Term Credit Bank
30.9	43.4	46.0	59.5	Deposit money banks

Source: KDB.

TABLE 13.11 Industrial Composition of KDB Loans
(per cents)

1964–73	1974–83	
0.1	0.6	Agriculture, forestry, and fishing
5.9	3.0	Mining
40.6	47.6	Heavy and chemical industries
11.3	6.1	Light manufacturing
41.1	42.7	Social overhead capital and others

Source: KDB.

TABLE 13.12 Number of KDB's Corporate Clients

1965	1970	1975	1980	1985	1990	1992
552	610	512	787	892	1,326	1,766

Source: KDB

There are two major factors behind KDB's rather close relationship with large corporations. First, the KDB was virtually the only institution from which large corporations could borrow long-term (especially foreign) capital for their plant and equipment investment. Until the 1970s, interest rates on KDB loans were lower than those on commercial banks loans, and until the early 1980s, KDB loans for long-term plant and equipment investments were larger than the total loans supplied by all commercial banks for the same purpose. Even though its share has decreased considerably during the 1980s, the KDB still remains the largest supplier of long-term credit. In addition, as the KDB established its credit in international financial markets much earlier than other Korean financial institutions, it could borrow or issue bonds there more easily, giving it a dominant position in the domestic foreign currency loan market. (The KDB guaranteed 49 per cent of total long-term foreign loans and 91 per cent of total foreign commercial loans during 1962–82. It also accounted for 45 per cent of total foreign bank loans and 74 per cent of foreign currency bond issues during 1970–81.)

The second factor is that borrowing from the KDB has not been subject to the credit control system. This favourable treatment reflects the government's desire to promote those industries considered vital for enhancing international competitiveness. For these reasons, large corporations value their relationship with the KDB more than their relationship with their principal transactions bank when it comes to carrying out large investment projects.

The KDB supplies long-term capital for plant and equipment investment of major public and private corporations through loans, equity investment, and repayment guarantees. In the course of financing large projects, it appraises their economic prospects and technical adequacy, maintaining close relationships with the borrowing corporations. Pohang Iron and Steel Company (POSCO) and Korea Electric Power Company are good examples of KDB financing through equity investment. The number of KDB's corporate clients increased only modestly, particularly until the mid-1980s, which suggests they are limited mostly to public and large private corporations (Table 13.12).

However, the role of the KDB in its relations with corporate clients has fallen short of that of Japanese main banks. Most importantly, the KDB does not monitor the overall business activities of clients. Its monitoring role is mainly limited to the projects it finances. Only when a client falls into serious financial trouble does the KDB begin to monitor its overall activities.

KDB loans are classified into five types as follows.

1 Policy loans provided at preferential interest rates for such activities as the purchase of domestically produced machinery, technology development, shipbuilding, and industry restructuring.
2 Loans of government funds extended mainly to state-run enterprises and local governments.
3 General fund loans provided mainly for working capital to corporations that have already borrowed from the KDB for plant and equipment.
4 Foreign currency loans for the import of capital goods and raw materials.

5 Loans from special purpose funds provided to industries or activities designated by the government, including loans from the National Investment Fund (NIF) to support heavy and chemical industries, and those from the Petroleum Business Fund for such activities as the supply of municipal gas and investments for improving efficiency of energy use.

There are two cases where KDB provides funds through equity investment. The first is when an investment project is considered very important for the economy but requires too much capital for private enterprises to accomplish, a new enterprise may be established to undertake the project. In this case, the KDB participates in the new enterprise on its own or the government increases KDB's equity capital which will then be invested in the new enterprise.

When a client faces serious financial difficulty, the KDB might convert its loans to equity to reduce the firm's financial burden. The purpose of KDB's investment is to support the start-up or survival of the corporation. Therefore, once operations are normalized, KDB's equity shares are sold to the public. POSCO, Korean Air Lines, and Korea Electric Power Corporation are good examples. Overall, during 1969–82, of the 22 corporations in which KDB had equity investment, 14 were sold off to the public and 6 were released from KDB's management control.

When a borrowing corporation becomes insolvent, the KDB designates it as a bank-managed corporation and directly participates in its management by providing priority financial support, dispatching KDB managers, reviewing business strategy and its implementation, readjusting production and profit targets, and conducting periodic management reviews. Thus, efforts to normalize troubled corporations require even closer relationships between the bank and the corporations than those observed in the Japanese main bank system: the KDB has not only monitored the general business activities of corporations, but also controlled their management. During 1974–82, 22 of the 28 corporations under bank management were normalized.

Supplying long-term capital to priority sectors that could contribute to economic development has been, and remains, the most important responsibility of the KDB. However, within that broad mission, the areas of emphasis and the relationship of the KDB with the corporate sector has undergone some changes. During the early stages of Korean development, the KDB supplied funds mostly to rehabilitation projects and infrastructure. During the rapid growth of the 1960s and 70s, the supply of long-term capital for facility investment, especially for the heavy and chemical industry, was the main responsibility of the KDB. At the same time, as inefficient investments resulted in insolvencies, the supervisory role or the role of delegated management gained importance.

Entering the 1980s, Korea faced an increasing need for restructuring inefficient industries and upgrading the industrial structure of the economy into a more sophisticated and technology-based orientation. The KDB played a major role in the industrial rationalization programmes of the mid-1980s, utilizing its close relationship with its clients. Currently, the KDB is concentrating its efforts on supporting industries with high growth potential and aiding technology development. In addition the KDB has been expanding its scope through subsidiaries in leasing, merchant banking and venture capital. Therefore, while its relative importance in the long-term capital market has decreased significantly, KDB is now offering more diversified financial services.

Case Study: POSCO

The KDB provided every possible means of support for Pohang Iron & Steel Company (POSCO) including loans, equity investment, and repayment guarantees. The KDB's share in POSCO's equity capital reached 50 per cent in 1968, but declined to 38 per cent in 1987, right before the 1988 listing of its shares on the Korea Stock Exchange, and to 15 per cent in September 1992. POSCO did not pay cash dividends to the KDB until 1987, which had a positive effect on POSCO's capital structure despite its continuing capacity enlargement. KDB lent to POSCO not only from its own funds but also from the NIF. The share of KDB's own funds in POSCO's total borrowing reached 16.5 per cent in 1974 and then declined to 4.6 per cent in 1981, when the share of NIF funds rose to 9.1 per cent. KDB also provided repayment guarantees for POSCO's foreign borrowings. This close relationship may make the KDB look similar to a Japanese main bank but, in at least two respects, it differs. First, KDB's roles were the product of government industrial policy and of the government-KDB relationship over which the government has complete control. Second, as a natural consequence of this, the KDB could not exert the sort of control as 'delegated monitor' that is implied by being a Japanese main bank.

The Korea Long-Term Credit Bank (KLCB)

Unlike the KDB, the Korea Long-Term Credit Bank (KLCB) has served as a supplier of long-term capital at the private level. The Korea Development Finance Corporation, established in 1968 as the first private institution to supply plant and equipment financing, was reorganized to become the KLCB in 1980. The KLCB supports enterprises by making facility loans of three years or more and related long-term working capital loans, underwriting bonds and share issues, issuing repayment guarantees, and providing management and technical consulting. The Korea Long-Term Credit Bank Act also requires it to allocate more than 30 per cent of its loans to small and medium firms. During 1980–88, 54.5 per cent of the KLCB's funds were allocated to support plant and equipment investment, 21.1 per cent for long-term working capital, and 6.4 per cent for security investment. Small and medium firms accounted for 32 per cent of KLCB loans for facility investment and long-term working capital.

There is a difference between KDB and KLCB in their relationships with clients. Since supplying policy loans has been the major function of the KDB, its choice of clients has been limited, which helped it maintain relatively stable relationships with them. The client relationship with the KLCB is formed on a project-by-project basis and is not as stable as in the case of the KDB. The average size of KLCB loans is much smaller than KDB's and it makes few policy loans. KLCB's clients may obtain policy loans from commercial and specialized banks and they also have accounts at commercial banks for other services, such as payment settlements. The success of the KLCB seems to be attributable largely to its strict evaluation of enterprises and projects. As such, the KLCB is rarely concerned with supplying emergency funds to save clients in financial difficulty.

A COMPARISON WITH JAPANESE MAIN BANKS

The characteristics of the principal transactions bank system become clearer when they are compared with those of the Japanese main bank system. First, the system in Korea is officially defined by the regulations of the Monetary Board, while the Japanese main bank system is defined by conventional customer relationships between banks and their client corporations.

Second, the main bank system represents a rather broad-based bank-enterprise relationship, with about 30 per cent of corporations having such relationship with their banks (Horiuchi, 1990). The system in Korea, however, applies only to corporations belonging to the 50 largest business groups in terms of borrowing from banks. At the end of April 1992, the number of such companies under the direct credit control of their principal transactions banks was 591. Other corporations must have banks that they have a closer business relationship with than with other banks. These banks, however, do not seem to play special roles deserving special definition.

Third, the principal transactions banks in Korea, in effect, function as a sub-structure or subordinate organization of the OBSE, controlling credit supply to clients and gathering and reporting information on their financial and credit situations. Like Japanese banks, the principal transactions banks in Korea are encouraged to form a consortium when providing a loan to a large project and to gather relevant information about the project. Also, the principal transactions banks sometimes play the role of an overall supervision of the debts of clients. However, while these are important functions of Japanese main banks, they are performed by Korean banks only in special circumstances, such as insolvency. This is due to the lack of confidence in a principal transactions bank as a serious evaluator of borrowing firms or investment projects. It may also reflect the fact that a principal transactions bank does not necessarily take a disproportionate share of the cost of rescuing or liquidating troubled firms. In fact, except for the Kukje case, where a whole group was broken up and taken over by other firms, there have been few incidents where a firm in the largest 30 *chaebol* was liquidated or rescued by its principal transactions bank.

Fourth, the relationship between corporations belonging to Japanese business groups and their main banks is based in part on mutual equity ownership. In Korea, however, no such relationship is found, even though banks are allowed to hold as much as 100 per cent of their own capital in the form of marketable securities. In the cases where a principal transactions bank holds shares in a client, it is only for the purpose of asset management. There are only six cases where a chaebol holds equity shares in its principal transactions bank (Table 13.3). Among these, three are holdings by their securities or insurance affiliates as part of their portfolio management. Also, the level of shareholding by those business groups is far lower than the 8 per cent limit that a stockholder can have in a nationwide commercial bank. This lack of interest in holding shares in principal transactions banks has resulted from the tight credit control of business groups, and government influence on bank management such as the appointment of top managers. (Until now the government has *de facto* appointed presidents and other executives of nationwide commercial banks; large shareholders have not had much influence in the matter. However, the government has announced it will no longer interfere in the appointment of top bank managers.)

While banks in the Japanese main bank system are often both lenders and shareholders, their Korean counterparts are limited to being lenders. In Japan the bank-enterprise relationship is a cooperative one in which both parties share mutual benefits by reducing information asymmetry. In Korea, it is typically a regulator-subject relationship.

Finally, although government-initiated industrial policies and interventions in credit allocation have existed in both Korea and Japan, the different roles of the banks appear to have resulted in a substantial difference in the efficiency of the private sector's resource allocation. In Japan, the main bank-enterprise relationship led to a double check mechanism regarding the credit-worthiness of borrowers, and the prospect of planned projects, as well as the sharing of investment risks between the banks and corporations. Korea's industrial policy was executed mainly in the form of direct financial support for the corporations involved, leaving little room for principal transactions banks to screen credit. The government selects the company to carry out a major industrial project and it is therefore difficult for the principal transactions bank to refuse to make a loan, even if the company's credit standing is poor. When a loan consortium is formed by several banks to meet a large investment requirement, the share of each bank usually has been allocated by the government. As a result of this lack of autonomy, banks have been more concerned about securing collateral than undertaking credit evaluation, and this in turn has led corporations to hold ever more real estate to offer as collateral. These differences in the roles of main banks, in the area of credit evaluation and risk sharing, must have led to different investment performances of the two countries.

Characteristics of the Korean System

The Korean principal transactions bank system is characterized by its emphasis on regulating the bank loans and investment activities of large corporations; this originated as a corrective device for the side effects of government-led development policies. If the Korean government had adopted a more balanced development policy in the 1970s, avoiding encouraging the growth of large corporations in comparison to small and medium firms, the credit control system with its strong regulatory characteristics would not have emerged. In addition, if the government had not been actively involved in bailing-out firms and mitigating the problems of non-performing loans of large corporations, justification for the credit control system would have been weak. The system has been operated as an institutional measure to minimize the socialization of corporate risk by reducing corporate insolvency and the deterioration of bank asset portfolio through government intervention.

As discussed earlier, the credit control system has evolved to meet the challenges the Korean economy has faced in the course of its development. The challenges include improvement of corporate capital structure, mitigation of the concentration of economic power, discouragement of real estate speculation and, more recently, the fostering of international competitiveness. The system has provided a regulatory framework that allows the government to impose policies on the corporate sector and control many of its activities. There have been continuous conflicts between the government and the corporate sector as a result.

The conflict has become more serious in recent years. The government insists that credit control is necessary to induce large chaebol to specialize and thus enhance the competitiveness of Korean industries. A chaebol operating in many different industries is assumed to be inefficient due to dispersion of managerial talent and diversion of financial resources from profit-making firms to those with financial difficulties. But the corporate sector argues that the credit control system impedes the ability of corporations to respond flexibly to a changing economic environment and is an obstacle to strengthening industrial competitiveness.

The government, banks, and enterprises seem to agree that the principal transactions bank system in Korea needs to be redefined in the light of the huge challenges the Korean economy faces, including liberalization and external opening. However, it is not clear what the role and nature of banks will be during the transition from a government-led to a more market-based regime of economic management. Serious concern remains that without a system of credit control, concentration of bank loans is inevitable. Unless the bank loan market is fully liberalized without interest rate regulations, banks prefer larger firms, which usually have smaller default risk and make bigger contributions to bank profitability with fee-generating business than do smaller firms. Nevertheless, it seems clear that the system's emphasis should be shifted from the regulation of the business sector to the efficient management of private resource flows. This new role should be accomplished through improvement in the capability of the principal transactions banks to conduct credit evaluation.

Recognizing that the current credit control system unduly restricts normal corporate activities, the government that took office in 1993 envisages a gradual relaxation of controls and realignment of related policies. As an initial step, credit control procedures will be simplified, and the guided debt-equity ratios, as well as the mode of basket control (credit ceiling), will be reviewed. Then the current system of approval by the principal transactions banks for corporate investment in other businesses and real estate will be phased out, and only the 10 largest chaebol will remain subject to credit control. The easing of excessive concentration of economic power and specialization of business groups in a few industries would be induced with the provisions of the Fair Trade Act and the Industrial Development Law. Speculation in real estate would be tackled by strengthening related tax laws and their implementation. Ultimately, the credit control system would focus on maintaining prudence and soundness in corporate banking operations. Credit ceilings would be established for groups based on their scale of operation as well as their capital structure.

LESSONS FROM THE KOREAN EXPERIENCE

The principal transactions bank system in Korea was introduced as a consequence of government-led economic development. In an effort to promote strategic industries and certain sectors, decisions on credit allocation were, in effect, made by the government, and banks simply carried them out. The principal transactions bank system is an institutional mechanism created to correct the side effects of government support for large corporations and to supervise their investment activities.

An evaluation of the principal transactions bank system is not favourable, even though it does not mean that some such system was not needed. It is difficult, in an economy where the government is directly involved in the allocation of bank credit, to find an alternative system to supervise corporate investment and financial activities. In such an economy, however, principal transactions banks cannot be efficient supervisors; they were not in a position to evaluate corporate investment plans in advance and merely conducted *ex post* oversight of predetermined projects. If the government had been less interventionist, principal transactions banks could have played a more positive role and prevented the gross inefficiencies that have resulted from government-led economic management.

The role of the principal transactions banks as suppliers of information to the government seems to be the major reason why the government still maintains the system in spite of the changing economic environment. As the government's financial support for the corporate sector is reduced, the need for corporations to supply information directly to the government also decreases. But the government still needs information from the corporate sector to monitor both aggregate economic activity and the concentration of economic power. Therefore, the principal transactions bank system in Korea now faces the task of meeting the government demand for information on corporate activities, while at the same time alleviating the adverse effects resulting from the regulatory nature of the system.

The Korean experience with its principal transactions bank system since the mid-1970s can be summarized as follows. First, it is difficult to imagine that a Japanese-style main bank system would have evolved even if there had been no credit control by the government. Due to the under-development of the banking industry in a fast-growing government-led economy, banks could not accumulate enough know-how and capability to guide corporations. It suggests that without government intervention, a main bank system cannot easily be established in a government-led developing economy.

Second, the credit control system has been effective in checking the concentration of bank loans and the economic power of large business groups. However, as the government used banks as a tool for controlling large corporations, the autonomy and efficiency of bank management suffered.

Third, despite some loopholes, the credit control system has been fairly effective in controlling corporate activities. This function of principal transactions banks, however, has been performed only passively as imposed by the credit control system.

Fourth, with continued economic development and the growing

inefficiency of government intervention in economic affairs, the credit control and principal transactions bank systems must change accordingly. The control function of principal transactions banks should give way to a normal bank-customer relationship. Without this change, the effectiveness of control will be weakened while the cost of control increases.

Korea's experience shows that a principal transactions bank system can play an important role in a developing economy as an institutional device to alleviate the side effects of government intervention in resource allocation. At the same time, it shows that this role of banks will be executed at the cost of impeding banks' autonomous credit-screening capabilities and restricting business activities. In a developing economy, the role and performance of the principal transactions banks should basically depend on the nature of the government-bank-enterprise relationship specific to that economy.

APPENDIX

List of Operations of Principal Transaction Banks

1. Provision of management guidance to business groups and individual corporations (Regulation on Credit Operations of Banking Institutions, Article 8; Operational Bylaw on Credit Control over Business Groups, Article 6)

- Encourage an adequate level of equity capital.
- Restrict investment in new business and encourage disposal of corporations in 'non-major' (that is, non-core) industries.
- Restrict real estate acquisition and encourage disposal of non-operating real estate.
- Curb excessive use of foreign loans.
- Consult on an annual plan for financing and its uses.
- Induce sound management.
- Encourage self-financing of investment in new business and real estate acquisition.
- Provide other management guidance for the improvement of capital structure.

2. Approval for corporate activities (Operational Bylaw on Credit Control over Business Groups)

- Give prior approval for investment in new business by member corporations of business groups (Article 11).
- Give prior approval for a real estate acquisition by large corporations (Article 13).
- Give prior approval for changes in the use of real estate owned by client corporations.

3. Acceptance of Report (Operational Bylaw on Credit Control over Business Groups, Article 20)

- Receive report about investment in new business by a group owner or by persons with special relations with the owner.

4. Report to the Office of Bank Supervision and Examination (OBSE)

- Annual report on the general situation of business groups at year-end, due by March of next year (Operational Procedure, Article 2.1).
- Monthly report on investment in new business by business groups that do not need approval of their principal transaction bank for such activity (Operational Procedure, Article 2.2).
- Consolidated financial statements of business groups, as reported by their principal corporations (Operational Bylaw, Article 6).
- Report on guided equity ratio and actual equity ratios of business groups and their member corporations (Operational Bylaw, Article 7).
- Report concerning the approval of Major Corporation's acquisition of other firms (Operational Bylaw, Article 8.3).
- Quarterly report on the result of *ex post* supervision of the use of funds provided to Major Corporations (Operational Bylaw, Article 9.2).
- Report on abuses of banks loans by Major Corporations reported by other banking institutions (Operational Bylaw, Article 9.4).

- Report concerning cases of 'window dressing' (Operational Bylaw, Article 31).
- Report on the designation and supervision of business groups put under special management guidance for the improvement of their capital structure (Operational Bylaw, Article 5.2).
- *Ex post facto* report on financing through self-help efforts and its uses (Operational Procedure, Article 9).

5. Sanctions against the Violation of Regulations

- Obligation to take appropriate actions, such as credit suspension, in case of non-compliance with the principal transactions bank's guidance for capital structure improvement (Regulation on Credit Operations of Banking Institutions, Article 8).
  - Levy of maximum interest rate (for loans in arrears) on the amount involved in the violation.
  - Application of 1.5 times the maximum fee for payment guarantees in domestic currency.
  - Ordering the restoration of the original state and imposing penalties for violation of regulations concerning prior approvals prescribed in the Operational Bylaws (Operational Bylaw, Article 27).

- Issuing warnings, ordering restoration of the original state, or suspending credit in cases of other violations (Operational Bylaw, Article 29).
- Ordering self-help financing of 50 per cent of the investment in new business made without proper report by the group owner or persons with special relations with the owner.

6. Other Administrative Operations

- Placing loan officers who are exclusively responsible for each business group (Operational Bylaw, Article 10).
- Conducting surveys at least once a year on the uses of real estate owned by client corporations (Operational Bylaw, Article 21).
- Encouraging disposal of non-operating real estate (Operational Bylaw, Article 22).
- Keeping track of local financing of overseas offices of client corporations and providing appropriate guidance (Operational Bylaw, Article 24).

Source: Compiled by the authors from 'Regulation on Credit Operations of Banking Institutions' and 'Operational Bylaws on Credit Control over Business Groups'.

JUNG, BYUNG-HYU and YOUNG-SIK

REFERENCES

Allied Press. 1991. 31 August.
Bank of Korea. Various issues. *Financial Statements Analysis.*
Bank Supervisory Board. 1991. Data submitted to the National Assembly. Seoul.
COLE, DAVID C. and YUNG-CHUL PARK. 1983. *Financial Development in Korea, 1945–1978.* Cambridge MA: Harvard University Press, for the Harvard University Council on East Asian Studies.
HORIUCHI, TOSHIHIRO. 1990. 'Management Structure of Japanese Banks and Their

Optimal Relationship with Firms as Mainbank.' Discussion Paper 309, Kyoto Institute of Economic Research, Kyoto University. December.

YANG. 1992. 'Hanguk Chaebol Bumun ui Kyungje Bunsuk' ('The Economic Analysis of Chaebols in Korea'). Korea Development Institute, Seoul.

KIM, DONG-WON. 1992. 'Unhaeng Daechul Shijang eseoui Jungbu, Unhaeng, Guiup Gwange ui Jaemosaek' ('Reconsideration of the Relationship between Government, Bank and Corporation in Bank Loan Market'). Korea Economic Research Institute, Seoul. January.

Korea Investors Service. 1981–90 (annuals). *Chaebol Bunsuk Bogoseo* (*Chaebol Analysis Report*).

Maeil Kyungje (newspaper). 7 May 1991, 31 March 1992, 16 October 1992.

Management Efficiency Research Institute. 1987. *Hanguk 50 Daegiup Group Jaemu Bunsuk Jaryojib* (*Analysis of Financial statements—Fifty Major Business Groups in Korea*). Seoul.

MIN, BYONG-KYUN. 1991. 'Keyulgiupgun Yushingwanrijedo Kaisun Bangan' ('Improving the Credit Control System on Business Groups'). In *Kumyung ui Kukjehwa wa Kyujewan hwa* (*Internationalization and Deregulation of Finance*). Research Paper 49–91–04, Korea Economic Research Institute, Seoul.

NAM, SANG-WOO. 1991. 'Korea's Financial Policy and Its Consequences.' Paper presented at the Workshop on Government, Financial Systems and Economic Development: A Comparative Study of Selected Asian and Latin American Countries, East-West Center, Honolulu HI, 18–19 October.

14

The Lead Bank Systems in India

V. V. BHATT

In both Japan and India the financial system was used after World War II as an instrument for rapid economic development, particularly through the accelerated pace of industrialization. The financial systems in both countries—in Japan until 1970 and in India until 1985—were largely bank-oriented. New projects and enterprises with no track record to facilitate financing through a market-oriented system, which can function only on the basis of detailed information about the actual performance of entrepreneurs and enterprises, therefore had to rely on bank financing. Further, in the initial post-war years in India, saving rates were low and, because of considerable uncertainty, savers were unwilling to assume the risk attached to market instruments. The policy environment in Japan also was not favourable for the functioning of a capital market. One of the mechanisms for making adequate finance available to new entrepreneurs and enterprises was the main bank system in Japan and the lead bank systems in India.

The objective of this chapter is to give a brief account of the lead bank systems in India and review their performance. These systems are, in the nature of financial innovations, somewhat similar to the universal banking system in Germany during the late nineteenth century and the main bank system in Japan with regard to their objectives (see Bhatt, 1988).

The plan of this chapter is as follows. A synoptic overview of the financial system in India is presented in the first section. The Indian lead bank systems and their characteristics are presented in the second section, and the reasons for their relative ineffectiveness are indicated in the third section. The relevance of the innovations represented by the lead bank systems in India and the main bank system in Japan for other developing countries and transforming socialist economies, and the pre-conditions for their effectiveness as an instrument for rapid industrialization, are discussed in the concluding section.

OVERVIEW OF THE FINANCIAL SYSTEM

The Indian financial system as it has evolved is comparable in many respects with the financial systems of the most advanced developing countries as well as some of the developed countries. It has a well-diversified structure of financial institutions and instruments and financial development has outpaced economic development (Bhatt, 1991 and World Bank, 1990).

Growth and Diversification

The financial system has developed at a fairly rapid pace since 1950 and its growth rate has exceeded that of gross domestic product and gross capital formation. The ratio of financial assets to gross domestic product has increased from 62 per cent in 1981 to 94 per cent in 1990, and the financial interrelations ratio (net increase in financial assets to net capital formation) has risen from 0.98 in 1965–66 to 2.50 in 1990; this *marginal* financial interrelation ratio is comparable with the *average* financial interrelations ratio in the United States (Bhatt, 1980, chapter 10). The household sector's gross saving in the form of financial assets has increased from 5.5 per cent of net domestic product in 1965–66 to 12.2 per cent in 1990. The population per bank branch has declined from 65,000 in 1969 to 11,000 in 1990. India's financial development is comparable to that of South Korea and the network of financial institutions as it functions at present does not appear have a parallel in any other part of the world. Tables 14.1–14.3 provide an overview of the system.

TABLE 14.1 Structure of Household Sector's Savings as a Percentage of Net Domestic Product

1982	1986	1990	1991	Form of savings
11.8	12.2	15.5	15.5	Net total savings
5.2	4.4	5.6	5.8	Physical assets
9.4	10.7	12.6	12.2	Financial assets
2.8	2.9	2.7	2.5	Financial liabilities
6.6	7.8	9.9	9.7	Net financial assets
56	64	64	63	Net financial assets as a percentage of net total savings

Data are for 31 March (fiscal year-end).

Source: Reserve bank of India, *Report on Currency and Finance* (1989–90); and *Annual Report* (1990–91).

TABLE 14.2 Gross Financial Assets of Financial Institutions as a Percentage of Total Assets and GDP

1981		1989		
Total Assets	GDP	Total Assets	GDP	
14	9	12	11	Reserve Bank of India
55	34	48	45	Banks
69	43	60	56	Banking system total
11	7	17	16	Specialized financial institutions
19	12	23	22	Social security institutions (insurance, pension and provident funds)
–	62	–	94	Financial system total assets

Source: Estimates computed by author from data in Reserve bank of India, *Report on Currency and Finance* (1989–90); and *Annual Report* (1989–90).

TABLE 14.3 Distribution of Total Gross Assets of Selected Financial Systems

Developed Countries (1985 average)	Advanced Developing Countries (1985 average)	South Korea (1984)	India (1989)	Financial Institution
5	24	12	12	Central bank
57	59	50	48	Deposit banks
14	11	33	17	Specialized lending institutions[1]
24	6	5	23	Contractual savings institutions

[1] Includes collective investment institutions.

Source: India: Reserve bank of India, *Report on Currency and Finance* (1989–90); and *Annual Report* (1990–91). Others: World Bank, *World Development Report* 1989.

The Central Bank

The Reserve Bank of India (RBI) is India's central bank. The RBI performs the traditional central banking roles of note issue, banker to the government and commercial banks. It formulates and manages monetary and credit policy by setting deposit and lending rates, and lending targets. It also manages the foreign exchange market and the exchange control system. The RBI regulates and supervises all commercial banks and manages the public sector commercial banks. It provides deposit insurance and credit guarantees for some bank loans through a subsidiary (the

Deposit Insurance and Credit Guarantee Corporation). The RBI established the Discount and Finance House of India (DFHI) in 1988 to encourage secondary trading in treasury and commercial bills and to facilitate open market operations. Finally, the RBI has played a developmental role by providing refinance lines. Two of them were later spun off into separate development finance institutions for industry (Industrial Development Bank of India) and agriculture (National Bank for Agriculture and Rural Development); its largest remaining refinance lines are for agriculture and exports.

Deposit Institutions

Commercial banks still dominate the financial system. Their widespread network of nearly 59,000 branches enables them to raise deposits countrywide. The large banks effectively operate as universal banks, taking in all types of deposits and offering many kinds of loans; in addition, some have established subsidiaries for leasing, underwriting, mutual funds, merchant banking and other corporate services.

Commercial banking is dominated by 20 public sector banks, (nationalized in 1969 and 1980) and 196 regional rural banks. Public banks account for over 90 per cent of commercial bank assets and deposits. The RBI controls the operations of all public sector banks through directives and guidelines and a comprehensive annual financial review. (Data in the section are for 1990.)

Private commercial banks consist of 29 Indian scheduled banks, 21 foreign banks and 3 small non-scheduled banks. (Scheduled banks have a minimum asset size, are limited companies and must abide by RBI and central government regulations. They are eligible for RBI refinance and licences to deal in foreign exchange.)

The Post Office Savings Bank also mobilizes deposits. Operating through post offices throughout the country, it caters mainly to lower-income groups and raises over 35 per cent of its deposits from rural areas. Traditional Post Office Savings deposits are equivalent to less than 2 per cent of broad money (currency in circulation plus all bank deposits). Other Post Office deposits and small saving instruments have been more successful because of their attractive interest rates and benefits; they amount to about 4.5 per cent of broad money and almost 7 per cent of the time deposit component of broad money. All of the resources mobilized by the Post Office Savings Bank go to the government.

Company deposits, which are term deposits with non-bank companies, are another important financial asset; they are equivalent to about 15 per cent of broad money and about 75 per cent of them are in non-financial companies. One-half of all company deposits are with government companies, representing security deposits for services and deposits of profitable public sector firms with unprofitable firms. Interest rates on these deposits are 13–14 per cent, making them both a low-cost source of funds for firms and more attractive than bank deposits for individuals. Large firms are allowed to take deposits of up to 35 per cent of their capital.

Term Lending and Apex

Table 14.4 lists the institutions that comprise India's financial system. Three important all-India industrial development finance institutions (DFIs) provide term finance to industry: the Industrial Development Bank of India (IDBI), the Industrial Credit and Investment Corporation of India (ICICI), and the Industrial Finance Corporation of India (IFCI). In addition, the Industrial Reconstruction Bank of India (IRBI) assists in restructuring firms experiencing operational and financial difficulties. At the state level there are state finance corporations (SFCs) and state industrial development corporations (SIDCs). There is also a Small Scale Industry Bank, providing refinance to financial institutions that provide credit to small industry. IDBI (established in 1964) acts as an apex and coordinating institution; about 30 per cent of its disbursements represent refinance. IDBI also holds equity positions in IFCI, IRBI, the Unit Trust of India (UTI) and SFCs. IDBI has taken a major role in promoting consortium finance for industrial projects, which currently govern about 90 per cent of all direct lending by DFIs. IDBI, IFCI and SFCs are all government-owned institutions, while ICICI is a semi-private institution.

The National Bank for Agriculture and Rural Development (NABARD) is the apex body for agricultural finance. Funded by the RBI and international agencies, it is owned by the central government. Its main responsibilities include extending loans and refinancing assistance to commercial banks, regional rural banks (RRBs) and state cooperative banks. It also coordinates the financing activities of constituent institutions and invests in their share capital and securities. In the last few years, NABARD has assumed additional tasks, including the rehabilitation of weak RRBs and cooperative banks.

The National Housing Bank (NHB) was established by RBI in 1988 to regulate and supervise housing finance. While NHB's role is still evolving, it currently sets interest rates for deposits and mortgage loans and provides refinance for small new houses.

The Life Insurance Corporation of India (LIC) and the General Insurance Corporation of India (GIC) were formed when the government nationalized life insurance companies in 1956 and took over the general insurance companies in 1972. Both are required to invest a substantial proportion of their portfolios in government securities or other approved instruments. They also invest part of their 'free' funds in industry through

TABLE 14.4 Financial Institutions in India, 1990

Central bank

    Reserve Bank of India (RBI)

Cooperative banks

    Central cooperative banks (354)
    Primary agricultural credit societies (87,000)
    Primary cooperative banks (1,331)
    State central land development banks (19)
    State cooperative banks (SBC) (28)

Term lending institutions

    All India

Industrial Development Bank of India (IDBI)
Industrial Credit and Investment Corporation of India (ICICI)
Industrial Finance Corporation of India (IFCI)
Industrial Reconstruction Bank of India (IRBI)
National Bank for Agriculture and Rural Development (NABARD)
Agricultural Finance Corporation (AFC)
Export-Import Bank of India (Exim Bank)
Small Industries Development Bank of India (SIDBI)
National Housing Bank (NHB)
Housing Development Finance Corporation Ltd. (HDFC)
Housing and Urban Development Corporation Ltd. (HUDCO)
Infrastructure Leasing and Financial Services Ltd. (ILAFS)
Risk Capital and Technology Finance Corporation Ltd. (RCTFC)
Tourism Finance Corporation of India Ltd. (TFCI)
The Technology Development and Information Company of India Ltd. (TDICI)

      State level

State financial corporations (SFCs)
State industrial development corporations (SIDCs)

Social Security and Investment Institutions

    Life Insurance Corporation of India (LIC)
    General Insurances Corporation of India (GIC)
    Employees Provident Fund (EPF)

the capital market, where they are important net buyers as well as underwriters. Moreover, some of the investment in industry consists of obligations of DFIs. LIC and GIC also purchase bonds issued by housing agencies and have recently established subsidiaries to finance housing directly.

Industrial exports are financed by commercial banks and the government-owned Export-Import Bank (Exim). The Exim Bank was formed in 1982, taking over many of the IDBI's functions as a supplier of credit to exporters. Despite the Exim Bank's growth, commercial banks still supply a significant portion of export credit.

Capital and Money Markets

India's capital market is among the largest in the developing world; it is composed of 22 regional exchanges trading long-term government debt, debentures, and shares. Nearly 6,800 firms are listed on Indian stock exchanges and there are about 15 million stockholders (March 1993 data); both numbers are more than any country other than the United States. Market capitalization of listed firms in 1987 was similar to Brazil, Malaysia, Singapore and Denmark, but much smaller than Korea. Until recently, the government security market was the largest segment of the capital market. In the 1980s, however, private issues have grown dramatically. Large companies now raise about 20 per cent of their new funding in the market; for them it has become a viable, low-cost source of funds and a way around the limits on credit and its high cost.

The Unit Trust of India (UTI), owned by the government, raises resources from sales of small denomination 'units' to households and invests the proceeds in the stock market and in private placements. In recent years, UTI has become a dominant player in the capital market. Several banks have established mutual funds as subsidiaries; so far there are seven mutual funds competing with the UTI.

The Indian money market is composed of transactions between financial intermediaries (call money, inter-bank funds, and rediscounting of bills), treasury bills and the inter-corporate market. The RBI has taken a major role in stimulating the development of the money market, and has actively sponsored new instruments. In 1988, to help banks even out liquidity, the RBI reintroduced participation certificates. In 1989, it introduced commercial paper and certificate of deposits.

Finance for Agriculture

Institutional finance for agriculture is provided to farmers by primary agricultural cooperative credit societies (PACs), which extend short- and medium-term credit to members; branches of cooperative land development banks (LDBs) provide term loans; and branches of commercial banks and RRBs provide credit of all maturities. Other credit, largely short term, comes from money lenders, input dealers, relatives and so forth; these informal market transactions are an extremely important aspect of agricultural finance as well as finance for all types of small enterprises. (See World Bank, 1990; and Bhatt, 1991.)

LEAD BANK SYSTEMS

In the late 1960s, India devised three types of lead banks with the explicit objective of raising the rate of financial saving, allocating financial resources on the basis of sound criteria to various sectors of the economy and improving investment and productive efficiency of assisted enterprises by providing entrepreneurial, managerial and technical assistance. The financial system since then has been expected to play a catalytic role in stimulating a process of rapid industrial and economic development. The lead bank systems had some of the characteristics of the main bank system, but the institutional and policy framework was quite different from that in Japan during 1950–70. The different characteristics of the Indian framework seem to have had an adverse effect on the functioning of lead bank systems.

There are three types of lead bank systems, each with a different function: (a) *lead development bank* for investment financing; (b) *lead commercial bank* for working capital finance; and (c) *lead commercial bank* in a district or simply the *lead bank* with the function of providing access to bank finance to small enterprises of all types in a district and promoting such enterprises through entrepreneurial, managerial and technical assistance.

Lead Development Bank

There are three all-India development banks: the Industrial Development Bank of India (IDBI), the Industrial Finance Corporation of India (IFCI), and the Industrial Credit and Investment Corporation of India (ICICI). At the state level, practically every state has a state financial corporation (SFC) and a state industrial development corporation (SIDC); there are 18 SFCs and 26 SIDCs.

The IDBI is an apex development bank with the function of coordinating the activities of the development banking system; its charter is broad and flexible and it can finance, directly or indirectly, any sound project, irrespective of its ownership, organization and size.

Inter-Institutional Meeting (IIM)

For coordinating the functions of the all-India development banks, the IDBI has devised an informal institution called Inter-Institutional Meeting (IIM), comprising as members the IDBI, IFCI, ICICI, Life Insurance Corporation of India (LIC), General Insurance Corporation (GIC), and the Unit Trust of India (UTI). The latter three are significant resource mobilizers; LIC and GIC account for about 8–9 per cent of the household sector's gross financial saving and the UTI for about 3 per cent. Since they are long-term investors, they also have an interest in providing finance to new sound enterprises by way of loans, purchase of bonds or equity; hence their participation in the IIM. The lead development bank function, however, is performed only by the development banks—the IDBI, ICICI, and IFCI.

Until about 1970, an IIM was held every month with the specific objective of (a) sharing and exchanging information on projects requiring finance, (b) forming a *collective* judgement about the soundness of the projects presented to each of them for financial assistance, and (c) arranging the required finance for each large project above a certain size through syndicated financial assistance.

This system reduced risk relating to adverse selection by pooling information on enterprises and projects available with each institution, mobilized adequate finance for new sound projects, and reduced each lender's risk by risk sharing. However, each enterprise had to submit a separate application form to each institution; each institution evaluated the applications and managed the legal formalities with respect to collateral separately. This process involved transaction costs to both institutions and borrowers. To reduce these costs, the institutions devised both a common application form and a system of a lead development bank after 1970. The institution, which is expected to be the largest lender, functions as a lead bank in this new system. A decision is taken at the IIM on which specific institution will function as a lead bank for investment finance, provided on a syndicated basis.

Syndicates are organized at the IIM, and the lead development bank is the first one to be approached by a firm. The project particulars are discussed at the IIM and the participants indicate what proportion of financing they can supply. Next, the firm's commercial banks are asked to indicate the size of long-term financing they can provide. For a large project, the commercial banks' participation has been crucial, but they provide long-term finance *only* on the basis of a project appraisal by the development banks; they are not permitted to provide long-term finance on their own to large projects. The real problem is that even when commercial banks participate in loan syndication, their monitoring responsibilities and exchange of information processes are not specified in advance. Ultimate monitoring responsibility rests with the lead development bank. It appears from available evidence that interim monitoring of project implementation and operation is not done effectively, as the lead development bank has not asked for assistance from the lead commercial bank.

Functions of the Lead Bank

The functions of the lead bank are the following:

* Appraising and evaluating the soundness of an enterprise or project on the basis of criteria collectively established by the institutions. The lead bank's appraisal is accepted by the other institutions before deciding their share of assistance to the project; the lead bank's share is the largest.
* Securing the required financial resources from participating institutions by issuing participation certificates. It is solely responsible for providing the financial package to the borrower.
* Managing the collateral on behalf of all the institutions; it is thus responsible for all legal formalities required for the purpose.
* Collecting interest payments and repayment of principal from the borrower; and paying each institution its share.
* Monitoring the project or enterprise and, for this purpose, deputing its own staff member to the board of the assisted enterprise; and obtaining information about the functioning of the enterprise by quarterly reports and periodical visits of its staff.
* Identifying financial and technical problems facing the enterprise, taking action to solve them, if necessary, by changing the management or in any other way with the help of the other institutions.
* Presenting a programme of action to the IIM for reconstructing or restructuring of sick enterprises or projects with accumulated arrears relating to interest and repayment of principal.

Impact on Transaction Costs and Risk

As in the case of the Japanese main bank system, the lead development bank system reduces the transaction costs of the borrower, as the borrower has to deal with only one institution for all matters relating to appraisal, documentation, disbursement, repayment, and sanction. The transaction costs of participant banks have been reduced, though the lead bank's transaction costs have increased. The overall transaction costs of lenders and borrowers taken together have been reduced; the risk of adverse selection is reduced as a result of shared information and critical appraisal of the enterprises and projects; and the moral hazard risk is reduced because of the lead bank's monitoring role and its representation on the board of the assisted enterprise.

The incentives for becoming a lead bank include (a) expanding business to include a portfolio of sound projects formulated by reliable firms; (b) gaining the prestige attached to being a lead bank—essential for business expanding; and (c) gaining a reputation as a sound development bank and thus creating a favourable impression on government authorities—essential for securing privileges.

Efficiency of the Lead Bank System

The lead bank system has ensured adequate long-term finance for sound industrial projects and has been responsible for the diversification of the industrial structure. Nearly all medium and large new projects and all major expansion and diversification projects have been financed to a significant extent by the development banking system. As a result, substantial production capacities have been built up in a large number of industries, not merely in traditional ones like textiles and food-processing, but also in chemicals, fertilizers, cement, industrial machinery, commercial vehicles, rubber, paper, metals, and metal products. This deliberate diversification of the industrial sector has contributed to the structural transformation taking place in India's manufacturing sector. The system has financed some 35–40 per cent of the project cost of assisted enterprises, and holds about 25 per cent of the equity and 62 per cent of debentures issued by assisted private sector companies. It is partly because of the development banking system that the annual growth rate of industrial output during 1950–51 to 1989–90 was about 6 per cent, which was much lower than in Japan, but still higher than the growth rate before 1950–51.

However, the lead bank system's performance in improving the investment and productive efficiency of assisted enterprises, and thus in reducing risk inherent in long-term financing, was not as good as in Japan during 1950–70. For example, in the case of the ICICI, which is the most efficient development bank in India, fewer than 50 per cent of the projects were completed on time, fewer than 60 per cent were completed without any cost over-run and fewer than 50 per cent were able to earn the anticipated return of 12 per cent or more (Table 14.5). The performance of the Korea Development Bank has been better in all these respects: of the assisted projects, 50 per cent were completed in time, 72 per cent had actual cost saving (that is, their costs were below anticipated costs), only 16 per cent made losses, and 90 per cent of the projects earned more than a 15 per cent return (Table 14.6) at constant prices (prices relevant at the project appraisal stage).

When judged in terms of the economic rate of return or exports to sales ratio of assisted projects, the performance of the Korea Development Bank has been much better than that of the development banks in India. This shows that the lead bank system has not performed

TABLE 14.5 Performance of Selected Projects and Companies Financed by the ICICI, 1981–87

Time over-run

	Sample size (number of projects)	Projects completed in time (per cent)	Projects with delays up to 12 months (per cent)	Projects with delays over 12 months (per cent)
(i)	113	47	37	16
(ii)	242	45	38	17

Cost over-run

	Sample size (number of projects)	Projects with cost over-run (per cent)	Aggregate cost over-run (per cent)	Average cost over-run for affected projects (per cent)
(i)	113	41	19	30
(ii)	242	42	13	25

Profitability

	Sample size (number of projects)	Projects with return of 12% or more (per cent)	anticipated making profits (per cent)	Projects incurring losses (per cent)	Projects yet to be completed (per cent)
(i)	53	45	59	41	–
(ii)	88	47	49	28	23

	Number of companies			
	Over 20%		10–19%	0.3–9%
Exports to sales ratio (per cent)	26	3	7	16

Source: World Bank, *Staff Appraisal Report: India, Industrial Finance and Technical Assistance Project*, 7 March 1988, Washington DC.

TABLE 14.6 Performance of Selected Projects Financed by the Korea Development Bank, 1976–85

	Sample size			
Time over-run		Projects completed ahead of schedule (per cent)	Projects completed in time (per cent)	Projects with delayed completion (per cent)
(i)	164	0.6	49	50.4
Cost over-run		Projects with cost saving (per cent)	Projects with cost over-run (per cent)	Project with anticipated costs (per cent)
		72	26	2
Financial performance		Projects with anticipated or more than anticipated return	Projects with below projected return	Projects with losses
		44	40	16
	Sample size (number of projects)	Projects with higher than 15% return (per cent)	Projects with below 15% return (per cent)	
Exports to sales ratio (per cent)	156	90	10	

Sources: World Bank (1989), *Staff Appraisal Report: Korea Development Bank,* (Washington DC: Annual Report of Korea Long Term Credit Bank 1990, Seoul.

well its functions of promoting viable import substitution and export pro-motion—the basic indicators of investment and productive efficiency—and efficient use of resources.

This is also reflected in the poor performance of the private corporate sector as a whole. The ratio of gross profits to sales of selected companies (most of them assisted by the development banking system) was only 10 per cent in 1981–82 and has been declining since (Table 14.7); the incremental capital-output ratio in the manufacturing sector is high and has been rising, going from 2.8 in 1950 to 6.2 in the 1970s; the growth rate of total factor productivity in the manufacturing sector during 1965–80 has been only 1 per cent per year in contrast to the rate of 2 to 5 per cent in several industrial and advanced developing countries; and manufacturing exports constitute only about 5 per cent of manufacturing output.

As a result, though the ICICI's administrative costs as a proportion of total assets was only 0.33 per cent in 1988–89—compared to about 0.59 per cent for the Korea Development Bank in 1987, and 0.96 per cent for the Korea Long-Term Development Bank in 1989—its provision for defaults as a proportion of total assets has increased from 0.87 per cent in 1981 to 1.79 per cent in 1988–89; while this was only 0.53 per cent for the Korea Development Bank in 1987, and 0.30 per cent for the Korea Long Term Development Bank in 1989 (Tables 14.8 and 14.9). This was largely the result of ICICI's loan recovery performance; it recovered only 70–75 per cent of repayment due in 1987–88 (Table 14.10).

Causes of Low Efficiency

This relatively poor performance reflects deficiencies in (a) project appraisal and evaluation, (b) monitoring and supervision of projects, and (c) mechanisms to anticipate problems and take a pro-active role in tackling them through timely managerial, technical or financial assistance to projects or enterprises that did not perform well.

In spite of lead bank representation on the boards of assisted companies and its holding of their equity, the monitoring and control mechanisms did not identify in time problems that emerged in the implementation of projects or in the functioning of assisted enterprises. Corrective action was delayed till the enterprise became 'sick'; and even then remedial measures were not well formulated; liquidation was seldom envisaged, owing to complicated legal procedures and government reluctance.[1]

One of the reasons for the lack of adequate monitoring of enterprises was the failure of the lead banks to evolve mechanisms of coordination

---

[1] A 'sick' industrial company, under the Sick Industrial Companies Act 1985, is one that has been registered for at least seven years, has accumulated losses equal to or exceeding the sum of its paid-up capital and free reserves, and has suffered cash losses, before providing for depreciation, in both the current and preceding financial years.

TABLE 14.7 Performance Indicators of Selected Companies

	Number of companies in the sample			Number of profit making companies (percentage of sample)			Return on capital employed (per cent)			Gross profits to sales (per cent)		
	81–82	84–85	87–88	81–82	84–85	87–88	81–82	84–85	87–88	81–82	84–85	87–88
1. RBI sample (i)	621	621	621	–	–	–	17.9	13.4	10.5	10.3	9.2	8.6
(ii)	1,720	1,867	621	–	–	–	11.2	8.7	8.3	9.3	8.3	8.6
2. IDBI sample	401	401	401	70	76	76	16.7	13.8	10.0	10.2	9.1	9.8
3. ICICI sample	417	417	417	84	79	82	17.7	15.3	13.3	10.6	10.1	9.6
4. Data base of capitaline series	–	542	824	–	81	77	–	5.55	3.51	–	6.35	7.26
5. Sample of Centre for Monitoring Indian Economy	–	–	–	–	–	–	–	9.8	8.3	–	7.6	7.2
6. Public sector companies (CMIE sample)	–	–	–	–	–	–	–	5.7	5.4	–	7.9	7.4
7. Average yield on ordinary shares	–	–	–	–	–	–	–	5.88	3.21	4.32	–	–
8. Government of India securities running yield	–	–	–	–	–	–	–	7.67	8.52	–	–	–

Source: Securities and Exchange Board of India, (1990) *State of the Capital Market—1989–90*; Centre for Monitoring Indian Economy, *Basic Statistics Relating to the Indian Economy*, August 1990.

TABLE 14.8 Industrial Credit and Investment Corporation of India (ICICI)
Spreads
(per cent of total assets)

	1981	1985	1988–89
Gross yield	11.01	12.66	12.55
Cost of funds	7.67	8.30	9.03
Gross spread	3.33	4.365	3.52
Risk*	0.87	1.64	1.79
Administrative cost	0.43	0.34	0.33
Risk plus administrative cost	1.30	1.98	2.12
Profits	2.03	2.38	1.40

* Risk is defined as gross risk before write-backs. (Provision for Risk.)

Source: World Bank, *Staff Appraisal Report: India, Industrial Finance and Technical Assistance Project*, 7 March 1988, Washington DC.

with the commercial banks. In India, development banks provide term finance for investment, while working capital finance is provided by commercial banks. The commercial banks are in a position to identify problems in time, as they deal with enterprises on a day-to-day basis and enterprise performance is reflected in their bank transactions. 'Although both the term lending institutions and the commercial banks broadly look for the same aspects as a part of follow-up, they monitor the performance separately without sharing the information systematically on an

TABLE 14.9 Korea Development Bank and Korea Long-Term Credit Bank
Spreads
(per cent of total assets)

Development Bank	Korea Development Bank		Korea Long-Term Credit Bank
	1985	1987	1989
Gross yield	8.80	8.50	8.30
Cost of funds	7.50	7.30	5.90
Gross spread	1.30	1.20	2.40
Administrative cost	0.60	0.59	0.96
Default risk provision	0.36	0.53	0.30
Administrative cost plus risk	0.96	1.12	1.26
Gross profits	0.34	0.08	1.14

Sources: World Bank (1989) *Staff Appraisal Report: Korea Development Bank*, Washington DC; Annual Report of Korea Long-Term Credit Bank (1990), Seoul.

TABLE 14.10 ICICI: Loan Recovery

	1982	1985	1987–88
1. Ratio of repayment of principal to repayment due (per cent) (collection ratio)	73.3	73.0	74.4
2. Collection ratio after rescheduling (per cent)	82.5	81.5	81.8
3. Arrears/total outstanding loans (per cent)	2.4	2.6	3.1
4. Arrears after rescheduling/total outstanding loans (per cent)	1.4	1.7	2.1

Source: World Bank, *Staff Appraisal Report: India, Industrial Finance and Technical Assistance Project*, 7 March 1988, Washington DC.

ongoing basis. This sometimes leads to duplication of efforts and results in the institutions working at cross purposes' (Reserve Bank of India, 1976). This was the finding of the Inter-Institutional Group appointed by the RBI. A relationship based on mutual trust among the participating institutions that was established in Japan did not evolve in India in the relationship between the lead development bank and the commercial banks concerned.

The lead bank and assisted enterprises in India face a greater degree of uncertainty and have much less freedom to adapt to changing circumstances than in Japan because of the direct controls regime and an institutional and policy framework that has been, to use the felicitous expression of Bhagwati, 'proscriptive' rather than 'prescriptive' (1988, pp. 98–102).

The lead development bank provides only *project financing*. The size of the project and its resource requirements—domestic and foreign exchange rather than the characteristics of the firm, determine which of the three all-India development banks a large firm will approach. If the project is large with significant resource requirements, a firm will approach the Industrial Development Bank (IDBI). If a firm requires only, or predominantly, foreign exchange financing, it will approach the Industrial Credit and Investment Corporation of India (ICICI). For projects of medium size and particularly for those located in North India, a firm may approach the Industrial Finance Corporation of India (IFCI). The relationship between the firm and the development bank in each case is quite participative and the bank tries to assist the firm in financial distress, but to a lesser extent than a main bank in Japan.

The problem of bad debt with respect to the development banks has arisen largely as a result of government directives—formal or informal—to assist sick industrial units, particularly in the textile sector which was not originally supported by the development banks. The other bad debts have arisen largely as a result of the unpredictability of government policies. Of course, some were due to imperfections in the project evaluation and supervision mechanisms of the development banks. The development banks require collateral, but to enforce the collateral provisions requires complex, lengthy, and costly legal formalities. There is a move to establish special tribunals for the recovery of debt, and this may help in enforcing the collateral conditions.

Lead Commercial Bank System

In order to prevent large borrowers—mostly 20 or so large business houses, similar to the business conglomerates in Japan and South Korea—from using excessive bank credit for purposes other than working capital finance, the RBI instituted a Credit Authorization Scheme (CAS) in 1965. Under the CAS, banks are expected to obtain prior authorization from the RBI before fresh or additional credit limits to large clients are sanctioned. However, since large borrowers borrowed from several banks (called the multiple banking system), it became difficult for the RBI to enforce credit discipline on them. Further, the transaction costs of borrowers increased as they had to submit information to each bank on their total credit requirements and the banks' transaction costs also increased as each had to collect this information. The RBI's transaction costs also increased as it had to collect information from each bank, consolidate it, and then appraise the credit proposed.

To reduce overall transaction costs, the RBI introduced a scheme in 1974 for consortium financing of large borrowers. Under this scheme, the Reserve Bank ruled that if the credit limit of a single borrower from any bank exceeded 1.5 per cent of that bank's deposits, then formation of a consortium was *obligatory* to reduce the bank's credit risk. Under the consortium arrangement, the largest lender has to act as a lead bank. The lead bank's responsibilities are the following:

- Credit appraisal, monitoring and supervision; legal formalities with respect to collateral; sanctioning and disbursement of consortium finance to the borrower on uniform terms and conditions; and collecting payment of interest and repayment of principal by the borrower on behalf of all participant banks.
- Sharing other banking business of the borrower with the participant banks in agreed proportions.
- Taking the lead in arranging for reconstruction or rehabilitation of assisted enterprises facing managerial, technical and financial problems.

The RBI also directed that in case of disagreement among the consortium members on the quantum of permissible bank finance, terms and conditions to be imposed, and the like, the view of the lead bank shall prevail; dissenting members must respect the lead bank's decision and may not leave the consortium. The basic objective of the RBI is to make the 'banks move towards a "single window" concept regarding delivery of credit, execution of documents, submission of data, and recoveries' (Reserve Bank of India, 1990, pp. 114–17), in order to reduce the transaction costs of the RBI, participant banks and borrowers, and to reduce the credit risk of each participant bank. Thus the lead commercial bank system's objectives are similar to those of the lead development bank system.

In practice, the system has not acheived its objectives for several reasons.

- The banks did not devise a mechanism, like the IIM of the lead development bank system, for taking decisions at the highest levels. This has led to delays in assistance to borrowers, and to avoidable transaction costs to participant banks, because of frequent meetings at various levels, none of which has the final authority to take decisions. The final authority rests with the bank's boards.
- The participating banks had no incentive to share information relating to a large borrower as each was reluctant to lose the other fee business of a credit-worthy customer. The lead bank has not been sharing customers' business with the participating banks either.
- Since each bank's share in that credit is small—in practice much less than 1.5 per cent of deposits—none of them takes the responsibility of monitoring the client's accounts. 'The lead bank does not enjoy the *de facto* status of a consortium leader and the observations, suggestions, and discussions of the consortium leader are not taken seriously by other banks. When an account gets into problems it becomes difficult to adopt a common approach *vis-à-vis* erring borrowers. Sometimes interests of an individual bank tend to gain precedence over common interests of all the involved banks' (Asian Development Bank, 1988, pp. 70–72). Since the system is in fact *imposed* by the RBI on the banks, the necessary trust and confidence among the participant banks are not established and each one tries to exploit the situation to its own advantage.
- Large borrowers have not liked the CAS because it causes delays in obtaining credit and makes it difficult to establish credit limits, which are deemed necessary by many borrowers. Hence a borrower has an incentive to obtain credit from several banks, avoiding the discipline of the CAS. A borrower is therefore unwilling to reveal its full credit needs to any single bank, and the banks have no incentive to share information with others since they are reluctant to lose profitable business. Because of the various credit allocation controls, only doing business with large borrowers is profitable for banks.

The failure of the system to attain its objectives is clearly brought out in a letter issued by the RBI to the commercial banks in 1987.

'. . . we regret to point out that even after the lapse of several years, we continue to get reports of non-implementation of the related guidelines by banks either in letter or in spirit. A quick study recently carried out by us has revealed that such deviations have been in various areas such as entering the formal consortium arrangements, joint appraisal, exchange of information, holding of meetings and the level of representation there at, sharing of business (including ancillary business) and stipulation of uniform terms and conditions. The non-compliance with our guidelines has resulted in inordinate delays and uncoordinated approach which have adversely affected the borrowers concerned. At times, borrowers have taken advantage of the lack of coordination amongst banks by obtaining additional credit facilities and/or concessions in terms and conditions for various facilities, affecting the overall health of the advances made to such borrowers.' (Reserve Bank of India, 1987.)

In 1988, the RBI moved from prior authorization of credit to large borrowers to post-sanction scrutiny in order to reduce delays in credit disbursement. It has, however, cautioned that if any bank is not enforcing the basic disciplines under the CAS, the RBI will instruct them to refer large cases to it for prior authorization. There does not seem to be much improvement in the implementation of the lead bank concept under consortium financing arrangements. The recent official committee, appointed by the Ministry of Finance, has recommended that the *mandatory* nature of the system should be given up and it should evolve on the basis of *voluntary* agreements among the banks.

The commercial banks provide only working capital finance on their own initiative. Historical links that existed between firms and banks before the nationalization of banks in 1969 have been weakened because of government and Reserve Bank allocation criteria and regulations. No commercial bank, lead or otherwise, feels responsible for assisting a firm in financial distress. A significant part of bad debts at commercial banks are a result of government and Reserve Bank credit allocation criteria and it is difficult to place responsibility on the banks' staff or top management. Where inefficiency can be proven, then of course the bank staff is punished in the sense that their chance of promotion is adversely affected; however, dismissal for inefficiency is rare because of trade union strength and government labour laws. The top management can, and has been, dismissed for gross inefficiency by the government, but because of complicated regulations, it is difficult to apportion blame. Politics has also been important in such decisions.

Lead Bank for District Development

From experience up to 1969, it was found that a bank with nationwide branches is unlikely to develop the intimate knowledge and feel of the local situation in a district (a unit of local government like a county in the United States) necessary to its development. Small district banks could have served the purpose, but given the structure and evolution of commercial banking, it was not practical to develop them. After national-ization of 14 commercial banks, the function of district development was assigned in 1969 to a commercial bank prominent in each district or region. Some districts were assigned to a lead bank whose function is to coordinate the policies of other local banks and financial institutions. Such a lead bank was expected to be more financially viable because of its nationwide operations and, for the same reason, would have at its dis-posal much larger resources than a small district bank. (Bhatt, 1972, chapter 1).

The main functions of a lead bank are to: (a) identify places in a dis-trict for branch expansion; (b) prepare a phased programme for branch expansion in the district to bring banking services within the reach of farmers and potential small enterprises in the entire area; (c) estimate the current requirement of credit and prepare a phased programme to meet it; (d) devise schemes of deposits and financial instruments which would prove attractive to the local people and effective for the purpose of mobi-lizing financial resources; (e) identify potential areas of agricultural and small-enterprise development and induce local entrepreneurs to undertake such development; (f) identify major bottlenecks in the development of the district and induce the appropriate agencies to take corrective action; and (g) encourage local entrepreneurs in agriculture and the small enter-prise sector to improve their productive efficiency.

The lead bank scheme has succeeded in its branch expansion pro-gramme and has provided access to credit to farmers and small enter-prises. The population per bank branch has declined from 65,000 in 1969 to 11,000 in 1990. Bank branches in rural areas are now 58 per cent of total branches as against 23 per cent in 1969. Bank credit to agriculture and small enterprises of all types now represents about 40 per cent of total bank credit as against 3–4 per cent in 1969. The system has also succeeded in mobilizing financial resources. The proportion of rural deposits to total deposits has increased from 3 per cent in 1969 to 15 per cent in 1990 and aggregate deposits of banks now form about 37 per cent of GNP.

However, the portfolio quality of the banks has deteriorated. In the farm sector, the proportion of loan recovery was only 57 per cent in 1988. The proportion of advances to sick small-scale industry to total advances to the small-scale industry sector had reached more than 15 per cent in 1990 (Table 14.11). The lead bank system has performed poorly with regard to appraisal, monitoring, and supervision of assisted small enterprises in the farm and the non-farm sector. This is reflected in Table 14.12 which shows the income and costs of public sector banks.

The system devised entrepreneur development programmes and also

TABLE 14.11 Indicators of the Quality of the Portfolio of Banks

	1986	1987	1988	1990
Recovery performance of direct agricultural advances: percentage of recoveries to demand	56.5	57.1	56.8	–
Loans outstanding to sick small-scale industry as a proportion of total loans to small scale industry (per cent)	–	17.7	17.6	15.6
Loans outstanding to sick non-SSI industry as a proportion of total loans to non-SSI industry (per cent)	–	–	12.0	11.9
Loans to all sick units as a percentage of total bank advances	–	9.4	9.7	9.2
Loans to all sick units as a percentage of bank advances to industry	–	18.1	18.2	17.4

Source: Estimates based on data given in the Reserve Bank of India, *Report on Trend and Progress of Banking in India, 1989–90*.

Note: A 'sick' industrial company, under the Sick Industrial Companies Act 1985, is one that has been registered for at least 7 years, has accumulated losses equal to or exceeding the sum of its paid-up capital and free reserves, and has suffered cash losses (before providing for depreciation) in both the current and preceding financial years.

TABLE 14.12 Income and Costs of Public Sector Banks (per cent of total assets)

	1987	1990
Interest income	7.23	8.50
Other income	0.67	0.82
Total income	7.90	9.32
Cost of funds	5.46	6.48
Gross spread	2.44	2.84
Administrative cost	2.31	2.68
Provision for risk or actual defaults	NA	NA
Administrative cost plus risk	2.31	2.68
Gross profits	0.13	0.16
Capital and reserves as a percentage of total advances	3.67	4.64
Non-performing advances as a percentage of total advances*	10–15	

* Estimated on the basis of the quality of portfolio relating to agricultural and industrial advances. See Table 14.11.

Source: 1. Estimates based on data given in Indian Banks' Association, Financial Analysis of Banks, 1987, volume I and 2. Reserve Bank of India, Report on Currency and Finance, 1987–88, 1989–90, and 1990–91.

established technical consultancy organizations to promote the development of non-farm small enterprises and improve their investment and productive efficiency; however, these mechanisms have not been effectively used for this purpose (Bhatt, 1981). The major reason for this failure has been the institutional and policy framework. The banks have been given targets for branch expansion and credit allocation to agriculture and small enterprises by the RBI and their principal effort has been concentrated on meeting these *quantitative targets* rather than in promoting sound schemes of farm and small-enterprise development. The credit allocation and subsidized interest rates through *directives* has weakened the top managements of the banks, and government ownership of banks has also led to political and bureaucratic intervention with regard to credit decisions and, as a result, corrupt practices.

INSTITUTIONAL AND POLICY FRAMEWORK IN INDIA

In contrast to the Japanese institutional and policy framework, the Indian framework has several characteristics adversely affecting the functioning of the banking system.

Macroeconomic Imbalances

There have been growing fiscal deficits financed by credit creation by the Reserve Bank which have led to inflationary pressures and payment imbalance. Wholesale prices increased at an annual rate of more than 7 per cent from 1960–61 to 1990–91 and are currently rising at about 7–8 per cent. The monetary and fiscal imbalances and the resulting inflationary pressures increased uncertainty and made it difficult for the lead development banking system and enterprises to appraise investment projects and monitor their performance. Further, relative prices have become distorted because of price and import controls; the price mechanism, in consequence, cannot perform the signalling function for resource allocation. In contrast, Japan achieved relative macroeconomic stability during its high growth period, 1950 to 1973.

Regulation and Control of the Banking System

The 20 major commercial banks and the development banks are under government ownership. The commercial banks are closely controlled by the Reserve Bank. Cash reserve and liquidity requirements take 53 per cent of deposits and priority sector lending to agriculture and small enterprises absorbs another 20 per cent. In addition, banks are compelled to finance special programmes. As a result, banks have discretion in allocating only 20 per cent of their resources, and even the free lending category is highly regulated. The RBI establishes credit limits for every significant borrower and prescribes norms for working capital loans by industrial sub-sector and firm location. The RBI also sets virtually all deposit and lending rates. The government and the RBI are responsible for banks' top management decisions.[2]

The commercial banks have hardly any operational autonomy (World Bank, 1990). Their position has been further weakened by political intervention in credit and recovery decisions. Management accountability, as a result, has been diluted, loan appraisal standards lowered, and collection efforts eased. Commercial banks' bad debts have increased and their profitability has declined.

The lead commercial banking system, devised by the RBI, has failed in attaining its objectives because banks have no incentive to implement it. Their discretionary allocation of resources relates only to large borrowers; only loans to large borrowers are profitable as the interest rates on them are the highest. Each bank has an interest in wooing large borrowers and no incentive to impose credit discipline on them. Borrowers can only gain from this inter-bank rivalry.

The system involves centralized decision-making through directives and direct controls on credit allocation; this does not leave adequate scope for experimentation, innovation and full use of widely dispersed information. Bank managements are concerned more with their dealings with the RBI and government than with good customer service and sound decision-making relating to credit transactions. In Japan, the financial institutions have operational autonomy and the Bank of Japan and the Ministry of Finance have adequate sanctions to ensure the soundness of the banking system.

Control Regime

An enterprise has to have an investment licence, import and foreign exchange licences, and a technology import licence, if it wants to undertake a new investment project or new expansion or diversification projects. Because of the uncertainty of obtaining licences, an enterprise has no incentive to formulate its project in detail at the time of application, which means the licensing system has to take decisions on the basis of inadequate information. Indeed, the system has no competence to

---

[2] Neither the government nor the Reserve Bank require banks to grant credit to *specific* industries or firms; allocation policy relates only to general strategy. Political and bureaucratic interference in favour of certain projects or firms and credit allocation quotas have led to corruption, affecting the entire banking system, but it has not been a frequent part of the general policy framework. The rent-seekers have been bank staff, politicians, and even firms. One serious case, attracting international attention, involved senior bank staff and certain stockbrokers speculating in the stock market (see the Reserve Bank of India, Annual Reports 1991–92, and 1992–93).

estimate the precise requirements for investment, imports, and foreign exchange. Despite this, once licences are approved, the main parameters of the project are determined.

It is only at this stage that the lead development bank appraises the project for financing. However good its appraisal, the bank has no discretion to alter the parameters—even if this would improve the project and its financial and economic viability. Its only option is not to finance the project; but that too cannot be done lightly if the necessary licences have been obtained. Both lead banks and enterprises have to function within these constraints.

Apart from constraints on project appraisal, neither the enterprise nor the lead bank has the freedom to alter the design of the project at the implementation or the operation stage with a view to adapting it to the emerging situation, even if the project faces problems. The system does not permit the lead bank to successfully perform its functions of appraisal, monitoring and supervision, and reconstruction or alteration of the project well.

Import Substitution Strategy

The main focus of the licensing system is the promotion of import substitution; this strategy does not permit domestic or international competition. The lead bank and the enterprise, denied competition, have neither the incentive nor the compulsion to improve investment and productive efficiency. Inevitably, a balance of payments problem becomes acute, as it has now in India. Japan, in contrast, actively encouraged export promotion and both government and Bank of Japan policies supported this dominant objective of strategic management.

Political and Bureaucratic Pressures

An export-oriented strategy imposes a certain discipline not only on the lead bank and the enterprise, but also on the government, whose policies have to be in accord. If this discipline is lacking, a situation is created where politicians and bureaucrats can interfere with the functioning of the licensing system and the banking system with impunity either for their own gain or to please vested interests: this is what happens in the Indian system. In Japan, there is less scope for corruption because a competent bureaucracy with proven integrity and the transparent and dominant objective of export performance provides an effective and unequivocal yardstick of performance of banks, firms, and government, and disciplines their strategies, policies and actions.

The characteristics of the Indian institutional and policy framework, unlike the Japanese system, have adversely affected the functioning of the lead banks. However, this framework has been liberalized since 1991 and, as a result, it is possible the system will be able to function as effectively and efficiently as the main bank system in Japan did during 1950–70. Of course, much depends on the evolving policy environment and the guidance and incentives provided by the Reserve Bank and the government, particularly the Ministry of Finance. They have yet to pay enough attention to the systems' critical roles. This means they have not created the pre-conditions for the effective and efficient functioning of lead banks.

Deregulation and Liberalization, 1991–93

After the payments crisis in 1991, several measures were taken to deregulate and liberalize financial sector policies as well as the other trade, industry, and foreign investment policies (Reserve Bank of India, 1992 and 1993).

With effect from 22 April 1992, the rates on term deposits of all maturities of 46 days and over are subject to a single prescription not exceeding 13.0 per cent a year. Banks are free to determine their maturity and deposit rates within this ceiling. Lending rates by banks are now only subject to a *minimum*, actual rates are left to the discretion of the banks, except for those applicable to some of the priority sectors, for which *maximum* rates have been fixed (presumably high enough to cover transaction costs, risk, and financial costs). All other interest rates are allowed to be determined by market forces.

Under the liberalized branch licensing policy, only those banks that have reached the revised capital adequacy norms (8 per cent for banks with international operations and 4 per cent, rising to 8 per cent in March 1996, for others) and prudential accounting standards have been given the freedom to open new branches and upgrade extension counters into full-fledged branches without the prior approval of the Reserve Bank. Provided they satisfy certain prudential norms, the private sector is permitted to start new banks.

On 1 March 1992, a Liberalized Exchange Rate Management System (LERMS) was introduced; this involved a dual rate system with one rate flexibly determined by the Reserve Bank (applicable to certain transactions) and a market rate (for all other transactions). The system provided an opportunity for the development of market-determined transactions in foreign exchange as a preparatory arrangement for unification of the two rates in early 1993. This is a step towards full convertibility on the current account, which is envisaged in the near future.

Since 1992, there has been a virtual abolition of the requirement of industrial licensing, except for a short list of industries, and the abolition of the concept of monopoly involving limits on the assets of large industrial houses for permitting industrial investment. The number of industries reserved exclusively for the public sector has been curtailed and competition between the public and private sectors has been encouraged.

The new policy substantially eliminates licensing, quantitative restrictions, and other regulatory and discretionary controls on imports. Exports and imports are allowed freely, subject only to a negative list of imports and exports. Restricted imports include mainly consumer goods which can be imported only against licences. Tariff rates have also been lowered.

Foreign direct investment of up to 51 per cent for foreign equity in 34 selected areas now receives automatic approval; other proposals are considered and approved on their merits by the Secretariat for Industrial Approvals and, more significantly, by a Foreign Investment Promotion Board specifically created to invite, negotiate, and facilitate substantial investment by international companies providing technology transfer and access to world markets.

In 1992, permission was given to companies with a good track record to issue convertible debentures or equity to investors abroad. Respectable foreign investors, such as pension funds, have also been allowed to invest in the Indian stock market, with suitable mechanisms to ensure that this does not threaten the loss of management control. Detailed information on the deregulation and liberalization measures is provided in the Reserve Bank of India Annual Reports for 1991–92 and 1992–93.

CONCLUSION

On the basis of the experience of the universal banks in Germany during the late nineteenth century, the main bank system in Japan in the 1950s and 60s, and the lead bank systems in India during 1970–91, the following conjectures are offered on the role of a bank-oriented system in initiating and sustaining a process of rapid industrialization and economic development in developing countries, as well as the transforming socialist economies and China (also see Bhatt, 1993).

First, to achieve industrial development, countries need to evolve a bank-oriented financial system with the nature and characteristics of the main bank system in Japan. (The Indian and the German systems have the same functions.) However, because of the shortage of qualified personnel, they should first concentrate on establishing development banks similar to the Industrial Bank of Japan (IBJ) or the Industrial Development Bank of India (IDBI) that can forge strong links with the banking system. Countries can then adapt the main bank system to meet their own criteria, under central bank guidance and supervision. The central bank itself should have a certain degree of autonomy and a development orientation with full powers of regulation and supervision of the banking system.

Second, in my opinion it is not possible for developing and transforming economies to have a *predominantly* market-oriented system for several reasons:

- The motive to save for most citizens of these countries is for transactional and precautionary purposes; their capacity to save is limited and they cannot afford to invest in risky market instruments.
- Enterprises can only issue market instruments such as equity and bonds when they are well established with a good track record, on the basis of which investors can make judgements about risk. In most of these countries, entrepreneurs and enterprises will inevitably be new; it is not possible for the market—even if it exists—to evaluate the degree of risk relating to their investments. In the transforming socialist economies, the existing enterprises have to be reconstructed or rehabilitated and the risk attached to them cannot be evaluated by investors.
- In most developing countries, capital markets have not developed well; they come into being only when enterprises mature, institutional investors like pension and provident funds, insurance companies, and mutual funds evolve, and people with a capacity to save more than what is required for transaction and precautionary purposes emerge. These conditions are still not met in most of these countries. They were met in Japan after 1970 and in India after 1985; but financing through the market is only possible for large enterprises and business houses. The market-oriented system is not geared to meet the financial requirements of small and medium enterprises, and new entrepreneurs and enterprises.

Third, the main bank system cannot perform its functions effectively if: (a) there is no macroeconomic stability and the price system is distorted; (b) the operational autonomy of banks is not ensured; (c) there is no prudential regulation of the financial system to ensure its safety and financial viability; (d) credit allocation decisions are governed by direct controls instead of decentralized management and incentives; and (e) there is a lack of trust and confidence among the main participants in the system.

Fourth, a central bank has to encourage development and should be prepared to lend to banks to overcome liquidity constraints; it should oversee directed credit allocation and ensure the viability and soundness of the financial system.

Fifth, appropriate credit allocation can also be ensured by promoting and supporting specialized, and even public sector, financial institutions to finance relatively risky investments in rehabilitating traditional or declining industries, investments in infrastructure, and small enterprises—farm and non-farm—which lack access to credit.

Sixth, credit allocation by institutions can be influenced by public agencies that provide information about investment opportunities and technology choice to enterprises and financial institutions.

Seventh, direct administrative intervention, if necessary for promoting efficient industrialization, should be minimal, strategic, selective, purposive, time bound, and market friendly. When the initial objectives are attained, the controls should be eliminated. The objective of controls should be to foster and promote entrepreneurial efforts. Domestic and international competition should be stimulated to provide enterprises with incentives to improve investment and productive efficiency.

Finally, a competitive environment can be created by an export-oriented or export-promoting strategy; this strategy would discipline policy-makers, financial institutions, and enterprises.

REFERENCES

Asian Development Bank. 1988. *Profile of Financial Sector in India*. Manila.

BHAGWATI, JAGDISH. 1988. *Protectionism*. Cambridge, Mass.: The MIT Press.

BHATT, V. V. 1972. *Structure of Financial Institutions*. Bombay: Vora & Co.

——. 1980. *Development Perspectives*. Oxford: Pergamon Press.

——. 1981. 'Financial Institutions and Technical Consultancy Services: The Indian Experiment in Small Industry Promotion.' Seminar Paper 24, Economic Development Institute, World Bank, Washington DC. Also in *Journal of Development Planning* 18, 1988.

——. 1988. 'Financial Innovations and Credit Market Evolution.' *World Development* 16(2).

——. 1991. 'On Improving the Effectiveness and Efficiency of the Financial System in India.' *Economic and Political Weekly* 26(41) (12 October).

——. 1993. 'Development Banks as Catalysts for Industrial and Financial Development.' *International Journal of Development Banking* 2(1).

Center for Monitoring Indian Economy. 1990 and 1991. *Basic Statistics Relating to the Indian Economy*. Bombay.

The Economist. 1992. 'Freeing India's Economy.' 23 May.

——. 1993. 'A Tiger Stirs.' 6 March.

Indian Banks' Association. 1987. *Financial Analysis of Banks*, vol 1. Bombay.

Industrial Finance Corporation. 1990. *Emerging Markets Data Base*. Washington DC.

Korea Long Term Credit Bank. 1990. *Annual Report*. Seoul.

Reserve Bank of India. 1976. *Coordination Between Term Lending Institutions and Commercial Banks*. Report of the Inter-Institutional Group. Bombay.

——. 1987. Letter by Chief Officer, Department of Bank Operations and Development to All Scheduled Commercial Banks. June 27.

——. 1989–93. *Report on Currency and Finance*. Bombay.

——. 1989–90. *Report on Trend and Progress of Banking in India*. Bombay.

——. 1990–91, 1991–92, 1992–93. *Annual Report*. Bombay.

——. 1990. *Manual for Bank Supervision*. Bombay.

——. 1991, 1992. *Bulletins*. Bombay.

Securities and Exchange Board of India. 1990. *State of Capital Market*. Bombay.

World Bank. 1988. *Staff Appraisal Report: India, Industrial Finance and Technical Assistance Project*. Washington DC.

——. 1989. *Staff Appraisal Report: Korea Development Bank*. Washington DC.

——. 1989. *World Development Report*. Washington DC.

——. 1990. *India—Financial Sector Report: Consolidation of the Financial System*. Washington DC.

15

The Reprivatization of Banking in Mexico

CLARK W. REYNOLDS

The experience of the Japanese main bank system provides a useful optic from which to view the role of banking in a developing country such as Mexico, illustrating how the specific structure of relations between financial intermediaries and non-financial enterprises can have an important impact on the efficiency, stability and growth of the real economy. The comparative institutional analysis approach used in this paper offers a framework permitting a complementary finance and development analysis by focusing on the microfoundations of real and financial sector decision-making in the context of evolving macroeconomic policies, market conditions and institutions. It is also possible to go beyond questions of ownership and control to issues of monitoring, allocative efficiency and stability of real-financial relationships under a range of institutional structures.

The Mexican model provides a useful case study of the role of institutions in the building of microfoundations of banking and financial relations in developing countries. The need for such countries to undertake institutional reforms to enhance their competitiveness and increase their rates of saving, investment and social participation in the development process, even while safeguarding their unique domestic character, gives a wide applicability to the Mexican experience.

Mexico is interesting because it also provides an example of the evolution from a closely held financial system linked to family and enterprise groups, to a state-owned banking system, to one in which ownership has reverted to the private sector—but on a more diversified basis and with important additional elements of regional supervision—all in about a decade. This chapter seeks to clarify the way in which the financial organizational structure has evolved and is operating in a developing and transforming economy that faces increased exposure to the international market.

The author wishes to acknowledge the valuable research assistance of Gerardo Teran, as well as the helpful comments of discussants and participants in the project's workshops, and a workshop at II University of Rome, Tor Vergata, in February 1993. Particularly helpful were perspectives provided by Patricia Armendariz de Hinestrosa, Theodor Baums, V. V. Bhatt, Hyung-ki Kim, Alfredo Phillips Olmedo, and Dmitri Vittas, as well as extensive written comments, full of insight, on an earlier draft by Hugh Patrick, and discussions with Masahiko Aoki and Paul Sheard.

Thus, this chapter looks at the relative merits of various approaches to real-financial sector relations, including those that restrict the degree of interaction between banks and non-financial groups, as in Mexico, and other approaches, such as the Japanese main bank system, in which inter-locking ownership permits banks to provide important services to their related business groups.

A COMPARATIVE INSTITUTIONAL APPROACH TO BANKING SYSTEM TYPOLOGIES

Organizational structure matters to the functioning of economic processes. In part this is because organizational structures and economic relationships reinforce each other over time. Recognizing this provides a range of approaches to market behaviour that goes beyond the conventional frameworks explicitly or implicitly assumed in the analysis of competitive market systems, and gives greater depth and explanatory power to the theory of rational choice.

Mexico is in a transition phase in terms of the types of banking systems presented by Aoki, Patrick and Sheard in the introductory chapter. They identify three types of relational banking systems. These are: (1) banks playing a dominant, controlling role over firms (German type); (2) banks and firms are on an equal footing, and endogenous syndications and mutual delegation of monitoring to particular banks take place (Japanese main bank system in its mature stage); and (3) industry-owned banks, which are susceptible to undiversified firm-specific risk and potential moral hazard problems.

The Mexican system has evolved from a type 3 system before nationalization to a more complex system since reprivatization. The current system has innovative patterns of control, power relations, and a greater regulatory role for the state. The original industrial groups (*grupos*), each of which had its own 'main' bank, lost their banks in the nationalization process of 1982.

The consolidated and reprivatized banks now have a new, wider constellation of owners. This is important even though many owners are the original industrial groups. There is a broader and more democratic constituency on the boards of directors and a greater national and regional voice in decision-making. Thus the result of privatization goes beyond a return to a type 3 system. Instead, the current regime combines all three types of relationship banking. Industry has repurchased the banks; reprivatized financial institutions are being encouraged to diversify in the direction of universal banking. At the same time, following the Japanese system, the 'main bank' of each group is positioned to increase monitoring of its non-financial affiliates without an exclusive lending role.

Political-Economic Issues in Organizational Structure

Institutions that developed in Japan during a period of relative isolation (especially of financial markets) facilitated the emergence and maintenance of 'especially Japanese' organizational and decision-making structures. For example, the Japanese interlocking shareholding system developed during the 1950s and early 60s as firms tried to re-establish relations with each other (Patrick, 1972), and was reinforced in the late 1960s and 70s in response to a perceived challenge from foreign direct investment and take-over (Aoki, 1988). While such institutions appear to have fostered the ability of Japanese firms to compete in the international market, they are themselves being challenged by pressures for change toward greater openness and financial sector liberalization. The current reprivatization of Mexico's banking system includes policy measures attempting to create 'especially Mexican' organizational and decision-making structures and to protect them from the threat of take-overs by larger and (initially) more competitive foreign banks, yet without losing the benefits of freer trade, investment and financial integration into North American and international markets.

Certainly this is an important lesson for countries such as Mexico and Canada during the NAFTA negotiation process, as both attempt to gain from fuller integration with the US while adapting their own legal and institutional systems to safeguard national interests in response to the social and political mandates of their domestic systems. The Japanese case suggests that it may be possible to increase the gains from exchange by adjusting domestic institutions to the exigencies of an ever more open and competitive international market, while still retaining features that give their own enterprises a competitive edge.

Institutional Structures and Organizational Quasi-Rents

The literature on directly unproductive rent-seeking has shown how markets may be distorted by such activity. For example, Latin American business and financial groups (*grupos*) are often selected to illustrate how barriers to competition are used to establish and preserve the private gains of certain elites at the expense of society at large.

The terms 'economic rent' and 'quasi-rent' as used in this chapter refer to an income over and above the normal rate of return on factor inputs. (In the case of capital it would be 'excess profits'.) Such a return can be positive or negative from the viewpoint of welfare and allocative efficiency. For example, rents can be generated from the presence of market barriers that reflect monopoly or monopsony power. This definition is employed by Krueger (1974) and others who refer to 'directly unproductive rent-seeking', often in association with state intervention.

There are also, however, positive forms of rent seeking, such as those in response to returns to natural resources, favouring the production of raw materials and primary products (*Ricardian rents*). Aoki has shown how certain institutional innovations may give rise to directly productive *organizational quasi-rents*, such as those arguably accruing to Japanese enterprises that profit from unique forms of labour, management and financial relations. In addition, there are two types of transitional rents. First are *innovation rents*, which accrue to product and process innovations before technology is fully diffused and pure competition is restored. These are the type of returns referred to by Schumpeter in his theory of development. They are an inducement for productive investment, giving rise to new sources of growth. The second are *market penetration rents*, which are generated during the process of market adjustment until new competitive equilibria are established. In all such cases, there is a place for public policy that favours directly productive rent seeking.

Insights from comparative institutional analysis suggest the possibility of forming interlocking real and financial groups, with the acquiescence of state regulatory authorities, that may actually enhance the generation of directly productive organizational quasi-rents available to be shared between capital and labour. (See the analysis of the J-type economy in Aoki, 1990.) The focus here on the gains from domestic institutional integration contrasts with the position of policy-makers in Mexico, Brazil and elsewhere in the Americas who, in the 1960s and 70s, supported the integration of national financial groups to enhance the economy's external bargaining power among highly concentrated international financial institutions.

Seen in broader comparative international perspective, concentration *per se* is not a problem, and may even enhance an economy's productivity and distribution. The difficulty is in avoiding the use of concentration to distort markets and to influence public policy for private gain. International opening reduces the scope for such abuses within the domestic system through the chastening effect of international competition.

Comparative institutional analysis may also be useful to developing countries in helping to bring about convergence in productivity and income through policies that favour innovative organizational and institutional structures. In Mexico, wide-ranging differences in productivity exist among enterprises, even within the same sector and region, leading to gaps in output per worker that are sometimes even greater than the differences between Mexico and advanced industrial countries. These gaps can be attributed in part to differences in transaction costs and other barriers to exchange, including imperfections in financial markets (see Stiglitz and Weiss, 1981). Organizational structures can facilitate or impede the pace of productivity diffusion during the development process. Increased market openness tends to favour gains from productive institutional innovations and to work against unproductive ones.

THE OLD MEXICAN BANKING SYSTEM

This section provides an historical overview of the pre-nationalization and nationalized periods, and analyses the effects of nationalization on financial savings and bank performance.

Before the Nationalization in 1982

Mexico's financial system in the 1960s has been regarded as a model of finance and development policy (Brothers and Solis, 1966). After the collapse of the banking system during the inflationary years of the revolution between 1910 and 1920, Mexico built a set of financial institutions that became a pattern for many developing countries. By the 1960s a private banking system had evolved characterized by a small number of major banks, some working closely with the government but all controlled by business groups, some regional, and some with networks throughout the country. In a typical business group there were several core firms, usually privately held, which maintained their own bank. These were situated in close proximity to the firms, usually in Mexico City, but also in other commercial and industrial centres such as Monterrey, Guadalajara and Chihuahua. The group's bank acted as a major intermediary among member firms, as well as benefiting from deposits of the local communities, providing short-term working capital and medium-term lines of credit to favoured borrowers that were rolled over for longer-term development.

In the 1960s, relying on a relatively independent central bank (Banco de Mexico) to enforce monetary stability, measures were taken to remove ceilings on nominal interest rates. This permitted real rates of interest that would more than cover inflationary expectations and compete with yields in the US and abroad at the time. The resulting increase in financial savings was channelled through the domestic capital market. The most attractive financial assets were *financiera* bonds—fully liquid instruments of investment banks having positive real interest rates that were purchased and redeemed by their issuers at par. Government commitment to fiscal stability and a fixed peso-dollar exchange rate minimized exchange rate risk and reduced inflationary pressures. The fact that monetary stability and increased financial liberalization were associated with rising rates of voluntary saving and investment caused the period to be labelled 'stabilizing development' (*desarrollo estabilizador*).

One important dimension of the Mexican stabilizing development model was the establishment of growing links between the state and commercial banks, as well as between the state and financieras, through the use of differential reserve requirements to channel financial savings toward loans for investment in favoured sectors and activities—along the lines of government indicative planning. The term-transformation problem of banks and financieras that were borrowing short (offering immediate redemption of bonds and deposits at par) while lending long was covered by the central bank, which acted as lender of last resort, guaranteeing the stability of financial institutions.

While the capture of funds reflected financial liberalization, the use of funds did not, as it responded to policies that favoured credit allocation at preferential borrowing rates for infrastructure and import-substituting industrialization. Notwithstanding arguments for credit rationing in conditions of thin markets, subject to moral hazard and adverse selection— justified subsequently by Stiglitz and Weiss (1981)—there may well have been abuse of the private banking system during this period through the diversion of credit to large groups able to take advantage of their lead banks. However, the increased use of the financial intermediation process by government and public sector enterprises to fund their large and growing operating deficits became a far greater problem in the 1970s.

Unfortunately, the combination of fiscal stability and monetary control did not endure. The period from 1970 to 1982 was one of increased concentration of banking in the hands of private sector groups, fiscal instability, state crowding out of private credit markets, and foreign borrowing. Already, by the end of the 1960s, there were pressures on the balance of payments as price increases generated by rising fiscal deficits put pressure on the fixed exchange rate; these problems that were offset somewhat by foreign borrowing.

After the change in administration in 1970, the government committed itself to a brief period of monetary stringency. Advocates of increased public expenditures to continue the growth of import-substituting industrialization and social programmes, however, won out over the independence of the central bank and advocates of fiscal discipline. Private savings were increasingly diverted into support of the current account deficits of the public sector. Inflation accelerated, causing the fixed peso-dollar exchange rate to become increasingly overvalued, lowering real interest rates to savers net of exchange risk, and causing capital flight (Gil-Diaz, 1988).

By 1976 the loss of reserves made it essential to free the peso for the first time in 22 years, resulting in a devaluation that had a considerable impact, especially on firms that had become increasingly exposed through foreign borrowing as government deficits crowded out domestic credit markets. Despite initial efforts of the incoming administration to re-establisdegree of fiscal stability and openness, the oil discoveries in the mid-1970s lubricated a new wave of government deficit spending and private sector borrowing. Borrowing abroad against the bonanza of expected oil rents was possible at extremely low real rates of interest. The private banking and financial system, always dominated by a few large banks linked to major industrial groups, became even more concentrated through creation of multiple banking institutions (*multibancos*). The peso became seriously overvalued in purchasing power parity terms, as devaluation lagged inflation, sustained by increased foreign borrowing that more than offset domestic capital flight. During the oil boom of 1978–81, with four successive years of 8 per cent real growth in GDP, the banking system prospered.

The Nationalized System, 1982–90

In August 1982 Mexico found itself facing the dual shocks of weakening oil prices and an unprecedented level of foreign debt with rising real interest rates. Capital flight accelerated and reserves disappeared, foreign lending dried up, and fiscal pressures became insupportable. Eventually, the president (in his final months in office), allowed the peso to fall, eliminated convertibility of 'Mexdollars' (dollar-denominated domestic deposits), and decreed the nationalization of all Mexican banks with the exception of the foreign-owned Citibank subsidiary (see Perez Lopez, 1987).

Under the nationalization of September 1982, the Ministry of Finance took immediate control of the banks with the power to dictate all aspects related to them. This included exchange controls, interest rates, debt-equity ratios and management. Each bank was provided with a new governing body responsible to the Ministry. Owners were partially compensated in the form of bonds.

With the change of administration in December 1982, there was more flexibility and regulatory decentralization, reflecting a new and more liberal economic policy regime that has operated ever since. Many of the lower and intermediate levels of bank management were kept relatively intact during the nationalization period. An extremely competent group of public officials, many of them familiar with economic policy-making, was chosen to head the nationalized banks.

At the time of nationalization there were 60 financial institutions including 34 multiple service banks (multibancos), 11 deposit banks, 9 financial corporations, 5 capitalization banks, and 1 mortgage bank. A significant number of the small banks sustained high operating costs with no economies of scale. The 3 largest banks controlled 54 per cent of assets and made 74 per cent of net profits; 9 institutions held 85 per cent of deposits.

The federal government decided to initiate a process of consolidation, mergers, and fusions of smaller with larger banks (see Soto Rodriguez, 1990). The goals were: increased economies of scale, consolidation of local banks on a regional basis, increased rates of return on capital, and the rescue of financially troubled banks. As a result of this process, the number of banks declined to 6 nationwide, 7 multi-regional, and 5 regional. The number of branches increased slightly between 1982 and 1989, from 4,438 to 4,506. Tables 15.1 and 15.2 show the increasing concentration.

TABLE 15.1 Number of Commercial Banks, Selected Years, 1975–89

Cumulative Share of Deposits (%)	1975	1979	1982	1989
60	4	4	3	3
75	10	6	6	5
85	21	12	9	8
100	139	100	60	18

Note: Calendar year-end. Throughout the period the two largest banks (Banamex and Bancomer) each held about 20% of deposits.

Source: Banco de Mexico, *Informe Anual*, various years.

TABLE 15.2 The Three Largest Banks' Share of Various Items, 1982 and 1989 (per cents)

Year	Total Assets	Capital Assets	Total Deposits	Total Credits	Past-due Credits	Employees	Net Profits
1982	53.7	65.8	57.7	47.8	53.0	48.7	74.3
1989	71.2	65.9	66.9	67.3	53.5	53.6	59.6

Note: The three banks, in order of importance, are Banamex, Bancomer, and Serfin.

Source: Banco de Mexico, *Indicadores Economicos*, various volumes; Comisión Nacional Bancaria y de Seguros, *Boletin Estadistico* (1982 and 1989).

Bank Nationalization and Financial Savings

As a consequence of weakened conditions in the domestic economy, combined with the increasing need for resources to finance the public sector deficit, the monetary aggregates show irregular behaviour during the 1980s. The financial system's total savings (total financial assets) as a share of GNP averaged 24.0 per cent for the period 1982–85, moving upward slightly to 25.4 per cent for 1986–89. The modest increase can be explained by the following factors: the issuing of highly accepted public instruments, such as treasury bonds, at market-determined interest rates; gradual economic recovery; return of flight capital and increased foreign direct investment due to improved economic expectations associated with macroeconomic stability and policy reforms; and the gradual rechannelling of 'informal financial sector' resources to formal credit institutions, due in part to the gradual liberalization of the financial system (including the nationalized banks).

Meanwhile, the structure of financial savings (financial assets) altered substantially. Government instruments trading in money markets increased from 8.8 per cent of total financial savings in 1982 to 29.9 per cent in 1989, while traditional instruments (which did not increase in absolute amounts) fell from 86.6 to 51.8 per cent. (Traditional instruments include bank deposits, non-interest-bearing cheque accounts and the like.) This dramatic shift in portfolio preference was almost certainly more attributable to the relative yield of government debt and other instruments linked to the rate of inflation and exchange risk than to any disincentive or discrimination associated with the change from private to public ownership of the banks.

Interest rates were not subject to ceilings, so the banks' failure to raise yields on highly liquid deposits to competitive levels may well have reflected the government's desire to minimize the cost of diverting bank deposits to the financing of its deficit. Treasury bills were in relatively small units, which made it easier to attract capital directly from the general public rather than through the banks.

Financing the public deficit since 1982 forced the federal government to increase its demand for savings in the form of money-market instruments, which led to a higher participation of the government in the reserves of its nationalized banks. These measures led to a decrease of bank deposits as a share of GNP between 1982 and 1990, as shown in Table 15.3.

Management of the debt created a vicious cycle because higher interest rates alone were unable to attract enough voluntary savings to finance both public and private sector borrowing. Hence the inflation tax had to cover the gap. The higher interest rates necessary to attract savings and repress demand in the economy meant greater financial costs. This meant additional financial resources were needed to cover the cost of debt service, which in turn pushed interest rates up still further. In addition, the instability of the peso and its continuous devaluations raised inflationary expectations and contributed to this process (Aspe, 1990).

From 1982 to 1989, total assets of banks remained at almost the same real levels, rising only 1.4 per cent over the period. However, towards the end of the decade total credits to the private sector increased by almost 28 per cent as the banking system was gradually liberated from the forced holding of government debt and as resources for private lending were made available. (See the data in Table 15.4.)

TABLE 15.3 Commercial Bank Deposits and Other Indicators, 1982–90 (per cent)

1982	1983	1984	1985	1986	1987	1988	1989	1990	Indicator
19.6	17.4	18.3	17.2	16.8	15.7	13.1	13.3	13.6	Bank deposits as a percentage of GNP
45.3	56.6	48.6	61.6	87.4	96.0	69.7	45.0	34.7	Nominal interest rate (28 day CTES)
-33.9	-3.7	1.3	15.3	13.4	-2.6	29.4	30.1	8.6	Real interest rate (nominal rate minus inflation)
-13.8	100.4	3.5	69.4	104.5	-13.5	32.0	65.5	15.5	Stock exchange index, real growth rate

Source: Banco de Mexico, *Informe Anual* and *Indicadores Economicos*, various issues; Banco de Mexico (1991).

TABLE 15.4 Commercial Bank Balance Sheets, 1982 and 1989

Nominal Annual Growth[1]	Real Increase[2]	1982	1989	Item
		(million new pesos)		
72.9	1.4	3,450	159,476	Assets
72.0	−2.5	3,355	149,136	Liabilities
95.4	138.9	95	10,341	Capital assets[3]
78.8	27.9	1,573	91,694	Total credits
79.5	31.8	1,504	90,375	Current credits
52.5	−57.9	69	1,319	Past-due credits
101.7	197.4	16	2,116	Net profits

[1] Median nominal annual growth rate in percentages.

[2] Overall percentage increase from 1982 to 1989 measured in real terms.

[3] 'Capital assets' is the literal translation of the Spanish for what is called 'shareholder equity' on English-language balance sheets.

Source: various issues of: Comisión Nacional Bancaria y de Seguros, *Boletin Estadistico*, Banco de Mexico, *Informe Anual*; Banamex, *Review of the Economic Situation of Mexico*, October (1991).

Conditions in financial markets reflected the instability of macroeconomic indicators and the speculative mentality associated with the volatile movement of yields on financial assets. Under the pressures of inflationary expectations and a lagged response to increased price stability, the monthly real rate of return on government debt (almost completely short term) rose from being negative (an average −0.62 per cent) in 1982–85 to being positive (0.35 per cent) in 1986–89. The real yield of money-market instruments increased from −0.37 per cent to +1.28 per cent in the same period.

By 1987 private savers were demanding that more profitable and liquid instruments be traded on the hitherto lacklustre Mexican stock exchange (Bolsa). However, the gains from share-price increases resulted largely from speculation rather than increases in the real return on capital (which continued to reflect the weakened condition of the domestic economy). In the first nine months of 1987 the MSE (stock exchange index) increased 470 per cent, generating a 300 per cent real rate of return. When the speculative bubble burst in the autumn of 1987 (in part in sympathy with the US stock market sell off) the resulting crash caused the Bolsa to end the year with a 70 per cent net loss.

To the extent brokerage firms had been using shareholder deposits to fund quasi-bank lending, which is illegal, the crash brought attention to the need for closer surveillance of the parallel credit market. This was only one indication of the need for the government to reconsider relations between the banking system and the private sector, and almost certainly contributed to the eventual reprivatization.

Performance of the Nationalized Banks

Profits doubled between 1982 and 1989. It should be remembered, however, that 1982 was troubled by domestic and foreign debt crises. Taking into account the fact that total assets remained practically unchanged, the increase in retained earnings meant a significant strengthening of the banks' capital resources. Balance sheet and financial ratio data are in Tables 15.4 and 15.5.

TABLE 15.5 Commercial Banks: Financial Indicators, 1982 and 1989 (per cent)

1982	1989	Indicator
2.75	6.48	Capital assets to total assets
64.81	92.52	Total credit to total deposits
4.37	1.44	Past-due credits to total credits
72.41	12.75	Past-due credits to capital assets
22.10	27.50	Net profits to capital assets
0.45	1.33	Net profits to total assets

Note: 'Capital assets' is the literal translation of the Spanish for what is called 'shareholder equity' on English-language balance sheets.

Source: Cómision Nacional Bancaria y de Seguros, *Boletin Estadistico* (1982 and 1989).

The process of nationalization, reorganization, and channelling of funds from the private to the public sector appears to have improved the quality, if not the quantity, of lending (from a bank profit perspective). Restructuring through the consolidation of banks (despite the increase in branches) has been consistent with a higher return on capital and improved levels of capitalization. The increase in capitalization was assisted by the government's reinforcement of the banks' position in the market, as almost all financial activities were channelled through the state-held banks and their subsidiaries.

In general, the banks were managed with sound business practices under the direction of disciplined professionals appointed by the state. In addition to some transfusion of capital from the government, asset revaluation due to a better economic environment in 1991 brought about an increase in book value.

As in other sectors of the economy, productivity gains were achieved by streamlining the employment structure rather than by increasing the real value of output. From 1982 to 1989—despite the unimpressive behaviour of real bank deposits—total deposits, resources, and net profits per employee and branch increased significantly, providing a crude measure of efficiency gains. Table 15.6 provides data.

Not surprisingly, the evolution of the nationalized banks in terms of income and costs was also favourable. In 1982 total costs represented 98.2 per cent of income, whereas by 1989 they had been reduced to 95 per cent. Increases in non-financial (administrative) costs were kept in check while financial margins remained practically the same. This was almost certainly related to personnel cutbacks and to falling real wages, not only for low-skilled labour but particularly for managerial and professional employees. However, during 1988 and 1989, as real wages began to recover and real interest rates declined, administrative costs moved upwards while financial costs decreased relative to income. For example, past due credits fell as a share of total credits and as a share of capital assets, owing primarily to better first-hand supervision by the government (see Tables 15.4 and 15.5).

TABLE 15.6 Commercial Banks: Performance Indicators, 1982 and 1989

1982	1989	Real Increase[1]	Indicator
(thousand new pesos)			
16.4	851	43.0	Deposits per employee
560.0	30,296	50.0	Deposits per branch
10.0	576	21.4	Credits per employee
354.0	20,472	26.7	Credits per branch
0.1	13.3	196.1	Net profit per employee
4.0	472.4	194.6	Net profit per branch

[1] Overall percentage increase from 1982 to 1989 measured in real terms.

Table 15.7 shows consolidated income, cost and profit figures for commercial banks for the years 1983 and 1989 in real terms. The share of non-interest costs covered by fees and commissions rose from 58.9 per cent to 75.4 per cent, indicating that charges for the provision of financial services had become an increasingly important source of income for the nationalized banking system.

However, the banks still show some weaknesses. There are low levels of investment in the development of information systems (2–5 per cent of budgets, as opposed to 10–15 per cent in more industrialized countries) and in employee training programmes (only 1 per cent of budget, as opposed to 4–6 per cent in other nations). This has contributed to poor growth in employee real wages, deficiencies in the quality of credit analy-

TABLE 15.7 Commercial Banks: Income Statement Data, 1982 and 1989
(million constant 1989 new pesos)

1983	1989	Increase (per cent)[1]	Indicator
4318	5056	17.1	Financial margin
4343	6460	48.8	Non-interest income
7273	8661	19.1	Non-interest costs
1389	2855	105.5	Pretax profits
682	1964	188.0	Net profits

Note: 1 new peso equals 1,000 old pesos. Data for 1983 are used because 1982 was a particularly bad year and 1983 was the first full year of operation after nationalization.

[1] Overall percentage increase from 1983 to 1989 measured in real terms.

Source: Comisión Nacional Bancaria y de Seguros, *Informe Anual* (1983 and 1989); Banamex, *Review of the Economic Situation of Mexico*, various issues.

sis and evaluation (also due to the recent economic instability and insufficient credit resources), and the fact that there are still too many employees relative to the value of resources managed, despite cutbacks in personnel. Overall, operating costs and financial margins (spreads) are high relative to international norms.

At the level of the banking system, a major weakness is the fact there are very few banks (only 18 at the time of this writing). Moreover, their branches and lending activities tend to be highly concentrated in major urban centres. Population per branch is 18,000, compared to 2,700 in Spain and 3,000 in France.

An analysis of the efficiency of the financial system during this period is complicated by the fact that macroeconomic adjustment included measures to increase the voluntary financing and gradual redemption of the internal and external debt. This called for increased access by the government to private sector deposits. On the one hand, the government assumed the external debt of private sector enterprises in exchange for peso-denominated obligations. On the other hand, the increasing cost of debt service falling on the government required it to make use of its newly nationalized banks to divert credit flows from the private to the public sector. Reserve requirements and other measures were used to increase the share of bank portfolios in government securities, these policies had the effect of crowding out the supply of credit to the private sector.

On the government expenditure side, fiscal stringency reduced aggregate demand which, together with devaluation, was particularly hard on the level of real wages and the wage share of GNP, but which also stemmed the growth of capital income. A sharp devaluation of the peso, required to turn Mexico's traditional post-war trade deficit into a surplus to service the foreign debt, combined with the funding of government deficits to trigger Mexico's first triple-digit inflation. Inflation, combined with interest-rate liberalization and government borrowing, led to a major increase in nominal interest rates, fuelled uncertainty about real interest rates, and dried up medium- and long-term lending by the domestic financial system.

The response to bank nationalization and the crowding out of credit markets was the formation of a parallel banking system. Private borrowers who had previously had access to commercial banks found it necessary to resort to new institutional mechanisms to attract and channel financial resources. An informal financial system emerged that included access to external lines of credit (often secured by transborder holdings of flight capital), the unauthorized use of deposits in stock brokerage houses for short-term lending, and other imaginative practices. Such measures were a reflection of the traditional rift between the state and private sector, a gap which widened considerably after the 1982 nationalization, and of the resistance of successive administrations to any return of the banks to their former owners, among other things (Perez Lopez, 1987).

To some extent, financial market failure is more likely to occur in thin credit markets where there are high transaction costs and the possibility of considerable multi-collinearity of incomes among producers of similar commodities (especially raw materials and primary products of artisanry and simple manufactures). This characterizes Mexico. The diffusion of growth in Mexico thus requires financial policies that provide a non-distorting support of regional banking and entrepreneurship, small-scale enterprise, and rural development—and that is not likely to occur through the highly concentrated and privatized banking system (Reynolds and Pessoa, 1991).

THE NEW PRIVATIZED SYSTEM

In the National Development Plan of 1989–94 the Salinas administration pointed to the need to change Mexico's financial structure in order to promote a more efficient and effective channelling of resources, increase the level of national savings, and further productive investment. In privatizing its commercial banks and supporting the formation of financial groups around them, the government aimed at strengthening the financial system by facilitating economies of scale, reducing costs, and providing a more effective and competitive system that would guarantee expanded and better services to the general public. In May 1990 a constitutional reform to remove the banking system from the public sector was announced and by July 1992 the process of privatization was complete (see Barnes, 1992).

The result is a pattern of ownership that opens up new relationships between banks and business groups by subjecting them to rules and regulatory procedures designed to capture the advantages of close real-financial sector linkages while avoiding opportunities for abuse. What is emerging appears to be a hybrid form of organization that combines several aspects of relationship banking. The regulatory authorities are still wrestling with the trade-off between the advantages of close relationships between financial and non-financial institutions (groups) and among banks and non-bank financial intermediaries (multi-banking) and the potential disadvantages of concentration. There is an additional attempt in the Mexican model to include state and regional participation in governance to facilitate the geographic diffusion of development.

Few countries have made such major changes in financial control in so short a time. The Mexican reprivatization process has the additional complication of occurring during a period of profound structural adjustment and international opening to the North American and global economies.

Reprivatization, 1991–92

In only 13 months during 1991–92, all 18 of Mexico's nationalized banks were auctioned to private groups of Mexican investors, for a total of over US$13 billion. Prices were well above expected levels, averaging three times book value (see Table 15.8).

The rules of bidding were set by the Ministry of Finance to guarantee Mexican majority ownership and control. The process made use of a series of auctions in which bidders were selected from a list of applicants. The criteria applied were designed to ensure that potential investors were 'experienced and of high moral standing and were able to make a positive contribution to the future growth of the banks' (*El Nacional* 7 July 1992, p. 15). Many Mexican business groups applied to participate and a number of them were accepted, but there was a clear tendency to avoid the return of banks to their original owners.

Under the initial process, bidding for a majority interest was restricted to nationals. Regulations subsequently appear to be relaxing, partly as a reflection of general tendencies toward capital market liberalization and partly as a result of NAFTA negotiations. However, formation of new domestic national banks still faces minimum size regulations, and the entry of foreign financial institutions is subject to a time lag and ceiling in terms of market shares. Meanwhile, credit unions, regional banks (subject to national ownership and control) and other financial institutions can be readily established, and there is no restriction on the opening of new branches of existing banks.

TABLE 15.8 Prices Paid When Nationalized (1982) and Reprivatized (1991–92)

Bank	Price in million US$		Multiple of book value		1991–92 price as percentage of 1982 price	Buyer
	1982	1991–92	1982	1991–92		
Atlantico	13.6	869.2	0.89	5.30	6,291	GBM
Banamex	219.2	3,188.0	1.36	2.62	1,354	Accival
Bancen	7.1	276.0	1.35	3.95	3,787	Multivalores
Bancomer	245.3	2,724.8	1.56	2.99	1,011	VAMSA
Bancreser	14.6	139.4	1.66	2.34	855	Roberto Alcantara
Banorie	3.4	73.5	1.29	4.03	2,062	Margen
Banoro	11.9	364.1	1.39	3.95	2,961	Estrategia Bursatil
Banorte	15.1	246.3	1.63	4.25	1,531	Roberto Gonzalez
BanPais	17.8	180.7	1.35	3.02	915	Mexival
BCH	20.7	285.6	1.49	2.67	1,280	Grupo Sureste
Comermex	13.6	869.2	0.43	3.73	6,291	Inverlat
Confia	11.4	293.9	1.69	3.73	2,478	Abaco
Cremi	4.6	247.8	0.49	3.40	5,287	Consorcio G
Internacional	18.3	479.6	1.12	2.95	2,521	Prime
Mercantil	20.6	202.9	1.72	2.66	885	Probursa
Promex	9.6	346.6	1.44	4.25	3,511	Finamex
Serfin	94.9	909.2	1.30	2.69	858	Obsa
Somex	17.8	475.1	1.38	4.15	2,569	Invermexico

Note: The 1982 prices include what was paid for any banks that were merged into a listed bank during the consolidation programme. The estimated number of years needed to return the amount invested, based on earnings, ranges from 22.2 (Banorie) and 21.8 (Cremi) to 10.3 (Banamex). The average is 15.7 years.

Source: National Banking Commission and Mexican stock market reports.

THE NEW ORGANIZATION OF MEXICO'S FINANCIAL SECTOR

In connection with bank privatization, the Financial Groups Law (FGL) was passed with the intention of creating an institutional framework to promote greater efficiency in the internal allocation of funds and resources, including exploitation of economies of scale, cross-marketing of products, and expansion into new areas. This section provides an overview of this peculiarly Mexican model, how it is working, or intended to work, to achieve these and other ends.

Institutional Features

One of the distinctive and rather innovative features of the new system and its intended economic organization has been the formation of a new type of financial group centred on business-controlled financial holding companies. What makes the system particularly interesting is the fact that the holding company and its subsidiaries provide a structure that is sufficiently concentrated to give it the financial strength to modernize its infrastructure and benefit from its extended services. Moreover, it provides an alternative to the take-over market that is missing in Mexico, at least in the financial sector. The structural organization of the system can be divided into three different levels of institutions, each having significant features and obligations.

At the top (*level I*) of financial corporate organization is the *controladora* (the controlling financial holding company). Many of these companies have adopted *Grupo Financiero* as the first part of their formal name. To use the second largest as an example, one thus sees references to GF Bancomer or simply GFB.

Each financial group is headed by a controladora that is business-controlled and readily identifiable. A key aspect of the system is that the core (controlling) investor group in a controladora is constrained by law from divesting its ownership. These investors hold Series A shares that they may only sell to each other except with prior approval from other Series A holders and the regulatory authorities. This almost eliminates a take-over market for financial institutions. The idea is that by providing security and certainty of control, the controlling group has an incentive to invest and plan its strategic moves with a long-term view. (Safeguards against opportunistic behaviour are addressed later.)

The FGL allows other, tradable, classes of stock so the controladora can raise equity capital from a larger group than its core members, and spread the (expected) benefits of its success. Foreigners are allowed to own shares, and the two largest controladora have issued stock that trades in the US market.

A controladora owns and manages at least 51 per cent of the capital shares of its subsidiaries, which must include at least three of the following: commercial bank, brokerage house, leasing company, factoring company, investment trust, insurance company, bonded warehouse company, foreign exchange dealer. It may not own more than one of each, and it may own only financial institutions.

Although the holding company (controladora) is a legal entity, separate and distinct from its group's anchor commercial bank group and from its subsidiaries, it is important to remember that the holding company and its subsidiaries are a financial group controlled by the same people. Moreover, these people can and do own industrial groups.

At least 20 individuals or corporations are needed to form a controladora because no one entity can hold more than 5 per cent of the Series A shares. There are typically many more. Banacci, the largest controladora, which controls Banamex, the country's largest bank, has some 800 investors. The principal institutional owner is Accival y Valores, a leading brokerage firm.

Special transition cases, where one individual may hold up to 10 per cent (subject to prior government approval) are allowed until the end of 1994. After that there will be no exceptions to the rule. However, there are many ways to agglomerate ownership and control within family and associational groups. For example, members of families can each hold 5 per cent, their non-financial company can hold 5 per cent, and those with close business relations tend to participate in ownership of the same financial institutions.

Because the Financial Groups Law (FGL) limits controladora activities to owning and managing the affairs of its subsidiaries, all of its revenues result from dividends paid by those subsidiaries. The board of directors determines the amount of dividends paid to the group's shareholders on the basis of earnings, financial condition, regulatory constraints, growth objectives, capital needs, and other factors deemed relevant by the controlling shareholders.

The holding company is responsible for the well functioning of each of its subsidiaries. As part of this, under the FGL, a controladora is responsible for the liabilities of its subsidiaries up to the amount of its own net capital. This means that controladoras focus on the collection, control, monitoring, evaluation, and transmission of information about their subsidiaries and their management. Subsidiaries have no exposure to the liabilities of the controladoras.

Level II includes all of the controladora's subsidiaries, each of which is at least 51 per cent owned, and thus controlled, by the controladora. They can offer a range of services under the (common) label of the financial group, and can exchange information among themselves. However, they are expected to operate in an individual manner. This means their services are to be complementary; they may not overlap. Each must maintain separate financial statements. Subsidiaries may not invest in the stock of the holding company or of each other. The intention of these provisions of the FGL is to prevent conflicts of interest within the group and the pyramiding of capital, as well as to diversify risk over a number of financial markets.

It is important to note that in the reprivatization process the government has paid special attention to the possibility of abuse of market power through excessive ownership concentration. One aspect of this is recognition of the fact there will be situations where the interests of a subsidiary differ from those of the controladora. Regulations exist to attempt to balance the controlling group with participation by a sufficiently large number of other investors and stakeholders.

This applies at both the controladora and individual subsidiary level. Each has a board of consultants selected from minority shareholders to represent their interests. In addition, each controladora of the 18 banks has a regional council that operates in a consulting capacity to monitor behaviour of the institution *vis-à-vis* the interests of the regional clients, as well as to provide advice and promote regional business development. Members of a bank's regional board, who are drawn from a list of bank clients in a region, also sit on the bank's regional credit committees.

These various boards provide an institutional forum for the controladora's senior executives to share information and experience with regard to strategic, operating, and financial issues, as well as to integrate activities in the various regions, and otherwise enhance operating synergies within the financial group. Members of these boards may also be elected as directors of the controladora or its subsidiaries.

While the first two levels are formal, *level III* is informal in that it represents *de facto* relationships. It is therefore not as explicitly regulated as the two previous levels. It covers related firms and businesses in which the controlling shareholders have interests, but which do not form part of their financial group.

Although both industrial corporations and controladora are often owned by the same people, there is a greater tendency for the owners of companies to monitor the banks than the other way round. This is because many of the major non-banking enterprises are privately owned and retain a high degree of confidentiality in their internal affairs, even with regard to the financial institutions in their group.

As in the Anglo-American model, Mexican banks cannot hold shares in non-financial enterprises, nor can controladoras. This means access to information is more restricted than when relationship banking allows equity ownership by banks. Eventually, one can expect that owners of banks and industrial enterprises will find it in their interests to facilitate two-way monitoring, having the effect of increasing the symmetry of relationship banking. Moreover, the Japanese and German cases indicate that as enterprises go public and ownership and management functions separate, the monitoring function of banks can occur somewhat independently of ownership, as part of the efficient operation of integrated groups.

Safeguards Against Self-Dealing and Opportunistic Behaviour

One of the main arguments for the 1982 nationalization was that business-owned commercial banks transferred profits to their owners through special access to lending (see Tello, 1984). The Financial Groups Law reflects concerns arising from this experience by regulating and limiting the transactions commercial banks are able to engage in with affiliates and 'privileged firms'. The rules cover loans to holders of 1 per cent or more of the stock, board members, and companies in which the bank or the controladora or their directors hold equity positions of 10 per cent or more. Such loans may be made only with explicit approval by the board of directors and the bank's credit committee. (Boards typically have several classes of directors, each of which must approve the transaction by majority vote.) Appropriate filings must be made with the National Banking Commission.

A commercial bank cannot loan more than 20 per cent of its portfolio (that is, the total value of outstanding loans) to related companies or provide more than 30 per cent of its loans to any single individual or corporation even if it is not related to the bank. This is quite high by international standards. While data are unavailable on the distribution by source of loans to specific firms, larger Mexican enterprises often go outside the domestic capital market for credit, and it is common for major corporations to use US and other international banks for syndications of major investment activities.

Because the controlling groups are largely insulated from the threat of take-over, they could behave opportunistically. However, the efficient and profitable functioning of its subsidiaries is in the primary interest of a controladora because it derives all its income from dividends paid by them and is responsible for their liabilities. Trying to pick up a few extra pesos by diverting profits is risky. Besides being monitored by the government, the activities of the controlling group and its subsidiaries are overseen by regional councils and consulting boards, as previously discussed. This sharply increases the risk of being caught.

Supervision and Regulation

The three primary bank regulatory authorities in Mexico are the Ministry of Finance, the central bank (Banco de Mexico, which is a legally autonomous agency that operates under the guidance of the Ministry), and the National Banking Commission (NBC, an agency of the Ministry).

The Ministry possesses broad powers over the banking system, and may require banks to provide almost any kind of information related to their financial position. The functions of the Banco de Mexico include the formulation and implementation of monetary policy, operation of the reserve bank, oversight of the clearing house for Mexican credit institutions, and regulation of the foreign exchange market. It also assists the NBC in monitoring the banks.

The principal functions of the NBC include the issue of regulations; supervision; approval of investment policies, fees, commissions and other charges; and approval of individuals elected to serve as directors of a bank or its financial-services holding company, and of individuals elected as senior officers of the bank. Special attention is given to capital adequacy, liquidity, earnings, loan loss experience, concentration of risks, the maturity structure of assets and liabilities, and potential exposures through equity association and international banking operations.

International Comparison

Other systems of relationship banking, such as the Japanese and German, not only permit significant cross shareholding by banks and non-financial enterprises, but are less hierarchical. For example, the Japanese system includes a main bank within a group of enterprises (including manufacturers) but without the bank or other financial institutions in the group being subordinated to a 'controlling financial holding company', which would be illegal in Japan. In the German case, the universal bank internalizes all financial services and does not represent a separate tier of ownership, monitoring, and control.

In both the Japanese and German systems of relationship banking, relations between financial and non-financial enterprises are sufficiently balanced and diversified in terms of management so that banks can act effectively as monitors without either dominating other members of the group or being dominated by them. Hence, although it shows important elements of relationship banking, in terms of separation of ownership, Mexico is more like the US system.

INFORMATIONAL ROLE OF THE CONTROLADORA

The cornerstone of the financial group system is the close information-sharing relationship that exists among the financial holding company, its subsidiaries, and their related non-financial firms (three levels). The owners and principal shareholders of a holding company are closely involved in the business and financial plans at each level. The holding company controls its subsidiaries, and although they are different commercial entities the law provides for information exchange and operation as complementary institutions. The process of information exchange is formalized by the Board of Regional Councils (which represent the regional client bases) and Board of Consultants (representing minority shareholders). Representatives of these boards also sit on the credit committees, offer advice on financial issues, and interact accordingly.

It is possible to view these business-related consulting boards as a complement to the kind of screening and monitoring institutions that are prevalent in other capital markets in the form of external auditors and credit-rating institutions. Furthermore, the organizational structure of the Mexican financial system provides that other security analysis agencies, such as brokerage houses and insurance companies, be members of the same financial group, thereby covering possible niches that could otherwise be missing in the bank's regular operations. Lenders have much less access to information on firms that are outside the group, although they do participate in syndicated loans—especially in the area of international trade. This increases the importance of the monitoring function of lenders within the group.

In Mexico the close association firms have with the financial group implies that the non-financial firms (and industries and regional borrower interests) have access to the internal decision-making process of the financial group. The effectiveness of the monitoring function in other forms of relationship banking depends on access by the group's bank to the related firms, allowing it to obtain information about the group and its management which might not be readily available to the external capital market.

In Mexico firms can be required to provide a wide range of information to their financial group. For example, any firm that requires a loan from its related bank will have to open its balance sheet to the credit analysis committees, and any firm that wants to go public on the Mexican stock exchange has to be evaluated by a brokerage house. Moreover, these operations are also monitored by the National Banking Commission. While credit analysis is reportedly not as sophisticated in Mexico as elsewhere, it can be used by minority partners to reject loans to group members.

The financial group structure exemplifies some important aspects of monitoring, such as the 'duplication problem' (Sheard, 1989). Since the costs of monitoring the financial group are basically fixed, there are gains from delegating the function of monitoring to a single institution (such as the main bank) to avoid duplication of effort. In the Mexican case, the controladora is the principal monitoring institution of its financial group, but it is not the only one. There is some coordination in monitoring and information gathering at different levels: the board of directors and regional councils engage in such coordination. In addition, the National Banking Commission and the Banco de Mexico also serve as monitors and maintain an information system throughout the entire banking system. In special cases they also employ teams to draw on the expertise of the group's subsidiaries.

It has been suggested that there might be an advantage to even more coordination and pooling of monitoring and information gathering in Mexico, as there is with the main bank's key role in Japan. While this might imply a risk of information loss through special relationships between banks and their groups, there appears to be sufficient diversification and decentralization in minority shares and regulations to prevent opportunistic behaviour by the controllers of the group.

Because a controladora derives all its income from dividends paid by its subsidiaries, it has a real incentive to monitor their activities, including ensuring they are monitoring their clients. This, incidentally, also addresses the 'free rider problem' of those who benefit from monitoring without sharing its costs, at least as far as the group controlling the controladora is concerned. For non-monitoring shareholders (that is, all the other investors) the problem is mitigated by the fact they cannot take control.

In times of extreme difficulty of a group firm, intervention is another aspect of the monitoring function that can be performed in a close relational banking arrangement such as the Japanese main bank system. This can substitute for a take-over market, especially in developing countries with incomplete capital markets or where hostile take-overs may impose greater social costs than does direct intervention in troubled firms by their group financial institution.

The ability of a commercial bank to intervene in the affairs of a non-financial enterprise has not yet been tested extensively. It will depend on the degree to which financial institutions have the authority to monitor the behaviour of firms owned by the same interests as the controladora and to intervene on a timely basis. This in turn depends on the symmetry of decision-making power between the bank and its affiliated customers. There is something of a bargaining (power) relationship present between the financial institutions and the non-financial firms controlled by the group, as well as between the controlling group's interests and those of its affiliates and the general public; it is not clear what might happen in specific instances. Clearly the capital market is not sufficiently developed to ensure that a competitive take-over market exists that could provide an efficient substitute for private sector intervention. The crisis of the 1980s has revealed the limitations of public sector intervention through receivership, or through actions of the government's own lending institutions.

POLICY IMPLICATIONS AND CONCLUSIONS

Mexico's reprivatized banking system represents an innovative approach to the design of financial institutions within a legal and regulatory framework that balances the advantages of relationship banking with safeguards against the abuse of financial institutions by industrial firms. With its new system, Mexico is positioning itself to develop two-way functions of shared finance, monitoring, control, and intervention that will enhance the economy's competitiveness in an increasingly open international trading and financial system.

It is too early to grasp fully the economic consequences of the new structures of ownership and the organizational implications, especially during the period of NAFTA negotiations and capital market opening. There are several key issues. Perhaps the most important is the potential of the new banks to create linkages with the private sector that facilitate generation of organizational quasi-rents, as well as the impact of the new structures on the distribution of such rents.

The banks (with links to foreign institutions) are now in a position to control the most important financial aspects of Mexico's economy, including those of the largest industrial groups. They facilitate market penetration of their associated enterprises, not so much through preferential credit terms as through greater access to credit of any kind for productive use, and the encouragement of innovative financial practices.

In this way, the seemingly exaggerated prices paid for the reprivatized banks may reflect expected returns derived from what might be termed an 'integration dividend'. The premiums also undoubtedly reflect expected returns from new forms of relationship banking over and above the rents from barriers to entry into the financial system which, according to regulatory authorities, will be relaxed progressively.

It is unlikely, however, given the present conditions of interlocking ownership and control, that banks in Mexico will be in a position soon to assume a monitoring role similar to that of main banks in Japan. Public policy fostering the strengthening of the monitoring of banks could do much to enhance the efficiency and competitiveness of enterprise and could speed up the diffusion of productivity within Mexico *vis-à-vis* its international competitors.

The projected opening of Mexico's financial system at home and abroad will also provide scope for lower-cost borrowing by enterprises and more efficient application of intermediation technology and management procedures. This will provide gains that will be less dependent on a past history of special relationships between domestic business and financial groups, and more responsive to the positive pressures of international competition. There are lessons here from the non-exclusive lending function but exclusive monitoring role in the Japanese case, as well as from other models of relationship banking.

So far profit-sharing considerations have not been central to corporate decision-making and labour relations, limiting the scope for consensus at the level of firm and industry. Still, the system is responsive to government macroeconomic policy leadership, given the acceptance in December 1987 by the (official) labour unions of the government's heterodox stabilization plan (Economic Solidarity Pact), which calls for voluntary restraints on wages and prices in order to bring about benefits to both labour and capital from lower inflationary expectations. The result has been a dramatic slowdown in inflation, return of flight capital, increased domestic and foreign investment, growth, and gradual recovery of real wages. The next step would be to develop real and financial sector institutions that favour longer-term rent sharing between labour and capital, as well as between domestic and international investors.

The banks must finance the restructuring and growth of Mexican firms in a highly competitive international market. This involves a shift from protection rent seeking to the earning of profits from new forms of organization, innovation, and market penetration.

It is a matter of concern among policy-makers how the banking system, comprised of a small number of large-scale financial groups, is going to provide capital to less-developed regions and to emerging small and medium enterprises—especially those in a position to penetrate export markets or supply exporting firms. The government is attempting to establish channels for wholesale financing of those banks and credit cooperatives willing to lend to small borrowers at rates of interest adequate to sustain and increase such services. However, there is much more to be done in this area, including the participation of foreign banks and non-bank financial intermediaries in the diffusion of financial services. Subject to appropriate financial policies to complete markets between domestic and international finance and among local regions, Mexico's emerging enterprises appear to have significant potential, not only in design and craft-based export industries, but in areas of greater technological sophistication (Ruiz Duran and Kagami, 1993).

Can Mexico develop non-hierarchical systems of coordination, while retaining hierarchical incentive structures? The needs of newly forming enterprises, and the flexibility that older firms require to restructure and achieve competitiveness under a new set of liberalized macroeconomic policy guidelines, argue in favour of new methods, procedures and institutions. The Mexican model offers important lessons to other newly industrializing countries and holds promise for its own future.

REFERENCES

AOKI, MASAHIKO. 1988. *Information, Incentives and Bargaining in the Japanese Economy.* Cambridge: Cambridge University Press.

——. 1990. 'Toward an Economic Model of the Japanese Firm,' *Journal of Economic Literature* 28: 1–27 (March).

AOKI, MASAHIKO, BO GUSTAFSON and OLIVER E. WILLIAMSON. 1990. *The Firm as a Nexus of Treaties.* London: Sage Publications.

Asociación Mexicana de Bancos. 1990. *Evolución Institucional.* Comisión Ejecutiva de Planeación Estrategica.

ASPE ARMELLA, PEDRO. 1990. 'Principios Fundamentales de la Desincorporación Bancaria.' *Comercio Exterior*, September.

——. 1991. 'La Banca: Un Instrumento de Impulso a la Producción.' *Comercio Exterior*, October.

Banco de Mexico. 1991 May. *The Mexican Economy 1991: Economic and Financial Developments in 1990, Policies for 1991.* Mexico City: Banco de Mexico.

BROTHERS, DWIGHT S., and SOLIS M. LEOPOLDO. 1966. *Mexican Financial Development.* Austin: University of Texas Press.

Comisión Nacional Bancaria y de Seguros. *Boletin Estadistico.* Various volumes.

——. *Informe Anual.* Various volumes.

EJEA, GUILLERMO, CELSO GARRDIO, CRISTIAN LERICHE, and ENRIQUE QUINTANA. 1991. *Mercado de Valores: Crisis y Nuevos Circuitos Financieros en Mexico, 1970–1990.* Universidad Autonoma Metropolitana, Division de Ciencias Sociales y Humanidades.

El Nacional, 7 July 1992, 'Concluyo la desincorporacion de 18 bancos: $38.6 billones' (and related articles). p. 1ff.

GARBER, PETER M., and STEVEN R. WEISBROD, 1991. 'Opening the Financial Services Market in Mexico.' Prepared for the conference on Mexico-US Free Trade Agreement, Brown University, October 18–19.

GIL-DIAZ, FRANCISCO. 1988 January. 'Macroeconomic Policies, Crisis, and Growth in the Long Run.' Draft prepared for World Bank, Research Project 673–99. Mexico City: Banco de Mexico.

Institutional Investor. 1989. 'Ranking the World's Largest Banks.' December 31.

Instituto Nacional de Estadistica, Geografia e Informatica (SPP). *Sistema de Cuentas Nacionales.* Mexico. Various volumes.

KRUEGER, ANNE O. 1974. 'The Political Economy of the Rent-Seeking Society.' *American Economic Review* 64: 291–303 (June).

PATRICK, HUGH. 1972. 'Finance, Capital Markets and Economic Growth in Japan.' In Arnold Sametz, ed., *Financial Development and Economic Growth.* New York: New York University Press.

PEREZ LOPEZ, ENRIQUE. 1987. *Expropiación Bancaria en Mexico y Desarrollo Desestabilizador.* Mexico: Editorial Diana.

REYNOLDS, CLARK W., and ANA PAULA PESSOA. 1991. 'The Promotion of Micro and Small Enterprise Development in Mexico: A Preliminary Report.' Draft presented to the Inter-American Development Bank, September.

RUIZ DURAN, CLEMENTE and MITSUHIRO KAGAMI. 1993. *Potencial Tecnologico de la Micro y Pequena Empresa en Mexico*. Mexico City: Nacional Financiera, Biblioteca de la micro, pequena, y mediana empresa 5.

SALINAS DE GORTARI, CARLOS. 1990. 'Reestablecimiento del Regimen Mixto de Banca y Credito.' *Comercio Exterior*, June.

——. 1990. 'Principios y Bases del Proceso de Desincorporación de la Banca.' *Comercio Exterior*, October.

——. 1991. 'La Banca en la Modernización Economica de Mexico: Hacia un Sistema Financiero Solido y Competitivo.' *Comercio Exterior*, October.

SHEARD, PAUL. 1989. 'The Main Bank System and Corporate Monitoring and Control in Japan.' *Journal of Economic Behavior and Organization*, 11: 399–422.

SOTO RODRIGUEZ, HUMBERTO. 1990. 'Los Nuevos Desafiós de la Banca.' *Comercio Exterior*, September.

——. 1991. 'Un Nuevo Perfil de las Instituciónes Financieras.' *Comercio Exterior*, October.

STIGLITZ, JOSEPH E. and ANDREW WEISS. 1981. 'Credit Rationing in Markets with Imperfect Information.' *American Economic Review* 71(3): 393–410 (June).

TELLO, CARLOS. 1984. *La Nacionalización de la Banca en Mexico*. Siglo Veintiuno Editores.

WEBB, TOMAS PENALOZA. 1992. 'Aspectos centrales de la banca mexicana 1982–1990.' *Comercio Exterior*, February.

16

Financial System Reform in China: Lessons from Japan's Main Bank System

YINGYI QIAN

China's economic reform is at a crucial moment. On the one hand, 14 years of economic reform have achieved considerable success. China's GNP grew at an average annual rate of 8.6 per cent between 1979 and 1991 and reached 12.8 per cent in 1992; exports grew even faster so that the export-GNP ratio increased from 4.7 per cent in 1978 to 19.3 per cent in 1991 and foreign reserves increased from US$1.6 billion to US$21.71 billion correspondingly (Table 16.1). Accompanying high growth, the living standards of the Chinese people have improved greatly. On the other hand, several key institutional aspects of a market system, including the fiscal system, the financial system, and the ownership and governance of enterprises, still wait for a major breakthrough before the benefits of the market can be fully realized. In October 1992 the Chinese government officially designated its reform goal as a 'socialist market economy', which opened ways for an all-round transition towards the market system. This could be an important new start.

This chapter studies financial system reforms in China with a focus on institutional restructuring. The achievements of the reforms in the financial sector in the past 14 years have been mixed: household bank deposits have risen to nearly 50 per cent of GNP; investment financing has gradually shifted from the government budget to bank loans; financial intermediaries have flourished; a nascent securities market made a quick start; and financial assets have multiplied to include choices of government, financial and enterprise bonds, as well as equity shares. However, old problems with the planning system remain and new problems have arisen: allocation of financial resources has been inefficient because credit was

The author has benefited greatly from discussions with Masahiko Aoki and Ronald McKinnon at Stanford University, and with several economists in China, especially Jiwei Lou of the State System Reform Commission, Jinglian Wu of the Development Research Center (DRC) of the State Council, Xiaoling Wu of the People's Bank of China, and Xiaochuan Zhou of the Bank of China. Yasushi Hamao, Akiyoshi Horiuchi, Hyung-Ki Kim, Diane McNaughton, Tetsuji Okazaki and Hugh Patrick also made valuable comments on the earlier version of the paper. This research is sponsored in part by the Center for Economic Policy Research (CEPR) at Stanford University. The author is solely responsible for all opinions and errors.

TABLE 16.1 China: Selected Macroeconomic Indicators, (1978–91)
(per cents)

	Growth of GNP	National Retail Price Index	Urban Cost of Living Index	Export /GNP	Foreign Reserves[1] (billion US$)
1978				4.67	
1979	7.6	2.0	1.9	5.31	0.84
1980	7.9	6.0	7.5	6.07	−1.30
1981	4.4	2.4	2.5	7.70	2.71
1982	8.8	1.9	2.0	7.97	6.99
1983	10.4	1.5	2.0	7.55	8.90
1984	14.7	2.8	2.7	8.34	8.22
1985	12.8	8.8	11.9	9.45	2.64
1986	8.1	6.0	7.0	11.16	2.07
1987	10.9	7.3	8.8	13.01	2.92
1988	11.0	18.5	20.7	12.60	3.37
1989	4.0	17.8	16.3	12.29	5.55
1990	5.2	2.1	1.3	16.88	11.09
1991	7.7	2.9	5.1	19.30	21.71

Note: Exports are calculated using the official exchange rate which may give the export-GNP ratio an upward bias.

[1] Central bank only.

Source: *Statistical Yearbook of China, 1992.*

allocated largely by quotas and interest rates played little role; 'soft budget constraint' problems have worsened, resulting in mounting bad loans and inter-enterprise arrears; and more seriously, inflationary pressure has threatened macroeconomic stability from time to time. Even worse, the government has no monetary instruments to deal with these problems, as the old method of credit control is becoming less effective.

The objective of financial reform is to establish a market for the mobilization and efficient allocation of financial resources, and to maintain macroeconomic stability. Fundamental institutional restructuring and change of control mechanisms are necessary to achieve this goal. In this regard, China faces a broad range of choices, and can learn from the experience of many other countries, in particular, from the experience of Japan.

Although China, Eastern Europe and the former Soviet Union are all making transitions from centrally planned to market economies, they face different types of economic, institutional and political constraints. Today's Chinese economy has already been decentralized in many ways. By the end of 1991, about 47 per cent of industrial output was already produced by the market-oriented non-state sector (including private businesses, joint ventures, cooperatives and collective enterprises), with the private sector accounting for about 10 per cent of the total (Qian and Xu, 1993). However, a dramatic departure from the past is very difficult, with the continuity of the current political system, as the government has a bias towards the status quo. For example, unlike Eastern Europe and Russia where mass privatization is imperative, centrally directed mass privatization of state-owned enterprises—let alone privatization of banks—is out of the question in China at the present time. This poses a special challenge to financial reform. Furthermore, most of the reforms in China so far have proceeded in an incremental, 'bottom-up' and decentralized fashion. More coherent action from the top is necessary for restructuring the financial system as a whole (as well as the fiscal system), which seems particularly difficult for China given its already decentralized structure and political constraints.

Discussion of the transformation of the Chinese financial sector and the lessons and relevance of the Japanese financial system is conducted bearing these facts in mind. The chapter is organized as follows. The first section reviews major changes in China's financial sector since 1979. The second section discusses the main institutional problems with the financial sector to the end of 1992. The third section analyses the relevance and limits of the Japanese financial system to Chinese reforms from both evolutionary and comparative perspectives. The fourth section suggests some essential aspects in the next stage of financial reforms, focusing on institutional restructuring.

MAJOR CHANGES IN THE CHINESE FINANCIAL SECTOR SINCE 1979

Before economic reform started in 1979, Soviet-type central planning was dominant in China, like all Central and Eastern European countries, where the financial sector (that is, the banking sector) played only a subordinate role in the economy. The planned economy was 'semi-monetized' (Kornai, 1992). Under central planning, the State Planning Commission made all the important decisions on investment, production and finance. There was only one bank, the People's Bank of China (PBC), which served both as the central bank and as a commercial bank; we can define this as a mono-bank system. The role of the PBC was very limited, as most long-term investment financing was not channelled to enterprises through the banking system, but through the state budget: all investment projects were financed with budgetary grants. The state bank was only responsible for providing working capital to enterprises. Therefore, it is not surprising that household savings were small relative to government savings—total household bank deposits were less than 6 per cent of GNP in 1978. The PBC followed cash and credit plans from the State Planning Commission, and its branches provided financial resources to enterprises according to the plan.

As in the other sectors of the Chinese economy, the financial sector has also undergone substantial changes since 1978. Generally speaking, more progress has been made on the deposit than on the lending side: the latter requiring not just policy adjustments, but also institutional changes, which is a more difficult task to achieve. A brief description of the major changes are given in this section, further analysis and evaluation of those changes follow in the next section. Detailed descriptions of the Chinese financial system can be found in Xie (1992) and World Bank (1988, 1991).

The Banking Sector

In 1978, the People's Bank of China (PBC) was separated from the Ministry of Finance and granted ministerial rank. Five years later, in 1983, the State Council granted the PBC the authority of a central bank and the PBC subsequently transferred its commercial operations to four specialized banks: the Agricultural Bank of China (ABC) for the rural sector; the Industrial and Commercial Bank of China (ICBC) for the industrial sector; the People's Construction Bank of China (PCBC) for long-term investment; and the Bank of China (BOC) for foreign exchange. In addition, the China Investment Bank (CIB) was established in 1981 to channel World Bank loans to China. Affiliated with the ABC are rural credit cooperatives whose main lending is to rural households' farming and township-village enterprises. Two additional universal banks were established in 1988: the Bank of Communications (BOCOM) and CITIC Industrial Bank. By 1990, the six banks had vast national networks, with more than 120,000 branches and more than 1.3 million employees. In addition, rural and urban credit cooperatives had 60,000 branches and more than half a million employees (State Statistical Bureau, 1992).

Since 1984, the four specialized banks have been allowed to compete for deposits and loans in each other's previously monopolized markets, and enterprises are allowed to open accounts with more than one bank (Zhou and Zhu, 1987). For example, the ABC is able to set up branches in cities and the ICBC is allowed to undertake foreign exchange business. However, all four banks have remained highly specialized in their operations. Unlike the industrial sector, by the end of 1992, the banking sector was characterized by the monopoly of state ownership dominated by the four big state banks.

The old way of financing projects with budgetary grants was phased out, and financing of fixed investment gradually shifted to bank loans and extra-budgetary funds of local governments and ministries (80 per cent of which are retained profits of enterprises). In 1978, fixed investment by state-owned enterprises, financed by the government, accounted for 12.7 per cent of GNP; this declined to only 3.6 per cent in 1991. Nevertheless, many investment projects still need to be approved by the central and local Planning Commissions (known as 'project registration' (*lixiang*)), although they are financed in a decentralized way. The share of bank financing of both fixed and working capital increased from 30 per cent in 1980 to 73 per cent in 1990 (Xie, 1992, table 3–11). Compared to the pre-reform era, the role of the banking sector in financing increased significantly.

Interest Rates Determination

Interest rates were fixed and adjusted periodically by the central bank. A positive real interest rate (that is, household one-year time deposit rate minus national retail price index) has been maintained for most years except 1988 and 1989 when the real rate turned very negative (Table 16.2). However, starting from the fourth quarter of 1988, indexation for time deposits with more than three years' maturity has been introduced. For example, for a three-year deposit, the annual rate was 9.72 per cent in the fourth quarter of 1988 and the annual rate of the cost of living allowance was 7.28 per cent, so the effective rate was 17.00 per cent (Table 16.3). Hence, for an indexed three-year time deposit, the real interest rate in 1989 was well above zero (the inflation rates from 1989 to 1991 were 17.8 per cent, 2.1 per cent and 2.9 per cent). The cost of living allowance was dropped to zero after June 1990, and the indexation scheme was eliminated in December 1991 (*Almanac of China's Finance and Banking*, 1992).

Floating rates in a narrow range based on rate standards provided by the central bank have been allowed by specialized banks and branches since 1984. For example, branches below the county level may increase deposit rates by 10 to 30 per cent and rural credit cooperatives by 70 per cent; the lending rate of banks may be adjusted upwards by 30 per cent and that of rural credit cooperatives by 100 per cent (*Almanac of China's Finance and Banking*, 1990).

Non-Bank Financial Intermediaries and Informal Financial Institutions

Before the reform, the only non-bank financial intermediary in China was the People's Insurance Company of China (PICC). Since 1979, numerous non-bank financial intermediaries were established. There are at least three major types of non-bank intermediaries other than the insurance

TABLE 16.2 China: Selected Real Interest Rates, 1980–91
(annual percentage rates)

	National Retail Price Index	Household 1-year Time Deposit (nominal)	Household 3-year Time Deposit (nominal)	Household 1-year Time Deposit (real)	Household 3-year Time Deposit (real)
1980	6.0	5.4	6.12	−0.60	0.12
1981	2.4	5.4	6.12	3.00	3.72
1982	1.9	5.76	6.84	3.86	4.94
1983	1.5	5.76	6.84	4.26	5.34
1984	2.8	5.76	6.84	2.96	4.04
1985	8.8	7.2	8.28	−1.60	−0.52
1986	6.0	7.7	8.28	1.70	2.28
1987	7.3	7.2	8.28	−0.10	0.98
1988	18.5	8.64	9.72[a]	−9.86	−8.78
1989	17.8	11.34	13.14[a]	−6.46	−4.66
1990	2.1	8.64	10.08	6.54	7.98
1991	2.9	7.56	8.28	4.66	5.38

Year-end figures.

[a] Cost of living adjustment allowance not included (see Table 16.3).

Source: *Statistical Yearbook of China, 1992* and *Almanac of China's Finance and Banking, 1990, 1992.*

companies: trust investment corporations established by the central and regional governments (China International Trust Investment Corporation, or CITIC, is the largest); trust investment corporations established by specialized banks and their branches; and finance companies of enterprise groups. In contrast to the six national banks under tight central control, these 'outside-the-plan' financial intermediaries are much less regulated.[1]

By the end of 1992, there were more than 1,000 trust investment corporations run by bank branches and government at all levels. The main reason for the rapid expansion of non-financial intermediaries is their ability to circumvent credit quotas imposed by the central bank on specialized banks and their access to a wide range of business alternatives. At a time the central bank still uses direct credit quotas as the main control instrument, the local branches of specialized banks, local governments and enterprises make use of loopholes and non-bank financial intermediaries to extend loans to meet the demand for fast growth.

[1] The phrase 'outside-the-plan' is used here for lack of a better term. Readers are cautioned that many financial institutions in this category are not entirely outside the plan, unlike outside-the-plan industrial firms.

TABLE 16.3 China: Interest Rates with Cost of Living Adjustments 1988:
IV–1990: IV
(per cent per year)

	Household 3-year Time Deposit (nominal)	Annual Rate of Cost of Living Adjustment Allowance	Effective Household 3-year Time Deposit (nominal)
1988: IV	9.72	7.28	17.00
1989: I	13.14	12.71	25.85
1989: II	13.14	12.59	25.73
1989: III	13.14	13.64	26.78
1989: IV	13.14	8.36	21.50
1990: 1	13.14	0.89	14.03
1990: 2	13.14	1.46	14.60
1990: 3	13.14	0	13.14
1990: 4	13.14	1.42	14.56
1990: 5	13.14	1.38	14.52
1990: 6	13.14	0	13.14
1990: III	10.08	0	10.08
1990: IV	10.08	0	10.08

Note: Roman numerals indicate calendar quarters; arabic numbers indicate months (I =
January, etc.).

Source: *Almanac of China's Finance and Banking, 1990, 1991.*

Informal financial institutions in China are widespread, especially in
rural areas, but documentation of their transactions is not always available. In rural areas, a major form of informal financial institutions are
'rural cooperative funds' (*nongcun hezuo jijinhui*) (RCFs). According to
Chen (1993) by 1991, there were 18,000 township-level RCFs (about one-
third of all townships) and 120,000 village-level RCFs (about one-sixth of
all villages). The initial funds of RCFs came mainly from receipts of sales
of grain and the collective assets of townships and villages. Chen gives
several reasons for the rise of independent rural cooperative funds outside
the state-controlled rural credit cooperatives (RCCs). First, there is generally inadequate credit provided for rural activities, and the formal banking system has the binding constraint of a credit limit; second, the
operation of the Agricultural Bank of China and the RCCs is still too
rigid and cannot meet the demands of rapid market development; and
third, RCCs are supervised closely by the Agricultural Bank of China,
and are not really cooperatives.

Capital Markets

With the issue of government bonds in 1981, capital market development in China has been relatively fast compared to the reform of the banking institutions. Capital market instruments now include not only government securities, but also financial bonds (bonds issued by financial intermediaries), enterprise bonds, and equities. The total volume of all instruments issued was estimated to be approximately 400 billion yuan from 1981 to 1991, with government securities amounting to 150 billion yuan and other instruments amounting to approximately 250 billion yuan (*Almanac of China's Finance and Banking*, 1992). The total volume of secondary market trading increased from about 100 million yuan in 1987 to over 40 billion yuan in 1991. The share of trading in treasury issues decreased from 92 per cent of total trading in 1988 to 80 per cent in 1991, and the share of trading in equities increased from less than 0.4 per cent in 1988 to 10 per cent in 1991. There are two stock exchanges, one in Shenzhen, the other in Shanghai. By the end of 1992, more than 70 publicly traded equity issues were available. In addition, with the introduction of the Securities Trading Automated Quotation System (STAQS), a computerized quotation and trading system links nine cities on-line through a central computer in Beijing. OTC trading started in December 1990, with both treasury bonds and shares trading in Shanghai and Shenzhen.

Capital market development got a big push from the emergence of a secondary market for government bonds. During most of the 1980s, the government ran a budget deficit, part of which was financed by issuing bonds. At the beginning, allocation of bonds was through mandatory planning and with very low interest rates: enterprises and households were forced to buy them. In the mid-1980s, some arbitrageurs found a profitable business in buying government bonds in rural areas at a discount and selling them to residents in urban areas. (One of Shanghai's security companies, Shanghai International, started by doing this type of trading.) A liquid government bond market then emerged. With the liquid secondary market, the government no longer allocated bonds by command; instead, bonds were offered at a slightly higher interest rate (about 1 per cent) than similar bank deposits. Starting from the late 1980s, shares and commercial bonds were also traded.

Household Financial Savings and Movements of Monetary Aggregates

China's national savings increased from 30 per cent of GNP in 1980 to around 35 per cent in 1991.[2] More significantly, major saving sources

---

[2] Since China's GNP figures may be underestimated, the savings-GNP ratio (and for that matter, all ratios using GNP as the denominator, for example, the M2-GNP ratio) may be upward biased.

have been shifted from the government to households and enterprises. A remarkable phenomenon of the 14 years of economic reform is the sustained and rapid increase of household financial savings. Total household bank deposits reached 911 billion yuan in 1991, or about 46 per cent of GNP, from merely 6 per cent in 1978 (Table 16.4). This translates into per capita household bank deposits increasing by more than 16 times in real terms. In 1979, household savings accounted for only 23 per cent, enterprises for 34 per cent and the government for 43 per cent of total saving. In 1991, household savings increased to 71 per cent, enterprise savings decreased to 26 per cent and the government savings fell to a mere 4 per cent of the total (Xie, 1992, table 3–13). Total household financial assets increased correspondingly from 87 billion yuan in 1980, or about 19 per cent of GNP, to 1,365 billion yuan in 1991, or about 70 per cent of GNP (Xie, 1992, table 3–8).

The sharp rise in household savings after the reforms has provoked a debate about whether or not it is forced saving. Two hypotheses were proposed in Qian (1988). One is the reflection of increasing disequilibrium or monetary overhang, which was the prevailing view at the time (see Feltenstein and others, 1986). An alternative hypothesis, which I favour, is increased monetization due to economic reforms. As more evidence accumulates, it becomes clear that savings continue to rise because of the rapid increase in personal income and monetization of the economy, especially the rapid entry and expansion of private and non-state businesses. Additional evidence supporting the voluntary savings hypothesis is the abundance of consumer goods on the market, and the fast increase in savings after interest rate indexing starting in the fourth quarter of 1988. Blejer and others (1991) conclude that monetary holdings of households are largely voluntary. However, the high degree of liquidity reflects the lack of less liquid assets for household portfolios, especially real assets such as housing. One policy implication is to increase the availability of less liquid assets like sales of government-owned housing (Qian, 1988).

China's financial sector became deeper and more liquid at a fast pace during the reform period (Table 16.5). The currency to GNP ratio rose from 6 per cent in 1978 to 16 per cent in 1991. M2 (broad money) increased from 61 per cent of GNP in 1985 to 72 per cent in 1988, and to 98 per cent in 1991. Monetary development in recent years has shown a faster increase in M1 and M2 than in loan credits from banks. In 1991, M2 increased by 27 per cent over the previous year, while loan credit increased by 20 per cent. In the first eight months of 1992, credit increased by 23 per cent over the same period of the previous year, but currency increased by 30 per cent, M1 by 36 per cent and M2 by 30 per cent (Table 16.6).

TABLE 16.4 China: Household Bank Deposits, 1978–91 (billion yuan)

	Total Household Deposits	Increase Over Previous Year (per cent)	Urban Household Deposits	Increase Over Previous Year (per cent)	Rural Household Deposits	Increase Over Previous Year (per cent)	Total Household Deposits as % of GNP
1978	21.06		15.49		5.57		5.87
1979	28.10	33.43	20.26	30.79	7.84	40.75	7.05
1980	39.95	42.17	28.25	39.44	11.70	49.23	8.94
1981	52.37	31.09	35.41	25.35	16.96	44.96	10.97
1982	67.54	28.97	44.73	26.32	22.81	34.49	13.01
1983	89.25	32.14	57.26	28.01	31.99	40.25	15.36
1984	121.47	36.10	77.66	35.63	43.81	36.95	17.45
1985	162.26	33.58	105.78	36.21	56.48	28.92	18.96
1986	223.76	37.90	147.15	39.11	76.61	35.64	23.08
1987	307.33	37.35	206.76	40.51	100.57	31.28	27.19
1988	380.15	23.69	265.92	28.61	114.23	13.58	27.12
1989	514.69	35.39	373.48	40.45	141.21	23.62	32.34
1990	703.42	36.67	519.26	39.03	184.16	30.42	39.77
1991	911.03	29.51	679.09	30.78	231.94	25.96	45.88

Source: Statistical Yearbook of China, 1992.

TABLE 16.5 China: Monetary Aggregates as Share of GNP
(per cent)

	Currency/GNP	M1/GNP	M2/GNP
1978	5.91		
1985	11.5	39.0	60.8
1986	12.6	43.6	69.3
1987	12.9	43.8	73.7
1988	15.2	42.5	71.8
1989	14.7	39.9	74.7
1990	14.9	43.0	86.4
1991	16.0	47.5	97.5

Households may not write cheques against their demand deposits, but enterprises and institutions may.

M1 = currency + enterprise and institution demand deposit
M2 = M1 + household bank savings deposit (demand and time) + enterprise and institution time deposit

Source: *Almanac of China's Finance and Banking, 1992.*

TABLE 16.6 China: Annual Monetary Expansion, 1986–92 (per cents)

	Credit	Currency	M1	M2
1986	29.4	23.3	26.7	29.3
1987	20.3	19.4	16.9	24.0
1988	17.0	46.7	21.0	21.2
1989	17.9	9.8	6.6	18.3
1990	22.8	12.8	19.2	28.0
1991	19.8	20.2	23.0	26.5
1992[a]	23.0	30.0	36.0	30.0

[a] First 8 months, preliminary, Lou (1993).

Source: *Almanac of China's Finance and Banking, 1992.*

FINANCIAL SECTOR PROBLEMS

Concerns for Inflation

With fast monetary expansion, inflation became a serious concern for the government. Fortunately, except for 1988 and 1989, China was able to control annual price increases within the single-digit range (Table 16.1). There are two institutional reasons that make controlling inflation in China difficult (and therefore costly), and both have to do with incomplete reforms. First, the central bank does not yet have monetary instruments that are more discriminating than credit quotas to manage aggregate demand, the second has to do with the fiscal reforms carried out in the 1980s.

With the introduction of the fiscal revenue-sharing scheme between the central and provincial–local governments in 1980, (consolidated) budget revenue declined steadily from about 35 per cent of GNP in 1978 to 18 per cent of GNP in 1991, and from 44 per cent to 33 per cent if extra-budgetary revenue is included (Sicular, 1992). At the same time, the official government budget deficit continued to rise and amounted to about 2–3 per cent of GNP. About half of the deficit was financed by government bond issues or by foreign loans and the other half by borrowing from the central bank (Table 16.7). Monetization of the budget deficit is clearly one possible source of inflation. Furthermore, under the current fiscal revenue-sharing system, the central government lost much of its ability to regulate aggregate demand through fiscal instruments. Even worse, since the fixed remittance by a local government is not indexed, the fiscal scheme tends to be pro-cyclical: in times of expansion, revenue remitted to the central government in real terms is reduced; in times of recession, it is increased. The fiscal sharing schemes also provide regional governments with strong incentives for fast expansion; the

TABLE 16.7 China: The Government Budgetary Deficit and Its Financing (per cents)

	Deficit/GNP	Foreign Loans	Financing by	
			Domestic Non-Bank Borrowing	Borrowing from the Central Bank
1978	(0.28)			
1979	5.15	17.5	0.0	82.5
1980	3.40	15.1	0.0	84.9
1981	1.21	55.2	84.5	−39.7
1982	1.48	−2.8	62.0	40.8
1983	1.64	11.5	43.8	44.8
1984	1.48	17.1	40.0	42.9
1985	0.50	2.4	148.8	−51.2
1986	1.82	28.3	3.7	67.9
1987	1.71	29.4	40.7	29.9
1988	2.17	31.8	36.5	31.8
1989	2.06	44.0	81.9	−25.9
1990	2.25			

Adjusted figures.

Source: Sicular, 1992; Tables 3 and 9.

central bank is often unable to resist the pressure from local governments, and this may lead to a loose monetary policy.

Three distinct periods can be identified as far as inflation is concerned. In the first half of the 1980s, the rapid increase in money supply did not lead to inflation and the price level was kept quite stable. Most Chinese economists agree that agricultural reforms and monetization of the rural sector played important roles in keeping the price level low. More specifically, McKinnon (1992a) argued that because rural households did not have access to credit, they had to build up their cash balance with the bank (or rural credit cooperatives) when they converted into production units. The government was then able to borrow from the banking system to capture the seigniorage without much inflationary effect.

This mechanism could not and in fact did not last long. In the second half of the 1980s, the price level started to rise; inflation grew out of control in 1988 and reached more than 50 per cent at an annual rate for several months in that year. Inflation, together with widespread corruption, led to a serious political crisis and caused a major disruption of economic development and reversal of economic reforms in 1989.

During 1990–92, the government deficit continued to climb and monetary expansion grew even faster, the price level nevertheless remained stable. During this period, rural income stagnated (showing an average 0.7 per cent annual increase between 1989 and 1991, and 4 per cent in 1992) and urban income soared. But the consumer goods markets were depressed, as were the producer goods markets because of the government's retrenchment programme. The clue to this puzzle probably lies in the change of expectations in urban areas. Unlike rural households, urban households do not own their houses and rely heavily on government for retirement, education, health and many other benefits. Therefore, the urban household savings propensity was much lower than that of the rural households (Qian, 1988). Following the political crisis in 1989—first concerning the uncertainty of the economy, and then anticipating the reforms in housing, health, and education—urban households had to increase their monetary balance in the absence of a credit market. A new wave of private businesses started in 1992 and this increased the demand for money. The fact that the rate of increase of urban household savings exceeds that of rural households since 1985 partially indicates a shift of monetization from rural areas to urban areas during this period (Table 16.4).[3] It is clear that this monetization process will not last forever. Whether and when the inflation crisis of 1988–89 will return is a question of great importance.

---

[3] Rural household savings deposits are deposits in rural credit cooperatives. Some farmers may deposit their savings in banks located in urban areas or in informal financial institutions like RCFs.

The Control Mechanism of the Central Bank

Three phases of control mechanism evolved between 1979 and 1992. Prior to 1983 when the specialized banks separated from the People's Bank of China, the control mechanism was essentially the same as in the pre-reform period. There were two separate plans for credit and cash each year, and cash was used only for wage payments and payments to rural households through the procurement of agricultural products; therefore, it was the cash plan that determined household demand. Because there was only one bank, no other financial intermediaries and no financial instruments other than credit, cash and credit controls were effective. From 1983 to the fourth quarter of 1988, while the old credit and cash plans were still in place, there was a gradual shift towards the use of indirect instruments such as reserve requirements (13 per cent, with an additional 5–7 per cent for excess reserve) and the deposit-lending ratio to achieve financial control. However, no capital requirement was imposed. During this period, specialized banks and their branches were allowed to float deposit and loan rates in a range 20–30 per cent wide around the rate set by the central bank.

Inflation in 1988 disrupted these experiments, and starting from the fourth quarter of 1988, strict credit quota controls were again imposed, except for credit cooperatives which were still under the deposit-lending ratio regulation. Interest rates were generally no longer allowed to float except in a few special areas. This mechanism was maintained until the end of 1992.

The credit quotas plan is the centre piece of the central bank's control mechanisms. Each year the PBC disaggregates credit quotas to each of the specialized banks, which in turn disaggregate to their branches. When strictly enforced, credit quotas are a binding constraint on specialized banks. (A branch director of the PBC in Sichuan province committed suicide in 1988 when facing the dilemma of extending the additional credit demanded by the local government while strict credit quotas were being imposed by the central government.) The second most important tool of the central bank is its credit to specialized banks. The central bank's claims on specialized banks account for more than two-thirds of its total assets (IMF, 1993). Indirect instruments of interest rates and reserve requirements do not yet play very important roles; there may be good reasons for this given the large size of the state sector. The last point is taken up in the fourth section.

Universal direct credit rationing results in misallocation of resources: some profitable projects may not be able to get finance, but less profitable ones may. Moreover, unlike indirect instruments such as interest rates, it is hard to achieve better macroeconomic demand management with credit quotas. The result of this situation is often the familiar 'stop-go' cycle with extreme swings in output: when the brakes are applied to slow down an overheated economy, there is a period of retrenchment before credit expands and the cycle continues. Even worse, evidence shows that it is mainly the non-state-owned enterprises like the township-village enterprises that get hurt most during a credit crunch, and these appear to be the more efficient and dynamic enterprises in China now (Qian and Xu, 1993).

Two new problems arose during the reform period. First, the boundary between the two monetary circuits, cash and credit, became increasingly blurred; because of the rise of non-state enterprises, business transactions used more cash than cheques. Even in the state sector, cash is used in order to avoid monitoring by the government (in particular for bonus payments and other benefits for employees). It is estimated that about 15 per cent of household savings is actually deposited by individual businesses and about 10 per cent by enterprises and institutions. Unlike enterprise deposit accounts, depositors with household accounts may withdraw cash with no questions asked. (Therefore enterprise and institutional deposits in household accounts will eventually end up in the hands of the individuals.) Second, with the faster pace of reform in other sectors due to the regional demand for high growth, using credit quotas imposed by the central bank becomes a less effective method of controlling the money supply. Local governments and bank branches found many ways to circumvent the limits (see below).

For several reasons, both the central bank and the central government were very reluctant to increase lending rates to cool off the economy. In 1992, interest rates on black market loans had soared to between 25 per cent and 30 per cent, more than 16 percentage points higher than the official rates. Some argue that the state sector, with its soft budget constraint problem, will not respond to increases in interest rates anyway. With the amount of decentralization and the rise of the non-state sector, the interest rate is not totally ineffective as it was in the past. Second, the government worries that the increased cost of capital as a result of interest rate hikes will make more state-owned firms lose money, which will require more subsidies from an already shrinking budget. The low interest rate for loans is in fact a subsidy through the banking system (rather than the government budget) for loss-making firms.

In recent years, the central government has restricted the banking sector from making major reforms assuming that this is perhaps the only leverage still at its disposal. During the 1990 retrenchment, the central government tried to revoke fiscal revenue-sharing schemes and to re-centralize investment decisions, but it failed after encountering strong opposition from the governors of the provinces. The only institutional reversal achieved during that period was the re-centralization of the banking system, moving back to credit quotas control, eliminating much of the floating interest rate, and re-centralizing personnel appointment and supervision from local government to the central bank. However, sticking to the old credit quotas system will not help in an already largely decentralized economy. Better financial control and a stable economy cannot be achieved unless the financial system is reformed and the control mechanism is changed.

Behaviour of State Banks

Chinese economists consider one of the most serious problems with state banks is the mixing of policy-oriented loans and profit-oriented loans in specialized banks. This is, by far, one of the most important institutional reasons for pervasive moral hazard problems in Chinese banking. Reform has set a clear objective for enterprises: to maximize profits (whether it is achieved is another matter), and incentives are offered to meet that goal. This is not the case in the banking sector. As the rest of the economy is focusing on how to make enterprises more profitable, the banks are debating whether they should maximize profits.[4]

Partly due to distorted prices and partly because of the importance of structural adjustment and priority industries, the government insists that loans should be granted not for reasons of profitability but as 'policy loans' (*zhengcexing daikuan*). The government is also concerned that it will suffer a loss of control if specialized banks become autonomous, profit-seeking commercial banks. This concern has increased given the already decentralized fiscal system mentioned above.

However, this practice appears to be responsible for the moral hazard problem and the loss of effective control in several ways. First, it becomes difficult to monitor diversion of funds from a less to a more profitable use if the same bank is responsible for both policy lending and commercial lending. This undermines the intention of structural adjustment and investments in priority industries because badly needed policy loans are not necessarily channelled to intended users. Instead, they are often diverted to other more profitable projects by banks. For example, agricultural credit is diverted for industrial use or for real estate, so that the government has to pay an IOU to farmers for grain procurement. This became a serious national problem in 1992.

Second, all levels of government constantly intervene in the operation of banks in the name of policy lending. The relationship between banks

---

[4] The governor of the PBC stated plainly in 1991 that: 'Banks are not only commercial entities conducting banking business but are also units empowered by the state to undertake policy lending—specialized banks are not supposed to operate for profit only or, rather, they are required to take on certain functions of macroeconomic regulation and control.' As late as in December 1992 when another new wave of economic reform was under way, the Chinese Premier still insisted that specialized banks should be responsible for structural adjustment and policy loans in the near future (*People's Daily*, 26 December 1992).

and the government is complicated due to the multi-layer multi-regional organization of China's economy—the deep 'M-form' hierarchy (Qian and Xu, 1993). Local bank branches are under so-called 'dual subordination' (*shuangchong lingdao*): they are subordinated to the banking hierarchy (to the higher level of the specialized bank and to the same level of the PBC branch), they are also under the leadership of the same level of local government. The influence of the local government can be seen at two points in time: *ex ante*, local governments are directly involved in credit plan formulation, in some cases, local governments are inclined to impose loans on specialized banks. *Ex post*, the local government can decide whether to let the enterprise pay back the loan or not; conflicts between the local finance department and bank branches may arise over this issue. The power of local governments comes from their power to make appointments and to allocate housing and other benefits.[5]

Third, an objective measurement of performance is difficult to achieve (if not impossible) when banks are obliged to extend loans to both money-losing and money-making projects, and their decisions are under constant government intervention. In such cases, if bank managers make loans to risky or bad projects, their incompetence can be easily disguised and their losses will most likely be excused. For this reason, bank managers often object to taking policy lending away from their banks, a seemingly paradoxical phenomenon. During 1985–90, specialized banks received credits from the PBC at a below-market rate which accounted for about a quarter to a third of their total assets (IMF, 1993). Heavy central bank lending is perhaps normal in a high growth period. But given the moral hazard problems described above, a high level of soft credit from the central bank may become an important source of soft budget problems at banks, which in turn become a source of soft budget problems at enterprises.

One of the alarming signals of the banking system is fast decapitalization, as both bad loans and the cost of capital increase, a result of imbalanced reform in favour of the deposit side together with the high remittance rate of bank profit to the Ministry of Finance (bank profits are taxed at 62 per cent). In only six years between 1985 and 1991, the capital to asset ratio of the specialized banks fell from 9.6 per cent to 6.1 per cent. Because Chinese banks are not allowed to write off bad loans easily, the net value of the state banks is questionable. Privately, Chinese economists estimated that bad loans account for more than 20 per cent of the total outstanding bank loans. If that is true and if all bad loans are

---

[5] In a survey of 10 cities experimenting with financial reforms, the ICBC found that local government officials imposed policy loans on local bank branches for 73 per cent of the category of technical renovation loans in 1986 (Wu, 1990). The Party branch affiliations of bank officials are with the local Party Committee, in which the organization department controls appointments. This system was changed after re-centralization in 1988.

written off, the net worth of every specialized bank would be negative. This may be less serious than it sounds because the banks are owned by the government anyway. Nevertheless, it poses a serious problem for the government's already troubled budget.

The Rise of 'Outside-the-Plan' Intermediaries

The rise of the outside-the-plan financial intermediaries has been a major event in financial institutional development in the past few years and could have profound consequences on the economy. Most of them are different from the state banks not so much because of ownership but because of control: they are generally subject to less regulation than state banks. Therefore, they are flexible in their financial activities, and have expanded quickly in recent years, especially in 1992.

Rural and urban credit cooperatives contribute to financing the non-state sector. The reserves-deposit ratio of rural credit cooperatives with the Agricultural Bank of China declined gradually from about 78 per cent in 1979 to about 34 per cent in 1991, and more loans are extended to township-village enterprises than to households (Table 16.8). Recently, foreign banks have been allowed to establish branches in some areas in China, but domestic non-state banks are not yet seen.

Most trust investment corporations are fully controlled subsidiaries of bank branches. Such a practice features what the Chinese call 'one

TABLE 16.8 China: Rural Credit Cooperative Activities
(billion yuan)

	Total Deposit	Loan to Households	Loan to TVEs	Loan to Collective Agriculture	Total Loans as a % of Total Deposits
1979	21.59	1.09	1.42	2.24	22.00
1980	27.23	1.60	3.11	3.45	29.97
1981	31.96	2.52	3.55	3.57	30.16
1982	38.99	4.41	4.23	3.48	31.08
1983	48.74	7.54	6.01	2.82	33.59
1984	62.49	18.11	13.5	3.84	56.73
1985	72.49	19.42	16.44	4.14	55.18
1986	96.23	25.80	26.59	4.46	59.08
1987	122.52	34.76	35.93	6.45	62.96
1988	139.98	37.24	45.61	8.01	64.91
1989	166.95	41.57	57.19	10.73	65.58
1990	214.49	51.82	76.07	13.41	65.88
1991	270.93	63.14	100.73	16.99	66.76

Source: *Statistical Yearbook of China, 1992.*

factory, two systems', that is, one part is under a planned system and the other is under a market system.[6] Although both banks and their affiliates remain state owned, the affiliated trust corporations are much less controlled by the government and are flexible in providing badly needed financing; they are, to a large extent, market led.

Qian and Stigliz (1993) found several interesting financial practices in the Pearl River delta of Guangdong province in their field studies in December 1992. For example, bank deposits were often diverted to the banks' affiliated trust investment corporations and loans were renamed 'trust investments'; bank branches or their trust investment corporations sometimes channelled funds directly between enterprises to avoid credit limits, so they provided a brokerage service; and banks helped firms by arranging bond financing, also to avoid credit quotas. Lou (1993) reported several other practices in China. In one incident, a bank-industry joint venture was formed in which the industrial enterprise deposited 50 million yuan and borrowed 80 million from the bank, but the amount borrowed was treated as an investment not as a bank loan. In another case, a bank affiliated trust investment corporation imposed fixed payments in a specific time period so that it was an investment in name, but a loan in practice. In fact, about 50 per cent of the financial sources of banks' affiliated trust investment corporations came from banks and other financial intermediaries and only 45 per cent came from direct trust deposits. The widespread practice of disguised credit expansion in the presence of credit quotas is reflected in the consolidated balance sheet of the banks in a curious way: a negative 150 billion yuan was registered on the liability side at the end of August 1992, which makes the amount of total assets look smaller.

From the microeconomic point of view, the rise of outside-the-plan financial intermediaries is an institutional innovation in response both to economic development and the constraints of the old system. At the same time, the moral hazard problems of bank managers are also pervasive: it is easy to divert state funds to private pockets to enable a spontaneous privatization. From the macroeconomic perspective, it may become a factor that destabilizes the economy if the central bank fails to react accordingly.

The Relationship Between Banks and State-Owned Enterprises

Financial system reforms cannot be separated from enterprise reforms. The failure of state-owned enterprises is partly a failure of the state bank-

---

[6] This practice started, and became quite common, in the industrial sector. State-owned enterprises set up fully controlled subsidiaries but register them as having collective ownership, or they establish joint ventures with another state or non-state-owned enterprise. These collectives and joint ventures are not under the control of the government. Similar practices in Hungary are called 'partial transformation', which is considered to have a tendency toward spontaneous privatization (Frydman and others, 1993).

ing system and vice versa. A great problem concerning state-owned enterprises is known as the problem of soft budget constraint (Kornai, 1992). The situation is a familiar one: when a state-owned enterprise is in financial trouble, the government, very often a state bank, steps in to rescue it by refinancing the investment or by rescheduling the overdue loans. Therefore, few bankruptcies of state-owned enterprises occur despite the passage of the Law on Bankruptcy by the People's Congress in December 1986. Managers in state-owned enterprises react to the soft budget constraint problem opportunistically: they undertake every possible investment project regardless of its profitability, which leads to 'investment hunger'. As a consequence of the soft budget constraint, investment is inefficient and completion of a project is slow.

Therefore, loss making and soft budget constraints are mutually supporting equilibrium phenomena: because of the soft budget constraint, there are more projects generating a loss; because of projects making a loss, subsidies are provided and the budget is soft. Most losses occur in the state sector. On paper, loss-making state-owned enterprises accounted for one-third of all state-owned firms; but the number may be underestimated, as there are many ways to disguise loss-making simply by playing accounting tricks. (For more information on China's loss-making firms, see Sicular, 1992.)

TABLE 16.9 China: Subsidies to Money-Losing Enterprises from the State Budget

	1986	1987	1988	1989	1990	1991
Subsidies (billion yuan)	32.48	37.64	44.65	59.89	57.89	50.64
As per cent of Budgetary Revenue	14.37	15.89	16.99	20.32	17.48	14.02

Source: Statistical Yearbook of China, 1992.

There are basically two channels for an enterprise to finance losses (or two sources for the soft budget constraint of enterprises): either through the state budgetary process (subsidies or reduction of taxes), or through the banking system. The annual subsidies to enterprises from the state budget account for more than 15 per cent of budgetary revenue each year since 1986, peaking at 20 per cent in 1989 (Table 16.9). As government budgetary revenue declined, the government increasingly pressed the banking system to take responsibility. Soft credit has become a main source of the soft budget constraint. A recent survey reveals that between 1986 and 1988, 229 of 403 (56.8 per cent) large and medium state-owned enterprises investigated had experienced difficulty in repaying loans.

TABLE 16.10 China: Methods of Bailing-Out Loss-Making Firms

Bailed-out firms	Loan repayment before taxes*	Extending repayment period	Rollover of the loans	Reducing the amount owed	Other methods
Number	98	60	24	3	18
Per cent	48.3	29.6	11.8	1.5	8.9

According to the Chinese tax law, there is no interest deduction, that is, loans should be repaid out of profit after tax. There are 229 firms in all.

Source: Survey sponsored by the Ford Foundation, 1990.

Furthermore, 203 enterprises had received assistance from their superiors, of which 48 per cent was loan repayment before taxes, 30 per cent was on extension of the repayment period, and 12 per cent was a roll over of loans. (Table 16.10).[7]

It is not surprising that overdue (*yuqi*) and non-performing loans (*daizhang*) grew rapidly. However, there is no published information; even worse, there is no clear definition of bad debts in the Chinese accounting system in the first place. The situation became much worse between 1989 and 1991. The increase of loss-making enterprises and weak market demand in 1989–91 also created a national problem of inter-enterprise arrears amounting to about 200 billion yuan: the government has injected 35 billion yuan into the economy to help settle this problem. Jump-starting the troubled enterprises is only a temporary solution, it also intensifies the problem of the soft budget constraint.

Unlike many financial rescue cases reported in Japan, no restructuring of state-owned firms (for example, replacement of management) has ever happened after financial assistance has been given in China—and the same symptoms are repeated. It is now widely recognized that the problem of soft budget constraint is a major obstacle to reform in virtually all socialist countries in transition, not just China. At the centre of the problem is the fact that the state bank is unable to make a credible commitment not to rescue enterprises in financial trouble. Although there are external reasons for the increase of loss-making—for example, the auster-

---

[7] The survey was conducted jointly by the Institute of Economics of the Chinese Academy of Social Sciences, Oxford University, University of Michigan and University of California (San Diego) under the sponsorship of the Ford Foundation.

In a separate study, Bowles and White (1989) identified numerous cases from the official newspapers and journal articles published in China in recent years about the soft credit relationship between state banks and state firms. They concluded that 'if the intention of the banking reforms has been to harden enterprise credit constraints by increasing the autonomy and commercial orientation of the banks, the evidence to date, after eight years of reform, suggests that this has not been realized. In fact, the credit constraint may have become softer.'

ity programme in 1989–91 in China—the fundamental reason is an institutional one, concerning the problems of ownership, control, and the governance structure of enterprises and banks, as is discussed later.

FINANCIAL REFORM FROM EVOLUTIONARY AND COMPARATIVE PERSPECTIVES

Despite considerable progress made in financial reforms during the past 14 years, the financial system in China as a whole has not yet been transformed into a market-oriented system. Major institutional restructuring is necessary now before it is too late. Compared to Eastern Europe and the former Soviet Union, China enjoys several advantages, but it also faces its own economic and political constraints. It is likely that institutional restructuring in the next five years must be carried out in an environment where most banks and large-scale enterprises remain state owned. The choice of the model financial system and the transitional path may affect not only the short-run cost but also the long-run performance of the economy. Careful evaluation and analysis of alternatives and their feasibility for China is important.

Development of Security Markets

For the past few years, China has experienced several waves of 'stock fever'. The enthusiasm (perhaps over-enthusiasm) for stocks and bonds in China has several reasons which are mainly related to incompleteness of reform. First, issuing undervalued stocks and bonds is a method of 'spontaneous privatization', and hence the stock market serves as a channel to transfer assets from the state to individuals and to capitalize the gains obtained from privatization. In such a process, employees are usually given the privilege of buying their own shares at a price discounted from face value (par), which is already much undervalued. Managers gain even more: turning a firm into a joint stock company and listing it on the stock market is more than fund raising, it is a way to avoid government interference in business and to get control rights to the company. As capital market discipline is unlikely in the near future, managers will get effective control and handsome rents if shareholding is widespread. Investors are also eager to buy shares in initial public offerings (but much less so in the secondary market) because, typically, stock is sold to the public at five to six times its face value, and its price rises to more than 10 times immediately after trading begins. At the initial experiment stage, all stock issues were carefully selected and they were the best projects available. Partly because these are experiments, the government feels obliged to back up the new institution.

Second, from the point of view of local governments and enterprises, direct financing from employees or the public is a practical way to meet the pressing need for raising funds for rapid development in the presence of an unreformed and inefficient state banking system. As an official from the Guangdong Provincial Government said 'Given the current institutional constraints, it is better to raise funds directly from investors than to rely on inefficient state banks.' This argument is reinforced by the fact that the central bank in China still relies on credit quotas as the main control mechanism. Hence direct financing through bonds and stocks is a way to circumvent credit limits imposed by the central government. Given the delay of reforms to the banking system, which needs the central government's initiative (local governments are not allowed to establish their own banks), direct financing through stocks and bonds is a natural response. Some economists are in favour of developing the stock market as a first priority for similar reasons: it is relatively easier to develop new institutions than to reform old ones (like banks) because the former do not require the central government's initiative and can be established in isolation from the rest of the system.

There is no doubt that China should develop security markets for both equities and bonds. However, it is unlikely that the stock market will play a major role in allocating financial resources in the next 10 years, because China is still at a low stage of development and a stock market takes a long time to become established. There are also special problems associated with transition, which makes it difficult for a stock market to work efficiently in the initial stage. First, the purpose of a stock market is to facilitate risk sharing and supply information that helps discipline management and increase profit opportunities. A key feature of transition from a planned to a market economy is the unusual degree of uncertainty. The absence of trained analysts and reliable accounting data deprives stock prices of most of their informational content in the noisy environment, and price fluctuations are unlikely to reflect the fundamental value of the company or measure managerial performance accurately. This disables the stock market's capacity to monitor and discipline managers. Garbled stock market prices may also give the wrong signals for restructuring (Tirole, 1991).

Second, the volatile nature of a stock market, plus the lack of regulation in the initial phase of transition, will attract scarce, talented people away from productive activities. Instead, they will be drawn to speculative and rent-seeking activities in security exchanges by using inside information, or by manipulating the market, or both. There is little social gain from such speculative trading in a noisy environment.

Third, many state-owned enterprises have accumulated a large amount of bad debts and it will be difficult to attract investors because, as residual claimants, they have low priority in claims. Therefore, for a majority of state-owned enterprises, going to the stock market is perhaps not a realistic option.

Nevertheless, market financing for those cream of the crop enterprises makes more sense. The recent successful initial public offerings by two Chinese state-owned enterprises on the New York Stock Exchange and the Hong Kong Stock Exchange demonstrated this potential. However, it should be noted that both enterprises are in the automobile industry, which is perceived to have great potential in China. Brilliance, Inc., which owns a company making mini-buses in Shenyang, was the first Chinese company listing on the New York Stock Exchange (October 1992). Denway Investment, which owns a car-manufacturing company in Guangzhou, was oversubscribed by 657 times on its initial public offering on the Hong Kong Stock Exchange in February 1993.

The Case for a Bank-Oriented Financial System in China

While development of a stock market is clearly important, the highest priority should be placed on the reform and adaptation of the commercial banking system (Corrigan, 1992). But reshaping the banking system is a more difficult task, and in this aspect, China can learn a lot from the Japanese experience. The Japanese development experience has been carefully studied by Chinese economists and government officials. Attention so far has been confined mainly to the roles of the Ministry of International Trade and Industry (MITI) for industrial policies, of the Economic Planning Agency (EPA) for indicative planning, and of the industrial grouping and interlocking shareholding inside a keiretsu. The experience of the Japanese financial system (including the main bank system) has yet to receive much attention.

It is important to realize that the Japanese main bank system has evolved in a market environment and was not imposed by the government (as in South Korea). Nevertheless, the Japanese government did play an important role in designing the institutional framework during the initial stage, such as setting up development banks and creating an environment that enabled commercial banks gradually to take over development bank loans. From both evolutionary and comparative perspectives, the Japanese experience is relevant for China's financial system reforms in several important aspects.

First, restructuring China's banking system by studying the Japanese experience can better utilize existing organizational capital; the transition can be made more gradually, and institutional transformation less costly. China's 14 years of reform have shown that a gradual and evolutionary approach in institutional transformation has the benefit of reduced risks and better use of existing organizational capital. The four specialized banks already have a vast number of branches throughout the country, and their personnel are learning market economics by practising economic reform. Even before the economic reforms, each PBC branch with whom an enterprise had a designated account had a responsibility to monitor enterprises on transactions, levels of inventory, wage and bonus bills, and the like, to ensure they were within the scope of the plan. This monitoring was very close before the reform. For example, bank branches had to make sure that every transaction over 50 yuan was conducted through a bank transfer, and that enterprises in areas where a bank branch was located did not hold more than three days' cash requirements. Of course, this monitoring was more gathering information than exercising control. Transforming the four specialized banks into commercial banks on the Japanese city bank model will be less costly and faster than destroying the existing system and building everything anew.

Second, scarcity of expertise and human capital in the financial sector is one of the major constraints in China. The Japanese financial system concentrates scarce expertise in the banking sector and uses it in an effective way. Integrated monitoring by the main bank uses scarce monitoring resources to better advantage (see Chapter 4 by Aoki). It also serves to reduce information asymmetry and to achieve better coordination in an environment where other institutional supports are lacking. In addition, repeated interactions between monitors and the monitored will help to develop reputations which are extremely valuable in the noisy environment of transition where enforcement of law and contracts needs time to develop.

Third, China demands a high growth rate, close to 10 per cent per year, for the next 5 to 10 years. This is not unrealistic, given that the average growth rate has been close to 9 per cent for the past 14 years and the continued high savings rate of more than 35 per cent of GNP. The Japanese financial system successfully supported double-digit growth from the 1950s to the mid-70s, and the Japanese government, mainly the Ministry of Finance and the Bank of Japan, played an important role in this. The Japanese development banks and long-term credit banks were instrumental in financing priority industries to avoid coordination failures of the market and to escape the under-development trap. The Japanese government also maintained a business-like relationship with banks; they tended to collaborate and cooperate with, rather than being hostile to, the banks. The government's involvement is particularly valuable and less costly at the initial stage of development, because this is the time when the market is less developed, when the task of catching up is relatively simple, and the technology used is not at the frontier. As the economy becomes more mature, the relative advantage of government intervention may recede.

Fourth, firms in China need to acquire new technology, to streamline the work force, and to develop new corporate governance structures.

Given the current political constraint, a Chinese-style ownership reform will mainly include: corporatization (reorganization of state-owned enterprises into limited liability or joint stock companies); joint ventures (between state-owned and foreign firms); mergers and acquisition (by non-state firms like township and village enterprises); and sales and repackaging of some small and medium firms into private, cooperative, or worker-controlled firms. A bank-oriented financial system is compatible with a variety of property ownership arrangements, and this flexibility is valuable in the transition period.

One feature of the Japanese main bank system is the bank's role in corporate governance. Banks use their expertise, resources, and information to help corporations in restructuring and investment decisions, particularly at critical times. In this context, the Japanese banking system, as opposed to arm's-length banking systems, is a useful model in two ways. One is for the bank to play a role in the transformation process itself; banks may contribute to evaluation of assets, settlement of bad loans, provision of ideas for new organizational forms, and the like. The other is the banks' role in corporate governance through taking equity positions.

Finally, historically, the current Japanese financial system evolved during and after the war-time economy, which shares several features with the contemporary Chinese economy: considerable concentration of the banking system; allocation of funds by government authorities; massive debts of firms; enormous demands for restructuring; and the critical situation of the government budget. Banks started to play an active role in corporate governance as a tight fiscal policy was imposed and the bad debts of corporations were removed in the post-war reconstruction period. The historical similarities suggest that China may benefit more from adopting features of the Japanese financial model than from other models in achieving its objective of restructuring the corporate sector while stabilizing its economy.[8]

Of course differences exist between Japan and China, which tend either to limit the scope of applicability of the Japanese experience to China, or to require China to take additional steps in order for the assumed benefits to be realized. First of all, banks in Japan, except for the development banks, are all privately owned, including the long-term credit

[8] In a different opinion, Scott (1992) recommended that the transitional objectives of restructuring enterprises be pursued by non-bank financial institutions (like mutual funds and trust companies), in order to ensure that the banking system achieved its fundamental objectives of maintaining the integrity of the payments system and the safety of depositors' savings. Maintaining the soundness of the banking system is indeed a primary concern for reforming the financial system. On the other hand, if banks lack managerial capacity and supervision skills for restructuring, as argued by Scott, it is even less clear how the newly established non-bank financial institutions acquire such capacity and skills in the short run other than by hiring foreign managers.

banks and city banks. Government agencies like the Ministry of Finance and Bank of Japan concentrate on regulatory issues; they do not have to worry about the profit motives of bank owners. Because all banks in China are state owned, bank managers' concern about profitability cannot be taken for granted. Governance structures must be created so that control will reside in those who benefit most from the banks' profits.

Second, the Japanese financial system has worked well in an environment of a sound fiscal system together with government budget surplus (up to 1975). In contrast, China's fiscal system still needs major reforms before the trend of declining government revenue can be halted and the government budget deficit comes under control. As mentioned earlier, the government's budget revenue has continued to decline and the deficit to rise in recent years. However, this is just part of the story. More frequently, governments at all levels tend to force the banks to make 'policy loans' for items that are supposed to be taken care of by the budget. Bad loans are less transparent than a budget deficit: this essentially has the effect of depleting bank capital, and will eventually show up in the government budget. Without a sound fiscal system and prudent fiscal policy, the functioning of the main bank system might be seriously undermined. Therefore, financial reform requires complementary reforms in the fiscal sector and a prudent fiscal policy to reduce pressure on the banking system.

Third, China is much larger than Japan and regional variations are much greater. Therefore, China needs more decentralization.

Finally, China's firms tend to be small scale and Chinese industries are not very concentrated. Also Chinese people are more family oriented and less organization oriented than the Japanese. For this reason, informal financial institutions may play a greater role in China.

RESTRUCTURING CHINA'S FINANCIAL SYSTEM: THE NEXT STAGE

Banks differ from ordinary manufacturing firms in that most of their claimholders, that is, depositors, are highly dispersed, which makes monitoring of bank behaviour extremely difficult. With private ownership, the owners of the bank (its capital account) care about returns to their assets, and therefore its profitability. Even in this case, government regulation and monitoring are required because owners may pursue investments contrary to depositors' interests, or if depositors are insured by the government, contrary to the public's interest. When the banks are owned by the state, the government itself may become a serious problem because it often has multiple objectives like macroeconomic stability, industrial policies, and employment, along with concerns for profitability. Hence, institutional re-arrangement is needed to mitigate agency costs and reduce the risks inherent in the financial system.

In this section, I make suggestions for institutional changes in the next stage of China's financial restructuring, to be completed, say, within three years from 1994 to 1996. This includes dividing responsibility for the fiscal sector and the financial sector; reorganizing the central bank and restructuring its control mechanism; and establishing decentralized multi-tier financial intermediaries. The last consists of development banks; commercialized national banks; second-tier regional banks and non-state banks; non-bank financial intermediaries; and informal financial institutions. (Other financial institutions, such as security companies and investment banks, are beyond the scope of this chapter.) The proposed institutional changes are intended to be realistic, practical, and implementable. At the same time, they also represent a pivotal and significant step in the transition to a market-oriented financial system.

Division of Responsibility between the Fiscal and Financial Sectors

In Japan, the Ministry of Finance, the Bank of Japan, and other regulatory agencies are all active in financial regulation but each has different responsibilities. With a sound fiscal system, the Ministry of Finance was able to maintain a budget surplus for a long period of time and therefore the government had no need to borrow from the central bank. Differing from many other countries, the Ministry of Finance played an important role in regulating banks and, in that context, it often exercised some rights of control as well, such as replacement of bank managers or granting more branch operations as a reward. But the Bank of Japan, like other central banks, operates through the market with the main objective of maintaining stability—stability in the purchasing power of the currency and stability of the workings of the financial system. The Bank of Japan did rediscount loans from commercial banks in support of some activities like exports, in particular in the high growth period when demand for money increased rapidly. Nevertheless, it was the responsibility of the commercial banks to make independent lending decisions.

In the current framework, the PBC combines the functions of a central bank, the government financial regulatory agency, and the supervising agency of the specialized banks exercising control rights on behalf of the state. The central bank's mission has at least two facets: it is responsible for macroeconomic management as well as for policy lending for structural adjustment (Lou, 1993). The central bank and its branches allocate the task of policy lending to specialized banks, and make policy loans directly in some cases as well. Recently, the central bank has even operated its own security companies. In the past 14 years China has moved from one extreme to the other: from the situation in which most finance comes from the state budget to one where most finance is bank loans.

In China, a clear division of responsibility between the fiscal and financial sectors should be a priority. A pre-condition for a good financial system is a sound fiscal system, and hence a reformed fiscal system is a prerequisite for financial reforms. First, the banking system should not assume fiscal responsibility. If there is no particular reason for policy lending (such as an important ongoing relationship), then subsidies should be channelled through the budget. The fiscal channel is much more transparent and therefore may be subject to better discipline. Nevertheless, such a change may mean an increase in the budget deficit in the short run, but that is no more than a transformation of implicit into explicit deficit. Second, tax reform is needed to ensure a sound base for government revenue. Third, in the case of a budget deficit, to avoid inflation, bond financing should be preferred to direct borrowing from the central bank.

It should be emphasized that the current definition of 'policy loans' in China is too broad. It essentially has two distinct categories: subsidies and loans for development purposes. The former includes subsidies to agricultural products through procurement and subsidies to state-owned enterprises due to price distortions or inefficient operation. Funds for the latter category should be used for infrastructure or priority industrial investment. The conceptual distinction between the two categories has important practical implications: a subsidy is a fiscal matter and should be financed from the budget and administered by an agency under the Ministry of Finance. Subsidies should not be treated as loans. Only loans for development purposes can be labelled 'policy loans', to be managed by development banks, as discussed below.

Finally, because China is much larger than Japan, more independent regulatory agencies might be needed to reduce the work load of the Ministry of Finance. In October 1992, regulation of security markets was transferred to a newly established agency, the State Security Exchange Commission, but regulation of security companies is still under the central bank. In fact, most security companies are subsidiaries of specialized banks or their branches. Furthermore, the People's Bank of China is also the supervising agency of the banks, which gives it the authority to exercise rights of control and to engage in micro intervention. This may undermine the central bank's ability to maintain stability. Therefore, ownership and control of the state banks should be shifted to an agency with strong profit motives, for example, the State Assets Management Commission (SAMC).

The Central Bank's Control Mechanisms in Transition

Eventually, the central bank will apply indirect monetary instruments to achieve macroeconomic management by adjustment of the discount rate and reserve requirements, and through open market operations. But it would be unwise to jump into that position in one step. There are two special problems in the case of China that Japan and many other developing countries do not have.

One problem has to do with the still large state sector. Although using credit quotas is a crude and indiscriminate mechanism, it is perhaps more effective in dealing with the state sector than any other instrument when the demand for investment is hard to curtail. It might well be the case that imposing credit quotas is the only effective way to constrain the state sector from expanding, because many state-owned firms are not sensitive to interest rates if they face a soft budget constraint. Enforcing strict credit quotas is one way to harden the budget constraint. Both Lau (1992) and McKinnon (1992a) are in favour of putting quota limits on state-owned firms' borrowing. The Bank of Japan for a long time used credit quotas, but as a supplementary, not as a main, control means.

Another unique situation in China is its fast process of monetization and financial deepening as the economy moves away from central planning to a decentralized market (Tables 14.5 and 14.6). As the velocity of money slows rapidly, setting a monetary target may be difficult, if not impossible. In this event, targeting a real interest rate is a better alternative (Lau, 1992). For example, the nominal interest rate can be indexed to the consumer price index, and targeted at say, 2 to 3 per cent above the inflation rate. Even in the United States, recent experience shows that adopting a monetary target may be less useful.

Another control instrument used by the central bank is lending to specialized banks (about a third of their total liabilities). During the high growth period, the central bank had to supply credit to meet increased demand for money. If the Japanese experience is relevant, the central bank should not be directly involved in policy lending or the direct supply of credit to specialized banks, instead, it should rediscount loans already made by the specialized banks.

Underlying the control mechanism is the institutional issue of the reorganization of the central bank. At the moment, the People's Bank of China has more than 160,000 employees and has branches down to the county level, the largest network in the world. The system is also very localized in the way the credit plan is balanced by regions through provincial branches of the PBC. Provincial branches of specialized banks hold reserves with provincial branches of the central bank; the reserve requirement and reallocation of credit are segmented across regions. This is rooted in the 'deep M-form' (the multi-layer-multi-regional form) of hierarchical organization in China (Qian and Xu, 1993). As a result, provincial branches of the central bank often form an alliance with provincial governments, and ignore instructions from Beijing.

To prevent localization of the central bank system by the provinces, a trans-province regionally based central banking system like the US Federal Reserve System could be a better choice for China. This means that the central bank establishes headquarters in seven or eight large regions (*daqu*) consisting of three or four neighbouring provinces. With such a scheme, a dramatic reduction in the number of employees and branches of the PBC is required. It seems appropriate to eliminate branches of the PBC at the county and municipality levels, and to consolidate provincial branches into large regional headquarters and their local offices.

Separation of Policy Lending from Commercial Lending: Establishment of Development Banks and Commercialization of Specialized Banks

One of the first priorities on the reform agenda is to remove policy lending from the portfolio of specialized banks and assign that task exclusively to newly established development banks. This is particularly important for China precisely because all other banks are also state owned. As analysed in the second section, pervasive moral hazard problems when policy and commercial lending are combined are the prime reasons for the inefficiency of the banking system at the current time. Because up to 40 per cent of loans are policy loans, it is impossible to impose a hard budget constraint on the specialized banks which, in turn, have no incentives to harden the budget constraints of firms.

Externalities and spill-over effects are strong at a low stage of economic development when the market is incomplete and selective policy lending (development loan) may become a catalyst for take-off. In Japan, development banks played an important role in transforming an economy with limited resources by setting priorities and performing indicative planning. An important point of the Japanese experience is that development bank loans were gradually taken over by commercial banks and there was an exchange of information between the Japan Development Bank and commercial banks (see Chapter 4 by Aoki).

The fact that the Chinese economy is still in the process of reform provides additional reasons for policy lending. Not only are some prices still distorted, but more significantly, there is a great demand for experimenting, for learning, and for building up the institutional infrastructure of the market system. To achieve this, there is an urgent need to establish one or several development banks with the explicit mission of lending for development and not for profit maximization. However, the amount of policy lending should be dramatically reduced from the current level of

40 per cent, given the moral hazard problems analysed above. At the present stage of economic development, the activities of development banks in China may include projects in transportation, communications, energy, and high risk, high tech industries, as well as for restructuring and building market institutions.[9]

China can learn from the Japanese experience in setting up development banks. The JDB was founded in 1951 with some employees transferred from the IBJ. It obtained trust funds from the government, which in turn obtained funds, in part, from the postal savings system. The average holding period of postal saving certificates was long, about 3.84 years in 1965, as opposed to 0.85 of a year for bank savings (Yasuda, 1992). China's new development bank could be built on the same basis as the People's Construction Bank of China and the six investment corporations under the State Planning Commission. Because China has already established a nationwide postal savings network, it is also possible to channel some of those funds to development banks. However, to the extent that loans of development banks are long term, they should be matched by long-term deposits.

With all policy lending removed, the four specialized banks should be made ordinary profit-seeking commercial banks. There are three aspects associated with this change. First, the central bank, as well as other central and local government agencies, should stop interfering with the detailed business activities of banks. In particular, the government and the central bank should not direct credit allocation and decisions. Banks can be incorporated into limited liability or joint-stock companies; the board of directors could be chosen from public institutions concerned with the profit and stability of banks, such as officials from the SAMC, as well as academic financial experts. Incorporation can to some degree shield the management of banks from frequent government intervention and also make the future transfer or sale of partial shares of the banks easy.

Second, banks should be held accountable for their actions, and a hard budget constraint should be placed on them. After having provided the initial capital, the government should not provide additional funds. Because of the expected fast growth in the next 5 to 10 years, credit from the central bank to commercial banks will continue, but that credit should be provided at the market interest rate and preferably in the form of rediscounting commercial loans. This is to ensure that no soft credit is given to the commercial banks by the central bank. There is an implicit

---

[9] The combined share of outstanding equipment loans by JDB and IBJ reached a peak at about 50 per cent in 1955, and were respectively 21.7 per cent and 18.1 per cent in 1960. The combined share declined to 22.4 per cent at the end of 1970. JDB loans were concentrated in transport, energy, and key industries like steel and chemicals (see Chapter 4 by Aoki).

deposit insurance under traditional state ownership of banks. However, an explicit deposit insurance programme is needed to safeguard depositors' funds after specialized banks are commercialized.

Third, in order to judge the managerial performance of banks, the state banks should be allowed to operate in overlapping business areas so that idiosyncratic uncertainty can be identified. Profitability should reflect good performance rather than random events, and reward or punishment can provide the correct incentives. This reflects the informational role of competition discussed in Holmstrom (1982). Overlapping business is also desirable for a bank's risk diversification as well as for mitigating the soft budget constraint problem of exclusive relational banking.

Decentralization of the Banking System: Establishment of Second-Tier Banking

Although commercialized national banks will be the core of the commercial banking system in China, there is plenty of room for regional banks and further expansion of non-state banks and credit cooperatives. At present, only some coastal provinces have regional banks; provincial branches of the Bank of Communication are joint stock banks with local governments holding significant interests and they are to a large extent regional banks. Several reasons support the proposition that regional banks are important for regional development: the huge size of the country; great regional variations; and local aspirations for regional development. Regional banks in Japan provided 14 per cent of short-term loans to listed firms in manufacturing and they play an even more important role in serving medium and small firms.

It is often heard that the state banking system in China is already over-decentralized, referring to the fact local governments usually have effective control over local branches of both the central bank and specialized banks. However, this should be more precisely referred to as fragmentation. China clearly needs a centralized central banking system and centralized control within each of the four specialized banks (the future national banks), but at the same time, China also needs truly decentralized regional banks.

The role of this second-tier banking, regional banks, non-state banks, and credit cooperatives, is not just limited to the contribution of funds. It is important for the sake of the decentralization of the banking system, now dominated by the four specialized national banks. Decentralization not only creates a competitive environment, it also provides an alternative device for mitigating soft budget problems.

When soft budgeting is seen as an agency problem, the central issue becomes the lack of commitment by banks to stop bad projects when they are discovered. The problem arises in situations where sunk costs make it more efficient to refinance a project *ex post* even though it is not efficient to do so *ex ante*. Dewatripont and Maskin (1990) argue that a decentralized competitive banking system can be used as a commitment device against the soft budget constraint. The reason is that when a bank is relatively small and is constrained by a lack of available funds (that is, the bank does not have a deep pocket), then additional financing must come from another bank. Inefficient *ex post* renegotiation between the new and old banks (due to asymmetric information) reduce the returns the new bank may receive, thereby reducing its incentive to refinance.

Qian and Xu (1991) suggest that even if banks are large, renegotiating projects financed by several banks is more difficult than renegotiating projects financed by a single bank, which makes additional financing less likely and the budget constraint harder. It is interesting to note that in Japan, although main banks' monitoring is exclusive, there is no exclusive financing. Rather, many banks together provide syndicated loans to firms and delegate monitoring to the main bank. From this perspective, a more important benefit of allowing foreign banks to operate in China would be the achievement of credible commitment and the imposition of harsh discipline on managers, rather than bringing in capital.

One practical method for achieving fast decentralization of the banking system is to establish regional commercial banks using the employees and facilities of branches of the People's Bank of China at the county and municipality levels. As discussed previously, after the recommended reorganization of the central bank, those lower level branches will be abolished and the personnel will be released. There are two possible options. One is to set up province-based regional commercial banks with the current facilities of the PBC as the initial investment by the central government. The provincial government then injects additional funds to maintain its controlling interest in the bank. Better, regional commercial banks could be established (serving, say, three to four provinces) with no single province having a controlling share. This has the advantage of facilitating capital flows across provinces and preventing regional banks from investing in projects that are only of provincial interest. Either way, the proposed method could make the best use of existing institutions, it could reduce the cost of re-employment by engaging the redundant central bank employees, and could create a competitive banking environment relatively quickly.

Banks' Roles in Corporate Governance

One of the benefits of the Japanese main bank system is the monitoring and information-collecting roles of main banks (city banks and regional banks alike). At present, most Chinese firms have only one designated bank branch for settlement of accounts and loans. For a more active role by the banks in corporate governance, institutional changes are needed; the newly commercialized banks may be allowed to hold some equity in newly incorporated state firms. This can be done through debt-equity swaps, as there are so many non-performing loans.

The presumed role of banks in corporate control is clearly dependent on the establishment of a new corporate governance structure, known as corporatization. The discussion on new governance structures of state-owned enterprises dates back to 1985 (World Bank, 1985, chapter 10). The main idea is to mimic corporations in capitalist economies with shares held by many financial intermediaries like pension funds, mutual funds, insurance companies and holding companies. (To a large extent, the first stage of Lipton-Sachs' proposal (1990) of privatization for Poland (corporatization or commercialization) has similar ideas.) Although individuals are also allowed to hold shares in these financial intermediaries, the majority of shares are expected to be held by the SAMC, to which the public delegates the rights of ownership. A major enterprise reform plan along these lines is under study in Shanghai with assistance from the World Bank.

The problems with this kind of plan are twofold: first, it is not clear how the soft budget constraint problem can be solved or mitigated, and second, the role of the banks is missing. There is little evidence in the market economy, at least to date, that mutual funds, pension funds and other institutional investors closely monitor or actively participate in the control of corporations in which they have large shareholdings, although there are some indications of growing activism by some public pension funds in the United States. Under the current Chinese plan, holding companies and other institutional investors (equity holders) are supposed to have the responsibility of monitoring, but their effectiveness is doubtful. Furthermore, all these institutions need to be built from scratch, which is both costly and time consuming.

However, there already are banking institutions, and it would be economic to make the best use of them. In fact, banks are uniquely positioned to play a monitoring role, and together with other institutional investors are able to provide better discipline. As large debt holders, banks are more likely to be tough on managers than equity holders would be. In addition, banks can access information on the flow of funds in and out of a firm and may threaten to withhold or cut off credit at any moment (Scharfstein, 1992). By comparison, a holding company cannot engage in close monitoring on a routine basis and does not have the tools to discipline unless things are really getting out of hand. Of course, the holding company, as an owner, can take many steps that banks cannot. The point is that, in restructuring the governance structure of state-owned enterprises, balancing power between banks and other large institutional investors is useful.

Development and Regulation of Non-Bank Financial Intermediaries and Informal Financial Institutions

As emphasized earlier, non-bank financial institutions in China rose rapidly in recent years as a response to strict credit quotas imposed by the central bank. The financial activities of trust investment corporations and enterprise finance companies alike played an important role in supporting fast regional growth, and most of their activities were perfectly legal. In order to maintain macroeconomic stability in China, there is an urgent need for regulation to ensure a proper balance between the two sectors. In particular, non-bank institutions should not be *de facto* banks; that is, their liabilities should not be deposits in disguise.

The non-state sector is producing nearly one half of China's national industrial output and even more in terms of GNP, and the township-village-private enterprises in rural areas already contribute to about a quarter to a third of total industrial output and export. Nevertheless, total lending from all banks and rural credit cooperatives to the non-state sector (including agriculture) was rather small, only about 20 per cent of total loans outstanding in 1989 (Table 16.11). Formal financial institutions can seldom satisfy demand from small firms in any country at a low development stage. At present, about 70 per cent of industrial output in China is contributed by medium and small businesses. To the extent that they are a dominant force of China's emerging non-state sector, informal financial institutions should not be prohibited, but should be supported by the government.

Taiwan's case may be relevant in this context. In Taiwan, up to half of the domestic financing of the private sector came from the informal financial system in its early period of development, with an average of more than a third between 1964 and 1989 (Shea and Yen, 1991, table 4). One

TABLE 16.11 China: Lending to the Non-State Sector As Percentage of Total Outstanding Loans

	Urban Collectives	Urban Individuals	TVEs	Agriculture	Total
1985	4.95	0.17	5.63	6.85	17.60
1986	5.11	0.13	6.82	6.78	18.74
1987	5.47	0.16	7.25	7.28	20.16
1988	5.58	0.17	7.59	7.19	20.53
1989	5.15	0.11	7.39	7.12	19.77
1990	4.93	0.09	7.42	7.17	19.61
1991	4.74	0.08	7.63	7.39	19.84

Source: *Almanac of China's Finance and Banking, 1992.*

of the old problems with informal contracts, as opposed to formal ones, is enforcement. Family bonds have been an important enforcement mechanism in Chinese society. What is particularly interesting in Taiwan is the use of post-dated cheques and the government's willingness to punish the bouncing of cheques by imprisonment. The Taiwanese experience shows that informal financial institutions have been helpful in mobilizing savings and financing the needs of those enterprises discriminated against by formal financial institutions. The government should set rules and create an environment for streamlining the operations of informal financial institutions to improve their efficiency in allocating loans in the curb market. It should also be pointed out that in Japan too local credit banks for small businesses, which grew out of the pre-war local credit cooperatives, have played a very important role in the regional development of small businesses.

McKinnon (1992) is in favour of China's adoption of a type of dual financial system following the establishment of a proper tax system. He argues that the extensive use of informal non-bank financial institutions has an additional advantage for maintaining confidence and stability of the monetary payment system, if the formal banking system finances only low-risk projects while the high-risk projects will be financed by the non-bank informal institutions. However, the informal system tends to divert funds away from the formal sector, which undermines the government's ability to borrow from the banking system and consequently endangers the financial stability of the economy if a proper tax system is not in place.

On the one hand, the market-oriented non-state firms (and reformed state firms) would not be allowed to borrow from the state banks and could only raise funds from retained earnings and from non-bank and informal institutions; but, un-reformed state-firms would still have access to bank credits, and their activities would be strictly limited and monitored. It is hoped that the 'within-the-plan' system (the state banks and unreformed state-owned firms) and the 'outside-the-plan' system (non-bank financial institutions and non-state firms) would be insulated from each other, and the former would be phased out eventually. As discussed above, it is important to limit the credit available to unreformed state firms. The main difficulty with this arrangement, however, is how the intended insulation between the two systems is implemented. In fact, many township enterprises (perhaps not village or private enterprises) relied heavily on bank credits to grow (Zhou and Hu, 1987), and cutting off their access to bank credits might lead to undesirable consequences.

CONCLUSION

This chapter makes a case for China to adopt several institutional elements of the Japanese financial system in its next stage of financial system reforms. But the Japanese model cannot be, and should not be, applied in its entirety because of the differences between the two countries. Perhaps the most important lesson China can learn from Japan is Japan's willingness and ability to adapt, rather than simply copy, institutions found in other countries which are useful to its own particular situation. Institutional changes are complex and it is impossible to have complete knowledge of the true benefits and costs of institutional alternatives in advance. Learning by experimenting is an effective way to reduce uncertainty and costs. In this regard, maintaining the flexibility of institutions and adopting pragmatic attitudes provide an option for corrections and changes at a later stage. Given the vast size of China, a more diverse and decentralized system than the Japanese one is not just necessary, it is also beneficial.

REFERENCES

Almanac of China's Finance and Banking, 1990, 1991, 1992, Beijing.

BLEJER, MARIO, DAVID BURTON, STEVEN DUNAWAY, and GYORGY SZAPARY. 1991 January. 'China: Economic Reform and Macroeconomic Management.' Occasional Paper 76, International Monetary Fund, Washington DC.

BOWLES, PAUL and GORDON WHITE. 1989. 'Contradictions in China's Financial Reform: The Relationship between Banks and Enterprises.' *Cambridge Journal of Economics* 17: 481–95.

CHEN, XIWEN. 1993. 'Dangqian nongcun jingji de ruogan xinqingkuang' ('Several Recent New Developments in Rural Economies'). *Journal of Comparative Economic and Social Systems* 2, Beijing.

CORRIGAN, E. GERALD. 1990. 'The Role of Central Banks in Emerging Market Economies.' *Federal Reserve Bank of New York Quarterly Review* 15(2) (Summer).

DEWATRIPONT, MATHIAS and ERIC MASKIN. 1990. 'Credit and Efficiency in Centralized and Decentralized Economies.' Harvard University, Cambridge MA.

FELTENSTEIN, ANDREW, D. LEBOW, and SWEDER VAN WIJINBERGEN. 1986. 'Savings, Commodity Markets Rationing, and the Real Rate of Interest in China.' Country Policy Department Discussion Paper, World Bank, Washington DC.

FRYDMAN, ROMAN, ANDRZEJ RAPACZYNSKI, and JOHN EARLE. 1993. *The Privatization Process in Central Europe*. Prague: Central European University Press.

HOLMSTROM, BENGT. 1982. 'Moral Hazard in Teams.' *Bell Journal of Economics*.

International Monetary Fund. 1993. *International Financial Statistics*, February.

Kornai, Janos. 1992. *The Socialist System*. Princeton University Press and Oxford University Press.

Lau, Lawrance. 1992 December. 'Macroeconomic Policies for Short-Term Stabilization and Long-Term Growth of the Chinese Economy.' Stanford University, Stanford CA.

Lipton, David and Jeffery Sachs. 1990. 'Privatization in Eastern Europe: The Case of Poland.' *Brookings Papers on Economic Activity* 2: 293–341.

Lou, Jiwei. 1993. '*Guanzhu huobi, gaishan tiaokong*' ('Improving macroeconomic management by tightly controlling money'). *Reform* issue 1, Chongqiang.

McKinnon, Ronald. 1992a. 'Financial Control in China's Transition to a Market Economy.' Stanford University, Stanford CA.

——. 1992b. 'Three Models of the Banking System, Which One Should China Choose?' *Journal of Comparative Economic and Social Systems* issue 6. In Chinese.

Qian, Yingyi. 1988. 'Urban and Rural Household Saving in China.' *International Monetary Funds Staff Papers* 35(4) (December).

Qian, Yingyi and Joseph Stiglitz. 1993. 'Institutional Innovations and the Role of Local Government in Transition Economies: The Case of Guangdong Province of China.' Stanford University, Stanford CA.

Qian, Yingyi and Chenggang Xu. 1991. 'Innovation and Financial Constraints in Centralized and Decentralized Economies.' Stanford University, Stanford CA.

——. 1993. 'Why China's Economic Reforms Differ: The M-Form Hierarchy and Entry/Expansion of the Non-State Sector.' *The Economics of Transition* 1(2): 135–70 (June).

Scharfstein, David. 1992. 'Japanese Corporate Finance and Governance: Implications for the Privatization of Eastern European Enterprises.' Massachusetts Institute of Technology, Cambridge MA.

Scott, David H. 1992 November. 'Revising Financial Sector Policy in Transition Socialist Economies: Will Universal Banks Prove Viable?' Working Paper Series 1034, Country Economics Department, World Bank, Washington DC.

Shea, Jia-Dong, and T. T. Yen. 1991 July. 'Comparative Experience of Financial Reforms in Taiwan and Korea: Implications for Mainland China.' Discussion Paper 9105, Institute of Economics, Academia Sinica, Taipai, Taiwan.

Sicular, Terry. 1992 November. 'Public Finance and China's Economic Reforms.' Harvard Institute of Economic Research Discussion Paper 1618, Cambridge MA.

State Statistical Bureau. 1992. *Statistical Yearbook of China*. Beijing.

Tirole, Jean. 1991. 'Ownership and Incentives in a Transition Economy.' Centre d'Enseignement et de Recherche en Analyse Socio-Economique (CERAS). Paris.

World Bank. 1985. *China: Long-Term Development Issues and Options*. Baltimore: Johns Hopkins University Press.

——. 1988. *China: Finance and Investment*.

——. 1991. *China: Financial Sector Policies and Institutional Development*.

Wu, Jinglian. 1990. 'China's Economic Reform and Financial Reform.' Development Research Center, Beijing.

Xie, Ping and others. 1992. *Zhongguo de Jinrong Shenhua yu Jinrong Gaige* (Financial Deepening and Financial Reform in China). Tianjin: People's Press.

YASUDA, AYAKO. 1992. 'The Performance and Roles of Japanese Development Banks.' Stanford University, Stanford CA.

ZHOU, QIREN and Z. HU. 1987. *'Fuzhai jingying de hongguan xiaoying'* (The Macroeconomic Consequences of Debt Financing), *Fazhan Yanjiu Tongxun (Development Research)*, May, Beijing.

ZHOU, XIAOCHUAN and LI ZHU. 1987. 'China's Banking System: Current Status, Perspective on Reform.' *Journal of Comparative Economics* 11: 399–409.

17

Financial System Reform in Poland: Lessons from Japan's Main Bank System

TAKEO HOSHI

ANIL KASHYAP

GARY LOVEMAN

Poland has, for more than three years, been engaged in a process of economic reform from a planned to a market economy, and as the first of the formerly communist eastern and central European countries to engage in the reform process, it has had to grapple with enormously complex problems without many meaningful precedents. The reform process in Poland can be characterized as having four central components: macroeconomic reform and stabilization; institutional reform to establish the basic legislative and structural mechanisms to support a market economy; financial system reform to separate the central bank from commercial banking, and to introduce intermediation into the economy; and privatization of state assets. When comparing the command planning system of Poland and its Warsaw Pact allies with the capitalist systems of the industrialized western countries, the differences are obvious and substantial. But when presented with the task of actually establishing some kind of market economy where there has been none for decades, it quickly becomes clear that there are a multitude of alternative arrangements within the general rubric of a 'market economy', each of which has compelling attributes that vary as a function of political and economic circumstances, transitional properties, and the need for complementarity amongst the four components of reform.

This chapter focuses on the choice facing Polish policy-makers on how

The authors thank Michael Gerlach, Rob Gertner, Peter Gourevitch, Simon Johnson, Toru Konishi, Morio Kuninori, Millard Long, Leonard Lynn, John McMillan, Hideaki Miyajima, Takafusa Nakamura, Barry Naughton, Tetsuji Okazaki, Hugh Patrick, Yingyi Qian, Tom Roehl, Gerard Roland, Paul Sheard, Satoshi Sunamura, Juro Teranishi and Kazuo Ueda as well as seminar participants at the Japan Export and Import Bank, the Japan Development Bank, Kyoto University, Osaka University, University of Tokyo and the World Bank Main Bank project for helpful comments. We also thank Yoshito Sakakibara and David Kotchen for research assistance. We received research support from the Federal Reserve Bank of Chicago, The University of Chicago IBM Faculty Research Fund, the National Science Foundation, and the Division of Research, Harvard Business School. The views in the chapter are strictly those of the authors.

to structure the financial system, and its relation to the privatization and restructuring of Polish industry. Financial sector reform has progressed painfully slowly in Poland despite its crucial role in enabling the revitalization of Polish industry. Indeed, more than three years after the introduction of the 'shock therapy' macroeconomic reforms on 1 January 1990, the banking system remains almost entirely state owned and operated and, more importantly, remains largely dysfunctional in collecting funds from depositors and allocating them to the most worthy borrowers.

As the Polish economy begins to emerge from a severe downturn, the failure of the financial system is widely viewed as a crippling impediment to recovery (see Berg and Blanchard, 1992). Taking a longer-term perspective, privatization and restructuring of Polish state enterprises will require careful valuations of companies and planned investment projects, large infusions of capital where warranted, and substantial financial expertise in the management of the privatized enterprises. In addition, the rapidly growing small private business sector in Poland also badly needs efficient and accessible intermediation to support further development. New legislation allows for the creation of private banks, and some have been established, but their share of banking activity remains quite low. Only a few foreign-owned banks have been established, and there has also been little foreign investment in Polish banks. Bankruptcy procedures exist, but they are cumbersome and often disadvantageous for creditors and, hence, are rarely used.

Meanwhile, the nine regional commercial banks that were spun-off from the National Bank of Poland continue to have the vast majority of the deposit and loan business. First steps toward the privatization of these nine banks have taken place, including their commercialization, the creation of a supervisory board overseeing the management of each bank, the classification of all outstanding loans into five categories on the basis of likelihood and timeliness of repayment, and the imposition of Ministry of Finance restrictions on further lending to state enterprises with existing non-performing loans.[1] As an incentive for improved management, the Ministry of Finance plans to privatize the banks in an order determined by their relative financial performance.

Although there is no precedent among eastern and central European countries for the problems of financial system reform, there are important lessons to be learned from the post-World War II experience of Japan. The post-war Japanese economy was faced with making the transition from extensive centralization and government intervention to support the war effort, including measures that directed funds and tangible resources to enterprises supplying the military, to a de-militarized, market

---

[1] Commercialization involves the conversion of a state-owned enterprise into a joint-stock company, in which the state initially owns all of the shares. Commercialization is a pre-condition for privatization.

economy. Post-war Japan, too, had severely limited productive capacity, a very high rate of inflation, and extremely close ties between large banks, large firms and government administrators. Japanese banks were left after the war with balance sheets full of munitions company loans that were initially guaranteed by the government, but following pressure from the Allies the guarantees were dropped and the loans were uncollectable. The large Japanese banks thus faced a balance sheet clean-up problem similar to that currently faced by the Polish banks, whose assets are almost entirely loans to state enterprises, the majority of which are likely to be uncollectable.

Rather than adopting a financial system based largely on financing through equity, bond markets, and arm's-length bank lending, as in the US and as currently contemplated for Poland, Japan developed a system dominated by financial intermediation through banks, in which banks also own some equity of the companies to whom they lend money. In the former system corporate control is exercised through the stock market by shareholders and their elected representatives and, in the latter, banks are more important, particularly in periods of financial distress when they often exercise control. In many cases, large Japanese firms pair off with a single bank that becomes the dominant lender to the firm. These main banks play a particularly active role in the governance and long-term financial needs of their large corporate customers.

Recent theoretical and empirical analysis suggests that the 'main bank' system has several advantages over the arm's-length banking relationships and reliance on securities market financing common in Anglo-Saxon countries, and these advantages are especially important for firms in financial distress. Concisely stated, the principle advantages are reductions in monitoring costs associated with long-term, closely integrated relationships, reductions in agency costs from significant bank ownership of debt and equity, coordination efficiencies from having one bank with a large stake as lead lender and reductions in rescue or liquidation costs for firms in financial distress.

There are clearly a number of important differences between post-war Japan and Poland in the early 1990s, but the parallels are sufficient to support further analysis of the virtues of the Japanese system for Poland. In particular, the circumstances facing Polish industry and the current condition of the Polish banking system raise additional challenges that seem well suited to the main bank structure: a complete lack of modern organizational and technological banking competence; the need for a long-term financial commitment to support restructuring of Polish enterprises; and the enormous information and credibility problems posed by an unstable economy with inexperienced and poorly trained managers.

Furthermore, Poland has embarked on a novel and highly complicated mass privatization programme aimed at rapidly privatizing hundreds of companies. Under the terms of this programme, the shares of the privatized companies would be held by roughly 20 management funds, and each fund would hold a substantial ownership share in a few companies (as much as 50–60 per cent). The management funds will have foreign investment banks and venture capitalists as advisers who are expected to behave as active investors, choosing and monitoring management, selling assets and facilitating restructuring through advice to management and the provision of capital. The management funds, in turn, are to be owned by the Polish citizenry, each of whom will receive one share in each fund. The management funds are intended to concentrate ownership and introduce scarce management expertise, thereby facilitating restructuring. The source of financing for these funds has been assumed to follow from the foreign advisers' access to capital markets. Since foreign direct investment in Poland has, to date, been far less than what is necessary to finance restructuring and investment on a large scale, substantial domestic funds will be required to support the privatization effort.

The main bank system presents a model for financial system reform that offers many benefits for the cluster of problems facing Poland's economy. The privatization and restructuring of Polish enterprises seems especially well suited to take advantage of the distinctive attributes of a main bank system. However, it is crucial to distinguish between the benefits of a main bank system for private Polish banks and the adoption of a main bank system under the current largely state-owned banking structure. The main bank system will work effectively if, and only if, the large commercial banks are privatized and well capitalized, and bank managers operate under profit-based incentives to prevent the lending of funds to unworthy borrowers. 'Soft budget constraints', a fundamental characteristic of banking under the communists, will not arise with a main bank system in which managers of banks are rewarded for the profitable use of private capital.

In the remainder of the chapter we examine the relative merits of the main bank system for Poland. The next section describes the problems facing Japan during the period when the main bank system emerged. The second section discusses how the system resolved these problems and the more general features of the modern main bank system. The third section describes the Polish situation in greater detail, and draws on the preceding sections to analyse the virtues of the main bank system for Poland. Our conclusions are then presented in the final section.

THE BACKGROUND LEADING TO THE DEVELOPMENT OF THE MAIN BANK SYSTEM IN JAPAN

This section reviews the pre-conditions that led to the development of the main bank system in Japan. Although the version of the Japanese main bank system that was operative during the high growth era (1955–73) has been widely studied and is nicely summarized in Chapter 1, it did not emerge instantly following World War II. It evolved from the financial system that was in place at the conclusion of the war through the process of dealing with the challenges associated with rebuilding the economy.

The analysis here will focus on four key economic conditions that contributed to the emergence of the main bank system. First, the manufacturing and financial sectors underwent an extreme concentration during the militarization of the economy. Second, the government arranged centralized financing by pairing banks and firms, and the bank was charged with taking care of the firm's financial needs. The end of the war brought with it two significant challenges. One problem was near hyperinflation that destroyed much of the country's wealth just as the economy needed to be rebuilt. A second difficulty was that Japanese banks and industrial firms were left with balance sheets full of war-time commitments that were ultimately repudiated. It will be argued that these four factors had a lasting effect on the banking system.[2]

Of course, there were other important factors that shaped the system, and it is important to recognize both the continuity and the shifts that occurred in the transition between the war-time and post-war financial system. For example, monitoring patterns in the war-time banking system differed significantly from those in the post-war system. Nevertheless, there are some similarities between the two systems; the purpose of this section and the next one is to explain how the transition occurred, and why the process of confronting the problems the economy faced after the war ultimately led to a system that was so successful during the high growth era.

One of the main effects of war was an increase in the concentration of the Japanese banking sector. From the onset of hostilities with China in 1937 to the end of World War II, the number of banks in Japan shrunk from 377 to 61. It appears that several laws passed by the government to assist in the war effort were largely responsible for this shift and for an increase in the concentration of the banking and industrial sectors of the economy.[3]

The first of these acts occurred in 1937 when a set of financial controls was designed to allocate funds preferentially to war-related industries. These industries tended to be located in the regional centres, (Teranishi, 1982, pp. 341–42), so that by discriminating against firms in non-

---

[2] In Chapter 2, Teranishi emphasizes another factor: the loan syndication arrangements that became prevalent during the war. He argues that these arrangements were instrumental in the development of the lending consortia that are an important characteristic of the main bank system.

[3] As Hoshi (1993a) describes, the government had previously passed other laws that led to considerable concentration in the bank sector—overall between 1901 and 1945, 98 per cent of the banks in Japan disappeared.

war-related industries, the policies generally hurt firms located outside the metropolitan areas. As these companies declined, so did the regional banks with whom they did business. Thus many regional banks eventually found that their best option was to merge with larger banks.

The war-time controls also were particularly advantageous to the largest banks because they had the most funds available to direct to the war effort. By acquiring small banks, the larger banks grew further during this period. Table 17.1 confirms this observation by showing time series information on the share of the five largest banks in various activities. Notice that even between 1940 and 1945, there was a considerable increase in concentration. By all conventional measures, the militarization of the economy left Japan with an incredibly concentrated banking sector.

TABLE 17.1 Shares of the Five Largest Banks in All Ordinary and Savings Banks (per cents)

End of Year	Paid-In Capital	Deposits	Lending
1900	5.4	15.1	10.6
1910	10.2	17.4	15.1
1920	13.9	20.5	16.5
1930	24.1	31.0	27.6
1940	31.6	35.4	44.7
1945	40.4	45.7	58.6

The five largest banks are Mitsui, Mitsubishi, Sumitomo, Dai-Ichi, and Yasuda until 1942. In 1943, Mitsui and Dai-Ichi were merged to form Teikoku, which then acquired Ju-Go Bank in 1944. Teikoku split back into Mitsui and Dai-Ichi, with the former Ju-Go branches belonging to Mitsui, in 1948.

Source: Teranishi (1982, p. 295).

Another way to measure the importance of the war effort is to note the compositional shift in output towards heavy capital-intensive industries at the expense of light industries. For instance, Hoshi (1993a) reports that between 1934 and 1942 the share of output coming from steel and metal and machinery industries increased from 27 per cent to 49 per cent, while the fraction of output produced in the food and textile industries declined from 42 per cent to 19 per cent. Along with this general shift towards heavy industry, the government also sought to shift production to certain favoured firms.

The result was that the zaibatsu firms significantly increased their importance in the economy over this period. For instance, Hadley (1970, pp. 48–55) reports that the Big Four zaibatsu (Mitsui, Mitsubishi,

Sumitomo and Yasuda) accounted for roughly 15 per cent of production in heavy industries (defined as mining, metal manufacturing, machine tools, shipbuilding and chemicals) in 1937 and 32 per cent of production by the end of the war. Apparently, many of the gains came because the Japanese army and navy routinely 'turned industrial and mining areas coming under Japanese jurisdiction over to Mitsui, Mitsubishi or Sumitomo to operate', (Hadley, 1970, p. 41). In fact, Hadley's data indicate that in the non-Japanese territory controlled by Japan, the Big Four zaibatsu accounted for over 60 per cent of production in heavy industries at the end of the war. Overall, the drive to convert the economy to prepare for war left both the manufacturing sector and financial sectors highly concentrated.

This reorientation of the manufacturing sector led to further changes in the credit flows. An examination of the sources of industrial funding during this period shows that with the increasing importance of capital-intensive sectors in the economy, firms were no longer able to rely on internally generated funds to finance their investment. These changes led to a pronounced aggregate increase in the demand for bank financing. For instance, the share of firm financing coming from banks more than tripled between 1936 and 1944—increasing from 18 per cent to 58 per cent—while the share of financing coming from internal funds fell by nearly half—from 47 per cent to 24 per cent. (See Ministry of Finance, 1978, pp. 462–63.)

To assist with this adjustment, another set of legal changes regarding the way that individual companies arranged their financing was implemented. Initially, these changes were made at the industry level. For instance, soon after Japan initiated the war with China, the Temporary Funds Adjustment Law was promulgated in order to guide the overall allocation of long-term funds and provide preferential allocations for war-related industries. Operationally, this meant that each industry was classified into one of three categories: those which were to get approval for most long-term funding requests, those which would sometimes get approval, and those which could generally not expect to get approval.

Over the next six years the government passed a series of laws that gave them increasing authority over the way funds would be allocated throughout the economy (see Hoshi, 1993a). During this period the demand for loans by war-related industries increased dramatically. The commercial banks responded to demand by forming lending consortia. Chapter 2 by Teranishi provides further details on this process and an argument for why these lending consortia may have had a lasting effect on lending arrangements in the post-war main bank system.

The financial controls reached the final phase when the government passed the Munitions Companies Act (October 1943) and the Munitions Companies Designated Financial Institutions System (January 1944). The

Munitions Companies Act put major companies that were considered strategically important under the direct control of the government, while the Munitions Companies Designated Financial Institutions System assigned a major bank to each munitions company to take care of the firm's financial needs. Large firms sometimes had more than one bank assigned to help them. In many cases, a lending consortium was formed around the designated bank to serve the munitions company. The Munitions Company Act also allowed managers to increase their power relative to shareholders by giving the managers much more autonomy provided that they were acting in the interests of the nation by trying to 'increase productivity'. (See Okazaki, 1991, pp. 392–93.) Hoshi (1993a) explains how this shift in power further contributed to the rise of a bank-led financing system.

Judging from the Selection Policy for Munitions Companies Designated Financial Institutions many of the designations are likely to have been based on the past relations through loans, shareholdings, and directorship. (Bank of Japan Research Bureau, 1973, p. 397 and Mitsubishi Bank, 1954, pp. 348–50.) Thus some assignments under the Munitions Companies Designated Financial Institutions System served only to reinforce pre-existing ties between banks and firms—especially in cases involving zaibatsu firms and banks.

But historical accounts of the matching process also suggest that there was competition among banks to receive designations for munitions companies. For example, in the corporate history of Mitsubishi bank, it is reported that the bank lobbied to obtain as many designations as possible because loans made to munitions companies were perceived to be riskless (see Mitsubishi Bank, 1954, pp. 349–50). Miyazaki and Itoh, in their review of the history of Fuji Bank, reach the same conclusion (1989, p. 202).

As a result of this process, some non-zaibatsu firms started to have close ties to zaibatsu banks. An interesting example is Ajinomoto, which changed its name to Dai Nippon Kagaku Kogyo during the latter stages of the war and then was designated as a munitions company and assigned to Mitsubishi Bank. Judging from the low levels of debt prior to the war, Ajinomoto does not appear to have had previous extensive relations with Mitsubishi (or any other bank) before the war. (Ajinomoto, 1971, vol. 1, Appendix, pp. 10–11.)[4] After the war, Ajinomoto gradually moved closer

---

[4] A further hint that suggests the lack of any prior ties between Ajinomoto and Mitsubishi is that another munitions company, Showa Nosan Kako, which was established by Ajinomoto to deal with alcoholic liquor business in 1934, was assigned Teikoku and Yasuda Banks as its designated institutions. Interestingly, Showa Nosan Kako, which changed its name to Sanraku Ocean after the war, had Mitsubishi Trust as its largest lender and the third largest shareholder in 1962. This suggests the ties established through government assignments were not as strong as the ties between a company and its former subsidiaries.

to the Mitsubishi group. For example, during the reconstruction period, Mitsuo Ogasawara of Mitsubishi Bank served as one of its five special managers charged with supervising the rebuilding of the firm. By 1962, Mitsubishi Bank was the largest lender to Ajinomoto and by 1972 had become both the largest lender and largest shareholder of Ajinomoto (Keizai Chosa Kyokai 1963, 1973). In addition to the financial ties, Ajinomoto and the Mitsubishi group developed close relations in intermediate product markets. For example, Ajinomoto's Tokai factory purchases raw materials from Mitsubishi Chemical, Mitsubishi Petro-Chemical, and Mitsubishi Monsanto (Ajinomoto, 1989, p. 281). Thus, even for the former zaibatsu banks there appear to have been new long-lasting relationships that formed because of the designation system.

For the non-zaibatsu banks that were far less likely to have had many long-standing ties to draw upon, the designation system may have been the key to establishing a number of new relationships. Hoshi (1993a) attempts to calibrate the importance of these designated arrangements by comparing the identity of a firm's main bank in 1962 with its designated lender during the war. Among 158 munitions companies that were assigned financial institutions during the first round of designation in 1944, he is able to track 112 of these companies and their successors. Of these 112 cases, the designated financial institution was both the largest lender and one of the ten largest shareholders in 1962 in 71 cases (63 per cent). In another 13 cases, the trust bank, or the life insurance company in the same enterprise group as the designated financial institution, is the main bank, so that the proportion rises to 75 per cent. Finally, there were 16 other cases where the designated financial institutions were the largest lenders but not one of the top 10 shareholders, so, by this 'looser' standard, the designations had a persistent effect on the financing patterns for 89 per cent of the former munitions companies.

To the extent these figures merely confirm the fact that many former-zaibatsu firms and banks stayed together after the war, they are not particularly noteworthy; among the 112 companies Hoshi studied, 42 are considered to have had close links to one of the zaibatsu even before the designation of financial institutions and therefore may be of less interest. A more important finding, however, is that the ties through the designated financial institutions system were long lasting, even for the other 70 firms which did not have close ties to zaibatsu. Out of 70, 61 companies (or 87 per cent) had their designated institution, or a financial institution in the same group, as their largest lender in 1962.

The same war-time controls that laid the groundwork for a strong bank-led financing system also caused some problems. The most important problem for the financial system was the paralysis of its monitoring function. Financial institutions were turned into organizations which merely followed the government's lending orders. The evaluation and monitoring of borrowers, which are central to a healthy banking system, were no longer the banks' business in the war-time economy. The following extract from a banker's memoirs shows what the banking business was like during the war:

'I was in charge of the loan business for the companies connected with production of top secret bombs: balloon bombs. My name was registered with the Army Headquarters for Weapon Administration, and my activities were a closely guarded secret. I dealt with all the loan documents related to balloon bombs, which was flagged by a letter "fu". ("fu" for "fusen", the Japanese word for balloon). Incidentally, the documents with a letter "ro" were for rocket bombs for Navy, and another person was in charge of these loans.

'My job was to make the loan immediately whenever a slip with a letter "fu" came to my desk. Lots of companies, such as paper manufacturers, producers of percussion caps, and *konnyaku* paste-makers (paste made from arum root), took part in the production of balloon bombs.' (Matsuzawa, 1985, p. 14.)

This absence of any monitoring was also reported in the corporate history of Mitsubishi Bank. For instance, Mitsubishi Bank (1954, pp. 351–53) notes that the managers of the munitions companies 'never had to worry about financing' and the banks 'could rarely use their own judgements regarding loan requests'. Ironically, the result of the massive intervention by the Japanese government to support the war effort seems to have left the financial system operating with a set of 'soft budget constraints'.[5]

With the conclusion of World War II, Japan found itself facing two additional problems (that more recently Poland has also had to confront). One problem arose because the war destroyed much of the capital stock. As Table 17.2 shows, during the war, Japan lost about 25 per cent of the total productive assets and 30 per cent of transportation-related durables and infrastructure. Until 1949, a major portion of the funds used to support the rebuilding effort came from the Reconstruction Bank, which raised the money by issuing Reconstruction Bonds. Unfortunately, in many instances, more than 60 per cent (and sometimes more than 90 per cent) of the bonds were bought by the Bank of Japan (Kosai, 1981), so that the Reconstruction Bank's financing fuelled inflation.

This inflation, in turn, destroyed much of the financial wealth in the economy. Table 17.3 shows the level of gross financial assets for the personal sector and corporations. Although the nominal value of financial assets increased during the period of 1946–54, the stock of financial assets fell substantially, relative to GNP, during the 1946–47 hyperinflation and still had not recovered by 1954.[6] Thus, like Poland 40 years later, Japan

---

[5] 'Soft budget constraints' is a term coined by Janos Kornai to describe the communist systems' willingness to subsidize poor performing companies and reluctance to press insolvent firms into bankruptcy and liquidation.

[6] Even afterwards, relative to the US, where comparable ratios at that time were around

TABLE 17.2 Damage of National Wealth by the War

	Total Damage	Wealth at 1945	Damage Ratio
Producer durables	19,838	59,689	24.9
Consumer durables	34,823	105,894	24.7
Transportation durables	9,617	23,269	29.2

The damage ratio is defined as (Total Damage)/(Total Damage + Wealth at 1945).

Source: Ministry of Finance (1978, pp. 14–15).

TABLE 17.3 Gross Financial Assets Held by Non-Financial Private Sectors

Year	Households (¥ million)	All Private (¥ million)	Households	Ratio to GNP All
1946	259,511	380,574	0.547	0.803
1947	259,811	655,097	0.351	0.501
1948	827,241	1,216,852	0.310	0.456
1949	929,101	1,384,109	0.275	0.410
1950	1,376,204	2,017,051	0.349	0.511
1951	1,887,053	2,796,976	3.443	5.103
1952	2,726,759	3,994,592	0.428	0.627
1953	3,547,437	5,195,570	0.475	0.690
1954	4,223,028	6,104,910	0.540	0.780

Source: Ministry of Finance (1978, pp. 424-41).

found itself trying to rebuild its economy with an acute shortage of domestic funds.

A second dilemma brought about by the end of the war was the extraordinary amount of war-time compensation the government owed the munitions companies. The Japanese government initially planned to pay compensation by collecting property taxes, but following pressure from the Allies, the government eventually decided to suspend compensation payments completely. (For a detailed description of negotiations between the Japanese government and the Allies, see Ministry of Finance, 1983a, pp. 183–347.) Since financial institutions obviously had high exposure to munitions companies, the suspension of war-time compensation also seriously damaged their balance sheets. To make the matter worse, the government also decided to drop its commitment to honour government guaranteed corporate bonds, most of which were held by financial institu-

1.5 for household financial assets and around 2 for private non-financial sector assets, the Japanese ratios seemed low. In fact, Hamada and Horiuchi (1987, p. 229) report that it took Japan another 30 years to catch up with the US in this respect.

tions, and to suspend compensation for the losses due to uncollectable government ordered loans to munitions companies.

The total losses stemming from the default were enormous. In October 1946 the government estimated the amount to be 66.9 billion yen (see Ministry of Finance, 1983b, p. 699). If one adds the losses due to the repudiation of government guaranteed bonds (19.8 billion yen) and the losses due to the suspension of compensation for losses arising from government ordered loans (5.0 billion yen), the total losses rise to an estimated 91.8 billion yen. This is almost one fifth of Gross National Expenditure in fiscal 1946 (474.0 billion yen) (Ministry of Finance, 1978, pp. 26–27).

To sum up, Japan was forced to rebuild its economy starting with a highly concentrated manufacturing sector that was receiving unmonitored credit from a highly concentrated, but nearly insolvent, banking sector. Moreover, losing the war had wiped out much of the capital stock, and the inflation after the war had wiped out much of the nation's wealth. Thus, credit during the early phase of the reconstruction was likely to be scarce. Against this backdrop the main bank system emerged. The next section investigates both the institutional and theoretical considerations that suggest that the main bank system was well suited to the challenge.

THE RATIONALE FOR THE MAIN BANK SYSTEM IN JAPAN

In this section it is argued that each of the major problems discussed in the last section—particularly, the pairing of specific banks and firms and the associated soft budget constraint problem, the massive amount of required rebuilding starting from a position of low wealth, and the significant balance sheet problems—played an important role in the selection of a bank-led financing system that eventually became the main bank system. Of course, the Japanese banking system was going through a major transition following the war, and these considerations were only some of the factors that ultimately led to the main bank system. Some of the other factors will be discussed at the end of this section.

In examining the Japanese system, two points deserve particular emphasis. On the one hand, it will be argued that a bank-led financing system was well suited to addressing the critical problems facing the economy. However, a second point is equally important: no other alternative to a bank-led financing system would have been likely to succeed. As discussed by Aoki, Patrick and Sheard in Chapter 1, the alternative to a main bank style financing system would be a securities market based system. In the latter, significant funding is obtained through equity and bond markets and the equity market plays a central role in the corporate governance structure. Throughout this discussion, it is important to recognize that while the main bank system may be imperfect it must be contrasted with a realistic alternative.

Perhaps the contrast between the relative strengths of a bank-led system and a securities market based system is sharpest in terms of the difficulties posed by the balance sheet problems that existed in Japan at the end of the war. The Japanese tackled these problems by freezing the balance sheets of both banks and industrial firms in August 1946. The rules were finalized in October of that year. The authorities hoped by taking these measures they could stop the accumulated war-related debts from choking the ongoing operations of the firms. Thus the policy-makers explicitly recognized that for any progress towards reconstruction to occur, the adverse incentive effects of the insolvency of lenders and borrowers had to be addressed.[7]

Because Polish banks now face a similar solvency problem it seems appropriate to review how the Japanese addressed this difficulty. (This discussion relies on Ministry of Finance, 1983b, pp. 213–327 and pp. 699–913.) For the financial institutions, their balance sheets were separated into a new account and an old account. Those assets that were expected to be uncollectable because of the suspension of war-time compensation were assigned to the old account and this account was expected to be reorganized. In the meantime, the banks were encouraged to continue operations using the new account. This new account included cash, government and municipal bonds, credits against the government other than bonds, credits against other financial institutions, and other assets specified by the Finance Minister. This meant that because most of the munitions company loans and government guaranteed bonds were expected to be uncollectable, they were placed in the old accounts.

The liabilities of the new account included a limited amount of deposits, tax obligations to central and local governments, loans from other financial institutions, and other liabilities specified by the Finance

---

[7] The initial laws were the Financial Institutions Accounting Temporary Measures Act (FIATMA henceforth) and Corporations Accounting Temporary Measures Act (COATMA) and the permanent laws were called the Financial Institutions Reconstruction and Reorganization Act (FIRRA) and Corporations Reconstruction and Reorganization Act (CORRA). See Teranishi (1991b, pp. 23–24) for a brief description of FIATMA and FIRRA.

The restructuring of financial institutions and industrial companies was only one of many changes that the Japanese financial system went through. The Japanese government, under the supervision of the Allies, implemented several other important financial reforms. Financial institutions in the former Japanese colonies (such as Taiwan Bank and Chosen Bank) and those for war-time controls (such as Wartime Finance Corporation) were completely shut down. The Munitions Companies Designated Financial Institutions System was formally abolished. New financial institutions which exclusively handled the distribution of long-term funds were created to replace the pre-war special banks. Financial institutions specializing in the financing of small and medium-sized firms and those for farmers were also established, and the Bank of Japan Act was partially reformed to increase the independence of the central bank from the government (see Kato, 1974).

Minister. Depositors were left with access to only a fraction of the money that they had put into the bank.[8] In aggregate, about half of the deposits were transferred to the old accounts where they were frozen and were at risk of being cancelled to cover the bad munitions company loans and government guaranteed bonds (Ministry of Finance, 1983b, p. 228). The banks' capital and retained earnings were also put in the old account and were, therefore, at risk. Differences between assets and liabilities in one account were recorded as an unsettled account against the other. For instance, if the liabilities of the new account happened to exceed its assets, the difference was entered as a credit against the old account.

If, in the course of doing business, a bank used assets (such as offices) in the old account, then compensation had to be paid from the new account to the old account. These sorts of payments generated some transfers to the old accounts. Finally, in March 1948, the assets were marked up to current prices and the losses due to suspension of war-time compensation were cancelled out.[9] This process was finished in May 1948 when new and old accounts were merged. Most banks were forced to reduce capital significantly and to cut into the frozen deposits to cover the losses. For example, 55 out of 61 ordinary banks reduced their capital by more than 90 per cent and had to default on some of the deposits. The capital was subsequently replenished by issuing new shares.

The restructuring of the non-financial corporations was done in a parallel fashion, but proved more difficult. The process began with the government letting the companies which were expected to be damaged by suspension of war-time compensation declare themselves 'special account companies' (*tokubetsu keiri gaisha*). These companies then had their balance sheets separated into new and old accounts on 11 August 1946, and were allowed to operate using the new account. In this case, the assets of the new account included only those assets that were deemed necessary to 'continue the current business and promote the post-war development' (Ministry of Finance, 1983b, p. 734). Meanwhile the firm's liabilities and other assets were moved into the old account and the total value of assets classified into the new account was recorded as the liabilities of the new account against the old account. The special account companies were prohibited from settling liabilities incurred before 11 August 1946, and

---

[8] In February 1946, in order to combat run-away inflation, the government prohibited withdrawals of deposits that exceeded the minimum amount assumed to be necessary for living. The Financial Institutions Accounting Temporary Act classified a limited amount of frozen deposits (per household) into the new account (these were termed 'first line frozen deposits'), and classified the rest into the old account ('second line frozen deposits'). Much of the second line frozen deposits were repudiated during the process of reorganization. See Teranishi (1991a) for more on frozen deposits.

[9] The following prioritization was used in the process: first, capital gains on assets; second, retained earnings; third, up to 90 per cent of the bank's capital; fourth, 70 per cent of the deposits that were at risk would be written down, followed by the remaining 10 per cent of the capital; and, finally, the remaining 30 per cent of the deposits would be written down.

were protected from seizure of their assets (in the old account). The companies were also forbidden to declare bankruptcy.

More importantly, this process included an important role for banks. Specifically, in the process of restructuring non-financial firms, each firm had to select a set of 'special managers' (*tokubetsu kanrinin*). As a rule, the special managers consisted of two of a company's own executives and two representatives of the firm's creditors. So, in almost all the cases, former munitions companies had representatives from their designated financial institutions as their special managers. For example, as pointed out earlier, Mitsuo Ogasawara of Mitsubishi Bank became a special manager of Ajinomoto.

Special managers played a central role in the restructuring process. For instance, it was their responsibility to determine which assets should be included in the new account. They were also required to draw up a restructuring plan and submit it to the Finance Minister for approval. Miyajima (1992, pp. 229–30) reports that drafting a restructuring plan required the special managers to assess the value of remaining assets, make plans for future production and finance, and create forecasts of balance sheets and income statements. Accordingly, the restructuring of special account companies gave the special managers (and, therefore, the banks) an excellent opportunity to acquire information about the companies. Indeed Miyajima (1992) argues that the 'banks accumulated information about borrowers during this period much more intensively than during the period of Designated Financial Institutions System, when the government legally forced loan contracts and basically guaranteed against the risk.' Ultimately, the accumulation of information and the responsibility associated with the restructuring process must have significantly enhanced the capabilities of banks. In effect, this process served to reverse the deterioration of bank monitoring skills that had been brought on by the war-time forced lending arrangements.

The restructuring of non-financial companies took much longer than the restructuring of financial institutions, and not until four years after the process began (in late 1950) had all the special account companies submitted their restructuring plans. The process was delayed because coordination with anti-trust measures was required. The implementation of the plans took even longer, and more than 20 per cent of the special account companies were still undergoing restructuring at the end of 1952. About 12 per cent of the companies seem to have disappeared without completing the restructuring. (See Ministry of Finance, 1983b, pp. 899–900.) The losses incurred by shareholders and creditors were not as large as expected. The profits of the old account, which included the proceeds from sales of assets, reached 45.9 per cent of the total losses, and the capital gains of assets covered another 21.3 per cent. Thus the losses of shareholders and creditors were 'limited' to 32.8 per cent of the total losses (or 30 billion yen). (See Ministry of Finance, 1983b, p. 902.)

In evaluating the entire restructuring process it is essential to recognize that the pivotal role played by banks was almost unavoidable. For instance, suppose authorities had opted for a securities market approach to restructuring where companies were instructed to issue equity to reliquify themselves. Given the complex web of debts between banks, the government, and firms, and the considerable uncertainty over how the various obligations would be resolved, it would have been hard to establish the value of a typical firm. But without accurate valuations, equity financing would have been very difficult to attract, since equity financiers have only a junior claim against the firm.

Attempts to rely in any significant way on equity financing would have been further complicated because most Japanese investors had only limited experience with the stock market. The pre-war market had been small. One of the goals of the Occupation forces in Japan was to break up the zaibatsu companies that were thought to have been responsible for encouraging military aggression (see Hadley, 1970). In the course of engineering this dissolution, the government decided to sell shares in the companies. However, the government and securities industries found that they had to educate potential investors about the opportunities associated with stock ownership.

Responding to this 'securities democratization' movement, many households put their savings into stocks. Other measures, such as low-interest loans for employees purchasing their own company's shares and permission to use frozen deposits to buy shares, also helped to create the demand. Although the stock exchange was closed, people actively traded shares through *shudan torihiki* (collective trading), whereby many securities companies gathered to offer over-the-counter trades. When the Tokyo Stock Exchange was re-opened in May 1949, it started with a boom but soon began to sag as the Dodge stabilization plan took hold and the economy slid into a recession. The composite index had lost more than 50 per cent by the end of the year. Thus, many investors were left with initial scepticism regarding the virtues of equity ownership. In our view, these sorts of difficulties with establishing an active securities market are probably unavoidable when an economy is beginning such a transition. Of course, this does not mean that a stock market cannot be useful in helping to redistribute ownership. Rather, given the fragile nature of the economy, it seems very unlikely that much new money can be raised to finance businesses.

The disinflation programme also had other important effects. For instance, by cutting off credit extensions from the Reconstruction Bank, the Dodge Stabilization Plan also led to a serious credit contraction. While documenting a credit crunch is always difficult, there is abundant anecdotal evidence suggesting that credit became quite tight. For example, Toshio Nakamura of Mitsubishi Bank recalled that 'shortage of funds made it difficult to lend to even keiretsu firms' during this period (Ohtsuki, 1987, p. 77). Research reports from the Bank of Japan between December 1947 to December 1951 also frequently discussed the shortage of funds. (These can be found in Bank of Japan Research Bureau, 1980, pp. 451–592.)

In response to these financing problems, many companies turned to banks, and the banks seem to have increased their power over industrial firms. Banks rescued many companies from the ensuing liquidity crisis, and sometimes directly intervened in their management. In his memoirs, Eiji Toyoda, who was president of Toyota Auto from 1967 to 1982, looks back on this time as the period when Toyota Auto reluctantly started to depend on banks, especially Mitsui Bank, and was forced to accept bank intervention in management (Nihon Keizai Shimbun-sha, 1987). Mitsui Bank and other banks helped Toyota through its liquidity crisis in 1950, but required substantial lay-offs and Toyota had to spin off its sales department as conditions for the rescue. Mitsui Bank also sent in a director, Fukio Nakagawa, who later served as president of Toyota.

This type of rescue operation seems to have been quite common during this period. Indeed, Miyajima (1992, pp. 233–35) argues that between 1949 and 1952 many banks regularly began sending their employees in as directors to the companies to which they were lending. He also finds that main bank dependence was negatively correlated with profitability during this period, but not during other periods. He interprets this correlation as evidence that the main banks were systematically taking on a higher fraction of distressed clients in the aftermath of the stabilization. Thus, the taming of inflation not only left the banks in a better position to monitor their clients, but also seems to have accelerated the practice of the banks intervening in cases of financial distress.

With the disinflation programme, however, the banks also suffered from a shortage of funds. For instance, Makoto Usami of Mitsubishi Bank recalled that 'the demand for funds came in continuously, but not the deposits' (Nihon Keizai Shimbun-sha, 1980). The recent memory of high inflation and the deposit freeze undermined the public's trust and reduced its willingness to let the banks manage its money. The situation was especially serious for large zaibatsu banks, which depended heavily on deposits by large zaibatsu companies. Because those companies were in the process of restructuring, they did not have much money available to deposit (Sumitomo Ginko, 1979, pp. 400–01; Miyajima, 1992, p. 229, tables 5–6). Thus, the large banks had to compete for inter-bank loans and Bank of Japan lending to make up for the shortage of deposits.

This competition among large banks also seems to have further helped the soft budget constraint problem that had characterized the war-time lending arrangements. Since the banks had their balance sheets cleaned up and were now solvent, they did not seem inclined to waste money on loans to friendly, but unworthy companies. The case of Mitsui Seiki described by Goro Koyama of Mitsui Bank is illustrative (see Edo, 1986, p. 129). Although Mitsui Seiki was *chokkei* (of direct lineage) of Mitsui and, therefore, considered a central Mitsui company, it got into trouble after the war because of loose management. Koyama argued that Mitsui Bank should help other firms that were trying hard, rather than instinctively helping Mitsui Seiki because it had the 'Mitsui' name. This argument persuaded President Sato of Mitsui Bank to let Mitsui Seiki go through restructuring under Kaisha Kosei Ho (Restructuring Law). Consequently, Mitsui Seiki became the first company to be restructured under that law.

As the economy emerged from the restructuring in the early 1950s, funding continued to be difficult to obtain and the possibility of facing financial distress was a concern for most companies. Against this backdrop, banking relations continued to evolve. By the middle of the decade many of the features of the main bank system were in place. In particular, three important patterns had emerged. First, banks were firmly established as the primary providers of external financing for firms. Second, banks had been permitted to hold equity (as well as debt) claims of their clients and were regularly taking an active role in corporate governance (for instance by serving on boards of directors). Finally, firms and banks were continuing to pair off, so that everyone could clearly identify the main bank of a particular firm.

As discussed in Chapter 1, these attributes are only a subset of the sorts of ties that characterize the main bank system. But in suggesting that Poland borrow from the Japanese experience, we think these attributes are essential and would have to be adopted for the system to be successfully implemented in Poland. We close this section with a discussion of how these three characteristics of banking relationships assist in the delivery of financing to firms in an economy with scarce capital, and assist in minimizing the costs of financial distress.

Starting with firms experiencing cash flow problems, the main bank system provides four distinct theoretical advantages over a US style system where banks' actions are more tightly controlled. First, concentrating the firm's financial obligations eases the type of coordination problems that typically accompany any reorganization effort and thus helps improve the delivery of financing. In most cases, different creditors will have very different incentives for providing relief or additional funding. In a system where there are few debt-holders with large stakes, the number of parties that must come to an agreement about the fate of the company can be (and often seems to be greatly) reduced. Indeed, in many unsuccessful workouts one of the major hurdles is securing agreements from small or marginal investors.

A second and related benefit is that by allowing debt-holders to take equity positions, one helps align the interests of the two parties. Thus, if some bargaining is required in the course of negotiating an agreement, the disparate interests of debt and equity holders are less likely to be a stumbling block. This effect can be relatively small unless the debt holders have significant equity positions, so as an empirical matter it is unclear whether this feature is particularly important.

On the other hand, in the US there are a number of legal impediments that limit a bank's incentive to intervene and try to bail-out one of its clients prior to the start of formal bankruptcy proceedings. For instance, the laws regarding the treatment of concessions offered by creditors differ depending on whether a firm has been declared bankrupt. Similarly, the nature of public debt contracts (where unanimity is effectively required to defer the payment of principal or interest) also makes it difficult for bargaining to take place outside bankruptcy proceedings. Overall, the considerable consolidation of claims and alignment of the interest of the creditors in Japan may lead to important differences in the efficiency with which these types of cases are resolved in the two countries.

A third benefit of the main bank system in cases of financial distress is that the main bank is well positioned to make informed judgements about whether additional assistance is prudent. In many cases, the inability to reach an agreement on the likely impact of an assistance package comes into play. Even if creditors can agree on what steps to take, assuming the benefits of these steps were certain, no single creditor is well enough informed to help the group come to a decision. The main bank, by virtue of its close ties to the firm, should be able to make such a decision and is likely to be looked to for leadership.

A fourth consideration closely related to the last point, and emphasized by Hoshi (1993b), is that the repeated participation of the same principal lenders across a number of deals helps facilitate workouts. If the largest creditors have previously been through rescues and know that they are likely to gain by cooperating in subsequent situations, these lenders may be better able to reach a compromise than would be true in a one-shot bargaining situation. In essence, the environment permits reputational factors to be deployed to help smooth over disagreements and may help to reduce the costs of financial distress.

In analysing the actual Japanese experience, one might debate whether this assistance is always efficient, since from an economy-wide perspective the rescues may lead to too few failures. The main bank system has one feature that does help on this front. Specifically, these bank-led assistance programmes often include significant managerial reorganizations.[10]

---

[10] Kaplan and Minton (1993) found in a sample of 121 large Japanese firms, taken during the 1980s, that the appointments of outside directors with bank experience tended to rise when the firm's cash flow deteriorated.

The well-known Sumitomo group rescue of Mazda provides an excellent example of this practice. The combination of the first OPEC oil shock and the low fuel efficiency of their new rotary engine vehicles left Mazda with serious financial problems. Worse yet, Mazda's management was already widely viewed as being ineffective. For instance, the company had the highest production costs of all Japanese car makers. As Pascale and Rohlen (1983, p. 223) put it, 'the oil crisis of 1973 did not *cause* Toyo Kogyo's (Mazda's Japanese name) problems, it simply *exposed* them'. Mazda's main bank, Sumitomo, stepped in and provided new cheap loans, wrote down some existing loans and convinced other lenders and suppliers to stick with the firm. Perhaps even more importantly, Sumitomo Bank sent Tsutomu Murai and four other employees as 'delegates' to Mazda and made them responsible for overhauling its management structure (see Pascale and Rohlen, 1983). This direct intervention by the bank was instrumental in transforming an inefficient company into an efficient company. As Sheard (1989, p. 399) wrote, 'The main bank system substitutes for the "missing" takeover market in Japan.'

A second set of features become relevant when assessing the ability of the main bank system to deliver funds to firms that are financially healthy. Here there are four distinct effects of the main bank system. The first effect is that the system helps prevent duplication of monitoring efforts. In other words, because the main bank has such a large stake at risk with the firm, it will have definite incentives to keep tabs on the firm. Because all other lenders recognize that this is the case, less monitoring is needed and the system will be more efficient than one in which multiple monitors might be required.

A second reinforcing effect arises due to the different channels of significant information flowing back and forth from the bank and its customer. The example cited earlier where Mitsui sent an employee to Toyota who later became a senior manager there appears to be quite common. For instance, Hoshi, Kashyap and Scharfstein (1990) report that in 1982, roughly 34 per cent of the firms listed on the Tokyo Stock Exchange had one internally appointed board member whose previous employer had been a bank that did business with the firm.[11] They also report that an additional 8 per cent of the firms had a board member who was currently employed by a bank. Through these sorts of informal ties the main bank can conduct its policing activities quite effectively, so that the monitoring that does take place uses fewer resources than would otherwise be necessary. (See Chapter 1, as well as Schoenholtz

[11] Kaplan (1992) reports, however, that in most cases, by the time a person is appointed to be a board member at the very largest Japanese firms, that person has typically been employed by the company for at least 7 years. It is not clear how to interpret this evidence. The data we reviewed are consistent with the following pattern: a person works for a bank for 25 to 30 years, then moves to the client company as a senior manager; and after another 7 to 10 years, this person becomes a board member.

and Takeda, 1985, and Sheard, 1989, for more discussion on these points.)

Another chance for informal information sharing occurs at the regular monthly meetings attended by the chief executive officers of the core companies in the *kigyo shudan*. These gatherings, commonly referred to as *shacho-kai* (Presidents Club) meetings, are generally described as being somewhat ceremonial and more oriented towards being an outlet for informal information sharing rather than for explicit strategic planning. (For details see Gerlach, 1992, chapter 4.) Nevertheless, the banks seem to play a central role when a joint decision among the members is made. For example, Toshio Nakamura, a former president of Mitsubishi Bank, reports that the bank was instrumental in the joint projects started by the Mitsubishi group, including Mitsubishi Cement (1954), Mitsubishi Petro-Chemical (1956), and Mitsubishi Atomic Power (1958). He also notes that the bank coordinated the group's effort to buy Mitsubishi Oil shares from Texaco after Texaco had acquired the shares by taking over Getty Oil (Ohtsuki, 1987, pp. 80–81). Similarly, Tsuda (1988, pp. 100–01) describes how Sumitomo Bank mobilized the Hakusui-kai (the Sumitomo Presidents Club) in its rescue plan for Sumitomo Machinery in 1954 when the manufacturer was financially distressed.

Hoshi, Kashyap and Scharfstein (1991) identify another channel by which a main banking system can be beneficial. This channel emerges because of standard asymmetric information problems that lead to a cost differential between internally generated funds and externally generated money. To the extent that investment opportunities are less cyclical than firms' cash flows, this cost differential may lead to under-investment. Hoshi, Kashyap and Scharfstein (1991) point out that a firm with an informed main bank may partially circumvent these difficulties. Indeed, they find the investment of firms with tight banking relationships is less sensitive to fluctuations in internal funds than is the investment of firms without tight bank relationships. These findings suggest the presence of a main bank may help insulate some Japanese firms from business cycles and other disturbances.

An additional effect comes from the interaction of the main bank system with the tax code. In Japan, like many other countries, interest payments on debt are tax deductible. Because of the previously mentioned lowered costs of financial distress, Japanese firms are able to load up on more debt than they otherwise would. From a purely corporate perspective, this is another advantage of the main bank system, although from society's point of view it is not clear whether this is desirable. Overall there appear to be a number of reasons why the main bank system has been advantageous for Japan.

Lastly, it is worth noting that while the banking system was very important in Japan, until very recently, securities markets remained fairly primitive. As mentioned earlier, in the immediate aftermath of the war the stock market was shut down, but even after it reopened in the 1950s it was not a terribly important source of funding for even the large corporations. Given the low level of wealth of most investors, it is perhaps not surprising that concerns about diversification might have led them to shy away from investing in particular companies. The alternative of pooling money with other investors by lending to a bank that can invest in many firms might have been much more attractive.

Regarding bond markets, one would also suspect that, in the initial, turbulent period following the war, unmonitored lending that was secured by a borrower's reputation would have been unlikely to succeed. Instead, investors would probably insist that firms either post collateral (which would mitigate the attractiveness of this borrowing strategy) or receive some sort of credit rating to guarantee their credit-worthiness. While this would have been difficult at the outset of the high growth era, one might have thought that as the economy matured a deeper bond market would develop. However, regulation seems to have prevented the growth of the bond market. In fact, until the early 1980s, bond issuance was tightly controlled, so firms had little choice as to where they would get their external funding. It is often asserted that the costs of raising funds in the Japanese equity markets also were unnecessarily high because of regulation (see Miller, 1992).

Since the restrictions have been eased, there has been a flurry of bond issuance among the largest, most successful Japanese companies—see Hoshi, Kashyap, and Scharfstein (1993). In advocating that Poland and other countries consider copying the main bank system, we want to be clear that we do not favour following the Japanese example with regard to the regulations pertaining to bond and equity markets. Our view is rather that until the economy reached a fairly mature state, the economic advantages of the main bank system described above would have made bank financing relatively attractive, even if the bond and stock markets were not so tightly controlled.

FINANCIAL REFORM IN POLAND

The preceding sections have described the emergence of the main bank system in post World War II Japan, and discussed research findings concerning the distinctive differences between the Japanese main bank system and the arm's-length separation of lending from ownership and control that characterize the US and British banking systems. This section considers whether the features of the main bank system are attractive for the ongoing reform process in Poland. The applicability of the main bank system depends on the existing institutional structure and economic

conditions in Poland, as well as the specific demands that the privatization and reform process places on the financial sector. These issues are
considered in turn.

The Economy and the Financial Sector in Poland

The first Solidarity-led government was installed in September 1989 under
Prime Minister Mazowiecki, and it moved quickly and with remarkable
resolve to implement a package of sweeping reforms, most of which
began on 1 January 1990:

- Essentially all price controls were removed (food prices had been liberalized in August 1989), and energy prices were increased by as much as
  500 per cent.
- The government budget was brought into balance through the reduction of subsidies to state enterprises and the elimination of tax credits;
- Current account convertibility was introduced and the zloty was pegged
  to the US dollar.
- Foreign trade was liberalized and government allocation of materials
  was eliminated.
- The 'excess wage' tax was increased and virtually all exemptions were
  eliminated in an effort to slow the growth of wages in response to rising prices.
- The National Bank of Poland (NBP) moved to establish positive real
  rates of interest after years of negative real rates and very high
  inflation.

The discontinuous nature of these reforms contrasted sharply with calls
for a gradual reform process, and earned the name of 'shock therapy'.
The effect of these reforms on the key macroeconomic variables is evident
in Table 17.4: the hyperinflation was stopped, the real interest rate
increased substantially, the government achieved a surplus, and output
fell precipitously. The substantial fall in industrial output was all
accounted for by state enterprises, and output in the state enterprise sector fell further in 1991, in part, because of the loss of the CMEA export
market.

Although the 'shock therapy' macroeconomic reforms were the most
dramatic and widely discussed of all, a distinguishing feature of the economy is a history of important reforms implemented by the communists
as early as 1982 in an effort to resuscitate the floundering Polish economy.[12] The National Bank of Poland (NBP) was separated from the
Ministry of Finance in 1982 and given independent authority to lend on
commercial criteria. Although this authority was rarely exercised, the

---

[12] The discussion of banking and macroeconomic reforms draws heavily on Corbett and
Mayer (1991) and Berg and Blanchard (1992).

TABLE 17.4 Poland: Basic Macroeconomic Statistics, 1989–91

	89:4	90:1	90:2	90:3	90:4	91:1	91:2	91:3	91:4
Industrial Sales	1.00	0.77	0.72	0.74	0.75	0.65	0.57	0.57	0.57
Employment	17.6				16.5				15.9
(State)	11.7				10.0				8.8
(Private)	1.8				2.3				3.0
Unemployment Rate	0%	2%	3%	5%	6%	7.1%	8.4%	10.4%	11.4%
CPI Inflation	31%	32%	5%	4%	5%	8%	3%	2%	3%
Exports									
Dollars	2,412	2,182	2,705	3,133	4,000	2,751	4,459	3,196	4,182
TR	3,910	2,688	3,110	2,305	3,011	561	560	84	175
Imports									
Dollars	2,182	1,573	1,465	1,825	3,391	3,050	3,457	3,047	4,692
TR	2,725	1,706	1,505	1,443	1,985	558	163	68	47
Markups	40%	31%	29%	28%	24%	16%	14%	19%	13%
Gvt surplus (% of GDP)	-3.6	1.6	3.4	1.7	-3.9	-2.4	-3.6	-3.8	-3.1
Refinance Rate	12%	22%	5.8%	2.8%	4.3%	5.5%	5.3%	3.8%	3.3%

The index of real sales is measured in the last month of each quarter. Employment is measured in thousands at the end of the year. Private employ-ment does not include agriculture. Unemployment is in the last month of each quarter, expressed as the share of the labour force. CPI inflation is the average monthly inflation for the quarter. Exports and imports are for the quarter, in millions of transferable rubles (TR) and US dollars. The markup is defined as (Sales - Costs)/Costs for the quarter, for the socialized sector. Government surplus is for the quarter, as a percentage of GDP. It is computed as the surplus as a share of expenditures, multiplied by the ratio of expenditures of GDP for the year. The refinance rate of the NBP is the average for the quarter in monthly rates. Some data are not (yet) available on a comparable basis for 1992. Real sales in industry are seasonally adjusted in 1992.

Source: Berg and Blanchard (1992).

independence of the NBP was an important first step in the separation of banking from the planning system. Five years later, in 1987, the State Savings Bank (PKO BP) was spun-off from the NBP, and given primary responsibility for personal savings deposits and housing loans.

The most important financial reform took place in January 1989 with the passage of the New Banking Law and Act on the National Bank of Poland. Under the terms of this legislation, the nine regional offices of the NBP became autonomous commercial banks and the NBP remained as a central bank with few commercial activities. The NBP continued to issue hard currency accounts and was involved in channelling credit from the PKO BP (savings bank) to the other commercial banks.

The 1989 Banking Law also authorized universal banking, although the concept has not yet been clearly defined in law or in practice. The new commercial banks inherited the assets and liabilities associated with the depositors and borrowers in their region and were expected to serve as generalists; that is, there was no specialization amongst the commercial banks. It is important to emphasize that although the banks were subsequently commercialized (turned into joint stock companies) in preparation for privatization, commercialization left ownership in the hands of the government, and the senior executives for each bank were appointed by NBP officials. Not surprisingly, there was little increase in competition amongst the banks for deposit or lending opportunities. The NBP, meanwhile, was left with conventional central banking responsibilities, and the imposition in 1989 of limits on credits to the government increased the NBP's capacity to operate as an independent institution. A Department of Bank Supervision was created within the NBP in May 1989 in an effort to begin building the capacity to monitor banks and ensure stability in the financial sector.

The 1989 legislation also amended the charters of three other special function banks that the communists had operated to allow these banks to engage in commercial banking. The Bank Handlowy serviced the needs of Polish state enterprises engaged in foreign trade, and the Bank PKO SA handled all foreign currency transactions for private persons. The Bank Gospodarki Żywnościowej (Bank of Food Economy), a collection of 1,500 small cooperative (but state-controlled) banks, served the many small Polish family farms. (Polish agriculture remained in private hands under the communists, and its small scale made centralized banking very difficult.) These specialized banks had been established by the government with non-overlapping scopes of activity to ensure that there was no competition; each had a monopoly over a sector of the economy. Consequently, the specialized banks, together with the NBP, held the vast majority of deposits in the banking sector.

The reform process begun in 1989 did little to change the level of concentration. New rules were implemented in July 1989 allowing enterprises to have deposit accounts at more than one bank, which were intended to increase competition amongst the banks. Nonetheless, nearly two years after the separation of the nine commercial banks from the NBP, the four specialized banks and the NBP still held more than 75 per cent of total Polish banking deposits (see Table 17.5), despite the fact that the nine commercial banks inherited the assets in their region.[13]

TABLE 17.5 Polish Banks by Balance Sum and Own Funds – Capital (at the end of 1990)
(billion zloty)

	Balance Sum	Own Funds
Total of all banks	481,782	29,379
Narodowy Bank Polski	145,147	2,079
Bank Handlowy w Warszawie SA	103,479	6,313
Bank Polska kasa Opieki SA	54,456	2,855
Powszechna kasa Oszczędności BP	38,700	686
Bank Gospodarki Żywnościowej	29,376	2,927
Państwowy Bank Kredytowy (W-wa)	14,522	1,845
Bank Śląski (Katowice)	12,673	2,122
Banki Spółdzielcze	11,583	884
Bank Przemysłowo-Handlowy (Kraków)	11,390	1,336
Powszechny Bank Gospodarczy (Łódź)	9,305	845

Source: The statistical data contained in this paper are taken from materials of Narodowy Bank Polski.

The Banking Law of 1982 permitted, in theory, the establishment of new banks with non-state capital. However, any new bank had to be approved by the Council of Ministers, who were free to decide on the scope of operations, location, and name of the bank. During the period 1982–89 no new banks were established as a result of this 'reform'.

The restrictions on the establishment of new banks were liberalized substantially in 1989, and have been amended subsequently. Permission from the president of the NBP to open a new bank requires that three conditions be met:

1. own capital (in 1990) of 70 billion zloty or US$2 million for Polish-owned banks; and, US$6 million for foreign-owned banks;
2. suitable premises for banking operations;
3. senior bank officials with suitable experience and training.

---

[13] The low level of deposits in the nine commercial banks spun-off from the NBP was clearly also a function of the financial circumstances facing state enterprises, who are their main customers.

By early 1993 there were more than 80 new private banks, including eight with at least partial foreign ownership. However, these new private banks were very small and accounted for less than 30 per cent of total banking assets. Capital requirements for new private banks had been lower in previous years—roughly $US100,000 in 1989—and most private banks were created under those less stringent conditions.

At this point, with the banks commercialized, the next step in banking reform in Poland is widely considered to be the privatization of the nine commercial banks. Several have already been twinned with western banks to develop greater banking skills and improved infrastructure. The critical actions that must be taken before privatization are rationalization of their loan portfolios to eliminate bad debts and recapitalization to assure solvency after cleaning up the balance sheets. Because banks did not face credit risk under the communist system, they had no reserves against loan losses. Therefore, in the absence of infusion of new funds, the writing off of bad loans would directly reduce the banks' capital.

The severe recession within the state sector in 1990 and 1991 (see Table 17.4) greatly worsened the quality of the banks' loan portfolios. The Ministry of Finance has recently overseen the review and categorization of all significant loans currently on the books of the nine commercial banks. Using a five-category hierarchy from very high to very low likelihood of collection, more than half the zloty value of the total loans were rated in the lower two categories. Although precise figures are hard to find, it is clear that cleaning-up balance sheets before privatization will be a time-consuming and costly process. As an incentive for improvement in bank balance sheets, the Ministry of Finance is committed to privatizing the nine banks in an order determined by the quality of their balance sheets.

The first bank privatization, the Wielkopolski Bank Kredytowy (WBK) in Poznon, finally took place in April 1993 when shares were issued on the Warsaw Stock Exchange. The Ministry of Finance judged WBK to have done the best job of the nine commercial banks in improving the quality of its balance sheet, mainly by curtailing lending to state enterprises and carefully increasing lending to private entrepreneurial companies. The WBK also distinguished itself by attracting a large deposit base of more than 250,000 people served by 44 branches around Poznon. The European Bank for Reconstruction and Development invested US$10.6 million to purchase 28.5 per cent of the newly issued shares.

Progress in privatizing state enterprises has also been agonizingly slow. There have been at least three mechanisms used to privatize industrial assets. First, in the few cases where large Polish enterprises were considered to have positive net worth and be viable in the near term, western consultants performed valuations and the firms were sold using initial public offerings (the British model). This process turned out to be very slow and extremely costly, with consultant fees occasionally exceeding the proceeds of the sale, and it has been used for fewer than 20 enterprises. Second, small companies have been sold on an *ad hoc* basis to incumbent managers or local business people. The vast majority of retail shops, restaurants, and the like, have been sold by local governments to private owners. Indeed, more than 60 per cent of wholesale and retail trade is now in private hands; Polish agriculture had remained largely in private hands under the communists. Third, a mass privatization programme (MPP) was developed and approved by the Parliament to privatize hundreds of industrial enterprises quickly.

The MPP was formulated as a means to achieve four goals simultaneously: speed, low administrative cost, concentration of control to facilitate restructuring, and broad-based ownership amongst the Polish citizenry. Clearly, the latter two goals require a novel solution, since concentration of control and broad-based ownership are difficult to reconcile using traditional mechanisms. The MPP was originally conceived as a means to privatize a substantial percentage of Poland's 8,000 industrial state enterprises. The scope of the MPP's initial activity, however, was restricted to the healthiest enterprises in an effort to learn from the most promising cases before tackling the more difficult ones. Thus far, only those firms with both positive net cash flow and positive operating profits have been allowed into the MPP. In early 1993, only roughly 600 enterprises met these criteria and were slated for inclusion in the MPP.

Under the complicated terms of the MPP, the 600 enterprises are first commercialized into joint-stock companies (for details, see Polish Ministry of Privatization, 1992). The shares are then allocated 30 per cent to the state, 10 per cent to the current work force, and 60 per cent to twenty management funds established under the MPP. Initially, roughly 30 per cent of each enterprise will go to one lead fund and the remaining 30 per cent will be evenly distributed amongst the remaining 19 funds. Funds will then be allowed to trade shares amongst themselves which, of course, is likely to lead to further concentration of ownership of the individual companies by a lead fund whose controlling interest can be used to facilitate the restructuring or the sale of assets. The management funds will engage western firms as advisors, or managers, under contract with the Ministry of Privatization. The fund managers have performance-based incentives and are empowered to borrow money and issue new shares in the funds.

Every Polish citizen of 18 years and above will receive a share in each of the 20 management funds. In an effort to forestall speculation and quick concentration of ownership among a few people, the shares will not be tradable for a period of at least several months. Since the shares in the enterprises themselves are not initially traded in a well-defined market, it will be difficult to value the citizens' ownership shares in the management funds. The plan foresees the management funds moving to public offerings for the enterprises in their portfolios when restructuring has proceeded to an appropriate extent, and gradually the enterprises would leave the management funds, the management funds would hold cash or tradable securities, and the citizens would have ownership shares with clearly defined market values. The MPP was to be implemented in the autumn of 1992, but after several setbacks in the Polish Parliament, it was finally approved in the spring of 1993, and is expected to be implemented in the very near future.

There has been little recognition of the connection between the privatization of the state industrial enterprises and financial sector reform. One important manifestation of this lack of connection is that responsibility for privatizing the banks rests with the Ministry of Finance, and the process has been kept almost entirely independent of the enterprise privatization process that is managed by the Ministry of Privatization and the Ministry of Industry. In addition, a number of schemes have been proposed for cleaning up bank balance sheets that involve debt-for-equity swaps in which the old debts of state enterprises are forgiven in exchange for equity in the new privatized company. Clearly, such an arrangement would have to be integrated into the other privatization processes—especially the MPP—but there has been little discussion of integrated solutions to these problems.

The much more rapid and dynamic road to private ownership in Poland has been the establishment and growth of private small businesses. Under the communists, legitimate private business was virtually non-existent outside the agricultural sector. Liberalization of the rules governing the formation of private cooperatives in 1982 marked the beginning of the explosion of private employment in Poland. Legal changes in 1985 for the first time in the communist era permitted the registration of private limited liability companies under the terms of the 1984 Code of Commerce. Finally, the 1989 New Law on Economic Activity removed most licensing and registration restrictions on self-employment and the establishment of unincorporated firms. The process for setting up joint ventures was also liberalized significantly in 1989.

The response to these reforms has been swift and dramatic. The first joint-venture company was registered in July 1986, and 52 more were registered in the next two years. Table 17.6 shows that since 1989, however, the number of private limited-liability companies, including joint-ventures has grown several fold. Also, Table 17.7 shows that the number of persons self-employed or with unincorporated businesses had grown to nearly 2.5 million by 30 September 1991. Total non-agricultural private employment was in excess of 3 million persons by the end of 1991.

The near absence of private businesses until recently in Poland meant that the state banking system had no experience with the needs of grow-

TABLE 17.6 The Number of Private Spółki in Poland: Domestic and Joint Venture

	31 Dec 1989	1 Dec 1990	30 Jun 1991
Industry			
Domestic	2,769	7,014	7,698
Joint venture	240	853	1,431
Construction			
Domestic	2,640	5,646	7,164
Joint venture	12	71	167
Agriculture			
Domestic	83	342	285
Joint venture	14	48	62
Forestry			
Domestic	10	36	39
Joint venture	3	4	5
Transportation			
Domestic	86	356	507
Joint venture	14	67	124
Telecommunication			
Domestic	18	56	80
Joint venture	–	5	7
Trade			
Domestic	1,759	8,661	12,598
Joint venture	32	198	475
Other branches of material production			
Domestic	2,979	7,098	5,837
Joint venture	80	258	296
Municipal economy			
Domestic	76	160	163
Joint venture	1	6	9
Nonmaterial production			
Domestic	1,273	3,870	4,145
Joint venture	33	135	264
Total	11,693	33,239	38,516
of which, joint venture	429	1,645	2,840

Spółki are firms in which private individuals have at least 51 per cent ownership.
Source: Johnson (1992).

ing small businesses. Indeed, the banking system was structured to allocate funds amongst large state enterprises according to the terms of the plan, and there were no incentives for bankers to consider even opening deposit accounts for small or private businesses. Data from small businesses that have been successful during the economic reform show that

TABLE 17.7 Employment in Unincorporated Firms in Poland

	31 Dec 1990	30 Jun 1991	30 Sept. 1991
Industry	334,613	339,291	348,803
Construction	165,541	165,428	170,618
Transportation	61,368	56,913	60,203
Trade	346,294	456,844	514,778
Catering & restaurant	22,511	30,443	34,845
Other material services	122,099	122,555	124,768
Nonmaterial services	83,066	100,923	111,629
Total	1,135,492	1,272,397	1,365,644

Source: Official Polish government statistics, see Johnson (1992).

their growth has been *in spite* of the banks' unwillingness to provide loans or, in most cases, even to provide simple transactions processing on a timely basis. (For evidence from the small business sector, see Johnson, 1992, and Johnson and Loveman, 1992.)

Irrespective of the details of future economic reforms in Poland, it is abundantly clear that the sustained growth of the private small business sector is vital for economic revitalization and job generation. Given the crucial role of external financing in small firm development, it is equally clear that the Polish financial sector must reform itself in a fashion that supports the needs of the small business sector *as well as* the restructuring of the large state enterprises.

Financial Restructuring and the Future of Reform in Poland

The preceding discussion has described the context in which competing financial reform proposals must be considered. The objectives for any financial system in Poland can now be stated concisely:

1. The provision of a credible and stable depository system that attracts domestic savings for investment.
2. Given the dysfunctional state of Polish accounting systems and budgeting procedures, and the lack of valuation mechanisms that follow from these systems and procedures, lenders must have the capacity to distinguish amongst prospective borrowers under conditions of poor information, scarce experience or credit history and unreliable projections of future earnings.
3. A long time horizon to support lending to enterprises in need of massive restructuring and small businesses whose profitability and growth may occur only several years after the first provision of financing.

4. The capacity to play an active role in helping borrowers to acquire badly needed general management expertise, especially with respect to management under conditions of financial distress and an inadequate supply of capital.
5. An absence of soft budget constraints: lenders must be willing to curtail lending to firms with inadequate prospects for future earnings and lend only to those that can deliver at least the market rate of return on borrowed funds.
6. An avoidance of inefficient liquidations; that is, the capacity to prevent the liquidation of any enterprises with positive net present values.

The first of these six criteria has relatively little to do with Poland's choices for banking reform, although in a country with low levels of financial assets, because of consumers' desire for diversification, bank-led financing systems may be superior to a securities market led system. The other five, however, can be used to distinguish powerfully between two distinct alternatives: the Japanese main bank system and the combination of equity, bond and arm's-length banking found in the United States and the United Kingdom. (The German system provides an intermediate case. See Corbett and Mayer, 1991, and Chapter 1 by Aoki, Patrick and Sheard.)

In assessing the merits of the main bank system for Poland, it is important to consider both the transition issues and the long-term, or steady-state, characteristics of the main bank system. There are two necessary transition conditions for the main bank system to succeed in Poland. First, the main banks must not offer soft budget constraints to enterprises. This concern is often voiced in Poland, where decades of lending without reference to ability to repay has led to a gross misallocation of funds. The best insurance against a soft budget constraint is competition amongst adequately capitalized private banks. Solvent private banks will not find it in their interest, as equity holders or otherwise, to lend to firms that lack the capacity to repay.[14] Therefore, the reform process must include privatization of the banks that will serve as main banks. Moreover, some large banks may need to be divided into multiple entities to enhance competitiveness.

Second, existing Polish banks lack many of the most fundamental banking and managerial skills. Consequently, there is understandable reluctance on the part of many people to give the banks any more power than is absolutely necessary in the reform process. One manifestation of this unwillingness to rely on the banks has been the separation of the

---

[14] Of course, as has been demonstrated by the US Savings and Loan crises, private ownership *per se* does not necessarily stop excessive risk taking. In the Polish case, once the bank recapitalization is completed, it will be important for the regulators promptly to close any institutions that subsequently become insolvent. Similarly, the central bank should not supply so much credit as to encourage expansive lending by banks.

banks from the MPP. Although the current lack of confidence in the banks is completely warranted, any reform process must include a massive effort to build basic banking competence quickly. If nothing else, one can confidently predict that it will be easier to regulate a concentrated main bank system.

The post-war Japanese financial sector, too, faced the problem of eliminating soft budget constraints between enterprises and their designated banks. The Dodge plan helped to stop the flow of easy credit to the banking system. The curtailment of inefficient lending in Japan was further reinforced by two key actions: the cleaning up of bank balance sheets to remove uncollectable loans, thereby removing any perverse incentives for further lending to uncredit-worthy borrowers; and the use of special managers from the banks to work-out existing loans to enterprises. Recall that in Japan the munitions companies were paired during the war with designated financial institutions. The restructuring of the former munitions companies was accomplished by special managers drawn from the debtor companies and the banks. The bankers involved in the restructuring gained invaluable familiarity with the debtor companies, and undoubtedly developed important monitoring skills that served them well as lenders in subsequent years.

Current Polish circumstances are also suited to having commercial bank managers involved in the resolution of enterprise debts, both to banks and to other enterprises. The use of special managers could develop badly needed monitoring expertise amongst Polish bankers while also generating enterprise-specific knowledge useful for future lending decisions. As in Japan, the restructuring process that featured special managers was premised on existing close relationships between an enterprise and a bank, and the process clearly facilitated the emergence of a main bank system. Given similar conditions, the same debt-restructuring process could be used as a mechanism for establishing a main bank system in Poland.

An examination of the substantive parallels between the post-war Japanese experience and the current Polish circumstances suggests that many of the conditions that led to the success of the main bank system exist in Poland. First, both economies had histories of centralized control of financial and non-financial assets. In Japan the war-time controls on the allocation of credit meant that the market mechanism for allocating funds to the most worthy borrowers failed to function. In Poland the problem is more severe, because the precedent and expertise necessary for market allocation of credit must be traced back more than 40 years.

Second, the Polish banks are themselves concentrated and have very close financial relationships with the highly concentrated industrial sector of the economy. If the soft budget constraint problem can be solved, then the evidence regarding the Japanese main bank system suggests that these relationships may actually be valuable. Given the existing web of financial ties between the banks and state enterprises, a banking system that builds on these connections, that is, the Japanese main bank system, would seem desirable.

Third, hyperinflation in Japan and Poland, along with other factors, left both economies with low levels of financial assets, while a largely destroyed (Japan) or woefully inefficient (Poland) industrial sector required large amounts of financing for reconstruction. Together, this combination of factors on the supply and demand sides of the credit markets suggests that careful allocation of credit will be crucial.

Finally, the problems associated with accurate valuation of companies and severe information and reputational inadequacies make the extensive use of equity financing quite difficult (see Lipton and Sachs, 1990). The Japanese stock market did not re-open until 1949; in Poland in early 1993, the fledgling Warsaw Stock Exchange had 17 listed securities and total market capitalization was about US$400 million. With privatization and equity markets in Poland in their infancy, there is little capacity for shareholders to exercise meaningful control over the management of industrial companies. Similarly, bond markets offer little hope for raising substantial sums of money for restructuring.

Lacking widespread access to equity markets, the issue for financial reform becomes focused on the best structure for banking, wherein banks will be the primary source of financing. Furthermore, since corporate control will not be exercised by shareholders, there is a vital need for another form of effective control. The main bank system, unlike arm's-length systems, provides a mechanism that can both deliver financing *and* exert substantial control over the managerial actions of its borrowers. As a substantial shareholder in the company, the main bank can act directly to influence the composition of the board of directors and, hence, the activities of senior management. Through its position as a large holder of debt *and* equity, the bank has an incentive to work diligently to increase the borrower's long-term performance. In Poland, where managerial expertise is currently very scarce, the provision of such skills from a bank would be an important resource, and such a conveyance of skills is much more likely under a main bank system. Moreover, as long as bankers are lending private money under profit-driven incentives, there is no reason to fear that soft budget constraints will lead to the ill-conceived lending practices of the communist system.

In sum, the main bank system has several virtues with respect to its control properties that recommend it for current Polish circumstances. But it is the economic efficiency properties, documented above from Japan, that make the strongest case for adoption of the main bank system in Poland. The results from research on Japan suggest that the main bank system is particularly well suited to meet the challenges associated with financial sector reform in Poland.

First, the main bank system has been shown to have a number of advantages in achieving the most efficient monitoring of borrowers. The close ties between the bank and the debtor firm, sustained over a long period of time, reduce information asymmetries and permit the bank to make more informed lending decisions. Thus the system saves on two margins, by both reducing duplication in monitoring and by increasing the efficiency of the monitoring that takes place. These savings are especially important in the Polish context, where information is poor, credit histories are non-existent, projections are inaccurate and few managers have significant reputations.

Evidence was presented in the second section that showed that main banks are especially preferable to arm's-length banking when the borrower is experiencing periods of financial distress. The main bank is better positioned, as a consequence of its monitoring efficiencies, to make decisions on additional lending. Inefficient liquidations are, therefore, less likely, and companies in financial distress are better able to undertake investment projects with positive net present values. Furthermore, the evidence from Japan suggests that even healthy firms were less reliant on internal funds for capital investments when they had a main bank relationship.

Since main banks accumulate substantial experience with their customers over time, they are better able to manage the working out of bad loans. In systems with arm's-length banking relationships, rescue plans for large debtors typically involve many lenders who may have widely varying incentives with respect to the disposition of the debts. A main bank relationship, conversely, reduces coordination costs by reducing the number of lenders *and* by providing very high quality information about the debtor and other creditors. In Japan, main banks have, on occasion, gone to the debtor's suppliers in effect to guarantee outstanding trade credits so that actions by suppliers will not bring the debtor into bankruptcy. Polish enterprises currently have a tremendous amount of trade credit that accumulated during the recession. Management of the outstanding trade credit by main banks would facilitate efficient decisions on the choice of enterprises that should be liquidated.

It is difficult to over-emphasize how important the monitoring efficiencies may be in Poland where state enterprises face such massive restructuring problems, and where such a large portion of the existing capital stock will require modernization and rationalization. It is difficult to imagine how a system based on diffused financing can succeed given the problems that will arise in trying to finance massive restructuring in Poland. Of course, it is also hard to imagine how a solvent and efficient decentralized banking system could be feasibly developed from the existing Polish banking system. In general, a bank-led financing system seems better suited to handling coordination problems in investment decisions than a securities market based financial system. Because of coordination problems, some analysts argue that it is important to develop specialized institutions to provide long-term financing. Packer discusses the impact of funding by long-term financial institutions on growth in Japan in Chapter 4.

A final important consideration favouring the selection of the main bank system for Poland stems from the long time horizons associated with equity ownership. There is no doubt that privatization and restructuring will require a period of several years before enterprises can reasonably expect to generate consistent profits. A key factor underlying the patience demonstrated by the main banks is that, as their clients mature, the banks' long-term commitments are rewarded with significant equity returns. The alignment of interests between debt and equity holders would greatly facilitate the flexibility needed by Polish managers to undertake comprehensive change and restructuring.

While the advantages of the main bank system for large Polish enterprises follow clearly from the Japanese precedent, there has been little research, and thus little evidence regarding main bank involvement with small businesses (see Chapter 8, and Horiuchi, 1988). Given the central role currently played by small businesses in Poland it is important to consider how the banking system can best serve their credit needs. Small businesses in Poland currently receive virtually no external financing from any source, and finance themselves largely from personal savings and retained earnings (see Johnson, 1992). Interestingly, many Polish small businesses began by providing services or other non-capital-intensive activities to generate sufficient cash flow to finance capital acquisitions, and then they gradually moved into manufacturing and construction (see Johnson and Loveman, 1992). The unavailability of credit to small businesses is a very large impediment to the growth and job generation process in Poland.

Financing for small businesses is often considered to be inadequate and poorly allocated even in western industrialized countries. Governmental entities such as the US Small Business Administration and venture capitalists play an important role in funding new businesses, while banks typically find new businesses to be too small or too risky to service profitably.

There is little evidence upon which to base an argument about the efficacy of a main bank system for Polish small businesses. On the one hand, small businesses share the need for careful monitoring, effective control and long-term financing experienced by large state enterprises. The proven ability of main banks to reduce the reliance of Japanese firms on internally generated funds bodes well for their application to small businesses, which often experience periods of severe cash shortages despite having many positive net present value projects. In this respect, the main bank system seems sensible. On the other hand, the sheer volume of small businesses could easily overwhelm the capacity of a concentrated banking sector to provide effective and profitable service. Whether or not a main bank system is chosen in Poland, it is clear that government policy must address the specific needs of small businesses so that their access to credit markets is given the proper priority. The growth of small private banks in Poland seems most promising in this respect, and policies should be considered to enhance the attractiveness of small bank lending to entrepreneurs.

Finally, the development of the MPP has proceeded with little direct involvement or consideration of the Polish banks. There is an important role for main banks to play in such a process, however, because the management funds could draw on the main banks for financing and assistance in the control of the constituent firms. The main banks need not be part of the MPP's formal structure, but at a minimum, the financial reform process must proceed at a pace that would permit main banks to be available to support the management funds in their restructuring efforts. Without direct bank support, the management funds will be dependent on raising funds through the sale of companies or their assets, internally generated funds from the companies, or solicitation from a number of banks in and outside Poland. None of these alternatives seems very likely to generate an adequate or consistent source of financing. Moreover, there has been little, if any, discussion of the Polish commercial banks being given access to shares in the management funds. This is due largely to the government's aim to distribute shares to individuals and workers as a right of citizenship, rather than to institutions. The exclusion of the banks is also a possible consequence of a desire to separate the planned restructuring of enterprises under the MPP from the unimpressive management and poor financial condition of the banks.

CONCLUSION

This chapter has examined the main bank system that developed in Japan after World War II as a model for the financial system reform in Poland. Pointing out some important similarities between the economic conditions in Poland today and Japan immediately after the war, we have argued that the main bank system is a preferred model for Poland due to both (a) the performance of the system and (b) the low implementation costs given the current situation in Poland.

We do not claim that we now have a concrete policy proposal for financial reform and privatization in Poland, although we believe that the main bank system should be an important component in such a proposal. In order to develop a specific policy toward financial reform, our analysis must be supplemented by additional considerations. For example, the main bank system does not have any clear implications for the deposits collection mechanism, which as was pointed out in the last section, is an important aspect of any financial system. Safety of deposits is especially important for an economy like Poland's, because each household holds a small amount of financial wealth. Analysis of regulatory mechanisms and deposit insurance that increase the safety (and hence supply) of the deposits must complement the analysis in this chapter.

Another consideration is the participation of international organizations and foreign banks in financial reform in Poland. The supply of expertise from foreign countries will be important in developing the human resources necessary to establish a well-functioning banking system. As the previous section points out, the lack of fundamental banking skills is a serious problem and may be considered especially damaging to a main bank approach to reform.

Similarly, we have ignored the political economy aspects of economic reform. In the immediate aftermath of World War II, the Allies were able to impose many reforms on the Japanese government. It is unclear how many of these changes would have been possible without this guidance or whether these reforms could have taken place without the help of the Japanese bureaucracy. Relative to Poland, there was a considerable amount of stability in the Japanese government during the period when the reform was taking place. While the political instability must make reform of any sort more difficult in Poland than it was in Japan, it is not obvious to us that this necessarily makes it much more difficult to move to a main bank style system rather than to an arm's-length banking system.

Nonetheless, we do not claim that the main bank system is an ideal financial system. While this chapter has focused almost exclusively on the benefits of the main bank system, in closing we want to emphasize that the system does have some limitations and is not necessarily appropriate for all types of economies. In particular, a major consideration in the design of the banking system is the list of possible alternative financing arrangements. For reasons that we have discussed above, both in Japan in the early 1950s and in modern-day Poland, the feasibility of a system that did not rely on bank financing seemed dubious. Thus the debate over the structure of the financial system is effectively limited to a discussion over which set of banking rules to adopt.

Obviously, in many other cases, a system based on security market financing is a completely viable alternative to a bank-led financing system. In comparing these two types of systems, one would probably be led to study a different set of contrasts than we have focused on in this chapter. For instance, to the extent that unmonitored lending can succeed, the associated savings in monitoring costs make it probable that bank lending will be a dominated form of financing. Of course, a firm's reputation is likely to be the central determinant of whether it can rely on public bond and equity markets to secure funding. Therefore, if an economy includes a significant number of firms that can circumvent bank dependence, then the financial system is likely to evolve to de-emphasize the role of banks. Indeed, one way to view the US economy is that by relying on public markets and exploiting firms' reputations, the United States is able to run a financial system that is much less dependent on bank financing than many other capitalist economies. An implication of this arrangement is that banks no longer seem the natural party to be involved with corporate governance. From this perspective, it is not surprising that the US system of corporate governance has been different from that of Japan in the 1950s and 60s.

An interesting recent development in Japanese corporate financing is that many large Japanese companies have begun to shift away from bank financing in favour of bond and equity financing. As Hoshi, Kashyap and Scharfstein (1993) discuss, this shift appears to be driven both by deregulation which has made the use of these instruments legal, and by the continued success and improved visibility of the companies that have made the securities attractive to investors. Ironically, although the major Japanese corporations may previously have been very well served by the type of main bank system that we have described, they may have outgrown it. In thinking about Poland, we think it also prudent to recognize that this type of evolution is possible, but it remains a long way down the road of economic reform.

REFERENCES

AJINOMOTO. 1971. *Ajinomoto Kabushiki Kaisha Sha-shi (Ajinomoto's Company History)*, vol. 1. Tokyo: Ajinomoto.

——. 1989. *Aji o Tagayasu: Ajinomoto Hachijunen-shi (Cultivating Tastes: Eighty Years' History of Ajinomoto)*. Tokyo: Ajinomoto.

Bank of Japan, Research Bureau. 1973. *Nihon Kin'yu-shi Shiryo: Showa Hen*, vol. 34 *(Data for Japanese Financial History: Showa Volumes)*.

——. 1980. *Nihon Kin'yu-shi Shiryo: Showa Zokuhen*, vol. 8 *(Data for Japanese Financial History: More Showa Volumes)*. Tokyo.

BERG, ANDREW and OLIVIER BLANCHARD. 1992. 'Stabilization and Transition: Poland 1990–1991.' Paper presented at NBER 'Conference on Transition in Eastern Europe,' Cambridge MA.

CORBETT, JENNY and COLIN MAYER. 1991. 'Financial Reform in Eastern Europe: Progress with the Wrong Model.' CEPR Discussion Paper 603, London.

EDO, HIDEO. 1986. *Watashi no Mitsui Showa-shi (My Showa History of Mitsui)*. Tokyo: Toyo Keizai Shimposha.

GERLACH, MICHAEL. 1992. *Alliance Capitalism: The Social Organization of Japanese Business*. Berkeley: University of California Press.

HADLEY, ELEANOR M. 1970. *Antitrust In Japan.* Princeton NJ: Princeton University Press.

HAMADA, KOICHI and AKIYOSHI HORIUCHI. 1987. 'The Political Economy of the Financial Market.' In Kozo Yamamura and Yasukichi Yasuba, eds., *The Political Economy of Japan*, vol 1: *The Domestic Transformation.* Stanford CA: Stanford University Press.

HORIUCHI, TOSHIHIRO. 1988. *Mein Banku Kyoso to Kashidashi Shijo (Main Bank Competition and Loan Market).* Tokyo: Toyo Keizai Shinposha.

HOSHI, TAKEO. 1993a. 'Evolution of the Main Bank System in Japan.' Macquarie University, Centre for Japanese Economic Studies, Working Paper 93–4.

——. 1993b. 'An Economic Model of the Main Bank System.' In preparation.

HOSHI, TAKEO, ANIL KASHYAP and DAVID SCHARFSTEIN. 1990. 'The Role of Banks in Reducing the Costs of Financial Distress in Japan.' *Journal of Financial Economics* 27: 67–88.

——. 1991. 'Corporate Structure, Liquidity and Investment: Evidence from Japanese Industrial Groups.' *Quarterly Journal of Economics* 106: 33–60.

——. 1993. 'The Choice Between Public and Private Debt: An Analysis of Post-Deregulation Corporate Financing in Japan.' Manuscript, Graduate School of Business, University of Chicago.

JOHNSON, SIMON. 1992. 'Private Business in Eastern Europe.' Paper presented at NBER 'Conference on Transition in Eastern Europe,' Cambridge MA.

JOHNSON, SIMON and GARY LOVEMAN. 1992. 'The Implications of the Polish Economic Reform for Small Business: Evidence from Gdansk.' In Zoltan Acs and David Audretsch, eds., *Entrepreneurship East and West.* Cambridge: Cambridge University Press.

KAPLAN, STEVEN N. 1992. 'Top Executive Rewards and Firm Performance: A Comparison of Japan and the US.' Manuscript, Graduate School of Business, University of Chicago.

KAPLAN, STEVEN N. and BERNADETTE MINTON. 1993. '"Outside" Intervention in Japanese Companies: Its Determinants and Implications for Managers.' Manuscript, Graduate School of Business, University of Chicago.

KATO, TOSHIHIKO. 1974. 'Kin'yu Seido Kaikaku' ('Reforms of Financial System'). In University of Tokyo, Social Science Research Institute, ed., *Sengo Kaikaku*, vol. 7: *Keizai Kaikaku (Post-War Reforms: Economic Reforms).* Tokyo: University of Tokyo Press.

KEIZAI CHOSA KYOKAI. 1963. *Keiretsu no Kenkyu (A Study of Keiretsu)* Tokyo: Keizai Chosa Kyokai.

——. 1973. *Keiretsu no Kenkyu (A Study of Keiretsu)* Tokyo: Keizai Chosa Kyokai.

KOSAI, YUTAKA. 1981. *Kodo Seicho no Jidai (The Age of Rapid Growth).* Tokyo: Nihon Hyoron-sha.

LIPTON, DAVID, and JEFFREY SACHS. 1990. 'Privatization in Eastern Europe: The Case of Poland.' Brookings Papers on Economic Activity 2: 293–333.

MATSUZAWA, TAKUJI. 1985. *Watashi no Ginko Showa-shi (My Showa Banking History).* Tokyo: Toyo Keizai Shinposha.

MILLER, MERTON H. 1992. 'The Economics and Politics of Index Arbitrage in the US and Japan.' Manuscript, Graduate School of Business, University of Chicago.

632   *The Comparative Context*

Ministry of Finance. 1976. *Showa Zaisei-shi: Shusen kara Kowa made*, vol. 12: *Kin'yu (1) (Financial History of Showa: War's End to Peace Treaty: Finance (1))*. Written by Takafusa Nakamura, Kaichi Shimura, and Shiro Hara. Tokyo: Toyo Keizai Shimposha.

———. 1978. *Showa Zaisei-shi: Shusen kara Kowa made*, vol. 19: *Tokei (Financial History of Showa: War's End to Peace Treaty: Statistical Data)*. Tokyo: Toyo Keizai Shimposha.

———. 1979. *Showa Zaisei-shi: Shusen kara Kowa made*, vol. 14: *Hoken Shoken (Financial History of Showa: War's End to Peace Treaty: Insurance and Securities)*. Written by Akira Inuta and Kaichi Shimura. Tokyo: Toyo Keizai Shimposha.

———. 1983a. *Showa Zaisei-shi: Shusen kara Kowa made*, vol. 11: *Seifu Saimu (Financial History of Showa: War's End to Peace Treaty: Government Debt)*. Written by Saburo Kato. Tokyo: Toyo Keizai Shimposha.

———. 1983b. *Showa Zaisei-shi: Shusen kara Kowa made*, vol. 13: *Kin'yu (2), Kigyo Zaimu, Mikaeri Shikin (Financial History of Showa: War's End to Peace Treaty: Finance (2), Corporate Finance, and Assistance Funds)*. Written by Toshimitsu Imuta, Osamu Ito, Shiro Hara, Masayasu Miyazaki, and Yoshimasa Shibata. Tokyo: Toyo Keizai Shimposha.

Mitsubishi Bank. 1954. *Mitsubishi Ginko-shi. (History of Mitsubishi Bank)*.

MIYAJIMA, HIDEAKI. 1992. 'Zaibatsu Kaitai' (Zaibatsu Dissolution). In Juro Hashimoto and Haruto Takeda, eds., *Nihon Keizai no Hatten to Kigyo Shudan (The Development of Japanese Economy and Industrial Groups)*. Tokyo: University of Tokyo Press.

MIYAZAKI, MASAYASU and OSAMU ITOH. 1989. 'Senji-Sengo no Sangyo to Kigyo' ('Industries and Enterprises in the War-time and the Post-war Period'). In Takafusa Nakamura, ed., *Nihon Keizaishi*, vol 7: *'Keikaku-ka' to 'Minshu-ka'. (Japanese Economic History: 'Planning' and 'Democratizing')*. Tokyo: Iwanami-Shoten.

NIHON KEIZAI SHIMBUN-SHA. 1980. *Watashi no Rirekisho: Keizai-jin*, vol. 14 (*My Personal History: Business People*). Tokyo: Toyo Keizai Shimposha.

———. 1987. *Watashi no Rirekisho: Keizai-jin*, vol. 22 (*My Personal History: Business People*). Tokyo: Toyo Keizai Shimposha.

OHTSUKI, BUNPEI. 1987. *Watashi no Mitsubishi Showa-shi* (My Showa History of Mitsubishi). Tokyo: Toyo Keizai Shimposha.

OKAZAKI, TETSUJI. 1991. 'Senji Keikaku Keizai to Kigyo' ('War-Time Planned Economy and Firms'). In University of Tokyo, Social Science Research Institute, ed., *Gendai Nihon Shakai*, vol 4: *Rekishi-teki Zentei (Contemporary Japanese Society: Historical Presumptions)*. Tokyo: University of Tokyo Press.

PASCALE, RICHARD and THOMAS P. ROHLEN. 1983. 'The Mazda Turnaround.' *Journal of Japanese Studies* 9: 219–263.

Republic of Poland (Ministry of Privatisation). 1992. 'Mass Privatisation: Proposed Programme, An Explanation.' Warsaw.

SCHOENHOLTZ, KERMIT and MASAHIKO TAKEDA. 1985. 'Joho Katsudo to Mein Banku sei' ('Informational Activities and the Main Bank System'). *Kin'yu Kenkyu* 4: 1–24.

SHEARD, PAUL. 1989. 'The Main Bank System and Corporate Monitoring and Control in Japan.' *Journal of Economic Behavior and Organization* 11: 399–422.

Sumitomo Ginko. 1979. *Sumitomo Ginko Hachi-Ju-nen-shi* (*Eighty Years' History of Sumitomo Bank*). Tokyo: Sumitomo Bank.

Teranishi, Juro. 1982. *Nihon no Keizai Hatten to Kin'yu* (*Japanese Economic Development and Financial System*). Tokyo: Iwanami Shoten.

——. 1991a. 'Inflation Stabilization with Growth—Japanese Experience during 1945–50.' Hitotsubashi University, Institute of Economic Research Working Paper 243.

——. 1991b. 'Financial System Reform after the War.' Institute of Economic Research Working Paper 244, Hitotsubashi University.

Tsuda, Hisashi. 1988. *Watashi no Sumitomo Showa-shi* (*My Showa History of Sumitomo*). Tokyo: Toyo Keizai Shimposha.

Yamazaki, Hiroaki. 1979. 'Senji-ka no Sangyo Kozo to Dokusen Soshiki (Industrial Structure and Monopolistic Organization during the War).' In University of Tokyo, Social Science Research Institute, ed., *Fascism-ki no Kokka to Shakai*, vol. 2: *Senji Nihon Keizai* (*State and Society under Fascism: War-Time Japanese Economy*). Tokyo: University of Tokyo Press.

INDEX OF AUTHORS

INDEX OF SUBJECTS

Note: Entries refer to the Japanese banking system unless otherwise stated and to banking systems in general.